Published by The Disinformation Company Ltd.
163 Third Avenue, Suite 108
New York, NY 10003
Tel.: +1.212.691.1605
Fax: +1.212.691.1606
www.disinfo.com

Designed by Greg Stadnyk

Printed in the United States of America

10 9 8 7 6 5 4 3 2 1

Library of Congress Control Number: 2008942907

ISBN: 978-1-934708-07-1

Distributed in the U.S. and Canada by:
Consortium Book Sales and Distribution
34 Thirteenth Avenue NE, Suite 101
Minneapolis MN 55413-1007
Tel.: +1.800.283.3572   Fax: +1.612.746.2606
www.cbsd.com

Distributed in the United Kingdom and Eire by:
Turnaround Publisher Services Ltd.
Unit 3, Olympia Trading Estate
Coburg Road
London, N22 6TZ
Tel.: +44.(0)20.8829.3000   Fax: +44.(0)20.8881.5088
www.turnaround-uk.com

Distributed in Australia by:
Tower Books
Unit 2/17 Rodborough Road
Frenchs Forest NSW 2086
Tel.: +61.2.9975.5566   Fax: +61.2.9975.5599
Email: info@towerbooks.com.au

YOU ARE $TILL BEING LIED TO

The REMIXED Disinformation Guide to Media Distortion, Historical Whitewashes and Cultural Myths

edited by **Russ Kick**

disinformation®

CONTENTS

THE SOCIAL FABRICATION

CONDEMNED TO REPEAT IT

TRIPPING

HOLY ROLLING

BLINDED BY SCIENCE

THE BIG PICTURE

INTRODUCTION

You Are Being Lied To was the first book that I created (edited or wrote) for The Disinformation Company. *You Are Being Lied To* was the first book that the Disinformation Company published. Our collaboration led to eight more books. Here we are years later, circling back to the beginning, closing the loop with a new edition of our maiden effort.

■ ■ ■ ■ ■ ■ ■ ■ ■

In 1998, I sent a copy of my second book, *Psychotropedia: Publications From the Periphery*, to Disinformation, hoping for a review, possibly an interview. Instead, I was hired to write for their website. (In those heady days of the dot-com bubble, it was actually possible to get paid for online writing.)

When I first talked to Disinformation's founders, they mentioned that at some point they were hoping to publish books, CDs, and DVDs. In early 2000, I reminded them of this, asking if they'd like to hear some book ideas I'd been percolating. They said yes, so I sent a proposal for a series of anthologies. Big anthologies. Huge. In an oversized format stuffed with at least twice as much material as a regular softcover.

Some of the anthologies, especially the early ones, would have a wide focus; the thread running through the articles would be that they questioned the status quo in some way, exposing lies, challenging cherished beliefs, toppling idols. They could focus on politics, current events, the media, law, history, science, religion, business…any field was fertile ground for questioning. (Later anthologies would focus on a single theme, like religion, sex, or history. Some of those have been published; others are in the pipeline; still others have a more nebulous future.)

Speculation was to be kept to a bare minimum, if not banished altogether. Sure, speculation is important, even vital, but there's a time and a place for it, and these anthologies— especially the unthemed ones—weren't it. I wanted facts, documented facts. What I'd discovered through my years of reading and research was that enough cold, hard, inconvenient facts were being ignored to easily fill volumes. That's what I set out to do.

As soon as I was told to get cracking on the first anthology, a title popped into my head, fully formed: *You Are Being Lied To*. Titles tend to come to me either early and in their final form, or not at all. I loved this one from the moment of its immaculate conception.

I'd been reading and reviewing non-mainstream, nonfiction books since my university days. My book-fetishism, my attraction to uncommon knowledge, and my distrust of authority melded in one explosive moment when I bought a copy of the *Amok Fourth Dispatch*, a monstrous compendium of subversive books. Soon I was reviewing such books for the free-speech magazine *Gauntlet* and the legendary *Factsheet 5*. Not content to just scratch the surface of the world of hidden knowledge and the books that revealed it, I wrote two books— *Outposts* and *Psychotropedia*—containing a total of 1,800+ short book reviews. My personal library of 3,000 volumes (and rapidly growing) clogged up my home.

So by the time *You Are Being Lied To* was being hatched, I already knew a bunch of potential contributors I wanted to approach, topics I wanted to cover, and specific pieces I wanted to include. A call for submissions went out; lots of acceptances came back. To my delight, even the big names— Noam Chomsky, Howard Zinn, Sydney Schanberg, and Riane Eisler among them—were climbing aboard. Most of Disinformation's regular crew submitted. I tapped acquaintances and colleagues, approached strangers, got directed to colleagues of colleagues. New subjects opened up, fascinating articles rolled in. Not everyone I approached wanted to take part—some didn't even respond—but more than enough did to fill a hulking volume.

Nor was everyone optimistic about the book. At the time, Disinformation was owned by Razorfish, a Web/new-media development/marketing/advertising/consulting/leveraging thingy of the type that was springing up like mushrooms during the dot-com boom. Razorfish's CEO bet Disinformation's president, Gary Baddeley, that *You Are Being Lied To* would flop. Savor that. The head of your publisher's parent company literally makes a personal wager that your book is going to be a failure. Gary, taking the bet, told me this at the time, and I assured him that the CEO was wrong. Not only did I believe this, I *knew* it. The time was right for a book like this.

Sure enough, with no marketing or advertising (or reviews), *You Are Being Lied To* found its audience, radiating outward in larger and larger circles as readers (and bookstore workers) discovered it and told other people about it. In what was a bold and unusual move at the time, Disinformation sent a PDF copy of the book to everyone who ordered a physical copy. This was in 2001, way before the Web 2.0 made social networking and interactivity so easy and prevalent. No MySpace, no YouTube, no wikis…and virtually no effort on our part, either. Gary collected on his bet.

■ ■ ■ ■ ■ ■ ■ ■

I edited two more unthemed volumes in the same vein: *Everything You Know Is Wrong* (another rousing success) and *Abuse Your Illusions* (not so much). After that, I wrote three books—*50 Things You're Not Supposed To Know*, its sequel, and *The Disinformation Book of Lists*—then started in on the hot-button-themed anthologies, one on sex, the next on religion.

Then I got sick. Really sick. I won't bore you with the details, but the upshots are 1) if you're ever living or working (or both, as I was) in a building infested with toxic mold, leave permanently the *second* you discover the fungal cause of your mysterious health problems, and 2) I'm damn lucky be alive.

Being in such a bad state, and then slowly recovering, meant that even though a fourth *You Are Being Lied To*-style anthology seemed like a good idea, I was too busy staving off the Grim Reaper to handle it. After seven years, sales of *You Are Being Lied To* had slowed, so Gary suggested a revised edition, obviously a much smaller project than creating a new collection from scratch. But this was still too much for me to handle, so Gary planned to put out an edition that would be lightly updated by the Disinformation staff. As I got better, I would be free to help as much as I wanted to. It was pretty late in the process before I was well enough to play a significant role, which kept expanding as the deadline bore down on us.

Originally, there was to be a smattering of new articles in this volume, but because of my insatiable need to stuff *more more more* into every anthology, around half of this edition is comprised of material that wasn't in the original. (And eleven of the pieces making a second appearance have been updated by their authors.)

■ ■ ■ ■ ■ ■ ■ ■

At this point, I could say something about how the need to question the status quo is at least as urgent as it's ever been (and it's *always* been urgent), but, well, I could also tell you that the sky is blue. I'd rather not state the obvious. And if you've bought, or at least picked up, this book, and if you've read this much of my self-indulgent intro, then chances are you already realize that there are so many fundamental and interlocking problems with the way things are done—politically, economically, legally, militarily, environmentally, educationally, socially, sexually, ethically, spiritually, scientifically, and so on—that it's a wonder the world keeps going at all, that society after society doesn't crumble and send us back to the hunter-gatherer stage. It's all held together by duct tape, inertia, and wishful thinking (or blind denial, if you prefer).

So, here's a little break in the storm, a dose of dangerous sanity in a Bizarro Wonderland.

A NOTE TO READERS

The beliefs (political, religious, etc.) of any contributor cannot be assumed simply because he or she appears in this anthology. If a contributor reveals his or her beliefs in the course of an article, that's obviously a different matter, but simply appearing here is not an indication of affiliation.

Similarly, bear in mind that no contributor necessarily agrees with the other contributors. In fact, I'm sure some would get into arguments if invited to the same dinner party. So, inclusion is not an indication of collusion.

ACKNOWLEDGMENTS

Thanks of a personal nature to my parents, my girls, Ruthanne & Raoul, Billy Dale, Darrell, Terrence & Beck, Mike Ravnitzky, Fred & Dorothy, Jeff & Christie, Z, and Dr. Miles. Many thanks also to the Disinfo crew: Gary Baddeley, Ralph Bernardo, Greg Stadnyk, Jacob Sloan, and Nimrod Erez. I greatly appreciate the efforts of Consortium, QPB, the printers, all booksellers, and Lora Fountain. Kisses to all the generous publishers who let me reprint material—AK, Chelsea Green, Grand Central, Seven Stories, and Soft Skull. I also want to highlight my continuing gratitude to those who played a role in the creation of the first edition, though they weren't around for this one: Anne Marie, Jennifer, Richard Metzger, Paul Pollard & Tomo Makiura, RSUB, Green Galactic, and former Disinfo staffers. And perhaps most crucial of all, I extend deep appreciation to all contributors: the original cast members who agreed to appear again in this edition; the newcomers; and those whose work from *You Are Being Lied To* was cut to make room for all the new stuff. Without you, there would be no anthologies.

–Russ Kick

KEYNOTE ADDRESS

Reality Is a Shared Hallucination
Howard Bloom

"Being here is a kind of spiritual surrender. We see only what the others see, the thousands who were here in the past, those who will come in the future. We've agreed to be part of a collective perception." —Don DeLillo

"We are accustomed to use our eyes only with the memory of what other people before us have thought about the object we are looking at." —Guy de Maupassant

"After all, what is reality anyway? Nothin' but a collective hunch." —Lily Tomlin

Once upon a time, the only libraries of information this planet's creatures passed down from generation to generation were the records of experience encoded in genes. Then, 2.5 million years ago, arose the first humans able to make stone tools— artificial claws and teeth. Roughly 2.4 million years later, those proto-humans invented something else brand-new—artificial memory. Language, sayings, stories, and clichés. The result was a whole new kind of reality—an artificially constructed reality. A man-and-woman-made reality. We call it "culture." And that artificial reality would play a key role in the emergence of a global intelligence—an intelligence whose full story you can read in my book *Global Brain: The Evolution of Mass Mind from the Big Bang to the Twenty-first Century*.

But there's an irony. If the group-brain's "psyche" were a beach with shifting dunes and hollows, individual perception would be that beach's grains of sand. However, this image has a hidden twist. Individual perception untainted by others' influence does not exist.

A central rule of large-scale organization goes like this: The greater the spryness of a massive enterprise, the more internal communication it takes to support the teamwork of its parts.[1] For example, in all but the simplest plants and animals only 5 percent of DNA is dedicated to DNA's "real job," manufacturing proteins.[2] The remaining 95 percent is preoccupied with organization and administration, supervising the maintenance of bodily procedures, or even merely interpreting the corporate rule book "printed" in a string of genes.[3]

In an effective learning machine, the connections deep inside far outnumber windows to the outside world. Take the cerebral cortex, roughly 80 percent of whose nerves connect with each other, not with input from the eyes or ears.[4] The learning device called human society follows the same rules. Individuals spend most of their time communicating with each other, not exploring ubiquitous elements of their "environment" such as insects and weeds which could potentially make a nourishing dish.[5] This cabling for the group's internal operations has a far greater impact on what we "see" and "hear" than many psychological researchers suspect. For it puts us in the hands of a conformity enforcer whose power and subtlety are almost beyond belief.

Which of your minds decides what to store in memory and what to toss away? Is it the rational you? Or is it the primitive you—the emotional you? If you guessed primitive, you're right. It's the brain's emotional center—the limbic system—that decides which swatches of experience to notice and tuck away in memory. Just how much does emotion's chokehold over memory matter? A whole lot more than you might think. Memory is the core of what we call reality.

Think about it for a second. What do you actually hear and see right now? This page. The walls and furnishings of the room in which you sit. Perhaps some music or some background noise. Yet you know as sure as you were born that out of sight there are other rooms mere steps away—perhaps the kitchen, bathroom, bedroom, and a hall. What makes you so sure that they exist? Nothing but your memory. Nothing else at all. You're also reasonably certain there's a broader world outside. You know that your office, if you are away from it, still awaits your entry. You can picture the roads you use to get to it, visualize the public foyer and the conference rooms, see in your mind's eye the path to your own workspace, and know where most of the things in your desk are placed.

Individual perception untainted by others' influence does not exist.

from *Global Brain: The Evolution of Mass Mind from the Big Bang to the 21st Century* by Howard Bloom.
© 2000 Howard Bloom.
Reprinted by permission of John Wiley & Sons, Inc.

The words of just one determined speaker had penetrated the most intimate sanctums of the eye and brain.

Then there are the companions who enrich your life—family, workmates, neighbors, friends, a husband or a wife, and even people you are fond of to whom you haven't spoken in a year or two—few of whom, if any, are currently in the room with you. You also know we sit on a planet called the earth, circling an incandescent ball of sun, buried in one of many galaxies. At this instant, reading by yourself, where do the realities of galaxies and friends reside? Only in the chambers of your mind. Almost every reality you "know" at any given second is a mere ghost held in memory.

Your limbic system, your emotional brain, is memory's gatekeeper and in a very real sense its creator. Your limbic system is also an intense monitor of others,[6] keeping track of what will earn their praise or their blame. By using cues from those around you to fashion your perceptions and the "facts" that you retain, your limbic system gives the group a say in that most central of realities, the one presiding in your brain. And it's the same for me. Other people fashion my reality.

Social experience literally shapes critical details of brain physiology, sculpting an infant's brain to fit the culture into which the child is born.

One of those people who shape my perception is Elizabeth Loftus, one of the world's premier memory researchers. Loftus is among the few who realize how powerfully the group remakes our deepest certainties. In the late 1970s, Loftus performed a series of key experiments. In a typical session, she showed college students a moving picture of a traffic accident, then asked after the film, "How fast was the white sports car going when it passed the barn while traveling along the country road?" Several days later when witnesses to the film were quizzed about what they'd seen, 17 percent were sure they'd spied a barn, though there weren't any buildings in the film at all. In a related experiment subjects were shown a collision between a bicycle and an auto driven by a brunette, then afterwards were peppered with questions about the "blond" at the steering wheel. Not only did they remember the nonexistent blond vividly, but when they were shown the video a second time, they had a hard time believing that it was the same incident they now recalled so graphically. One subject said, "It's really strange because I still have the blond girl's face in my mind

and it doesn't correspond to her [pointing to the woman on the video screen]…It was really weird." These experiments gave us a glimpse of how information from others nudges us as we piece together the collage of memory. Loftus concluded that hints leaked to us by fellow humans, even when they're leaked in questions, override the scene we're sure we've "seen with our own eyes."[7]

Though it got little public attention, research on the slavish nature of perception had begun at least 20 years before Loftus' work. It was 1956 when Solomon Asch published a classic series of experiments in which he and his colleagues showed cards with lines of different lengths to clusters of their students. Two lines were exactly the same size and two clearly were not—the dissimilar lines stuck out like a pair of basketball players at a Brotherhood of Munchkins brunch. During a typical experimental run, the researchers set up nine shills. They asked nine volunteers, nine co-conspirators, to pretend they were innocent experimental subjects. They asked these collaborators to act as if they didn't have a clue about the nature of the research going on. Then they told these conspirators to claim that two badly mismatched lines were actually the same, and that the real twin was a misfit. Now came the nefarious part. The researchers ushered a real unknowing student, a real innocent experimental subject, into a room filled with the collaborators and gave him the impression that the crowd already there knew just as little as he did about what was going on. Then a white-coated psychologist passed the cards around. One by one he asked the pre-drilled shills to announce out loud which lines were alike. Each dutifully declared that two lines of preposterously different length, a long line and a short line, were the same. By the time the scientist prodded the unsuspecting newcomer to pronounce judgment, he usually went along with the bogus consensus of the crowd. In fact, a full 75 percent of the clueless experimental subjects bleated in chorus with the herd. Asch ran the experiment over and over again. When he quizzed his victims after their ordeal was over, it turned out that many had done far more than simply go along to get along. They had actually *seen* the mismatched lines as equal. Their senses had been swayed more by the views of the multitude than by the actuality. Peer pressure had squeezed their vision out of all whack with reality.

Psychologist Paul Ekman has demonstrated that the faces we make recast our moods, reset our nervous systems, and fill us with the feelings the facial expressions indicate.

To make matters worse, many of those whose vision hadn't been deceived had also become inadvertent collaborators in the praise of the emperor's new clothes. Some did it out of self-doubt. They were convinced that the facts their eyes reported were wrong, the herd was right, and that an optical illusion had tricked them into seeing things. Still others realized with total clarity which lines were identical but lacked the nerve to utter an unpopular opinion.[8] Conformity enforcers had tyrannized everything from visual processing to honest speech, revealing some of the mechanisms that wrap and seal a crowd into a false belief.

Another series of experiments indicates just how deeply social suggestion can penetrate the neural mesh through which we think we see a hard-and-fast reality. Students with normal color vision were shown blue slides. But one or two stooges in the room, shills, collaborators with the experimenter, declared the slides were green. In a typical use of this procedure, only 32 percent of the students ended up going along with the vocal but totally phony proponents of green vision.[9] Later, however, the subjects were taken aside, shown blue-green slides and asked to rate them for blueness or greenness. Even the students who had refused to see green where there was none a few minutes earlier showed that the insistent greenies in the room had colored their perceptions. They rated the new slides more green than pretests indicated they would have otherwise.

More to the point, when asked to describe the color of the afterimage they saw, the subjects often reported it was red-purple—the hue of an afterimage left by the color green. Afterimages are not voluntary. They are manufactured by the visual system. The words of just one determined speaker had penetrated the most intimate sanctums of the eye and brain.

When it comes to herd perception, this is just the iceberg's tip. Social experience literally shapes critical details of brain physiology,[10] sculpting an infant's brain to fit the culture into which the child is born. Six-month-olds can hear or make every sound in virtually every human language.[11] But within a mere four months, nearly two-thirds of this capacity has been cut away.[12] The slashing of ability is accompanied by ruthless

alterations in cerebral tissue.[13] Brain cells remain alive only if they can prove their worth in dealing with the baby's physical and social surroundings.[14] Half the brain cells we are born with rapidly die. The 50 percent of neurons which thrive are those which have shown they come in handy for coping with such cultural experiences as crawling on the polished mud floor of a straw hut or navigating on all fours across wall-to-wall carpeting, or comprehending a mother's words, her body language, stories, songs, and the concepts she's imbibed from her community. Those nerve cells stay alive which demonstrate that they can cope with the quirks of strangers, friends, and family. The 50 percent of neurons which remain unused are literally forced to commit preprogrammed cell death—preprogrammed cell suicide.[15] The brain that underlies the mind is jigsawed like a puzzle piece to fit the space it's given by its loved ones and by the larger framework of its culture's patterning.[16]

When barely out of the womb, babies are already riveted on a major source of social cues.[17] (Newborns to four-month-olds would rather look at faces than at almost anything else.[18]) Rensselaer Polytechnic's Linnda Caporael points out what she calls "micro-coordination," in which a baby imitates its mother's facial expression, and the mother, in turn, imitates the baby's.[19] The duet of smiles and funny faces indulged in by Western mothers or scowls and angry looks favored by such peoples as

Unconsciously, the conversationalists began to coordinate their finger movements, eye blinks, and nods.

New Guinea's Mundugumor[20] accomplishes far more than at first it seems. Psychologist Paul Ekman has demonstrated that the faces we make recast our moods, reset our nervous systems, and fill us with the feelings the facial expressions indicate.[21] So the baby imitating its mother's face is learning how to glower or glow with emotions stressed by its society. And emotions, as we've already seen, help craft our vision of reality.

There are other signs that babies synchronize their feelings to the folks around them at a very early age. Emotional contagion and empathy—two of the ties that bind us—come to us when we are still in diapers.[22] Children less than a year old who see another child hurt show all the signs of undergoing the same pain.[23] The University of Zurich's D. Bischof-Köhler concludes

Even in our most casual moments, we pulse in synchrony.

from one of his studies that when babies between one and two years old see another infant hurt they don't just ape the emotions of distress, they share it empathetically.[24]

More important, both animal and human children cram their powers of perception into a conformist mold, chaining their attention to what others see. A four-month-old human will swivel to look at an object his parent is staring at. A baby chimp will do the same.[25] By their first birthday, infants have extended this perceptual linkage to their peers. When they notice that another child's eyes have fixated on an object, they swivel around to focus on that thing themselves. If they don't see what's so interesting, they look back to check the direction of the other child's gaze and make sure they've got it right.[26]

One-year-olds show other ways in which their perception is a slave to social commands. Put a cup and a strange gewgaw in front of them, and their natural tendency will be to check out the novelty. But repeat the word "cup," and the infant will dutifully rivet its gaze on the old familiar drinking vessel.[27] Children go along with the herd even in their tastes in food. When researchers put two-to-five-year-olds at a table for several days with other kids who loved the edibles they loathed, the children with the dislike did a 180-degree turn and became zestful eaters of the dish they'd formerly disdained.[28] The preference was still going strong weeks after the peer pressure had stopped.

At six, children are obsessed with being accepted by the group and become hypersensitive to violations of group norms. This tyranny of belonging punishes perceptions that fail to coincide with those of the majority.[29]

Even rhythm draws individual perceptions together in the subtlest of ways. Psychiatrist William Condon of Boston University's Medical School analyzed films of adults chatting and noticed a peculiar process at work. Unconsciously, the conversationalists began to coordinate their finger movements, blinks, and nods.[30] When pairs of talkers were hooked up to separate electroencephalographs, something even more astonishing appeared—

some of their brain waves were spiking in unison.[31] Newborn babies already show this synchrony[32]—in fact, an American infant still fresh from the womb will just as happily match its body movements to the speech of someone speaking Chinese as to someone speaking English.

As time proceeds, these unnoticed synchronies draw larger and larger groups together. A graduate student working under the direction of anthropologist Edward T. Hall hid in an abandoned car and filmed children romping in a school playground at lunch hour. Screaming, laughing, running, and jumping, each seemed superficially to be doing his or her own thing. But careful analysis revealed that the group was rocking to a unified beat. One little girl, far more active than the rest, covered the entire schoolyard in her play. Hall and his student realized that without knowing it, she was "the director" and "the orchestrator." Eventually, the researchers found a tune that fit the silent cadence. When they played it and rolled the film, it looked exactly as if each kid were dancing to the melody. But there had been no music playing in the schoolyard. Said Hall, "Without knowing it, they were all moving to a beat they generated themselves…an unconscious undercurrent of synchronized movement tied the group together." William Condon concluded that it doesn't make sense to view humans as "isolated entities." They are, he said, bonded together by their involvement in "shared organizational forms."[33] In other words, without knowing it individuals form a team. Even in our most casual moments, we pulse in synchrony.

No wonder input from the herd so strongly colors the ways in which we see our world. Students at MIT were given a bio of a guest lecturer. One group's background sheet described the speaker as cold. The other group's handout praised him for his warmth. Both groups sat together as they watched the lecturer give his presentation. But those who'd read the bio saying he was cold saw him as distant and aloof. Those who'd been tipped off that he was warm rated him as friendly and approachable.[34] In judging a fellow human being, students replaced external fact with input they'd been given socially.[35]

The cues rerouting herd perception come in many forms. Sociologists Janet Lynne Enke and Donna Eder discovered

Every word we use carries within it the experience of generation after generation of men, women, families, tribes, and nations, often including their insights, value judgments, ignorance, and spiritual beliefs.

that(in gossip, one person opens with a negative comment on someone outside the group. How the rest of the gang goes on the issue depends entirely on the second opinion expressed.)If the second speechifier agrees that the outsider is disgusting, virtually everyone will chime in with a sound-alike opinion. If, on the other hand, the second commentator objects that the outsider is terrific, the group is far less likely to descend like a flock of harpies tearing the stranger's reputation limb from limb.[36]

Crowds of silent voices whisper in our ears, transforming the nature of what we see and hear. Some are those of childhood authorities and heroes, others come from family[37] and peers.[38]

All too often when we see someone perform an action without a name, we rapidly forget its alien outlines and tailor our recall to fit the patterns dictated by convention…and conventional vocabulary.

The strangest emerge from beyond the grave. A vast chorus of long-gone ancients constitutes a not-so-silent majority whose legacy has what may be the most dramatic effect of all on our vision of reality. Take the impact of gender stereotypes. These are notions developed over hundreds of generations. They've been repeated, reinterpreted, embellished, and passed on by literally billions of humans during our march through time. In one study, parents were asked to give their impression of their brand-new babies. Infant boys and girls are completely indistinguishable aside from the buds of reproductive equipment between their legs. Their size, texture, and the way in which newborns of opposite sex act are, according to researchers J.Z. Rubin, F.J. Provenzano, and Z. Luria, completely and totally the same. Yet parents consistently described girls as softer, smaller, and less attentive than boys.[39]

The crowds within us resculpt our gender verdicts over and over again. Two groups of experimental subjects were asked to grade the same paper. One was told the author was John McKay. The other was told the paper's writer was Joan McKay. Even female students evaluating the paper gave it higher marks if they thought it was from a male.[40]

The ultimate repository of herd influence is language—a device that not only condenses the opinions of those with whom we share a common vocabulary, but sums up the perceptual approach of swarms who have passed on. Every word we use carries within it the experience of generation after generation of men, women, families, tribes, and nations, often including their insights, value judgments, ignorance, and spiritual beliefs. Take the simple sentence, "Feminism has won freedom for women." Indo-European warriors coined the word *dh[=a]*, meaning to suck, as a baby does on a breast. They carried this term from the Asian steppes to Greece, where it became *qu^sai*, to suckle, and *theEIE*, nipple. The Romans managed to mangle *qh^sai* into *femina*—their word for woman.[41] At every step of the way, millions of humans mouthing the term managed to change its contents. To the Greeks, *qh^sai* was associated with a segment of the human race on a par with domesticated animals—for that's what women were, even in the splendid days of Plato (who preferred young boys to women). In Rome, on the other hand, *feminae* were free and, if they were rich, could have a merry old time behind the scenes sexually or politically. The declaration, "Feminism has won freedom for women," would have puzzled Indo-Europeans, enraged the Greeks, and been welcomed by the Romans.

Freedom—the word for whose contents many modern women fight—comes from a men's-only ritual among ancient German tribes. Two clans who'd been mowing each other's members down made peace by invoking the god Freda[42] and giving up ("Freda-ing," so to speak) a few haunches of meat or a pile of animal hides to mollify the enemy and let the matter drop.[43] As for the last word in "Feminism has won freedom for women"—*woman* originally meant nothing more than a man's wife (the Anglo-Saxons pronounced it "wif-man").

"Feminism has won freedom for women"—over the millennia new generations have mouthed each of these words of ancient tribesmen in new ways, tacking on new connotations, denotations, and associations. The word *feminine* carried considerable baggage when it wended its way from Victorian times into the twentieth century. Quoth *Webster's Revised Unabridged Dictionary* of 1913, it meant: "modest, graceful, affectionate, confiding; or…weak, nerveless, timid, pleasure-loving, effeminate." Tens of millions of speakers from a host of nations had heaped these messages of weakness on the Indo-European base, and soon a swarm of other talkers would add to the word *feminine* a very different freight. In 1895 the women's movement changed *feminine* to *feminism*, which they defined as "the theory of the political, economic, and social equality of the sexes."[44] It would take millions of women fighting for nearly 100 years to firmly affix the new meaning to syllables formerly associated with the nipple, timidity, and nervelessness. And even now, the crusades rage. With every sentence on feminism we utter, we thread our way through the sensitivities of masses of modern humans who find the word *feminism* a necessity, a destroyer of the family, a conversational irritant, or a still open plain on which to battle yet again, this time over whether the word *femina* will in the future denote the goals of eco-feminists, anarcho-feminists, amazon feminists, libertarian feminists, all four, or none of the above.[45]

The hordes of fellow humans who've left meanings in our words frequently guide the way in which we see our world. Experiments show that people from all cultures can detect subtle differences between colors placed next to each other. But individuals from societies equipped with names for numerous shades can spot the difference when the two swatches of color are apart.[46] At the dawn of the twentieth century, the Chukchee people of northeastern Siberia had very few terms for visual hues. If you asked them to sort colored yarns, they did a poor job of it. But they had over 24 terms for the patterns of reindeer hide, and could classify reindeer far better than the average European scientist, whose vocabulary didn't supply him with such well-honed perceptual tools.[47]

Physiologist/ornithologist Jared Diamond, in New Guinea, saw to his dismay that despite all his university studies of nature, illiterate local tribesmen were far better at distinguishing bird species than was he. Diamond used a set of scientific criteria taught in the zoology classes back home. The New Guinean natives possessed something better: names for each animal variety, names whose local definitions pinpointed characteristics Diamond had never been taught to differentiate—everything from a bird's peculiarities of deportment to its taste when grilled over a flame. Diamond had binoculars and state-of-the-art taxonomy. But the New Guineans laughed at his incompetence.[48] They were equipped with a vocabulary, each word of which compacted the experience of armies of bird-hunting and bird-munching ancestors.

All too often when we see someone perform an action without a name, we rapidly forget its alien outlines and tailor our recall to fit the patterns dictated by convention…and by conventional vocabulary.[49] A perfect example comes from nineteenth-century America, where sibling rivalry was present in fact, but

according to theory didn't exist. The experts were blind to its presence, as shown by its utter absence from family manuals. In the expert and popular view, all that existed between brothers and sisters was love. But letters from middle-class girls exposed unacknowledged cattiness and jealousy.

Sibling rivalry didn't begin to creep from the darkness of perceptual invisibility until 1893, when future Columbia University professor of political and social ethics Felix Adler hinted at the nameless notion in his manual *Moral Instruction of Children*. During the 1920s, the concept of jealousy between siblings

Almost every reality you "know" at *any* given second is a mere ghost held in memory.

finally shouldered its way robustly into the repertoire of conscious concepts, appearing in two widely-quoted government publications and becoming the focus of a 1926 crusade mounted by the Child Study Association of America. Only at this point did experts finally coin the term "sibling rivalry."

Now that it carried the compacted crowd-power of a label, the formerly nonexistent demon was blamed for adult misery, failing marriages, crime, homosexuality, and God knows what all else. By the 1940s, nearly every child-raising guide had extensive sections on this ex-nonentity. Parents writing to major magazines cited the previously unseeable "sibling rivalry" as the root of almost every one of childraising's many quandaries.[50]

The stored experience that language carries can make the difference between life and death. For roughly 4,000 years, Tasmanian mothers, fathers, and children starved to death each time famine struck, despite the fact that their island home was surrounded by fish-rich seas. The problem: Their tribal culture did not define fish as food.[51] We could easily suffer the same fate if stranded in their wilderness, simply because the crowd of ancients crimped into our vocabulary tell us that a rich source of nutrients is inedible, too—insects.

The perceptual influence of the mob of those who've gone before us and of those who stand around us now can be mind-boggling. During the Middle Ages, when universities first arose, a local barber-surgeon was called to the lecture chamber of famous medical schools like those of Padua and Salerno year after year to dissect a corpse for medical students gathered from the width and breadth of Europe. While this lowly combination barber-surgeon carved away at the body in the theatrical pit, an august scholar on a raised platform discoursed about the revelations unfolding before the students' eyes. The learned doctor would invariably report a shape for the liver radically different from the form of the organ sliding around on the surgeon's blood-stained hands. He'd verbally portray jaw joints which had no relation to those being dis-

Brain cells remain alive only if they can prove their worth in dealing with the baby's physical and social surroundings.

played on the trestle below him. He'd describe a network of cranial blood vessels that were nowhere to be seen. But he never changed his narrative to fit the actualities. Nor did the students or the surgeon ever stop to correct the book-steeped authority. Why? The scholar was reciting the "facts" as found in volumes over 1,000 years old—the works of the Roman master Galen, founder of "modern" medicine. Alas, Galen had drawn his conclusions, not from dissecting humans, but from probing the bodies of pigs and monkeys. Pigs and monkeys do have the strange features Galen described. Humans, however, do not. But that didn't stop the medieval professors from seeing what wasn't there.[52] Their sensory pathways echoed with voices gathered for a millennium, with murmurings of a crowd composed of both the living and the dead. For the perceptual powers of Middle Age scholars were no more individualistic than are yours and mine. Through our sentences and paragraphs, long-gone ghosts still have their say within the collective mind…and within yours and mine.

Endnotes

1. Waller, M.J.C. (1996). Personal communication, May; Waller, M.J.C. (1996). "Organization theory and the origins of consciousness." *Journal of Social and Evolutionary Systems*, 19(1), p 17–30; Burns, T. & G.M. Stalker. (1961). *The management of innovation*. London: Tavistock Publications, pp 92–93, 233–234. **2.** Doolittle, Russell F. "Microbial genomes opened up," pp 339–342. **3.** Bodnar, J.W., J. Killian, M. Nagle & S. Ramchandani. (1997). "Deciphering the language of the genome." *Journal of Theoretical Biology*, November 21, pp 183–93; Kupiec, J.J. (1989). "Gene regulation and DNA C-value paradox: a model based on diffusion of regulatory molecules." *Medical Hypotheses*, January, p 7–10; Knee, R. & P.R. Murphy. (1997). "Regulation of gene expression by natural antisense RNA transcripts." *Neurochemistry International*, September, pp 379–92; Sandler, U. & A. Wyler. (1998). "Non-coding DNA can regulate gene transcription by its base pair's distribution." *Journal of Theoretical Biology*, July 7, pp 85–90; Hardison, R. (1998). "Hemoglobins from bacteria to man: Evolution of different patterns of gene expression." *Journal of Experimental Biology*, April (Pt 8), pp 1099–117; Vol'kenshten, M.V. (1990). "Molecular drive." *Molekuliarnaia Biologiia*, September-October, p 1181–99.; Cohen, Jack & Ian Stewart. (1994). *The collapse of chaos: Discovering simplicity in a complex world*. New York: Viking, 1994, p 73. **4.** Szentagothai, Janos. (1989). "The 'brain-mind' relation: A pseudoproblem?" In *Mindwaves: Thoughts on intelligence, identity and consciousness*. Edited by Colin Blakemore & Susan Greenfield. Oxford: Basil Blackwell, p 330; Douglas, Rodney J., Christof Koch, Misha Mahowald, Kevan A.C. Martin, Humbert H. Suarez. (1995). "Recurrent excitation in neocortical circuits." *Science*, 18 August, p 981. **5.** Caporael, Linnda R. (1995). "Sociality: Coordinating bodies, minds and groups." *Psycoloquy*. Downloaded from <www.ai.univie.ac.at/cgi-bin/mfs/31/wachau/www/archives/

Psycoloquy/1995.V6/0043.html?84#mfs>, 95/6/01. **6.** Bower, Bruce. (1994). "Brain faces up to fear, social signs." *Science News*, December 17, p 406; Kandel, Eric R. & Robert D. Hawkins. (1992). "The biological basis of learning and individuality." *Scientific American*, September, pp 78–87; LeDoux, Joseph E. "Emotion, memory and the brain." *Scientific American*, June, pp 50–57; Blakeslee, Sandra. (1994). "Brain study examines rare woman." *New York Times*, December 18, p 35; Emde, Robert N. "Levels of meaning for infant emotions: A biosocial view." In *Approaches to emotion*, edited by Klaus R. Scherer & Paul Ekman. Hillsdale, NJ: Lawrence Erlbaum Associates, p 79; Stein, Kathleen. "Mind reading among the macaques: How the brain interprets the intentions of others." *Omni*, June, p 10. **7.** Loftus, Elizabeth. (1980). *Memory: Surprising new insights into how we remember and why we forget*. Reading, MA: Addison Wesley, pp 45–49; Loftus, Elizabeth. (1992). "When a lie becomes memory's truth: Memory distortion after exposure to misinformation." *Current Directions in Psychological Science*, August, pp 121–123; Loftus, Elizabeth F. (1997). "Creating false memories." *Scientific American*, September, pp 70–75; Roediger, Henry L. (1996). "Memory illusions." *Journal of Memory and Language*, April 1, v 35 n 2, p 76; Roediger III, Henry L. & Kathleen B. McDermott. (1995). "Creating false memories: Remembering words not presented in lists." *Journal of Experimental Psychology*, July, v 21 n 4, p 803. **8.** Asch, Solomon E. (1956). "Studies of independence and conformity: I. A minority of one against a unanimous majority." *Psychological Monographs*, 70, p 9 (Whole No. 416); Raven, Bertram H. & Jeffrey Z. Rubin. (1983). *Social Psychology*. New York: John Wiley and Sons, pp 566–9, 575. **9.** Faucheux, C. & S. Moscovici. "Le style de comportement d'une minorité et son influence sur les réponses d'une majorité." *Bulletin du Centre d'Études et Recherches Psychologiques*, 16, pp 337–360; Moscovici, S., E. Lage, & M. Naffrechoux. "Influence of a consistent minority on the responses of a majority in a color perception task." *Sociometry*, 32, pp 365–380; Moscovici, S. & B. Personnaz. (1980). "Studies in social influence, Part V: Minority influence and conversion behavior in a perceptual task." *Journal of Experimental Social Psychology*, 16, pp 270–282; Raven, Bertram H. & Jeffrey Z. Rubin. *Social Psychology*, pp 584–585. **10.** Eisenberg, L. (1995). "The social construction of the human brain." *American Journal of Psychiatry*, 152(11), pp 1563–1575; Leonard, Christiana M., Linda J. Lombardino, Laurie R. Mercado, Samuel R. Browd, Joshua I. Breier, & O. Frank Agee. (1996). "Cerebral asymmetry and cognitive development in children: A magnetic resonance imaging study." *Psychological Science*, March, p 93; Goldman-Rakic, P. & P. Rakic. (1984). "Experimental modification of gyral patterns." In *Cerebral dominance: The biological foundation*, edited by N. Geschwind & A.M. Galaburda. Cambridge, MA: Harvard University Press, pp 179–192; Pascual-Leone, A. & F. Torres. (1993). "Plasticity of the sensorimotor cortex representation of the reading finger in Braille readers." *Brain*, 116, pp 39–52; Recanzone, G., C. Schreiner, & M. Merzenich. (1993). "Plasticity in the frequency representation of primary auditory cortex following discrimination training in adult owl monkeys." *Journal of Neuroscience*, 13, pp 97–103. **11.** Skoyles; John. (1998). "Mirror neurons and the motor theory of speech." *Noetica*. <psy.uq.edu.au/CogPsych/Noetica/OpenForumIssue9/>. **12.** Werker, Janet F. & Renee M. Desjardins. (1995). "Listening to speech in the 1st year of life: Experiential influences on phoneme perception." *Current Directions in Psychological Science*, June, pp 76–81; Werker, Janet F. (1989). "Becoming a native listener." *American Scientist*, January-February, pp 54–59; Werker, Janet F. & Richard C. Tees. (1992). "The organization and reorganization of human speech perception." *Annual Review of Neuroscience*, 15, pp 377–402; Werker, J.F. & J.E. Pegg. (In press). "Infant speech perception and phonological acquisition." *Phonological development: Research, models and implications*, edited by C.E. Ferguson, L. Menn & C. Stoel-Gammon. Parkton, MD: York Press; Werker, Janet F. (1995). "Exploring developmental changes in cross-language speech perception." In D. Osherson (series editor), *An invitation to cognitive science*: L. Gleitman & M. Liberman (volume editors) *Part I: Language*. Cambridge, MA: MIT Press, pp 87–106. **13.** Eisenberg, L. (1995). "The social construction of the human brain." *American Journal of Psychiatry*, 152 (11), pp 1563–1575. Segall, M.H., D.T. Campbell & M.J. Herskovitz. (1966). *The influence of culture on visual perception*. Indianapolis: Bobbs-Merrill; Shi-xu. (1995). "Cultural perceptions: Exploiting the unexpected of the other." *Culture & Psychology*, 1, pp 315–342; Lucy, J. (1992). *Grammatical categories and cognition: A case study of the linguistic relativity hypothesis*. Cambridge: Cambridge University Press; Berridge, Kent C. & Terry E. Robinson. (1995). "The mind of an addicted brain: Neural sensitization of wanting versus liking." *Current Directions in Psychological Science*, June, p 74; Lancaster, Jane B. (1968). "Primate communication systems and the emergence of human language." *Primates: Studies in adaptation and variability*, edited by Phyllis C. Jay. New York: Holt, Rinehart and Winston, pp 451–453; Emde, Robert N. "Levels of meaning for infant emotions: A biosocial view." *Approaches to Emotion*, p 79; Belsky, Jay, Becky Spritz & Keith Crnic. (1996). "Infant attachment security and affective-cognitive information processing at age 3." *Psychological Science*, March, pp 111–114; Bower, Bruce (1995). "Brain activity comes down to expectation." *Science News*, January 21, p 38; Op cit., Caporael (1995); Nisbett, R. & L. Ross. (1980). *Human inference: Strategies and shortcomings* *of social judgment*. Englewood Cliffs, NJ: Prentice-Hall; Shweder, R.A. & R.G. D'Andrade. (1980). "The systematic distortion hypothesis." *Fallible Judgment in Behavioral Research. New Directions for Methodology of Social and Behavioral Science*, 4 1980, pp 37–58. For neural plasticity in non-humans, see: Nottebohm, F., M.E. Nottebohm & L. Crane. (1986). "Developmental and seasonal changes in canary song and their relation to changes in the anatomy of song-control nuclei." *Behavioral and Neural Biology*, November, pp 445–71. **14.** Ruoslahti, Erkki "Stretching Is Good For A Cell," pp 1345–1346. **15.** Gould, Elizabeth. (1994). "The effects of adrenal steroids and excitatory input on neuronal birth and survival." In *Hormonal Restructuring of the Adult Brain: Basic and Clinical Perspective*, edited by Victoria N. Luine, Cheryl F. Harding. *Annals of the New York Academy of Sciences*, Vol. 743, p 73. New York: The New York Academy of Sciences; Vogel, K.S. (1993). "Development of trophic interactions in the vertebrate peripheral nervous system." *Molecular Neurobiology*, Fall-Winter, pp 363–82; Haanen, C. & I. Vermes. (1996). "Apoptosis: Programmed cell death in fetal development." *European Journal of Obstetrics, Gynecology, and Reproductive Biology*, January, pp 129–33; Young, Wise, June Kume-Kick & Shlomo Constantini. "Glucorticoid therapy of spinal chord injury." In *Hormonal restructuring of the adult brain: Basic and clinical perspective*, p 247; Nadis, Steve. (1993). "Kid's brainpower: Use it or lose it." *Technology Review*, November/December, pp 19–20. Levine, Daniel S. (1988). "Survival of the synapses." *The Sciences*, November/ December, p 51. Elbert, Thomas, Christo Pantev, Christian Wienbruch, Brigitte Rockstroh & Edward Taub. (1995). "Increased cortical representation of the fingers of the left hand in stringed players." *Science*, October 13, pp 305–307. Barinaga, Marsha. (1994). "Watching the brain remake itself." *Science*, Dec, p 1475; Pascual-Leone, A. & F. Torres. (1993). "Plasticity of the sensorimotor cortex representation of the reading finger in Braille readers." *Brain*, 116, pp 39–52. Holden, Constance (1995). "Sensing music." *Science*, 13 October, p 237; Korein, Julius, M.D. (1988). "Reality and the brain: The beginnings and endings of the human being." In *The reality club*, edited by John Brockman. New York: Lynx Books, p 94; Changeux, J.P. (1985). *The biology of mind*. Translated by Laurence Garey. Oxford: Oxford University Press, pp 217–218; Aoki, C. & P. Siekevitz. (1988). "Plasticity in brain development." *Scientific American*, June, pp 56–64; Bagnoli, P.G., G. Casini, F. Fontanesi & L. Sebastiani. (1989). "Reorganization of visual pathways following posthatching removal of one retina on pigeons." *The Journal of Comparative Neurology*, 288, pp 512–527; DePryck, Koen. (1993). *Knowledge, evolution, and paradox: The ontology of language*. Albany: State University of New York Press, pp 122–125; Black, I.B. (1986). "Trophic molecules and evolution of the nervous system." *Proceedings of the National Academy of Sciences of the United States of America*, November, pp 8249–52. **16.** Leonard, Christiana M., Linda J. Lombardino, Laurie R. Mercado, Samuel R. Browd, Joshua I. Breier, & O. Frank Agee. (1996). "Cerebral asymmetry and cognitive development in children: A magnetic resonance imaging study." *Psychological Science*, March, p 93; Scarr, S. (1991). "Theoretical issues in investigating intellectual plasticity." In *Plasticity of development*, edited by S.E. Brauth, W.S. Hall & R.J. Dooling. Cambridge, MA: MIT Press, 1991, pp 57–71; Goldman-Rakic, P. & P. Rakic. (1984). "Experimental modification of gyral patterns." In *Cerebral dominance: The biological foundation,* edited by N. Geschwind & A.M. Galaburda. Cambridge, MA: Harvard University Press, pp 179–192. For brilliant insights on the role of culture in the way the brain is used, see: Skoyles, Dr. John R. (1997). "Origins of Classical Greek art." Unpublished paper. <www.users.globalnet.co.uk/~skoyles/index.htm>. **17.** Without training, guidance, or positive reinforcement, newborns automatically begin to imitate their fellow humans during their first hours out of the womb. (Wyrwicka, W. (1988). "Imitative behavior. A theoretical view." *Pavlovian Journal of Biological Sciences*, July-September, p 125–31.) **18.** Fantz, R.L. (1965). "Visual perception from birth as shown by pattern selectivity." *Annals of the New York Academy of Sciences*, 118, pp 793–814; Coren, Stanley, Clare Porac & Lawrence M. Ward. (1979). *Sensation and perception*. New York: Academic Press, 1979, pp 379–380. **19.** *Op cit.*, Caporael. (1995). A baby begins imitating others when it is less than a week old. Bower, T.G.R. (1977). *A primer of infant development*. New York: W.H. Freeman, p 28. **20.** Mead, Margaret. (1977). *Sex and temperament in three primitive societies*. London: Routledge and Kegan Paul. **21.** Ekman, Paul. (1992). "Facial expressions of emotion: an old controversy and new findings." *Philosophical Transactions of the Royal Society of London. Series B: Biological Sciences*, January 29, pp 63–69; Levenson, R.W., P. Ekman & W. Friesen. (1997). "Voluntary facial action generates emotion-specific autonomic nervous system activity." *Psychophysiology*, July, pp 363–84; Ekman, Paul. (1993). "Facial expression and emotion." *American Psychologist*, April, p 384–92. **22.** Hoffman, M.L. (1981). "Is altruism part of human nature?" *Journal of Personality and Social Psychology*, 40(1), pp 121–137; Raven, Bertram H. & Jeffrey Z. Rubin. *Social Psychology*, pp 311–312. **23.** Hoffman, M.L. (1981). "Is altruism part of human nature?" *Journal of Personality and Social Psychology*, 40(1), pp 121–137; *Op cit.*, Bertram & Rubin. **24.** Bischof-Köhler, D. (1994). "Self object and interpersonal emotions. Identification of own mirror image, empathy and prosocial behavior in the 2nd year of life." *Zeitschrift fur Psychologie Mit Zeitschrift fur Angewandte Psychologie*, 202:4, pp 349–77. **25.** Hood, Bruce M., J. Douglas Willen & Jon Driver. (1998). "Adult's eyes trigger shifts of visual attention in human infants." *Psychological Science*, March, p 131–133; Terrace Herbert. (1989). "Thoughts without words." In *Mindwaves: Thoughts on intelligence, identity and consciousness*, edited by Colin Blakemore & Susan Greenfield. Oxford: Basil Blackwell, pp 128–9. **26.** Bruner, Jerome. (1986). *Actual minds, possible worlds*. Cambridge, MA: Harvard University Press, pp 60, 67–68; Frith, Uta. (1993). "Autism." *Scientific American*, June, pp 108–114. **27.** Kagan, Jerome. (1989). *Unstable ideas: Temperament, cognition and self*. Cambridge: Harvard University Press, pp 185–186. In the body of psychological literature, the effect we're discussing is called "social referencing." According to Russell, et al., "it is a well-documented ability in human infants." (Russell, C.L., K.A. Bard & L.B. Adamson. (1997). "Social referencing by young chimpanzees (*Pan troglodytes*)." *Journal of Comparative Psychology*, June, pp 185–93.) For more on social referencing in infants as young as 8.5 months old, see: Campos, J.J. (1984). "A new perspective on emotions." *Child Abuse and Neglect*, 8:2, pp 147–56. **28.** But let's not get too homocentric. Rats flock just as madly to the imitative urge. Put them with others who love a beverage that they loathe and their tastes will also change dramatically. (Galef, B.G., Jr, E.E. Whiskin & E. Bielavska. (1997). "Interaction with demonstrator rats changes observer rats' affective responses to flavors." *Journal of Comparative Psychology*, December, pp 393–8.) **29.** Kantrowitz, Barbara & Pat Wingert. (1989). "How kids learn." *Newsweek*, April 17, p 53. **30.** Condon, William S. (1986). "Communication: Rhythm and structure." *Rhythm in psychological, linguistic and musical processes*, edited by James R. Evans & Manfred Clynes. Springfield, IL: C.C. Thomas, pp 55–77; Condon, William S. (1970). "Method of micro-analysis of sound films of behavior." *Behavior Research Methods, Instruments & Computers*, 2(2), pp 51–54. **31.** Condon, William S. (1999). Personal communication. June 10. For information indicating the probability of related forms of synchrony, see: Krams, M., M.F. Rushworth, M.P. Deiber, R.S. Frackowiak, & R.E. Passingham. (1998). "The preparation, execution and suppression of copied movements in the human brain." *Experimental Brain Research*, June, pp 386–98; Lundqvist, L.O. "Facial EMG reactions to facial expressions: a case of facial emotional contagion?" *Scandinavian Journal of Psychology*, June, pp 130–41. **32.** Condon, William S. & Louis W. Sander Louis. (1974). "Neonate movement is synchronized with adult speech: Interactional participation and language acquisition." *Science*, 183(4120), pp 99–101. **33.** Hall, Edward T. (1977). *Beyond culture*. New York: Anchor Books, pp 72–77. Several others have independently arrived at similar conclusions about the ability of shared activity to bond humans. Psychologist Howard Rachlin has called the process "functional bonding," and historian William McNeill has called it "muscular bonding." (Rachlin, Howard. (1995). "Self and self-control." In *The self across psychology: Self-recognition, self-awareness, and the self concept*, p 89; McNeill, William H. (1995). *Keeping together in time: Dance and drill in human history*. Cambridge, MA, p 4.) **34.** Kelley, H.H. (1950). "The warm-cold variable in first impressions of persons." *Journal of Personality*, 18, pp 431–439; Raven, Bertram H. & Jeffrey Z. Rubin. *Social Psychology*, pp 88–89. **35.** Our susceptibility to social input is so powerful it can kill. Knowing someone who's committed suicide can increase your chances of doing yourself in by a whopping 22 thousand percent. The impulse to imitate others sweeps us along. (Malcolm, A.T. & M.P. Janisse. (1994). "Imitative suicide in a cohesive organization: observations from a case study." *Perceptual and Motor Skills*, December, Part 2, pp 1475–8; Stack, S. (1996). "The effect of the media on suicide: Evidence from Japan, 1955–1985." *Suicide and Life-threatening Behavior*, Summer, pp 132–42.) **36.** Eder, Donna & Janet Lynne Enke. (1991). "The structure of gossip: Opportunities and constraints on collective expression among adolescents." *American Sociological Review*, August, pp 494–508. **37.** Psychologist Daniel Goleman calls the family "a conglomerate mind." (Goleman, Daniel, Ph.D. (1985). *Vital lies, simple truths: The psychology of self-deception*. New York: Simon and Schuster, p 167. See also pp 165–170.) **38.** Andersen, Susan M., Inga Reznik & Serena Chen. "The self in relation to others: Motivational and cognitive underpinnings." In *The self across psychology: Self-recognition, self-awareness, and the self concept*, pp 233–275. **39.** Rubin, J.Z., F.J. Provenzano & Z. Luria. (1974). "The eye of the beholder: Parents' views on sex of newborns." *American Journal of Orthopsychiatry*, 44, pp 512–9; Raven, Bertram H. & Jeffrey Z. Rubin. *Social Psychology*, p 512. **40.** Goldberg, P.A. (1968). "Are women prejudiced against women?" *Transaction*, April, pp 28–30; Raven, Bertram H. & Jeffrey Z. Rubin. *Social Psychology*, p 518. **41.** *Webster's Revised Unabridged Dictionary* (G & C. Merriam Co., 1913, edited by Noah Porter), The DICT Development Group <www.dict.org>, downloaded June 1999. **42.** Freda is better known in his Norse incarnation as Freyr. Northern European mythology—that of the Germans, Goths, and Norse—can be confusing. Freyr has a twin sister Freyja. In some stories it is difficult to keep the two straight. Some have suggested that Freyr and Freyja represent the male and female sides of the same deity. (Carlyon, Richard. (1982). *A guide to the gods*. New York: William Morrow, pp 227–9.) **43.** Friedman, Steven Morgan. (1999). "Etymologically Speaking." <www.westegg.com/etymology/>, downloaded June 1999. **44.** Merriam-Webster, Inc. <www.m-w.com/netdict.htm>, downloaded June 1999. **45.** n.a. "feminism/terms." Version: 1.5, last modified 15 February 1993, downloaded June 11, 1999. **46.** Bruner, Jerome S. (1995). *Beyond the information given: Studies in the psychology of knowing*, pp 380–386; van Geert, Paul. (1995). "Green, red and happiness: Towards a framework for understanding emotion universals." *Culture and Psychology*, June, p 264. **47.** Bogoras, W. *The Chukchee*. New York: G.E. Stechert, 1904–1909; Bruner, Jerome S. *Beyond the information given: Studies in the psychology of knowing*, p 102–3. **48.** Diamond, Jared. (1989). "This fellow frog, name belong-him Dakwo." *Natural History,* April, pp 16–23. **49.** *Op cit.*, Caporael (1995). **50.** Stearns, Peter N. (1988). "The rise of sibling jealousy in the twentieth century." In *Emotion and social change: Toward a new psychohistory*, edited by Carol Z. Stearns & Peter N. Stearns. New York: Holmes & Meier, pp 197–209. **51.** For many examples of similar phenomena, see: Edgerton, Robert B. (1992). *Sick societies: Challenging the myth of primitive harmony*. New York: Free Press. **52.** Boorstin, Daniel J. (1985). *The discoverers: A history of man's search to know his world and himself*. New York: Vintage Books, pp 344–357.

THE NEWS MEDIA AND OTHER MANIPULATORS

What Makes Mainstream Media Mainstream
Noam Chomsky

From a talk at Z Media Institute, June 1997.

Part of the reason I write about the media is that I am interested in the whole intellectual culture, and the part of it that is easiest to study is the media.

It comes out every day. You can do a systematic investigation. You can compare yesterday's version to today's version. There is a lot of evidence about what's played up and what isn't and the way things are structured.

My impression is that the media aren't very different from scholarship or from, say, journals of intellectual opinion. There are some extra constraints, but it's not radically different. They interact, which is why people go up and back quite easily among them.

If you want to understand the media, or any other institution, you begin by asking questions about the internal institutional structure. And you ask about their setting in the broader society. How do they relate to other systems of power and authority? If you're lucky, there is an internal record from leading people that tells you what they are up to. That doesn't mean the public relations handouts, but what they say to each other about what they are up to. There is quite a lot of interesting documentation.

Those are major sources of information about the nature of the media. You want to study them the way, say, a scientist would study some complex molecule. You take a look at the structure and then make some hypothesis based on the structure as to what the media product is likely to look like. Then you investigate the media product and see how well it conforms to the hypotheses.

Virtually all work in media analysis is this last part—trying to study carefully just what the media product is and whether it conforms to obvious assumptions about the nature and structure of the media.

Well, what do you find? First of all, you find that there are different media which do different things. For example, entertainment/Hollywood, soap operas, and so on, or even most of the newspapers in the country (the overwhelming majority of them) are directed to a mass audience, not to inform them but to divert them.

There is another sector of the media, the elite media, sometimes called the agenda-setting media because they are the ones with the big resources; they set the framework in which everyone

The real mass media are basically trying to divert people.

else operates. The *New York Times*, the *Washington Post*, and a few others. Their audience is mostly privileged people.

The people who read the *New York Times* are mostly wealthy or part of what is sometimes called the political class. Many are actually involved in the systems of decision-making and control in an ongoing fashion, basically as managers of one sort or another. They can be political managers, business managers (like corporate executives and the like), doctrinal managers (like many people in the schools and universities), or other journalists who are involved in organizing the way people think and look at things.

The elite media set a framework within which others operate. For some years I used to monitor the Associated Press. It grinds out a constant flow of news. In the mid-afternoon there was a break every day with a "Notice to Editors: Tomorrow's *New York Times* is going to have the following stories on the front page." The point of that is, if you're an editor of a newspaper in Dayton, Ohio, and you don't have the resources to figure out what the news is, or you don't want to think about it anyway, this tells you what the news is. These are the stories for the quarter-page that you are going to devote to something other than local affairs or diverting your audience. These are the stories that you put there because that's what the *New York Times* tells us is what you're supposed to care about tomorrow. If you are an editor of a local newspaper you pretty much have to do that, because you don't have much else in the way of resources. If you get out of line and produce stories that the elite press doesn't like, you're likely to hear about it pretty soon. What happened recently at *San Jose Mercury News* (i.e. Gary Webb's "Dark Alliance" series about CIA complicity in the drug trade) is a dramatic example of this. So there are a lot of ways in which power plays can drive you right back into line if you move out. If you try to break the mold, you're not going to last long. That framework works pretty well, and it is understandable that it is a reflection of obvious power structures.

The real mass media are basically trying to divert people. "Let them do something else, but don't bother us (us being the people who run the show). Let them get interested in professional sports, for example. Let everybody be crazed about professional sports or sex scandals or the personalities and their problems or something like that. Anything, as long as it isn't serious. Of course, the serious stuff is for the big guys. 'We' take care of that."

What are the elite media, the agenda-setting ones? The *New York Times* and CBS, for example. Well, first of all, they are major, very profitable, corporations.

Furthermore, most of them are either linked to, or outright owned by, much bigger corporations, like General Electric, Westinghouse, and so on. They are way up at the top of the power structure of the private economy, which is a tyrannical structure. Corporations are basically tyrannies, hierarchic, controlled from above. If you don't like what they are doing, you get out. The major media are part of that system.

What about their institutional setting? Well, that's more or less the same. What they interact with and relate to is other major power centers: the government, other corporations, the universities. Because the media function in significant ways as a doctrinal system, they interact closely with the universities. Say you are a reporter writing a story on Southeast Asia or Africa, or something like that. You're supposed to go over to the university next door and find an expert who will tell you what to write, or else go to one of the foundations, like

Brookings Institute or American Enterprise Institute. They will give you the preferred version of what is happening. These outside institutions are very similar to the media.

The universities, for example, are not independent institutions. There are independent people scattered around in them (and the sciences in particular couldn't survive otherwise), but that is true of the media as well. And it's generally true of corporations. It's even true of fascist states, for that matter, to a certain extent. But the institution itself is parasitic. It's dependent on outside sources of support, and those sources of support, such as private wealth, big corporations with grants, and the government (which is so closely interlinked with corporate power that you can barely distinguish them)—they are essentially the system that the universities are in the middle of.

People within them, who don't adjust to that structure, who don't accept it and internalize it (you can't really work with it unless you internalize it, and believe it)—people who don't do that are likely to be weeded out along the way, starting from kindergarten, all the way up. There are all sorts of filtering devices to get rid of people who are a pain in the neck and think independently.

Those of you who have been through college know that the educational system is highly geared to rewarding conformity and obedience; if you don't do that, you are a troublemaker. So, it is kind of a filtering device which ends up with people who really, honestly (they aren't lying) internalize the framework of belief and attitudes of the surrounding power system in the society. The elite institutions like, say, Harvard and Princeton and the small upscale colleges, for example, are very much geared to socialization. If you go through a place like Harvard, a good deal of what goes on is a kind of socialization: teaching how to behave like a member of the upper classes, how to think the right thoughts, and so on.

I'm sure you've read George Orwell's *Animal Farm*, which he wrote in the mid-1940s. It was a satire on the Soviet Union, a totalitarian state. It was a big hit. Everybody loved it. Turns out he wrote an introduction to *Animal Farm* which wasn't published. It only appeared 30 years later. Someone found it in his papers. The introduction to *Animal Farm* was about "Literary Censorship in England," and what it says is that obviously this book is ridiculing the Soviet Union and its totalitarian structure, but free England is not all that different. We don't have the KGB on our neck, but the end result comes out pretty much the same. People who have independent ideas or who think the wrong kind of thoughts are cut out.

He talks a little, only two sentences, about the institutional structure. He asks, why does this happen? Well, one, because the press is owned by wealthy men who only want certain things to reach the public. His second observation is that when you go through the elite education system, when you go through the proper schools (Oxford, and so on), you learn that there are certain things it's not proper to say and there are certain thoughts that are not proper to have. That is the socialization role of elite institutions, and if you don't adapt to that, you're usually out. Those two sentences more or less tell the story.

When you critique the media and you say, look, here is what Anthony Lewis or somebody else is writing, and you show that it happens to be distorted in a way that is highly supportive of power systems, they get very angry. They say, quite correctly, "Nobody ever tells me what to write. I write anything I like. All this business about pressures and constraints is nonsense because I'm never under any pressure." Which is completely true, but the point is that they wouldn't be there unless they had already demonstrated that nobody has to tell them what to write because they are going to keep to the rules. If they had started off at the Metro desk and had pursued the wrong kind of stories, they never would have made it to the positions where they can now say anything they like.

The same is largely true of university faculty in the more ideological disciplines. They have been through the socialization system. Okay, you look at the structure of that whole system. What do you expect the news to be like? Well, it's not very obscure. Take the *New York Times*. It's a corporation and sells a product. The product is audiences. They don't make money when you buy the newspaper. They are happy to put it on the World Wide Web for free. They actually lose money when you buy the newspaper. The audience is the product. For the elite media, the product is privileged people, just like the people who are writing the newspapers, high-level decision-making people in society. Like other businesses, they sell their product to a market, and the market is, of course, advertisers (that is, other businesses). Whether it is television or newspapers, or whatever else, they are selling audiences. Corporations sell audiences to other corporations. In the case of the elite media, it's big businesses.

Well, what do you expect to happen? What would you predict about the nature of the media product, given that set of circumstances? What would be the null hypothesis, the kind of conjecture that you'd make assuming nothing further?

The obvious assumption is that the product of the media, what appears, what doesn't appear, the way it is slanted, will reflect the interest of the buyers and sellers, the institutions, and the power systems that are around them. If that wouldn't happen, it would be kind of a miracle.

Okay, then comes the hard work. You ask, does it work the way you predict?

Well, you can judge for yourselves. There's lots of material on this obvious hypothesis, which has been subjected to the hardest tests anybody can think of, and still stands up remarkably

> The first World War was the first time that highly organized state propaganda institutions were developed.

well. You virtually never find anything in the social sciences that so strongly supports any conclusion, which is not a big surprise, because it would be miraculous if it didn't hold up given the way the forces are operating.

The next thing you discover is that this whole topic is completely taboo. If you go to the media department at the Kennedy School of Government or Stanford, or somewhere else, and you study journalism and communications or academic political science, and so on, these questions are not likely to appear. That is, the hypothesis that anyone would come across without even knowing anything that is scarcely expressed, and the evidence bearing on it, scarcely discussed. There are some exceptions, as usual in a complex and somewhat chaotic world, but it is rather generally true. Well, you predict that, too.

If you look at the institutional structure, you would say, yeah, sure, that's likely to happen because why should these guys want to be exposed? Why should they allow critical analysis of what they are up to? The answer is, there is no reason why they should allow that and, in fact, they don't.

Again, it is not purposeful censorship. It is just that you don't make it to those positions if you haven't internalized the values and doctrines. That includes what is called "the left" as well as the right. In fact, in mainstream discussion the *New York Times* has been called "the establishment left." You're unlikely to make it through to the top unless you have been adequately socialized and trained so that there are some thoughts you just don't have, because if you did have them, you wouldn't be there. So you have a second order of prediction which is that the first order of prediction is not allowed into the discussion—again, with a scattering of exceptions, important ones.

The last thing to look at is the doctrinal framework in which this proceeds. Do people at high levels in the information system, including the media and advertising and academic political science and so on, do these people have a picture of what ought to happen when they are writing for each other, not when they are making graduation speeches? When you make a commencement speech, it's pretty words and stuff. But when they are writing for one another, what do these people say?

There are several categories to look at. One is the public relations industry, you know, the main business propaganda industry. So what are the leaders of the PR industry saying internally? Second place to look is at what are called public intellectuals, big thinkers, people who write the op-eds and that sort of thing. The people who write impressive books about the nature of democracy and that sort of business. What do they say? The third place to look is the academic sector, particularly that part that has been concerned with communications and information, much of which has been a branch of political science for many years.

So, look at these categories and see what leading figures write about these matters. The basic line (I'm partly quoting) is that the general population are "ignorant and meddlesome outsiders." We have to keep them out of the public arena because they are too stupid, and if they get involved they will just make trouble. Their job is to be "spectators," not "participants." They are allowed to vote every once in a while, pick out one of us smart guys. But then they are supposed to go home and do something else like watch football or whatever it may be. But the "ignorant and meddlesome outsiders" have to be observers, not participants. The participants are what are called the

"responsible men" and, of course, the writer is always one of them. You never ask the question, why am I a "responsible man" and somebody else, say Eugene Debs, is in jail? The answer is pretty obvious. It's because you are obedient and subordinate to power and that other person may be independent, and so on.

But you don't ask, of course. So there are the smart guys who are supposed to run the show and the rest of them are supposed to be out, and we should not succumb to (I'm quoting from an academic article) "democratic dogmatisms about men being the best judges of their own interest." They are not. They are terrible judges of their own interests so we have do it for them for their own benefit.

Actually, it is very similar to Leninism. We do things for you, and we are doing it in the interest of everyone, and so on. I suspect that's part of the reason why it's been so easy historically for people to shift up and back from being sort of enthusiastic Stalinists to being big supporters of US power. People switch very quickly from one position to the other, and my suspicion is that it's because basically it is the same position. You're not making much of a switch. You're just making a different estimate of where power lies. One point you think it's here, another point you think it's there. You take the same position.

How did all this evolve? It has an interesting history. A lot of it comes out of the first World War, which is a big turning point. It changed the position of the United States in the world considerably. In the eighteenth century the US was already the richest place in the world. The quality of life, health, and longevity was not achieved by the upper classes in Britain until the early twentieth century, let alone anybody else in the world. The US was extraordinarily wealthy, with huge advantages, and, by the end of the nineteenth century, it had by far the biggest economy in the world. But it was not a big player on the world scene. US power extended to the Caribbean Islands, parts of the Pacific, but not much farther.

During the first World War, the relations changed. And they changed more dramatically during the second World War. After the second World War the US more or less took over the world. But after the first World War there was already a change, and the US shifted from being a debtor to a creditor nation. It

By manufacturing consent, you can overcome the fact that formally a lot of people have the right to vote.

wasn't a huge actor in the international arena, like Britain, but it became a substantial force in the world for the first time. That was one change, but there were other changes.

The first World War was the first time that highly organized state propaganda institutions were developed. The British had a Ministry of Information, and they really needed it because they had to get the US into the war or else they were in bad trouble. The Ministry of Information was mainly geared to sending propaganda, including fabrications about "Hun" atrocities, and so on. They were targeting American intellectuals on the reasonable assumption that these are the people who are most gullible and most likely to believe propaganda. They are also the ones that disseminate it through their own system. So it was mostly geared to American intellectuals, and it worked very well. The British Ministry of Information documents (a lot have been released) show their goal was, as they put it, to control the thought of the entire world—which was a minor goal—but mainly the US. They didn't care much what people thought in India. This Ministry of Information was extremely successful in deluding leading American intellectuals, and was very proud of that. Properly so, it saved their lives. They would probably have lost the first World War otherwise.

In the US there was a counterpart. Woodrow Wilson was elected in 1916 on an anti-war platform. The US was a very pacifist country. It has always been. People don't want to go fight foreign wars. The country was very much opposed to the first World War, and Wilson was, in fact, elected on an anti-war position. "Peace without victory" was the slogan. But he decided to go to war. So the question was, how do you get a pacifist population to become raving anti-German lunatics so they

When you go to college, you don't read the classics about how to control people's minds.

want to go kill all the Germans? That requires propaganda. So they set up the first and really only major state propaganda agency in US history. The Committee on Public Information, it was called (nice Orwellian title); it was also called the Creel Commission. The guy who ran it was named Creel. The task of this commission was to propagandize the population into jingoist hysteria. It worked incredibly well. Within a few months the US was able to go to war.

A lot of people were impressed by these achievements. One person impressed, and this had some implications for the

future, was Hitler. He concluded, with some justification, that Germany lost the first World War because it lost the propaganda battle. They could not begin to compete with British and American propaganda, which absolutely overwhelmed them. He pledges that next time around they'll have their own propaganda system, which they did during the second World War.

More important for us, the American business community was also very impressed with the propaganda effort. They had a problem at that time. The country was becoming formally more democratic. A lot more people were able to vote and that sort of thing. The country was becoming wealthier and more people could participate and a lot of new immigrants were coming in, and so on. So what do you do? It's going to be harder to run things as a private club.

Therefore, obviously, you have to control what people think. There had been public relations specialists, but there was never a public relations industry. There was a guy hired to make Rockefeller's image look prettier and that sort of thing. But the huge public relations industry, which is a US invention and a monstrous industry, came out of the first World War. The leading figures were people in the Creel Commission. In fact, the main one, Edward Bernays, comes right out of the Creel Commission. He has a book that came out a few years afterwards called *Propaganda*, which became kind of a manual for the rising Public Relations industry, in which he was a prominent figure. The term "propaganda," incidentally, did not have negative connotations in those days.

It was during the second World War that the term became taboo because it was connected with Germany and all those bad things. But in this period, the term "propaganda" just meant information or something like that.

So he wrote a book called *Propaganda* in the late 1920s. He explains that he is applying the lessons of the first World War. The propaganda system of the first World War and this commission that he was part of showed, he says, that it is possible to "regiment the public mind every bit as much as an army regiments their bodies." These new techniques of regimentation of minds, he said, had to be used by the "intelligent minorities" in order to make sure that the slobs stay on the right course. We can do it now because we have these new techniques.

This was an important manual of the public relations industry.

Bernays was a kind of guru. He was an authentic Roosevelt/Kennedy liberal. He also engineered the public relations effort behind the US-backed coup which overthrew the democratic government of Guatemala.

His major coup, the one that really propelled him into fame in the late 1920s, was getting women to smoke. Women didn't smoke in those days, and he ran huge campaigns for Chesterfield. You know all the techniques—models and movie stars with cigarettes coming out of their mouths, symbolizing the free, liberated modern woman. He got enormous praise for that. So he became a leading figure of the industry, and his book was an important manual.

Another member of the Creel Commission was Walter Lippmann, the most respected figure in American journalism for about half a century (I mean serious American journalism, serious think pieces). He also wrote what are called progressive essays on democracy, regarded as progressive back in the 1920s. He was, again, applying the lessons of propaganda very explicitly. He says there is a new art in democracy called "manufacture of consent." That is his phrase. Edward Herman and I borrowed it for our book, but it comes from Lippmann. So, he says, there is this new art in the practice of democracy, "manufacture of consent." By manufacturing consent, you can overcome the fact that formally a lot of people have the right to vote. We can make it irrelevant because we can manufacture consent and make sure that their choices and attitudes will be structured in such a way that they will do what we tell them, even if they have a formal way to participate. So we'll have a real democracy. It will work properly. That's applying the lessons of the propaganda agency.

Academic social science and political science come out of the same kind of thinking. One of the founders of the field of communications in academic political science is Harold Lasswell. One of his first achievements was a study of propaganda. Writing in an Encyclopedia of Social Science he says, very frankly, the things I was quoting before about not succumbing to "democratic dogmatisms." That comes from academic political science (Lasswell and others).

Again, drawing the lessons from the war-time experience, political parties drew the same lessons, especially the conservative party in England. Their documents from the period, just being released, show they also recognized the achievements of the British Ministry of Information. They recognized that the country was getting more democratized and it wouldn't be a private men's club. So the conclusion was, as they put it, politics has to become political warfare, applying the mechanisms of propaganda that worked so brilliantly during the first World War towards controlling people's thoughts. That's the doctrinal side, and it coincides with the institutional structure.

It strengthens the predictions about the way the thing should work. And the predictions are well confirmed. But these conclusions, also, are not supposed to be discussed. This is all now part of mainstream literature, but it is only for people on the inside. When you go to college, you don't read the classics about how to control people's minds.

Just like you don't read what James Madison said during the constitutional convention about how the main goal of the new system has to be "to protect the minority of the opulent against the majority," and has to be designed so that it achieves that end. This is the founding of the constitutional system, but it is scarcely studied. You can't even find it in the academic scholarship unless you look hard.

That is roughly the picture, as I see it, of the way the system is institutionally, the doctrines that lie behind it, the way it comes out. There is another part directed to the "ignorant and meddlesome outsiders." That is mainly using diversion of one kind or another. From that, I think, you can predict what you would expect to find.

We Were Silenced by the Drums of War

Jeff Cohen

September 11th made 2001 a defining year in America's history. But 2002 may have been the strangest. It began with all eyes on Osama bin Laden and ended with Osama bin Forgotten—as the White House turned its attention to Iraq. Bush's January 2003 State of the Union speech mentioned Saddam Hussein seventeen times, but bin Laden not once.

Networks that normally cherished shouting matches were opting for discussions of harmonious unanimity.

I was hired by the cable news channel MSNBC seven months after the 9/11 attacks. My job was twofold: on-air pundit and senior producer of MSNBC's new primetime show hosted by Phil Donahue. Since I'd founded the media-watch group FAIR in the 1980s and had been a vociferous critic of TV news, taking this fulltime job inside the belly of the corporate media beast—at a channel owned by General Electric—was an Alice-in-Wonderland experience.

As it turned out, everything about my tenure at MSNBC occurred in the context of the ever-intensifying war drums over Iraq. The drums grew louder as D-Day approached, until the din became so deafening that rational journalistic thinking could not occur. Three weeks before the Iraq invasion, MSNBC suits terminated *Donahue*. At the time it was cancelled, it was their most-watched program.

For nineteen weeks, I had appeared on MSNBC in on-air debates almost every afternoon—the last weeks heavily focused on Iraq. I adamantly opposed an invasion. I warned that it would "undermine our coalition with Muslim and Arab countries that we need to fight Al Qaeda" and would lead to a "quagmire."

In October 2002, my debate segments were terminated. There was no room for me after MSNBC launched *Countdown: Iraq*—a daily show that seemed more keen on glamorizing a potential war than scrutinizing or debating it. The show featured retired colonels and generals resembling boys with war toys as they used props, maps, and glitzy graphics to spin invasion scenarios. They reminded me of pumped-up ex-football players doing pre-game analysis.

It was excruciating to be silenced while myth and misinformation went unchallenged. Military analysts typically appeared unopposed; they were presented as neutral experts, not advocates. But their closeness to the Pentagon often obstructed independent, skeptical analysis.

When Hans Blix led UN weapons inspectors back into Iraq in November 2002 after a four-year absence, the host of *Countdown: Iraq* asked an MSNBC military analyst, "What's the buzz from the Pentagon about Hans Blix?" The retired colonel declared that Blix was considered "something like the Inspector Clouseau of the weapons of mass destruction

It's telling that in the run-up to the war, no American TV network hired any on-air analysts from among the experts who questioned White House WMD claims.

inspection program…who will only remember the last thing he was told—and that he's very malleable."

Retired General Barry McCaffrey (Bill Clinton's "drug czar") was the star military analyst on NBC and MSNBC—a hawk who pushed for an invasion every chance he got. After the war began, McCaffrey crowed, "Thank God for the Abrams tank and the Bradley fighting vehicle." Unknown to viewers, McCaffrey sat on the board of a military contractor that pocketed millions for doing God's work on the Abrams and Bradley.

Soon after the Iraq invasion, CNN news president Eason Jordan admitted that his network's military analysts were government-approved:

> I went to the Pentagon myself several times before the war started. I met with important people there and said, for instance, at CNN, here are the generals we're thinking of retaining to advise us on the air and off about the war. And we got a big thumbs-up on all of them. That was important.

Besides military analysts, each news network featured "weapons experts"—usually without opposition or balance—to discuss the main justification for war: Iraq's alleged weapons of mass destruction. The problem for US media was that there was wide disagreement among WMD experts, with many skeptical about an Iraqi threat. The problem only worsened when UN inspectors returned and could not confirm any of the US claims.

How did MSNBC and other networks solve the problem? Management favored experts who backed the Bush view—and hired several of them as paid analysts. Networks that

MSNBC suits decreed that if we booked one guest who was anti-war on Iraq, we needed two who were pro-war.

normally cherished shouting matches were opting for discussions of harmonious unanimity. This made for dull, predictable TV. It also helped lead our nation to war, based on false premises.

CNN and other outlets featured David Albright, a former UN inspector who repeatedly asserted before the war that Iraq possessed chemical and biological weapons. Asked later about his assertions, Albright pointed his finger at the White

Soon after the Iraq invasion, CNN news president Eason Jordan admitted that his network's military analysts were government-approved.

House: "I certainly accepted the administration claims on chemical and biological weapons. I figured they were telling the truth."

Another CNN expert was former CIA analyst Ken Pollack, who fervently pushed for war. He warned Oprah's viewers that Saddam could use WMDs against the US homeland and was "building new capabilities as fast as he can." Later, he blamed his errant remarks about Iraq's WMDs on a "consensus" in the intelligence community: "That was not me making that claim; that was me parroting the claims of so-called experts."

Not every weapons expert had been wrong. Take ex-Marine and former UN inspector Scott Ritter. In the last months of 2002, he told any audience or journalist who would hear him that Iraqi WMDs represented no threat to our country. "Send in the inspectors," urged Ritter. "Don't send in the Marines."

It's telling that in the run-up to the war, no American TV network hired any on-air analysts from among the experts who questioned White House WMD claims. None would hire Ritter.

Inside MSNBC in 2002, Ritter was the target of a smear that he was receiving covert funds from Saddam Hussein's government. The slur was obviously aimed at reducing the media appearances of one of the most articulate, informed critics of an invasion. It surfaced like clockwork at MSNBC when we sought to book Ritter as a guest on *Donahue*.

The irony is that at MSNBC, I regularly debated an analyst who was soon to become a recipient of covert government funds. The covert funder was the Bush administration. I'm talking about pundit Armstrong Williams, who pocketed nearly a quarter of a million dollars to promote Bush's No Child Left Behind Act. At the time, I had no inkling of Bush's No *Pundit* Left Behind program, which was apparently more fully funded than No Child Left Behind.

After we featured Ramsey Clark as a *Donahue* guest—he

argued against invading Iraq—we were told it wasn't supposed to happen. MSNBC bosses had the former US Attorney General on some sort of network blacklist.

As the Iraq invasion neared, MSNBC suits turned the screws even tighter on *Donahue*. They decreed that if we booked one guest who was anti-war on Iraq, we needed two who were pro-war. If we booked two guests on the left, we needed three on the right. At one staff meeting, a producer proposed booking Michael Moore and was told she'd need three right-wingers for political balance.

After the war began, Ret. Gen. McCaffrey crowed, "Thank God for the Abrams tank and the Bradley fighting vehicle." Unknown to viewers, McCaffrey sat on the board of a military contractor that pocketed millions for doing God's work on the Abrams and Bradley.

I thought about proposing Noam Chomsky as a guest, but our stage couldn't accommodate the 28 right-wingers we would have needed for balance.

It's says a lot about TV news that people like Phil Donahue, who correctly questioned the Iraq war, were banished from the system. Yet I'm unaware of a single TV executive, host, pundit, or "expert" who lost his or her job for getting such a huge story so totally wrong, as almost all of them did. Indeed, many were promoted.

Americans like to say that they favor meritocracy—where one's advancement is based on ability or achievement. What I found inside today's corporate media is the opposite. The dictionary has a word for it: *kakistocracy*. Literally, it means "rule by the worst"—where the least qualified and most unprincipled rise to the top. In such a media system, lethal myths and lies will flourish.

The Puppets of Pandemonium
Sleaze and Sloth in the Media Elite
Howard Bloom

Everything you've ever heard about pack journalism is true. In fact, it's an understatement. Though journalists pride themselves on their intellectual independence, they are neither very intellectual nor even marginally independent. They are animals. In fact, they operate on the same herd instincts that guide ants, hoofed mammals, and numerous other social creatures.

In 1827, well before the sciences of ethology and sociobiology had been invented, historian and essayist Thomas Carlyle said that the critics of his day were like sheep. Put your walking stick at knee level across the path as a lead sheep goes by, wrote the sage, and the beast will jump over it. Remove the stick, and each following sheep in line will jump at precisely the same spot...even though there's no longer anything to jump over! Things haven't changed much since then. If the key critics at the *New York Times*, the *Village Voice*, and *Rolling Stone* fall in love with a musical artist, every other critic in the country will follow

My fellow publicists liked riding waves. I preferred the more difficult task of making them happen.

their lead. On the other hand, if these lead sheep say an artist is worthless, every other woolly-minded critic from Portland to Peoria will miraculously draw the same conclusion.

When I was out on tour with ZZ Top in 1976, I remember sitting at one of the group's concerts between the critics from Minneapolis' two major dailies. At the time, I was also handling a group called Dr. Buzzard's Original Savannah Band. The lead sheep in the press hated ZZ Top, but they loved Dr. Buzzard. So it had been fairly easy to land major features lauding the Original Savannah Band in the *New York Times* and the *Village Voice* during the same week. As I sat between Minneapolis' two finest models of journalistic integrity and independent judgment in the moments before the lights dimmed and ZZ Top hit the stage, one was reading the *New York Times'* article on Dr. Buzzard and the other was reading

the *Voice*'s. Both were hungrily snorfing up the latest hints on how they should feel about the music of the month.

Not surprisingly, when the concert ended and the duo returned to their typewriters, they cranked out copy with identical judgments. ZZ Top, whose music the *Village Voice*, in a blaring headline, had recently said sounded like "hammered shit," was roundly panned, despite the fact that both critics admitted grudgingly in print that via some collective descent into tastelessness, the crowd had gone wild. Then both turned their attention to slaveringly sycophantic paeans to Dr. Buzzard, thus echoing the opinions they'd absorbed from their fashionable reading earlier in the evening.

If I sound like I despise such attitudes, it's because I do. An appalling number of the acts the press (and the publicists who fawn over journalistic dictates) dislikes have tremendous validity. I always felt it was my job to do for erring writers what Edmund Wilson, the literary critic, had done for me. When I was a teenager, I couldn't make head nor tails of T.S. Eliot. His poetry utterly baffled me. So I came to the conclusion that Eliot's work was an elaborate hoax, a pastiche of devices designed to fool the pretentious into thinking that if they admitted a failure to understand all of his erudite references, they'd make themselves look like fools.

Then along came Edmund Wilson (or at least one of his books), and gave me the perceptual key that unlocked Eliot's poetry. Now that I finally understood the stuff, I fell in love with it. What's more, I started giving public readings of Eliot's work, and "The Love Song of J. Alfred Prufrock" became one of the biggest influences on my 16-year-old life.

My task as a publicist was to provide similar perceptual keys. It was to read every lyric an artist had ever written, listen to his or her album 20 or 30 times, and immerse myself in his work until I understood its merit. Then my job was to impart that understanding to a hostile press. In other words, my fellow publicists liked riding waves. I preferred the more difficult task of making new tsunamis.

What's more, I felt my job was to act as a surrogate journalist. I studied everything that had ever been written (quite literally) about a new client in English (or sometimes French, my only other tongue), then subjected the artist to an interview that lasted anywhere from six hours to three days. My goal was to find the interesting stories, the things that would amaze, the facts that would make sense out of the music, the angles that would make for unrejectable feature stories, and the tales that would give some insight into the hidden emotional and biographical sources of the performer's creations.

After one of these interviews, John Mellencamp, a natural-born talker, was literally so exhausted that he couldn't croak more than a sentence or two to his wife and fell asleep in the living room chair he'd been sitting in through the entire interview (we'd been going since ten in the morning, and it was now four in the afternoon).

At any rate, this may explain why it was not Dr. Buzzard's Original Savannah Band—the group with the automatic popularity—that I spent six years working on, but ZZ Top, the band the press either refused to write about altogether or put down with some variation of Robert (*Village Voice*) Christgau's "hammered shit" verdict. It took three years to turn the press around. Creating that about-face involved a process I used to call "perceptual engineering." ZZ Top had authenticity and validity out the kazoo. My task was to

While millions were being killed in the Soviet Union, Western journalists participated in the cover-up.

do everything in my power to reverse the direction of the herd's stampede and to make the critics see the substance they had overlooked. For the first few years, the press continued to sneer whenever the group's name came up. But gradually, I got a few lead sheep by the horns (do sheep have horns?) and turned them around. The rest of the herd followed. One result: For the next ten years, ZZ Top became one of the few bands of its genre to command genuine, unadulterated press respect.

Eventually, the group didn't need me anymore. They don't to this day. The press is now ZZ Top's best publicist. Say something nasty at a press party about this band, and those in the

know will turn around and snarl, forgetting that over a decade ago they would have growled if you'd even confessed to listening to one of the Texas band's LPs.

■ ■ ■ ■ ■ ■ ■ ■ ■ ■

Public relations taught me a good deal more about why facts were not, after all, what a good reporter wanted. He wanted a story that would either titillate his audience, fit his own clique's political prejudices, or replicate a piece of reportage he'd read somewhere else.

If you really want to have your blood curdled, ask for the tale of the day that two members of the paparazzi, using a fast car, chased Michael Jackson's van down a crowded highway, jumped a divider, raced at 60 miles an hour against traffic on a two-way highway, thus endangering lives, then jumped the divider again and spun at a ninety-degree angle, blocking the highway and nearly causing Jackson's van to crash. The photographers exited their vehicle, cameras in hand, smugly thinking they'd cornered Jackson and would get a highly prized photo. They didn't show any identification and could easily have been nut jobs attempting to pull what was threatened in a large pile of daily mail Jackson received—an assassination.

Hence, Jackson's security guards—LAPD officers on leave—exited the van, which had been forced to a screeching halt in mid-highway. Not knowing what they were up against, one of the guards armed himself with a truck iron. Seeing this weapon, one of the photographers (this is not a joke or exaggeration) pulled a gun. Then the two photographers hightailed it to a telephone, called their editor at the New York *Daily News*, and reported that they'd been threatened for no reason by Michael Jackson's bodyguards. The editor then prepared a front-page headline story about the violent way in which Michael Jackson's toughs had just manhandled innocent press folk. It was on its way to press.

I did some quick research (not easy on a Sunday afternoon), found out that the photographer who had waved his firearm had been arrested on two felony charges for similar behavior, got on the phone, pried the paper's publisher from a golf course, and gave him the real details of the story. It took two hours of threatening the man with the nasty facts to convince the publisher to yank the story. On normal occasions there is no one to stop a falsified tale of this nature from hitting the headline of a publication thirsting for tabloid blood.

I suspect a similar race to avoid a pack of rabid paparazzi was in full sprint the night Princess Di was killed in a car crash.

■ ■ ■ ■ ■ ■ ■ ■ ■ ■

That these principles of press misconduct are regularly applied in the world of pop music doesn't really matter much. It will have hardly any effect on the fate of the world. But the same principles at work in the field of politics have wreaked havoc. In fact, they made the media one of the most egregious collaborators in mass murder from beginning to end of the twentieth century.

While millions were being killed in the Soviet Union, Western journalists participated in the cover-up. Walter Durante of the *New York Times*, who was supplied by the People's Government with a luxurious apartment in Moscow and a good supply of caviar, said nothing about Stalin's murderous rampage. Reporting the truth might have endangered his cozy relationship with the Soviet authorities. Hundreds of other journalists visited the Soviet Union without reporting on the slaughter. Lincoln Steffens, an influential American newspaperman, said: "I have seen the future and it works." This didn't fit the facts, but it did fit Steffens' political preconceptions. He was an admirer of one of the bloodiest of all the Marxist Revolutionaries—Leon Trotsky. Writers with similarly idealistic beliefs tried to

Only one page on the Lebanese atrocities appeared in the *New York Times* during a four-year period.

give the impression that while the West was decomposing, the Soviet Union was showing the way to a brave new world.

More than mere idealism was involved. Writers were determined to remain politically fashionable. They didn't want to be snubbed by their peers. After all, the bright lights of high culture were pro-Soviet. George Bernard Shaw had gone to the Soviet Union and had said it was ushering in a thousand bright tomorrows. He'd read his own dreams into this land of horror. Critic Edmund Wilson, the man who'd opened my eyes to T.S. Eliot, had said the death chamber of the Soviet state was "a moral sanctuary where the light never stops shining." Writers

who attempted to tell the truth were viciously attacked as enemies of progressive humanitarianism. Meanwhile, shielded by a dishonest Western press, Soviet authorities killed over 25 million men, women, and children—shooting, starving, torturing, or working them to death.

Now the press is doing it again. This time in its coverage of Israel's showdown with the Islamic world. In 1989, when the offices of *Omni* magazine were picketed by Arabs for four days because of an article I'd written, I was forced to dive into Jewish issues. I discovered, to my horror, that vast areas of fact were being violently distorted by the media in a subtly anti-Semitic manner, and that no one was getting the truth out.

Take the following instance. In the early 1970s, the Palestine Liberation Organization had created so much havoc in Lebanon that Jordan's non-Palestinian Hashemite government decided to throw the PLO out.

The PLO moved its operations to southern Lebanon, where the Islamic population welcomed the Organization's members as brothers. But the PLO were not in a brotherly mood. They turned their visit into a military occupation, confiscating Lebanese homes and autos, raping Lebanese girls, and lining up groups of Lebanese who didn't acquiesce quickly enough, then machine-gunning them to death.

The PLO was even harsher to Lebanon's 2,000-year-old Christian population. Using Soviet-supplied heavy artillery, the PLO virtually leveled two Christian cities, Sidon and Tyre, and carried out massacres in smaller Christian villages. Only one page on the Lebanese atrocities appeared in the *New York Times* during a four-year period. No articles whatsoever showed up in the *Times* of London.

Why didn't the press cover any of this? You can infer some of the reasons from the comments on press behavior I mentioned above. For one thing, there's the slavish herd impulse that drives the press (see Evelyn Waugh's brilliant novel *Scoop* for a satirical view of the press at work as Waugh saw it when he was covering Mussolini's expected invasion of Ethiopia in 1936). It had become chic among media types to run away from Israel and into the arms of the Arabs. For another, there's the unerring tendency of the press to make the cause of mass murderers politically fashionable. And finally, there's the fact that the PLO had done its best to make sure it got every story covered its own way.

Yasir Arafat's kindly organization killed six Western journalists who strayed from the PLO line. Yasir's boys took an "uncooperative" Lebanese newspaper publisher captive, dismembered him one joint at a time, and sent a piece of the corpse to each of the Beirut foreign press corps with a photo of the man being tortured alive. The message was self-explanatory.

The Associated Press (AP), United Press International (UPI), and the major American newspapers had long been frantic to maintain a foothold in Beirut. After all, Syria, Iraq, and most of the other Arab countries wouldn't let their correspondents in. Beirut was their only toehold in the Arab world. So each outlet bargained sycophantically with the PLO. They promised not to publish stories on PLO atrocities—including the military seizure of southern Lebanon. The major news organizations submitted credentials on all journalists sent to the area for PLO approval. They agreed to headquarter their reporters in a PLO-controlled hotel. And they let the PLO assign a "guide"—that is, a censor, watchdog, and feeder of disinformation—to each writer. Within a short amount of time, only PLO sympathizers were covering Middle Eastern news.

In the early 1980s, Israel sent forces into Lebanon. Every 24 hours or so, the PLO threw a conference at which it rolled out its version of the day's events. The press dutifully printed what it had been given. PLO spokesmen handed out photos of Israeli tanks rolling through the two Christian cities the PLO had leveled several years earlier with captions "explaining" that the PLO-caused damage clearly visible in the pictures had been inflicted by the Israelis. The press printed these distortions as fact.

The PLO distributed photos of a Beirut infant wrapped in bandages with a caption declaring that the baby had been burned over 75 percent of its body by Israeli shelling. Most major newspapers ran the story on page one. President Reagan was so moved that he kept the picture on his desk for days. Later, UPI was forced to issue a retraction. It turned out that the PLO press release accompanying the photos had contained several minor inaccuracies. The child had been injured not by an Israeli shell but by a PLO rocket, and 75 percent of the baby's body had not been burned; the infant had suffered a sprained ankle. The PLO had been aware of these facts before it ever wrote up its caption.

But pictures are what counts. No one registered the correction. Everyone remembered the mislabeled image.

By sifting through tens of thousands of pages of information—including ten years' worth of the *New York Times* and the *Times* of London—by digging up some very obscure books, and by working my way through a maze of little-known experts, I found that the Arab countries have a massive campaign of media and press manipulation at work in the United States. They've endowed university chairs from coast to coast to give academic credibility to their spokesmen. One result: When the

The Israel lobby spends a penny per year for every man, woman, and child in America. That's a lot of pennies. How much does the Islam lobby spend? $13.13 for every American man, woman, and child.

Ayatollah called for the death of Salman Rushdie in 1989, the head of UCLA's Middle East studies program said he'd be happy to fire the gun himself. So the Middle East "experts" interviewed everywhere from the *Washington Post* to PBS' *Newshour* have an increasing tendency to speak up on the Arab side, defending gross distortions as gospel truths.

In addition, the Arabs pull strings in Washington through top-ranking firms like Bechtel and Aramco. Bechtel, in fact, used its military contacts to obtain top-secret US surveillance photos of Israel's border deployments before the 1948 war of liberation and passed them to the Saudis. In addition, companies like Ford, General Electric, and numerous other lobbies woo the press actively on behalf of the Arabs under the umbrella of the Arab American Chamber of Commerce.

Meanwhile, journalists shout loudly about the Israel lobby, while pretending that an Islamic lobby dwarfing it in size and resources does not exist. When the Iranian government—owned English-language global TV news channel Press-TV asked me to appear in 2008 to discuss the controversy over John Mearsheimer and Stephen Walt's 2006 book *The Israel Lobby*, I researched the subject and made a discovery that stunned me. The Israel lobby spends a penny per year for every man, woman, and child in America. That's a lot of pennies. How much does the Islam lobby spend? $13.13 for every American man, woman, and child. Walk into your corner candy store with a penny and how much can you buy? Now walk in with $13.13 and see what you can buy. Washington is a candy store. So is the press.

The Islam lobby is supported by the budgets of 57 Islamic nations with a total population of roughly 1.5 billion. The Israel lobby is supported by a total world population of 13 million Jews. Yes, there are 1,200 Muslims for every Jew on this planet. From the propaganda, you'd imagine it's the other way around.

The treasuries of many of the Islamic nations funding the Islam lobby are pumped by oil money. And it shows. Just one of the nations supporting the Islam lobby, Saudi Arabia, has spent close to $80 billion since 1970 to bring its extremist form of Islam—Wahabism—to the world. A lot of this money has been spent to deceive the West with what Hussein Ibish, former PR Director of the American-Arab Anti-Discrimination Committee and Senior Fellow at another organization supported by the Islam lobby—the American Task Force on Palestine—calls "sophistry"—arguments that cloak extremist Islam in the Western vocabulary of human rights. Has this PR onslaught worked? The result is stunning.

"I found that I was more likely to get on the CBS *Evening News* with a black militant talking the language of 'Burn, baby burn!' than with moderates appealing for a Marshall Plan for the ghetto."

First of all, the campaign has succeeded in hushing up the very existence of the Islam lobby. But there's more.

Until 1948, more Jews than Arabs lived in Baghdad, yet no reporter champions the rights of Baghdad's Jewish refugees. 800,000 Jews fled Arab countries in which their families had lived for centuries—sometimes for millennia—with only the clothing on their backs, yet the press never writes about them. And many of the Palestinian refugees the media are so concerned for are not Palestinians at all. The United Nations Relief and Works Agency for Palestinian Refugees in the Near East was long ago pressured into defining as "Palestinian" any Arab who had lived in Palestine for a minimum of two years.

Yet the press has adopted the slogan, "Land for peace." Israel has given up the land of Gaza. But no Arab country has offered genuine peace. For decades, none talked seriously about stopping the boycott of Israel, which in terms of international law constituted an act of war. Few have offered to drop their official state of war against Israel. And none has ceased the rhetoric in its official newspapers, calling for or implying the need for the annihilation of Israel, the genocidal destruction of Israel's citizens, and, in some cases, the elimination of worldwide Jewry.

Just as in the case of Stalin's Soviet Union and Mao's China, the media has chosen sides. And the side it likes the best is that of the mass murderers.

■ ■ ■ ■ ■ ■ ■ ■ ■ ■

In 1964, while writing a position paper on the Viet Nam war for a congressional candidate in Buffalo, NY, I reviewed a tremendous percentage of the material being written on the war in Viet Nam at the time—everything from articles in *Time* and *Newsweek* to the speeches of the President and his leading cabinet members. I turned vehemently against our participation in the bloodbath. It wasn't until 26 years later, while reading a novel by a South Korean who'd participated in the war—an author whose moral stance was neutral and whose work was published by a house whose owners were as much against the war as I had been—that I learned the Viet Cong had regularly enforced discipline in "liberated" villages by tying recalcitrant families—men, women, and children—to kegs of dynamite and blowing them up in the town square as a lesson to anyone else who might disagree with the new form of Viet Cong freedom. Somehow the American and French press—which I'd also followed fairly carefully—were diligent in their reporting of American atrocities. But the atrocities of the Viet Cong were airbrushed out of existence. And my impression these days is that the Viet Cong's outrages were the worse of the two.

■ ■ ■ ■ ■ ■ ■ ■ ■ ■

Print journalists have traditionally been accomplices in mass violence. Television journalists have gone a step further; they have become instigators of violence. Highly respected former CBS reporter and Senior News Analyst for National Public Radio Daniel Schorr, who started his career with Edward R. Murrow and reported on everything from the Soviets and the CIA to Watergate, confesses:

> [M]ost of us in television understood, but did not like to think about, the symbiotic relationship between our medium and violence…. In the mid-Nineteen Sixties, covering urban unrest for CBS, I perceived that television placed a premium on violence and the threat of violence. I found that I was more likely to get on the *CBS Evening News* with a black militant talking the language of 'Burn, baby burn!' than with moderates appealing for a Marshall Plan for the ghetto. So, I spent a lot of time interviewing militants like Stokely Carmichael and H. Rapp Brown.
>
> In early February 1968, the Reverend Martin Luther King Jr. came to Washington to announce plans for a "poor people's march" on Washington in the Spring. It was envisaged as a challenge to America's social conscience at a time when the Vietnam War was escalating. The civil rights community was sharply divided over whether the campaign should be completely peaceful or resort to disruptive action, like unlicensed demonstrations and blocking the bridges into the capitol. Dr. King was having trouble sustaining his policy on nonviolence. On February 6, the evening before his planned news conference, the civil rights leader expressed his despair to a rally, "I can't lose hope, because when you lose hope, you die." Only dimly aware of the pressures on Dr. King, I came to his news conference with a CBS camera crew prepared to do what TV reporters do—get the most threatening sound bite I could in order to insure a place on the *Evening News* lineup. I succeeded in eliciting from him phrases on the possibility of "disruptive protest" directed at the Johnson Administration and Congress.
>
> As I waited for my camera crew to pack up, I noticed that Dr. King remained seated behind a table in an almost-empty room, looking depressed. Approaching

> him, I asked why he seemed so morose. "Because of you," he said, "and because of your colleagues in television. You try to provoke me to threaten violence, and if I don't then you will put on television those who do. By putting them on television, you elect them our leaders. And, if there is violence, will you think of your part in bringing it about?" I was shaken, but not enough to keep me from excerpting the news conference film from the evening news…. I never saw Dr. King again. Less than two months later, he was assassinated."[1]

■ ■ ■ ■ ■ ■ ■ ■ ■ ■

Jonathan Swift, the author of *Gulliver's Travels*, was an early pioneer of the kind of not-so-subtle moral corruption of the press that I constantly bumped my nose against during my fifteen years working with journalists. Swift came along at just the time when coffee had been introduced to London. The stuff became a rage and made men unbelievably jumpy and talkative. So they gathered to work off their energies by gossiping in a hot new form of eatery (or drinkery)—the coffeehouse. Out of the coffeehouses and the men who entered them to swap political and economic tidbits came another pair of fashionable new items— the newspaper and the magazine. (The news broadsheet had already been around for nearly 200 years, as had the pamphlet, which Christopher Columbus used to good effect after he got back from America, and which Martin Luther tossed around like dynamite to set off a cultural avalanche in Europe.)

At any rate, Swift made it from Ireland to London just in time to cash in on the power of the newborn press to sway public opinion and to make or break political careers. One of the most influential politicians when Swift arrived was Robert Walpole, First Earl of Orford—a man accustomed to doing things in the old way. He was smooth as a mink at making connections in court circles, but he would by no means lower himself to hobnob with those ghastly writers swamping their stomachs with coffee. So though Walpole met with Swift once, he treated him rather rudely. Swift retaliated by writing a broadsheet filled with phony allegations that ran the man who'd spurned him through the muck and helped to permanently damage his reputation.

On the other hand, Walpole's leading political opponent—Robert Harley, First Earl of Oxford—could see a promising new possibility when it raised its head. He met regularly with Swift, leaked torrents of inside news to him, solicited his advice on major decisions, and made him feel like a co-conspirator, a partner in the process of government. (Of course he also hid vast amounts of fact from Swift, something Jonathan never seems to have caught on to.) This swelled Swift's ego like a blimp, and our boy Jonathan wrote reams of prose that made Harley look like an indispensable mainstay of the state.

■ ■ ■ ■ ■ ■ ■ ■ ■ ■

The newspapers of the American colonies weren't any better. They went into fits of hysteria when the British tried to get the colonists to pay part of the costs of the English troops that had been defending Massachusetts, New York, New Jersey, and Pennsylvania against the French and the Indians. Why did the press blow the minor taxes the Brits levied out of all proportion and help precipitate a revolution? Because the method of taxa-

Benjamin Franklin's unresearched diatribes helped kill off thousands of innocents.

tion the English chose raised the cost of paper and shaved a few farthings off publishers' profits.

Meanwhile, one of Benjamin Franklin's first journalistic forays was a virulent attack on Cotton Mather. What did Franklin lace into Mather for? Advocating a controversial technique for the prevention of the small pox epidemics that continually ravaged the colonial cities. The method Mather favored was an early version of inoculation. Franklin's unresearched diatribes helped kill off thousands of innocents by scaring them away from inoculation. Nothing much has changed since then. Ah, how heroic is the press in a free society!

■ ■ ■ ■ ■ ■ ■ ■ ■ ■

Back in the mid-nineteenth century, when something like eleven newspapers were fighting ferociously for circulation in New York City, a young part-time journalist named Edgar Allan Poe carried out a secret mission for the *New York Sun*. He wrote up a group of British adventurers who had built a propeller-driven balloon, had taken off to cross the English Channel, had run into contrary winds, and had been blown across the Atlantic to a beach in Virginia, thus effecting the first aerial transatlantic

crossing. This was big news. The *Sun*'s unnamed correspondent was the first to reach Virginia's coast and interview the intrepid airmen about their perilous flight across the ocean.

The *Sun* ran new stories of the balloonist's adventures on the front page every day, and circulation leaped mightily, leaving New York's remaining papers in the dust. So all of them "sent reporters" down to Virginia and began cranking out their own exclusive interviews with the Brits. There was only one small problem: There was no balloon, no balloonists, and no transatlantic crossing. But the papers were no more concerned with truth than they'd been in Ben Franklin's day. They just wanted a hot story, even if they had to make it up by rewriting what had appeared someplace else.

■ ■ ■ ■ ■ ■ ■ ■ ■ ■

When Fidel Castro launched one of his Keystone Comedy–style invasions of Cuba, his rather rusty ship got bogged down in the mangrove roots about a mile offshore, so it was impossible to unload the supplies and ammunition. Castro's men, all 30 or so of them, had to wade 5,270 feet in water up to their necks to get ashore, seriously moistening their gunpowder and their weapons in the process. By the time they reached the beach they were exhausted.

Then Batista's troops spotted them as they crawled inland, and the dictator's soldiers managed to wipe out all but three of the would-be revolutionaries—Castro and two others. The trio of survivors took refuge in a cane field, but the Batista troops knew they were in there somewhere. So they combed one row of cane after another, while Fidel and his two companions lay still on their bellies and avoided even a belch or a whisper to elude detection. Then the Batista folks got fed up and started to set the fields on fire. Unfortunately for history, they missed the one in which Fidel and his somewhat diminished army of two were ensconced.

That night, when the Batista boys decided to get some sleep, Fidel counted heads—which took about half a second—and inventoried his arsenal. There was one rifle left. The future "savior" of Cuba (poor Cuba) was elated. He spent the rest of the night lecturing his unfortunate duo of followers in an intense whisper. The theme of his exuberant, though hushed oration? "We have won the Revolution!!!!" I am not kidding. (Neither was Fidel.) How ironic that this real-life Ayn-Randian hero—Fidel Castro—turned out to be a Leninist monster.

But you haven't heard the last of Fidel yet. Once the wily leader had escaped the sugar field, he managed to triple the size of his army—bringing it up to a grand total of seven. Then some of his supporters persuaded the *New York Times* to send a reporter down to the Sierra Madres for a week of interviews. Fidel ordered his men to change costumes and identities every hour or two, then report for duty, supposedly as the heads of massive brigades camped out in the neighboring hills. Each time one of his septet reappeared as a supposedly different member of the revolutionary corps, the entrant would say something like, "Comrade exigente, I have 1,000 men stationed three miles away. Do you want me to move them farther from the urinals?"

After seven days of this, the *New York Times* reporter was convinced that the Maximum Leader had roughly 10,000 hard-bitten soldiers salted away among the pine trees, and that the revolutionary force was unbeatable. The scribe wrote up this "indisputable fact" in a highly touted series on the "Cuban insurrection." Journalists, being an independent-minded lot, immediately scrambled to Cuba to replicate the *Times'* scoop. *Life, Look*, and all three networks sent in their best reporters. Fidel repeated the costume-changing trick. The result: Every media outlet in sight parroted the *Times'* conclusion that Fidel and his massive army had practically taken Cuba already. A year later, when Cuba's dictator, Batista, finally couldn't stand being made a fool of by the American press anymore, he decamped. Then the *New Yorker* ran a cartoon with a picture of Fidel and the caption, "I got my job in the *New York Times*." "I got my job in the *New York Times*" was the tagline of an advertising campaign the *Times* was running for its job-wanted section. I doubt that many people understood the precision of the joke.

■ ■ ■ ■ ■ ■ ■ ■ ■ ■

Watch the weekend talk shows in which Washington "reporters" swap their "insider" data. Note the pools from which their data is gathered: press conferences, not-for-attribution briefings (meaning more press conferences), and "my sources." In other words, each reporter is simply picking up scraps that government PR people and the officials they serve have pre-packaged—or manufactured from scratch—for the Washington press corps. The diligent and independent journalists are regurgitating what they've been handed on a platter. Not a one is reporting (with the exception of Georgie Anne Geyer, who stays out of Washington). None is digging. None is going underground. None is moving from the level of what's offered for official presentation to the level of what's held in secrecy. None is piercing the veil, as I had to when researching my story on the kids of New York's private schools. Okay, granted that my story led to threats of ending my publishing career. The threats were made by some of the wealthiest and most influential men in the Big Apple, the core of the publishing world. The gentlemen using phrases like, "You are putting your head in the noose, Mr. Bloom," were on the boards of New York's most prestigious schools for the elite. But isn't wading your way through threats and attacks part of the job?

Granted that each Washington reporter knows that to retain access to press conferences, briefings, and sources, he or she must abide by a set of unwritten and shamefully unreported rules, rules which seriously constrain what he or she can say. Also granted that without this access, a reporter would no longer have a standard Washington career. But whoever said that journalism is about following a standard pattern? Isn't reporting

> Fidel ordered his men to change costumes and identities every hour or two, then report for duty, supposedly as the heads of massive brigades camped out in the neighboring hills.

all about rule-breaking to pierce the shroud and uncover what's really going on? Isn't it about discovering those well-kept secrets and soaring insights most likely to have an impact on our lives and to explain the hows, whats, whens, wheres, and whys? If not you, as a reporter, then who? And if not now, when?

■ ■ ■ ■ ■ ■ ■ ■ ■ ■

"Karl Marx held that history is shaped by control of the means of production. In our times history is shaped by control of the means of communication." —Arthur Schlesinger, Jr.

"Public sentiment is everything. With public sentiment, nothing can fail. Without it, nothing can succeed. He who molds public sentiment goes deeper than he who executes statutes or pro-

The Puppets of Pandemonium
Sleaze and Sloth in the Media Elite   Howard Bloom

35

nounces decisions. He makes statutes or decisions possible or impossible to execute." —Abraham Lincoln

■ ■ ■ ■ ■ ■ ■ ■ ■

It's not enough to invent something fantastic, you have to "promote" it.

A nineteenth-century Floridian, John Gory, tried to keep the town of Apalachicola's population from contracting a fever that racked its multitudes every summer. In 1850, Gory invented refrigeration and air conditioning. Alas, the clever tinkerer was better at inventing than at promoting his invention. He was blind to the necessity of creating a climate of belief that gets all the members of a skittish herd moving in the same direction. Normal human beings are afraid of straying from the pack. They are frightened at the thought of finding merit in something they might be ridiculed for championing. Gory and his air conditioners were ridiculed by no less an authority than the writers of the *New York Times*, the lead

None is moving from the level of what's offered for official presentation to the level of what's held in secrecy.

animals in the herd. So a man whose gizmos could have improved many a Southerner's life died in abject poverty. Air conditioning and refrigeration were denied to mankind until a German inventor more skillful at manipulating the perceptions of the herd came along.

Charles Darwin was far less naïve than Gory. He didn't just theorize and marshal evidence, then leave it at that. Darwin marshaled support, working hard to line up the backing of the top scientists of his day. Darwin already had one herd-head-turner going for him. His family was scientifically illustrious. The famous evolutionary theorist Erasmus Darwin was his grandfather. Anything with the Darwin name on it had an automatic attraction for the scientific sheep of the day. Yet Darwin worked methodically to court the friendship of scientific opinion-makers. He mounted a PR campaign, writing a target list of the taste-makers—the lead sheep—he would have to win over to his cause, then checking them off one by one as he and his "bulldog," Thomas Henry Huxley, won them over to the Darwinian point of view. When Alfred Russel Wallace showed up in England having already written up ideas Darwin had only penciled in, Darwin's influential friends lined up to support

Darwin's prior claim to the concepts. They turned down the claims of Wallace, a stranger to them.

When Darwin finally published *On the Origin of Species by Means of Natural Selection* in 1859, he relied on Huxley to publicize his ideas. Said Huxley, "I am sharpening up my claws and beak in readiness." The father of evolution knew that science is more than a struggle for truth, it's a struggle for social influence, a game of manipulating the herd.

Dante was equally savvy. He became known as a great poet through unabashed self-promotion. Thirteenth-century poets were poor, anonymous creatures. But Dante Alighieri lusted after the kind of fame poets had had in the long-lost days of Rome. So he wrote a poem of epic proportions and made himself the hero. Then he structured the plot to leave the impression that the greatest of all earthly poets was, well, who else? Dante Alighieri. Now watch carefully as the Florentine wannabe makes the bunny of renown emerge from a hat. The Roman poet Virgil was widely acknowledged as the greatest versifier who had ever lived. But Dante was a relative unknown. So when he wrote *The Divine Comedy*, Dante made himself the lead character and portrayed Virgil as his fictional guide through hell and purgatory, thus putting himself in Virgil's league. When the pair reached heaven, Virgil had to stay behind. Only Dante was allowed in. The implication: that Dante picked up where Virgil had left off, and that the lad from Florence had transcended the old Roman entirely.

This flagrant act of self-promotion worked. In fact, it snowballed. After he died, Florence promoted a surprising new claim—that Dante was the world's greatest poet. Why? To promote Florence as a leading city of the arts and an all-round admirable town.

■ ■ ■ ■ ■ ■ ■ ■ ■

"The press has become the greatest power within the Western countries, more powerful than the legislature, the executive, and the judiciary." —Aleksandr Solzhenitsyn

"Hostile newspapers are more to be dreaded than a hundred thousand bayonets." —Napoleon

"The press leads the public." —Japanese saying

"The conscious and intelligent manipulation of the organized habits and opinions of the masses is an important element in democratic society. Those who manipulate this unseen mechanism in society constitute an invisible government which is the true ruling power of our country…. It is they who pull the wires which control the public mind, who harness old social forces and contrive new ways to bind and guide the world." —Edward Bernays

"He who molds public sentiment goes deeper than he who executes statutes or pronounces decisions." —Abraham Lincoln

■ ■ ■ ■ ■ ■ ■ ■ ■ ■

We see what we're *told* is there, not what is. A 1989 survey showed that drug use and crime were on a par in the US and Canada. But Americans ranked drugs as their number-one problem and crime as their third. Canadians saw drugs as insignificant and ranked crime a lowly twentieth on the list of their dilemmas. The facts were the same, but the perceptions were different. Why? Because the headlines in the two countries were different.

■ ■ ■ ■ ■ ■ ■ ■ ■ ■

Molly Ivins, a highly respected journalist who worked for the *New York Times*, among other papers, wrote in the *Houston Journalism Review*:

You can find out more about what's going on at the state capitol by spending one night drinking with the capitol press corps than you can in months of reading the papers those reporters write for. The same is true of City Hall reporters, court reporters, police reporters, education writers, any of us. In city rooms and in the bars where newspeople drink you can find out what's going on. You can't find it in the papers."[2]

■ ■ ■ ■ ■ ■ ■ ■ ■ ■

Then there are the many cases in which the press manufactures or manipulates the news. According to the *New York Times Book Review*, Oliver North "describes being in the office of the Reagan aide Pat Buchanan, working on an announcement of the capture of the *Achille Lauro* terrorist [an Islamic terrorist who led a gang that hijacked a cruise ship and killed a passenger, an elderly Jew in a wheelchair, then threw him into the sea], when Niles Latham, an editor at the *New York Post*, called to ask Mr. Buchanan to make the President say, 'You can run, but you can't hide,' so the paper could use it as the front page headline. Mr. Buchanan obligingly wrote the line into the President's remarks."[3]

■ ■ ■ ■ ■ ■ ■ ■ ■ ■

From 1968 to 1988, the average length of a TV news sound bite allotted to a presidential candidate fell from 43 seconds to 9.8. Meanwhile, pictures of the candidates with *none* of his words tripled. This gave the TV producer nearly total power to reshape or distort a candidate's message.

■ ■ ■ ■ ■ ■ ■ ■ ■ ■

A 1990 survey showed that an astonishing number of Congressmen and other elected officials believed that the pyramids may have been built by aliens. Even worse, one of the groups that came out with the highest levels of general ignorance was newspaper editors. Over 50 percent of these media leaders felt that dinosaurs and humans had inhabited the earth at the same time. (Humans, in fact, didn't show up until some 65 million years after the dinosaurs had abandoned their bones and departed from the scene.) The bottom line: The men and women spooning facts into the brains of most Americans have apparently gotten their scientific education from the Flintstones.

Writes Molly Ivins: "One of the most depressing aspects of reporters as a group is that they tend to be fairly ignorant themselves. There is no excuse for it, and there is a complete cure for it. Read, read, read."[4]

Further muddling the information we receive from overseas is the fact, reported by historian and former *New York Times* journalist Robert Darnton, that "few foreign correspondents speak the language of the country they cover."[5] So-called foreign reporters simply regurgitate preconceptions. English correspondents write as if they are visiting a long-gone England, "the England of Dickens," and those in France portray a France that no longer exists, "the France of Victor Hugo, with some Maurice Chevalier thrown in." What justifies this? Says Darnton: "Newspaper stories must fit a culture's preconceptions of news."

Anyone who's been interviewed by the press knows that her so-called quotes will be wild distortions of her original statements, yet writers refuse to check the accuracy of their notes

The men and women spooning facts into the brains of most Americans have apparently gotten their scientific education from the Flintstones.

with the source. Why? Says one former investigative reporter for the *New York Times*, AP, and the *Wall Street Journal*, Thomas Goldstein: "We don't like to be confronted with our own mistakes." What's more, we "are tired of the story and don't want to do more work."[6]

■ ■ ■ ■ ■ ■ ■ ■ ■

Writers respond to the world with a kind of herd instinct. They see which direction the animals on either side of them are rushing, and don't bother to notice the real world through which the pack is moving. Yet they pretend to report on the real world. What's worse, they often fool their readers into believing that this is true.

So I am angry at the press. I am angry at its dishonesty. I am infuriated by its moral corruption. I am disgusted with its laziness and lack of intellectual independence. I am sickened by its phony self-image. And I am furious that I was lied to in my youth. I hate the wonderful progressive magazine I read in my teens, the *Reporter*, for telling me about Chiang Kai Check's atrocities while hiding the atrocities of Mao. I hate the *Village Voice*, a publication I swore by in my twenties, for telling me about the despicable My Lai Massacre our troops carried out in Viet Nam without informing me that the standard Viet Cong procedure for winning the hearts and minds of villagers was to take the most prominent village family—usually a dozen or more grandparents, uncles, aunts, mothers, fathers, children, and infants—tie them to a few canisters of dynamite in the town square, then detonate the charge. I hate the press for turning me into a war protester against Nixon and Johnson when I should have been shouting just as loudly against Ho

Chi Minh. And, worse, when I should have been shouting against the genocide of between one and three million of my fellow human beings that Pol Pot was pulling off in Cambodia. And I am disconcerted that the tribe the press have slated for the next Cambodian-style unreported annihilation is my own, the Jews.

Today, I read 30 different publications, most of them obscure periodicals from both the left and right. I never want to be deceived again. And I don't want to see my own people victimized. Though I can't for the hell of me figure out how to stop it.

I could give you numerous other examples from personal experience and subsequent research, but it's a long story and will have to wait for some other time. The surprising part is that just like Jonathan Swift, today's journalists regard themselves as not only the guardians of honesty, morality and truth, but think they're incorruptible. Human nature is so peculiar. In fact, it's a bit worse than that—it's downright dangerous. And the press is among the most dangerous of all.

Well, I see I've put you to sleep. But just remember, all you need is an automatic weapon and a sharp knife and you too can use Yasir Arafat's keys to publicity success. If you handle them properly, the press will fall for anything. Especially if it promises to spill a lot of blood.

Endnotes

1. Schorr, Daniel. (1992). Confessions of a newsman. *World Monitor*, May, pp 40–1. **2.** Ivins, Molly. (1991). *Molly Ivins can't say that, can she?* New York: Random House, p 235. **3.** Dowd, Maureen. (1991). The education of Colonel North (a review of *Under Fire: An American Story* by Oliver L. North). *New York Times Book Review*, November 17, p 12. **4.** *Op cit.*, Ivins, p 237. **5.** Darnton, Robert. (1990). *The kiss of Lamourette*. New York: WW Norton & Co, p 92. **6.** Goldstein, Tom. (1985). *The news at any cost: How journalists compromise their ethics to shape the news*. New York: Simon & Schuster, p 204.

The New Rules for the New Millennium

Gary Webb

When the newspaper I worked for in Kentucky in the 1970s, *The Kentucky Post*, took the plunge and hiked its street price from 20 cents to a quarter, the executive editor, Vance Trimble, instructed our political cartoonist to design a series of full-page house ads justifying the price increase. One of those ads still hangs on my wall. It depicts an outraged tycoon, replete with vest and felt hat, brandishing a copy of our newspaper and shouting at a harried editor: "Kill that story, Mr. Editor…or else!"

We were worth a quarter, the ad argued, because we weren't some "soft, flabby, spineless" newspaper. We'd tell that fat cat to take a long walk off a short pier.

"Our readers would be shocked if any kind of threat swayed the editor," the ad declared. "If it happens, we print it. Kill a story? *Never!* There are no fetters on our reporters. Nor must they bow to sacred cows. On every story, the editor says: 'Get the facts. And let the fur fly!' Our reporters appreciate that. They are proud they can be square-shooters."

The newspaper for the most part held to that creed. When the executive editor was arrested for drunk driving, a photographer was dispatched to the city jail and the next day the paper carried a picture of our disheveled boss sitting forlornly in a holding cell. The newspaper had done the same thing to many other prominent citizens, he reminded the stunned staff after his release. Why should he be treated any differently?

How quaint that all sounds 20 years later. And how distant that post-Watergate era seems. Today, we see corporate news executives boasting not of the hardness of their asses, but of the value of their assets. We witness them groveling for public forgiveness because something their reporters wrote offended powerful interests or raised uncomfortable questions about the past. Stories that meet every traditional standard of objective journalism are retracted or renounced, not because they are false—but because they are true.

The depth of this depravity (so far) was reached the day New York attorney Floyd Abrams decided CNN/Time Warner should retract its explosive report on a covert CIA operation known as Tailwind, which was alleged to have involved the use of nerve gas against American deserters in Southeast Asia in the 1970s. I saw Abrams on a talk show afterwards arguing that the ultimate truth of the Tailwind story was irrelevant to CNN's retraction of it.

"It doesn't necessarily mean that the story isn't true," Abrams insisted. "Who knows? Someday we might find other information. And, you know, maybe someday I'll be back here again, having done another report saying that, 'You know what? It was all true.'"

Stop and savor that for a moment. Let its logic worm its way through your brain, because it is the pure, unadulterated essence of what's wrong with corporate journalism today. Could anyone honestly have dreamed that one day a major news organization would retract and apologize for a story that even it acknowledges could well be true?

For that matter, who could have envisioned the day when a veteran investigative reporter would be convicted of a felony for printing the voicemail messages of executives of a corporation that was allegedly looting, pillaging, and bribing its way through Central America? Yet, like CNN producers April Oliver and Jack Smith, *Cincinnati Enquirer* reporter Mike Gallagher was fired, his work "renounced" as his editors ludicrously wrote in a front-page apology, and he has been uniformly reviled in the mass media as a fabricator for his devastating exposé of Chiquita Brands International. So far, however, no one has shown that his stories contain a single, solitary inaccuracy. Again, the truth seems irrelevant, a sideshow not worthy of serious discussion.

In 1997 Florida television reporters Steve Wilson and Jane Akre, both highly respected journalists, tried to air a series on the dangers of a growth hormone injected into most of Florida's dairy cows to stimulate milk production. After receiving threatening letters from Monsanto, the makers of the growth hormone, Wilson and Akre were ordered to rewrite their script more than 80 times, yet at no time were they told that anything they had reported was inaccurate. Finally, their bosses ordered them to run a watered-down story the reporters felt was misleading, untrue, and heavily slanted towards the chemical giant, and threatened to fire them if they didn't. Instead, they quit and sued the Fox station. In August 2000, Jane Akre won a jury verdict of more than $400,000. Amazingly, the press reports portrayed the verdict as a vindication for Monsanto and the TV station that fired Akre and Wilson.

Astute readers may well wonder what the hell is going on, and the answer is this: The rules are being changed, and they are being changed in such a way as to ensure that our government

Stories that meet every traditional standard of objective journalism are retracted or renounced, not because they are false —but because they are true.

and our major corporations won't be bothered by nettlesome investigative journalists in the new millennium.

When I started in the newspaper business the rules were simple: Get as close to the truth as you possibly can. There were no hard and fast requirements about levels of proof necessary to print a story—and there still aren't, contrary to all the current huffing and puffing about "journalistic standards" being abused. I worked as a reporter for nearly 20 years, wrote for dozens of different editors, and each had his or her own set of standards. Generally, if you diligently investigated the issue, used named sources, found supporting documentation, and you honestly believed it was true, you went with it. Period. That was the standard that gutsy editors used, at any rate. Some—like Ben Bradlee during Watergate, for example—occasionally went with less because instinct and common sense told them the story was right even if everything wasn't completely nailed down.

Nervous editors, on the other hand, used different standards. "Raising the bar" was the usual trick they used to avoid printing troublesome news. The squeamish demanded an admission of wrongdoing (preferably written) or an official government report confirming the story's charge.

What that means, of course, is that stories about serious, unacknowledged abuses never get printed, and eventually reporters learn not to waste their time turning over rocks if no one will officially confirm when something hideous slithers out. And once that happens, they cease being journalists and become akin to the scribes of antiquity, whose sole task was to faithfully record the pharaoh's words in clay.

It is this latter standard that was championed by Abrams in the Tailwind case and to some extent by *San Jose Mercury News* editor Jerry Ceppos in the case of my "Dark Alliance" series in 1996. Under these new rules, it isn't enough anymore for a reporter to have on-the-record sources and supporting documentation. Now they must have something called "proof." Investigative stories must be "proven" in order to reach the public; having "insufficient evidence" is now cause for retraction and dismissal.

"Having read all your stuff, as much as I can about this…I can't see where you prove it," CNN commentator Bill Press whined to former CNN producer April Oliver. "None of your sources add up to that."

"What is the standard of proof in a black operation where everyone's supposed to deny, or information is tightly compartmentalized?" Oliver demanded.

Her question, which cuts to the heart of the debate, went unanswered. But judging from Abrams' report, "proof" apparently is a statement no one disagrees with, or something that can be demonstrated, as Ted Turner phrased it, "beyond a reasonable doubt"—the courtroom standard of proof.

Some, including Turner, say this is good for journalism, that it will keep unsubstantiated stories out of public circulation, and there's no doubt about that. But it will also have the same muffling effect on a lot of important stories that happen to be true. Such a standard would have kept Watergate out of the papers. Love Canal, the CIA's mining of Nicaragua's harbors, the El Mozote massacre in El Salvador—all would have been suppressed. Don't believe it? Consider the Iran-Contra scandal. It was only after Ronald Reagan and Edwin Meese held their famous press conference and confessed that something funny had been going on in the White House basement that the Washington press corps felt emboldened enough to start covering the scandal seriously. Until then, the idea of a secret parallel government had been sneeringly dismissed as some left-wing conspiracy theory.

What is devious about these standards of proof is that they sound so eminently responsible. They are doubly handy because they can be applied after publication, when the heat comes down. Then, as CNN/Time Warner did, lawyers and former government operatives can be called in to produce palliative reports bemoaning the lack of "proof," and the bothersome story can be interred without further ado. (Few will question the validity of these reports because, after all, they come straight from the top.)

But somewhere along the way it's been forgotten that journalism was never meant to be held to courtroom standards of proof. As investigative reporter Pete Brewton once put it: "I'm not in the proof business. I'm in the information business." Unlike police and prosecutors, reporters don't have the power to subpoena records or wiretap phone conversations. We can't conduct 24-hour surveillances or pay informants for information. We write what we can find on the public record (which becomes less public all the time). Or at least we used to.

Fortunately, there are still some reporters and editors out there who consider an official denial to be a starting point, rather than the end, of a promising story. It is these men and women who are the true journalists, the ones who will carry on where the giants of yesterday—George Seldes, I.F. Stone, and the late Jonathan Kwitny—left off. Though many of them toil in relative obscurity, for little money and even less appreciation, their work contributes more to our lives than the million-dollar celebrity-correspondents that we see on the nightly news.

Back in 1938, as fascism was sweeping across Europe, George Seldes presciently observed: "It is possible to fool all the people all the time—when government and press cooperate."

Today, such mass deception is possible on a scale that Seldes never could have imagined. That is why it is more important than ever to support the journalists with backbones. If these few bits of illumination should ever sputter and disappear, out of neglect or frustration or censorship, we will be enveloped by a darkness the likes of which we've never seen.

Digital Seductions
Norman Solomon

The Web has been extensively integrated into the commercial twenty-first-century Zeitgeist—reflecting, hyping, and boosting a consumer culture—to the point that the notion of the Internet as an "information superhighway" now sounds antiquated.

During the late 1960s, a popular psychedelic poster appropriated and mocked a DuPont advertising motto—"Better Living Through Chemistry." More than forty years later, there's no need for a "Better Living Through Technology" poster. Everyone but a complete dunderhead understands that we live in a wondrous technological era with fantastic vistas ahead.

It's stunning to consider what has happened since the days when DOS and floppy disks were the PC standard. And, as fabulous as computer advances have been since the 1980s, even more incredible is the kind of techno-future that we can extrapolate. When "progress" is gauged in merely technical terms—celebrating huge leaps in memory, broadband capacity, and miniaturization, along with incessant marketing to consumers—a new manifest destiny beckons.

In media realms, no doubt some self-congratulation is in order. Without the Internet, the media landscape would be much bleaker; the corporate hammerlock on most real-time news, held for many decades by big-money outlets, would be even worse than it is today. Fortunately, many people are making creative use of the Web and its endless permutations.

The everyday benefits of digital technologies are apparent and real enough. But beyond complaints about various snafus, we hear little mention of the downsides. The media storyline is that the march of progress has gone digital and global. No one can dispute that the worldwide spread of digital technology is sure to continue—but the specter of inevitability should not blind us to dubious aspects of social digitization.

The Web has been extensively integrated into the commercial twenty-first-century Zeitgeist—reflecting, hyping, and boosting a consumer culture—to the point that the notion of the Internet as an "information superhighway" now sounds antiquated.

The last half of the 1990s saw a steady shift in media framing and expectations of the Web. Along that line, I found some telling statistics via the Nexis media database:

■ In 1995, media outlets were transfixed with the Internet as an amazing source of knowledge. Major newspapers in the United States and abroad referred to the "information superhighway" in 4,562 stories. Meanwhile, during the entire year, articles mentioned "e-commerce" or "electronic commerce" only 915 times.

■ In 1996, coverage of the Internet as an "information superhighway" fell to 2,370 stories in major newspapers, about half the previous year's level. At the same time, coverage of electronic commerce nearly doubled, with mentions in 1,662 articles.

■ For the first time, in 1997 the news media's emphasis on the Internet mainly touted it as a commercial avenue. The quantity of articles in major newspapers mentioning the "information superhighway" dropped sharply, to just 1,314. Meanwhile, the references to e-commerce gained further momentum, jumping to 2,812 articles.

■ In 1998, despite an enormous upsurge of people online, the concept of an "information superhighway" appeared in only 945 articles in major newspapers. Simultaneously, e-commerce became a media obsession, with those newspapers referring to it in 6,403 articles.

■ In 1999, while Internet usage continued to spike upwards, the news media played down "information superhighway" imagery, with a mere 842 mentions in major papers. But media mania for electronic commerce exploded. Major newspapers mentioned e-commerce in 20,641 articles.

How did America's most influential daily papers frame the potentialities of the Internet? During the last five years of the 1990s, the annual number of *Washington Post* articles mentioning the "information superhighway" dropped from 178 to 20, while such *New York Times* articles plummeted from 100 to 17. But during the same half-decade, the yearly total of stories referring to electronic commerce zoomed, rising in the *Post* from 19 to 430 and in the *Times* from 52 to 731.

Today—despite the rampant commercialization of the Web—online digital technology is proving to be extremely useful for large numbers of people who are pursuing information and civic engagement. In some admirable ways, the Internet has been a fabulous boon to real-time transmission of news, analysis, and images. Meanwhile, in contrast to printed pages, the financial barrier to entry for publishing online is low to nonexistent. We've partially realized how digital technologies can serve as tools for quality journalism and grassroots activism.

But too much confidence has been placed in digital media as the key to fulfilling democratic potential. History tells cautionary tales.

After the first rudimentary telegraph went into operation during the late eighteenth century in Europe, media analyst Armand Mattelart says, "long-distance communication technology was promoted as a guarantee of the revival of democracy." During the next several decades, a powerful concept took hold—"the ideology of redemption through networks."

In his book, *Networking the World, 1794–2000*, Mattelart points to assumptions that have spanned continents and centuries. "Each technological generation provided a new opportunity to propagate the grand narratives of general concord and social reconciliation under the aegis of Western civilization." Whether the instruments of unprecedented change were railroads, undersea cables, or electric patents, promoters spoke of wondrous horizons. But the gaps were huge between "promises for a better world due to technology" and "the reality of struggles for control of communication devices." Elites routinely won those struggles.

In recent decades, he adds, technology has often appeared to offer the means for global solutions. "At the end of the 1970s, the nation-state was being attacked on two fronts: it was accused of being(too large to solve small problems of human existence and too small to solve big ones)... As a way out of this dual impasse, information and communication networks had become the panacea."

But hucksterism kept tightening its grip. "Advertising, which initially seemed little more than a modernized sales technique, gradually became the vector of the commercialization of the entire mode of communication and, as such, a key feature of the public sphere," Mattelart writes. These days, it's a facile corporate feat to conflate democratic decision-making with global shopping. "The advertising industry strives to con-

Whether the instruments of unprecedented change were railroads, undersea cables, or electric patents, promoters spoke of wondrous horizons.

struct vast transnational communities of consumers who all share the same 'socio-styles,' forms of consumption, and cultural practices."

We're now hearing the latest versions of what Mattelart calls "messianic discourses about the democratic virtues of technology." Serving as smoke screens for inordinate privilege and consolidated power, such rhetorical exercises commonly tout "globalization"—corporate globalization—as an obvious, commonsense way of stimulating prosperity and encouraging democracy. "The idea has taken root in free trade rhetoric that the spread of products of the entertainment industry automatically leads to civil and political freedom, as if the status of the consumer were equivalent to that of the citizen." Mattelart notes "the rapidity with which Asian and Latin American countries have adapted to digital technology and the advantage they have taken of it." But there's a grim flip side. "We cannot deny, however, that these new sources of modernity coexist—

Digital Seductions
Norman Solomon

43

as the second side of the coin—with a galloping process of impoverishment and exclusion of large sections of the population." In effect, a New Mediaspeak equates the universal with the marketable.

These days, it's a facile corporate feat to conflate democratic decision-making with global shopping.

While conveying a sense of inevitability, the momentum of digital communications is offering exponential profits in tandem with divine efficiency. "In an age of advanced technology," Aldous Huxley foresaw, "inefficiency is the sin against the Holy Ghost." Digital technology is nothing if not tremendously efficient. Yet it always functions within social context.

Along the way, the ubiquitous presence of media technologies in the workaday world has facilitated chronic employer demands for greater "productivity." While a new digital gizmo may serve the worker, that worker is still expected to serve management's drive for profits, more efficiently than ever. So, in newsrooms across America, we now have a profusion of superb digital technology in conjunction with a notable scarcity of human beings. Layoffs occur in tandem with computer upgrades.

It's easy enough to equate technical breakthroughs with human breakthroughs. And news media have not hesitated to glorify the new achievements of digital wonders. But whether we're really living better through technology is another matter.

The Media and Their Atrocities

Michael Parenti

For the better part of a decade the US public has been bombarded with a media campaign to demonize the Serbian people and their elected leaders. During that time, the US government has pursued a goal of breaking up Yugoslavia into a cluster of small, weak, dependent, free-market principalities. Yugoslavia was the only country in Eastern Europe that would not dismantle its welfare state and public sector economy. It was the only one that did not beg for entry into NATO. It was—and what's left of it, still is—charting an independent course not in keeping with the New World Order.

Targeting the Serbs

Of the various Yugoslav peoples, the Serbs were targeted for demonization because they were the largest nationality and the one most opposed to the breakup of Yugoslavia. But what of the atrocities they committed? All sides committed atrocities in the fighting that has been encouraged by the Western powers over the last decade, but the reporting has been consistently one-sided. Grisly incidents of Croat and Muslim atrocities against the Serbs rarely made it into the US press, and when they did they were accorded only passing mention.[1]

Meanwhile, Serb atrocities were played up and sometimes even fabricated, as we shall see. Recently, three Croatian generals were indicted by the Hague War Crimes Tribunal for the bombardment and deaths of Serbs in Krajina and elsewhere. Where were the US television crews when these war crimes were being committed? John Ranz, chair of Survivors of the Buchenwald Concentration Camp, USA, asks: Where were the TV cameras when hundreds of Serbs were slaughtered by Muslims near Srebrenica?[2] The official line, faithfully parroted in the US media, is that Bosnian Serb forces committed all the atrocities at Srebrenica.

Are we to trust US leaders and the corporate-owned news media when they dish out atrocity stories? Recall the 500 premature babies whom Iraqi soldiers laughingly ripped from incubators in Kuwait—a story repeated and believed until exposed as a total fabrication years later. During the Bosnian war in 1993, the Serbs were accused of pursuing an official policy of rape. "Go forth and rape," a Bosnian Serb commander supposedly publicly instructed his troops. The source of that story never could be traced. The commander's name was never produced. As far as we know, no such utterance was ever made. Even the *New York Times* belatedly ran a tiny retraction, coyly allowing that, "[T]he existence of 'a systematic rape policy' by the Serbs remains to be proved."[3]

Bosnian Serb forces supposedly raped anywhere from 25,000 to 100,000 Muslim women, according to various stories. The Bosnian Serb army numbered not more than 30,000 or so,

> Of the various Yugoslav peoples, the Serbs were targeted for demonization because they were the largest nationality and the one most opposed to the breakup of Yugoslavia.

many of whom were involved in desperate military engagements. A representative from Helsinki Watch noted that stories of massive Serbian rapes originated with the Bosnian Muslim and Croatian governments and had no credible supporting evidence. Common sense would dictate that these stories be treated with the utmost skepticism—and not be used as an excuse for an aggressive and punitive policy against Yugoslavia.

The "mass rape" propaganda theme was resuscitated in 1999 to justify the continued NATO slaughter of Yugoslavia. A headline in the *San Francisco Examiner* (April 26, 1999) tells us: "Serb Tactic Is Organized Rape, Kosovo Refugees Say." No

> An Albanian woman crossing into Macedonia was eagerly asked by a news crew if she had been forced out by Serb police. She responded: "There were no Serbs. We were frightened of the [NATO] bombs."

evidence or testimony is given to support the charge of organized rape. Only at the bottom of the story, in the nineteenth paragraph, do we read that reports gathered by the Kosovo mission of the Organization for Security and Cooperation in Europe found no such organized rape policy. The actual number of rapes were in the dozens, "and not many dozens," according to the OSCE spokesperson. This same story did note in passing that the UN War Crimes Tribunal sentenced a Bosnian Croat military commander to ten years in prison for failing to stop his troops from raping Muslim women in 1993—an atrocity we heard little about when it was happening.

A few-dozen rapes is a few-dozen too many. But can it serve as one of the justifications for a massive war? If Mr. Clinton wanted to stop rapes, he could have begun a little closer to home in Washington, DC, where dozens of rapes occur every month.

> While Kosovo Albanians were leaving in great numbers—usually well-clothed and in good health, some riding their tractors, trucks, or cars, many of them young men of recruitment age—they were described as being "slaughtered."

Indeed, he might be able to alert us to how women are sexually mistreated on Capitol Hill and in the White House itself.

The Serbs were blamed for the infamous Sarajevo market massacre. But according to the report leaked out on French TV, Western intelligence knew that it was Muslim operatives who had bombed Bosnian civilians in the marketplace in order to induce NATO involvement. Even international negotiator David Owen, who worked with Cyrus Vance, admitted in his memoir that the NATO powers knew all along that it was a Muslim bomb.[4]

On one occasion, notes Barry Lituchy, the *New York Times* ran a photo purporting to be of Croats grieving over Serbian atrocities when in fact the murders had been committed by Bosnian Muslims. The *Times* printed an obscure retraction the following week.[5]

The propaganda campaign against Belgrade has been so relentless that even prominent personages on the left—who oppose the NATO policy against Yugoslavia—have felt compelled to genuflect before this demonization orthodoxy, referring to unspecified and unverified Serbian "brutality" and "the monstrous Milosevic."[6] Thus they reveal themselves as having been influenced by the very media propaganda machine they criticize on so many other issues. To reject the demonized images of Milosevic and of the Serbian people is not to idealize them or claim that Serb forces are faultless or free of crimes. It is merely to challenge the one-sided propaganda that laid the grounds for NATO's aggression against Yugoslavia.

The Ethnic Cleansing Hype

Up until the NATO bombings began in March 1999, the conflict in Kosovo had taken 2,000 lives altogether from both sides, according to Kosovo Albanian sources. Yugoslavian sources put the figure at 800. Such casualties reveal a civil war, not genocide. Belgrade is condemned for the forced expulsion policy of Albanians from Kosovo. But such expulsions began in substantial numbers only after the NATO bombings, with thousands being uprooted by Serb forces, especially from areas where KLA mercenaries were operating.

We should keep in mind that tens of thousands also fled Kosovo because it was being mercilessly bombed by NATO, or because it was the scene of sustained ground fighting between Yugoslav forces and the KLA, or because they were just afraid and hungry. An Albanian woman crossing into Macedonia was eagerly asked by a news crew if she had been forced out by Serb police. She responded: "There were no Serbs. We were frightened of the [NATO] bombs."[7] I had to read this in the *San Francisco Guardian*, an alternative weekly, not in the *New York Times* or *Washington Post*.

During the bombings, an estimated 70,000 to 100,000 Serbian residents of Kosovo took flight (mostly north but some to the south), as did thousands of Roma and others.[8] Were the Serbs ethnically cleansing themselves? Or were these people not fleeing the bombing and the ground war? Yet, the refugee tide caused by the bombing was repeatedly used by US warmakers as justification for the bombing, a pressure put on Milosevic to allow "the safe return of ethnic Albanian refugees."[9]

While Kosovo Albanians were leaving in great numbers—usually well-clothed and in good health, some riding their tractors, trucks, or cars, many of them young men of recruitment age—they were described as being "slaughtered." It was repeatedly reported that "Serb atrocities"—not the extensive ground war with the KLA and certainly not the massive NATO bombing—"drove more than one million Albanians from their homes."[10] More recently, there have been hints that Albanian Kosovar refugees numbered nowhere near that figure.

Serbian attacks on KLA strongholds or the forced expulsion of Albanian villagers were described as "genocide." But experts in surveillance photography and wartime propaganda charged NATO with running a "propaganda campaign" on Kosovo that lacked any supporting evidence. State Department reports of mass graves and of 100,000 to 500,000 missing Albanian men "are just ludicrous," according to these independent critics.[11] Their findings were ignored by the major networks and other national media. Early in the war, *Newsday* reported that Britain and France were seriously considering "commando assaults into Kosovo to break the pattern of Serbian massacres of ethnic Albanians."[12] What discernible pattern of massacres? Of course, no commando assaults were put into operation, but the story served its purpose of hyping an image of mass killings.

An ABC *Nightline* show made dramatic and repeated references to the "Serbian atrocities in Kosovo" while offering no specifics. Ted Kopple asked a group of angry Albanian refugees what they had specifically witnessed. They pointed to an old man in their group who wore a wool hat. One of them reenacted what the Serbs had done to him, throwing the man's hat to the ground and stepping on it—"because the Serbs knew that his hat was the most important thing to him." Kopple was appropriately horrified about this "war crime," the only example offered in an hour-long program.

A widely-circulated story in the *New York Times*, headlined "US Report Outlines Serb Attacks in Kosovo," tells us that the State Department issued "the most comprehensive documentary record to date on atrocities." The report concluded that there had been organized rapes and systematic executions. But as one reads further and more closely into the article, one finds that State Department reports of such crimes "depend almost entirely on information from refugee accounts. There was no

Unsubstantiated references to "mass graves," each purportedly filled with hundreds or even thousands of Albanian victims, repeatedly failed to materialize.

suggestion that American intelligence agencies had been able to verify, most, or even many, of the accounts…and the word 'reportedly' and 'allegedly' appear throughout the document."[13]

British journalist Audrey Gillan interviewed Kosovo refugees about atrocities and found an impressive lack of evidence or credible specifics. One woman caught him glancing at the watch on her wrist, while her husband told him how all the women had been robbed of their jewelry and other possessions. A spokesman for the UN High Commissioner for Refugees talked of mass rapes and what sounded like hundreds of killings in three villages, but when Gillan pressed him for more precise information, he reduced it drastically to five or six teenage rape victims. But he had not spoken to any witnesses, and admitted that "we have no way of verifying these reports."[14]

Gillan notes that some refugees had seen killings and other atrocities, but there was little to suggest that they had seen it on the scale that was being reported. One afternoon, officials in charge said there were refugees arriving who talked of 60 or more being killed in one village and 50 in another, but Gillan "could not find one eyewitness who actually saw these things happening." Yet every day Western journalists reported "hundreds" of rapes and murders. Sometimes they noted in passing that the reports had yet to be substantiated, but then why were such unverified stories being so eagerly reported in the first place?

The Disappearing "Mass Graves"

After NATO forces occupied Kosovo, the stories about mass atrocities continued fortissimo. The *Washington Post* reported that 350 ethnic Albanians "might be buried in mass graves"

The team lugged 107,000 pounds of equipment into Kosovo to handle what was called the "largest crime scene in the FBI's forensic history," but it came up with no reports about mass graves.

around a mountain village in western Kosovo. They "might be" or they might not be. These estimates were based on sources that NATO officials refused to identify. Getting down to specifics, the article mentions "four decomposing bodies" discovered near a large ash heap.[15]

It was repeatedly announced in the first days of the NATO occupation that 10,000 Albanians had been killed (down from the 100,000 and even 500,000 Albanian men supposedly executed during the war). No evidence was ever offered to support the 10,000 figure, nor even to explain how it was arrived at so swiftly and surely while NATO troops were still moving into place and did not occupy but small portions of the province.

Likewise, unsubstantiated references to "mass graves," each purportedly filled with hundreds or even thousands of Albanian victims, repeatedly failed to materialize. Through the summer of 1999, the media hype about mass graves devolved into an occasional unspecified reference. The few sites actually unearthed offered up as many as a dozen bodies or sometimes twice that number, but with no certain evidence regarding causes of death or even the nationality of victims. In some cases there was reason to believe the victims were Serbs.[16]

On April 19, 1999, while the NATO bombings of Yugoslavia were going on, the State Department announced that up to 500,000 Kosovo Albanians were missing and feared dead. On May 16, US Secretary of Defense William Cohen, a former Republican senator from Maine now serving in President Clinton's Democratic Administration, stated that 100,000 military-aged ethnic Albanian men had vanished and might have been killed by the Serbs.[17] Such widely varying but horrendous figures from official sources went unchallenged by the media and by the many liberals who supported NATO's "humanitarian rescue operation." Among these latter were some supposedly progressive members of Congress who seemed to believe they were witnessing another Nazi Holocaust.

On June 17, just before the end of the war, British Foreign Office Minister Geoff Hoon said that "in more than 100 massacres" some 10,000 ethnic Albanians had been killed (down from the 100,000 and 500,000 bandied about by US officials)."[18] A day or two after the bombings stopped, the Associated Press and other news agencies, echoing Hoon, reported that 10,000 Albanians had been killed by the Serbs.[19] No explanation was given as to how this figure was arrived at, especially since not a single war site had yet been investigated and NATO forces had barely begun to move into Kosovo. On August 2, Bernard Kouchner, the United Nations' chief administrator in Kosovo (and organizer of Doctors Without Borders), asserted that about 11,000 bodies had been found in common graves throughout Kosovo. He cited as his source the International Criminal Tribunal for the Former Republic of Yugoslavia (ICTY). But the ICTY denied providing any such information. To this day, it is not clear how Kouchner came up with his estimate.[20]

As with the Croatian and Bosnian conflicts, the image of mass killings was hyped once again. Repeatedly, unsubstantiated references to "mass graves," each purportedly filled with hundreds or even thousands of Albanian victims, were publicized in daily media reports. In September 1999, Jared Israel did an Internet search for newspaper articles, appearing over the previous three months, including the words "Kosovo" and "mass grave." The report came back: "More than 1,000—too many to list. " Limiting his search to articles in the *New York Times*, he came up with 80, nearly one a day. Yet when it came down to hard evidence, the mass graves seemed to disappear.

Thus, in mid-June, the FBI sent a team to investigate two of the sites listed in the war-crimes indictment against Slobodan Milosevic, one purportedly containing six victims and the other 20. The team lugged 107,000 pounds of equipment into Kosovo to handle what was called the "largest crime scene in the FBI's forensic history," but it came up with no reports about mass graves. Not long after, on July 1, the FBI team returned home, oddly with not a word to say about their investigation.[21]

A Spanish forensic team was told to prepare for at least 2,000 autopsies, but found only 187 bodies, usually buried in individual graves, and showing no signs of massacre or torture.

Forensic experts from other NATO countries had similar experiences. A Spanish forensic team, for instance, was told to prepare for at least 2,000 autopsies, but found only 187 bodies, usually buried in individual graves, and showing no signs of massacre or torture. Most seemed to have been killed by mortar shells and firearms. One Spanish forensic expert, Emilio Perez Puhola, acknowledged that his team did not find one mass grave. He dismissed the widely publicized references about mass graves as being part of the "machinery of war propaganda."[22]

In late August 1999, the *Los Angeles Times* tried to salvage the genocide theme with a story about how the wells of Kosovo might be "mass graves in their own right." The *Times* claimed that "many corpses have been dumped into wells in Kosovo.... Serbian forces apparently stuffed...many bodies of ethnic Albanians into wells during their campaign of terror."[23] Apparently? Whenever the story got down to specifics, it dwelled on only one village and only one well—in which one body of a 39-year-old male was found, along with three dead cows and a dog. Neither his nationality nor cause of death was given. Nor was it clear who owned the well. "No other human remains were discovered, " the *Times* lamely concluded. As far as I know, neither the *Los Angeles Times* nor any other media outlet ran any more stories of wells stuffed with victims.

In one grave site after another, bodies were failing to materialize in any substantial numbers—or any numbers at all. In July 1999, a mass grave in Ljubenic, near Pec (an area of concerted fighting)—believed to be holding some 350 corpses—produced only seven after the exhumation. In Djacovica, town officials claimed that 100 ethnic Albanians had been murdered, but there were no bodies because the Serbs had returned in the middle of the night, dug them up, and carted them away, the officials seemed to believe. In Pusto Selo, villagers claimed that 106 men were captured and killed by Serbs at the end of March, but again no remains were discovered. Villagers once more suggested that Serb forces must have come back and removed them. How they accomplished this without being detected was not explained. In Izbica, refugees reported that 150 ethnic Albanians were executed in March. But their bodies were nowhere to be found. In Kraljan, 82 men were supposedly killed, but investigators found not a single cadaver.[24]

The worst incident of mass atrocities ascribed to Yugoslavian leader Slobodan Milosevic allegedly occurred at the Trepca mine. As reported by US and NATO officials, the Serbs threw 1,000 or more bodies down the shafts or disposed of them in the mine's vats of hydrochloric acid. In October 1999, the ICTY released the findings of Western forensic teams investigating Trepca. Not one body was found in the mine shafts, nor was there any evidence that the vats had ever been used in an attempt to dissolve human remains.[25]

In contrast to its public assertions, the German Foreign Office privately denied there was any evidence that genocide or ethnic cleansing was ever a component of Yugoslav policy.

By late autumn of 1999, the media hype about mass graves had fizzled noticeably. The many sites unearthed, considered to be the most notorious, offered up a few-hundred bodies altogether, not the thousands or tens of thousands or hundreds of thousands previously trumpeted, and with no evidence of torture or mass execution. In many cases, there was no certain evidence regarding the nationality of victims.[26] No mass killings means that the Hague War Crimes Tribunal indictment of Milosevic "becomes highly questionable," notes Richard Gwyn. "Even more questionable is the West's continued punishment of the Serbs."[27]

No doubt there were graves in Kosovo that contained two or more persons (which is NATO's definition of a "mass grave"). People were killed by bombs and by the extensive land war that went on between Yugoslav and KLA forces. Some of the dead, as even the *New York Times* allowed, "are fighters of the Kosovo Liberation Army or may have died ordinary deaths"—as would happen in any large population over time.[28] And no doubt there were grudge killings and summary executions as in any war, but not on a scale that would warrant the label of genocide and justify the massive death and destruction and the continuing misery inflicted upon Yugoslavia by the Western powers.

■ ■ ■ ■ ■ ■ ■ ■ ■ ■

We should remember that the propaganda campaign waged by NATO officials and the major media never claimed merely that atrocities (murders and rapes) occurred. Such crimes occur in every war and, indeed, in many communities during peacetime. What the media propaganda campaign against Yugoslavia charged was that mass atrocities and mass rapes and mass murders had been perpetrated, that is, genocide, as evidenced by mass graves.

In contrast to its public assertions, the German Foreign Office privately denied there was any evidence that genocide or ethnic cleansing was ever a component of Yugoslav policy: "Even in Kosovo, an explicit political persecution linked to Albanian ethnicity is not verifiable.... The actions of the [Yugoslav] security forces [were] not directed against the Kosovo-Albanians as an ethnically defined group, but against the military opponent and its actual or alleged supporters."[29]

Still, Milosevic was indicted as a war criminal, charged with the forced expulsion of Kosovar Albanians and with summary executions of a hundred or so individuals—again, alleged crimes that occurred after the NATO bombing had started, yet were used as justification for the bombing. The biggest war criminal of all is NATO and the political leaders who orchestrated the aerial campaign of death and destruction. But here is how the White House and the US media reasoned at the time: Since the aerial attacks do not intend to kill civilians, then presumably there is no liability and no accountability, only an occasional apology for the regrettable mistakes—as if only the intent of an action counted and not its ineluctable effects. In fact, a perpetrator can be judged guilty of willful murder without explicitly intending the death of a particular victim—as when the death results from an unlawful act that the perpetrator knew would likely cause death. George Kenney, a former State Department official under the Bush Administration, put it well: "Dropping cluster bombs on highly populated urban areas doesn't result in accidental fatalities. It is purposeful terror bombing."[30]

In sum, through a process of monopoly control and distribution, repetition, and image escalation, the media achieve self-confirmation, that is, they find confirmation for the images they fabricate in the images they have already fabricated. Hyperbolic labeling takes the place of evidence: "genocide," "mass atrocities," "systematic rapes," and even "rape camps"—camps which no one has ever located. Through this process, evidence is not only absent, it becomes irrelevant.

So the US major media (and much of the minor media) are not free and independent, as they claim; they are not the watchdog of democracy but the lapdog of the national security state.

They help reverse the roles of victims and victimizers, warmongers and peacekeepers, reactionaries and reformers. The first atrocity, the first war crime committed in any war of aggression by the aggressors is against the truth.

Endnotes

1. For instance, Bonner, Raymond. (1999). "War crimes panel finds Croat troops 'cleansed' the Serbs." *New York Times*, March 21, a revealing report that has been ignored in the relentless propaganda campaign against the Serbs. **2.** John Ranz in his paid advertisement in the *New York Times*, April 29, 1993. **3.** Anonymous. (1993). "Correction: Report on rape in Bosnia." *New York Times*, October 23. **4.** Owen, David. (1997). *Balkan odyssey*. Harvest Books, p 262. **5.** Lituchy, Barry. "Media deception and the Yugoslav civil war," in *NATO in the Balkans*, p 205; see also *New York Times*, August 7, 1993. **6.** Both Noam Chomsky in his comments on Pacifica Radio, April 7, 1999, and Alexander Cockburn in *The Nation*, May 10, 1999, describe Milosevic as "monstrous" without offering any specifics. **7.** Biggs, Brooke Shelby. (1999). "Failure to inform." *San Francisco Bay Guardian*, May 5, p 25. **8.** *Washington Post*, June 6, 1999. **9.** See for instance, Robert Burns, Associated Press report, April 22, 1999. **10.** For example, *New York Times*, June 15, 1998. **11.** Radin, Charles & Louise Palmer. (1999). "Experts voice doubts on claims of genocide: Little evidence for NATO assertions." *San Francisco Chronicle*, April 22. **12.** *Newsday*, March 31, 1999. **13.** *New York Times*, May 11, 1999. **14.** Gillan, Audrey. (1999). "What's the story?" *London Review of Books*, May 27. **15.** *Washington Post*, July 10, 1999. **16.** See for instance, Gall, Carlotta. (1999). "Belgrade sees grave site as proof NATO fails to protect Serbs." *New York Times*, August 27. **17.** Both the State Department and Cohen's figures are reported in the *New York Times*, November 11, 1999. **18.** *New York Times*, November 11, 1999. **19.** Associated Press release, June 18, 1999. Reuters (July 12, 1999) reported that NATO forces had catalogued more than 100 sites containing the bodies of massacred ethnic Albanians. **20.** Stratfor.com, Global Intelligence Update. (1999). "Where are Kosovo's killing fields?" *Weekly Analysis*, October 18. **21.** Irvine, Reed & Cliff Kincaid. (1999). "Playing the numbers game." Accuracy in Media Website <www.aim.org/mm/1999/08/03.htm>. **22.** *London Sunday Times*, October 31, 1999. **23.** *Los Angeles Times*, August 28, 1999. **24.** Op cit., Stratfor.com. **25.** Richard Gwyn in the *Toronto Star*, November 3, 1999. **26.** Op cit., Gall. **27.** Op cit., Gwyn. **28.** *New York Times*, November 11, 1999. **29.** Intelligence reports from the German Foreign Office, January 12, 1999, and October 29, 1998, to the German Administrative Courts, translated by Eric Canepa, Brecht Forum, New York, April 20, 1999. **30.** Teach-in, Leo Baeck Temple, Los Angeles, May 23, 1999.

The Martin Luther King You Don't See on TV

Jeff Cohen and Norman Solomon

It's become a TV ritual: Every year in mid-January, around the time of Martin Luther King's birthday, we get perfunctory network news reports about "the slain civil rights leader."

National news media have never come to terms with what Martin Luther King, Jr. stood for during his final years.

The remarkable thing about this annual review of King's life is that several years—his last years—are totally missing, as if flushed down a memory hole.

What TV viewers see is a closed loop of familiar file footage: King battling desegregation in Birmingham (1963), reciting his dream of racial harmony at the rally in Washington (1963), marching for voting rights in Selma, Alabama (1965), and finally, lying dead on the motel balcony in Memphis (1968).

An alert viewer might notice that the chronology jumps from 1965 to 1968. Yet King didn't take a sabbatical near the end of his life. In fact, he was speaking and organizing as diligently as ever. Almost all of those speeches were filmed or taped. But they're not shown today on TV.

Why?

It's because national news media have never come to terms with what Martin Luther King, Jr. stood for during his final years.

In the early 1960s, when King focused his challenge on legalized racial discrimination in the South, most major media were his allies. Network TV and national publications graphically showed the police dogs and bullwhips and cattle prods used against Southern blacks who sought the right to vote or to eat at a public lunch counter.

But after passage of civil rights acts in 1964 and 1965, King began challenging the nation's fundamental priorities. He maintained that civil rights laws were empty without "human rights"—including economic rights. For people too poor to eat at a restaurant or afford a decent home, King said, anti-discrimination laws were hollow.

Noting that a majority of Americans below the poverty line were white, King developed a class perspective. He decried the huge income gaps between rich and poor, and called for "radical changes in the structure of our society" to redistribute wealth and power.

"True compassion," King declared, "is more than flinging a coin to a beggar; it comes to see that an edifice which produces beggars needs restructuring."

By 1967, King had also become the country's most prominent opponent of the Vietnam War, and a staunch critic of overall US foreign policy, which he deemed militaristic. In his "Beyond Vietnam" speech delivered at New York's Riverside Church on April 4, 1967—a year to the day before he was murdered—King called the United States "the greatest purveyor of violence in the world today."

In his last months, King was organizing the most militant project of his life: the Poor People's Campaign.

From Vietnam to South Africa to Latin America, King said, the US was "on the wrong side of a world revolution." King questioned "our alliance with the landed gentry of Latin America," and asked why the US was suppressing revolutions "of the shirtless and barefoot people" in the Third World, instead of supporting them.

In foreign policy, King also offered an economic critique, complaining about "capitalists of the West investing huge sums of money in Asia, Africa, and South America, only to take the profits out with no concern for the social betterment of the countries."

You haven't heard the "Beyond Vietnam" speech on network news retrospectives, but national media heard it loud and clear back in 1967—and loudly denounced it. *Life* called it "demagogic slander that sounded like a script for Radio Hanoi." The *Washington Post* patronized that "King has diminished his usefulness to his cause, his country, his people."

King called the United States "the greatest purveyor of violence in the world today."

In his last months, King was organizing the most militant project of his life: the Poor People's Campaign. He crisscrossed the country to assemble "a multiracial army of the poor" that would descend on Washington—engaging in nonviolent civil disobedience at the Capitol, if need be—until Congress enacted a poor people's bill of rights. *Reader's Digest* warned of an "insurrection."

King's economic bill of rights called for massive government jobs programs to rebuild America's cities. He saw a crying need to confront a Congress that had demonstrated its "hostility to the poor"—appropriating "military funds with alacrity and generosity," but providing "poverty funds with miserliness."

How familiar that sounds today, more than forty years after King's efforts on behalf of the poor people's mobilization were cut short by an assassin's bullet.

 In this nation of immense wealth, the federal government continues to accept the perpetuation of poverty and an absurdly bloated military budget. So do most corporate media. Perhaps it's no surprise that big media outlets tell us so little about the last years of Martin Luther King's life.

Treacherous Words
Normand Baillargeon

"Words, words, words."

—William Shakespeare

"What is well-conceived is easily articulated
And the words to say it come easily."

—French poet and critic Nicola Boileau, from his *Art of Poetry*

This section invites you to show great vigilance with regard to words, a vigilance that should equal the attention that those who know how to use words effectively to convince, deceive, and indoctrinate shrewdly pay them. I will begin by introducing an important distinction between the verbs "denote" and "connote."

1.1.1 To Denote/To Connote

Our spontaneous conception of language is often quite naïve. It is based on the idea that words designate objects in the world, objects to which we could otherwise point. One minute of reflection shows that it is far from being that simple. Many words do not have such referents: (They are abstract, imprecise, vague, and they change meaning depending on the context. Still others reify, transmit emotions, and so forth.) yes!

It is useful to distinguish between what words denote (the objects, people, facts, or properties to which they refer) and their connotations, that is, the emotional reactions that they elicit. Two words can thus denote the same thing but have very different connotations, positive in one case, negative in the other. Knowing this is crucial, because in this way one can glorify, denigrate, or neutralize that of which one speaks, as the case may be, merely by choosing one's words. Thus, it is different to talk about a car, a cruiser, or a beater: Each of these terms denotes a motor vehicle designed for individual trans-

port, but each also carries with it connotations and elicits very different emotional reactions. So it is advisable to be attentive to the words used to describe the world—especially in all the polemical and contested categories of social life. Think, for example, about the vocabulary used to speak about abortion. The protagonists in that debate refer to themselves as being pro-life or pro-choice. That is no accident: Who would want to be anti-life or anti-choice? Whether an activist is more willing to speak of a fetus or a baby is not accidental either. Think also about Wal-Mart employees, who are referred to as associates. Or again, think about comedian Roseanne Barr's joke: "I've found a fail-proof way of making sure that the kids eat healthily: the health mix. One spoonful of M&Ms and two of Smarties. The kids love it. You know it's good for them: Hey! It's a health mix!"

Look, too, at the use of what are known as euphemisms, which are words used to mask or at least minimize a disagreeable idea by referring to it with a word with less negative connotations. They are a good illustration of how this property of language can be used to mislead an audience.

Think about the following case, reported and studied by Sheldon Rampton and John Stauber.[1] It shows how groups with specific interests can use language to their advantage. In 1992, the US International Food Information Council (IFIC) was concerned about the public perception of food biotechnology. So they launched a vast research project to determine how to talk to the public about these technologies. Some words were identified as carrying positive baggage, and it was strongly recommended that they be used exclusively. For

Excerpted from *A Short Course in Intellectual Self-Defense* by Normand Baillargeon (Seven Stories Press, 2007).

example: beauty, abundance, children, choice, diversity, earth, organic, heritage, hybrid, farmer, flowers, fruits, future generations, hard work, improve, purity, soil, tradition, and whole. On the other hand, others were absolutely proscribed, notably: biotechnology, DNA, economy, experimentation, industry, laboratory, machine, manipulate, money, pesticides, profit, radiation, security, and researcher.

As one might easily guess, war is another domain particularly propitious to the use of euphemisms, as shown by the following table.[2] In the first column, you will find several examples of vocabulary that have been used to talk about war from Vietnam to our day. The second column suggests a translation of what is likely referred to by each of the words or expressions.

Collateral damage	Civilian deaths
Pacification center	Concentration camp
Caribbean peacekeeping force	The army, marines, and air force that invaded Grenada
US Department of Defense	Ministry of Aggression?
Operation Desert Storm	War on Iraq
Operation Provide Relief/ Operation Restore Hope	Entry of American troops into Somalia
Incursion	Invasion
Surgical strike	Bombing hoped to be precise because of the proximity of civilians
Defensive strike	Bombing
Strategic withdrawal	Retreat (ours)
Tactical redeployment	Retreat (the enemy's)
Advisors	Military officers or CIA agents —before the US admitted to its involvement in Vietnam
Terminate	Kill
Particular explosives	Napalm

The Demonstrations Against the Quebec Summit in Spring 2001, As Seen by Mario Roy

People dressed up as dolphins or sea-turtles—or even cows, as they were at the meeting of the Finance Ministers of the Americas in Toronto. Street musicians and dancers. Placards and posters. Rants and songs. Slogans and flyers. A demonstrator offers a flower to a police officer, as in that photo from the 1960s that was broadcast around the world and became an icon for the same reasons as Che.

A poster that says: Capitalism sucks! Like in 1970.

Everywhere, lanky teenagers and young adults race to the party, for the sole reason that you have to be where the action is, with your friends, whether it is Seattle or Quebec. For them, at night after the demo, once the placards have been stacked along the wall, there will be music and pot, love and wine….

We're not talking here about professional demonstrators, often paid by big unions or "community" organizations, who are leashed to the State, and who are completely uninteresting. Nor about the hooligans, the word we use in these instances for the little bums, who are scarcely less so.

Not at all.

We're talking about the big anonymous crowd of youth brimming with hormones and enthusiasm who go to the WTO or to the Summit of the Americas for the same reasons that other young people went to Woodstock, or to "McGill français," or to the Sorbonne for the big show in May of '68.

It's normal. And it's healthy. Don't you remember being eighteen?

Editorial, *La Presse*, April 14, 2001, A18.

1.1.2 On the Virtues of Imprecision

If words are often used to express precise and clear ideas, they can also be vague and imprecise. This property is sometimes even very useful. Thanks to it, something can be affirmed with such vagueness that there is little chance that an interpretation of the facts can confirm the affirmation.

Or, again, a thorny question can be answered with generalities that don't commit to anything specific, precisely because they say nothing specific.

> Q: Mr. President, critics of your proposed bill on interrogation rules say there's another important test—these critics include John McCain, who you've mentioned several times this morning—and that test is this: If a CIA officer, paramilitary, or special operations soldier from the United States were captured in Iran or North Korea, and they were roughed up, and those governments said, well, they were interrogated in accordance with our interpretation of the Geneva Conventions, and then they were put on trial and they were convicted based on secret evidence that they were not able to see, how would you react to that, as Commander-in-Chief?
>
> THE PRESIDENT: David, my reaction is, is that if the nations such as those you named, adopted the standards within the Detainee Detention Act, the world would be better. That's my reaction. We're trying to clarify law. We're trying to set high standards, not ambiguous standards.[3]

Nostradamus' Predictions

Michel de Notre-Dame, the doctor and astrologer who came to be known as Nostradamus, was born in Saint-Rémy-de-Provence, France, in 1503.

In 1555, he published his first collection of enigmatic quatrains, entitled *Centuries*, that immediately became immensely popular and are still held by his followers to be extraordinarily accurate predictions. The second edition of *Centuries* appeared in 1558: It was dedicated to King Henry II, to whom Nostradamus wished "a happy life." Henry II died the following year of a wound received in a tournament.

Was the visionary's sight clouded? Not at all, reply his sycophants, who maintain that the prediction of Henry II's death is, on the contrary, one of the clearest of all of Nostradamus' predictions. For Henry II died in a tournament held in Paris (on Saint-Antoine Street), hit by the Count of Montgomery's lance, which shattered and then penetrated his skull.

Nostradamus did indeed write the following:

> The young lion will overcome the older one,
> On the field of combat in a single battle;
> He will pierce his eyes through a golden cage,
> Two wounds made one, then he dies a cruel death.

Let us first note that such predictions are always formulated explicitly after the fact, which means they are not really predictions. For example, the events of September 11, 2001, could certainly be read into Nostradamus, but only starting on September 12, 2001.

But let's look more closely at this exemplary prediction/postdiction. This is the way James Randi analyzes the quatrain about King Henry II:

1. Speaking of "young" and "old" is questionable here because the two men were only a few years apart in age.

2. "On the field of combat" refers to a battlefield, but that is not how one would refer to the location of a jousting tournament, which is a sports competition.

3. "Golden cage": no piece of armor and no helmet were made of gold, because it is a soft metal.

4. "He will pierce his eyes": no witness at the time spoke of a pierced eye.

5. The lion was not the emblem of the King of France at the time, nor was it ever before or has it been since.

The moral of the story: Use vague words and put together obscure sentences—there will always be someone to read something into them and to exalt your gifts.

(James Randi. *The Mask of Nostradamus: The Prophecies of the World's Most Famous Seer* (Buffalo, NY: Prometheus Books, 1993), 170–176.

1.1.3 Sexism and Political Correctness

A language reflects the particular ideologies of the society by which it is spoken. It also reflects the transformations in these ideologies. A number of years ago, we became more sensitive to the sexist dimensions of our spoken language (which discriminate according to gender), but also to its classist, ageist, and ethnocentric dimensions (which discriminate according to social class, age, and society or culture, respectively). We have tried to get rid of them, because language can be a powerful vehicle of more and less subtle forms of exclusion and discrimination.

The story that follows is well-known. A man is traveling in a car with his son. There is an accident, and he is killed on the spot. The child is brought to the hospital emergency room. In the operating theater, however, the doctor declares: "I can't operate on this child; he's my son." How do you explain this perfectly true affirmation? The answer is obviously that the doctor is his mother.
Below are some examples of non-sexist rewriting.[4]

ORIGINAL: If the researcher is the principal investigator, he should place an asterisk after his name.
GENDER-NEUTRAL: Place an asterisk after the name of the principal investigator.

> The moral of the story: Use vague words and put together obscure sentences—there will always be someone to read something into them and to exalt your gifts.

ORIGINAL: Repeat the question for each subject so that he understands it.
GENDER-NEUTRAL: Repeat the question for all subjects so that they understand it.

ORIGINAL: The effect of PCBs has been studied extensively in rats and man.
GENDER-NEUTRAL: The effect of PCBs has been studied extensively in rats and humans.

ORIGINAL: The governor signed the workmen's compensation bill.
GENDER-NEUTRAL: The governor signed the workers' compensation bill.

Let us conclude by noting that some authors argue that these modes of expression sometimes limit us to excessive political correctness, which they decry as irritating, pernicious, and even harmful. Diane Ravitch,[5] for example, denounces what she calls the "language police" on American campuses and sees in them a threat to freedom of expression and the free exploration of all subjects and questions.

> It is useful to distinguish between what words denote (the objects, people, facts, or properties to which they refer) and their connotations, that is, the emotional reactions that they elicit.

Here, for example, are two cases reported by the author. A text dealing with the (true) story of a blind man who successfully climbed to the summit of a mountain was declared offensive, because the story of a mountain discriminates against people who live in flat cities and regions, and because the story suggests that being blind is a handicap. Further, an article affirming that there were rich and poor people in ancient Egypt was declared offensive to poor people today.

1.1.4 The Art of Ambiguity: Equivocation and Amphibology

In every language there are many words that are polysemous, which is to say that they have many meanings. It is this use of a word to mean one thing and then to subtly alter its meaning that produces the sort of equivocation considered here.

This property of words can, of course, be used to humorous effect. For example: Everyone agreed that the actor, who had played a hostage, had given a captivating performance. Or: The dead batteries were given out free of charge.

In both cases, the play is with the equivocal character of a word: A "captive" is a hostage or a prisoner; "captivating" means something that keeps an audience's attention. "Charge" can refer to both a quantifiable property of electricity and the act of taking money in exchange for something else.

But equivocation is not always easy to detect. Thus, it can be used to muddle people rather than to make them smile. For example: You have no trouble accepting the miracles of science; why do you suddenly become so critical when it comes to those in the Bible? After thinking a little, one will see that the word "miracle" is used in two clearly different ways. But if that goes unnoticed, one might think that the argument deserves a reply.

Newspaper headlines provide us with others: Red Tape Holds Up New Bridge.

Charlatans have known for a long time how to take full advantage of amphibology. The first known use probably goes back to Greek antiquity. King Croesus consulted the Delphic Oracles to know if he would be victorious in a war against the Persians. The Kingdom of Persia was separated from Croesus' own by the Halys River. The king received this answer: "If Croesus crosses the Halys, he will destroy a great empire." Croesus interpreted this to mean that he would win. But the prediction is ambiguous. Do you see why?

A text dealing with the (true) story of a blind man who successfully climbed to the summit of a mountain was declared offensive, because the story of a mountain discriminates against people who live in flat cities and regions, and because the story suggests that being blind is a handicap.

Let me give a final example. Some pedagogues place the concept of interest at the center of their thinking on education. But this word is an equivocal word that can be understood in at least two different ways: On the one hand, it can mean what does in fact interest the child, and on the other hand, it can mean that which is in the child's interest. It may well be that what interests the child is not in her interest and that that which is in her interest does not interest her.

Not specifying what one means by a pedagogy founded on interest can thus give way to a number of hard-to-detect equivocations. And thus do all those empty pedagogical slogans flourish. The rhetorical construction that enables the production of statements with multiple interpretations is called amphibology. Such statements are sometimes very funny and committed unbeknownst to their authors. Because people are trying to express themselves using a minimal number of words, classified ads are an endless sources of examples.

Croesus waged the war, convinced that he would be victorious. He was defeated. Taken prisoner by the king of Persia, he sent messengers to complain to the Oracle about her bad prediction. In Herodotus's account, the Pythia answered him thus:

> Croesus recriminates without reason. Loxias predicted that if he went to war against the Persians, he would destroy a great empire. In light of this answer, he should have asked the god which empire he spoke of, his own or that of Cyrus. He didn't understand what we told him, he didn't ask any further: let him reproach himself.[6]

So the Oracle's prediction was ambiguous and would be confirmed no matter who was defeated, which would be a great kingdom in either case.

> —Dog to give. Eats everything and adores children.
> —Renting superb sailboat twenty meters recent with comfortable sailor, well-equipped.
> —Dresser for ladies with curved feet.

A Dangerous, Invisible Killer

The following text was written in 1988 before being posted on the Web a few years later by Eric Lechner, one of its authors. It had more than once been presented as a petition and passed to random people in various public places to sign. Each time, it was signed by many people—which obviously has no scientific value. Be that as it may, it is a good read, as you will see, and an attentive read is an amusing critical thinking exercise.

The Invisible Killer

Dihydrogen monoxide is colorless, odorless, tasteless, and kills uncounted thousands of people every year. Most of these deaths are caused by accidental inhalation of DHMO, but the dangers of dihydrogen monoxide do not end there. Prolonged exposure to its solid form causes severe tissue damage. Symptoms of DHMO ingestion can include excessive sweating and urination, and possibly a bloated feeling, nausea, vomiting, and body electrolyte imbalance. For those who have become dependent, DHMO withdrawal means certain death.

Dihydrogen monoxide
• is also known as hydroxyl acid, and is the major component of acid rain;
• contributes to the "greenhouse effect";
• may cause severe burns;
• contributes to the erosion of our natural landscape;
• accelerates corrosion and rusting of many metals;
• may cause electrical failures and decreased effectiveness of automobile brakes;
• has been found in excised tumors of terminal cancer patients.

Contamination Is Reaching Epidemic Proportions!

Quantities of dihydrogen monoxide have been found in almost every stream, lake, and reservoir in America today. But the pollution is global, and the contaminant has even been found in Antarctic ice. DHMO has caused millions of dollars of property damage in the Midwest, and recently California. Despite the danger, dihydrogen monoxide is often used
• as an industrial solvent and coolant;
• in nuclear power plants;
• in the production of Styrofoam;
• as a fire retardant;
• in many forms of cruel animal research;
• in the distribution of pesticides—even after washing, produce remains contaminated by this chemical;
• as an additive in certain junk foods and other food products.

Companies dump waste DHMO into rivers and the ocean, and nothing can be done to stop them because this practice is still legal. The impact on wildlife is extreme, and we cannot afford to ignore it any longer!

The Horror Must Be Stopped!

The American government has refused to ban the production, distribution, or use of this damaging chemical due to its "importance to the economic health of this nation." In fact, the navy and other military organizations are conducting experiments with DHMO, and designing multi-billion dollar devices to control and utilize it during warfare situations. Hundreds of military research facilities receive tons of it through a highly sophisticated underground distribution network. Many store large quantities for later use.

The hoax continues on a hilarious site <www.dhmo.org> that promotes banning dihydrogen monoxide. Luckily, the effort has so far been completely in vain.

1.1.5 Accentuation

This rhetorical strategy relies on the fact that it is possible to change the meaning of a statement simply by changing the tone with which one pronounces certain words. For example, take the following maxim: "A person should not speak ill of her friends." Its meaning is clear and its interpretation generally unproblematic. But one can say it and mean that one can speak ill of those who are not one's friends, simply by emphasizing the last word: "A person should not speak ill of her *friends*." And one can also say it and make it understood that one can speak ill of others' friends: "A person should not speak ill of *her* friends." In a certain context, one would be able to say in insinuating that, if one cannot speak ill of one's friends, one can nevertheless do them ill: "A person should not *speak* ill of her friends."

There is a written equivalent of this oral strategy that consists of emphasizing certain parts of a message. Advertisements often employ this strategy, announcing in big letters, for example, "PERSONAL COMPUTER FOR $300"—and in very small print stating that the monitor is not included in the price.

The rhetorical construction that enables the production of statements with multiple interpretations is called amphibology.

A similar yet distinct strategy involves selectively presenting only certain passages from a text, thereby giving the impression that one thing was stated when in fact the original text said, if not the exact opposite, at least something entirely different. I suggest that we call this procedure *eduction*.[7]

To offer a fictitious example, here is what was written in the review of a play by Marvin Miller.

> The new play by Marvin Miller is a monumental failure! Presented by the producers as an adventure full of twists and turns and suspense that recounts the events of an arctic expedition, the only suspense, for this writer, was in finding out whether he would manage to stay until the end of the first act of this pitiful show. To tell the truth, the only interesting thing about this play is its musical accompaniment, superb and spellbinding, composed by Pierre Tournier.

And here is what one could extract to advertise the show:

> ...monumental!... an adventure full of twists and turns and suspense...superb and spellbinding.

1.1.6 Weasel Words

The weasel, charming animal that it is, attacks eggs in bird nests using a very particular method: It pierces them and sucks them, then leaves them there. The mama bird thinks she sees her egg, but it is only the shell emptied of its precious contents.

Weasel words do the same thing, but with propositions. Thus, one can be under the impression that a statement is full of rich content, but the presence of a little word has emptied it of substance.

Advertising often relies on this strategy; an attentive observer will find a great number of incidences. Who hasn't received an envelope marked, "You could have won $1,000,000"?

Here are a few other examples:

> A product *can* produce such-and-such effect.
> A product diminishes or augments something *up to* such-and-such level.
> A product *helps* to…
> A product *contributes* to…
> A product is a *component* of…
> A product makes you feel *like*…
> A product is *like*…
> A product is *in some ways*…
> *Some* researchers say that…
> Research *suggests* that…
> Research *tends* to demonstrate…
> *It is claimed* that…
> A product is *almost*…

Advertising, however, is hardly the only domain in which these weasel words are used. A critical thinker has to know how to recognize them right away in order not to misinterpret the message. At the same time, one must remember that, in certain cases, it is important to nuance one's thinking. But that should not be confused with using weasel words in a conscious effort to deceive or mystify.

"Dihydrogen monoxide is colorless, odorless, tasteless, and kills uncounted thousands of people every year."

1.1.7 Jargon and Pseudo-Expertise

It is sometimes necessary and altogether legitimate to use specialized vocabulary to express certain ideas clearly. One cannot, for example, seriously discuss quantum physics or Kant's philosophy without making use of technical words and precise vocabulary that allow one to engage in an exchange about complex ideas. This vocabulary, which a neophyte doesn't understand, serves to raise and clarify genuine problems, and yet one can generally give interested neophytes some idea of the meaning of these concepts and of the issues that they raise. With that glimpse, they can decide if they want to advance and deepen their knowledge. Should this be the case, they will have to acquire both the specialized vocabulary and the totality of knowledge which corresponds to it.

"Intellectuals have a problem: they have to justify their existence."

Yet one sometimes gets the impression that, far from revealing real problems, and allowing them to be studied and understood more clearly, vocabulary is used to make rather simple things artificially complicated, or to mask poor thinking. I concede that the dividing line between the first and second categories is not always easy to see—but it exists nonetheless. That which comprises the second category is called jargon.

There is a wide variety of jargon, and many terms have been suggested for it. For example, lawyers' jargon would be *legalese*; in fact, in the United States, there are groups that work to counter this juridical obscurantism and offer translations of legal documents into everyday language. Education studies jargon is called *educando*; to my knowledge no one has yet broached the Herculean task of translating those texts into language that is comprehensible to mortals.

Here is an example of academic jargon. It is an excerpt from a sociology Ph.D. thesis defended at the Sorbonne by a well-known French astrologer. According to the experts who read it, the thesis was unbelievably vacuous, and was intended to be an attempt to introduce astrology into the university curriculum.

The crux and the heart of astrology, that mirror of the profound unicity of the universe, reminds us of the *unus mundis* of the ancients, in which the cosmos was considered to be a massive indivisible Whole. With the rationalism and its Enlightenment, a schism of the heart, soul, and spirit took place—a schism between reason and feeling. It was a socio-cultural schism that went hand in hand with the duality to which our Western culture is still wedded, despite the apparent paradigm shift of the past few years....

However, a new paradigm is generating a growing interest in the stars, in spite of a residual rejection that endures and is basically linked to the confusion and elision of practices such as clairvoyance, tarot readings, and others. In light of our experience, a fundamental element of the outlook of any comprehensive sociology, whether Weberian or Simmelian, we wanted to privilege the phenomenon of the media, reflective as it is of the social, given our more than twenty years of experience in this area, within and beyond the Hexagon.... We have tried to analyze this de facto ambivalence between attraction and rejection; but also to define, by means of a social survey, what the epistemological situation of astrology is today....

Such a dialogue [between scientists and astrologers] could only ever be established around a complex thought, that which governs the New Scientific Spirit and also the astrological paradigm—think of A. Breton's discussion of the multi-dialectical game that astrology necessitates. We have largely practiced that openness, that flexibility of spirit on an empirical plane, to the point of becoming monomaniacal—or rather, metanoic (Pareto).[8]

The above passage is a perfect example of jargon and manages to condense into a few lines the worst imaginable contrivances: pseudo-wise terms used for no reason at all, and artificial references to concepts, theories, and prestigious authors.

No doubt such jargon has many functions. Some perceive it as a smokescreen intended to procure prestige for those who use it. Noam Chomsky sees it, at least in part, as a way for intellectuals to hide the vacuity of their work:

> Intellectuals have a problem: they have to justify their existence. Now, there are few things about the world that are understood. Most of the things that are understood, except perhaps for in certain areas of physics, can be explained with very simple words and in very short sentences. But if you do that, you don't become famous, you don't get a job, people don't revere your writing. There's a challenge there for intellectuals: to take what is rather simple and make it appear to be something very complicated and very profound. Groups of intellectuals interact that way. They speak amongst each other, and the rest of the world is supposed to admire them, treat them with respect, etc. But translate what they are saying into simple language and you'll often find either nothing at all or truisms, or absurdities.[9]

Learning to draw the line mentioned above, and thus to recognize jargon, is not always easy. In fact, it is a long-term task that requires a great deal of knowledge, rigor, and modesty in the face of one's own ignorance, as well as openness to new ideas.

To conclude, I would like to call to mind the results of an amusing study[10] that sought to demonstrate some of the effects of the recourse to jargon in the academic context. Although it is unique and does not allow for meaningful conclusions to be drawn, I will cite it here nonetheless, because it is one of the rare studies to try to deal with this topic.

At the beginning of the 1970s, Dr. Fox gave a talk on three different occasions, entitled "Mathematical Theory of Games and its Application in the Training of Doctors." He spoke in front of a total of 55 people, all highly educated: social workers, educators, administrators, psychologists, and psychiatrists. His exposition lasted an hour and was followed by a half-hour-long discussion. Then a questionnaire was distributed to the audience to find out what those present thought of the doctor's presentation. All the participants found it clear and stimulating; none of them noticed that the talk was a mess of nonsense—which it was.

Dr. Fox was actually an actor. He looked very distinguished and spoke authoritatively and with conviction. But the text he spoke, which he had learned by heart and which had to do with a topic he knew absolutely nothing about, was laden with vague words, contradictions, bogus references, knowledgeable references to concepts that had nothing to do with the topic at hand, empty concepts, and so on. In short, it was nothing but hot air, contradictions, and pompous meaninglessness.

Those who pulled off the hoax—which calls to mind Sokal's[11] a few years ago—formulated what they call the Fox hypothesis, according to which an unintelligible speech, if given by a legitimate source, will tend in spite of everything else to be accepted as intelligible. A corollary of this idea is that using vocabulary that gives even the illusion of profundity and erudition can contribute to increasing the credibility of a message.

1.1.8 Defining

> "There's glory for you!"
>
> "I don't know what you mean by 'glory,'" Alice said.
>
> Humpty Dumpty smiled contemptuously. "Of course you don't—till I tell you. I meant 'there's a nice knock-down argument for you!'"
>
> "But 'glory' doesn't mean 'a nice knock-down argument,'" Alice objected.
>
> "When I use a word," Humpty Dumpty said, in rather a scornful tone, "it means just what I choose it to mean—neither more not less."
>
> "The question is," said Alice, "whether you can make words mean so many different things."
>
> "The question is," said Humpty Dumpty, "which is to be master—that's all."
>
> —Lewis Carroll, *Through the Looking-Glass*

Anyone who has ever been sucked into a discussion that got bogged down this way knows some arguments are actually misunderstandings based on the imprecision of a meaning of a given word, or go on because each interlocutor has a different definition for one or more of the terms being used. Obviously, in such cases, it is necessary to produce a definition on which everyone can agree. But defining is no small task.

The first temptation is to rely on the dictionary. Sometimes this is entirely legitimate. Nevertheless, it must be remembered that the dictionary often provides what are essentially a society's conventions in relation to the use of words—conventions that are clarified through the use of synonyms. This is certainly not without value. For example, if you don't know what your interlocutor means by "quadruped," the dictionary will provide you with a useful synonym which will enlighten you sufficiently to be able to continue the conversation: "a four-footed animal, esp. a four-footed mammal." Another example: If you don't know what an author means by "Dearborn," a nineteenth-century English dictionary will tell you that at that time it was the name of a kind of covered wagon.

In the West, we can say that philosophy was born, at least in part, of the desire to resolve problems related to conceptual definitions, the immense difficulty of formulating them, and their numerous consequences.

This type of definition, however—which is called linguistic—is generally not what is required. Suppose that you were discussing whether a given practice is just: Appealing to a dictionary to learn that "just" means "acting or done in accordance with what is morally right or fair" will not help you very much. You would immediately want to know what "right or fair" means, if that "accordance" is necessary and why, and a thousand other things. If you were having a conversation with someone about whether the creations of Christo—who wrapped the Reichstag in Berlin, the Pont Neuf in Paris, and Central Park in New York—are art or not, the linguistic definition of "art" would not help you very much.

These problems are not purely theoretical. On the contrary, they are vital and fraught with all kinds of consequences. For example, it is difficult to define terms like "terrorism," "life," "death," "abortion," "war," "genocide," "marriage," "poverty," "theft," or "drugs." Think for just a moment about the repercussions of using of one definition rather than another.

In these cases, what has to be produced is called a conceptual definition. In the West, we can say that philosophy was born, at least in part, of the desire to resolve problems related to conceptual definitions, the immense difficulty of formulating them, and their numerous consequences. Socrates' name is still associated with all of this. He urged his contemporaries to adopt an approach that involved arriving at a conceptual definition of a problematic term by way of induction, that is to say, through the examination of a particular case. This approach is still valuable; it is often advantageous to try to clarify the concepts we use in this way. What are the necessary and sufficient conditions that must be satisfied to be able to talk of terrorism? Are these conditions found in every case that is currently understood to be terrorism? And if not, what needs to be revised, our use or our definition of the term?

One old but useful way of proceeding is to look for the general type (genus) and the specific difference (differentia) of what we want to define. For example, imagine we want to define "bird." The genus is animal; the specific difference is that by which birds—and they alone—differ from other animals (which we could say is having feathers). Try it with "drug": You'll see that the exercise is not as easy as it seems. Science and specialized knowledge often provide definitions that can be helpful to us.

Undertaking such exercises in definition, some people appeal to etymology, the study of the roots of words. Here again, a warning is necessary: The origin of a word is not necessarily illuminating, since the meaning it had yesterday, in its original form, is not necessarily identical to the meaning it has in its new form. Often it is even very distant, such that etymology tells us almost nothing at all. The word "role," for example, comes from the medieval Latin rotulus, which referred to a rolled parchment on which a text was written. That is not exactly a big help.

What could be called an "etymological fallacy" can sometimes be pushed quite a distance. Thus, partisans of a liberal conception of education have claimed that the word "education" comes from educere, etymology that invites a conception of education as an act of leading (*induco*) out of (*ex*) ignorance—which conforms to the liberal notion of education. On the other side are those who favor a notion of education understood as nourishing and, more broadly, furnishing the conditions necessary for a person's development. They invoke a second etymological hypothesis, according to which "education" comes from *educare*, which means "nourish" or "raise." And still others maintain that education is an indeterminate concept and support their thesis with the very uncertainty of the etymology. You see that etymology, as illuminating as it sometimes is, cannot, in any instance, resolve problems of conceptual definition on its own.

Sometimes we have to agree to a stipulative definition, that is to say a contextual definition. Concepts like "overweight" and "obese," for example, belong to a continuum of excess weight: The line between normal weight, overweight, and obesity are drawn with the help of a body mass index, which provides a stipulative definition of those concepts.

As for science, it often relies on two sorts of definitions, which are important to know.

First, operational definitions. These show the sequence of stages to follow in order to observe the concept that constitutes the object of study. The recipe for a Black Forest cake is an operational definition of the concept of Black Forest cake. Of course, the operational definitions used in science are much more complex.

Secondly, consider indexes. The approach involves a number of steps. Take concept X. We would begin by making ourselves an image representation of the concept: Here in this phase, knowledge, sensitivity, and creativity come into play. The next step is the specification of the concept, in which we would clarify its dimensions. The third phase is when we would choose the indications of those dimensions, the observable characteristics that make them visible. To finish, we would carry out a weighted synthesis of these dimensions according to a unique scale, which comes to constitute the index. To finish, I would note how easy it is to succumb to the temptation of reification, which grants a reality and autonomous existence to an index that is nothing more than one possible or hypothetical construction. The Intellectual Quotient (the infamous IQ) is just such an index; everyone knows how easily it can be reified.

Endnotes

1. Rampton, Sheldon, and John Stauber. (2001). *Trust us, we're experts*. New York: Jeremy P. Tarcher/Putnam, ch 3. **2.** Adapted from Kahane, Howard (1984). *Logic and contemporary rhetoric: The use of reason in everyday life*, 4th ed. Belmont CA: Wadsworth, p 137. **3.** White House press conference, 15 Sep 2006. Transcript at <whitehouse.gov>. **4.** These examples were taken from the Writing Center at Rensselaer Polytechnic. **5.** Ravitch, Diane. (2003). *The language police: How pressure groups restrict what students learn*. New York: Knopf, pp 10, 13. **6.** Herodotus. *Histories I*, p 91. **7.** Education is an ancient term in philosophy that is seldom used today, referring to the act through which an efficient cause, acting on "matter," gives it a determined form, or removes the surplus, so that a specific form can emerge. **8.** Tessier, É. (No date). *Situation épistémologique de l'astrologie à travers l'ambivalence fascination rejet dans les sociétés postmodernes*. Doctoral dissertation, La Sorbonne. **9.** Baillargeon, Normand, and David Barsamian. (2002). *Entretiens avec Chomsky*. Montreal: Editions écosociété, pp 45–6. **10.** Armstrong, J. Scott. (1980). Unintelligible management research and academic prestige. *Interfaces* 10.2, pp 80–6. **11.** At this point, there is ample literature concerning the Sokal affair. Briefly, Alan Sokal, a physician, succeeded in getting a text advancing the critiques of science and rationality common in certain academic disciplines published in a cultural studies journal. But his article was riddled with significant stupidities and falsities concerning science, which the editors missed. By doing this, Sokal was trying to suggest that in those milieus, some people had virtually no knowledge of the science they were so blithely critiquing. You can read more on the topic in Sokal, A., and A Bricmont. (1999). *Impostures intellectuelles*. Paris: Odile Jacob.

Treacherous Words
Normand Baillargeon

School Textbooks

Unpopular History vs. Cherished Mythology?

Earl Lee

One of the most pervasive and yet poorly understood influences on American society is the high school textbook. Thanks to the virtual monopoly of public education, textbook publishers have a wide-ranging power to shape the ideas of young people. Textbooks do more to misinform and mislead than almost any other print media. Some of our most basic beliefs,

> Major textbook publishers will not include content that might offend powerful political and religious constituencies, both national and local.

including our conception of ourselves as Americans, are shaped and distorted by the school textbook.

Looking at the areas of history, literature, and science, it is easy to see how textbooks fail. First, history textbooks typically focus on names, dates, and places, rather than on the conflict of political and economic interests. Second, literature textbooks create a censored and bowdlerized version of our literary heritage. Third, science textbooks present a detail-based version of science that often very deliberately shies away from broader concepts.

The reason for this is obvious. Textbook publishers want to sell textbooks to as many schools as possible. The key to doing this is marketing, which means printing bright, shiny book covers, pages filled with lots of color pictures, and an eye-catching layout. Creating a visually interesting layout is fairly easy and safe—unless you make the mistake, as happened in 1999, of printing a picture of General Washington in too-bright colors, so that his watch fob could be mistaken for an exposed penis—then all hell can break out! At least this is what happened in Muscogee County, Georgia, where school officials, fearful of the "disruptive element" that would be created by fifth-graders who might notice the exposure of General Washington's fob, decided to alter the picture in 2,300 copies of the textbook.[1] (Ironically, given the publicity over this picture and knowing the nature of fifth-grade boys, the students will probably draw brand-new cartoon penises on every single copy of the history text, so that within a few years all 2,300 pictures of General Washington will sport an enormous (and anatomically incorrect) "John Thomas" in place of the missing watch fob.)

In spite of such occasional errors, the real problem with textbooks is not in the illustrations but in the written content. Major textbook publishers will not include content that might offend powerful political and religious constituencies, both nationally and locally—from the local chamber of commerce to the Church of Christ. Offending these groups could be a serious obstacle to selling books.

Schools go to great lengths to avoid buying books that have dangerous ideas. In some states, a government agency takes over the role of censor by creating lists of "approved" texts. In a state the size of Texas, getting a textbook on the "approved" list means a potential gain of millions of dollars in sales for the publisher. Thus textbook publishers are motivated to search for the lowest possible threshold of political offensiveness.

In some areas, teachers have to select textbooks from a locally approved list. In these situations, the school board appoints a committee to take over the task of weeding out any

> In a state the size of Texas, getting a textbook on the "approved" list means a potential gain of millions of dollars in sales for the publisher.

textbooks that contain offensive ideas. This list is often submitted to a principal or superintendent who can make further cuts. Also, in recent years a number of organizations have come forward to "help" school boards and state agencies by identifying dangerous textbooks that should be avoided. Controversial ideas must be cut out to avoid offending the feelings, not only of the "educators" who select textbooks, but of the parents of students, and even people who have no school-age children but have self-appointed themselves as watchdogs for "community values."

For example, Mel and Norma Gabler, a husband and wife from Texas, have had a strong influence on the choice of textbooks for public schools nationwide. Over a period of 30 years, until their deaths in 2004 and 2007, the Gablers helped to bring about the rejection, or significant revision of, one-half to two-thirds of the textbooks proposed for use in Texas.[2] More recently, their organization, Educational Research Analysts, has made major inroads in influencing the selection of textbooks in California. Given the economics of textbook publishing, they and similar advocacy groups have had a ripple effect across the country. Such groups often include in their guidelines for textbooks that these should "encourage loyalty" and avoid "defaming" the nation's founders, and avoid material that might lead students to criticize their parents. In one of his more revealing statements, Mel Gabler criticized textbooks, saying, "Too many textbooks and discussions leave students free to make up their minds about things."

In 1975, this campaign got particularly ugly. The Gablers helped several local ministers in Kanawha County, West Virginia, protest the use of several new language-arts textbooks in the local schools. A leader of the protest claimed that the textbooks were "filthy, disgusting trash, unpatriotic and unduly favoring blacks."[3] The conflict over textbooks soon led to a school boycott and a riot, and one minister was later jailed for his part in a conspiracy to burn several elementary schools and even bomb school buses.[4]

In addition to Educational Research Analysts, an organization founded by the Gablers and which continues their work, there are dozens of other similar right-wing groups. But there are also left-wing groups who lobby textbook publishers, and some of these have been very successful in getting publishers to add more material favorable toward women and minorities, while also getting publishers to cut "expressions containing racial or ethnic statements that might be interpreted as insulting and stereotyping of the sexes, the elderly, or other minority groups or concerns."[5] Of course the word "might" here leaves a hole big enough to drive a truck through. This statement implies that material should be cut that might through some misinterpretation be considered racist. This means bowdlerizing the word *nigger* out of *Huckleberry Finn* and "fixing" the lower-class slang, or, better yet, not teaching the book at all.

Overall, the public school textbook is designed to avoid controversy and perpetuate ideas that are safe, comfortable, and uncomplicated. To an outsider looking at the goals of public education, it is clear that the primary goal of public schools must be to instill in students conventional and conformist hab-

> The possibility that people might view government as an instrument of the public will, much less take up arms to oppose entrenched power, is a dangerous idea that must be squelched on all levels.

its of thought. Textbook authors recognize this fact and do their part to assist in the goal of creating a lazy conformity in students. Of course, this is hardly a new observation. Back in the 1870s, French novelist Gustave Flaubert, in notes for his *Dictionary of Accepted Ideas*, commented on the tendency of French schoolbooks to direct students toward the acceptable ideas about French history. "French textbooks repeat the same views, offer the same extracts, and lest the student should rashly venture on a perception of his own, guide him with footnotes to the correct criticism of the text." This has the effect of creating in the student "a compound of error, pedantry, misplaced scorn, fatuous levity, and ignorance of its ignorance."[6]

There have been a lot of complaints in the media in recent years about the dumbing down of textbooks. However, most of these complaints point to lower standardized test scores as evidence of a failure in education. In fact, whether or not students can come up with the names of military leaders in the Civil War, or the correct location of Lexington on a map, or the dates for the passage of Amendments to the Constitution— these factoids are of little real importance. It is far more important for students to understand *why* the Civil War started, *why*

School Textbooks Unpopular History vs. Cherished Mythology?
Earl Lee

65

the Battle of Lexington took place, and *why* the Bill of Rights and other Amendments to the Constitution were necessary. But these concepts are not easily measured on a standardized test. Yet the corporate-controlled media focus almost exclusively on standardized test results when they criticize public education. This philosophy of education was pretty well summed up by Mel Gabler when he said, "Allowing a student

> By claiming that we live in a democracy, school textbooks help to deceive us about the basic functions of American government.

to come to his own conclusions about abstract concepts creates frustration. Ideas, situation ethics, values, anti-God humanism—that's what the schools are teaching. And concepts. Well, a concept never will do anyone as much good as a fact."[7] Unfortunately, this reliance on "just the facts" is central to President Bush's No Child Left Behind program, which relies heavily on standardized tests, published by the same companies who create the textbooks. In recent years the reliance on testing as a measure of success has only increased.

In the real world, people tend to remember the things that engage their senses and their imaginations.[8] People are compelled by the interplay of ideas and personalities, not by the names and dates of historic events. The meaning of the Magna Carta is not in the date when it was signed, but rather in its origins. It has meaning as the result of the conflict that led to its creation and the personalities that brought it into existence. But in the classroom, the significance of the Magna Carta is obscured by factoids and the trivial pursuit of names and dates. Similarly, John Locke's *Two Treatises of Government*, which is the foundation of modern political ideas, is cited only as a dead fact, not a living idea.

> In some cases the Anti-Federalists are mentioned, though their concerns about the powers granted a new federal government are always dismissed as unfounded.

In 1999, when the Kansas State Board of Education voted to remove evolution from state standards, it caused a nationwide furor. Yet ironically, when this same board voted to move away from using essay questions and toward relying on multiple-choice questions in evaluating students, virtually nothing was said. Board members stated that this decision was based on the fact that the results of multiple-choice tests are easy to measure. Clearly the goal of twenty-first-century education is memorization, not understanding.

History

In theory, one of the main functions of public education is to help create a citizenry that understands the functions of government and is able to make informed judgments about how public policy will affect future generations. It is a basic justification for studying history, often repeated by historians, that those who fail to learn about the past are doomed to repeat it. This was certainly the view of many leaders of the American Revolution. We study history in order to understand how humans have responded in the past to similar events and situations. As a society, we have a compelling interest in making sure that people understand how government functions, within the context of our history.

But, at the same time, there are powerful commercial interests who see an informed citizenry as a direct threat to corporate power. These corporations would rather have a citizenry that is easily influenced to accept whatever message is given them by the corporate-controlled media. For this reason, they find the topics of the American Revolution and the Civil War to be particularly dangerous. The possibility that people might view government as an instrument of the public will, much less take up arms to oppose entrenched power, is a dangerous idea that must be squelched on all levels.

One of the most blatant frauds found in textbooks is the idea of "democracy." All students are taught, from a very early age, that the United States is a democracy and has a democratic form of government. However, anyone who bothers to examine our system of government objectively can quickly see that it is a republic, not a democracy. At the time of the Constitutional Convention, Ben Franklin declared that "we have a republic, if we can keep it," and any nineteenth-century schoolboy could have told you this in an instant. This is why we have "The Battle Hymn of the Republic" and not "The Battle Hymn of the Democracy." The United States continued to think of itself as a republic through the end of the nineteenth century. After the

Civil War, according to the newly written Boy Scouts' Pledge of Allegiance, we were well on our way to becoming a homogenized "one nation, indivisible," but the American flag still represented "the republic, for which it stands."

Ironically, "democracy" was not always as cherished a concept as it is today. In the early years of the republic, "democracy" was a dirty word, in part because of its association with Cromwell and the Puritan Revolution in England. Thomas

Most textbooks struggle to avoid an honest assessment of Washington's military leadership.

Jefferson, who today is one of the major icons of the Democratic Party, never identified himself as a "democrat" in his speeches or writings. Many other American leaders also avoided the "democratic" label. It wasn't until WWI that the term "democracy" lost its bad associations. During WWI, President Woodrow Wilson began pushing "democracy" as an idea that needed to be defended in Europe.[9] But it is pretty clear that Wilson, and those who followed his lead, used "democracy" as a vague euphemism for Americanism, meaning the Anglo-American form of government.

Thanks to Wilson, following WWI "democracy" stopped being a form of government and became, instead, a vague and loosely defined expression meaning "The American Way." It is in this sense that the United States has exported "democracy" to Latin America, Southeast Asia, and other areas worldwide. Over the decades since WWI, our history textbooks have helped to reinforce this idea and have helped to homogenize the American federal and state powers into a democracy that isn't one. Today, most people incorrectly use "democracy" in place of "suffrage"—meaning the right of citizens to vote in elections. This confusion over "democracy" makes it easier for politicians to obscure the way our government really functions. Looking at how the word is used, people must think that "democracy" means a free-market economy where people get to vote in elections. And even though most young people today have only a vague idea of what our "democracy" stands for, they are apparently willing to fight and die in various regional wars in order to promote this form of government in Eastern Europe, the Middle East, and Africa.

What textbooks do not teach us about government is this: There are very few truly democratic governments in existence in North America, much less the world. Even though politicians

claim that the United States is a democracy, espouses democracy and democratic values, and promotes democracy worldwide—this is probably the greatest con game (bait-and-switch) in history. We may claim to be a government "of the people, by the people, for the people," but in fact we are ruled by a government made up of our "legal representatives" who were anointed by the mass media and voted into office with the help of money from lobbyists and PACs. Except for the few states that allow referenda, voters have no direct say in legislative decisions. And this situation is unlikely to change because, in the view of politicians and lobbyists, a republic works much better than a government "of the people," especially since it is very hard to lobby, much less buy off, "the people." By claiming that we live in a democracy, school textbooks help to deceive us about the basic functions of American government.

Looking at the American Revolution and the Civil War, we can see that there are several ideas that are typically obscured, avoided, downplayed, or distorted. A history textbook can be easily be judged by how it deals with these problem issues:

1. **How does the textbook deal with the Anti-Federalists and the opposition to the Constitution?**

In some cases the Anti-Federalists are mentioned, though their concerns about the powers granted the new federal government are always dismissed as unfounded. This is the standard view of historians, although a convincing argument can be made that this increased federal power under the new Constitution led to a whole series of terrible consequences, from the extermination of native peoples to the Civil War. But, given the current political climate in this country, no existing school textbook is likely to (1) question the decision to create a new federal power, or (2) clearly explain why banks and other commercial interests strongly supported creating this new centralized power.

It is worth noting, too, that even though the thirteen colonies had just defeated the most powerful empire on earth over the issues of taxation and maintaining a standing army, the Federalists now wanted the power to levy taxes and establish a powerful federal army. The purpose of this army was clear: to put down internal conflicts, like Shay's Rebellion. And what was the cause of Shay's Rebellion? Heavy taxes, unfair banking practices, and the resulting farm foreclosures!

School Textbooks Unpopular History vs. Cherished Mythology?
Earl Lee

67

2. How does the text explain the origins of the Bill of Rights?

It is common for textbooks to gloss over the Bill of Rights, as if these first ten Amendments were a natural outgrowth of the Constitution. In actuality, many Federalists did not want a Bill of Rights, and these Amendments to the Constitution were passed largely due to the insistence of

Textbook authors don't like to write about events where anyone could be blamed for anything.

"old revolutionaries" like Jefferson. Earlier, during the debates over the Constitution, several states agreed to adopt the Constitution with the understanding that a Bill of Rights would be added. Although several dubious methods were used to get the Constitution ratified, not carrying through with the promise of a Bill of Rights would have been a public-relations disaster for the new government, and so passing the Bill of Rights was later supported, grudgingly, by many Federalists. It is important for today's students to understand that the passage of the Bill of Rights was not, by any means, a sure thing.

3. How quickly does the textbook gloss over the Alien and Sedition Acts?

The passage of these legislative measures is a touchy point in American history. This was the closest we came, early on, to establishing a monolithic oligarchy. Most textbooks rush to point out that the public reaction against the acts led to Jefferson's election as president. They also often point out that only a few people were actually imprisoned or deported under the acts, which makes as much sense as the more recent claim that the Patriot Act affects only a few people or affects only "suspected terrorists." With the earlier acts, the decision of whom to spy on, arrest, and prosecute was left solely in the hands of Federalists, who used it to harass and jail their critics. Despite the obvious relevance today, the Alien and Sedition Acts, which very nearly destroyed this country, are given little (if any) coverage in many textbooks.

4. How does the textbook handle George Washington?

Most textbooks struggle to avoid an honest assessment of Washington's military leadership. Washington is often present-

ed as the first person to lead the country (ignoring the earlier leaders of the Continental Congress, like John Hancock and Richard Henry Lee). It would be more honest to say that Washington was the first leader of the new federal government under the Constitution. In spite of the fact that the Continental Congress successfully led us through the Revolution, this body is typically described as "weak and ineffective." But what does this really mean? To be more historically precise, the Continental Congress was too weak from the point of view of Eastern banks and other commercial interests who wanted a strong federal government. And Washington became the spokesman for this new federal power. He also supported a strong federal army that could put down internal conflicts, like Shay's Rebellion.

Additionally, in terms of Washington's military leadership, it is worth noting that the Iroquois knew George Washington as "the destroyer of towns" because his Indian policy was to starve them out by burning their villages and corn fields, rather than fighting them on the battlefield. But this fact will certainly never find its way into textbooks.

5. How does the textbook explain the origins of the Civil War?

Most textbooks focus on slavery as the main issue of the Civil War, even though slavery was really one of several broader political and economic conflicts between North and South. Lincoln himself appeared to have mixed feelings about the issue, as his Emancipation Proclamation freed only the slaves living in the Confederacy, and then only the slaves living in those areas still under control of rebel forces. From a legal point of view, the Emancipation Proclamation was based on the idea that slaves were property used in the act of rebellion and could therefore legally be seized (under the Confiscation Act). Ironically, after the end of the war many newly freed slaves moved north, becoming a cheap source of labor for Northern factories. As former slaves moved north they often exchanged their former status as chattel slaves for the position of wage slaves in factories. One former slave, years later, described slavery as "a snake pointed south" and emancipation as "a snake pointed north." Of course, this fact is unlikely to find its way into history textbooks, which are more concerned with the effects of Reconstruction.

6. **Does the textbook mention the hardships and privations suffered by civilians as the result of the conflict, and especially Sherman's March to the Sea?**

William Tecumseh Sherman was the first American general to use "total war." By this it is meant that Sherman destroyed food supplies necessary for the survival of many Southerners. People today, who can go to a grocery to buy food, have no idea just how terrible Sherman's March was in its very real consequences for the civilian population in Georgia, white and black. Before this time, American soldiers had not waged this type of war on civilian populations, except for several Native American tribes.

7. **How does the textbook deal with Reconstruction?**

Under the influence of Southern states, many of whom had laws requiring the use of the term "War Between the States" rather than "Civil War" in educational materials, textbook publishers have come over the years to adopt a pro-Southern take

graft) during Rockefeller's mini-Reconstruction were outraged. The new two-party system in Arkansas later produced a US President and several contenders for the job, including Hillary Clinton and Mike Huckabee. This should probably be taken as a sign of the more healthy political give-and-take which now exists in the state.

8. **How does the textbook deal with race riots, lynching, and the widespread growth of racial violence in the early part of this century?**

This aspect of American history has never been dealt with very well in history textbooks. This is in large part because textbook authors don't like to write about events where anyone could be blamed for anything. One the one hand, when you write about the Alien and Sedition Acts, it's easy to emphasize that President Adams was hesitant to enforce the legislation, and only a few dozen people were deported or imprisoned, while the reaction led to Jefferson's election. On the other hand, how do you write about the Tulsa Race Riot of 1921? It is impossible to write about this horrendous event without blaming the white population. It is hard for textbook authors to

> As with history, the study of literature often descends into a trivial pursuit of facts and data, things easily measured in multiple-guess questions.

on this topic. The Reconstruction era is virtually always portrayed as a period when greed and political corruption ran rampant in the South.[10] In the first years after the war, many Southerners did suffer severe hardships, but over time Reconstruction was generally successful. Reconstruction ushered in an era of relatively honest and fair government.

The effects of Reconstruction can be compared with more recent history to make this process clear. In 1966 when Winthrop Rockefeller was elected the first Republican Governor of Arkansas since Reconstruction, his election marked the end of decades of one-party rule, characterized by cronyism, graft, and corruption on a massive scale. For example, when the former Governor Orval Faubus left office in 1967, he was able to buy a house worth more than $100,000 even though, as governor, he had earned only $10,000 a year in salary. After taking office, Gov. Rockefeller began a massive overhaul of the corrupt state prison system. He did this largely by bringing in experts (i.e., carpetbaggers) from outside of Arkansas to clean up and manage the prisons (as dramatized in the 1980 film *Brubaker*). Of course, the locals who lost their jobs (and

find a silver lining in an act of pure hatred, when white mobs attacked and burned out all the black businesses in the city. And so it is difficult to find the Tulsa Race Riot even mentioned.

On the other hand, the Civil Rights movement of the 1960s does have genuine heroes who can be the main characters of the drama. At the same time, when it is covered in history texts, Civil Rights history is often written so that the whites who opposed integration come off as well as possible, usually as victims of a Southern racist upbringing. The KKK is a handy bad guy, though it is considered bad manners to mention that the KKK was a powerful political force in Northern states, too. In the 1920s, the Klan had over 300,000 members in Indiana alone, which works out to about a third of all the adult white males in that state. Yet, in our history books, the Civil Rights workers are put center stage, opposed by police dogs and fire hoses, while the earlier lynching and the brutal beatings and murders are kept far in the background. After all, in trying to cover American history, textbook publishers have to keep one eye on the large textbook markets in Florida and Texas.

School Textbooks Unpopular History vs. Cherished Mythology?
Earl Lee

69

In a very real sense, the reconciliation of North and South depends on a set of "collective lies."[11] This is the cherished mythology reflected in our textbooks. Similarly, the reconciliation of blacks and whites, after centuries of political and economic oppression, is based on a decision not to discuss what happened in the early part of the century and instead focus on

Swift's *Gulliver's Travels* is the original source for the expression "a piece of ass."

a few heroic figures in the 1960s Civil Rights movement. Unfortunately, this deliberate censorship of a large chunk of history leaves many whites in the position where they can pretend to be the injured party, which helps to further inflame racist conflicts today.

■ ■ ■ ■ ■ ■ ■ ■ ■

There are literally dozens of other questions one could ask: How does the textbook deal with labor history? Does it mention the struggle for the 8-hour day and the minimum wage at all? Does it mention Eugene Debs, the International Workers of the World (IWW), the Socialist Party, the Haymarket Martyrs, the AFL and CIO, the trials of pacifists in WWI, the women's riots over unsafe factories, etc., etc., etc.?

The problem is, of course, that high school history textbooks tend to give a heavily pro-corporate "consensus" view of history. In this version of history, it is important to develop a cherished mythology rather than an accurate nuts-and-bolts view of historical events. Creating a cherished mythology means that textbooks avoid all the unpopular "revisionist" histories, as textbook publishers particularly dislike the idea of abandoning popular ideas for more pragmatic views of historical events. This resistance to "unpopular" history is also common to public history, meaning the history put forth in museums and public exhibits.

For example, in 1995, when the Smithsonian Institution tried to put on an *Enola Gay* exhibit, the whole project came under considerable criticism from veterans' groups that objected to graphic photographs of the human casualties of the atomic bombing of Hiroshima. Interestingly enough, an earlier exhibit on the use of the V2 bombs by the Nazis, including graphic

photographs of the human devastation in London, did not provoke a reaction (although if a similar exhibit were held in a Berlin museum, it would probably draw fire). The *Enola Gay* exhibit was quickly withdrawn and replaced by a more politically expedient exhibit. Richard Kurin, in his book *Reflections of a Culture Broker*, says that the curators "naïvely believed that there is an absolute historical truth." Indeed, many academic historians believe that being historically accurate is a reasonable defense from criticism. The curators at the Smithsonian forgot that the use of the atomic bomb is still a major part of our nation's military capability and should not be criticized by publicly funded institutions.

It also happens that museum exhibits can be put forward for purely political reasons. In 1998, the Library of Congress opened an exhibit called "Religion and the Founding of the American Revolution." The exhibit was based on research by James Hutson, chief of the Library's Manuscript Division. This exhibit went to great lengths to try to present Jefferson's statement on the Separation of Church and State as an empty political exercise, rather than Jefferson's statement of policy. The exhibit opened, interestingly enough, just as the House of Representatives was preparing to vote on the Religious Freedom Amendment, which would do a great deal to cancel recent Supreme Court pro-separation decisions. Additionally,

"It is truly enough said that a corporation has no conscience...."

in California, a member of the Academic Standards Commission cited this exhibit in an effort to remove references to church-state separation from proposed statewide history guidelines for public schools.[12]

Religious history is potentially the most dangerous, politically, for the textbook publishers. And, regrettably, they tend to omit all reference to religion, except in the most broad and general terms. Students do not, for example, know the difference between a Pilgrim and a Puritan. Most learn a bit about Thomas Paine, but they don't learn that Thomas Paine, like many of the Founding Fathers, was a deist. Nor do they learn that Teddy Roosevelt once called Paine "a dirty little atheist." They are almost certainly ignorant of the fact that Abraham Lincoln was both an admirer of Paine's deistic ideas and, rather oddly, the first President to suggest that politics should be influenced by Christian values. And students never hear about the 1838 Mormon War, the anti-Catholic riots of 1844, or any other violent conflict involving religious sects. Many areas of the American religious experience are left unexplored—deism, congregationalism, spiritualism, communalism, the origins of various religious denominations in the nineteenth century. Richard Shenkman's popular book, *I Love Paul Revere, Whether He Rode or Not*, contains more information in one chapter on religion in American history than most schools teach from kindergarten through the twelfth grade.

The goal of history textbooks is to convey a "cherished mythology"—a consensus view of history full of inaccuracies and misrepresentations. In public schools, history becomes what the majority of people think it is. And even though there has been a good deal of progress in terms of expanded coverage of women and minorities, many of the dirty little secrets are left secret.

Literature

As with history, the study of literature often descends into a trivial pursuit of facts and data, things easily measured in multiple-guess questions. This has been true for many years, as I can remember being asked on a test in high school English what the Nun ate for dinner in *The Canterbury Tales*. This obsession with trivia hasn't changed in the intervening 35 years.

Helping students to come to a real understanding of our cultural history is not a goal of public education, largely because there are a lot of dangerous ideas in there. As with history, there are "problems" that textbook editors tend to handle very gingerly and avoid altogether when possible. In this case, literature anthologies have a decided advantage. It is fairly easy to "select" particular works as essential parts of the established literary canon, while ignoring the more dangerous stuff.

It is easy to criticize literature anthologies for not including enough minorities or women. This is a common (and valid) criticism to make. Recently, some publishers have tried hard to correct this defect. However, it is perhaps more interesting to look at how "major" authors are bowdlerized and distorted in these textbooks. We are all familiar with how Shakespeare is "adapted" for school textbooks, but how is this done for other authors?

For example, most people reading the poetry of Emily Dickinson, as she is anthologized in school textbooks, would assume that she was a nature poet. Her more questionable works are easily omitted. After all, what would a high school student make of her poem "Wild Nights" or, worse yet, "I Held a Jewel"? (Several recent interpretations suggest that Dickinson's "jewel" was, obviously, her clitoris.) The same problem is true of Wordsworth, Byron, Keats, and the other English Romantic poets, as some of their best poetry, like Byron's *Don Juan*, might be considered too erotic for the classroom. Most of these poets were also sympathetic toward the revolutions of their time, both political and religious. But these revolutionary and/or erotic impulses, like Shelley's atheism, can easily be omitted from the anthologies.

A good litmus test for a textbook on English literature is to examine how it deals with William Blake. That is, does the anthology include his poetry critical of English society? Does the book deal with his unorthodox religious views? On the other hand, Charles Dickens' *A Tale of Two Cities* is a popular choice for school textbooks, especially since it criticizes the French and the lower classes who dared to revolt against their betters. But there are a number of land mines, even in popular classics of English literature. For example, Dickens' *Oliver Twist* has a boy called Master Bates who is continually jingling the change in his pocket. And, worse yet, some schoolboys might find in Swift's *Gulliver's Travels* the expression "a piece of ass's flesh."[13]

> We will never live to see selections from Steinbeck's boldly pro-union *In Dubious Battle* taught in schools.

There are, of course, many texts that will probably never make it into a school textbook. For example, what textbook publisher today would even consider adding selections from de Quincey's *Confessions of an English Opium-Eater*? Or worse yet, selections from anti-authoritarian fiction, like Alan Sillitoe's story "The Loneliness of the Long Distance Runner." In fact, any book that celebrates resistance to authority is, like General Washington's penis, a likely candidate for exclusion from school textbooks.

School Textbooks Unpopular History vs. Cherished Mythology?
Earl Lee

71

In terms of American literature, a good litmus test is looking at how the text handles Walt Whitman. Does the anthology include poetry from the first edition of *Leaves of Grass*, or does it use verse from the later versions? The first version of *Leaves* was very powerful, often even erotic (in a nineteenth-century sort of way). Over time Whitman kept rewriting and editing the text, with one eye on his future reputation as a poet. The later versions of *Leaves* are the work of an old man, mainly concerned with becoming a mainstream poet who would be remembered and anthologized, and to that purpose he was very successful. In looking at Whitman, an even more interesting question would be to ask how many school textbooks include Whitman's "A Sun Bath Nakedness," in which he describes going naked near a secluded stream. What high school anthology would dare to make reference to his naturist views, much less to his sexual orientation?[14]

A good deal of the literature that was added in the 1970s because it held echoes with the 1960s generation was

The publisher of *Kansas: The Prairie State Lives* decided to cut the entire first chapter of the textbook, which included references to fossils and the inland sea that once covered what is now Kansas.

removed from textbooks in the 1990s. And there is plenty of material from that era that will never find its way into a textbook. After all, what textbook publisher would consider adding selections from books like *Who Walk in Darkness* by Chandler Brossard, *The Monkey Wrench Gang* by Edward Abbey, or John Holmes' *Go*? These books, along with many others that celebrate the lower classes, environmentalism, and subcultures—in other words, any work that gives alternatives to the middle-class view of what America should be—are excluded from textbooks.

Like Emily Dickinson, Ralph Waldo Emerson is often included in literature anthologies for his views on nature and his philosophical views on nineteenth-century America. His religious views, however, are too scandalous to be included in any school anthology. Emerson was not anti-Christian, but he was certainly anti-religion, and in his "Divinity School Address" he bluntly said that going to church on the Sabbath was a poor way to get in touch with the divine.

Even more important is Henry David Thoreau, especially in terms of his influence on Dr. Martin Luther King, Jr., and Mahatma Gandhi. But although his work "Civil Disobedience" was a major intellectual force in history, it is also problematic in an era where school administrators are obsessed with classroom control. Can a school culture where George Washington's watch fob can be erased as a "disruptive element in the classroom" manage to accommodate Thoreau? This is a case where, although "Civil Disobedience" is too important to be left out of anthologies, one might fairly ask how much of it is printed.

Looking at the reader *Elements of Literature, Fifth Course*, we find that it includes Thoreau's work, but cut very drastically to remove a number of objectionable passages.[15] This textbook includes his essay complete through the middle of the fourth paragraph—including a strong libertarian statement against government regulation—but cutting a large section beginning, "It is truly enough said that a corporation has no conscience...." It's not hard to see how the editors might have been urged to cut this statement. Shortly after, Thoreau begins a passage that could be viewed as disrespectful of the military, describing marines as "a mere shadow and reminiscence of humanity," mere walking machines without judgment or moral sense. He then expands this description to include "legislators, politicians, lawyers, ministers, and office-holders." This sentiment might have been left intact, satisfying the censors, except for his including ministers and soldiers in this group.

Then, Thoreau is unkind enough to describe his home state of Massachusetts, using the verse:

A drab of state, a cloth-o'-silver slut, To have her train borne up, and her soul trail in the dirt.

This is not exactly the kind of sentiment you'd find engraved on a state commemorative quarter! Thoreau uses this verse to attack the merchants of Massachusetts for profiting from slavery and the war with Mexico. He then follows this with a criticism of voting, saying, "All voting is a sort of gaming, like checkers or backgammon, with a slight moral tinge to it, a playing with right and wrong." This is followed by a damning condemnation of political conventions and men without backbone who live by the principles of what is easy and expedient.

Generally speaking, the editor of this textbook has left the intellectual argument in place, while cutting out the guts of the essay. All that might be objected to has been removed. The people of Massachusetts can sleep safe, knowing that the editors have erased a terrible insult against them. And the people of Massachusetts will, in turn, buy lots of textbooks.

Shortly after the Columbine massacre, a school official claimed that the murders might not have happened if the Ten Commandments had been posted on the wall at Columbine High School. This idea seems laughable to most intelligent people. After all, how could the violent "eye for an eye" ethic of the Old Testament have deterred anyone from committing violence? However, one might seriously ask if the Columbine attack would have happened had the principles of nonviolent protest, embodied in Thoreau's "Civil Disobedience," been taught *in its original form* in the English classes at Columbine.

Another popular text that has fairly recently fallen on hard times is Shirley Jackson's story "The Lottery." This story, written at the end of WWII, portrays a rural community where, each year, a person is selected in a lottery and then stoned to death. The community continues this practice because it is traditional and, some residents say, important to the fertility of the crops. The lottery is, obviously, a religious ritual, and the story can also be read as an oblique criticism of the Red Scare. Although this story was once quite popular in literature anthologies, it has been cut out of recently editions, largely because it associates religion with violence.[16]

On the other hand, you can count on the literary canon to include texts that cover long-dead political controversies. For example, Melville's *Billy Budd* is anthologized fairly often, especially now that sailors are rarely ever whipped or hanged at sea. Similarly, selections from *Moby-Dick* are a popular choice, especially as no one today is likely to object to a ship full of whale killers meeting a watery grave. Like Coleridge's *Rime of the Ancient Mariner*, this novel teaches an exemplary attitude toward animals.

More problematic are Melville's anti-war poems and his novels *Typee* and *The Confidence Man*. *Typee* was based on his

experiences in the South Pacific, and in the original version, published in England, the novel contains criticism of both missionaries and American imperialism. The revised American edition of *Typee*, published by John Wiley, cut out these references, along with references to the venereal diseases which Americans and Europeans spread among the native population. The expurgated version of *Typee* is still being reprinted, in large part because it renders the novel into a safe "children's adventure story." Similarly, *The Confidence Man* casts an unfavorable light on American boosterism and commercialism, much like Sinclair Lewis' *Babbitt*, which is also an unlikely choice for a high school literature anthology. And Lewis' *Elmer Gantry*—don't even think it! His hilarious satire of evangelical Christianity would not go over well in most communities.[17] Similarly, Robert Heinlein's *Stranger in a Strange Land* is unlikely to be taught in public schools today.[18]

Upton Sinclair's *The Jungle* is considered a classic novel, but it is rarely taught in schools or included in anthologies. Some of the problems Sinclair describes in the meatpacking industry are still very much alive today—so much so that when a recent unexpurgated version of his novel, called *The Lost First Edition of Upton Sinclair's The Jungle*, was published in 1988, it was quietly suppressed by the meatpacking industry through some backdoor dealings, much the same way they tried to suppress the original 1905 publication.[19] Largely excluded from the literary anthologies, today Sinclair's classic novel has become little more than a footnote in history books.

We are far enough removed from the Great Depression to accommodate Steinbeck's *The Grapes of Wrath*, but we will never live to see selections from his boldly pro-union *In Dubious Battle* taught in schools. In fact, although many socialist and pro-union books and novels were published in the early part of this century, very few such books—especially novels—are published today. And virtually no "leftist" material is included in the literary canon or in the literary anthologies. The lack of fiction dealing with the laboring classes also has another drawback in that many of these working-class novels were written by women, including Meridel Le Sueur, Rebecca Harding Davis, Theresa Malkiel, Agnes Smedley, Mary Heaton Vorse, Catherine Brody, Josephine Herbst, Ruth McKenney, Josephine Johnson, Beatrice Bisno, Leane Zugsmith, and Mari Sandoz. When women authors are included in the literary canon, they are frequently those authors who wrote about the middle and upper classes.

School Textbooks Unpopular History vs. Cherished Mythology?
Earl Lee

73

Science

Science is probably the most difficult area to judge for the layman, especially since most people have a fairly limited understanding of the implications of bad science. It is worth noting that in 2000 the American Association for the Advancement of Science gave its harshest criticism ever of math and science textbooks. They gave unsatisfactory ratings to all ten of the major high school biology textbooks that they reviewed. "At their best, the textbooks are a collection of missed opportunities," according to Dr. Jo Ellen Roseman, director of the study. "While most contain the relevant content on heredity and natural selection, for example, they don't help students to learn it or help teachers to teach it."[20]

Although the books all had bright, colorful graphics, they all fell short in terms of four basic ideas: how cells work, how matter and energy flow from one source to another, how plants and animals evolve, and the molecular basis of heredity. The books spent more time on vocabulary words, naming the parts of cells, etc., than on understanding concepts of biology. Generally speaking, the critics claimed that these textbooks were "obscuring with needless detail" the principle ideas of biology. The textbooks did not relate science to everyday life or provide for hands-on experience.

Publishers quickly responded to this criticism by accusing state standards of being responsible for this problem. The people who write the standards, in turn, complained that textbook publishers were not giving them what they asked for. In reality, a major part of the problem is the fact that science textbook publishers are desperately trying to avoid being caught up in the creation vs. evolution controversy.

Several states have been involved in that controversy. In August 1999, the Kansas State Board of Education voted to remove references to evolution from state standards, replacing them with standards written with the help of a creationist organization. As a result of this controversy, the publisher of *Kansas—The Prairie State Lives* decided to cut the entire first chapter of the textbook, which included references to fossils and the inland sea that once covered the plains of what is now Kansas. The publishers candidly stated that they were concerned about criticism from creationists, most of whom believe that the earth is only a few thousand years old.[21] In 2005, the board approved a draft proposal that made it a requirement that "intelligent design" be given equal time in classrooms.

Later in 2006, the creationist majority was voted out of office, and the new board has since reversed these earlier decisions, restoring the old definition of science as "the search for natural explanations for what is observed in the universe." I mention this small victory because, in the twenty-first century we must celebrate any kind of progress in the face of powerful religious fundamentalists and their lobbies.

■ ■ ■ ■ ■ ■ ■ ■ ■ ■

Mel and Norma Gabler, who were major critics of school textbooks, were also supporters of both creationism and home-schooling. This is fairly typical, as many conservative critics of public schools are supporters of various right-wing causes, including home-schooling and voucher programs. It would be fair to say that they support any change that would give them more power over the content of education, public and private. Many of these critics approach textbook reform, not as friends of public education, but as enemies who ultimately want to see public education moved to private control. Influencing the content of textbooks in public schools is, in reality, only a temporary position to be maintained until they can get more direct control over education.

Manipulating the content of textbooks is only one small step toward the goal of completely changing public education as it exists today. Failing that, they are more than willing to undermine the whole system in the hopes of someday replacing it with a loose system of home schools, parochial schools, and semi-religious private "charter" schools. And mandated standardized test scores, deeply flawed though they are, provide their main justification for funding these alternatives. Teachers in both public and private schools are forced to "teach to the test" in order to chase state and federal funding. Finding ways to stop schools from manipulating test results is already a serious problem.

Ultimately, in spite of the pressures from special interest groups, textbook publishers must take responsibility for producing a bad product. Unfortunately, we probably won't see any mass litigation, as we have with the tobacco industry. Even so, it seems that textbook publishers should take full credit for creating a bad product. And the educators and editors who put together these textbooks should be held accountable for their failures.

Even more important, many educational associations and government agencies need to get involved in promoting good textbooks. The National Education Goals Panel, for example, sponsored a paper by Harriet Tyson called "Overcoming Structural Barriers to Good Textbooks" and has made the paper available on its website.[22] Similarly, the Association of Departments of English has promoted research on the censorship of literary texts. These groups can do a great deal to counter the influence of right-wing groups and, perhaps someday, restore a more balanced and open-minded approach to education.

Endnotes

1. Reed, Kwofi. Censorship foes: Altering painting of Washington crosses the line. *Free!: The Freedom Forum Online* <www.freedomforum.org>. **2.** DelFattore, Joan. (1986). Contemporary censorship pressures and their effect on literature textbooks. ADE Bulletin, spring, pp 5–40. **3.** See Wikipedia article, "Kanawha County textbook controversy." **4.** Michael, Kay. (1974). County schools closed in face of text fight. *Charleston gazette*, Sep 13. **5.** *Op cit.*, DelFattore. **6.** Flaubert, Gustave. (1954). *Flaubert's dictionary of accepted ideas*. London: Max Reinhardt. **7.** *Op cit.*, DelFattore. **8.** This was demonstrated recently when President Bush met with the President of the Philippines. The only fact he was able to bring to mind about her country was that he enjoyed their cooking. **9.** Shenkman, Richard. (1988). *Legends, lies & cherished myths of American history*. New York: HarperPerrenial. **10.** Loewen, James W. (1995). *Lies my teacher told me*. New York: New Press. **11.** Conniff, Richard. (2005). *The ape in the corner office*. New York: Crown. **12.** Unsigned. (1998). Library of Congress questions Jefferson's "wall" letter. *Church & state*, Jul/Aug, p 18. **13.** The passage reads: "...this leader had usually a favorite as like himself as he could get, whose employment was to lick his master's feet and posteriors, and drive the female YAHOOS to his kennel; for which he was now and then rewarded with a piece of ass's flesh" (Chapter 34). This sexual expression is usually described as "a 19th century schoolboy term of uncertain origin." However, in several editions of Swift's book, the line on the page ends with "a piece of ass's" and the word "flesh" is carried over onto the next line. It's very likely some imaginative schoolboys, taking this in its obvious sexual context, promptly adopted the phrase. **14.** Abrams, Sam. (1993). *The neglected Walt Whitman: Vital texts*. New York: Four Walls Eight Windows. **15.** *Elements of literature, fifth course: Literature of the United States*. Austin: Holt, Rinehart & Winston; HBJ, 1993. **16.** *Op cit.*, DelFattore. **17.** His *Main Street* is considered a safe choice for schools. I am rather sympathetic toward *Elmer Gantry* because my own religious satire *Raptured!: The Final Daze of the Late, Great Planet Earth* will probably also end up in the dustbin of history. **18.** Published in 1961, it was popular in the 1970s, but is largely forgotten today. **19.** Sinclair, Upton. (2003). *The jungle: The uncensored, original edition*. Tucson: See Sharp Press. **20.** Project 2061. (2000). Big biology books fail to convey big ideas, reports AAAS's Project 2061. Project 2061 press release, June 27. <www.project2061.org>. **21.** Amazingly, many of these people believe that humans once lived in harmony with the dinosaurs, as in the *Alley Oop* and *B.C.* comics. It's worth noting that Johnny Hart, the author of *B.C.*, is often praised for his "creationist friendly" comics. **22.** Tyson, Harriet. (1997). Overcoming structural barriers to good textbooks. Washington, DC: National Education Goals Panel. <govinfo.library.unt.edu/negp/>.

For Further Reading

Apple, Michael W., and Linda K. Christian-Smith. (1991). *Politics of the textbook*. New York: Routledge.

Crabtree, Charlotte A. (1994). *National standards for United States history: Exploring the American experience*. Los Angeles: National Center for History in the Schools, Univ. of Calif.

Davis, O. L. (1986). *Looking at history: A review of major US history textbooks*. Washington DC: People for the American Way.

Graves, Patrick K. (1999). Education board honors controversial textbook critics: Five members protest resolution, accuse Mel and Norma Gabler of racism. *Corpus Christi caller times*, May 8.

Lee, Earl. (1998). *Libraries in the age of mediocrity*. Jefferson, NC: McFarland, 1998.

Loewen, James. (1999). *Lies across America: What our historic sites get wrong*. New York: New Press.

Nash, Gary B. (1997). *History on trial: Culture wars and the teaching of the past*. New York: Knopf.

Shenkman, Richard. (1991). *I love Paul Revere, whether he rode or not*. New York: HarperPerrenial.

School Textbooks Unpopular History vs. Cherished Mythology?
Earl Lee

75

The Information Arms Race
Douglas Rushkoff

In any Information War, we human beings lose by definition. For the moment communication becomes information, it is no longer alive. As living beings, when we accept a role in the InfoWar, we also lose the home field advantage—the defensive capability offered any indigenous population.

When we are fooled into believing the battle over information is, in fact, a battle over our reality, we have already lost the war.

Communication Only Occurs Between Equals

Television broadcasting is not communication. Neither are radio news, magazines, or even this little essay. These are all one-way distribution of content. However vital, realistic, or

Even the so-called "interactive" media, like computer games and most Websites, simply allow for the user to experience a simulation of free choice.

engaging a movie or book, it is not interactive or participatory in any real sense. Unless we can have just as much of an effect on the director, writer, producer, or journalist as he has on us, we are not involved in a communication. We are merely the recipients of programming.

Even the so-called "interactive" media, like computer games and most Websites, simply allow for the user to experience a simulation of free choice. The creator of the simulation is no longer present. If a player creates a sequence of moves that has never been played before, or a reader moves through an interactive story along a path that has never been followed before, this still does not count as communication. It is merely a unique and personalized experience of essentially dead

data. Multimedia CD-ROMs are not interactive, because the user is not interacting with anyone.

This is not so terrible in itself. Stories, movies, and video games are all great storage media. The enduring values of many indigenous cultures are passed down from generation to generation through myths and stories. The artist, philosopher, and scientist alike have published their findings in one form or another for the consumption of others. For centuries, we have willingly submitted to the performances and writings of great thinkers, and have been enriched as result. They are what allow for a cumulative human experience over time, greater than any single life span.

But we should not confuse such experiences with communication. However lifelike it may feel, unless we are in a position to influence the presenter as much as he can influence us, we are not involved in a living exchange. In other words, to be aroused by a pornographic tape is not to make love.

For like lovemaking, communication is a living exchange between equal partners. No matter how much our world's nihilists might like to deny it, there is an energy inherent to such exchanges: a living space of interaction. And this is the zone where change—and all its inherent dangers—can occur.

Just as lovemaking presents the possibility of new genetic combinations, communication initiates the process of cultural mutation. When equals are communicating, nothing is fixed. Honest participation means everything is up for grabs.

Information Wants To Be Preserved

The so-called "Communications Departments" of most major universities would have us believe otherwise. The study of

Today, "communications" is the science of influence.

mass media has little to do with mass participation in the design of cultural values. Students do not learn how to foster the living interaction among a society's members. There are few courses in promoting media literacy or creating online groups to solve problems collectively.

Today, "communications" is the science of influence. Mass communication is the study of how governments and corporations can influence their populations and customers—the so-called "masses." The tools they employ are rhetoric, the ancient art of influence,[1] and information, the modern science of control.[2]

But wherever real communication is occurring, there is life. Like the new buds on a tree, the places where communication takes place are the most effective leverage points in a culture from which to monitor and direct new growth. Those hoping to direct or, as is most often the case, stunt the development of cultural change, focus on these points. By imitating the qualities we associate with living communication, and then broadcasting fixed information in its place, the mass media manipulator peddles the worldview of his sponsors.

Anthropology and Religion

Most anthropology is carried out in service of a nation or corporation. The anthropologist is the research half of the "R & D" for cultural manipulation. Historically, the anthropologist is sent to a new territory ripe for commercial, religious, or political colonization. He looks for the gaps or inconsistencies in the culture's mythology, so that these "soft spots" may be hardened with strong, imported data.

For example, sixteenth-century Christian missionaries to the New World first studied the indigenous people in order to appraise their pantheistic belief system, as well as gain their

trust. They observed local rituals to learn about particular beliefs associated with each god. Then they converted people by associating local gods with the closest corresponding Catholic saints or deities. The native god for animals, the people were taught, is really just St. Francis. The drinking of chicken's blood is really just a version of the Communion. And so on, until a local, hybridized version of Christianity evolved.

In the 1500s, Franciscan brothers studied the language and religion of the people of Tenochtitlàn before choosing to build the hilltop basilica of the Virgin of Guadalupe on the site of an Aztec temple dedicated to the earth goddess Tonatzin. In its new incarnation, the mountaintop church became an homage to Mary, who is pictured stepping on the stars and moon, the symbols of her pagan predecessor. She overlooks what is now called Mexico City. These missions were not generally sponsored by the Church, but by the monarchy. As a result, the visiting missionary served the dual role of converter and intelligence gatherer. Ultimately, both functions simply prepared the target population for its inevitable co-option by force.

This is the two-millennium-old process by which Christianity absorbed the rituals and beliefs of the peoples it converted. The Christmas tree began as a solstice ritual practiced by Germans to light the darkest night of the year. Smart missionaries of the time realized that this was the superstitious ritual developed to address the people's fear of the darkness of winter. The missionaries did a fairly advanced job of cultural analysis for the time, keying in on the local people's doubt in the rejuvenation of the coming spring season. The *tannenbaum* exposed their deepest fear—and most fertile ground for conversion.

By identifying the tree with the rood and the birth of Christ, the missionaries augmented the pagan ritual, and redirected the sense of hope that the ritual fostered away from pagan forces and towards their own messiah. They filled a living ritual with dead information.

Similarly, churches and cathedrals were most often placed on local pagan "power spots" and ley lines—not because the priests believed that these locations offered any magical leverage, but because the people believed they did. What better way to get people into your church than to build it on the same spot where they already did their praying? Ironically, the "black masses" that were conducted illicitly by pagans on church altars were not meant as a statement against Christianity at all. The unconverted people were merely attempting to carry out their pre-Christian ceremonies in the locations where they believed they would work.

In the years preceding World War II, anthropologists studied the cultures of the South Seas so they could more easily be turned to the "Allied" cause against the Japanese once these territories were to become a war zone. Whether or not these well-meaning cultural researchers knew it, the governments funding them had more than pure science in mind when they chose which expeditions to fund.

After World War II, Air Force Brigadier General Edward G. Lansdale emerged as the preeminent "counterinsurgency" strategist for the CIA. Over a period of three decades, he developed a wide range of intelligence and propaganda theories that were employed and refined in the field. His principal strategy was first to engage in qualitative anthropological research to discover a target audience's underlying belief systems, and then exploit these beliefs mercilessly in the pursuit of military gains.

For example, in the 1950s as part of his counterinsurgency campaign against the Huk rebels of the Philippines, Lansdale began by conducting research into local superstitions. He learned that the Huk battleground was believed to be inhabited

with symbols that can be more easily controlled.

This is the same process by which today's target marketers research and co-opt new cultural strains. Even the language of marketing, in which new populations are called "targets" reveals the war-like precision and hostility with which these marketers attack their new prospects.

When a public relations person reduces a group of human beings to a target market, he has effectively removed himself from the equation. Feedback and user surveys do not put us in communication with anyone; they simply make us the subjects of scrutiny and the victims of an eventual assault. The PR person is the lone gunman at the top of the tower, intentionally isolated so as to get a better shot. When the gun goes off, we panic down in the plaza. Someone is out to get us.

The reticence of the generation formerly known as "X" to belong to anything at all can be traced directly to the corrosive effects of target marketing on our society. In fact, the "slacker" ethic was little more than reaction to the segmentation of a culture based on demographic leanings. No sooner do young people find a new style of music, clothing, or attitude, than marketers sieze on it as a trend to be exploited. The kids rush from style to style, but only stay until they sense the target marketer's sites closing in on them. Then they rush to find something different, and maintain their anomalous behavior until it is recognized and tagged.

The reticence of the generation formerly known as "X" to belong to anything at all can be traced directly to the corrosive effects of target marketing on our society.

by an "asuang," or vampire figure. To capitalize on this mythology, his "psywar" units would follow Huk patrols and then quietly ambush the last man on the trail. They would kill the soldier by means of two punctures on the neck, drain him of his blood, and then leave him to be found the next morning. On encountering the victim, the Huks in the area would retreat for fear of further vampire attacks.

Such information campaigns depend on concretizing living myth with fixed data. They invariably mine the most fertile cultural soil for inherent inconsistencies, and then replace them

When "GenX" adopted the anti-chic aesthetic of thrift-store grunge, for example, it was in an effort to find a style that could not be so easily identified and exploited. Grunge was so self-consciously lowbrow and depressed that it seemed, at first, impervious to the hype and glamour applied so swiftly to trends of the past. But sure enough, grunge anthems found their way onto the soundtracks of television commercials, and Dodge Neons were hawked by kids in flannel shirts saying "whatever." The superstardom and eventual shotgun suicide of Kurt Cobain—lead singer of the seminal grunge group Nirvana—bore witness to the futility of giving chase to the target marketers. Symbolically—at least for his fans—Cobain set his rifle's sites on himself rather than be subjected to the crosshairs of someone else's. Then the kids moved on to other genres.[3]

Advertising as Info-War

The development of advertising throughout this century can best be understood as the process by which marketers find ways to attack our sense of well-being. While advertising may have begun as a way to publicize a new brand or invention, the surfeit of "stuff" with little or no qualitative difference from its competition forced advertisers to find ways of distinguishing their products from that of their competitors.

Advertising quickly became about creating needs rather than fulfilling them. Commercials took the form of coercive teaching stories. We are presented with a character with whom we identify. The character is put into jeopardy, and we experience vicarious tension along with him. Only the storyteller holds the key to our release.

Imagine a man in his office. The boss tells him his report is late. His wife calls to tell him their son is in trouble. His co-worker is scheming to get him fired. What is he to do? He opens his desk drawer: inside is a bottle of Brand X aspirin. He takes the pills and we watch as a psychedelic array of color fills his body. Whether or not we really believe that the aspirin could solve his problems—or cure his headache—we must accept the sponsor's solution if we want to be relieved from tension.

This simple form of programming has been used since Aristotle's day. Create a character, put him in danger, and then choose the method by which he will be saved. The remedy can be Athena or a new brand of sport shoe. The audience must submit.

Because television is not a communicator's medium but the programmer's (why do you think they call the stuff on TV "programming" anyway?), it depends on a passive, captive audience. There is no room for interaction, or the programmer's advantage will be lost.

This is why the remote control has wreaked such havoc on traditional coercive advertising. Although it doesn't allow for feedback, it does allow for escape. A regular television viewer, feeling the rising and uncomfortable tension of a coercive story, would have to walk all the way up to his television set to change the channel. His brain makes the calculation of how many calories of effort this would cost, and instructs the man to sit and bear the momentary anxiety.

A person armed with a remote control, on the other hand, can escape the dilemma with almost no effort at all. One simple click and he's free. The less reverence he feels for the television image, the less hesitation he'll have to click away. Video games help in this regard. The television tube's pixels, which used to be the exclusive province of the programmer, can now be manipulated by the user. Simply moving Super Mario across the screen changed our relationship to the television image forever. The tube is now a playground. It can be changed.

The viewer armed with a remote control becomes an armchair postmodernist, deconstructing images as he sees fit. The shorter his attention span, the less compelled he feels to sit through coercive or tension-inducing media. In fact, Attention Deficit Disorder—an ailment for which millions of parents are now giving their children medication—may just be a reaction to relentless programming. If everywhere you look someone is attempting to program you, you will quickly learn not to look anywhere for too long.

The most skilled viewers have become amateur media semioticians. They maintain an ironic distance from the media they watch so as not to fall under the programmer's influence. Young people watch shows in groups, constantly talking back to the screen. They protect one another from absorption by the image.

Watching television skillfully means watching for the coercive techniques. Watching television with ironic distance means not to watch television at all, but rather to watch "the television." The new entertainment is a form of media study: What are they going to try next? The viewer remains alive and thinking by refusing to surrender to any of the stories he sees.

Unfortunately, it didn't take advertisers long to develop a new set of coercive techniques for their postmodern audience. The state of ironic detachment that young people employ to remain immune to the programming spell is now their greatest liability.

New advertising intentionally appeals to this postmodern sensibility. "Wink" advertising acknowledges its viewers' intelligence. These commercials readily admit they are manipulative, as if this nod to their own coercive intentions somehow immunizes the audience from their effects. The object of the game, for the audience, is to be "in" on the joke.

Sprite commercials satirize the values espoused by "cool" brands like Coke and Pepsi, then go on to insist that, "Image is nothing, thirst is everything." A brand of shoes called "Simple" ran a magazine ad with the copy: "advertisement: blah blah blah…name of company."

By letting the audience in on the inanity of the marketing process, such companies hope to be rewarded by the thankful viewer. Energizer batteries launched a television campaign where a "fake" commercial for another product would be interrupted by their famous pink Energizer bunny marching through the screen. The audience was rescued from the bad commercial by the battery company's tiny mascot. The message: The Energizer Bunny can keep on going, even in a world of relentless hype.

Of course the marketers haven't really surrendered at all. What's really going on here is a new style of marketing through exclusivity. Advertisers know that their media-savvy viewership prides itself on being able to deconstruct and understand the coercive tactics of television commercials. By winking at the audience, the advertiser is acknowledging that there's someone special out there—someone smart enough not to be fooled by the traditional tricks of the influence professional. "If you're smart enough to see our wink and get the joke, then you're smart enough to know to buy our product."

Where this sort of advertising gets most dangerous is where there's really no joke at all. Diesel Jeans launched a billboard campaign with images designed to provoke a "wink" response, even though no amount of semiotic analysis would allow its audience to "get" the joke. In one print ad, they showed a stylish couple, dressed in Diesel clothing, in a fake billboard advertisement for a brand of ice cream. The advertisement-within-the-advertisement was placed in a busy district of North Korea.

What does this advertisement mean, and why was it placed amongst bicycling North Koreans? Who knows? The meta-advertisement attacks the hip viewer. He must pretend that he understands what's going on if he wants to maintain his sense of ironic detachment. The moment he lies to himself in order to turn the page, he has actually admitted defeat. He has been beaten at his own game by the advertiser, who has re-established himself as the more powerful force in the information war.

The Co-option of Cyberspace

The Internet posed an even greater threat to culture's programmers than channel zappers. For the first time, here was a mass medium that no longer favored broadcasters.

A true communications medium from the start, the Internet was as much about sending as receiving. The early Internet was a text-only technology. Users would send email, join in live chats, or participate in asynchronous discussions on bulletin boards and Usenet groups. For those of us lucky enough to have engaged in this style of contact, we sensed liberation.

The viewer armed with a remote control becomes an armchair postmodernist, deconstructing images as he sees fit.

The early Internet spurred utopian visions because it was the first time that real people had the opportunity to disseminate their ideas globally. The Internet was less about the information itself than contact. Networked together through wires and computers, the Internet community—and it really was a community—was a living cultural experiment.

To some, it was as if the human race was hardwiring its members together into a single, global brain. People talked about the Internet as if it were the realization of the Gaia Hypothesis—the notion that all living things are part of the same, big organism.[4] Many believed that the fledgling communications infrastructure would allow for the beginning of global communication and cooperation on a scale unimagined before.

Even if these dreams were a bit more fantastic than the reality of an Internet society, they indicated the underlying experience essential to this interconnectivity. The interactive communications infrastructure was merely the housing for a collective project in mutual understanding. It was not about information at all, but relationships. We were not interacting with data, but with one another.

This is why the Internet seemed so "sexy." It was not that pornography was available online. It felt and looked sexy because people and their ideas could commingle and mutate. A scientist sharing his new research would be challenged and provoked. A philosopher posing a new idea would be forced to defend it. Nothing was safe, and nothing was sacred—except, perhaps, the idea that everyone shared an equal opportunity to give voice to his or her opinions.

As more people turned off their TVs and migrated online, the question for influence professionals became clear: How do we turn this communications nightmare into a traditional, dead, and controllable mass medium?

Their great trick was to replace communication with information. The works of futurists like Alvin Toffler were twisted to proclaim that we were on the cusp of the Information Age,

speed and modem baud rates do nothing for communication. They do, however, allow for the development of an increasingly TV-like Internet.

The ultimate objective of today's communication industry is to provide us with broadcast-quality television images on our computers. The only space left for interactivity will be our freedom to watch a particular movie "on demand" or, better, to use the computer mouse to click on an object or article of clothing we might like to buy.

Only by killing its communicative function could the Web's developers turn the Internet into a shopping mall.

forever confusing a revolution in communication with an expansion of the propaganda machine. No, the Internet was not a medium for interpersonal exchange, but data retrieval. And it was tricky and dangerous to use. *Wired* magazine's hip graphics and buzzword-laden text convinced newcomers to the world of "hi-technology" that the Internet was a complex and imposing realm. Without proper instruction (from the likes of *Wired* editors), we would surely get lost out there.

Now that the Internet was seen as a dangerous zone of information, best traveled with the advice of experts, it wasn't long before the World Wide Web became the preferred navigational tool. Unlike bulletin boards or chat rooms, the Web is—for the most part—a read-only medium. It is flat and opaque. You can't see through it to the activities of others. We don't socialize with anyone when we visit a Website; we read text and look at pictures. This is not interactivity. It is an "interactive-style" activity. There's nothing participatory about it.

Instead of forging a whole new world, the Web gives us a new window on the same old world. The Web is a repository for information. It is dead. While you and I are as free to publish our works on the Web as Coke is to publish its advertising or The Gap is to sell its jeans, we have given up something much more precious once we surrender the immediacy of a living communications exchange. Only by killing its communicative function could the Web's developers turn the Internet into a shopping mall.

The current direction of Internet technology promises a further calcification of its interactive abilities. Amped-up processing

Promoting the Fixed Reality

Once we have reduced the living exchanges that these new media promise to one side or other in an information war, we have given up the only advantage we really have: to evolve unpredictably.

The enemy of the coercer is change. Coercion and influence are simply the pushing of a fixed point of view. In this sense, the coercer is promoting death. The messy fertility of a living system is the information coercer's greatest obstacle. But it is also our greatest strength as a developing culture.

Finally, the conflict between "them and us" is fictional. The culture war is just a battle between those who see the need for change, and those would hope to prevent it. Those in power, obviously, seek to preserve the status quo. The only time they feel the need to make an adjustment is when they are hoping to absorb a unique new population, or when the populations already under their control have grown immune to the current styles of influence.

And, to be sure, the preservation of certain status quo values is crucial to the maintenance of organized society. Just as there are certain genes in the body with no function other than to resist mutation, there are institutions in our society that work very hard to resist change.

Since the chief agents of change are interaction and communication, these will be the activities that the enemies of evolution will want to keep in check. But when an over-whelming proportion of our world community seeks a referendum on the human project, we must not allow our efforts to be derailed by those who would prevent such a movement by any means necessary.

More importantly, we cannot let ourselves be fooled into thinking that simply having the right to select our data with the click of a computer mouse instead of a TV remote means we have won the Information Arms Race.

Endnotes

1. See Aristotle, 1954. **2.** See Wiener, 1967; see also Chomsky, 1991; Crossen, 1994; Kelly, 1998; Schwartz & Leydon, 1997; Simpson, 1994; Stauber & Rampton, 1995. **3.** For more on the ideas presented in this section, see Carlisle, 1993; Chomsky, 1989; Cialdini, 1993; and Watson, 1978 (which is excerpted at Psywar Terror Tactics Website at <www.parascope.com>). **4.** See Lovelock, 1987.

References

Aristotle. (1954). *Rhetoric* (W. Rhys Roberts, Trans.). New York: The Modern Library.

Carlisle, J. (1993, Spring). Public relationships: Hill & Knowlton, Robert Gray, and the CIA. *Covert Action Quarterly*.

Chomsky, N. (1991). *Media control: The spectacular achievements of propaganda*. Westfield, NJ: Open Magazine Pamphlet Series.

Chomsky, N. (1989). *Necessary illusions: Thought control in democratic societies*. Boston: South End Press.

Cialdini, R. B. (1993). *Influence: The psychology of persuasion*. New York: William Morrow.

Crossen, C. (1994). *Tainted truth: The manipulation of fact in America*. New York: Simon & Schuster.

Kelly, K. (1998). *New rules for the new economy*. New York: Viking.

Lovelock, J.E. (1987). *Gaia : A new look at life on earth*. New York: Oxford University Press.

Schwartz, P. & P. Leydon. (1997, July). The long boom. *Wired*.

Simpson, C. (1994). *Science of coercion: Communication research and psychological warfare, 1945–1960*. New York: Oxford University Press.

Stauber, J. & S. Rampton. (1995). *Toxic sludge is good for you!: Lies, damn lies, and the public relations industry*. Monroe, ME: Common Courage Press.

Toffler, A. (1980). *The third wave*. New York: Morrow.

Watson, P. (1978). *War on the mind: The military uses and abuses of psychology*. New York: Basic Books.

Wiener, N. (1967). *The human use of human beings: Cybernetics and society*. Boston, MA: Avon.

ONE NATION, UNDER THE CORPORATION

The Truth About Corporations

Where They Came From, How They Took Over and What You Can Do About It

Agent J

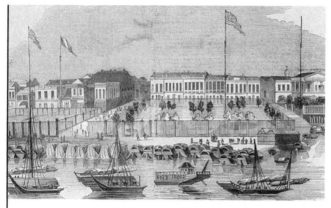

One of the first successful "joint-stock companies" was the British East India Company, formed by royal charter in 1600. ...it was the most powerful corporation that has ever existed...a private company so unaccountable that it conducted its own criminal trials and ran its own jails,...possessed an army larger than any other organized force in the world, and...squeezed the economy of the richest country in the world (India) until observers reported that some regions had been "bled white."[1]

One of the big reasons for the American Revolution was colonial opposition to corporate power.[2]

1600

...the Virginia colony (established by the Virginia Company) ...was a deadly work camp for the English poor and...the starting place for the 244-year holocaust of African slavery, but gets credit as a "cradle of democracy" for establishing the first legislative body among Europeans in America.[3]

Top: Crest of the British East India Company

You Are Still Being Lied To

According to Adam Smith, a core flaw of the corporation as an institutional form was the intrinsic lack of functional accountability caused by separating ownership from management.[4]

Among British and French thinkers, corporate enterprise was considered synonymous with monopoly—a way for privileged elites to profit at the expense of the general public.[5]

Under the early American system, corporate charters tended to be granted sparingly, in keeping with the widespread belief that the potential for corporations to accumulate power rendered them inherently dangerous to democracy.[6]

Little-known facts about corporations:

☠ *The Founding Fathers intentionally left corporations out of the Constitution.*

☠ *Thomas Jefferson, Adam Smith, Abraham Lincoln, Henry Adams, Theodore Roosevelt, Franklin Roosevelt, and Dwight Eisenhower all warned of the power of corporations and their threat to democracy.*

☠ *With the help of state legislatures and the courts, corporations have acquired more rights than people.*

☠ *Corporations receive over three times more in government "welfare" payments than people do.*

☠ *You are 50 times more likely to be robbed by a corporation than by a person.*

☠ *You are six times more likely to be killed by a corporation than by a person.*

1670

Only when truly modern-style general incorporation, with no restrictions, was introduced (in the late nineteenth century)…did it become impossible for states to control corporations…[7]

The **Boston Tea Party** was a highly pragmatic economic rebellion against an overbearing corporation (the East India Company)…Or more accurately, it was a rebellion against a corporation and a government that were thoroughly intertwined.[8]

In 1773, a parliamentary committee investigating the **East India Company** wrote, "In the East, the laws of society, the laws of nature have been enormously violated. Oppression in every shape has ground the faces of the poor defenseless natives; and tyranny in her bloodless form has stalked abroad." The company's representatives responded by bribing members of Parliament and providing open-ended loans to the monarch.[9]

From 1820 to 1900, state legislatures granted corporations the rights of limited liability, perpetual existence, virtual location, and indefinite entity:

limited liability: investors are not held legally liable for the actions of the corporation.

perpetual existence: a corporation is allowed to exist indefinitely (even beyond the lifespans of its founding shareholders and managers).

virtual location: a corporation may operate outside the state where it was originally chartered.

indefinite entity: a corporation is able to change by conglomerating (buying other companies), changing its structure (creating or selling divisions), or just renaming itself.

1750

Left to its own devices, the "free" market always seeks a work force that is hungry, desperate, and cheap—a work force that is anything but free.[10]

The founding fathers' vision was to subordinate corporations to democratic oversight, then make use of this tamed institution as a tool for meeting the pent-up need for infrastructure such as roads and bridges.[11]

We need a "three strikes" law for bad corporations.

"…we've seen the results of **capitalism without conscience; the pollution** of the air we breathe, the water we drink, and the food we eat; the **endangerment** of workers; and the sale of **dangerous products**—from cars to toys to drugs. **All in the pursuit of greater profits."**
—Arianna Huffington

"I hope we shall crush in its birth the aristocracy of our monied corporations which dare already to challenge our government to a trial of strength, and bid defiance to the laws of our country."
—Thomas Jefferson, 1816

1820

Of the **US-transnationals** with assets over $100 million, **37% paid no US federal taxes at all in 1991**, and the average tax rate for those that did pay was just 1% of gross receipts!…**they avoid paying tax by concealing how much profit they make.**[12]

Profited from African slave labor:

American International Group

Bank of America

Brown Brothers Harriman

Brown and Williamson Tobacco

CSX

Gannett

JPMorganChase

Lehman Brothers Holdings

Liggett Group

Lloyds of London

Loews Corporation

Norfolk Southern Railroad

Union Pacific Railroad

WestPoint Stevens

RJ Reynolds Tobacco Holdings

The Tribune Company

WESTPOINT STEVENS

 Liggett Group Inc.

 LLOYD'S

You Are Still Being Lied To

"As a result of the war, corporations have been enthroned and an era of corruption in high places will follow, and the money power of the country **will endeavor to prolong its reign by working upon the prejudices of the people until** all wealth is aggregated in a few hands and **the Republic is destroyed."**
—Abraham Lincoln (attributed), 1864

Following the Civil War, **bribery by railroad lobbyists** was rampant among Senators and congressmen…Among the fruits of these expenditures by railroad interests were immense land grants…they acquired two hundred million acres of land—**a tenth of the area of the entire country.**[13]

1855   1890

"corporations…will ultimately succeed in directing government itself. Under the American form of society, there is no authority capable of effective resistance."
–Henry Adams, 1870

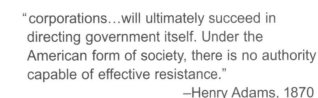

"There can be no effective control of corporations while their political activity remains. To put an end to it will be neither a short nor an easy task."
—Theodore Roosevelt, 1910

Back in the 1930s…General Motors…began buying up streetcar systems, tearing out the tracks, buying buses from itself and then selling the new, polluting bus systems back to the cities…GM was soon joined by Greyhound, Firestone Tire and Rubber, Standard Oil of California (also called Chevron) and Mack Trucks. In 1949—after these companies had destroyed more than 100 streetcar systems in more than 45 cities, including New York, Los Angeles, Philadelphia, San Francisco, Oakland, Baltimore, St. Louis and Salt Lake City—GM, Chevron and Firestone were convicted of a criminal conspiracy to restrain trade. They were fined $5,000 each and the executives who organized the scheme were fined $1 each.[14]

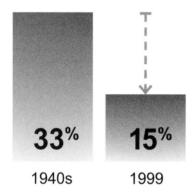

33% 1940s **15%** 1999

Corporate share of federal taxes[15]

1900   1935

Loss, Waste & Fraud: $224B

Federal Military Spending in 2003 ($393 Billion)

56% was **lost, wasted or stolen**[16]

"The American press, which is controlled mostly by vested interests, has an excessive influence on public opinion."
—Albert Einstein, 1921

Profited from slave labor during WWII:

BASF	IBM
Bayer	General Motors
BMW	Mitsubishi
Daimler	Mitsui
Deutsche Bank	Siemens
Ford	Volkswagen

DAIMLER

As of 2006, 2.4% of the U.S. population was on welfare.[17]

$193 Billion

Social Welfare
2004

[18]

$815 Billion

Corporate Welfare
2004

"…at the end of another century we shall have all American industry controlled by a dozen corporations, and run by perhaps a hundred men. Put plainly, we are steering a steady course toward economic oligarchy, if we are not there already."

—Franklin Roosevelt, 1932

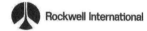

Rockwell International

Paid fines for allegedly defrauding the U.S. Government:

Boeing

Cubic

Hughes

General Electric

Grumman

Hazeltine

Litton

Lockheed

Loral

LTV

McDonnell Douglas

Northrop

Raytheon

RCA

Rockwell

Teledyne

Unisys

United Technologies

Whittaker

"In the councils of government, we must guard against the acquisition of unwarranted influence by the military-industrial complex."

—Dwight D. Eisenhower, 1961

1930

1965

THE WORLD BANK

INTERNATIONAL MONETARY FUND

You Are Still Being Lied To

$200 Billion [19]

$4 Billion

Corporate "White-Collar" Crime

Burglaries, Robberies & Muggings

———— 1995 ————

Yearly deaths in the US (est.) [20]

A. Murder 24,000

B. Medical negligence 120,000

C. On-the-job accidents, occupational diseases . . . 66,800

D. Dangerous or defective products 28,000

B+C+D   A

…nearly a third of all cancer deaths are due to carcinogens in the workplace. [21]

67% of the adults requesting emergency food aid are people with jobs.
—America's Second Harvest, 2000

-37%

1968   2003

Minimum Wage [22]

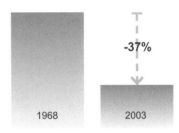

From 1886 to 1986 the Supreme Court granted corporations the following Constitutional rights:

• First Amendment right of free speech

• Fourth Amendment right against unwarranted searches

• Fifth Amendment right against double jeopardy

• Sixth Amendment right to a jury trial in a criminal case

• Seventh Amendment right to a jury trial in a civil case

• Fourteenth Amendment rights to due process and equal protection

+362%

1983   2003

Profits for the world's 200 richest companies [23]

In 2007 the US child poverty rate was 37 percent— the highest in the developed world. [24]

37%

Unlike every other industrialized nation, the US still lacks comprehensive healthcare for all its citizens—thanks to Big Insurance. We pay more (per capita) than anyone else in fhe world. So we could easily afford to cover every American if we could just get rid of the greedy corporations. We'd be healthier and we'd save a ton of money, too.

AOL

BERTELSMANN
media worldwide

Just a few of the many corporate-sponsored public policy and/or disinformation programs:

American Enterprise Institute

American Conservative Union

American Legislative Exchange Council

Annapolis Center for Science-Based Public Policy

Business Roundtable

Cato Institute

Center for the Study of CO_2 and Global Change

Center for Tobacco Research

Committee for a Constructive Tomorrow

Competitive Enterprise Institute

Consumer Alert

The Cooler Heads Coalition

The Environmental Education Working Group

Family Research Council

Heartland Institute

Heritage Foundation

Hoover Institution

George C. Marshall Institute

Media Research Center

Project for a New American Century

The Rand Corporation

Science and Environmental Policy Project

…the World Bank, the IMF and the WTO…have become integral to the expansion of transnational corporations, especially in the Third World.[25]

TimeWarner   SONY   VIVENDI UNIVERSAL

"Ten multinational corporations own virtually all broadcast, Internet, or print media in this country—**General Electric, Viacom, AOL/Time Warner, Disney, AT&T, News Corp, Liberty, Sony, Bertelsmann, and Vivendi.**"

—*Baton Rouge Advocate*, 1/11/02

VIACOM.   at&t   DISNEY

News Corporation

Ronald Reagan abolishes the **Fairness Doctrine** for American broadcast media.

1980

? →

NAFTA ——— WORLD TRADE ORGANIZATION

Organized resistance:

THE CENTER FOR PUBLIC INTEGRITY

Slow Food®

GLOBAL Exchange

You Are Still Being Lied To

"**The corporate grip on opinion in the United States is one of the wonders of the Western world.** No First World country has ever managed to eliminate so entirely from its media all objectivity—much less dissent."

—Gore Vidal

" **...corporations spend millions of dollars manipulating public policy** in their favor... But **ordinary people can** stand up to deadly and dangerous corporate practices and **bring about change.**"

—Kathryn Mulvey, CAI

Licking and Porter, PA...**decreed that** within their townships, **"Corporations shall not be considered to be 'persons'** protected by the Constitution of the United States."[26]

👍 Minnesota has introduced a state constitutional amendment **eliminating corporate personhood.**

👍 The Arizona Green Party is campaigning for a similar amendment in their state.

👍 Point Arena, CA passed nonbinding resolutions in opposition to corporate personhood.

👍 Iowa, Kansas, Minnesota, Missouri, Nebraska, Oklahoma, North Dakota, South Dakota, and Wisconsin have all passed laws **outlawing corporate ownership of farms.**[27]

"A state can revoke a company's charter, distribute their assets and put them out of business."

—Robert Benson, Attorney

YOU WRITE WHAT YOU'RE TOLD!

© Micah Ian Wright & AntiWarPosters.com

THANKS, CORPORATE NEWS!
We Couldn't Control The People Without You

A MESSAGE FROM THE MINISTRY OF HOMELAND SECURITY

A proposed **constitutional amendment:**

"This amendment enshrines the sanctity of the individual and establishes the presumption that **individuals are entitled to a greater measure of constitutional protection than corporations.**

For purposes of the foregoing amendments, **corporations are not considered 'persons,'** nor are they entitled to the same Bill of Rights protections as individuals. Such protections may only be conferred by state legislatures or in popular referenda."

—Carl J. Mayer

What can you do to fight back?

Democratic strategies and tactics:

1. Shop small, local, and responsible.
Boycott the Wal-Mart, the McDonalds, the Starbucks, the Home Depot, the Winn-Dixie. Shop at locally owned stores selling locally produced goods.

2. Spread the word.

Become an expert on an issue related to the larger struggle for democracy. Then consult with the government, politicians, and the media.

Get published. Write letters to the editor of your newspaper. Submit articles and ideas to magazines, websites, and TV shows.

Volunteer. Join an activist organization. Man a table. Hand out literature. Stuff envelopes.

Organize an event. Start a discussion group. Present a film series. Hold a vigil.

Get material into your local library. Most libraries encourage requests.

Ask the ACLU to reject corporate personhood. The American Civil Liberties Union is a fantastic organization. But on this issue, they just got it wrong.

Always choose democratic language. A language of tolerance, acceptance, and understanding. Never hateful, dehumanizing or divisive.

3. Support revolutionary change.
Spend your time and money on the root cause of our problems, not just the damage control. We will be unable to solve any of the crises we face unless we can wrest control of our government from rich and powerful corporations.

4. Get involved in politics.

Run for office. Start with your co-op board, the community board, the school board, the city council.

Support electoral reform. Fight for public financing. All corporate money must be removed from politics.

Support media reform. Campaigns are expensive because of high advertising costs. All broadcast media companies should be required to provide free advertising to political candidates in exchange for public financing.

M. WUERKER

Propose an ordinance or resolution eliminating corporate personhood. Our founding fathers never intended for corporations to have more rights than human beings.

Reject "privatization" of our common spaces, natural resources, and critical services. Protect the public commons for everyone. Remove commercialism from our schools. Preserve the ecosystem we all depend upon.

Fight corporate subsidies. No more tax abatements or government handouts for giant corporations. Let's support our local small businesses and entrepreneurs.

Restrict corporate chain stores and restaurants. Use your local zoning laws to keep out the big box developments.

Preserve family farms. Support or propose a statute banning corporate farm ownership.

Ban predatory corporations. Propose a "3-strikes" statute in your town or county. Don't let the company or the managers off the hook.

Endnotes:

1. Nace, Ted. (2005). *Gangs of America: The rise of corporate power and the disabling of democracy.* Berrett-Koehler Publishers, p 24. **2.** *Ibid.*, p 39. **3.** *Ibid.*, p 35. **4.** *Ibid.*, p 40. **5.** *Ibid.*, p 39. **6.** *Ibid.*, p 48. **7.** *Ibid.*, p 72. **8.** *Ibid.*, p 42. **9.** *Ibid.*, p 29. **10.** Schlosser, Eric. (2004). *Reefer madness: Sex, drugs and cheap labor in the American black market.* Houghton Mifflin Harcourt, p 108. **11.** *Op cit.*, Nace, p 46. **12.** Zepezauer, Mark. (2004). *Take the rich off welfare* (expanded edition). South End Press, p 29. **13.** *Op cit.*, Nace, p 93. **14.** *Op cit.*, Zepezauer, p 139. **15.** *Op cit.*, Nace, p 199. **16.** *Op cit.*, Zepezauer, pp 54, 74. **17.** US Deptartment of Health and Human Services. 2007 Annual Report of the SSI Program. **18.** *Op cit.*, Zepezauer, pp 1, 142. **19.** *Ibid.*, p 134. **20.** *Ibid.*, p 134. **21.** *Ibid.*, p 134. **22.** *Op cit.*, Schlosser, p 217. **23.** Moore, Michael. (2001). *Stupid white men.* HarperCollins, p 52. **24.** National Center for Children in Poverty <nccp.org>. **25.** *Op cit.*, Nace, p 190. **26.** Kaplan, Jeffrey. (2003). Consent of the governed. *Orion*, Nov/Dec. **27.** *Ibid.* **28.** Women's International League for Peace and Freedom website <wilpf.org>.

Recommended Reading:

Adbusters Magazine

Bill Moyers on America, Bill Moyers

A Civic Arousal, Ralph Nader

Confessions of an Economic Hitman, John Perkins

Executive Excess 2007: The Staggering Cost of U.S. Business Leadership, Sarah Anderson, John Cavanagh, Chuck Collins, Mike Lapham and Sam Pizzigati

Fast Food Nation, Eric Schlosser

How to Overthrow the Government, Arianna Huffington

The Nation Magazine

Nickle and Dimed, Barbara Ehrenreich

No Logo, Naomi Klein

Other People's Money: The Corporate Mugging of America, Nomi Prins

The People's Business: Controlling Corporations and Restoring Democracy, Lee Drutman and Charlie Cray

A People's History of the United States, Howard Zinn

Pigs at the Trough, Arianna Huffington

The Progressive Magazine

Perfectly Legal: The Covert Campaign to Rig Our Tax System to Benefit the Super Rich—And Cheat Everyone Else, David Cay Johnston

Taming the Giant Corporation: How the Largest Corporations Control Our Lives, Ralph Nader, Mark Green and Joel Seligman

Vice Magazine

28

Organized Resistance:

ACORN
acorn.org

Business Ethics Network
businessethicsnetwork.org

Center for American Progress
americanprogress.org

Center for Economic and Policy Research
cepr.net

Center for Public Integrity
publicintegrity.org

Citizen Works
citizenworks.org

Common Cause
commoncause.org

Consumer Federation of America
conserfed.org

Corporate Accountability International
stopcorporateabuse.org

CorpWatch
corpwatch.org

Demos: A Network for Ideas & Action
demos.org

Economic Policy Institute
epi.org

Fairness and Accuracy in Reporting
fair.org

Free Press
freepress.net

Global Exchange
globalexchange.org

Inequality.org

Multinational Monitor
multinationalmonitor.org

Polaris Institute
polarisinstitute.org

Program on Corporations, Law and Democracy
poclad.org

Program on Inequality and the Common Good
Institute for Policy Studies
ips-dc.org

ReclaimDemocracy.org

Slow Food
slowfood.org

United for a Fair Economy
faireconomy.org

War Resisters League
warresisters.org

Women's International League for Peace and Freedom
wilpf.org

Chemicals Are Killing You
Terri Mitchell

People who undergo stomach bypass surgery for obesity have a problem. Hazardous waste bubbles up in their blood. It keeps surfacing for years after surgery, to the point where it reaches levels similar to those found in people involved in industrial spills. Fourteen different "polychlorinated biphenyls" and eleven different pesticides have been documented so far in the blood of these formerly obese patients. There are hundreds more.[1] The chemicals contain chlorine—as in chlorine bleach.[2]

One of the most notorious chlorine chemicals is dioxin. Dioxin is the stuff Victor Yushchenko was poisoned with. It's the toxin in Agent Orange. Dioxin is so toxic that it sets the standard for other chemicals. So toxic, it's measured in *parts per trillion* (as opposed to *parts per billion* like other chemicals). Dioxin is in every person on earth. It's also in Kentucky Fried Chicken,

> Dioxin is the stuff Victor Yushchenko was poisoned with. It's the toxin in Agent Orange. Dioxin is so toxic that it sets the standard for other chemicals. So toxic, it's measured in *parts per trillion* (as opposed to *parts per billion* like other chemicals). Dioxin is in every person on earth.

Pizza Hut pizza, McDonald's Big Macs, and Häagan-Daz ice cream.[3] Dioxin is in hot dogs, luncheon meat, fish, cheese, eggs, butter, chicken, pork, especially beef, and most especially farmed catfish. It's in vegan diets and baby food, too.[4,5] It's not supposed to be there. It's not okay that it's there, despite what you've heard from your government.

Along with several dozen versions of dioxin, America's food is contaminated with an unknown number of other POPs (persistent organic pollutants). They're known as "endocrine disruptors" because they block, mimic, and otherwise destroy the endocrine system.[6] What is the endocrine system? It's the body's communication network. It's glands and hormones.

Think pancreas, thyroid, estrogen, insulin. It's important.

Normally, the body creates infinitesimally small amounts of endocrine hormones. The whole system is self-regulating. Normally.

Breast Cancer and Corporate Secrets

If it weren't for a couple of researchers at Tufts University, the endocrine-destroying effects of manmade chemicals might still be a "corporate secret." Drs. Carlos Sonnenschein and Ana Soto were working with breast cancer cells, looking for a cancer inhibitor. One morning Dr. Soto was stunned to discover the cells multiplying. Normally, only estrogen would cause such a thing. She did the experiments over. And over. No estrogen was present—why were the cells growing? Four months later, the two researchers narrowed it down to the test tubes they were using. Something in the plastic tubes was fueling breast cancer. They contacted the manufacturer (Corning), and a meeting was set up. At the meeting, Corning representatives refused to disclose what's in the company's test tubes that fuels cancer growth. That—they told Soto, Sonnenschein, and representatives from Tufts—is a corporate secret.[7]

It was impossible to simply ignore something that makes cancer cells multiply. So the two researchers abandoned their research and devoted all their time to uncovering the identity of the breast-cancer promoter that Corning didn't want anybody to know about.

Two years later, they found it. Nonylphenol is a manmade chemical used in the manufacture of pesticides, laundry detergent, and plastic. It's banned in the European Union. In the US, women use a version of it as a contraceptive cream (Nonoxynol-9). They also ingest it. It migrates into food encased in plastic wrap and styrofoam.[8]

American women also wash clothes in it. Although what's in Tide laundry detergent is also a "corporate secret," the product reportedly contains a version of nonylphenol. Tide was a gift to mankind from Chevron Oil. In the late 1940s, this chemical wonder replaced natural soaps. It's made from coal tar derivatives. There was no oversight to stop toxic products like Tide from coming onto the market and polluting America's water. There still isn't. Tide originally contained benzene, which is a gasoline additive.[9] Products like Tide end up in sewage sludge that is being spread all over American crops as "fertilizer." Food crops soak up chemicals like nonylphenol.[10]

Researchers claim they can't figure out what causes breast cancer. Some say it's "genes" or refusing to have kids at a young age.[11] They advise women at high risk to take a cancer-causing chemical to prevent it.[12] It's called tamoxifen (brand name: Nolvadex), and it causes endometrial cancer.[13] Mainstream medicine never tells women about fake-estrogen chemicals in plastic that make cancer cells grow. Maybe that's because Western medicine is based on chemicals. They're called "drugs."

Some girls are now getting breasts and pubic hair at age three.[14] Some teenage boys are having mastectomies.[15] An 11-year-old girl in Italy had to have her massive breasts removed so she could breathe. They weighed one-quarter of her entire body weight.[16] These things are a mystery. Care for a hamburger and shake?

> Nonylphenol is a manmade chemical used in the manufacture of pesticides, laundry detergent, and plastic. It's banned in the European Union. In the US, women use a version of it as a contraceptive cream (Nonoxynol-9).

> DEHP can be used as a pesticide or an insect repellant. The FDA approved it for food wrap in 1968. Some plastic food wraps are 40 percent DEHP.

Plastic Poison

NHANES stands for National Health and Examination Survey. It sounds grandiose because it *is* grandiose. A big study, it's designed to get a handle on Americans' health issues. Blood and urine samples from tens of thousands of people are being analyzed in dozens of laboratories.

In one of the studies, researchers at the University of Rochester report that the big, fat stomachs of American men correlate with the amount of phthalate in their urine.[17] The fatter the stomach, the more phthalate. Phthalates are petroleum-based chemicals. Billions of pounds are produced every year to combine with PVC (polyvinyl chloride) to make it soft and flexible. Throwaway drink bottles and milk jugs with "PET" or "PETE" stamped on the bottom contain phthalate (polyethylene terephthalate). So do many other things—shampoos, deodorants, paints, pesticides, pacifiers, garden hoses, hair mousses, after-shaves, auto interiors, packaging for food, building materials, shower curtains, pet-food packaging, suntan lotions, body lotions, perfumes, cosmetics, printing ink, floorings, wall papers, carpet tiles, insect repellants, gloves, clothing, and much more.[18]

The most notorious phthalate is DEHP (di(2-ethylhexyl) phthalate). DEHP can be used as a pesticide or insect repellant.[19] The FDA approved it for food wrap in 1968. Some plastic food wraps are 40 percent DEHP. That's a problem because DEHP can migrate out of plastic and into whatever is around. Like plastic soft-drink bottles and food wrapped in plastic.[20]

In the early 1970s, microwave ovens became a feature of many American kitchens, and food heated in plastic became a feature of American cooking. At the time, the Food and Drug Administration knew that DEHP and other phthalates migrate out of plastic. The agency also knew that phthalate leaches out faster/better when heated. The FDA didn't say a word when people started nuking their lunches in plastic wrap.

Chemicals Are Killing You
Terri Mitchell

Blood and I.V. bags have a stamped warning that they contain DEHP. Check it out next time you're in the emergency room getting blood. DEHP is in most all plastic hospital paraphernalia including the bags that deliver chemotherapy drug solution straight into a person's arteries.

■ ■ ■ ■ ■ ■ ■ ■ ■ ■

When chemicals get into humans, they don't magically disappear. They do things. They stick around. Build up. Make you sick. The older a person is, they more saturated they become. The fatter a person is, the more they're lugging around. Fat is the storage depot for many petroleum-based chemicals in the human body.[21] When fat is reduced, chemicals move into the bloodstream and organs. They do not move out. They persist in the environment; they persist in the human body. The health effects of generations of exposure to billions of pounds of petroleum-based chemicals are just now beginning to be discovered.

Here's some late-breaking news the plastic industry doesn't want you to hear. Phthalates cause testicles to shrivel. They block sex hormones. Men with fat stomachs have abnormally low testosterone levels. Phthalates interfere with normal sugar metabolism.

When the FDA was made aware that phthalates were leaching into milk, into humans, into stored blood, into rivers—into most everything—the agency trotted out its usual excuses and threats on behalf of the petroleum industry. This was way back in 1972. When forced to respond to overwhelming data,

A 2005 study in *Science* showed that the fertility-lowering effects of a fungicide called vinclozolin last for three generations after the mother is exposed.

Associate Commissioner for Science Lloyd B. Tepper indicated that he was concerned about the costs to industry, should the FDA take any action. Anybody who doesn't understand that profits are as important as public health, he warned, is a simple-minded demagogue. He went on to threaten scientists who dared publish anything negative about plastic. Their data

would be retracted and they would be publicly humiliated if it was later discovered that manmade chemical phthalates leaching into everything are actually a natural part of the human body.[22]

Despite the FDA's threats against anyone or anything attempting to compete against plastic manufacturers, nontoxic, DEHP-free blood bags and other hospital equipment were developed.

Phthalates cause testicles to shrivel.

Such items have been available for decades, but most American hospitals are still pumping toxic phthalates into patients (as are veterinary clinics into companion animals).

Plastic and pesticides affect brain and behavior. Bisphenol A, a chemical in plastic water bottles, causes mother mice to spend less time mothering their babies.[23] A new line of research suggests that hyper-aggression and the inability to learn in males is caused by chemical destruction of normal estrogen activity.[24] Estrogen puts a lid on male aggression, counteracts anxiety, and is critical for learning.

The toxic effects of at least some chemicals are inherited. A 2005 study in *Science* showed that the fertility-lowering effects of a fungicide called vinclozolin last for three generations after the mother is exposed.[25] Vinclozolin is used in vineyards. It blocks androgen. Insecticides such as methoxychlor (brand name: Maralate) and fenitrothion also block androgen.[26] The abnormalities passed down for generations are invisible: The animals look perfectly normal.

When European health ministers found a connection between skyrocketing rates of learning and behavioral abnormalities in children and the phthalates in plastic, they passed an emergency ban on six of them. That was in 1999. America did nothing. The safety picture for phthalates is worsening. Most Americans are not aware that pacifiers and other items kids put in their mouths contain toxic chemicals that leach out. American toddlers have higher levels of phthalates than adults. Americans don't know that the plastics industry uses lead and cadmium to manufacture plastic. They think kids get high levels of lead from old paint.

Autistic kids have abnormal brain cells. The ends, where one neuron interacts with the next one are, essentially, fried. In some autistic kids, the part called the "axon" is too short.[27] How could that happen?

Americans love pesticides. They purchase gallons, blanketing their yards and houses with the smelly chemicals. One all-American favorite is Dursban. Dursban is the market name for a chemical known as chlorpyrifos. Chlorpyrifos is an organo-phosphate that attacks the nervous system. Dursban was "banned"—wink, wink—in 2000. (It's still with us.) If Dursban is put on brain cells when they're growing, the axons end up too short.[28]

Most Americans are not aware that pacifiers and other items kids put in their mouths contain toxic chemicals that leach out. American toddlers have higher levels of phthalates than adults.

Coke and Pepsi claim that small amounts of DDT and other pesticides in their products are not harmful to consumers. That argument was part of an effort by the companies to get the High Court in India to reverse its ruling that they have to list the ingredients—including pesticides and chemicals—of soft drinks on the labels. The issue came up after it was reported that farmers in India use Coca-Cola as a pesticide. High levels of malathion, DDT, lindane, Dursban, and now benzene have been found in Indian Coke products. Coke and Pepsi claim that what's in their products is a "corporate secret." China recently banned Coke's Fanta for containing high levels of benzoic acid, a chemical that converts to benzene, a cancer-causing gasoline additive.[29] The FDA knew in 1990 that soft drinks contain high levels of the cancer-causing chemical, but it hasn't taken any action to protect the public. Coke and Pepsi have been sued over benzene contamination.

The issue came up after it was reported that farmers in India use Coca-Cola as a pesticide.

Quick. Name 25 chemicals commonly found in American groundwater.

acetone
aroclor 1260
arsenic
benzene
cadmium
carbon tetrachloride
chlorobenzene
chloroform
chromium
1,1-dichloroethane
1,2-dichloroethane
1,1dichloroethylene
1,2-trans-dichloroethylene
di(2-ethylhexyl) phthalate
ethylbenzene
lead
mercury
methylene chloride
nickel
phenol
tetrachloroethylene
toluene
1,1,1-trichloroethane
trichloroethylene
xylenes

This list was made by the Environmental *Protection* Agency.[30] If you expand the list by h-u-n-d-r-e-d-s more, you'll begin to get an idea of what's in the water you drink and bathe in. I say "begin to" because no one actually knows how many chemicals are in your water. The number of chemicals *potentially* in your water is about 80,000—that's how many are manufactured and sold—billions of pounds of plastic every year alone. Don't worry, though—all of these chemicals have "safe" levels.

Scotchgard and Diacetyl—Yum

Take Scotchgard, for example. This is the stuff that "resists stains." Carpet, couches, and babies' night clothes are "treated" with it. "Scotchgard" is a catchy euphemism for perfluorooctanoic acid (PFOA). There are many different versions of PFOA. What they all have in common is fluorine and carbon.

The only chemicals required to be tested before they're sold to the public are drugs. …All chemicals, except those designated as "drugs," are presumed safe unless the government can prove otherwise.

Scotchgard was first marketed by 3M in 1956. The company also sold PFOA to DuPont to make Teflon. The first tests on the health effects of these products were begun in *1997*. Both 3M and DuPont knew, as early as 1961, that PFOA is hazardous. (The only chemicals required to be tested before they're sold to the public are drugs. The manufacturer does the testing—not the government. All chemicals, except those designated as "drugs," are presumed safe unless the government can prove otherwise. Regulatory agencies put in place to protect the public from manufacturers were defunded and gutted during the Reagan era of "deregulation." The preeminence of profit over health and environment was adopted into law during this time. This policy has since been strengthened, especially under George W. Bush, the petroleum president.)

In 2002, the Minnesota Pollution Control Agency set the "safe level" of PFOA at 7 ppb (parts per billion). At that point, the Agency's new commissioner was Sheryl Corrigan. She had left 3M to become head of the state environmental agency. The Republican governor who appointed her felt she would have a "business perspective" on the environment. She did. She made sure Minnesota did absolutely nothing about Scotchgard contaminating parts of Minnesota and the Mississippi River.

The Agency, under Corrigan's leadership, had set the "safe level" of PFOA at 7 ppb. DuPont had established the "safe level" at 1 ppb eleven years earlier. As the dangers began surfacing in media reports, her agency lowered the "safe level" to 1 ppb. In 2007, it was lowered again to 0.5 ppb. In reality, there is no "safe level" of perfluorooctanoic acid, or any other fluorine-based chemical, in human beings. "Safe levels" are set by manufacturers. They're artificially created for the sole purpose of keeping dangerous products on the market. There was no scientific basis for Minnesota's "safe levels" of PFOA. In fact, Corrigan blocked research on Scotchgard/PFOA, claiming that state environmental agencies shouldn't employ research scientists.

PFOA has been used as an industrial detergent for over 50 years.[31] Now that it's in people, there's a "safe level" for humans to eat. It's in carpet, dental floss, pizza containers, hamburger containers, toilet bowl cleaner, microwave popcorn packages, pet food packages, "easy care" bedding, blue jeans, car seats, insecticides, and thousands of other products. PFOA, like all other chemicals, is *unregulated*. Under existing law, manufacturers are supposed to inform the government of any toxicity they discover regarding their products. The EPA had to *sue* DuPont for failing to tell the government that Teflon/PFOA is toxic. Seriously. There is no oversight. There is no one protecting the public.

Unlike chlorine-based chemicals that hole up in a person's fat, fluorine-based chemicals like PFOA circulate continuously between organs and the bloodstream. It sticks around for about eight years. It's everywhere. It's in every ocean on earth, and probably food crops. Antarctic birds were tested for ten versions of it, and it's in them, too. It's predicted that hundreds of years from now, Scotchgard/Teflon-type chemicals will still be in soil treated with sewage sludge that American food crops are grown on.[32]

Unlike chlorine-based chemicals that hole up in a person's fat, fluorine-based chemicals like PFOA circulate continuously between organs and the bloodstream.

Only because of a class-action lawsuit by very sick people did the facts about Scotchgard and Teflon come out. With industry subject to no regulation, there is no other avenue for information about the hazards to become public.

PFOA and other fluorine chemicals may be even scarier than chlorine chemicals such as dioxin. Already it's known that little kids have the highest amounts of anyone in their bodies—at a time when their brains are supposed to be developing. These chemicals are brain-toxic. They cause "deranged" behavior including hyperactivity and hypoactivity.[33] Babies exposed to PFOA during pregnancy have small heads and low birth weights.[34]

Among the "corporate secrets" revealed in the Teflon/PFOA lawsuit: DuPont scientists told DuPont that anybody *potentially* exposed to PFOA should wear protective clothing and a breathing device. When PFOA vaporizes off of nonstick frying pans,[35] and popcorn heated to 375° F in an enclosed office, shouldn't people be wearing breathing devices?

Butter-flavored microwave popcorn. De-li-cious. That smell is yet another petroleum product. Diacetyl is a chemical that was originally developed as an antidote to nerve poison. Now they

Only because of a class-action lawsuit by very sick people did the facts about Scotchgard and Teflon come out.

use it as the "butter flavor" in popcorn and commercial "baked goods." Diacetyl is FDA-approved under the FDA's GRAS list ("Generally Recognized As Safe"). Eat as much as you want.

The National Institute for Occupational Safety and Health (NIOSH) started looking into this FDA-approved chemical after young, healthy people working in a popcorn-packaging plant developed a killer lung disorder called *bronchiolitis obliterans*. *Bronchiolitis obliterans* is something akin to a pack-a-day smoker on asbestos. The agency exposed rats to this FDA-approved safe "butter flavor" for six hours. The results were *"the most dramatic cases of cell death ever seen."* Their lungs were toast. This NIOSH study reportedly confirms an earlier one where rats exposed to four hours of intense diacetyl fumes all died.

People who work with "artificial butter flavor" are supposed to wear a serious respirator—the kind designed for toxic gas. If "artificial butter flavor" (diacetyl) is spilled, *"Do not reenter the contaminated area until the Safety Officer (or other responsible person) has verified that the area has been properly cleaned."*

Missouri's Department of Health contacted the Occupational Safety and Health Administration (OSHA) to investigate the first microwave popcorn-packaging plant where ten workers had been diagnosed with the deadly *bronchiolitis obliterans* ("popcorn lung") in 1999. An inspector named David Fine was sent to the Jasper Popcorn Company. He wrote in his report

that "in his professional opinion it would be ludicrous" to sample the dust in the work area because he didn't see any. He also determined that there was no danger from any oil mist because he didn't see that either. He characterized the cases of "popcorn lung" documented by the Missouri Department of Health as "alleged." This is deregulation. It gets worse.

OSHA subsequently entered into an alliance with the Popcorn Board, a front for a company called Smith Bucklin, which is a front for the popcorn industry. An agreement was signed between OSHA and the popcorn industry establishing a "collaborative relationship."

Although OSHA made it clear that it would do everything possible to protect popcorn profits against people poisoned by diacetyl, NIOSH continued its investigation into "popcorn lung" and "artificial butter flavor." It took eight years to write a report.

Part of that report is an account of how microwave popcorn is made. It's an eye-opener about the food-like, chemical-laced products lining the shelves of American "supermarkets."

When it arrives at the plant, the corn is treated with an organophosphate insecticide. It's then put in silos. When it's taken out of the silo, it's cleaned with air and screened. Corn destined to be unflavored popcorn is then put in polyethylene bags, stacked and wrapped in plastic. Butter-flavored popcorn is made by mixing the insecticide-treated kernels with a mixture of heated, hydrogenated soybean oil, diacetyl, artificial colorings, and salt.

NIOSH detected over 100 volatile organic compounds (VOCs) in one popcorn plant, including diacetyl, methyl ethyl ketone, 2-nonanone, acetoin, acetaldehyde, and acetic acid. Methyl ethyl ketone is a solvent used in varnishes and paint remover. 2-nonanone is used in the synthesis of pesticides. Acetoin is a sister compound to diacetyl. According to Wikipedia, it and diacetyl are added to margarine; otherwise it would be tasteless. It's also one of 599 additives in cigarettes. Acetaldehyde is what damages an alcoholic's liver. It's also created by auto-

Diacetyl is a chemical that was originally developed as an antidote to nerve poison. Now they use it as the "butter flavor" in popcorn and commercial "baked goods."

NIOSH detected over 100 volatile organic compounds (VOCs) in one popcorn plant.

mobile exhaust. Acetic acid is what gives vinegar its smell. The petroleum industry manufactures acetic acid for use in PET (PETE) (phthalate) for plastic drink bottles. What are these chemicals doing in a food plant?

Seven years after the FDA, OSHA, NIOSH, and state regulatory agencies refused to do anything but "study the problem" of "butter flavor," the *Seattle Post-Intelligencer*, under the guidance of consumer advocate Andrew Schneider, commissioned a study on diacetyl in commercial kitchens. Millions of people are exposed to an unknown amount of diacetyl fumes everyday when things such as 30-pound blocks of margarine are melted and fired up on hot griddles in restaurants. The newspaper found diacetyl in everything it tested.

Unite Here, a labor union representing 440,000 kitchen workers, asked NIOSH to find out how much diacetyl kitchen workers are inhaling. The agency is working on it. Meanwhile, it advises people working in popcorn-packaging plants to wear respirators that supply oxygen. What about people working in office buildings?

Microwave popcorn is the poster child for unregulated dietary chemicals. This artificial food-like product contains two killer

ed odds ratio for a normal-weight person with a high level of chemicals is 19.8. The adjusted odds ratio for an overweight person with a low level of chemicals is 11.5. Chemicals or fat? You be the judge.

Relax, you've got enough on your mind without having to worry about toxic petroleum products. Have you ever wondered why a hot shower is so relaxing? It might be the chloroform. This anesthetic shows up in a person's blood within ten minutes of stepping into a shower.[36] It comes from the chlorine added to American water supplies. When the chlorine combines with chemicals already in the water, it creates a chemical stew that's absorbed through the skin, inhaled, and ingested. It then spreads throughout the body through the bloodstream. On any given day, a bath or shower may include rocket fuel, arsenic, fluoride, dry-cleaning fluid, pesticides, prescription drugs like tranquilizers and birth control pills, and much more. The longer you steam, the more you absorb. Going for a swim? Making tea with tap water? Doing dishes over a steamy sink? Eight glasses of tap water a day? Only if you want to increase your risk of bladder cancer.[37]

Chemicals eaten as "food additives," "flavorings," "colorings," and "coatings" do not magically disappear. The body does not ignore PFOA and diacetyl heated to 375° and served up with pesticides. The chemicals are not in such tiny amounts that they're "nothing." One of the scariest findings about petroleum-

On any given day, a bath or shower may include rocket fuel, arsenic, fluoride, dry-cleaning fluid, pesticides, prescription drugs like tranquilizers and birth control pills, and much more.

chemicals ("butter-flavor" diacetyl and the Scotchgard-like PFOA). It's the most hazardous food-like product ignored by the greatest number of regulatory agencies thus far.

Your Daily Dose of Chemicals—Take it and Shut Up

"Hazardous waste" courses through the veins of more than 80 percent of Americans tested in one of the NHANES study. The hazardous waste in question is chlorine/dioxin chemicals. These chemicals, plus three pesticides and two PCBs, dramatically increase the risk of developing diabetes. The adjust-

based chemicals is that they have some of their worst effects at low levels.

Organic. Vegan. Vegetarian. Bottled water. No, no, no, and no. They will not save you from chemicals. America's water, soil, air, food, atmosphere—everything you eat, everything you touch, every breath you take—is contaminated with petroleum-based chemicals. The earth is enclosed in a plastic Baggie full of pollution and tied securely with a twist-tie. Thirty-five years ago, FDA's Lloyd B. Tepper commented that certain bodies of water in America had levels of phthalates approaching the entire amount ever manufactured. *Petroleum chemicals do not go away.* The *billions of pounds* of chemicals manufactured in

America *every year* are in you, your kids, your animals, food, air, water, house, yard—you name it. And will continue until people put a stop to it.

The American Dream is Plastic

The American dream, as envisioned by the petroleum industry, is an artificial world of plastic and pesticides, fake food and early death. Everything in this version of life is patented, owned, and controlled by petroleum profiteers—every piece of DNA, every plant on earth—everything. Fake estrogen from plastic Gatorade bottles? You ain't seen nuthin' yet. The latest from the chemical industry is fake similes of every living thing made from "nanos."

Smaller than a single cell, nanos are already being released into the environment without any oversight. Nanotechnology is a creative new use of life-destroying chemicals. A recent attempt to make a fake spider web used the following: dibutyltin—a version of tributyltin, which the EPA says is the most toxic chemical ever deliberately put into the oceans; naphthalene—the highly toxic chemical used to make plastic phthalates and moth balls; chloroform—the major toxic chlorine chemical that forms in hot tap water; ethylene; hexamethylene diisocyanate; cyclohexane; tetrahydrofuran…. Do we really want to keep swimming in this junk so a small group of profiteers can maintain its stranglehold on Western society? Isn't it enough that the petroleum industry has destroyed the atmosphere, warmed the globe, and caused wetlands to sink under the ocean?

Say Bye-Bye to the Petroleum People

By the 1960s, the dangers of WWII-era chemicals became so alarming that for a brief time environmental degradation overshadowed almost everything else in America. Legislation was passed under Nixon that forced the petroleum industry to submit to some oversight. Regulatory agencies were created. It seemed the masses would gain some control over the profiteers. What hadn't been destroyed would be protected.

It lasted a mere 20 years. In 1980, Americans voted to have oversight dismantled. Embracing the philosophy that *greed is*

good, and *profits over people*, they relinquished control of their government to the profiteers. A corporate-looking white daddy, former lifeguard, and talking head for General Electric became President. He began dismantling the regulatory agencies by "Executive Order," staffing them with industry, and cutting off funding. Americans put him in office to get the lowlifes off welfare, and get the regulatory agencies off the backs of corporate America so everyone could get rich. Americans didn't get rich: They got poisoned.

The American government is "monitoring" the levels of toxic chemicals in Americans' bodies. The purpose of this "monitoring" is to enable scientists to set "appropriate levels of exposure." Historically, the "appropriate level of exposure" is above the level already found in us. It changes according to the marketing needs of the petroleum industry. Since 2000, the Centers for Disease Control (CDC) has "monitored" 148 toxic

> The American government is "monitoring" the levels of toxic chemicals in Americans' bodies. The purpose of this "monitoring" is to enable scientists to set "appropriate levels of exposure."

chemicals. That's about 18 chemicals a year. There are about 80,000 more chemicals to go, and more being dumped into the environment every year.

While government "monitors" the levels of toxic chemicals in human beings, and "studies the effects," the clock is ticking. Only a demented species would believe that there's a "safe level" of toxic chemicals in humans, oceans, and everything on earth. Only a severely compromised creature would believe it can destroy everything on earth except itself and still live. Only a dying species would ignore the accumulating evidence of its own demise. And only a short-lived species would allow itself to be led by creatures so devoted to profit that they would cut down entire forests rather than allow another of their own kind to make one dime.* That time it was only beavers. This time it's only humans. The Petroleum People didn't last very long.

And you thought Neanderthals were stupid.

---

* For 200 years, a private company owned and ruled one-quarter of North America. The Hudson's Bay Company was a monopoly run by a handful of

families who divvied up the vast riches among themselves. Fiercely devoted to profit as the highest achievement of mankind, this group enriched itself by exterminating the fur-bearing animals of North America. As with all profiteers, the Hudson's Bay Company was convinced that the world, and everything in it, existed for its own exploitation. When seven brothers moved onto the company's "property" and began trading lumber for pelts with the indigenous people, the Hudson's Bay Company had every tree in the entire area cut down so the brothers would have nothing to trade. It took the company three years to cut down every tree within one mile of the lake where the brothers had set up shop.[38]

Endnotes

1. Third national report on human exposure to environmental chemicals 2005. <www.cdc.gov/exposurereport>. 2. Hue, O., et al. Increased plasma levels of toxic pollutants accompanying weight loss induced by hypocaloric diet or by bariatric surgery. Ob Surg 16: 1145–54. 3. Schecter, A., and L. Lingjun. Dioxins, dibenzofurans, dioxin-like PCBs, and DDE in U.S. fast food, 1995. Chemosphere 34: 1449–57. 4. Schecter, A. Intake of dioxins and related compounds from food in the U.S. population. J Tox Environ Health, Part A 63:1–18. 5. Schecter, A., et al. Dioxins in commercial United States baby food. J Toxicol Environ Health A 65: 1937–43. 6. Sanderson, J.T. The steroid hormone biosynthesis pathway as a target for endocrine-disrupting chemicals. Tox Sci 94: 3–21. 7. Colborn, Theo, Dianne Dumanski, and John P. Myers. (1996). Our stolen future. New York: Dutton. 8. Fernandes, A.R., et al. 4-Nonylphenol (NP) in food-contact materials: analytical methodology and occurrence. Food Add Contam 235: 364–72. 9. <www.acswebcontent.acs.org/landmarks/landmarks/tide/time.html>; <www.tide.com>; <en.wikipedia.org/wiki/Nonylphenol>; <en.wilipedia.org/wiki/Dodecyl_benzene>; Yoshitake, J., et al. Suppression of NO production and 8-nitroguanosine formation by phenol-containing endocrine-disrupting chemicals in LPF-stimulated macrophages: involvement of estrogen receptor-dependant or –independent pathways. Nitric Oxide 18:223–28; Krüger, T., et al. Plastic components affect the activation of the aryl hydrocarbon and the androgen receptor. Toxicology 246:112–213; Chen, M.L., et al. Quantification of prenatal exposure and maternal-fetal transfer of nonylphenol. Chemosphere 26 Apr 2008. 10. Sjostrom, A.E., et al. Degradation and plant uptake of nonylphenol (NP) and nonylphenol-12-ethoxylate (NP-12EO) in four contrasting agricultural soils. Env Pollution 21 Apr 2008. 11. Gail, M.H., et al. Projecting individualized probabilities of developing breast cancer for white females who are being examined annually. J Natl Cancer Inst 81: 1879–86. 12. Fisher, B., et al. Tamoxifen for prevention of breast cancer: report of the National Surgical Adjuvant Breast and Bowel Project P-1 Study. J Natl Can Inst 90: 1371–88. 13. I have an 8-inch file on Tamoxifen, including a transcript of the FDA hearing and correspondence with corrupt researchers. Fishter, B., et al. Endometrial cancer in tamoxifen-treated breast cancer patients: findings from the National Surgical Adjuvant Breast and Bowel Project (NSABP) B-14. J Natl Cancer Inst 86: 527–37. 14. Herman-Giddens, M.E., et al. Secondary sexual characteristics and menses in young girls seen in office practice: a study from the pediatric research in office settings network. Pediatrics 99: 505–12. 15. Shozu, M., et al. Estrogen excess associated with novel gain-of-function mutations affecting the aromatase gene. NEJM 348: 1855–65. 16. Fiumara, L., et al. Massive bilateral breast reduction in an 11-year-old girl: 24% ablation of body weight. J Plast Reconstr Surg 2008 Feb 19. 17. Stahlhut, R.W., et al. Concentrations of urinary phthalate metabolites are associated with increased waist circumference and insulin resistance in adult U.S. males. Env Health Persp 115: 876–82. 18. Aggregate Exposures to Phthalates in Humans. Health Care Without Harm. July 2002; Pretty Nasty; www.SafeCosmetics.org; Not Too Pretty: Phthalates, Beauty Products and the FDA. Houlihan J, Brody C and B Schwan. July 8, 2002. <www.healthcarewithoutharm.org>. 19. Graham, P.R. Phthalate ester plasticizers—why and how they are used. Environ Health Persp Jan 1973: 3–10. 20. Nazir, D.J., et al. Di-2-ethylhexyl phthalate in bovine heart muscle mitochondria: its detection, characterization, and specific localization. Environ Health Persp January 1973: 141–8; Wildbrett, G. Diffusion of phthalic acid esters from PVC milk tubing. Environ Health Persp January 1973: 29–35. 21. Mullerova, D., and J. Kopecky. White adipose tissue: storage and effector site for environmental pollutants. Physiol Res 56: 375–81; Schildkraut, J.M., et al. Environmental contaminants and body fat distribution. Cancer Epidem Biomarkers Prev 8: 179–83. 22. Tepper, L.B. Phthalic acid esters—an overview. Environ Health Persp January 1973: 179–82. 23. Palanza, P., et al. Exposure to a low dose of bisphenol A during fetal life or in adulthood alters maternal behavior in mice. Environ Health Persp 110 (Suppl 3): 415–22. 24. Nomura, M., et al. Estrogen receptor-beta gene disruption potentiates estrogen-inducible aggression but not sexual behaviour in male mice. Eur J Neurosci 23: 1860–68; Bobo, C., and E.F. Rissman. New roles for estrogen receptor beta in behavior and neuroendocrinology. Front Neuroendocrinol 27: 217–32; Patisaul, H.B., and H.L. Bateman. Neonatal exposure to endocrine active compounds or an ERbeta agonist increases adult anxiety and aggression in gonadally intact male rats. Horm Behav 53: 580–8. 25. Anway, M.D., et al. Epigenetic transgenerational actions of endocrine disruptors and male fertility. Science 308: 1466–9. 26. Tamura, H., et al. Androgen receptor antagonism by the organophosphate insecticide fenitrothion. Tox Sci 60: 56–62. 27. Weidenheim, K.M., et al. Etiology and pathophysiology of autistic behavior: clues from two cases with an unusual variant of neuroaxonal dystrophy. J Child Neurol 16: 809–19; Bouley, D.M., et al. Spontaneous murine neuroaxonal dystrophy: a model of infantile neuroaxonal dystrophy. J Comp Path 134: 161–70. 28. Howard, A.S., et al. Chlorpyrifos exerts opposing effects on axonal and dendritic growth in primary neuronal cultures. Tox Appl Pharmacol 207: 112–24; Yang, D., et al. Chlorpyrifos and chlorpyrifos-oxon inhibit axonal growth by interfering with the morphogenic activity of acetylcholinesterase. Tox Appl Pharm 228: 32–41. 29. <www.indiaresource.org>. 30. Yang, R. NTP technical report on the toxicity studies of a chemical mixture of 25 groundwater contaminants administered in drinking water to F344N rats and B6C3F mice. Toxic Rep Ser 35: 1. 31. Tao, L., et al. Perfluorooctanesulfonate and related fluorochemijcals in albatrosses, elephant seals, penguins, and polar skuas from the southern ocean. Environ Sci Technol 40: 7642–48. 32. vanZelm, R., et al. Modeling environmental fate of perfluorooctanoate and its precursors from global fluorotelomer acrylate polymer use. Environ Toxicol Chem 18 Apr 2008. 33. Johansson, N., et al. Neonatal exposure to perfluorooctane sulfonate (PFOS) and perfluorooctanoic acid (PFOA) causes neurobehavioural defects in adult mice. Neurotox 29: 160–9. 34. Fei, C., et al. Fetal growth indicators and perfluorinated chemicals: a study in the Danish National Birth Cohort. Am J Epidemiol 5 May 2008. 35. DuPont claims that it uses PFOA only to manufacture Teflon, that it's not in Teflon. That's a lie. See Sinclair, E., et al. Quantification of gas-phase perfluoroalkyl surfactants and fluorotelomer alcohols released from nonstick cookware and microwave popcorn bags. Environ Sci Technol 41: 1180–5. 36. Backer, L.C., et al. Exogenous and endogenous determinants of blood trihalomethane levels after showering. Environ Health Persp 11 October 2007. 37. Villanueva, C.M., et al. Total and specific fluid consumption as determinants of bladder cancer risk. Int J Cancer 118: 2040–7. 38. Galbraith, J.S. (1957). The Hudson's Bay Company as an imperial factor, 1821–1869. University of California Press, p 34.

Cheap, Crappy Food = A Fat Population
How Corporations and the US Government Create the Obesity Epidemic

Steven Greenstreet, Bryan Young, and Elias Pate

If the rates of obesity in the United States continue to increase at about the same rate they have been, 75 percent of the population will be overweight and 41 percent will be obese by the year 2015.[1] Obesity causes at least 111,000 deaths per year in the United States,[2] and some researchers place that number at over 400,000.[3] Add to these figures the cases of cancer and heart disease—brought on or worsened by obesity—and the cases of type 2 diabetes caused by obesity and resulting in death, and you have the single largest killer of Americans.

For years, the government has been fighting any meaningful stance on obesity by repeating over and over their two favorite mantras: "Exercise personal responsibility," and, "Exercise more." Certainly each of these recommendations has a certain amount of validity, but taken from a government that does far more to *cause* obesity than to prevent it, these quiet calls for the individual to take action are hardly enough (and somewhat a slap in the face). When it comes to powerful lobbyists and moneyed corporations influencing the government to implement policies that endanger the health and safety of its citizens, the issues surrounding obesity are no exception. From how we support our farm and agriculture system to how we regulate nutrition standards in schools and all points in between, the government takes an extremely damaging and passive-aggressive role in contributing to a national health crisis that former US Surgeon General Richard Carmona called "more pressing than 9/11 or any other terrorist event you can point out to me."[4]

We've spent two years researching the causes of obesity for our documentary film, *Killer at Large*, and have been floored by the degree of culpability on the part of government policy and by government-industry collusion in regards to our national obesity crisis. One expects such things from the healthcare industry, big tobacco, and defense contractors, but the pro-obesity lobby is just as big and just as ardent in protecting its monetary interests.

The following sections briefly detail some of the more flagrant instances we've uncovered, where government and industry have joined hands to institute or perpetuate policies and practices that have reshaped our food system in ways that overwhelmingly benefit business.

Fast, Cheap, and Irresistible

It is very important for one to realize before analyzing the problem of obesity at any length that we, as humans, are not nearly as clever as we give ourselves credit for being. Despite advances in technology, breakthroughs in science, or successes in business, we're still a species of hunter-gatherers with simple needs and desires. Namely, lots of food and lots of sex. While these compulsions are largely responsible for insuring our continued existence as a species over millions of years, lately they've made us easy targets to manipulate and have gotten us into quite a bit of trouble—most notably regarding the quality, availability, and price of our food.

> When it comes to powerful lobbyists and moneyed corporations influencing the government to implement policies that endanger the health and safety of its citizens, the issues surrounding obesity are no exception.

There is plenty of health information out there for anyone who cares to look, but when it comes to food, the mind is willing but the flesh is weak. Despite the advice of your doctor or the promise of the heartburn and constipation to come, too many of us (against our better judgment) are springing for fast food. But with a 30-minute lunch break and

Cheap, Crappy Food = A Fat Population
How Corporations and the US Government Create the Obesity Epidemic
Steven Greenstreet, Bryan Young, and Elias Pate

107

five bucks in your pocket; who can blame you? You're not a nutritionist or a culinary critic—you're a hunter searching for easy prey and enough fuel to get you through the day. With

turned into either feed for beef or processed into high-fructose corn syrup (HFCS), in short, solving the mystery of that unnaturally cheap burger and soda at the drive-thru.

In a bizarre world where one salad can cost as much as five burgers, and water costs more than soda, all biological and economic incentives seem to line up against the healthy options.

that in mind as you peruse the menu board at the drive-thru, the odds are already stacked in favor of the fatty, salty, calorie-loaded burger, not only because your body craves it, but your pocketbook demands bang for its buck. In a bizarre world where one salad can cost as much as five burgers, and water costs more than soda, all biological and economic incentives seem to line up against the healthy options.

Try as we might in this battle against junk food, we're hopelessly outgunned. But before lashing out at the purveyors of junk food, no matter how predatory their tactics, it would be far more productive to pull back the curtain and expose those who are supplying the ammo. Surely, all known laws of nature or economic theory would scoff at the idea that five hamburgers could be as cheap to produce as a pile of leaves and a handful of vegetables. Someone is clearly bending the rules, and though industry is the clear benefactor and the consumer the clear victim, the United States Department of Agriculture provides the impetus.

Since 1972, under Richard Nixon's Secretary of Agriculture Earl Butz, the USDA has poured billions of dollars into the pockets of corn and soy farmers across the country to produce as much as possible, no matter how egregious the surplus. As overproduction sends the cost of corn through the floor, the federal government picks up the slack, writing farmers a check ensuring them a small profit, ensuring continued overproduction, and ensuring that food processors pack in an endless source of calories.[5] As most of the corn produced in the US is not fit for human consumption, the vast majority of the grain is

Certainly there are other factors at play here, but with nearly 65-billion tax dollars from 1995 to 2005 paid directly to corn and soy farmers,[6] the United States Farm Bill has had the largest singular effect on transforming our food landscape, as well as the physical landscape of the farm belt. Where once upon a time, crop diversity was the key to insuring a healthy and sustainable food supply, the small family farm has all but been snuffed out, swallowed by an endless sea of corn. Why chance vegetable-crop failure when drought-resistant, genetically-modified corn—saturated in hydrogen fertilizer—will guarantee you a substantial government check at the end of the year? Where once upon a time, grocery stores were filled with simple (read: healthful) foods that required imagination and effort to prepare, everything from bread, soup, frozen dinners, and all points in between is ready-made and loaded with corn-derived preservatives and sweeteners. You've no doubt noticed that as of 1997 the average American consumed 60.4 pounds of HFCS per year.[7] That translates into 200 calories per person per day, which roughly translates into 20 extra pounds per year.

Aside from the beverage industry, the meat industry has benefited most from the endless supply of cheap corn, and with most USDA chiefs, employees, and committee members either coming from or ending up on the payroll of the meat industry, it should come as no surprise. For every pound of fattened beef, it takes six pounds of corn to produce it. It's not exactly the most efficient means of producing food unless the feed is cheaper than dirt, literally. Corn-fed American beef is not only fattier but many times cheaper and much more prevalent than its non-corn-fed counterparts, a fact punctuated by statistics showing that meat consumption in America has risen from 144 pounds per person per year in 1950 to 222 pounds per person per year in 2005.[8]

Unfortunately, the effects of these USDA subsidies don't end at

Since 1972, under Richard Nixon's Secretary of Agriculture Earl Butz, the USDA has poured billions of dollars into the pockets of corn and soy farmers across the country to produce as much as possible, no matter how egregious the surplus.

When nutritionists want to say, "Eat less meat and restrict sugar intake as much as possible," but industry wants to say, "Consume as much meat and sugar as you can, just exercise more," then the government has to get tricky with its language.

the drive-thru and your expanding waistline. Rather, they provide the spark in the seemingly endless cycle of industry profiting from our poor health with the government's blessing and funding.

As long as the USDA is subsidizing the burger instead of the salad, the cheapest meal is guaranteed to be the least healthful, even with the current rate of rising food prices.

Pyramid Scheme

Knowing that it's hard to pick the right thing to eat and keep you healthy, the government offers dietary recommendations like the food pyramid. Generally, it's as simple as how many servings of what you should have in a day for a healthy, balanced diet. One would think it's based on sound, current nutritional science, but it's actually the target of some of the fiercest lobby efforts in the government. Why? Because these companies will stop receiving all the farm subsidies the government gives them if people stop buying all of the over-processed, bad-for-you foods they produce.

The simple fact of the matter is that the best science dictates that our diet should consist of a wide variety of foods, not too much, mostly plants. Unfortunately, if you eat mostly plants, then you have to eat less meat, soda, candy, and processed foods, and the producers of meat, soda, candy, and processed foods don't want you to hear that. These "food" producers simply can't stand the idea of the government endorsing a reduction of consumption in their products, since they've done such a good job—and spent a lot of money—getting us to eat more of their products. (For example, as stated above, the average consumption of meat per person in the US has risen from 144 pounds a year in 1955 to 222 pounds a year today. Soda used to be an occasional treat in an 8-ounce serving, but is now a daily ritual in excess of 44 ounces for millions of Americans.[9])

In order to please industry and provide the illusion of clearing up the "what-to-eat" debate for us, the USDA compromises on all of the scientific recommendations it makes. When nutritionists want to say, "Eat less meat and restrict sugar intake as much as possible," but industry wants to say, "Consume as much meat and sugar as you can, just exercise more," then the government has to get tricky with its language. "Avoid sodium," has become, "Choose a diet moderate in salt and sodium." "Maintain your ideal weight," has become, "Balance the food you eat with physical activity—maintain or improve your weight."[10] "Decrease consumption of meat," and, "Restrict sugar to 15 percent of calories," were changed to, "Choose more lean meats," and, "Avoid too much sugar."[11] Even the dairy lobby has come into the debate: Regardless of race, age, sex, or level of lactose tolerance, the government recommends three glasses of milk a day.[12]

The problems, however, don't stop there. When the government comes out with a fairly helpful recommendation like, "Eat more whole grains," you get companies like General Mills putting one gram of dietary fiber into every serving of Trix and slapping a seven-inch "Made With Whole Grain" banner on the front of each box.

What's worse, our government allows the export of this corporate-profit-fueled lunacy to the rest of the world.

The sugar industry, which was suffering a 4.3 percent drop in sales at the time, launched an all-out war to bury the report.

Exporting American Obesity

In 2004, the World Health Organization (WHO) presented a study called "Global Strategy on Diet, Physical Activity and Health," in which 30 renowned scientists suggested that sugar should account for no more than 10 percent of a person's daily caloric intake. The study warned that poor diets and lack of exercise are the leading causes of cardiovascular disease,

Cheap, Crappy Food = A Fat Population
How Corporations and the US Government Create the Obesity Epidemic
Steven Greenstreet, Bryan Young, and Elias Pate

109

type 2 diabetes, and certain cancers. It went on to say that such illnesses account for nearly 60 percent of 56.5 million deaths each year, and that these deaths were deemed preventable.

The sugar industry, which was suffering a 4.3 percent drop in sales at the time, launched an all-out war to bury the report.

> "The job of the Surgeon General is to be the doctor of the nation not the doctor of a political party. The reality is that the nation's doctor has been marginalized and relegated to a position with no independent budget and with supervisors who are political appointees with partisan agendas." —former US Surgeon General Richard Carmona

The sugar industry first organized a coalition of other food-industry groups (which had given nearly $200,000 to George W. Bush's 2000 campaign) and had them write angry letters to then–Secretary of Health Tommy Thompson and then–Secretary of Agriculture Ann Veneman (former CEO of a food company herself), asking them to have the WHO report withdrawn. The industry went on to recruit US Senators Larry Craig and John Breaux to put further pressure on Secretary Thompson.[13]

When letter-writing seemed only to delay the publishing of the WHO report instead of quashing it completely, the sugar industry wrote to WHO Director General Gro Harlem Brundtland,[14] saying that it would "exercise every avenue available" to permanently kill the health study. Taking things a step further, the industry then hired top Washington lobbyists to pressure Congress into removing the US's $406 million funding to the WHO.

WHO insiders commented at the time that threats like this were "tantamount to blackmail." In *Killer at Large*, Marion Nestle, author of *Food Politics*, said that most "felt this move was extremely crass, especially since during that same time the World Health Organization was working miracles in dealing with the SARS virus."

It was obvious to everyone involved (with the exception of the Sugar Association) that a removal of WHO funding from the US would have been disastrous.

The Bush Administration caved to the sugar industry's demands and, in the end, all mention of sugar restrictions were removed from the final WHO health report. William Steiger, a special assistant to Secretary Thompson and godson to former President George H.W. Bush, called for far weaker, unspecified policy approaches, like "better data and surveillance, and the promotion of sustainable strategies that focus on energy balance, individual responsibility, and strong public health approaches." In effect, he shifted the onus of responsibility onto the people and away from governments and industry.[15]

"People need to be empowered to take responsibility for their health," he said. But many health groups responded to the Bush Administration by stating that people cannot be "empowered to take responsibility" when the facts and information that would influence their decisions are censored or removed.

Continued Censorship

Three years later, it was discovered that the Europe-based WHO wasn't the only entity being bullied and shut up by the US government. On July 10, 2007, Dr. Richard Carmona, who had recently resigned his position as the US Surgeon General, testified before the House Oversight Committee that during his 2002–2006 tenure, he had been censored, muzzled, and oft times prohibited by the Bush Administration from releasing his health and science reports to the American public.

"The job of the Surgeon General is to be the doctor of the nation not the doctor of a political party. The reality is that the nation's doctor has been marginalized and relegated to a position with no independent budget and with supervisors who are political appointees with partisan agendas," Carmona stated. "Anything that doesn't fit into the political appointee's ideological, theological, or political agenda, is often ignored, marginalized, or simply buried."[16]

Among the evidence presented to the Committee was a report called "The Surgeon General's Call to Action," which Carmona had drafted based on his research and scientific data. The report had been given to William Steiger (yes, the same guy) at Health and Human Services who then, in turn, edited, trimmed, and deleted portions of the report. In addition to changing scientific content about topics like sexual contraception and adding the words "Iraq" and "President Bush" over a dozen times (seriously), Steiger had completely removed Carmona's section on obesity and obesity-related illnesses.[17]

Carmona testified: "I was often instructed what to say or what not to say. I did the best I could to speak out on issues. But I was blocked at every turn; I was told the 'decision has already been made,' 'Stand down,' 'Don't talk about it.'"[18]

Frustrated, Carmona resigned his post as Surgeon General. In response to his testimony before the House Oversight Committee, the Bush White House issued this statement: "As Surgeon General, Dr. Carmona was given the authority and had the obligation to be the leading voice for the health of all Americans. It's disappointing to us if he failed to use his position to the fullest extent…"[19]

Obesity is proof that food marketers are doing their jobs properly.

Healthy Population vs. Healthy Economy

What it comes down to is simple: Obesity is good for the gross domestic product (GDP).

In a consumer culture, obesity is the physical representation of overconsumption. Obesity is proof that food marketers are doing their jobs properly.

After paying big agriculture to make you fat and depressed, you then pay big pharma to make you feel better so the cycle can continue. And, so long as success in this country is measured in dollars, the cycle will never end.

Endnotes

1. Wang, Dr. Youfa, and Dr. May A. Beydoun. (2007). The obesity epidemic in the United States—gender, age, socioeconomic, racial/ethnic and geographic characteristics: A systematic review and meta-regression analysis." *Epidemiologic reviews* 29(1): 6–28. 2. Flegal, Katherine, Ph.D. (2005). Excess deaths associated with underweight, overweight and obesity. *Journal of the American Medicine Association*, Apr 20. 3. Mokdad, Ali H., Ph.D. (2004). Actual causes of death in the United States, 2000. *Journal of the American Medicine Association* Mar 10. 4. Carmona quoted in *Killer at Large*. Dir. Steven Greenstreet, 2008. 5. Pollan, Michael. (2003). The way we live now: The (agri) cultural contradictions of obesity. *New York Times Magazine*, Oct 12. 6. Environmental Working Group. Farm subsidy direct payment database. <farm.ewg.org>. Accessed 1 Jun 2008. 7. Philpott, Tom. (2006). I'm hatin' it: How the feds make bad-for-you-food cheaper than healthful fare. *Grist*, Feb 22. 8. Economic Research Service, US Department of Agriculture. (2006). Farm animal statistics, 30 Nov. 9. *Op cit.*, *Killer at large*. 10. Davis, Carole, and Etta Saltos. (1999). Dietary recommendations and how they have changed over time. In *America's eating habits: Changes and consequences*. Elizabeth Frazao, editor. Washington, DC: United States Department of Agriculture. 11. Nestle, Marion. (2002). *Food politics*. University of California Press, pp 40–1. 12. Chef Ann Cooper, quoted in *Killer at Large*. 13. Documents obtained for *Killer at Large*. 14. *Ibid*. 15. Center for Science in the Public Interest. (2004). Bush Administration trying to bury WHO obesity report. Jan 16. 16. US House of Representatives, Committee on Oversight and Government Reform. (2007). The Surgeon General's vital mission: Challenges for the future. 110th Congress, 1st session, Jul 10. 17. *Ibid*. 18. *Ibid*. 19. Lee, Christopher. (2007). Ex-Surgeon General says White House hushed him. *Washington post*, Jul 11.

Cheap, Crappy Food = A Fat Population
How Corporations and the US Government Create the Obesity Epidemic
Steven Greenstreet, Bryan Young, and Elias Pate

111

Fields of Fuel
Change Your Fuel, Change The World
Josh Tickell

In my eco-documentary, *Fields of Fuel*, I shuttle audiences on a revelatory, fast-paced journey to unravel America's addiction to oil as I track the domination of the petrochemical industry, beginning with Rockefeller's strategy to halt ethanol use in Ford's first cars. I show how the oil industry's tactics have shaped US politics, energy use, and the environment. The following is excerpted from *Fields of Fuel*.

■ ■ ■ ■ ■ ■ ■ ■ ■

My journey began at a young age when I moved from Melbourne, Australia, to Baton Rouge, Louisiana. As a hub of oil processing, Louisiana has over 150 polluting oil refineries dotting its landscape. The contrast between the pristine environment of wildlife in Australia and the "Don't Swim Here" signs neighboring Louisiana waters was shocking to me. But this was not nearly as shocking as watching members of my family get sick and die from diseases caused by the toxic air and water pollution from the local oil refineries. That experience set me on a lifelong quest to find the truth about our energy and to find a new course for America—away from oil addiction.

Oil companies have a long history of misinformation campaigns, beginning with the Standard Oil Company. Founded in 1870 by John D. Rockefeller, Standard Oil actively discouraged the use of alternative energy. One notable case of Standard Oil Company propaganda is *The Louisiana Story*, a film all Louisiana students watch during history class. The film showcases the story of a young Cajun boy and his family. The plot starts when an oil derrick moves into his neighborhood. The oil people are friendly. They give the local residents money. The oil company hits a gusher, caps the well, and then leaves the place almost better than they found it.

One little detail that we were never told: The film was funded by Standard Oil. This film misinforms the public and misrepresents the oil industry's actions. Behind the happy scenes of the film, the oil companies were actually going into Louisiana and ripping the bayous open, creating a toxic cesspool.

Louisiana has the highest production rate of gasoline in the nation. As a result of the subsequent pollution, residents are suffering. The rate of birth defects has increased significantly amongst women raised in the midst of the refineries. This section of Louisiana, known as "Cancer Alley," has the highest incidence of the disease in the United States.

It is common knowledge that John D. Rockefeller used underhanded and unethical practices to secure Standard Oil's dominant position in the emerging US marketplace. One of Rockefeller's first targets was contemporary rival Henry Ford, the visionary father of the modern auto industry. Ford designed the Model-T to run on ethyl alcohol (ethanol), a fuel that can be created from biomass. Consequently, Ford accounted for 25 percent of the fuel market in the Midwest. An agriculturally produced fuel threatened Rockefeller's empire, prompting him to fund the drive for a new Constitutional Amendment, which would become known as Prohibition. The law shut down all alcohol production in the United States, including that of ethanol alcohol. For twelve of the thirteen years of Prohibition, Ford continued to produce ethanol-compatible cars. And then he gave up. One year later, Prohibition was lifted.

> This section of Louisiana, known as "Cancer Alley," has the highest incidence of the disease in the United States.

Rockefeller's practices were so criminal that President Teddy Roosevelt broke up Standard Oil in 1911. The two largest frac-

> According to the Center for Public Integrity, the oil industry spent more than $420 million between 1998 and 2004 funding politicians and political parties.

tions were called Exxon and Mobil. Eighty-eight years later Exxon and Mobil would reunite, forming the largest oil conglomerate in history.

With the precedent set by Rockefeller, the oil industry has continued to practice backdoor business policies. In 2001, executives of Exxon-Mobil, Conoco, Shell, and BP secretly met with Vice President Dick Cheney to help develop a national energy policy. To this day, what was discussed in those meetings remains a mystery. In fact, the oil companies' CEOs denied the meetings ever took place. When the oil executives were called to testify at a congressional hearing with the Commerce, Science, and Transportation Committee on the nature of the meetings, they were not sworn in. Consequentially, they couldn't be held accountable for anything they had said, and could lie at the hearing without any repercussions. Several Senators at the hearing, including Barbara Boxer (D-CA) and Maria Cantwell (D-WA), motioned to have the executives testify under oath, but Chairman Senator Ted Stevens (R-AL) overruled the motion because it was "out of order."

Actions like those of Senator Stevens are not surprising given Congress' heavy financial support from oil companies. According to the Center for Public Integrity, the oil industry spent more than $420 million between 1998 and 2004 funding politicians and political parties. The industry's subsequent influence on politics has undermined the democratic process. Democratic Senator Barbara Boxer of California believes that "what we are seeing is a government run for the oil companies." Michael Nobel is the executive director of Fresh Energy, a nonprofit organization leading the transition to clean, efficient, and fair energy systems. He makes the candid observation that "the oil companies, the coal companies, and the auto companies that run the energy policies in this country [have] gone from bad to worse."

Oil companies have failed to disclose the toxic nature of the chemicals they use. Some companies have sent memos to field workers addressing health and safety issues of Polyvinyl Chloride (PVC), a chemical that contains toxic compounds and is used in building materials. The memos claim that PVC is a non-hazardous material and that PVC dust is non-toxic. The memos were distributed even though it appears that the company was aware that these statements are false. The law offices of Baggett, McCall, Burgess, Watson & Gaughan in Lake Charles, Louisiana, possess internal documents from an oil company that states: "If we don't tell what we know, it could be construed as evidence of an illegal conspiracy on the part of industry to withhold vital information from the government." William Baggett, a partner at the firm, believes that the oil industry itself is aware of the actions taken to cover up toxic working and living conditions.

Despite the devastating impacts of fossil fuels on society and the environment, the petrochemical industry remains entrenched in Louisiana. With so many oil refineries in the state, Hurricane Katrina hit New Orleans with disastrous consequences. During Katrina, nine million gallons of toxic oil spread into the bayous, rivers, and swamps—all of it crude oil, all of it from the oil industry. This wasn't reported by the media. This spill is almost as big as the *Exxon Valdez* disaster. While American taxpayers paid for the restoration of coastal Louisiana, the wealthiest corporations in the world did not pay a dime.

Michael Nobel states, "All of these environmental problems are as serious as a heart attack. This is not a problem that's 200 years away. This is a problem that's now. The children that are

> During Katrina, nine million gallons of toxic oil spread into the bayous, rivers, and swamps—all of it crude oil, all of it from the oil industry.

coming into the world now are going to face a radically different climate. In the next President's administration, they must limit CO_2 emissions that systematically leads to carbon neutrality. That's what the American people want. That's what the economy requires. That's what the climate requires. And that's what our national security requires."

The petrochemical industry has conspired with the government to perpetuate environmentally destructive energy policies for over a century. They have persuaded the public to pur-

Fields of Fuel Change Your Fuel, Change The World
Josh Tickell

chase fossil fuel for their main mode of transportation—to the detriment of the environment, national security, and the overall health of the nation. But this is not a permanent way of life. We have the power to change this situation with the choices we make as conscious consumers and knowing citizens.

While average citizens have exercised their power by using biodiesel, corporate media outlets have confused the issue by

Unlike ethanol produced from corn, biodiesel production uses little water and *increases* food supplies (because it is made only from oil, leaving the rest of the plant).

changing the dialogue, switching from alternative fuels to the hot-button issue known as the "food versus fuel" debate. Opponents of biodiesel argue that because it can be derived from soybeans and other edible, oil-producing crops, using biodiesel decreases the availabilty of food and increases the cost of food, thus depriving impoverished people of necessary staples. However, this idea is woefully generalized and only includes carefully extrapolated information.

The word *biofuel* has become falsely synonymous with *biodiesel*. Understanding the distinction between the two is crucial. Biofuel refers to any fuel derived from organic matter; whereas biodiesel is a specific type of biofuel made from the oils of crops or other sources. The most hotly discussed biofuel, ethanol, is not biodiesel—it's derived from corn. Ethanol has aroused debate largely because of the increase in corn prices in 2008. Unlike ethanol produced from corn, biodiesel production uses little water and *increases* food supplies (because it is made only from oil, leaving the rest of the plant).

Biodiesel is composed of 80 percent organic oil and 20 percent alcohol, usually methanol. It can be locally produced from a variety of sources, ranging from soy beans to algae to beef tallow. It has a closed carbon cycle, meaning that the amount of carbon dioxide released to the atmosphere when biodiesel is burned is almost as much as the original crop absorbed when grown (70–80 percent). Biodiesel also significantly reduces emissions of sulfur dioxide and other greenhouse gasses that contribute to global warming. By switching to biodiesel, you can support a different type of oil company and become familiar with the source of your fuel.

Former head of Sun Microsystems, Vinod Khosla, articulates the vastly generalized criticisms of biodiesel use: "Calling all these fuels biofuels, independent of their source, is a little bit like saying aspirin and cocaine are both drugs. Now, are drugs good or bad? You can't tell me until I tell you which drug."

Don't let corporate media misinformation fool you. It is possible to reduce our dependence on big oil and maintain a clean and self-sufficient environment. I believe the answer depends less on technology and more on how we educate ourselves. Multiple options for sustainable energy use exist today, be it wind, solar, or biodiesel. Thus, both the challenge and the tools for change are in our hands. America was not built by people afraid to change; neither is this revolution.

Here are the top ten things you can do *right now*:

- **Buy a wind turbine or invest in wind energy.**

- **Buy solar panels or invest in solar energy.**

- **Grow trees.**

- **Invest in algae biodiesel companies.**

- **Buy an electric car.**

- **Buy a diesel car and use biodiesel.**

- **Conserve your energy usage <www.currentenergy.com>.**

- **Vote for leaders who support green energy.**

- **Go carbon neutral <www.nativeenergy.com>.**

- **Learn more: read *Biodiesel America* and visit <www.FieldsofFuel.com>.**

Why Did the Iraqi Government Want Blackwater Banned?

Jim Marrs

According to a 2007 report by the US House Committee on Oversight and Government Reform, since 2005, employees of Blackwater USA, a security company that many call a private army, were engaged in about 200 incidents in Iraq, the majority of cases involving drive-by shootings.

In late September 2007, the Iraqi Government announced that it would ban Blackwater from working in the country. A spokesman for Iraq's Ministry of Interior, Brig. Gen. Abdul Karim Khalaf, said the government had canceled the company's license to operate and might seek to prosecute some employees.

This break with Blackwater, which held contracts to protect top US officials in war-torn Iraq, came after an incident that September 16 in which gunfire from an American convoy left about seventeen Iraqis dead and more than two dozen wounded.

Later in the week, US Secretary of State Condoleezza Rice called Iraq's Prime Minister Nuri Kamal al-Maliki to express her regret "over the death of innocent civilians that occurred during the attack on an embassy convoy." Her use of the term "attack" buttressed claims from Blackwater that the "civilians" killed were actually enemy combatants and that "Blackwater professionals heroically defended American lives in a war zone."

She also reported that she and the Prime Minister had agreed that a "fair and transparent investigation" would be conducted. The more cynical observers noted that a call from Rice was not necessary to assure a fair investigation and that the call more likely was to rein in the Iraqi attempts to oust Blackwater. Apparently it worked.

Apparently, a law issued by the American authorities before sovereignty was returned to the Iraqis, Order No. 17, gives Blackwater immunity from Iraqi law.

With great irony, officials of the United States, reportedly in Iraq to bring "freedom and democracy," said that no official ban had been received by the State Department and they did not foresee the private force leaving the country. Apparently, a law issued by the American authorities before sovereignty was returned to the Iraqis, Order No. 17, gives Blackwater immunity from Iraqi law. Maliki agreed to suspend the Blackwater ban pending further investigation.

Details of the September 16th incident were confusing. Initial reports from the American Embassy said a convoy of US State Department officials had come under fire in Nisour Square, a commercial area in west Baghdad. It was an area clogged with traffic as well as construction and concrete blocks. The Embassy said that one of the convoy's vehicles was "disabled" in the incident but did not report if the attendant security guards fired their weapons.

Iraqi sources said that a car bomb had exploded about the time of the convoy's passage but denied that any gunfire was directed at the convoy. They claimed that the convoy apparently became stuck in traffic and that Blackwater security men began firing into the crowded square. The account of a car bomb was confirmed by US Embassy spokesperson Mirenbe Nantongo, who said, "Our people [Blackwater] were responding to a car bombing."

But the bombing was not in the square but about a mile northeast, near a meeting of officials from the US Agency for International Development.

The US convoy was carrying officials away from the meeting but apparently four sport utility vehicles running ahead of the convoy became caught in a traffic snarl. Guards exited the vehicles and took up defensive positions. Shortly after noon, one guard shot and killed Ahmed Haithem Ahmed, who was driving his mother to a nearby hospital where his father worked as a pathologist. More shots were fired, killing Ahmed's mother. A grenade or flare then set the car on fire.

A traffic officer at the scene, Ali Khalaf, told Agence France-Presse that the shooting continued;

> The Americans fired at everything that moved, with a machinegun and even with a grenade launcher. There was panic. Everyone tried to flee. Vehicles tried to make U-turns to escape. There were dead bodies and wounded people everywhere. The road was full of blood. A bus was also hit and several of its occupants were wounded.

Khalaf added that two small, black helicopters hovering overhead dropped and sprayed the square with machinegun fire. This account was supported by nearby grocery owner Abu Muhammad.

Afrah Sattar was seated next to her mother on the bus when a bullet struck her mother in the head, killing her instantly. "They are killers," Sattar said of the Blackwater force. "I swear to God, not one bullet was shot at them. Why did they shoot us? My mother didn't carry a weapon."

A 50-year-old Iraqi attorney, Hassan Jaber Salma, who suffered eight gunshot wounds in the incident, said he and others were trying to clear a path for the American convoy when the Blackwater guards "strafed the line of traffic with gunfire."

Iraqi Prime Minister Maliki stated, "This is a big crime that we can't stay silent in front of." One American official in Baghdad said the Blackwater shooting incident "will be the true test of diplomacy between the State Department and the government of Iraq."

But it appears that a cover-up began to take shape. A joint American-Iraqi board of inquiry was created between the State Department and the Iraqi Ministry of Defense. Maliki dropped his demands that Blackwater be banished from the country, saying he would await the outcome of the inquiry. However, by September 29, this inquiry board still had not

met and had not responded to Iraqi government requests for information.

The Nisour Square incident was only the latest questionable Blackwater activity.

On September 9, 2007, just more than a week before the Nisour shooting, a clerk in the Iraqi customs office, Batoul Mohammed Ali Hussein, walked out of the customs building as a Blackwater-protected convoy passed. According to the *Seattle Times*, rocks were thrown when Blackwater guards ordered some construction workers to move back. The guards then sprayed the intersection with gunfire, one round striking Hussein in the leg. When she tried to struggle to her feet, a Blackwater guard shot her several times, killing her.

On Christmas Eve, 2006, a drunken Blackwater employee shot and killed an Iraqi guarding the country's Vice President. The man was fired but quickly hustled out of the country and nothing to date has been done, as there is confusion over what laws might be applied. According to the 2007 House report, US State Department officials initially were prepared to pay the dead man's family $250,000 in restitution, but another official argued that such a high figure might "cause incidents with people trying to get killed by our guys to financially guarantee their family's future." Blackwater ended up paying $15,000.

"It's hard to read these emails [concerning restitution] and not come to the conclusion that the State Department is acting as Blackwater's enabler," declared California Democrat Henry Waxman, Chairman of the House Oversight and Government Reform Committee.

Most Americans recall the horrid images of four American contractors who were killed in Falluja and their dismembered bod-

"The Americans fired at everything that moved, with a machinegun and even with a grenade launcher."

ies hung from a bridge. What was not reported was that the four were Blackwater employees and, again, accounts of the incident varied greatly depending on whose version was offered.

According to Blackwater vice president Patrick Toohey, the men were "lured into a carefully planned ambush by men they believed to be friendly members of the Iraqi Civil Defense Corps…"

Toohey's statements were soon countered by Jim Steele, a deputy to Paul Bremer, the head of the Coalition Provisional Authority, i.e. occupation forces. Steele, who was sent to Falluja to recover the bodies, told the *New Yorker* magazine that "there was no evidence that the Iraqi police had betrayed the contractors." A video reportedly made by Iraqi insurgents stated that an informant had reported "a group of CIA will pass through Falluja…They will have no bodyguards with them and they will wear civilian clothes—thus to avoid being captured by the mujahideen [who had pledged that] every American that passes through Falluja will be killed."

The four Blackwater contractors were escorting empty trucks. They were to pick up kitchen equipment on the other side of the city, the focal point of recent harsh fighting. Despite the warnings, they were sent into a hotbed of anti-American sentiment and armed insurgents.

Firms other than Blackwater supplying private contractors to Iraq include DynCorp, Triple Canopy, and the British firms Aegis Security and Erinys International.

Although hard numbers are hard to come by, the estimated 186,000 private contractors operating in Iraq by mid-2007 still outnumbered the 160,000 American soldiers, even after being reinforced by the 30,000-troop "surge" earlier that year.

On Christmas Eve, 2006, a drunken Blackwater employee shot and killed an Iraqi guarding the country's Vice President.

Since the *New Webster Encyclopedic Dictionary of the English Language* (1971 edition) defines as a mercenary anyone who provides troops or services for hire, many people feel that Blackwater's armed hirelings should rightly be seen as mercenaries, and well-paid ones at that.

Blackwater employees, who provide services to the US military as well as private security for American officials, are reportedly paid as much as $1,000 a day, more income than a four-star general in the Army.

This pay disparity coupled with the trigger-happy antics of Blackwater mercenaries, who sometimes accompany US combat troops, has caused friction even with American soldiers.

In 2005, Marine Col. Thomas X. Hammes reported that Blackwater activities tended to counteract efforts to win the support of the Iraqi population. "The problem is in protecting the principal they had to be very aggressive, and each time they went out they had to offend locals, forcing them to the side of the road, being overpowering and intimidating, at times running vehicles off the road, making enemies each time they went out," Hammes told PBS.

Besides the obvious cozy relationship between Blackwater and the State Department, concern has been voiced over the connection between Blackwater founder and chairman Erik Prince and President George W. Bush.

Prince, a former Navy SEAL and major contributor to Bush's campaigns, has repeatedly denied any wrongdoing on the part of Blackwater. "I believe we acted appropriately at all times," Prince told the House committee in 2007.

Prince, who founded Blackwater in 1997, refused to discuss his company's finances at the House hearing, claiming it would give his competitors an unfair advantage. He did reveal that his salary in 2006 was more than $1 million.

Committee Chairman Waxman admonished David Satterfield, the Iraq coordinator for the State Department, stating, "We've had a better response from Blackwater than we've had from the State Department in getting information. Doesn't that bother you as much as it bothers me?"

The rise of private armies of mercenaries began in earnest after former Secretary of Defense Donald Rumsfeld in 2002 published an article in *Foreign Affairs*, an organ of the Council on Foreign Relations, entitled "Transforming the Military." Rumsfeld called for the widespread use of mercenaries in all aspects of war, including combat.

Overnight, Blackwater evolved from a small private security firm to one of the largest private armed forces in the world. "[I]t represents the realization of the life's work of the officials who formed the core of the Bush administration's war team," noted Jeremy

> "We've had a better response from Blackwater than we've had from the State Department in getting information."
> —Congressman Henry Waxman

Scahill, *New York Times*–bestselling author of *Blackwater: The Rise of the World's Most Powerful Mercenary Army*.

According to Scahill, by 2007 Blackwater employed more than 2,300 troops deployed in nine countries including the United States, and could draw upon 21,000 former Special Forces troops, soldiers, and law enforcement personnel, plus 20 aircraft, including helicopter gunships and a surveillance blimp division.

As pointed out by Scahill, "Blackwater is a private army, and it is controlled by one person: Erik Prince, a radical right-wing Christian mega-millionaire who has served as a major bankroller not only of President Bush's campaigns but of the broader Christian-right agenda."

Prince's father Edgar, a self-made millionaire in auto parts, supported the Family Research Council (FRC), a right-wing fundamentalist Christian group close to the Bush administration. Edgar's widow served on the boards of FRC and another heavyweight Christian right organization, James Dobson's Focus on the Family. She runs the Edgar and Elsa Prince Foundation, of which Erik is a vice president. The foundation gave more than $1 million to the Christian right from July 2003 to 2006.

Incredibly, Congressman Dennis Kucinich, a self-styled "Wellstone Democrat" and presidential candidate who voted against the US invasion of Iraq, found that while American soldiers are subject to prosecution under the military's rules of engagement, Blackwater mercenaries are not. "Think about what that means," Kucinich told Pentagon procurement chief Shay Assad. "These private contractors can get away with murder."

Operating out of a 7,000-acre compound in Moyock, North Carolina, Prince's private army, which has been compared to Hitler's "Brownshirts," includes scores of Chilean mercenaries who operated under the brutal dictator Augusto Pinochet. Blackwater President Gary Jackson praised these men as "very, very professional and they fit within the Blackwater system."

Michael Ratner, president of the Center for Constitutional Rights, pointed out the basic problem with private armies like Blackwater by telling author Scahill:

The increasing use of contractors, private forces or as some would say "mercenaries" makes wars easier to begin and to fight—it just takes money and not the citizenry.

To the extent a population is called upon to go to war, there is resistance, a necessary resistance to prevent wars of self-aggrandizement, foolish wars and, in the case of the United States, hegemonic imperialist wars. Private forces are almost a necessity for a United States bent on retaining its declining empire. Think about Rome and its increasing need for mercenaries [the Praetorian Guard]. Likewise, here at home in the United States. Controlling an angry, abused population with a police force bound to obey the Constitution can be difficult—private forces can solve this problem.

Many question whether a large, well-equipped mercenary force could be restrained from operating against American citizens should they be so ordered by political or corporate leaders. As one online writer fears, "These fascistic mercenary elements are being groomed to be thrown against workers and youth in the US who resist the escalating attacks on their living standards and democratic rights."

In the wake of the 2007 congressional report on Blackwater and other firms, the Senate approved a defense policy bill that included the establishment of an independent commission to investigate private contractors in both Iraq and Afghanistan.

However, considering the vast amounts of money involved and the closeness of Blackwater to the Bush administration, many observers have little confidence in impartial investigations or true justice.

You Are Still Being Lied To

The War on Bugs: Pesticide Spray Devices, Household Poisons, and Dr. Seuss

Will Allen

The following article is chapter fourteen of Will Allen's huge, profusely illustrated book The War on Bugs *(Chelsea Green Publishing, 2008). In its introduction, he writes: "The War on Bugs outlines how the industrialists changed US agriculture, first with imported guano fertilizer, then with arsenic, lead, synthetic fertilizer, cyanide, DDT, methyl bromide, nerve poisons, antibiotics, growth hormones, and, currently, genetically manipulated products. The facts presented here serve to indict corporate chemical advertisers, farm magazines, university scientists, and the government as enablers of the poisonous changeover in agriculture and the destruction of rural communities in the United States. This book also tracks the parallel development of organic agriculture and farmer resistance to chemical farming."*

Immediately after chemical firms began to promote pesticides to American families for house and farm use, equipment manufacturers began to produce and advertise pesticide applicators. Unbelievable contraptions appeared by the mid-1870s, invented or adapted to spread pesticide dusts and sprays. The marketing of chemicals became inextricably linked with the development of effective spray devices to apply the poison on the plant, on the pest, or under the sink.

Pump applicators supplemented this primitive arsenal in the 1880s, facilitating the spread of poisons at home and in the fields. Only slightly different from a bicycle pump, they increased efficiency and range significantly. Pumps came with a variety of attachments that could accommodate numerous poisons and different applicator needs. For the next 40 years, manufacturers endlessly modified these canister pumps, especially for household use.

The earliest pesticide applicator was a folded piece of paper or cardboard from which a person literally blew the poison onto the plants.

The earliest pesticide applicator was a folded piece of paper or cardboard from which a person literally blew the poison onto the plants. This, however, was not a sufficient or efficient system, since an accidental cough or an inhalation could prove deadly.

The need to spread dust over a wider area led to the use of simple flour sifters, or, as we saw with arsenic, makeshift box dusters with milk screens nailed on the bottom. The lovable fireplace bellows was the next household item to be jerry-rigged as a pesticide duster. Modified and enlarged, the bellows could be ordered with attachments for fumigation and animal-pest control. This enabled farmers and gardeners to blow poison dust wherever and on whatever needed it.

Fabricators and farmers developed crank and lever pumps sometime before the turn of the twentieth century. The ad-makers advertised a safe and civilized lever pump, with graphics implying that one could wear a hat and tie while dusting one's crops or garden with arsenic.

Preparations for spraying were elaborate by this time, as can be seen in the photo below.

Here the horses pull the spray rigs through the orchard, and interestingly, some of the horses wear more protection than the poison applicators. Similar two-man pumps supplied gangs of workers in the late 1800s. Workers climbed ladders or sprayed poisons from long hoses on the backs of wagons.

In addition to the stationary spray devices, there was an enormous array of sprayers—some motorized, some with hand pumps—that were pulled by horses through vegetable rows, melon patches, cotton fields, vineyards, and orchards.

Most types of pumps that we have today were available to American farmers, nurserymen, and gardeners by the early 1900s. By the 1910s compressed-air and gas sprayers became more widely used. But pesticide sprayers were not used only by farmers; householders also used spray rigs and chemical poisons. As the US population urbanized, domestic households became an increasingly important market for the chemical merchants.

Frank Presbrey in *The History and Development of Advertising* and Roland Marchand in *Advertising the American Dream*, along with several other authors, point out how advertisers linked chemical cleanliness with being American in the 1920s.[1] American interest in technology was stimulated by the press, and by advertisers who applauded, defended, and marketed each new "scientific" breakthrough in pest control. Each concoction was heralded as the product that could eradicate all household pests.

Many American cities, however, continued to have only patchwork programs of sanitation and unclean water-supply systems. Without well-designed systems to deliver freshwater and carry away wastes, disease continued to be a constant reality of American cities. Filth, rats, and fear of the plague still drove buyers to get rat poisons or call the exterminator, since most people felt that rats carried almost any disease that would come along for the ride.

Preying on these real but often media-exaggerated fears, pest-control and chemical-advertising agencies turned out creative and dramatic campaigns that really stimulated the market. Of course, such campaigns were successful because there were always too many rats, flies, mosquitoes, and roaches. For the pest exterminators at the turn of the century, there was a greatly expanding market!

No. 8 Pint Sprayer

Made in Tin only.
Pump Chamber: 10 in. by 1½ in.
Tank: 4 in. by 3 in.
Capacity: One pint.

Double seamed tank, strong and durable. Provided with drip cup, preventing liquid soiling floor or carpet. For disinfecting purposes, for killing flies, lice, cockroaches, water bugs, etc.
Packed 1 dozen in case. Shipping weight 11 lbs.

No. 10 Half-Pint Sprayer

Made in Tin only.
Pump Chamber: 10 in. by 1¼ in.
Tank: 3 in. by 3 in.
Capacity: One-half pint.

Air chamber is set into reservoir and thoroughly soldered there, making the sprayer compact and exceptionally strong throughout. Throws fine mist spray. Used extensively for spraying disinfectants, for killing flies, cockroaches, lice, water bugs, etc.
Packed 1 dozen in case. Shipping weight 10 lbs.

Eleven

Savage Dry Powder Duster
(Continued)

The nozzle tube may be raised up or down for spraying short or tall plants or trees. Does not discharge poison in "chunks" or "gobs" but thoroughly breaks it up and dusts evenly. Feed lever adjusted from 1 to 20 pounds per acre, which is a wonderful improvement over any duster made.

Construction: Heavy sheet metal; brass; aluminum fan and housing; rubber nozzle; ball bearings throughout; nicely finished.

Weight: When empty 9½ pounds. Packed one in case. Shipping weight 14 pounds.

Hopper: Capacity 7 to 10 pounds of poison, depending on density.

Full directions for operating each Duster.

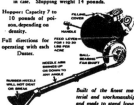

Built of the finest material and workmanship and made to stand long, hard service.

No. 19 Quart Glass Sprayer

Pump Chamber: 18 in. by 1½ in.
Reservoir: Quart Mason fruit jar.

Has two spray tubes. The reservoir is a quart Mason fruit jar, and may be easily replaced if broken. Easily filled. Body of sprayer is heavy tin nicely painted. Very substantial, neat and attractive.
Packed 1 dozen in case. Shipping weight 26 lbs.

No. 12 Dry Powder Duster

Made of heavy Tin, enameled red.
Pump Chamber: 14 in. by 2 in.
Tank: 6½ in. by 4 in.
Capacity: 1½ quarts.

The reservoir is filled with dry powder, such as Paris Green, Arsenate of Lead, Savol, etc. Size of spray depends upon operation of plunger. Funnel and elbow are reversible, to spray up or down.
Packed 1 dozen in case. Shipping weight 14 lbs.

Twelve

No. 36 Lightning
COMPRESSED AIR SPRAYER

Pump inside of tank is always out of way

For spraying all garden vegetables, potatoes, plants, cotton, shrubbery, vines, tobacco plants, carbola, disinfectants, etc. The brass nozzle provided with brass elbow so that nozzle will not clog. It is fitted with brass elbow so that nozzle may be turned in any direction desired. By detaching elbow, nozzle may be screwed directly to shutoff, which throws spray straight ahead. A slight pressure of the fingers on the lever automatically throws a broad, fine mist, or coarse spray; by releasing the fingers the nozzle shuts off instantly, thereby no liquids are wasted. The carrying handle is enameled black and sprayer is attractively finished.

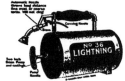

Tank: 11 in. by 7½ in. galvanized steel, double seamed; strong.
Capacity: Two gallons.
Pump: 2-in. seamless brass, screws in tank head.
Pump Castings: Heavy brass.
Nozzle: Brass, automatic, for three different sprays. Will not clog.
Elbow: Brass with union end. For spraying up or down.
Packed 1 case, Shipping weight 7 lbs.

No. 20 Quart Glass Sprayer

Pump Chamber: 16 in. by 1½ in.
Reservoir: Quart Mason fruit jar.

No. 20 is well made, and has an exceptionally large pump chamber, insuring plenty of air with each stroke of the handle, to produce a large, broad mist spray. Has two spray tubes. The screw cap for filling is brass. This will not corrode or rust. The reservoir is a Mason quart glass fruit jar, quickly detached if necessary and may be easily replaced if broken. Sprayer is nicely finished in red enamel as shown by illustration.

For spraying garden vegetables, house plants, shrubbery, disinfectants, etc.
Packed 1 dozen in case. Shipping weight 30 lbs.

SMITH BANNER COMPRESSED AIR SPRAYER
No. 22

This handle easily locks into pump-head for quickly loosening or tightening pump, also for carrying sprayer in hand. With this same handle, a few strokes of the pump charges the tank with compressed air.

Fill tank here through large opening by easily detaching pump. Pump is brass 2 in. diameter, provided with brass casting with machine cut threads for screwing into tank. Nothing to corrode, rust or wear out.

Adjustable strap with snap ends. For carrying sprayer over the shoulder.

2 feet heavy hose, detachable for cleaning. Spring wire to prevent breaking.

Golden Automatic brass spray nozzle. Long distance fine mist or coarse spray. No liquids. Wasted.

Heavy 4-gallon galvanized steel tank, well riveted, to stand heavy pressure. Also made entirely of brass.

As cities grew and the problems worsened, customers began to complain about the ineffectiveness

As the US population urbanized, domestic households became an increasingly important market for the chemical merchants.

WHAT TO DO WHEN FLIES WON'T STAY DEAD?

SPRAY WITH BIF— IT'S MADE FROM A POWERFUL FORMULA DEVELOPED BY SCIENTISTS

Bif not only stuns flies—it kills them. Developed by research chemists after countless tests with actual flies.

The research men of the Unacal Company made literally hundreds of tests at the "fly farm" in their Wilmington laboratories before Bif's formula satisfied them. When you try Bif, you'll be surprised to find how really *effective* a scientific fly spray can be. Bif is no half-remedy. It's quick, positive, dependable —and economical. It's safe. Stainless to walls, furnishings and clothing. Pleasantly scented. For results—with flies, mosquitoes, ants or moths—get *Bif.*

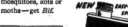

COMPLETE FLY FARM was established at Unacal laboratories for scientific tests which produced Bif's powerful *High-Kill* Formula.

KILLS ALL FOUR. Being effective against flies, Bif makes short work of lesser insects, including clothes moths. Mosquitoes hate it! To halt or prevent ant "raids" *safely*, spray baseboards and doorways with Bif.

NEW EASY-POURING SPOUT

bif INSECT SPRAY *kills* FLIES·ANTS·MOTHS AND MOSQUITOES

AT NEIGHBORHOOD STORES

GUARANTEED BY UNACAL PRODUCTS INC.

---

sprayer had a half-pint, pint, or quart reservoir with a bicycle-like pump attached to spray the poison. By the early 1930s, this pump became popularly known as the "Flit gun." Although Flit was the name of Standard Oil's bug spray, it also became the generic name for this type of pump, due to the popularity of the bug spray. The Flit campaign was so successful that by the mid-1930s airplane crop dusters were called "flying Flit guns."

Standard Oil, which John D. Rockefeller started as a commodities brokerage house in the 1830s, had grown to dominate the world's petroleum industry. In the late 1920s, the company needed a distinctive advertising campaign to make Flit rise above the sea of advertisements for other bug killers. Standard Oil was used to being number one in sales with its pesticide spray, and the company wanted to remain on top. After seeing two 1927 cartoons that featured Flit guns as props, Standard Oil hired the cartoonist, Theodore Seuss Geisel, to create Flit advertisements. Geisel subsequently came to be known as Dr. Seuss. For the next fifteen years, Seuss' humorous ads, which were really commercials in the

and danger of the products. To deal with this consumer skepticism, advertisers increased their propaganda to convince families that they needed chemicals and spray devices that they could use at home.

Pesticide advertising flared out of control after World War I. The United States was awash in ads, with practically every rock, barn, and flat space covered with promotions and propaganda. Amidst this visual assault, corporate advertisers desperately sought gimmicks to make their products leap out at the consumer and rise above the crowd.

As cities grew, advertisers hit on a few pivotal strategies that dramatically and permanently expanded the market demand of both city and country residents.[2] One of the most successful and innovative pesticide sales campaigns was for Flit, a fly and mosquito killer.

In the 1920s, America's most common household spray device was a hand-pump sprayer with a pressurized canister. Each

Danger!

"The fly is a little insect but a great spreader of disease," says the U. S. Public Health Service. "Thousands of people die every year from diseases transmitted by them. Remember! No filth, no flies, *less disease.*"

Kill flies! Buy Flit at once and get rid of all flies and other disease-carrying pests—roaches, mosquitoes, bed bugs, fleas.

Flit will kill every insect in the house. It has greater killing power. Guaranteed to kill all household insects or money back.

Flit is deadly to insects, but harmless to people and Flit vapor will not stain. Spray Flit on clothing to repel insects outdoors, while hunting, fishing, camping! Follow directions on the Flit can and use the improved Flit sprayer.

Most People Prefer FLIT *because*

1 It kills quicker.
2 It is guaranteed to kill all insects indoors, or money back.
3 It repels insects outdoors.
4 It can't stain fabrics.
5 It has a pleasant, clean smell.
6 It is the largest selling insecticide in the world.
7 It is easy to use, especially with the inexpensive Flit sprayer.
8 It is absolutely harmless to people — perfectly safe to use where there are children.

FLIT Kills Flies Mosquitoes Moths Bed Bugs Roaches Ants

"The yellow can with the black band" will not stain

The War on Bugs: Pesticide Spray Devices, Household Poisons, and Dr. Seuss
Will Allen

form of cartoons, appeared in thousands of weekly and hundreds of daily newspapers and magazines.

At the time of his hiring, Seuss was a well-known but underpaid "screwball" cartoonist writing humorous copy and drawing cartoons for the *Judge*, a national humor magazine. With his cartoons for Standard's bug killer, Dr. Seuss turned Flit and the Flit gun into household necessities. His success, which kept Flit in the leadership position in the marketplace, also made the incredibly prolific Geisel economically comfortable and afforded him enough freedom to gestate his later cartoon masterpieces.

Adelynne Whitaker, the author of *A History of Pesticide Regulation in the US*, contends that the Dr. Seuss cartoon campaign had the effect of increasing pesticide use tenfold for the nation's families.

ourselves while we went about poisoning things. In the process, the public grew comfortable with the myth that pesticides were absolutely necessary.

The Flit campaign was an advertising stroke of genius, and luck. Why luck? Because Seuss had actually considered using FlyTox or Bif for the name of the bug spray in his 1928 cartoons. The Rockefellers were twice lucky: Dr. Seuss chose to help sell Flit and several other Standard Oil products. And the public loved it!

Gradually, American householders came to depend on their Flit guns. Whether filled with Flit, Bif, Black Leaf 40, or arsenic, the home-spray device had become an essential tool in the public's mind. The petroleum solvent that Seuss was selling as Flit, however, was very dangerous and probably carcinogenic in large doses, though mild when compared to the World War II chemicals that would be sprayed from Flit guns on everything from bedbugs to flies, mosquitos, and humans after the end of the war.

"Don't worry, Papa. Willie just swallowed a bug, and I'm having him gargle with Flit!"

The Seuss taglines—"Quick Henry, the Flit!," "Swat the Fly!," "Kill the Tick!"—became nationally known slogans. Seuss helped America become friendly with poisons; we could laugh at

Considering the reverence with which Dr. Seuss is held today, it is difficult to envision him as a pivotal figure in the public acceptance of poisonous pesticides. Nevertheless, some historians feel that his campaign was largely responsible for popularizing dangerous pesticides to the American public.

Standard Oil was used to being number one in sales with its pesticide spray, and the company wanted to remain on top.

Adelynne Whitaker, the author of *A History of Pesticide Regulation in the US*, contends that the Dr. Seuss cartoon campaign had the effect of increasing pesticide use tenfold for the nation's families.[4]

One of Seuss' later books, *The Lorax*, with its save-the-environment theme, is ironic when compared to impact of the Flit cartoons. Perhaps Dr. Seuss realized his earlier mistakes and indiscretions with Standard Oil's Flit and tried to make amends with *The Lorax*.

Geisel must have known that Flit's cartoons and his World War II cartoons for DDT had an enormous impact on the public's use of pesticides and acceptance of DDT. Seuss was proud of his success as a pesticide salesman. For most of his life, however, Seuss was a reformer, a progressive, and a patriot—as his World War II cartoons for the government attacking Nazi Germany and the American right wing illustrate.

Endnotes

1. Marchand, Roland. (1985). *Advertising the American dream: Making way for modernity, 1920–1940*. University of California Press, pp 162, 210; Presbrey, Frank. (1929). *The history and development of advertising*. Doubleday & Co, p 616. **2.** The rural population remained large until well after World War II, still accounting for more than 40 percent of the citizenry at the start of World War II. **3.** Chemically, Flit was a petroleum fraction—a dimethyl phthalate. **4.** Whitaker, Adelynne Hiller. (1974). *A history of federal pesticide regulation in the US to 1947*. Ph.D. dissertation, Emory University.

In the spring of 1933 a fifteen year old girl from Billings, Montana died from eating fruit with high residues of arsenic.

This was followed in the summer of 1933 in Los Angeles, California by one of the worst episodes of arsenic poisoning in the U.S.

Dozens of people suffered from stomach poisoning.

Cramps, vomiting, diarrhea, high fever, bloody urine, bloody stool, bloody vomit, cold sweats, irregular pulse and exhaustion were common symptoms.
Tests revealed that the cabbage eaten by the poison victims had thirty five times the level of arsenic allowed by the government.

Pears eaten by some of the victims had fifty-four times the limit of safety.

These examples were quoted by James Whorton in *Before Silent Spring* (Princeton: Princeton University Press, 1974). By the early 1930s almost everyone in the United States was suffering from arsenic and lead poisoning.

The Ambush

The War on Bugs: Pesticide Spray Devices, Household Poisons, and Dr. Seuss

Will Allen

Pharmaceutical Crimes and Misdemeanors

Peter Rost, M.D.

Formerly a vice president at Pfizer, Peter Rost, M.D., is the first executive to publicly reveal the inner workings of the pharmaceutical industry via 60 Minutes, *opinion pieces for leading newspapers, new conferences with members of Congress, and an exposé,* The Whistleblower: Confessions of a Healthcare Hitman *(Soft Skull, 2006).*

In chapter four of The Whistleblower, *below, he discusses his tenure as a vice president at another drug company, Pharmacia, at the time it was purchased by Pfizer.*

From the beginning of my time at Pharmacia, the flagship drug of my endocrinology franchise had been Genotropin, a human growth hormone. Though we sold it for use in both short children and adults with growth hormone deficiency, the big market was children—they had to inject the drug daily for many years until they reached their adult height. A patient base like that made for stable sales that didn't fluctuate a lot. Our only worries were our three major competitors, each with their own genetically engineered growth hormone, virtually identical to ours.

This situation resulted in an unusual practice called "rotation," in which doctors played "eeny meeny miney mo," giving the first patient our drug, the second patient a competitor's drug, and so on. They did this so that they could enjoy the meetings, travel, and other incentive programs that all pharmaceutical companies provided. "Why go to an exotic resort only once a year when you can go four times?" appeared to be the general motto among physicians. This was one of my first concerns as I started my new job back in the summer of 2001. I found out that we paid for many hundreds of physicians to go to wonderful locations in the Caribbean and Mexico. Against American Medical Association (AMA) guidelines, we paid their way, and we even allowed spouses to attend for a very low price. The way this was explained to me was that Pharmacia didn't consider them to be regular doctors. They were "investigators." Needless to say, few of them did any real studies. To become an investigator was all too simple: Fill out a form with information about how much Genotropin they had given a particular patient, write down a few patient measurements, send it to Pharmacia and—*voila*—you're an "investigator." I asked Darren

McAllister about this in the fall of 2001, and he told me that Pharmacia's legal department had approved the program.

An Unusual Memo

Darren McAllister apparently had his own concerns about my area of responsibility, and one of the first documents he gave me was a memo he had written to all the foreign affiliates and to our US sales department, with a copy to Pharmacia's senior management. It was titled "Growth Hormone in Aging Patients."[1]

The memo went on to explain that there had been much media attention about the use of growth hormone in elderly patients to reduce the impact of aging. The memo stated in bold letters that, "Pharmacia does not, may not and will not promote or encourage the usage of our products outside of the approved labeling."

Anyone who works in pharmaceutical marketing knows that it is illegal to promote a product beyond the FDA-approved labeling. A company can't say the drug works for a disease or use which has not been approved by the Food and Drug Administration. Companies that have been caught doing so

"Why go to an exotic resort only once a year when you can go four times?" appeared to be the general motto among physicians.

have paid hundreds of millions of dollars in fines. The question in my mind was simple: Since everyone knew this basic fact of pharmaceutical sales and marketing, why the memo?

My worries increased as my first months with Pharmacia passed. I discovered more and more details about our business that concerned me.

I knew that Darren was the epitome of integrity, so I didn't believe for a second that he would do anything wrong, but he had taken responsibility for my area only recently. Who knew what had been the practice before he came on? Or what people might *still* have been doing? I would get many opportunities during the coming years to reflect on these initial concerns.

More Discoveries

My worries increased as my first months with Pharmacia passed. I discovered more and more details about our business that concerned me. I researched the situation and learned that giving a rebate to doctors who did off-label prescriptions could be regarded as an improper incentive, which could be a violation of anti-kickback statutes.[2] I also learned that we could be even worse off if we provided free drugs. Cold chills started to creep down my spine. We were giving all kinds of rebates to all kinds of centers, including doctors that specialized in anti-aging. We were also giving away free drugs to virtually *all* new patients for the first few months, before they got approval for insurance coverage. (This was a very expensive drug costing $20,000 per year—not something patients simply picked up in a pharmacy.)

My primary concern, however, was not sales we shouldn't have made, but how to increase overall sales. After all, that was my job—to be a healthcare hitman. Exploring my options led to the next anomaly: 90 percent of our sales went to pediatric patients, and only 10 percent to adult patients. But our sales efforts didn't reflect this ratio: Half our sales force focused on the adult area, and seventeen of the top twenty bonus payouts went to sales reps targeting the adult area.[3]

This made no sense from a business point of view. Why give bonuses mainly to the sales people that generated just 10 percent of the business? Why push sales to the adult market?

Did its potential really justify the expense?

The reason most sales went to children was that they needed very high doses, costing a lot of money, for many years. Adults, on the other hand, used very low doses and often stopped treatment after only a few months. Based on the doctors who wrote adult prescriptions, dosing and length of treatment, we concluded that most of the adult sales were being prescribed for off-label anti-aging treatments.

Bonus Formulas That Didn't Make Sense

I got even more concerned when I saw how we calculated bonuses. We rewarded sales representatives per new patient, not per sales dollar. In this way, a rep who called on a doctor who brought in hundreds of low-paying adult patients could make much more money than a rep who sold to a doctor with a few high-paying pediatric patients.

Suspicious, I tried to compare how profitable these two areas were. Apparently no one had ever done such an exercise, and I had a hard time extracting this information from my US marketing team. When we finalized the analysis, I was in for a shocker: We made *no* money on the adult franchise. We also projected that we wouldn't make any money over the next five years. It was time for some major change in how we ran our business, and it was time to tell the Pharmacia lawyers what I had learned.[4]

Criminal Liability

But the surprises didn't stop there. One day a Pharmacia lawyer left a document I had never seen before on my desk. As I read the words, the hair on the back of my neck stood straight up.

> The 21st paragraph of the United States Code 333(f) states that: "…whoever knowingly distributes, or possesses with intent to distribute, human growth hormone for any use in humans other than the treatment of a disease or other recognized medical condition, where such use has been authorized by the Secretary of Health and Human Services under 21 U.S.C. 355 and pursuant to the order of a physician, is guilty of an offense punishable by not more than 5 years in prison."

Anyone who works in marketing knows that off-label marketing is illegal and can result in fines for the company, but I had never before heard of any drug where illegal distribution could result in jail. I looked at my business card. It said, "Peter Rost, M.D., Vice President, Endocrine Care, Healthcare Hitman." Actually, it didn't say the last two words, but it could have. To be a vice president, I thought, would be enough to put me in a bad position if the Feds came looking at our business. I had to take action.

The Internal Investigation

I spent the following months working closely with Pharmacia's legal department, and many of the employees in the US group were interviewed. By the time we were done, we had new people in the US marketing department and had created a new sales incentive system that didn't reward off-label sales. We also stopped giving all those rebates to the anti-aging centers and all kinds of other rebates to various wholesalers and pharmacy benefit managers. The effect didn't take long to appear—Genotropin sales went through the roof.

As a direct result of these changes, in 2003 Genotropin became the best performing product vs. budget, if products with sales of more than $100 million were compared. We increased sales by 46 percent and came in more than 30 percent over forecast.[5] This was the best performance in the history of Genotropin.

But I still had concerns. Pharmacia's legal department had helped us stop many questionable practices, but they hadn't stopped all of them. Now we had new bosses from Pfizer, so we set out to inform them about what had been going on and perhaps get them to agree to take additional action.

Breaking the News to Pfizer

On a beautiful day in October 2002,[6] a small group from my department went to Pfizer's headquarters in Manhattan to discuss our programs and concerns. (None of us had yet been offered jobs with Pfizer.)

Pfizer's offices were shoddy in comparison to Pharmacia's headquarters. The corridors were small and cramped, and the carpet looked like it hadn't been replaced in thirty years. Even Pfizer's vice presidents were squeezed into offices so small they could stand and touch virtually everything in their room. It didn't look like a fun environment to work in; it reminded us of a beehive.

They put us in a dinky conference room, and when the last one of us had arrived, the Pfizer people joined. Their employees appeared different too: tense, harried, and stressed. Many were quite old in relation to the positions they held—promotions were few and far between. Compared to Pharmacia, this was a different country.

I had a lot on my mind, not all of which I got a chance to discuss. After some of my US marketing people had departed six months earlier, I went through their files, which were treasure troves of illegal marketing. I found contracts that paid $50,000 to individual anti-aging physicians for "consulting" services; I discovered an outfit in Canada that was going to help establish business for these physicians, to which we paid a $10,000 monthly retainer. Sales people came forward telling us how they had been forced to do off-label promotion. One sales person in Chicago had been terminated because he had refused. In the years past, Pharmacia had conducted an annual ethics certification of our sales reps and many had stated that they had been forced to do off-label promotion. It

> After some of my US marketing people had departed six months earlier, I went through their files, which were treasure troves of illegal marketing.

was bad, really bad, and I wasn't sure if Pharmacia's legal department had done everything it could.

Pens on Fire

What really scared Pfizer were the business practices still in place at Pharmacia, the ones that I had warned Pharmacia's legal department about but that they hadn't stopped. We divulged the "investigator" meetings and Caribbean trips, and we described the program that supplied everyone with free drugs for several months, which could easily be seen as an inducement to off-label sales. We called this the Bridge program, since it bridged the time period until the patient got reimbursement from his insurance company with free drugs, and though fundamentally this was a well-meaning program, it could be abused. All of us had a strong incentive to explain what we had done to stop inappropriate practices, since we didn't want to be associated with any of this.

We could see the Pfizer people writing as if their pens were on fire, and they immediately requested a second meeting to review the Bridge program in detail. They were visibly shaken, and after the meeting they sent a flurry of email requests for more information. We actually felt pretty good about all this— we had put the cards on the table, and we hoped our forthright-

> The fact that Pharmacia paid for and included many off-label patients in their database was of particular concern to them.

ness, and the fact that we had addressed many of the problems, would help us land new jobs within Pfizer.

A Promise

I didn't just have legal issues on my mind during this time period; most of all I was concerned about my own future. After having done a number of presentations to Pfizer, I thought it was a good time to ask them what my situation with the company would be. The response came back very quickly from Pfizer's new Senior Vice President for Global Marketing. "There is no issue whatsoever on our side with your being considered for several positions,"[7] Wyler Jennings wrote.

I was relieved. I knew there weren't too many vice president positions out there in a shrinking industry, especially with all the Pharmacia employees now looking for jobs. I was also confident that Pharmacia's management would give me a strong endorsement for a new job with Pfizer. In fact, Gertrude Hawk, Pharmacia's president, had written an email to me saying, "You have made outstanding contributions to our organization that surpass by far the length of your tenure, and I sincerely hope you'll have a long career with the new company. If I can be of any assistance to you, now or in the future, please don't hesitate to call me."[8]

While I didn't have a specific job offer in my hand yet, things were moving in the right direction, and I started to feel com-

fortable. It was also a relief to have reviewed some of the legal concerns we had with Pfizer; hopefully, this would make them understand how responsibly we had managed the situation and how we could assist them in resolving some of the remaining issues.

Pharmacia's CEO Receives a Warning

Later in 2003, I got another piece of alarming news. One of the most famous professors in the endocrinology area told me that a group of renowned endocrinologists around the world had been very worried a couple of years earlier about the direction the Genotropin franchise was taking in the US. The fact that Pharmacia paid for and included many off-label patients in their database was of particular concern to them.

They had been so worried, in fact, that they had written a letter directly to Fred Hassan—Pharmacia's CEO. I asked if I could see the letter. Lo and behold, back on August 21, 2000, one year before I started my new job at Pharmacia, he and many others had indeed spelled out their concerns to Fred.[9]

Dear Fred Hassan,

Since you had personally devoted much interest into the KIGS/KIMS [Pharmacia International Growth/ Metabolic Database] process we take the liberty to address you directly without considering in-house aspects of hierarchy.

We—the members of the Strategic Planning Committee of KIGS and KIMS—would like to express our most sincere concerns about pending decisions by the management of Pharmacia which will have major adverse implications for these databases.

One relates to the intention to incorporate patient groups other than those with GHD or short stature into the existing databases.

KIGS and KIMS were two outcomes databases that tracked patients. GHD was an abbreviation for "growth hormone deficiency," a condition for which the FDA had approved Genotropin. A competing drug was approved for short stature a year after this letter. So when this professor asked Fred not to include patients with other indications, he was referring to all the indications for which Genotropin *was not approved*. The professor also wrote in an email to me, "I told them that it was first when you joined that my confidence in Pharmacia returned. I told them about your predecessor's off-label marketing."[10]

What I didn't discover until later when I started to connect many loose documents, was that on January 14, 2000, Fred had received a letter from a prominent anti-aging physician. The letter was written on the "The Renaissance Longevity Center" stationary and invited Hassan to a "strategic alliance" for the "most aggressive ethical campaign ever launched for the marketing of growth hormone injections."

Fred sent the letter with an annotation in his own handwriting, "Please follow-up/ack, etc., FH," to his direct reports, and it ended up on the desk of the person responsible for Genotropin at that time. On February 3, 2000, the same anti-aging physician wrote a two-page letter to the Vice President of Endocrine Care, summarizing a telephone conference they had on January 28, 2000. Among other things he wanted to discuss were the ability for the longevity centers to purchase growth hormone at quantity discount prices and other benefits that Pharmacia could provide them. On May 1, 2000, the US marketing director for Genotropin signed a "$50,000" consulting agreement with the anti-aging physicians, and the rest is history; sales of Genotropin for anti-aging purposes took off.

Endnotes

1. McAllister, Darren. (2001). Growth hormone in aging patients. 21 May. **2.** The federal health care Anti-Kickback statute, 42 U.S.C.§1320a-7b(b) prohibits any person or entity from making or accepting payment to induce or reward any person for referring, recommending, or arranging for the purchase of any item for which payment may be made under a federally funded healthcare program. **3.** Adult GHD Sales & Marketing Strategy Presentation, 27 Feb 2002. **4.** *Ibid*. **5.** Pfizer 31 Dec 2003 sales report. **6.** Meeting Pfizer, New York, 28 Oct 2002. **7.** Jennings, Wyler. (2002). Email to Peter Rost, 13 Nov. **8.** Hawk, Gertrude. (2002). Email to Peter Rost, 17 Sep. **9.** Letter from Professors Michael B. Ranke, Edinburgh; Kerstin Albertsson-Wikland, Gothenburg; Pierre Chatelain, Lyon; David Antony Price, Manchester; Roger Abs, Antwerp; Bengt-Ake Bengtsson, Gothenburg; Ulla-Feldt-Rasmussen, Copenhagen; John P. Monson, London to Mr. Fred Hassan, 21 Aug 2000. **10.** Bengtsson, Professor Bengt-Ake. (2003). Email to Peter Rost, 12 Sep.

POLITRICKS

John McCain and the POW Cover-up
The "War Hero" Politician Buried Information About POWs Left Behind in Vietnam
Sydney H. Schanberg

Senator John McCain, who has risen to political prominence on his image as a Vietnam POW war hero, has, inexplicably, worked very hard to hide from the public stunning information about American prisoners in Vietnam who, unlike him, didn't return home. Throughout his Senate career, McCain has quietly sponsored and pushed into federal law a set of prohibitions that keeps the most revealing information about these men buried as classified documents. Thus the war hero whom people would logically imagine as a determined crusader for the interests of POWs and their families has become instead the strange champion of hiding the evidence and closing the books.

Almost as striking is the manner in which the mainstream press has shied from reporting the POW story and McCain's role in it, even as the Republican Party made McCain's military service the focus of his presidential campaign. Reporters who had covered the Vietnam War turned their heads and walked in other directions. McCain doesn't talk about the missing men, and the press never asks him about them.

> Thus the war hero whom people would logically imagine as a determined crusader for the interests of POWs and their families has become instead the strange champion of hiding the evidence and closing the books.

The sum of the secrets McCain has sought to hide is not small. There exists a telling mass of official documents, radio intercepts, witness depositions, satellite photos of rescue symbols that pilots were trained to use, electronic messages from the ground containing the individual code numbers given to airmen, a rescue mission by a special forces unit that was aborted twice by Washington—and even sworn testimony by two Defense Secretaries that "men were left behind." This imposing body of evidence suggests that a large number—the documents indicate probably hundreds—of the US prisoners held by Vietnam were not returned when the peace treaty was signed in January 1973 and Hanoi released 591 men, among them Navy combat pilot John S. McCain.

Mass of Evidence

The Pentagon had been withholding significant information from POW families for years. What's more, the Pentagon's POW/MIA operation had been publicly shamed by internal whistleblowers and POW families for holding back documents as part of a policy of "debunking" POW intelligence even when the information was obviously credible.

The pressure from the families and Vietnam veterans finally forced the creation, in late 1991, of a Senate Select Committee on POW/MIA Affairs. The chairman was John Kerry. McCain, as a former POW, was its most pivotal member. In the end, the committee became part of the debunking machine.

One of the sharpest critics of the Pentagon's performance was an insider, Air Force Lieut. Gen. Eugene Tighe, who headed the Defense Intelligence Agency (DIA) during the 1970s. He openly challenged the Pentagon's position that no live prisoners existed, saying that the evidence proved otherwise. McCain was a bitter opponent of Tighe, who was eventually pushed into retirement.

Included in the evidence that McCain and his government allies suppressed or sought to discredit is a transcript of a senior North Vietnamese general's briefing of the Hanoi politburo, discovered in Soviet archives by an American scholar in 1993. The briefing took place only four months before the 1973

There exists a telling mass of official documents, radio intercepts, witness depositions, satellite photos of rescue symbols that pilots were trained to use, electronic messages from the ground containing the individual code numbers given to airmen, a rescue mission by a special forces unit that was aborted twice by Washington—and even sworn testimony by two Defense Secretaries that "men were left behind."

who had not died from illness or hard labor or torture—were eventually executed.

My own research, detailed below, has convinced me that it is not likely that more than a few—if any—are alive in captivity today. (That CIA briefing at the agency's Langley, Virginia, headquarters was conducted "off the record," but because the evidence from my own reporting since then has brought me to the same conclusion, I felt there was no longer any point in not writing about the meeting.)

peace accords. The general, Tran Van Quang, told the politburo members that Hanoi was holding 1,205 American prisoners but would keep many of them at war's end as leverage to ensure getting war reparations from Washington.

Throughout the Paris negotiations, the North Vietnamese tied the prisoner issue tightly to the issue of reparations. They were adamant in refusing to deal with them separately. Finally, in a February 2, 1973, formal letter to Hanoi's premier, Pham Van Dong, Nixon pledged $3.25 billion in "postwar reconstruction" aid "without any political conditions." But he also attached to the letter a codicil that said the aid would be implemented by each party "in accordance with its own constitutional provisions." That meant Congress would have to approve the appropriation, and Nixon and Kissinger knew well that Congress was in no mood to do so. The North Vietnamese, whether or not they immediately understood the doubletalk in the letter, remained skeptical about the reparations promise being honored—and it never was. Hanoi thus appears to have held back prisoners—just as it had done when the French were defeated at Dien Bien Phu in 1954 and withdrew their forces from Vietnam. In that case, France paid ransoms for prisoners and brought them home.

In a private briefing in 1992, high-level CIA officials told me that as the years passed and the ransom never came, it became more and more difficult for either government to admit that it knew from the start about the unacknowledged prisoners. Those prisoners had not only become useless as bargaining chips but also posed a risk to Hanoi's desire to be accepted into the international community. The CIA officials said their intelligence indicated strongly that the remaining men—those

For many reasons, including the absence of a political constituency for the missing men other than their families and some veterans' groups, very few Americans are aware of the POW story and of McCain's role in keeping it out of public view and denying the existence of abandoned POWs. That is because McCain has hardly been alone in his campaign to hide the scandal.

The Arizona Senator, and two-time Republican candidate for President, has actually been following the lead of every White House since Richard Nixon's and thus of every CIA Director, Pentagon chief, and National Security Advisor, not to mention Dick Cheney, who was George H.W. Bush's Secretary of Defense. Their biggest accomplice has been an indolent press, particularly in Washington.

Hanoi thus appears to have held back prisoners—just as it had done when the French were defeated at Dien Bien Phu in 1954 and withdrew their forces from Vietnam.

McCain's Role

An early and critical McCain secrecy move involved 1990 legislation that started in the House of Representatives. A brief and simple document, it was called "the Truth Bill" and would have compelled complete transparency about prisoners and missing men. Its core sentence reads:

John McCain and the POW Cover-up
Sydney H. Schanberg
The "War Hero" Politician Buried Information About POWs Left Behind in Vietnam

131

> [The] head of each department or agency which holds or receives any records and information, including live-sighting reports, which have been correlated or possibly correlated to United States personnel listed as prisoner of war or missing in action from World War II, the Korean conflict and the Vietnam conflict, shall make available to the public all such records held or received by that department or agency.

Bitterly opposed by the Pentagon (and thus McCain), the bill went nowhere. Reintroduced the following year, it again disappeared. But a few months later, a new measure, known as "the McCain Bill," suddenly appeared. By creating a bureaucratic maze from which only a fraction of the documents could emerge—only records that revealed no POW secrets—it turned the Truth Bill on its head. (As an example of its influence, the Pentagon cited McCain's bill in rejecting a Freedom of Information Act request.) The McCain bill became law in 1991 and remains so today. So crushing to transparency are its provisions that it actually spells out for the Pentagon and other agencies several rationales, scenarios, and justifications for not releasing any information at all—even about prisoners discovered alive in captivity. Later that year, the Senate Select Committee was created, where Kerry and McCain ultimately worked together to bury evidence.

McCain was also instrumental in amending the Missing Service Personnel Act, which had been strengthened in 1995

"This is a man not at peace with himself."

by POW advocates to include criminal penalties, saying: "Any government official who knowingly and willfully withholds from the file of a missing person any information relating to the disappearance or whereabouts and status of a missing person shall be fined as provided in Title 18 or imprisoned not more than one year or both." A year later, in a closed House-Senate conference on an unrelated military bill, McCain, at the behest of the Pentagon, attached a crippling amendment to the act, stripping out its only enforcement teeth, the criminal penalties, and reducing the obligations of commanders in the field to speedily search for missing men and to report the incidents to the Pentagon.

About the relaxation of POW/MIA obligations on commanders in the field, a public McCain memo said: "This transfers the bureaucracy involved out of the [battle] field to Washington." He wrote that the original legislation, if left intact, "would accomplish nothing but create new jobs for lawyers and turn military commanders into clerks."

McCain argued that keeping the criminal penalties would have made it impossible for the Pentagon to find staffers willing to work on POW/MIA matters. That's an odd argument to make. Were staffers only "willing to work" if they were allowed to conceal POW records? By eviscerating the law, McCain gave his stamp of approval to the government policy of debunking the existence of live POWs.

A year later, in a closed House-Senate conference on an unrelated military bill, McCain, at the behest of the Pentagon, attached a crippling amendment to the act, stripping out its only enforcement teeth, the criminal penalties, and reducing the obligations of commanders in the field to speedily search for missing men and to report the incidents to the Pentagon.

McCain has insisted again and again that all the evidence—documents, witnesses, satellite photos, two Pentagon chiefs' sworn testimony, aborted rescue missions, ransom offers apparently scorned—has been woven together by unscrupulous deceivers to create an insidious and unpatriotic myth. He calls it the "bizarre rantings of the MIA hobbyists." He has regularly vilified those who keep trying to pry out classified documents as "hoaxers," "charlatans," "conspiracy theorists," and "dime-store Rambos."

Some of McCain's fellow captives at Hoa Lo prison in Hanoi didn't share his views about prisoners left behind. Before he died of leukemia in 1999, retired Col. Ted Guy, a highly admired POW and one of the most dogged resisters in the camps, wrote an angry open letter to the Senator in an MIA newsletter—a response to McCain's stream of insults hurled at MIA activists. Guy wrote: "John, does this [the insults] include Senator Bob Smith [a New Hampshire Republican and activist on POW issues] and other concerned elected officials? Does this include the families of the missing where there is overwhelming evidence that their loved ones were 'last known alive'? Does this include some of your fellow POWs?"

It's not clear whether the taped confession McCain gave to his captors to avoid further torture has played a role in his post-war behavior in the Senate. That confession was played endlessly over the prison loudspeaker system at Hoa Lo—to try to break down other prisoners—and was broadcast over Hanoi's state radio. Reportedly, he confessed to being a war criminal who had bombed civilian targets. The Pentagon has a copy of the confession but will not release it. Also, no outsider I know of has ever seen a non-redacted copy of the debriefing of McCain when he returned from captivity, which is classified but could be made public by McCain. (The Pentagon rejected my attempt to obtain records of this debriefing via a Freedom of Information Act request.)

All humans have breaking points. Many men undergoing torture give confessions, often telling huge lies so their fakery will be understood by their comrades and their country. Few will fault them. But it was McCain who apparently felt he had disgraced himself and his military family. His father, John S. McCain II, was a highly regarded rear admiral then serving as commander of all US forces in the Pacific. His grandfather was also a rear admiral.

In his bestselling 1999 autobiography, *Faith of My Fathers*, McCain says he felt bad throughout his captivity because he knew he was being treated more leniently than his fellow POWs, owing to his high-ranking father and thus his propaganda value. Other prisoners at Hoa Lo say his captors considered him a prize catch and called him the "Crown Prince," something McCain acknowledges in the book.

Also in this memoir, McCain expresses guilt at having broken under torture and given the confession. "I felt faithless and

couldn't control my despair," he writes, revealing that he made two "feeble" attempts at suicide. (In later years, he said he tried to hang himself with his shirt and guards intervened.) Tellingly, he says he lived in "dread" that his father would find out about the confession. "I still wince," he writes, "when I recall wondering if my father had heard of my disgrace."

He says that when he returned home, he told his father about the confession, but "never discussed it at length"—and the Admiral, who died in 1981, didn't indicate he had heard anything about it before. But he had. In the 1999 memoir, the Senator writes: "I only recently learned that the tape…had been broadcast outside the prison and had come to the attention of my father."

In 1996, McCain roughly pushed aside a group of POW family members, including a mother in a wheelchair, who had waited outside a hearing room to appeal to him.

Is McCain haunted by these memories? Does he suppress POW information because its surfacing would rekindle his feelings of shame? On this subject, all I have are questions.

Many stories have been written about McCain's explosive temper, so volcanic that colleagues are loathe to speak openly about it. One veteran Congressman who has observed him over the years asked for confidentiality and made this brief comment: "This is a man not at peace with himself."

He was certainly far from calm on the Senate POW committee. He browbeat expert witnesses who came with information about unreturned POWs. Family members who have personally faced McCain and pressed him to end the secrecy also have been treated to his legendary temper. He has screamed at them, insulted them, brought women to tears. Mostly his responses to them have been versions of: How dare you question my patriotism? In 1996, he roughly pushed aside a group of POW family members, including a mother in a wheelchair, who had waited outside a hearing room to appeal to him.

But even without answers to what may be hidden in the recesses of McCain's mind, one thing about the POW story is clear: If American prisoners were dishonored by being written off and left to die, that's something the American public ought to know.

John McCain and the POW Cover-up
Sydney H. Schanberg
The "War Hero" Politician Buried Information About POWs Left Behind in Vietnam

133

10 Key Pieces of Evidence That Men Were Left Behind

1. In Paris, where the Vietnam peace treaty was negotiated, the United States asked Hanoi for the list of American prisoners to be returned, fearing that Hanoi would hold back some prisoners. The North Vietnamese refused, saying they would produce the list only after the treaty was signed. Nixon agreed with Kissinger that they had no leverage left, and Kissinger signed the accord on January 27, 1973, without the prisoner list. When Hanoi produced its list of 591 prisoners the next day, US intelligence agencies expressed shock at the low number. Their number was hundreds higher. The *New York Times* published a long, page-one story on February 2, 1973, about the discrepancy, especially raising questions about the number of prisoners held in Laos, only nine of whom were being returned. The headline read, in part: "Laos POW List Shows 9 from US—Document Disappointing to Washington as 311 Were Believed Missing." And the story, by John Finney, said that other Washington officials "believe the number of prisoners [in Laos] is probably substantially higher." The paper never followed up with any serious investigative reporting—nor did any other mainstream news organization.

2. Two Secretaries of Defense who served during the Vietnam War testified to the Senate POW committee in September 1992 that prisoners were not returned. James Schlesinger and Melvin Laird, both speaking at a public session and under oath, said they based their conclusions on strong intelligence data—letters, eyewitness reports, even direct radio contacts. Under questioning, Schlesinger chose his words carefully, understanding clearly the volatility of the issue: "I think that as of now that I can come to no other conclusion…some were left behind." This ran counter to what President Nixon told the public in a nationally televised speech on March 29, 1973, when the repatriation of the 591 was in motion: "Tonight," Nixon said, "the day we have all worked and prayed for has finally come. For the first time in twelve years, no American military forces are in Vietnam. All our American POWs are on their way home." Documents unearthed since then show that aides had already briefed Nixon about the contrary evidence.

> Two Secretaries of Defense who served during the Vietnam War testified to the Senate POW committee in September 1992 that prisoners were not returned.

Schlesinger was asked by the Senate committee for his explanation of why President Nixon would have made such a statement when he knew Hanoi was still holding prisoners. He replied: "One must assume that we had concluded that the bargaining position of the United States…was quite weak. We were anxious to get our troops out and we were not going to roil the waters…." This testimony struck me as a bombshell. The *New York Times* appropriately reported it on page one, but again there was no sustained follow-up by the *Times* or any other major paper or national news outlet.

3. Over the years, the Defense Intelligence Agency has received more than 1,600 first-hand sightings of live American prisoners and nearly 14,000 second-hand reports. Many witnesses interrogated by CIA or Pentagon intelligence agents were deemed "credible" in the agents' reports. Some of the witnesses were given lie-detector tests and passed. Sources provided me with copies of these witness reports, which are impressive in their detail. A lot of the sightings described a secondary tier of prison camps many miles from Hanoi. Yet the DIA, after reviewing all these reports, concluded that they "do not constitute evidence" that men were alive.

4. In the late 1970s and early 1980s, listening stations picked up messages in which Laotian military personnel spoke about moving American prisoners from one labor camp to another. These listening posts were manned by Thai communications officers trained by the National Security Agency (NSA), which monitors signals worldwide. The NSA teams had moved out after the fall of Saigon in 1975 and passed the job to the Thai allies. But when the Thais turned these messages over to Washington, the intelligence community ruled that since the intercepts were made by a "third party"—namely Thailand—they could not be regarded as authentic. That's some Catch-22: The US trained a third party to take over its role in monitoring signals about POWs, but because that third party did the monitoring, the messages weren't valid.

Here, from CIA files, is an example that clearly exposes the farce. On December 27, 1980, a Thai military signal team picked up a message saying that prisoners were being moved out of Attopeu (in southern Laos) by aircraft "at 1230 hours." Three days later a message was sent from the CIA station in Bangkok to the CIA Director's office in Langley. It read, in part: "The prisoners…are now in the valley in permanent location (a prison camp at Nhommarath in Central Laos). They were transferred from Attopeu to work in various places…. POWs were formerly kept in caves and are very thin, dark and starving." Apparently the prisoners were real. But the transmission was declared "invalid" by Washington because the information came from a "third party" and thus could not be deemed credible.

5. A series of what appeared to be distress signals from Vietnam and Laos was captured by the government's satellite system in the late 1980s and early 1990s. (Before that period, no search for such signals had been put in place.) Not a single one of these markings was ever deemed credible. To the layman's eye, the satellite photos, some of which I've seen, show markings on the ground that are identical to the signals that American pilots had been specifically trained to use in their survival courses—such as certain letters, like X or K, drawn in a special way. Other markings were the secret four-digit authenticator numbers given to individual pilots. But time and again, the Pentagon, backed by the CIA, insisted that humans had not made these markings. What were they, then? "Shadows and vegetation," the government said, insisting that the markings were merely normal topographical contours like saw-grass or rice-paddy divider walls. It was the automatic response—shadows and vegetation.

On one occasion, a Pentagon photo expert refused to go along. It was a missing man's name gouged into a field, he said, not trampled grass or paddy berms. His bosses responded by bringing in an outside contractor who found instead, yes, shadows and vegetation. This refrain led Bob Taylor, a highly regarded investigator on the Senate committee staff who had examined the photographic evidence, to comment to me: "If grass can spell out people's names and secret digit codes, then I have a newfound respect for grass."

6. On November 11, 1992, Dolores Alfond, the sister of missing airman Capt. Victor Apodaca and chair of the National Alliance of Families, an organization of relatives of POW/MIAs, testified at one of the Senate committee's public hearings. She asked for information about data the government had gathered from electronic devices used in a classified program known as PAVE SPIKE.

The devices were motion sensors, dropped by air, designed to pick up enemy troop movements. Shaped on one end like a spike with an electronic pod and antenna on top, they were designed to stick in the ground as they fell. Air Force planes would drop them along the Ho Chi Minh trail and other supply routes. The devices, though primarily sensors, also had rescue capabilities. Someone on the ground—a downed airman or a prisoner on a labor gang—could manually enter data into the sensor. All data were regularly collected electronically by US planes flying overhead.

Alfond stated, without any challenge or contradiction by the committee, that in 1974, a year after the supposedly complete return of prisoners, the gathered data showed that a person or people had manually entered into the sensors—as US pilots had been trained to do—"no less than 20 authenticator numbers that corresponded exactly to the classified authenticator numbers of 20 US POWs who were lost in Laos." Alfond added, according to the transcript: "This PAVE SPIKE intelligence is seamless, but the committee has not discussed it or released what it knows about PAVE SPIKE."

McCain attended that committee hearing specifically to confront Alfond because of her criticism of the panel's work. He bellowed and berated her for quite a while. His face turning anger-pink, he accused her of "denigrating" his "patriotism." The bullying had its effect—she began to cry.

Over the years, the Defense Intelligence Agency has received more than 1,600 first-hand sightings of live American prisoners and nearly 14,000 second-hand reports.

After a pause Alfond recovered and tried to respond to his scorching tirade, but McCain simply turned away and stormed out of the room. The PAVE SPIKE file has never been declassified. We still don't know anything about those twenty POWs.

John McCain and the POW Cover-up
Sydney H. Schanberg
The "War Hero" Politician Buried Information About POWs Left Behind in Vietnam

135

7. As previously mentioned, in April 1993, in a Moscow archive, a researcher from Harvard, Stephen Morris, unearthed and made public the transcript of a briefing that General Tran Van Quang gave to the Hanoi politburo four months before the signing of the Paris peace accords in 1973.

In the transcript, General Quang told the Hanoi politburo that 1,205 US prisoners were being held. Quang said that many of the prisoners would be held back from Washington after the accords as bargaining chips for war reparations. General Quang's report added:

> This is a big number. Officially, until now, we published a list of only 368 prisoners of war. The rest we have not revealed. The government of the USA knows this well, but it does not know the exact number…and can only make guesses based on its losses. That is why we are keeping the number of prisoners of war secret, in accordance with the politburo's instructions.

The report then went on to explain in clear and specific language that a large number would be kept back to ensure reparations.

The reaction to the document was immediate. After two decades of denying it had kept any prisoners, Hanoi responded to the revelation by calling the transcript a fabrication.

Similarly, Washington—which had over the same two decades refused to recant Nixon's declaration that all the prisoners had been returned—also shifted into denial mode. The Pentagon issued a statement saying the document "is replete with errors, omissions and propaganda that seriously damage its credibility," and that the numbers were "inconsistent with our own accounting."

Neither American nor Vietnamese officials offered any rationale for who would plant a forged document in the Soviet archives and why they would do so. Certainly neither Washington nor Moscow—closely allied with Hanoi—would have any motive, since the contents were embarrassing to all parties, and since both the United States and Vietnam had consistently denied the existence of unreturned prisoners. The Russian archivists simply said the document was "authentic."

8. In his 2002 book, *Inside Delta Force*, retired Command Sgt. Major Eric Haney described how in 1981 his special forces unit, after rigorous training for a POW rescue mission, had the mission suddenly aborted, revived a year later, and again abruptly aborted. Haney writes that this abandonment of captured soldiers ate at him for years and left him disillusioned about his government's vows to leave no men behind.

Haney writes: "Years later, I spoke at length with a former highly placed member of the North Vietnamese diplomatic corps, and this person asked me point-blank: 'Why did the Americans never attempt to recover their remaining POWs after the conclusion of the war?'" He continued, saying that he came to believe senior government officials had called off those missions in 1981 and 1982. (His account is on pages 314 to 321 of my paperback copy of the book.)

9. There is also evidence that in the first months of Ronald Reagan's presidency in 1981, the White House received a ransom proposal for a number of POWs being held by Hanoi in Indochina. The offer, which was passed to Washington from an official of a third country, was apparently discussed at a meeting in the Roosevelt Room attended by Reagan, Vice President Bush, CIA Director William Casey, and National Security Advisor Richard Allen. Allen confirmed the offer in sworn testimony to the Senate POW committee on June 23, 1992.

Allen was allowed to testify behind closed doors, and no information was released. But a *San Diego Union-Tribune* reporter, Robert Caldwell, obtained the portion of the committee transcript relating to the ransom offer and reported on it. The ransom request was for $4 billion, Allen testified. He said he told Reagan that "it would be worth the president's going along and let's have the negotiation." When his testimony appeared in the *Union-Tribune*, Allen quickly wrote a letter to the panel, this time not under oath, recanting the

In the late 1970s and early 1980s, listening stations picked up messages in which Laotian military personnel spoke about moving American prisoners from one labor camp to another.

ransom story and claiming his memory had played tricks on him. His new version was that some POW activists had asked him about such an offer in a meeting that took place in 1986, when he was no longer in government. "It appears," he said in the letter, "that there never was a 1981 meeting about the return of POW/MIAs for $4 billion."

But the episode didn't end there. A Treasury agent on Secret Service duty in the White House, John Syphrit, came forward to say he had overheard part of the ransom conversation in the Roosevelt Room in 1981, when the offer was discussed by Reagan, Bush, Casey, Allen, and other cabinet officials.

General Quang said that many of the prisoners would be held back from Washington after the accords as bargaining chips for war reparations.

Syphrit, a veteran of the Vietnam War, told the committee that he was willing to testify but that they would have to subpoena him. Treasury opposed his appearance, arguing that voluntary testimony would violate the trust between the Secret Service and those it protects. It was clear that coming in on his own could cost Syphrit his career. The committee voted 7 to 4 not to subpoena him.

In the committee's final report, dated January 13, 1993 (on page 284), the panel not only chastised Syphrit for his failure to testify without a subpoena ("The committee regrets that the Secret Service agent was unwilling…"), but noted that since Allen had recanted his testimony about the Roosevelt Room briefing, Syphrit's testimony would have been "at best, uncorroborated by the testimony of any other witness." The committee omitted any mention that it had made a decision not to ask the other two surviving witnesses, Bush and Reagan, to give testimony under oath. (Casey had died.)

10. In 1990, Colonel Millard Peck, a decorated infantry veteran of Vietnam then working at the DIA as chief of the Asia Division for Current Intelligence, asked for the job of chief of the DIA's Special Office for Prisoners of War and Missing in Action. His reason for seeking the transfer, which was not a promotion, was that he had heard from officials throughout the Pentagon that the POW/MIA office had been turned into a waste-disposal unit for getting rid of unwanted evidence

about live prisoners—a "black hole," these officials called it.

Peck explained all this in his telling resignation letter of February 12, 1991, eight months after he had taken the job. He said he viewed it as "sort of a holy crusade" to restore the integrity of the office but was defeated by the Pentagon machine. The four-page, single-spaced letter was scathing, describing the putative search for missing men as "a cover-up."

Peck charged that, at its top echelons, the Pentagon had embraced a "mind-set to debunk" all evidence of prisoners left behind. "That national leaders continue to address the prisoner of war and missing in action issue as the 'highest national priority,' is a travesty," he wrote. "The entire charade does not appear to be an honest effort, and may never have been…. Practically all analysis is directed to finding fault with the source. Rarely has there been any effective, active follow through on any of the sightings, nor is there a responsive 'action arm' to routinely and aggressively pursue leads."

"I became painfully aware," his letter continued, "that I was not really in charge of my own office, but was merely a figurehead or whipping boy for a larger and totally Machiavellian group of players outside of DIA…. I feel strongly that this issue is being manipulated and controlled at a higher level, not with the goal of resolving it, but more to obfuscate the question of live prisoners and give the illusion of progress through hyperactivity." He named no names but said these players are "unscrupulous people in the Government or associated with the Government" who "have maintained their distance and remained hidden in the shadows, while using the [POW] Office as a 'toxic waste dump' to bury the whole 'mess' out of sight." Peck added that "military officers…who in some manner have 'rocked the boat' [have] quickly come to grief."

Peck concluded:

From what I have witnessed, it appears that any soldier left in Vietnam, even inadvertently, was, in fact, abandoned years ago, and that the farce that is being played is no more than political legerdemain done with "smoke and mirrors" to stall the issue until it dies a natural death.

John McCain and the POW Cover-up
Sydney H. Schanberg
The "War Hero" Politician Buried Information About POWs Left Behind in Vietnam

137

The disillusioned Colonel not only resigned but asked to be retired immediately from active military service. The press never followed up.

My Pursuit of the Story

I covered the war in Cambodia and Vietnam but came to the POW information only slowly afterward, when military officers I knew from that conflict began coming to me with maps and POW sightings and depositions by Vietnamese witnesses.

I was then city editor of the *New York Times*, no longer involved in foreign or national stories, so I took the data to the appropriate desks and suggested it was material worth pursuing. There were no takers. Some years later, in 1991, when I was an op-ed columnist at *Newsday*, the aforementioned special Senate committee was formed to probe the POW issue. I saw this as an opening and immersed myself in the reporting.

At *Newsday*, I wrote 35 columns over a two-year period, as well as a four-part series on a trip I took to North Vietnam to report on what happened to one missing pilot who was shot down over the Ho Chi Minh trail and captured when he parachuted. After *Newsday*, I wrote thousands more words on the subject for other outlets. Some of the pieces were about McCain's key role.

Though I wrote on many subjects for *Life*, *Vanity Fair*, and *Washington Monthly*, my POW articles appeared in *Penthouse*, the *Village Voice*, and APBnews.com (now defunct). Mainstream publications just weren't interested. Their disinterest was part of what motivated me, and I became one of a very short list of journalists who considered the story important.

Serving in the Army in Germany during the Cold War and witnessing combat first-hand as a reporter in India and Indochina led me to have great respect for those who fight for their country. To my mind, we dishonored US troops when our government failed to bring them home from Vietnam after the 591 others were released—and then claimed they didn't exist. And politicians dishonor themselves when they pay lip service to the bravery and sacrifice of soldiers only to leave untold num-

bers behind, rationalizing to themselves that it's merely one of the unfortunate costs of war.

John McCain—who campaigned for the White House as a war hero, maverick, and straight shooter—owes the voters some explanations. The press were long ago wooed and won by McCain's seeming openness, Lone Ranger pose, and self-deprecating humor, which may partly explain their ignoring his record on POWs. In the numerous, lengthy McCain profiles that appeared during the 2008 campaign in papers like the *New York Times*, the *Washington Post*, and the *Wall Street Journal*, I may have missed a clause or a sentence along the way, but I have not found a single mention of his role in burying information about POWs. Television and radio news programs have been similarly silent.

Reporters simply never ask him about it. They didn't when he ran unsuccessfully for the Republican nomination in 2000. They haven't now, despite the fact that we're in the midst of another war—a war he supports and one that has echoes of Vietnam.

> "Years later, I spoke at length with a former highly placed member of the North Vietnamese diplomatic corps, and this person asked me point-blank: 'Why did the Americans never attempt to recover their remaining POWs after the conclusion of the war?'"

The only explanation McCain has ever offered for his leadership on legislation that seals POW files is that he believes the release of such information would only stir up fresh grief for the families of those who were never accounted for in Vietnam. Of the scores of POW families I've met over the years, only a few have said they want the books closed without knowing what happened to their men. All the rest say that not knowing is exactly what grieves them.

Isn't it possible that what really worries those intent on keeping the POW documents buried is the public disgust that the contents of those files would generate?

How the Senate Committee Perpetuated the Debunking

In its early months, the Senate Select Committee on POW/MIA Affairs gave the appearance of being committed to finding out the truth about the MIAs. As time went on, however, it became clear that they were cooperating in every way with the Pentagon and CIA, who often seemed to be calling the shots, even setting the agendas for certain key hearings. Both agencies held back the most important POW files. Dick Cheney was the Pentagon chief then; Robert Gates, now the Pentagon chief, was the CIA Director.

Further, the committee failed to question any living president. Reagan declined to answer questions; the committee didn't contest his refusal. Nixon was given a pass. George H.W. Bush, the sitting president, whose prints were all over this issue from his days as CIA chief in the 1970s, was never even approached.

Troubled by these signs, several committee staffers began asking why the agencies they should be probing had been turned into committee partners and decision makers. Memos to that effect were circulated. The staff made the following finding, using intelligence reports marked "credible" that covered POW sightings through 1989: "There can be no doubt that POWs were alive…as late as 1989." That finding was never released. Eventually, much of the staff was in rebellion.

This internecine struggle continued right up to the committee's last official act—the issuance of its final report. The "Executive Summary," which comprised the first 43 pages, was essentially a whitewash, saying that only "a small number" of POWs could have been left behind in 1973 and that there was little likelihood that any prisoners could still be alive. The Washington press corps, judging from its coverage, seems to have read only this airbrushed summary, which had been closely controlled.

But the rest of the 1,221-page Report on POW/MIAs was quite different. Sprinkled throughout are pieces of hard evidence that directly contradict the summary's conclusions. This documentation established that a significant number of prisoners was left behind—and that top government officials knew this from the start. These candid findings were inserted by committee staffers who had unearthed the evidence and were determined not to allow the truth to be sugar-coated.

If the Washington press corps did actually read the body of the report and then failed to report its contents, that would be a scandal of its own. The press would then have knowingly ignored the steady stream of findings in the body of the report that refuted the summary and indicated that the number of abandoned men was not small but, rather, considerable. The report gave no figures, but estimates from various branches of the intelligence community ranged up to 600. The lowest estimate was 150.

Highlights of the report that undermine the benign conclusions of the Executive Summary:

■ **Pages 207–209:** These three pages contain revelations of what appear to be either massive intelligence failures or bad intentions—or both. The report says that until the committee brought up the subject in 1992, no branch of the intelligence community that dealt with analysis of satellite and lower-altitude photos had ever been informed of the specific distress signals US personnel were trained to use in the Vietnam war, nor had they ever been tasked to look for any such signals at all from possible prisoners on the ground.

"Rarely has there been any effective, active follow through on any of the sightings, nor is there a responsive 'action arm' to routinely and aggressively pursue leads."

The committee decided, however, not to seek a review of old photography, saying it "would cause the expenditure of large amounts of manpower and money with no expectation of success." It might also have turned up lots of distress-signal numbers that nobody in the government was looking for from 1973 to 1991, when the committee opened shop. That would have made it impossible for the committee to write the Executive Summary it seemed determined to write.

The failure gets worse. The committee also discovered that the DIA, which kept the lists of authenticator numbers for pilots and other personnel, could not "locate" the lists of these codes for Army, Navy, or Marine pilots. They had lost or destroyed the records. The Air Force list was the only one intact, as it had been preserved by a different intelligence branch.

John McCain and the POW Cover-up
Sydney H. Schanberg
The "War Hero" Politician Buried Information About POWs Left Behind in Vietnam

139

The report noted:

> In theory, therefore, if a POW still living in captivity [today], were to attempt to communicate by ground signal, smuggling out a note or by whatever means possible, and he used his personal authenticator number to confirm his identity, the US Government would be unable to provide such confirmation, if his number happened to be among those numbers DIA cannot locate.

It's worth remembering that throughout the period when this intelligence disaster occurred—from the moment the treaty was signed in 1973 until 1991—the White House told the public that it had given the search for POWs and POW information the "highest national priority."

■ **Page 13:** Even in the Executive Summary, the report acknowledges the existence of clear intelligence, made known to government officials early on, that important numbers of captured US POWs were not on Hanoi's repatriation list. After Hanoi released its list (showing only ten names from Laos—nine military men and one civilian), President Nixon sent a message on February 2, 1973, to Hanoi's Prime Minister Pham Van Dong, saying: "US records show there are 317 American military men unaccounted for in Laos and it is inconceivable that only ten of these men would be held prisoner in Laos."

Nixon was right. It was inconceivable. Then why did the President, less than two months later, on March 29, 1973, announce on national television that "all of our American POWs are on their way home"?

On April 13, 1973, just after all 591 men on Hanoi's official list had returned to American soil, the Pentagon got into step with the President and announced that there was no evidence of any further live prisoners in Indochina (this is on page 248).

Though I wrote on many subjects for *Life*, *Vanity Fair*, and *Washington Monthly*, my POW articles appeared in *Penthouse*, the *Village Voice*, and APBnews.com.

■ **Page 91:** A lengthy footnote provides more confirmation of the White House's knowledge of abandoned POWs. The footnote reads:

> In a telephone conversation with Select Committee Vice-Chairman Bob Smith on December 29, 1992, Dr. Kissinger said that he had informed President Nixon during the 60-day period after the peace agreement was signed that US intelligence officials believed that the list of prisoners captured in Laos was incomplete. According to Dr. Kissinger, the President responded by directing that the exchange of prisoners on the lists go forward, but added that a failure to account for the additional prisoners after Operation Homecoming would lead to a resumption of bombing. Dr. Kissinger said that the President was later unwilling to carry through on this threat.

When Kissinger learned of the footnote while the final editing of the committee report was in progress, he and his lawyers lobbied fiercely through two Republican allies on the panel—one of them was John McCain—to get the footnote expunged. The effort failed. The footnote stayed intact.

■ **Pages 85–86:** The committee report quotes Kissinger from his memoirs, writing solely in reference to prisoners in Laos:

> We knew of at least 80 instances in which an American serviceman had been captured alive and subsequently disappeared. The evidence consisted either of voice communications from the ground in advance of capture or photographs and names published by the Communists. Yet none of these men was on the list of POWs handed over after the Agreement.

Then why did he swear under oath to the committee in 1992 that he never had any information that specific, named soldiers were captured alive and hadn't been returned by Vietnam?

■ **Page 89:** In the middle of the prisoner repatriation and US troop-withdrawal process agreed to in the treaty, when it became clear that Hanoi was not releasing everyone it held, a furious chairman of the Joint Chiefs of Staff, Admiral Thomas Moorer, issued an order halting the troop withdrawal until Hanoi complied with the agreement. He cited in particular the known prisoners in Laos. The order was retracted by President Nixon the next day. In 1992, Moorer, by then retired, testified under oath to the committee that his order had received the approval of the President, the National Security Advisor, and the Secretary of Defense. Nixon, however, in a letter to the committee, wrote: "I do not recall directing Admiral Moorer to send this cable."

The staff made the following finding, using intelligence reports marked "credible" that covered POW sightings through 1989: "There can be no doubt that POWs were alive…as late as 1989." That finding was never released.

The report did not include the following information: Behind closed doors, a senior intelligence officer had testified to the POW committee that when Moorer's order was rescinded, the angry Admiral sent a "back-channel" message to other key military commanders telling them that Washington was abandoning known live prisoners. "Nixon and Kissinger are at it again," he wrote. "SecDef and SecState have been cut out of the loop." In 1973, the witness was working in the office that processed this message. His name and his testimony are still classified. A source present for the testimony provided me with this information and also reported that in that same time period, Moorer had stormed into Defense Secretary Schlesinger's office and, pounding on his desk, yelled: "The bastards have still got our men." Schlesinger, in his own testimony to the committee a few months later, was asked about—and corroborated—this account.

"According to Dr. Kissinger, the President responded by directing that the exchange of prisoners on the lists go forward, but added that a failure to account for the additional prisoners after Operation Homecoming would lead to a resumption of bombing."

■ **Pages 95–96:** In early April 1973, Deputy Defense Secretary William Clements "summoned" Dr. Roger Shields, then head of the Pentagon's POW/MIA Task Force, to his office to work out "a new public formulation" of the POW issue; now that the White House had declared all prisoners to have been returned, a new spin was needed. Shields, under oath, described the

meeting to the committee. He said Clements told him: "All the American POWs are dead."

Shields said he replied: "You can't say that."

Clements shot back: "You didn't hear me. They are all dead."

Shields testified that at that moment he thought he was going to be fired, but he escaped from his boss' office still holding his job.

■ **Pages 97–98:** A couple of days later, on April 11, 1973, a day before Shields was to hold a Pentagon press conference on POWs, he and Gen. Brent Scowcroft, then the Deputy National Security Advisor, went to the Oval Office to discuss the "new public formulation" and its presentation with President Nixon.

The next day, reporters right off asked Shields about missing POWs. Shields fudged his answers. He said: "We have no indications at this time that there are any Americans alive in Indochina." But he went on to say that there had not been "a complete accounting" of those lost in Laos and that the Pentagon would press on to account for the missing—a seeming acknowledgement that some Americans were still alive and unaccounted for.

The press, however, seized on Shields' denials. One headline read: "POW Unit Boss: No Living GIs Left in Indochina."

■ **Page 97:** The POW committee, knowing that Nixon taped all his meetings in the Oval Office, sought the tape of that April 11, 1973, Nixon-Shields-Scowcroft meeting to find out what Nixon had been told and what he had said about the evidence of POWs still in Indochina. The committee also knew there had been other White House meetings that centered on intelli-

John McCain and the POW Cover-up
Sydney H. Schanberg
The "War Hero" Politician Buried Information About POWs Left Behind in Vietnam

141

gence about live POWs. A footnote on page 97 states that Nixon's lawyers said they would provide access to the April 11 tape "only if the Committee agreed not to seek any other White House recordings from this time period." The footnote says that the committee rejected these terms and got nothing. The committee never made public this request for Nixon tapes until the brief footnote in its 1993 report.

In the numerous, lengthy McCain profiles that appeared during the 2008 campaign in papers like the *New York Times*, the *Washington Post*, and the *Wall Street Journal*, I may have missed a clause or a sentence along the way, but I have not found a single mention of his role in burying information about POWs.

McCain's Catch-22

None of this compelling evidence in the committee's full report dislodged McCain from his contention that the whole POW issue was a concoction by deluded purveyors of a "conspiracy theory." But an honest review of the full report, combined with the other documentary evidence, tells the story of a frustrated and angry President, and his National Security Advisor, furious at being thwarted at the peace table by a small, much less powerful country that refused to bow to Washington's terms. That President seems to have swallowed hard and accepted a treaty that left probably hundreds of American prisoners in Hanoi's hands, to be used as bargaining chips for reparations.

for keeping the truth about this matter hidden. Yet he says he's the right man to be the Commander-in-Chief, and his credibility in making this claim is largely based on his image as a POW hero.

On page 468 of the 1,221-page report, McCain parsed his POW position oddly: "We found no compelling evidence to prove that Americans are alive in captivity today. There is some evidence—though no proof—to suggest only the possibility that a few Americans may have been kept behind after the end of America's military involvement in Vietnam."

"Evidence though no proof." Clearly, no one could meet McCain's standard of proof as long as he is leading a government crusade to keep the truth buried.

The committee also discovered that the DIA, which kept the lists of authenticator numbers for pilots and other personnel, could not "locate" the lists of these codes for Army, Navy, or Marine pilots.

To this reporter, this sounds like a significant story and a long-overdue opportunity for the press to finally dig into the archives to set the historical record straight—and even pose some direct questions to the perennial candidate.

Maybe Nixon and Kissinger told themselves that they could get the prisoners home after some time had passed. But perhaps it proved too hard to undo a lie as big as this one. Washington said no prisoners were left behind, and Hanoi swore it had returned all of them. How could either side later admit it had lied? Time went by and as neither side budged, telling the truth became even more difficult and remote. The public would realize that Washington knew of the abandoned men all along. The truth, after men had been languishing in foul prison cells, could get people impeached or thrown in jail.

Which brings us to today, when the failed Republican candidate for President is the contemporaneous politician most responsible

Mission Rejected: Clifton Hicks
"I'll Be Home Soon"
Peter Laufer

We're sitting at the Holiday Inn in Heidelberg, Germany, just before the Heidelberg Volksfest, and Clifton Hicks is telling me some horrific tales from his time in Iraq. The son and grandson of soldiers, Clifton was not yet nineteen when he found himself working as a gunner on a Humvee on the dusty roads of Baghdad.

"The first time that I really saw some shit go down that really freaked me out, we were driving around at night," he begins to tell me. "There were all these packs of wild dogs all over Baghdad, they chased the Humvees, and they yipped and yapped. This one night the headlights went over a pack of dogs and they're eating something. They were eating a cou-

> "This one night the headlights went over a pack of dogs and they're eating something. They were eating a couple of dead people that had been picked down to the rib cage."

ple of dead people that had been picked down to the rib cage. I was eighteen and a half, had never even been to a funeral before, had never killed anything other than a raccoon or a possum, get grossed out going to a butcher's market or a fish store.

"And here I'm seeing a rib cage, bare. And a bunch of dogs eating it."

For Clifton, being in the Army was the fulfillment of a childhood dream. Born in Jacksonville, Florida, he grew up in Tampa and Savannah before moving back to Tampa when his parents divorced. In early 2003, armed with a high school diploma he earned via correspondence courses, he joined the Army. He always wanted to "be a tanker," to drive a tank and fight in a war. He expected to enjoy a military career as a lifer, through to retirement.

Just weeks after graduating from basic training at Fort Knox, Clifton shipped out to Germany, where he "received some ramshackle training." A couple of weeks later he was on a plane to Kuwait, and then was sent on to Iraq. Within a few more weeks he was driving Humvees and tanks on patrol, and working as a gunner on Humvees. "I didn't know how to use the weapon yet—the machine gun," he says. "But they had me up there gunning on it. I learned pretty quick." For the next ten months he was a gunner on a Humvee and a tank driver in the 1st Squadron, 1st US Cavalry Regiment. "Most of the time I was just standing on the gunner's hatch of a Humvee, looking back and forth."

The duty was mostly a dismal routine for Clifton. "We'd go out and nine days out of ten you'd just be sitting up there and it'd be raining," he recalls. "You'd drive through these flooded streets, and get shit-splashed—literally—I'm talking about shit water with people walking through it. It'd splash in your face and your eyes, and you get sick from it. You're covered in human feces. You're sitting around just bored and miserable, wishing you weren't there. You sing a song or you talk to yourself. Make fun of each other. Let your mind wander. Fall asleep standing up. I would volunteer for night missions. The most dangerous job for a gunner would be a night mission on the tail Humvee. The Humvees go out in pairs, one in front with a guy standing in front, and one in back with a guy watching over the rear. I'd volunteer to do that. It was the most dangerous job; nobody wanted to do it. I would do that at night just so I could go to sleep. I would sit up there on the gun and sleep standing up, the whole four hours. Most of the time it was pure boredom, but every once in a while...."

Seeing the dogs picking at the human rib cage is clearly among his many vivid memories. Clifton looks drawn as we talk; his eyes are piercing when he tells his war stories, as if he is reliving the moments he's describing.

Outside, Heidelberg's perfectly preserved Renaissance neighborhoods bustle with activity in the shadow of its magnificent castle overlooking the Neckar River. Posters for the fair are spotted all around the storybook-looking city, decorated with the American flag and including the English line, WITH A TASTE OF AMERICA, plus the promise, in the hyphenated German style, of the US-ARMY-BAND.

Heidelberg, long a US Army headquarters city and home to one of Germany's important universities, is accustomed to Americans in its midst. Clifton is stationed a couple of hours' drive north, in Büdingen, "a one-horse town, just a horrible place," he says.

During much of Clifton's Iraq tour, the scene was calm when he was on patrol. It was after the initial invasion and before the insurgency developed into a consequential threat to US forces. "There were occasional poorly made explosives on the side of the road; you could usually spot them and get rid of them," he says. "Occasionally some guy would get drunk and decide he wanted to shoot us. He'd go up on his roof and he'd ra-tat-ta-ta-ta-ta-da, and run away. It was like being a police officer in a really bad neighborhood."

Clifton is a good storyteller, and his tough GI lexicon mixes freely with a sophisticated interpretation of his ten months in Iraq. His speech is staccato as he recounts one of the first events that began to turn him against the war.

"We were driving around one night in the Humvees in Baghdad, nothing out of the ordinary," he begins. "We got out there and immediately this drunk guy got pissed off and threw something at the Humvee. I thought it was a hand grenade at first. I was just about to shoot this guy. It was a bottle and broke on the back of the Humvee. I was not going to shoot this guy for throwing a bottle. I was kind of shaken from that."

The patrol continued. And things got worse. "We heard a lot of gunfire up ahead and you could tell it wasn't just a couple AK-47s; it was some US weapons firing back," he recounts. "We knew somebody was in a fight up there. We race ahead down the street, and there's an 82nd Airborne infantry platoon, and they're all parked in their Humvees—about four Humvees packed with guys. There's a house with the lights on, and people are all around the place. There's a big fuss going on.

"We pull up and we say, 'What's going on? We heard some shooting up here.' And they're like, 'Yeah, we got ambushed just now.' They started clearing buildings to find out who was firing at them. They kicked in this first door, and there's a wedding party going on. What they do in Baghdad, when there's a wedding, they shoot into the air. These people were up on their roof, probably a little sauced up, happy there's a wedding, and I guess Grandpa is up on the roof shooting off his rifle at the same time as this 82nd patrol drives by and is engaged by insurgents from a field. They returned fire in both directions, and I think most of them returned fire on the wedding party. They returned fire on the wedding party, and they shot three people, three people at a wedding party. Because somebody was shooting into the air to celebrate, these guys wanted to kill him."

He always wanted to "be a tanker," to drive a tank and fight in a war. He expected to enjoy a military career as a lifer, through to retirement.

Clifton watched as soldiers searched the field for the enemy and found nothing but some AK-47 shell casings. "The insurgents were fine, not a scratch on them. They made it just fine. The innocent people who were partying, just trying to celebrate a wedding, three of them had been shot. One man had been shot in the arm, a girl had been shot in the leg, and one younger girl who was about six was dead—laying on the ground, dead. She was six years old, laying on the ground, face down, palms up, in a little flowery dress. She was stone dead. Mothers and women are all bawling and crying. The men are all standing in shock. We bandaged up the one guy. The one little girl was crying, she was maybe ten, shot in the leg. Everyone is sitting around like, 'Yeah, they fucking killed some little kid.' I'm like, 'What the fuck? That's pretty shitty.'

"The 82nd called it up to their guys, and their command said, 'Charlie Mike [military parlance for "Continue the mission"], just keep going.' They packed up and drove off. So we just hopped in our Humvees and we drove off too.

"And that was the end of it. They applied first aid to the people who had been shot. The girl who was dead, they just left her there on the floor. We drove off and continued the mission."

Clifton looks shell-shocked in the Holiday Inn lobby as he tells the story, distraught and puzzled and disturbed all at the same time. "Continue the mission? I was like, 'What the fuck is that all about?' We're supposed to be here to rebuild this country, to help these people, and we just shot three people. We just killed somebody's daughter. And we drove off. That's never going to be reported in the news. No one is ever going to know about it except people who were there."

The dead girl was the beginning of Clifton's epiphany. After just a few months in the midst of the post-invasion Iraq, he began to question the war. He became convinced the US policy was counterproductive. He saw his role as a waste of time, and he decided to simply work at staying alive until he completed his Iraq tour of duty. He read books sent from home, kept up his diary, and sent some plaintive emails: "Please write and let me know what's going on around home. I'm always worrying in the back of my mind that I'll return home to find everything dramatically changed, that everyone hates me and I've been disowned or some crap."

Finally, departure day arrived for his squadron. They loaded the tanks onto flatbed trucks and drove south to Kuwait. "We crossed the border. The first tank that crossed, they started cheering. And then the next tank cheers. The whole convoy is just screaming and yelling. We're like, 'Yeah! We got the fuck out of there!' We're in Kuwait. We're safe. We can put our weapons down because no one is going to kill us in Kuwait."

The euphoria was short-lived. They enjoyed the relative luxury of the base—"There's a Subway, there's a Baskin-Robbins, there's a damn Pizza Hut, there's a swimming pool," reports Clifton—as they prepared their gear for the trip back to their

135 of our soldiers were killed in April. One of them was a Staff Sergeant who I had met in Germany. We flew into Iraq together side by side on the same C-130. At one point the crew noticed that a guided missile had been fired at us and we all hung on for dear life as the plane banked left and right, discharging its anti SAM [shoulder-to-air missile] thermal flares in a thankfully successful attempt to save our hides.

Staff Sergeant "R" was on top of his tank getting an MRE and some water for his loader (who happened to be a good friend of mine from basic training) when they came under attack. Haj shot an RPG [rocket-propelled grenade] at them, the rocket missed the tank, but it hit SSG. "R" square in the chest and split him right down the middle. The loader (who's name and rank I won't mention at all) jumped up on the loader's M240 and fired into a crowd of civilians who were standing there, killing and maiming a large number of them. He told me that he just "freaked out," I guess he didn't know what else to do.

I myself saw a number of people killed and wounded in Iraq. All but one of them were unarmed Iraqis. The one guy who could be considered an "enemy combatant" blew his own hand off trying to hang mortar rounds on us, but besides him they were all innocent as far as I know. Sometimes they got shot, sometimes they got run over by humvees or tanks. Sometimes they were just laying there dead and nobody knew what had killed them.

"We're supposed to be here to rebuild this country, to help these people, and we just shot three people. We just killed somebody's daughter. And we drove off."

home base in Germany. But it was April 2004, and security in Iraq was deteriorating fast. US forces were struggling in their attempts to contain the growing violent opposition to their occupation. Clifton and the 1-1 Cav were ordered back to Iraq.

It was a brutal time, and Clifton wrote home with details:

The military doesn't like Clifton Hicks, and Clifton Hicks doesn't like the military. That became clear to both sides when Clifton's father posted one of his letters home on the family's blog, where his commanders read it carefully. It was April 2004 when Clifton's fingers flew over the keyboard and punched SEND after composing a diatribe.

First, he described how his unit was in Kuwait after their tour of duty in Iraq, waiting to go home, when they were sent back to Iraq to quell uprisings. Morale, Clifton said, had "plummeted from 'pretty low' to 'non-existent.'" His "elite" unit was the QRF (quick reaction force), which meant whenever "they've got some dirty work, we have to go there." Then Clifton's note revealed some shocking details:

Just got out of some miserable town that had been blown to pieces, 700–900 dead (all "enemies" right?). The battle was over and the bodies cleaned up by the time we got there. It's like being invited to a party when it's already over and when you get there the guy who invited you says, "Here, I need you to clean up all these beer cans for me. Somebody puked in the bathroom too, and can you mow my grass when you're done?" Fuck you General Abizaid.[1] There were a lot of dead cows and horses that we used to zero our weapons, and I ran over a couple cars (on purpose this time). Everyone is so pissed about this stupid crap that they just want to get the anger out. We'd like to spit in the President's face, and tell all the Generals to go fuck themselves, but we can't do that (because the damn cowards aren't here) so instead we take it out on (most likely) innocent Iraqis. Running over cars, or even throwing trash on the side of the road makes you feel good. It's really fun to take a shit in an MRE [Meals Ready to Eat] bag and throw it out to the people who are begging for food, who then fight over it. That's not even the worst that I've seen or done. The whole thing is disgusting.

So basically that's all we're doing. They sent us back to help fix Iraq, but all any of us are doing is trying to have fun, mostly at the expense of the country we are supposed to be helping. Congratulations you stupid Generals, what an excellent plan. I guess I sound really bitter and pissed off, and I guess I am, but now I've progressed past that, I've detached myself, because that's the only way you can get by without losing it and doing something stupid. We had a platoon meeting today and they told us about our new mission and how much it was going to suck, everyone else looked like they'd just seen Old Yeller bite the dust but I was smiling because me and Slater were going to watch The Goonies (for the second night in a row) on his DVD player afterwards. I've learned to pay more attention to the simple pleasures rather than the

complex miseries which occupy my current existence. There's no sense in being miserable about it, I was depressed for a few days, was even thinking about shooting a hole through my foot or something stupid like that, but it passed.

Anyhow, it's almost midnight here and I've got about a mile hike to get home so I must be going. Please send me mail!

Once Clifton's Army commanders read that letter, he suffered a Field Grade Article 15, charged with OPSEC—operations security—violations and disrespecting officials and superior commissioned officers, which, he says, "nearly landed me in jail for treason and dishonorably discharged."

He woke up one morning as his commanding officers kicked his cot. "They told me to get the fuck up. They had this big stack of papers in front of me with my name all over it." It was material from the blog, criticism of the military and the mission. "Stuff I had written. They read the whole thing to me." He acknowledged that the words were his. "They were going to throw me in jail for treason. They were going to kick me out of the Army." Instead he lucked out with a slap: demotion to private, a fine of some $800, and a couple of months' extra duty. His response to the punishments was to file for conscientious objector (CO) status.

"I myself saw a number of people killed and wounded in Iraq. All but one of them were unarmed Iraqis."

Clifton survived the redeployment, and once back in Germany he filed an AR 600-43, his official application to be discharged from the Army as a conscientious objector. His statement on the form was succinct: "It is against my moral and religious beliefs to take human life under any circumstances; I am opposed to war in any form. As long as I live, I will never attempt to kill another living person. I am seeking classification as a conscientious objector and separation from the military."

The form requires the applicant to explain how his beliefs changed or developed, and Clifton noted his deadly experiences in Iraq, such as the inadvertent assault on the wedding party. He detailed an event when his patrol in Baghdad came under fire. "I identified where the firing was coming from and returned fire, the enemy firing stopped immediately and nothing more became of it, the incident was never reported. This was a major turning point in my life, I was thoroughly repulsed by what I had done and prayed that I would never have to try to kill a fellow human being again."

> "It's really fun to take a shit in an MRE [Meals Ready to Eat] bag and throw it out to the people who are begging for food, who then fight over it."

Clifton summed up his position with a preemptive written strike against any critics who would dismiss his CO application as a device to attempt an early discharge from the Army. "There are those who remain skeptical of my claims; I am thought of by some of my superiors as a liar, an idiot, and a coward. They and those who think alike are entitled to their beliefs, just as I am entitled to mine. If only they knew how much honesty, intelligence and courage it takes to pursue such beliefs, thus enduring the persecution and hatred of such a multitude of naysayers. My actions in the past and at present have well proven that I am not a coward, for a coward will never do what he believes to be right when those around him say that he is wrong, he will simply be bullied into submission. I expect that none of us would have found ourselves in disagreement with Abraham Lincoln when he said, 'To sin by silence when they should protest makes cowards of men.' I intend to live my own life in a way that will affirm the lives of others, not destroy them."

Not that Clifton was counting on the Army to approve his CO application. "If I don't get it? I have other avenues of approach to get home," he tells me. "I've told them I am not going to go back to Iraq." He says he'd rather go to prison than back to the war. "It won't come to that, though, because I think I'm too smart for that to happen to me. Civil disobedience is an option—just refuse to put the uniform on. Maybe a hunger strike. There's all kinds of things you can do. It's looking like they'll approve it. But if they don't, I have Plan B, Plan C, all the way up to desertion."

He exhibits calm about his circumstances. He's made up his mind. "It's not that I won't go back," he says about Iraq, "it's that I *can't* go back. I just hate that place so much. The sad thing is that I hate those people. I hate the reason we're there." He's spitting the words out now. "The whole place is just so foul. It's a cesspool of pure evil. The insurgents are evil, but we're evil too. The insurgent who's killing me, he's being used just like I am. They say these guys are mindless—look at us. Shit, we joined up too. We're both volunteers fighting each other. Once we volunteer, we can't leave. We become conscripts. We're just pawns. We're being used."

It's a war, says Clifton Hicks, fought for "filthy rich bastards too cowardly to do it themselves" who want more money, fought by "us, the masses of uneducated fools killing each other."

> "It is against my moral and religious beliefs to take human life under any circumstances; I am opposed to war in any form. As long as I live, I will never attempt to kill another living person."

■ ■ ■ ■ ■ ■ ■ ■ ■ ■

Early in November 2005, I received a celebratory email from Clifton. "I just found out that my [CO] application has been approved and I've been recommended for honorable discharge by the Commanding General." The note starts out like a dry recitation of the facts, with no emotion. "So I'm good to go I guess," and he adds, "I'll be home soon." And then a line of understated reflection, "It's been a really tough period in my life." And finally a cry of relief, "I nearly fell over like a sack of potatoes when they gave me the news, I could hardly contain myself!"

Endnote

1. General John Abizaid was Central Command's [CENTCOM] commander-in-chief while Clifton Hicks served in Iraq.

Dear Deluded Mass Media, North American Union Agenda Exists

Alex Jones and Steve Watson

The media campaign to deny the reality of the move towards a North American Union—a merging of the economies of the United States, Canada, and Mexico in the same vein as the European Union—continues with a sharp focus on attacking Texas Congressman (and overachieving 2008 Republican presidential candidate) Ron Paul, who has spoken about the move on numerous occasions.

The North American Union issue came to the fore in late 2007 when Congressman Paul was sardonically asked during the CNN GOP debate if he believed in it, as his many supporters have suggested he does.

Dr. Paul put the record straight by explaining that it is ludicrous to call the very real NAU movement a conspiracy theory.

"The CFR [Council on Foreign Relations] exists, the Trilateral Commission exists," Paul explained. "And it is a, quote, 'conspiracy of ideas.' This is an ideological battle. Some

> The linchpin of the North American Union is a cross-border North American Free Trade Agreement (NAFTA) super-highway that stretches from southern Mexico, through the United States, and up to Montreal, Canada.

people believe in globalism; others believe in national sovereignty. And there is a move on toward a North American Union, just like early on there was a move for a European Union that eventually ended up. So we have NAFTA and a move toward a NAFTA highway; these are real things."

Despite Ron Paul's explanation, and despite overwhelming and manifestly provable evidence to support his assertions, the hacks at CNN spent much of their post-debate coverage attacking the Congressman on the issue as if he were insane.

Congressman Paul has reiterated that plans for the NAU and an accompanying highway exist in reality despite the continued mind-numbing denials by the federal government and the mainstream media.

The linchpin of the North American Union is a cross-border North American Free Trade Agreement (NAFTA) superhighway that stretches from southern Mexico, through the United States, and up to Montreal, Canada.

The organization overseeing the implementation of the highway is NASCO, North America's SuperCorridor Coalition Inc., which describes itself as a "non-profit organization dedicated to developing the world's first international, integrated and secure, multi-modal transportation system along the International Mid-Continent Trade and Transportation Corridor to improve both the trade competitiveness and quality of life in North America."[1]

NASCO has received $250 million in earmarks from the US Department of Transportation to plan the NAFTA Super Highway as a 10-lane, limited-access road (five lanes in each direction), plus passenger and freight rail lines running alongside pipelines laid for oil and natural gas. One glance at the map of the NAFTA Super Highway as produced by NASCO makes it clear that the design is to connect Mexico, Canada, and the US into one transportation system.

Toll roads are to be placed upon existing roads in so-called Security Prosperity Partnership agreements that bypass Congress, agreements between the bureaucracies of the US and Mexican governments, to raise capital to build the super highway that will travel south of the American border in Texas and into Mexico.

Security Prosperity Partnership documents reveal that out of 85 interstate highways, 83 are slated to fall under this agreement, and toll roads are being created on them already. The money from this operation will further fund the dismantling of US sovereignty by seizing the infrastructure at its very heart in a bloodless coup.

The highway is to be linked to the Trans-Texas Corridor, the first leg of the highway, which will connect Mexico with the United States. This is being overseen by the Texas Department of Transportation (TxDOT), a member of NASCO.[2]

The NAFTA corridor movement also involves CANAMEX, another trade organization that promotes a Western trilateral route utilizing I-19, I-10, I-93, and I-15 in the states of Arizona, Nevada, Utah, Idaho, and Montana to link the three countries in trade.

Another non-profit group, the North American Forum on Integration (NAFI), identifies four bands of NAFTA corridors

> The North American trade corridors are bi- or tri-national channels for which various cross-border interests have grouped together in order to develop or consolidate the infrastructures. The North American corridors are considered multimodal in the sense that they bring into play different modes of transport in succession.
>
> The infrastructures may include roads, highways, transit routes, airports, pipelines, railways and train stations, river canal systems and port facilities, telecommunications networks and teleports.[3]

The architects of this unification are not just merging the agencies and the laws and the regulations in name only—they are physically getting rid of the borders by buying off and lobbying the politicians at the state level, who then hand the roads over to international bodies and their subsidiary companies.

NASCO has received $250 million in earmarks from the US Department of Transportation to plan the NAFTA Super Highway as a 10-lane, limited-access road (five lanes in each direction), plus passenger and freight rail lines running alongside pipelines laid for oil and natural gas.

In January 2007, it was reported that one of the foreign toll-road conglomerates, Macquarie Group of Australia, had agreed to buy dozens of newspapers in Texas and Oklahoma that were, until then, harsh critics of the Trans-Texas Corridor super-highway.[4] This indicates a clear

(Pacific, West, East, and Atlantic), all relying primarily upon internationalizing existing north-south interstate highways into NAFTA trade corridors.

The NAFI website states the following:

> Following the implementation of NAFTA, coalitions of interest have been formed in order to promote specific transport channels, to develop the infrastructures of these channels and to propose jurisdictional amendments to facilitate the crossing of borders. These coalitions include businesses, government agencies, civil organizations, metropolitan areas, rural communities and also individuals, wishing to strengthen the commercial hubs of their regions.

example of influence-peddling pointing to racketeering, and a desperate lunge to silence dissent against the sellout of American infrastructure and the formation of a North American Union.

The further incontrovertible evidence for a NAU agenda is so abundant that one could write volumes on the subject.

President Bush, Mexican President Vicente Fox, and Canadian Prime Minister Paul Martin signed the initial Security and Prosperity Partnership agreement on March 23, 2005, in Waco, Texas. It established working groups, under the North American Free Trade Agreement office.[5]

Security and Prosperity Partnership (SPP) documents released under the Freedom of Information Act (FOIA) show that a wide range of US administrative law is being rewritten in stealth under this program to "integrate" and "harmonize" with administrative law in Mexico and Canada, just as has become commonplace within the EU.[6]

The documents contain references to upwards of thirteen working groups within an entire organized infrastructure drawn from officials within most areas of administrative government, including the US Departments of State, Homeland Security, Commerce, Treasury, Agriculture, Transportation, Energy, and Health and Human Services, and the office of the US Trade Representative.[7]

Further documents from a 2006 SPP meeting in Banff, Alberta, which were obtained by Judicial Watch under the Freedom of Information Act, refer to an "evolution by stealth" agenda for the SPP, explaining that Congress and the American people would not willingly go along with such a move.[8]

This stealth agenda has also been carefully pointed out in a Hudson Institute White Paper entitled *Negotiating North America: The Security and Prosperity Partnership*:

> The most important feature of the SPP design is that it is neither intended to produce a treaty nor an executive agreement like the NAFTA [North American Free Trade Agreement] that would require congressional ratification or the passage of implementing legislation in the United States. The SPP was designed to function within existing administrative authority of the executive branch.[9]

The paper also states "mobility across the border is central to the idea of an integrated North American economic space." The Hudson White Paper also reminds us that the 2005 Council on Foreign Relations (CFR) document called *Building a North American Community* bragged that its recommendations are "explicitly linked" to SPP.[10] The CFR document called for establishing a "common perimeter" around North America by 2010, the development of a biometric North American border pass, and the adoption of a North American tariff.

Further, the CFR report revealed that the group wants to "establish private bodies that would meet regularly or annually to buttress North American relationships, along the lines of the Bilderberg conferences."[11] (Bilderberg members are the power brokers behind the formation of the EU and the single European currency.)

During the secretive SPP meetings, an advisory council cre-

Security and Prosperity Partnership (SPP) documents released under the Freedom of Information Act (FOIA) show that a wide range of US administrative law is being rewritten in stealth under this program to "integrate" and "harmonize" with administrative law in Mexico and Canada, just as has become commonplace within the EU.

ated in 2006—known as the North American Competitiveness Council—met on issues including border regulation and competitiveness in the automotive, transportation, manufacturing, and services sectors.[12] The Council is expected to meet annually with security and prosperity ministers and will engage with senior government officials on an ongoing basis.

A 2007 SPP meeting in Canada also saw the US Army enforcing a huge 25-kilometer (15-mile) security perimeter, as well as cracking down on protests, barring the media, and shutting down public forums in the vicinity of the event.[13]

Eighteen states have introduced resolutions calling on their federal representatives to halt work on the North American Union (they include Virginia and South Carolina). Three of these states (Idaho, Montana, and Oklahoma) have passed their resolutions.

Oklahoma, which is in the path of the superhighway component of the North American Union, passed its resolution 97–0 in the State Senate.

This came after it was revealed that the Mayor of Oklahoma City, with the approval of 90 other officials, signed a document endorsing an economic and political integration of the US with Canada and Mexico.[14]

Twenty-two US Congressmen, including North Carolina's Virginia Foxx and Walter Jones, along with all three Republican Congressmen running for the presidency in 2008, signed on as cosponsors of H.Con.Res 40,[15] calling on the executive branch to end all work on the North American Union and the proposed superhighway.

Even the Sierra Club of Canada is sounding the alarm against the North American Union.[16]

The standardization and centralization of policy into a North American Union framework is very real, a fact we personally came face to face with in 2007 when our office received a letter from the Texas Workforce Commission demanding that we provide business information for the purposes of assigning a North American Industry Classification System (NAICS) code to our location.

The NAICS website—located within the US Census Bureau's website—reveals:

> The North American Industry Classification System has replaced the US Standard Industrial Classification (SIC) system. NAICS will reshape the way we view our changing economy.
>
> NAICS was developed jointly by the US, Canada, and Mexico to provide new comparability in statistics about business activity across North America.

The fact that we received this letter and that businesses across America are being forced to submit census information for the purposes of registration in a North American database that includes Mexico and Canada is no "conspiracy theory"—it's another documented step on the road to full harmonization and integration. (According to the NAICS website, the US agencies implementing the NAICS are the Census Bureau, the Internal Revenue Service, the Bureau of Labor Statistics, the Bureau of Economic Analysis, and the Small Business Administration.)

The planned introduction of the amero, a pan-American currency often lambasted as a conspiracy theory, is common knowledge amongst all financial analysts worth their salt. Steve Previs of Jeffries International talked about it on a CNBC segment in November 2006, saying it's "the one thing that

nobody's talking about that I think is going to have a big impact on everybody's life in Canada, the US, and Mexico."[17]

In November 2007, renowned money manager Stephen Jarislowsky told a parliamentary committee in Canada that "we

Former Mexican President Vicente Fox himself admitted the plan for a North American "euro-dollar" currency during an appearance on *Larry King Live* in October 2007.

have to really seriously start thinking of the model of a continental currency just like Europe," as he advocated the creation of a North American currency to replace the Canadian dollar, the US dollar, and the peso.[18]

American University professor Robert Pastor, one of the architects of the plan for a regional government, has authored a book (*Toward a North American Community*) and speaks at confabs in front of governmental officials, promoting the adoption of the amero as a common monetary currency to replace the dollar and the peso.

Former Mexican President Vicente Fox himself admitted the plan for a North American "euro-dollar" currency during an appearance on *Larry King Live* in October 2007.[19]

A new wave of media attacks came on the back of a *Boston Globe* piece entitled "The Amero Conspiracy," the latest in a long line of public relations stunts on behalf of the establishment to attempt to hoodwink Americans into thinking that the NAU is crackpot conspiracy fodder on a par with Bigfoot, when in reality a plan for merging the Americas is on the record and its proponents have long bragged about their goal to destroy US sovereignty in pursuit of world government.[20]

The ultimate goal, to bring together the Pan American Union, the Asian Union, and the European Union into a structure of world government, is also often scoffed at by the media as another conspiracy theory, but the agenda to end US sovereignty in the interests of centralizing global power is a concept that has been pushed forward by elitists for decades, and their intentions to continue to do so are on the record.

Here are just a handful of quotes from top power brokers attesting to that fact, as well as warnings from those who oppose it.

"In the next century, nations as we know it will be obsolete; all states will recognize a single, global authority. National sovereignty wasn't such a great idea after all." —Strobe Talbot, who became President Clinton's Deputy Secretary of State, as quoted in *Time* magazine, July 20, 1992.

"If instant world government, Charter review, and a greatly strengthened International Court do not provide the answers, what hope for progress is there? The answer will not satisfy those who seek simple solutions to complex problems, but it comes down essentially to this: The hope for the foreseeable lies, not in building up a few ambitious central institutions of universal membership and general jurisdiction as was envisaged at the end of the last war, but rather in the much more decentralized, disorderly and pragmatic process of inventing or adapting institutions of limited jurisdiction and selected membership to deal with specific problems on a case-by-case basis…. In short, the 'house of world order' will have to be built from the bottom up rather than from the top down. It will look like a great 'booming, buzzing confusion,' to use William James' famous description of reality, but an end run around national sovereignty, eroding it piece by piece, will accomplish much more than the old-fashioned frontal assault." —Richard N. Gardner, in *Foreign Affairs*, April 1974.

"Ultimately, our objective is to welcome the Soviet Union back into the world order. Perhaps the world order of the future will truly be a family of nations." —President George Bush, Texas A&M University, 1989.

"There does exist and has existed for a generation, an international…network which operates, to some extent, in the way the radical right believes the Communists act. In fact, this network, which we may identify as the Round Table Groups, has no aversion to cooperating with the Communists, or any other groups and frequently does so. I know of the operations of this network because I have studied it for twenty years and was permitted for two years, in the early 1960s, to examine its papers and secret

records. I have no aversion to it or to most of its aims and have, for much of my life, been close to it and to many of its instruments. I have objected, both in the past and recently, to a few of its policies…but in general my chief difference of opinion is that it wishes to remain unknown, and I believe its role in history is significant enough to be known." —Professor Carroll Quigley, in his book *Tragedy and Hope* (1966).

"The Trilateral Commission is intended to be the vehicle for multinational consolidation of the commercial and banking interests by seizing control of the political government of the United States. The Trilateral Commission represents a skillful, coordinated effort to seize control and consolidate the four centers of power, political, monetary, intellectual and ecclesiastical. What the Trilateral Commission intends is to create a worldwide economic power superior to the political governments of the nationstates involved. As managers and creators of the system, they will rule the future." —US Senator Barry Goldwater in his book *With No Apologies* (1979).

Every time the agenda for full political and economic integration is advanced one step further, whether by treaties, lawfully binding agreements, or rhetoric about what the next step will be, the establishment media steps in to scoff at such patently observable developments and label them "conspiracy theories."

Other media hit pieces against the North American Union "conspiracy" seem to hinge on the notion that the globalists pushing for it don't call it a "union" but a "community."

We have seen articles in a variety of major publications that exactly mirror each other in denying the existence of the NAU. The establishment media has promoted this consistent hoax and repeatedly engaged in mass public deception.[21]

This tactic of smearing anyone who attempts to raise the issue and to categorically deny reality comes directly from those who are pushing the NAU.

Some media hit pieces surmise that the entire subject of the North American Union is an urban myth that "feeds on American fear of immigration and globalization." Other media hit pieces against the North American Union "conspiracy" seem to hinge on the notion that the globalists pushing for it don't call it a "union" but a "community." This is akin to when David Rockefeller dismissed the notion that he was aiding the creation of a global government, instead asserting only that he believed in "global governance." The media are basically ninnying about how many angels can dance on the head of a pin.

Whatever you want to call it, a plan for political, economic, and social integration of the Americas is afoot, and it is being rammed through with little or no say from Congress or the American people.

However, as the old saying goes, any kind of publicity is good publicity. The rapid move toward a North American Union is finally attracting mainstream attention, as witnessed by the increased effort on behalf of the corporate media to deny its reality and implement the usual technique of branding it a myth or baseless conspiracy theory. As the attacks become more pronounced, the clearer it will become that the move toward a NAU is a very real prospect.

Endnotes

1. NASCO website <www.nascocorridor.com>. **2.** "Trans-Texas Corridor" <keeptexasmoving.com/index.php/ttc>. **3.** North American Forum on Integration website <www.fina-nafi.org/eng/integ/corridors.asp>. **4.** Halyard Capital press release. (2007). Halyard Capital sells American Consolidated Media for $80 million to Macquarie Media Group. PR Newswire, 24 Jan; Corsi, Jerome R. (2007). Texas newspapers sold to Australian interests. WorldNetDaily, 29 Jan. **5.** White House Office of the Press Secretary. (2005). Joint statement by President Bush, President Fox, and Prime Minister Martin. 23 Mar. **6.** Unsigned. (2006). Documents disclose "shadow government." WorldNetDaily, 26 Sep. **7.** Documents obtained by Judicial Watch <www.judicialwatch.org/archive/2006/SPPFOIADocsSecl.pdf>. **8.** Documents obtained by Judicial Watch <www.judicialwatch.org/archive/2007/POLADBoltonNotesBanff.pdf>. **9.** Anderson, Greg, and Christopher Sands. (2007). *Negotiating North America: The Security and Prosperity Partnership*. Hudson Institute, summer. **10.** *Ibid*. **11.** Manley, John P. (2005). *Building a North American community*. Council on Foreign Relations. **12.** Leadlay, Christina. (2007). Meet the powerful business members of the North American Competitiveness Council. *Embassy* (*Canada's foreign policy newsweekly*), 13 Jun. **13.** Watson, Steve. (2007). Military to crackdown on North American Union protesters. InfoWars.net, 25 Jul. **14.** Watson, Paul Joseph. (2007). No "conspiracy theory": OKC Mayor signed North American Union document. InfoWars.net, 25 Jul. **15.** H.Con.Res. stands for House Concurrent Resolution. This type of measure must pass both the House and Senate but does not become public law. **16.** Eaton, Janet M., Ph.D. *Threats to our water: NAFTA, SPP, super-corridors, Atlantica*. Sierra Club Canada. **17.** Interview with Steve Previs. (2006). CNBC, 27 Nov. Video available at YouTube and Google Video. **18.** Chase, Steven, (2007). Consider a continental currency, Jarislowsky says. *Globe and mail* (Toronto), 23 Nov. **19.** Watson, Paul Joseph. (2007). Vicente Fox admits plan for single NAFTA currency. InfoWars.net, 9 Oct. **20.** Lane, Tim. (2007). The amero conspiracy. *Boston globe*, 25 Nov. **21.** Watson, Steve. (2007). Debunkers deny existence of NAU, JFK conspiracy. InfoWars.net, 22 May; Ratcliffe, R.G. (2007). Perry's push for highway raises conspiracy buzz. *Houston chronicle*, 18 Aug; Sanchez, Marcela. (2007). Stop, stop! A North American Union! *Washington post*, 13 Jul.

Colony Kosovo
Not So Pretty
Christian Parenti

Choked by almost 800,000 souls, Pristina, Kosovo, a city of tower blocks rising from a parched valley floor, now holds twice as many people as it was built for. The air reeks of exhaust and burning garbage. All day a hot wind blows ghostly airborne litter and clouds of gritty dust from the huge mountain of mine tailings that lies a dozen miles due west. At night one still hears the snap of gunfire and the next day, rumors of another unsolved murder.

Despite the city's hyper-modernist aesthetic (the place was rebuilt from scratch after an earthquake in 1963), Pristina has no public transportation nor any systematic refuse collection.

Water and electrical services are intermittent, but several cybercafes and brothels operate around the clock.

All the most impressive modernist buildings of the downtown now stand as bombed-out relics. Adding to the *Blade Runner* feel of the place are throngs of cellphone-wielding crowds and streams of new Mercedes and Audis that clog the streets below the charred towers. Water and electrical services are intermittent, but several cybercafes and brothels operate around the clock.

Welcome to ground zero of NATO's reincarnation of what Secretary of State Madeline Albright has called "a force for peace from the Middle East to Central Africa."

Billed by almost all media, right-wing and liberal, as the greatest humanitarian intervention since World War II, the UN/NATO occupation of Kosovo doesn't look so noble up close. Rather than a multiethnic democracy, Kosovo is shaping up to be a violent, corrupt, free-market colony erected on the foundation of a massive lie.

The first fact to establish is this: Despite the shrill and frantic cries about genocide that paved NATO's road to Kosovo, forensics teams from Spain and the FBI found less than 2,500 bodies. As it turned out, this was the total body count from the Serbs' brutal, but hardly genocidal, two-year counterinsurgency campaign against the KLA. A horror and a brutal war fueled by ethnic hatred on all sides? Yes. Genocide? No.

Humanitarian Imperialism

The Albanians here may talk about "their country," but foreign aid workers in official, white SUVs call the shots. After NATO's 78-day bombing—done with radioactive, depleted-uranium-tipped ordnance—the United Nations Mission in Kosovo (UNMIK) was created to act as an "interim administration." The UN in turn has opened Kosovo to a kaleidoscopic alphabet soup of subsidiary governmental and nongovernmental organizations ranging from Oxfam to obscure evangelical ministries. All municipalities and state agencies are run by UN personnel or UN appointees, and deutsch marks are the legal tender.

At the apex of it all sits Bernard Kouchner, the Secretary General's Special Representative in Kosovo. Founder of Médecins Sans Frontiéres and a former socialist, Kouchner took a sharp right in the 1980s when he began to champion the use of Western (particularly American) military intervention to

Rather than a multiethnic democracy, Kosovo is shaping up to be a violent, corrupt, free-market colony erected on the foundation of a massive lie.

protect human rights. Kouchner's left-wing critics—who correctly point out that American and European corporate and military power are the main causes of human rights violations internationally—see Kouchner as a Clinton-Blair "third way" hypocrite. Meanwhile many mainstream right-wing commentators cast the wiry Frenchman as a publicity-seeking autocrat.

In Kosovo, Kouchner's responsibilities range from censoring the local press when it offends him, to appointing all local government personnel, to unilaterally ditching the Yugoslavian dinar for the mark. Adding muscle to these sorts of executive caprice are about 4,000 so-called UNMIK police, many of whom are transplanted American cops. For the really heavy lifting, Kouchner counts on the 40,000 international soldiers that make up KFOR—the Kosovo Implementation Force.

"This place is a shithole. All the young people I meet, I tell 'em: Get out! Go to another country."

Along with putting down the occasional ethnic riot, protecting convoys of refugees, and guarding the few small Serb enclaves remaining in Kosovo, KFOR and the UNMIK police occasionally uncover caches of weapons that belong to the officially disarmed Kosovo Liberation Army. Such operations are usual followed up with robust statements by KFOR spokespeople reaffirming their commitment to "building a multiethnic society." Strangely, the ethnic cleansing—this time Albanian against Serb and Roma (Gypsies)—never stops.

Violence Still

"This is an amazing place. The people are so resilient, so creative. I've made so many friends," enthuses an American aid worker named Sharon who is helping to set up an Albanian radio station. When asked about the continuing Albanian-on-Serb violence, she chalks it up to the Albanian culture of revenge feuds. It's a typical dismissal, but not all internationals approach the issue with such equanimity.

"This place is a shithole. All the young people I meet, I tell ' em: Get out! Go to another country," booms Doc Giles, a tanned, muscled American cop who speaks in a thick south Jersey accent. A longtime narc-officer from hyper-violent Camden, New Jersey, Giles has spent the last year working homicide in Pristina with UNMIK. The pack on his bike sports a "Daniel Faulkner: fallen not forgotten" button. (Faulkner was the cop that death-row inmate and journalist Mumia Abu Jamal may, or may not, have murdered eighteen years ago in Philadelphia.)

Giles' maggot-eye view of inter-ethnic relations is sobering:

"Look, all the perps are oo-che-kaa," says Giles, using the Albanian form for the Kosovo Liberation Army's acronym. "They're fucking gangsters. I don't care what anyone says—they're an organized crime structure. And all the judges are either scared or pro-KLA. They're like: You shot an 89-year-old Serb grandmother? Good for you. Get out of jail."

Of the province's 276 judges, only two are Serb, so Albanian hit squads operate with near total impunity. Among their favorite targets during the last year have been Orthodox churches and monasteries, over 85 of which have been burned, looted, or demolished according to both the UN and a detailed report by the Serbian Orthodox Church.

By the end of one of Giles' rants about fifteen-year-old Maldovan girls "turned out" as prostitutes and KLA thugs ganging-up on their Serb and Roma victims five-to-one, you'll almost agree with his proscription: "What they should've done was put this place under martial law, get a bunch of American cops from cities like Philly, Dallas, and Denver to come in here and just kick the shit out everyone for a few months. Then turn it over to your NGO's, or whatever."

Terrified merchants also tell stories of KLA thuggery. "Ten percent. They take ten percent of everything you make. And you pay or it's kaput," says a hushed and nervous restaurateur in Prizren, an ancient town near the Albanian border. He's a Kosovar Turk whose great-grandparents probably moved here during the twilight of the Ottoman Empire, but when he gets enough money he says he's taking his two children to Canada.

Privatization

While Giles and his comrades recycle Albanian "perps" through a non-working judicial system, the UN's paper-pushers and its partner organizations are hard at work trying to turn Kosovo into a free-market paradise.

"We must privatize so as to secure investment and new technology. There is no alternative," explains Dianna Stefanova, director of the European Agency for Reconstruction's office on privatization, which is working under the auspices of UNMIK and Kouchner.

"They're like: You shot an 89-year-old Serb grandmother? Good for you. Get out of jail."

There's only one problem with this plan: The industries located in Kosovo are not UNMIK's to privatize. Nor does the wording of Security Council resolution 1244—the document defining the UN's role in Kosovo—give UNMIK the power to sell off local industries. And when Kouchner made his pitch for mass privatization to the Security Council in late June, he met stiff opposition from the Russians.

Bizarrely, resolution 1244 recognizes Kosovo as an integral province of Yugoslavia. So technically the dinar should be the currency, trials should proceed according to Yugoslavian law, Yugoslav officials should be free to travel and should control the borders, and Yugoslav state assets shouldn't be sold by the UN.

To get around the awkward parts of resolution 1244, Kouchner has devised a useful bit of legerdemain. The UN isn't actually selling off assets—they are just offering ten- and fifteen-year leases to foreign transnationals. The first industry to go was the huge Sharr Cement factory, leased to the Swiss firm Holderbank. "Sharr could produce all the cement needed for reconstruction and even export to Macedonia," explains Roy Dickinson, a privatization specialist with the European Agency for Reconstruction.

The next assets on the block are a series of vineyards and wine cooperatives, but the ultimate prize is the gargantuan Trepca mining and metallurgical complex that sprawls across northern Kosovo and into the mountains of southern Serbia. Since Roman times, foreign armies have targeted these massive mineral deposits. Hitler took Trepca in 1940, and thereafter the mines—some of the richest in the world—supplied German munitions factories with 40 percent of their lead inputs.

Trepca contains all of Yugoslavia's nickel deposits and three-quarters of its other mineral wealth; during the 1990s the 42 mines and attendant factories were one of Yugoslavia's leading export industries.

The Belgrade government and a private Greek bank that has also invested in the mines insist that Trepca shall not change hands. The UN isn't so sure. "The question of who gets what will be settled by a panel of judges that UNMIK is still setting up," says a coy Stefanova. In the meantime UNMIK is drawing up plans to downsize local industries and streamline enterprise so as to make them more attractive to foreign investors. But there's another piece of the equation: Who controls the land above the mines? That of course brings us back to the issue of ethnic cleansing.

Balkan Belfast

The swift and shallow river Ibar, bisecting the town of Mitrovica, is the front line in an unfinished war that pits Albanians against Serbs and Roma. All non-Albanians have been expelled from south of the Ibar, and all Albanians driven from its northern bank. Thus crossing into north Mitrovica is much like entering Serbia: The language, the music, and the beer are all Serbian, and people use the dinar. This is also the heart of the Trepca complex.

Here, despite occupation by French troops, the Belgrade government still pays salaries and pensions and still provides health care. And if even a fraction of UN and KFOR accusations are true, then some of the hard men with mobile phones who lounge

"We're in a prison, and under attack."

at the Dolce Vita Cafe on the banks of the Ibar are probably undercover cops from Serbia (some of whom, you will recall, have been indicted by the International Tribunal on War Crimes at the Hague and could be arrested by KFOR).

"We're in a prison, and under attack. What you see is all we have," says a young Serb Branislav who is hanging out near a north Mitrovica newsstand selling Serbian papers. "If I cross that bridge I'll be killed." This, it seems, is the future: An ethnically "pure" and therefore "stable" Albanian Kosovo in the south, with huge NATO installations like the sprawling 775-acre American base, Bondsteel, which hosts 4,000 GIs on the plains of Kosovo's southeast. While in the north, astride some small part of the Trepca mines, and in a few other spots, Serb and Roma ghettos will remain, possibly as parts of Serbia. In the places where these communities overlap, there will be trouble and therefore "humanitarian work" for NATO troops and, thus, a plausible—and more importantly, palatable—reason for the West to maintain its long-term military presence.

Moral Imperialism and the Iron Logic of War

Stan Goff

"A revolution is not a dinner party, or writing an essay, or painting a picture, or doing embroidery; it cannot be so refined, so leisurely and gentle, so temperate, kind, courteous, restrained and magnanimous. A revolution is an insurrection, an act of violence by which one class overthrows another."

—Mao Zedong, from *Report on an Investigation of the Peasant Movement in Hunan*, March 1927

"Unfortunately, the class struggle does not always pit a plucky guerrilla band in white hats against a villainous Uncle Sam, in some kind of latter-day version of Robin Hood. Far more often you end up with a much more complex drama involving shades of gray. If your sole criteria for offering solidarity to those struggling against imperialism is morality blended with esthetics, it is very easy to lose your way."

—Louis Proyect, 2003

Acteal, Mexico, 1997:

It began in a church. The quiet tension of the occupied territory was broken by automatic weapons fire. Lives were extinguished, and lives next to them were changed forever with the instantaneous absence of friends, relatives, parents, children. Life was reduced to the inescapable right-now and the necessity to run. Mourning was slammed into a box in the heart, deferred until survival was secure. Running blindly down the dirt streets, between houses of clay and straw, with the dry metal taste of terror in their mouths, one after another fell from the physical shock of tissue cavitation, shattered bone, shredded organs, the personal Armageddon of high-velocity ammunition.

The Chiapas Rebellion entered a new phase in Acteal, December 22, 1997.

Since the uprising of Mexico's southern indigenous peoples in 1994, around 500 murders had been committed against rebels, rebel sympathizers, and those suspected of being sympathizers. But the massacre at Acteal was a qualitative escalation. Foreigners were expelled to rid the terrain of witnesses.

The relative circumspection of the rebel operations, the astonishing initial successes they had against shocked government troops, and the gnome-like, charismatic spokesperson for the rebels, known as Subcomandante Marcos, had given the rebellion a mystique. Chiapas had become a *cause célèbre* in left-liberal circles in the United States and around the world. The David-and-Goliath tenor of the conflict is partly responsible for the popularity of the rebellion. But another reason the rebellion has been embraced by many has been the ability of the rebels to defend a certain moral high ground, refraining from the more brutal and repugnant activities of war. They shed little blood, and thereby avoided the kinds of crossfires, military and political, where everyone is transformed into a combatant.

Until Acteal.

The last century was filled with examples of what happened in Chiapas in 1998, the marriage of violence and capital. The 45 massacred Tzotzil civilians represented a deliberate escalation of hostilities designed to attain the objectives of the Mexican political patriarchs who ordered the attack. Much attention would be paid to the phony investigation that the federal government conducted,[1] and to Jacinto Arias Cruz, mayor of Chenalho, who was accused with 23 others of perpetrating the action. Little attention was paid to the net result of this and smaller actions; the land which produces the wealth, and which the rebellion was designed to preserve for its original inhabitants, was then "willingly" vacated. Mission accomplished.

The government had agreed in 1996 to refrain from sending government representatives or armed forces into Acteal and environs. Pure fraud. Government-tolerated death squads did the job much more efficiently with terror, terror sponsored by the economic elite that needed to liberate the capital locked in the rich coffee lands upon which these bothersome Indians resided. History should have taught us, and the Zapatistas, that a belief that the invisible captains of the land-grab might be reformed or contained is a pious fantasy. They would destroy the indigenous rebels, or the rebels would destroy them.

The action of December 23, wherein the 45 terrified residents of Acteal met their extinction, was the next logical step for the ruling class in Mexico. And their logic was as clean and cold as a scalpel. That is why the Zapatistas could no longer afford circumspection and restraint, except at the service of a logic as cold and calculating as their enemy's. The struggle had moved to another level. They would make war, real war, or they would be systematically dismantled as a viable force.

Hesitation under these circumstances would be fatal. The rebels had to fight. To fight, they would need weapons, many weapons, and ammunition, and communications equipment… all the luggage of war. There is only one way for an isolated force with no outside sponsorship to acquire that materiel. When I worked in Special Forces, it was called "battlefield recovery." They would have to wage frequent, audacious, and deadly assaults on small police and military elements simply to seize their weapons and equipment.

The people they would have to destroy would have families, parents, grandparents, spouses, and children. The starkest reality of war is that the enemy is never really a monster, never inhuman. Warriors have often tried to reduce their foes to subhumans to prop up their denial, but the fact is the enemy is someone who dreams, someone who loves, someone who just needed a job, someone who is just waiting for a break to take a leak or eat his supper: a full-fledged human just like us.

To conduct such operations would require central coordination and the refinement of a general staff to both direct operations and determine the disposition of new troops and equipment. They needed to become an even more disciplined, secretive, decisive, vigilant force. The only principles they would be capable of embracing in every situation would be the principles of war. They would cease looking like pastoral heroes and begin to gain the hard edges of soldiery.

History should have taught us, and the Zapatistas, that a belief that the invisible captains of the land-grab might be reformed or contained is a pious fantasy.

They would encounter spies, collaborators. Those must be dealt with summarily and ruthlessly. Failure to do so would result in loss of security and therefore the loss of precious combatants. Mistakes would be made. If and when victory approached, seasoned combatants would have committed excesses. Every soldier is the same fallible breed of human that we are. The making of war, even the most necessary and "just" war, hardens human hearts. War has its own internal logic, one that is icily cruel and impervious to refinement.

These warriors would have no nation to which they might appeal for aid. The Soviet Union and the Cuba that provided support for African national liberation fights and the Soviet-Chinese-Vietnamese partnerships that supported the latter's anti-colonial struggle are no more.

The rebels of Chiapas now depended upon the outside world, in the most critical way, for solidarity in their political struggle. More than anything, they needed us to understand the necessity of what they would have to do. They needed international recognition and unwavering support for the ultimate justice of their fight, a solidarity that would weather the brutality into which they were being inexorably pulled to secure that justice.

And they choked. Neither they nor their international base had the will for what was necessary.

■ ■ ■ ■ ■ ■ ■ ■

The paramilitaries were organized by Grupo Aerotransportado de Fuerzas Especiales (GAFE), a Mexican Special Forces group trained at the School of the Americas and the JFK Special Warfare School in Ft. Bragg, and were materially assisted by members of the Guatemalan military—who maintain close ties to the US foreign policy establishment as well. The massacre was portrayed as "senseless," but my point is that military operations, when they are successful, are anything but senseless. Acteal had a purpose. The purpose was to accelerate the depopulation of key terrain in the conflict area, and it worked very well.

The tiny, ineffectual remains of the Zapatista military force are now confined in the Lacondon (forest), cut off from all outside lines of communication, encircled and effectively neutralized. This cannot be romanticized away. It is a fact on the ground.

Just to remain fair, however, it is important to point out that military success is not measured in linear ways. It's not a football game. It has to be measured against political objectives, and the Zapatistas have always been a reformist movement. They never sought military victory or state power. This

The making of war, even the most necessary and "just" war, hardens human hearts. War has its own internal logic, one that is icily cruel and impervious to refinement.

accounts for their popularity even in some chic metropolitan coffee houses where class war is anathema.

It also accounts for their incremental destruction as a guerrilla movement.

An interesting read on this comes from the 1995 US Army Command and General Staff College publication *Insurrection: An Analysis of the Chiapas Uprising*, by Major Grady G. Reese, US Army. It is an extremely well-documented account of the insurrection up to the time of the report with a great deal of detail, albeit with a scrupulous evasion of the informal connections between landowners, political structures, the *guar-*

dias blancas, and the Mexican armed forces. The US military hates talking about political stuff. We all hate talking about our weaknesses.

From the executive summary:

> The Zapatista Army of National Liberation (EZLN) limited its objectives to the betterment of the Indian condition. The desired end-state was an Indian community with a greater share of the national wealth. Not wanting to necessarily overthrow the central government, the Zapatistas were deliberate in designing their strategy to force the government into negotiations. Their military operations supported the strategic objectives until they made the error of trying to capture Rancho Nuevo. The EZLN leadership timed the campaign well. The greatest strategic error was to underestimate the readiness of the government to negotiate. At the point that the government declared a unilateral cease-fire, the EZLN lost the strategic initiative.

The Mexican government, under the Partido Revolucionario Institucional (PRI) and Vicente Fox, played a decade-long game of diplomatic and military bait-and-switch with the Zapatistas. Political concessions have been repeatedly made then abrogated, and with each high-publicity withdrawal of the official Mexican armed forces from Chiapas, Guerrero, and Oaxaca, more substantial and less legally constrained paramilitary forces—composed of former *guardias blancas* and PRI paramilitaries, among others, now integrated with the armed forces—have filled the void. The Zapatistas are allowed to march by the thousands on Distrito Federal unmolested, and the *chilangos* welcome them as folk heroes, but in Chiapas, they have been slowly squeezed into the mountains and encircled. Viable Zapatista military forces were cut off from their popular base, and that base, subjected to intense military and economic pressure, including forced dislocation, has broken out into a series of interethnic rivalries. All that remains for the Mexican government now is to seize the moment when international political support for the EZLN is diverted or neutralized.

Armed struggle has to be weighed carefully against political objectives. As the Reese paper indicates, without itself fully grasping its own implications, a political objective short of the seizure of state power can fence in combatants and cause them to lose that intangible with the greatest material force in war—initiative.

There is a naïve and dangerous faith among people of good will in the churches and coffeehouses and campuses of America and Europe that "righteousness" will win out. Failing to grasp the full context of the nonviolent struggle against British colonialism in India and against Jim Crow in the US, where neither could have happened except against the backdrop of a well-armed socialist bloc, there is an ahistorical faith in nonviolent resistance, combined with moral imperialism, which leads progressives to distance themselves from aggressive armed resistance. Support for the Zapatistas has been so broad precisely *because* the EZLN has limited its objectives and avoided combat. Liberals and many anarchists are down with that. For entirely different reasons, each of these constituencies opposes any contest for state power. This is lethal when it is the state that is bent on your extermination. And it's why I'm not and never will be a progressive.

The charm of the Zapatistas has been their refusal to engage in any but defensive operations and their scrupulous avoidance of Marxist rhetoric. They have become the "good guerrillas," as opposed to the Fuerzas Armadas Revolucionarias Colombianas–Ejercito del Pueblo (FARC-EP) in Colombia, who are now seen by limousine liberals and parlor socialists as the "bad guerrillas."

The Zapatistas' refusal to engage in offensive operations, to ramp up their political objectives from reform to revolution, and with it all the implications regarding military objectives is the central error that is leading to their political defeat—no matter its PR value, no matter what *moral* high ground it gains them.

One cannot defend oneself against an unleashed army from "moral" high ground. One needs *real* high ground—as in key terrain—and one needs cover and concealment, well-covered avenues of approach, well-appointed automatic weapons, appropriate tactics, and reliable logistics. The Mexican government has all but won, and Zapatista allies here can do little but wail and fume and cling to their denial.

When any conflict, regardless of its social and political content, escalates to war, war itself asserts a stark logic. All other objectives are sublated into the choice between destroying the enemy's capacity and will to fight or perishing as a viable military

> There is a naïve and dangerous faith among people of good will in the churches and coffeehouses and campuses of America and Europe that "righteousness" will win out.

force. Military operations are shaped and directed by political objectives—a fact the US military has yet to grasp in all its complexity—but the conduct of war is brutally physical. It is the desolate and hideous application of physical laws to the project of open and absolute destruction. When a people or a movement is the target of that destruction, it must employ the same cold pragmatism in its defense, or it will drown in its own blood.

I once saw a little plaque in English on the desk of a South Korean general. It said, "God favors the strong." Those who are strong can be patient. But strength in war is not solely determined by mass or technology. The great guerrilla leaders have shown that *initiative* is the key. When you have it, you are ahead, and when you lose it, you are behind.

Reese again:

> The military performed well in supporting the national strategy. It mobilized and deployed rapidly. It used combined arms in joint operations and quickly gained the initiative. The success of operations in the field allowed the government to pursue a negotiated settlement from a position of relative strength.

Warfare is a temporal process. Time matters. Speed matters. Getting inside your enemy's decision-making cycle and seizing the initiative matters. Taking the offensive matters. There is no due process. There are no time-outs.

And there is no perfection.

Armed forces, both oppressive and liberatory, are organizations that, once committed to active combat, must administer themselves, supply themselves, train themselves, protect themselves, and replace themselves…by any means necessary, *while in the conduct of inherently chaotic conflict*. With what is available. Here is where an established state military is different from the guerrilla. The guerrilla cannot go to the state with its hand out. The guerrilla has no recognized courts or well-funded press with which to legitimize itself in the eyes of well-fed foreigners. And the guerrilla, once committed, cannot stop.

One cannot defend oneself against an unleashed army from "moral" high ground.

Failure to escalate quickly and to consolidate and expand guerrilla control in the wake of Acteal has spelled a complete loss of battlefield initiative. The Zapatistas are no longer a viable military force. Their "armed struggle" is now utterly symbolic.

Let me compare that to the FARC-EP.

Like the Zapatistas, the FARC-EP began in a struggle for land. After World War II, Colombian liberals supported the development of several peasant self-defense militias that clamored for land redistribution and limited autonomy. By the FARC-EP's own account, they employed a strategy that is eerily similar to that of the EZLN: an armed resistance, combined with appeals for national and international solidarity.[2] The war became far more brutal, on both sides, and the Colombian government offered a negotiated settlement in 1952. This offer of diplomacy was accepted by the Liberal Party and by their followers among the militia.

But a small group of peasants led by peasant communist Pedro Antonio Marin refused to stand down. Marin had none of the coffeehouse charm of Subcomandante Marcos, but he had a hard head for military matters. He would have understood Mao's little essay on Hunan peasants very well.

Like the Zapatistas, the FARC-EP began in a struggle for land.

When you do what is necessary, you will be called "terrible," and you will have "gone too far." "No revolutionary comrade should echo this nonsense,"[3] said Mao. Yet many still do.

Marin was convinced of the duplicity of the government, including the Liberals, and he continued to organize self-defense units among the peasantry. So effective did these militias become that the government began to refer to peasant communities as "independent communist republics," and in 1964—with urging from the US government—launched a sudden and unprecedented attack against the peasant militia at Marquetelia.

Marin, who had since changed his name to Manuel Marulanda Vélez, led the successful resistance to this massive military assault *with 48 guerrilla fighters*.

Thereafter, this guerrilla band took the name Feurzas Armadas Revolucionarias Colombianas. Marulanda, who put a high premium on marksmanship as a core skill for guerrillas, and who was himself legendary for his skill with a rifle, became affectionately known as Tiro Fijo, or Sureshot.[4]

The FARC recognized that the battle had been decisively engaged and that there was no turning back. The struggle would now end with state power or defeat. They launched one audacious attack after another and perfected the ability to quickly concentrate and then diffuse their forces, massing for quick strikes, then disappearing in small teams back into the countryside, delivering one pinprick tactical victory after another, acquiring materiel and recruits along the way.

I have been questioned as to whether I really believed the FARC is winning. I do. From this 48-person core, they have grown into a 20,000-strong political and military organization, on seven regional fronts, in more than 60 independently maneuverable military organizations. In the past two years, they have decimated the paramilitaries, destroying at least 10 percent of their forces (probably substantially more). They have survived and counterattacked one of the most well-financed military offensives in this hemisphere, even after losing the *despeje*, or autonomous demilitarized zone, when the Pastrana government was pressured by the right wing in Colombia (and the US Embassy) to scrap peace talks.[5]

Without US aid to the ever more-fascistic Colombian government, the FARC would achieve state power in less than five years, and that's conservative. The paramilitaries are neither the FARC-EP's equal on the battlefield, nor do they command any loyalty from the population. And the Colombian armed forces are largely conscripts, led by a venal and corrupt officer corps suffering the daily stings of class resentment and blistering racism. The FARC-EP is racially diverse, and 30 percent female.

Without air support from the US and its surrogates there, the Colombian armed forces cannot match the FARC's military prowess, and they have no popular base outside the urban petit-bourgeois and ruling classes.

The metropolitan anticommunist left are now claiming that the FARC has evolved into some kind of authoritarian monstrosity that now oppresses the people just like the government, or that it has become some criminal enterprise, or that it fails to bargain in good faith. They are now "terrible" and have "gone too far." This is a classic case of the left falling for the slanders of the mainstream press, assisted in their fall by the "bourgeois right" (as opposed to wrong, not left), or moral imperialism—the convenient morality of the fed and the fat in the imperial cores who've never known war and who never tire of telling all those brown people what the right thing is to do.

The FARC stood down from the armed struggle in 1984, forming an electoral wing called the Patriotic Union (UP), calling a truce, and agreeing to engage in electoral politics. Four thousand UP members were summarily assassinated by death squads. This was their one flirtation with the "bourgeois right." They are in a war, and they understand the iron logic of war, especially after 1984.[6]

In 2002, after the Colombian military was ordered into the *despeje*, where their offensive fizzled out, paramilitaries began a savage campaign against civilians around Bojaya. The Colombian armed forces secured passage of the parmilitaries into the area. The paramilitaries were met by a surprise counteroffensive from the FARC, who killed over 500 paramilitaries, losing approximately 130 guerrillas, mostly due to support from the Colombian military in the form of an attack helicopter and one fixed-wing aircraft. Paramilitaries fell back on the pueblo of Bojaya, taking up positions around a public health center and a church. The FARC fired an expedient mortar that fell short

onto the church, where civilians had taken refuge from the fighting, and killed dozens of those inside.

When this was reported, it was not reported by the mainstream press as a battle between the FARC and the paramilitaries. It was not reported that the paramilitaries were bent on violence against the civilians there. Military complicity was not reported. The huge tactical defeat of the paramilitaries was not reported. The FARC mortar attack that destroyed the church and killed the civilians inside was reported, not as the unintentional loss of civilian life in combat, but as a FARC massacre.[7]

The FARC admitted the terrible error, as they have consistently done. They have studied the assassinated Cape Verdean revolutionary Amilcar Cabral, who warned comrades to "mask no difficulties, mistakes, failures."[8]

Weapons, equipment, and "the luggage of war" might be provided to the imperial soldier, but it must be gained through "battlefield recovery" by most insurgents, and in some cases improvised like the propane mortars used by the FARC. They will not be perfect or standardized weapons and equipment. Frontline soldiers, logicians, medical cadre, commanders, and staffs are recruited (or conscripted) from the finite pool of people in areas of operation; all are trained with the resources and skill sets available, and all of those lost to attrition must be replaced. They will inevitably be people of varying native ability, varying consciousness, varying motivations, varying character, and they will perform in variable and unpredictable ways. They will not operate with perfect oversight from top to bottom. And the situations at the bottom will never be clear to the top, and far less clear to those who are outside the armed conflict altogether.

Over time, including the coherence of the political program behind the organization, the strategy, the discipline, the agility and flexibility, the resources, the quality of intelligence, the soundness of the tactics, the leadership skills, and, last but

> When you do what is necessary, you will be called "terrible," and you will have "gone too far."

> The FARC stood down from the armed struggle in 1984, forming an electoral wing called the Patriotic Union (UP), calling a truce, and agreeing to engage in electoral politics. Four thousand UP members were summarily assassinated by death squads.

certainly not least, the sheer size of the organization, will emerge through these other daily doses of overdetermination and leave a victor.

So when we judge the armed struggles of the left around the world, we need to be mindful of Sherman's statement that "war is cruel and cannot be refined." No commander worth a damn can ever measure decisions using the ethical tools of peacetime. Either the struggle is worth a war or it is not. We can't

Either the struggle is worth a war or it is not.

have it both ways. The political goal is paramount, not the accolades of pacifists in the imperial centers, not the approval of liberal media, not the blessing of those who should be allies but who are not there and cannot comprehend the urgency that sometimes leads to terrible mistakes, sometimes even crimes.

So I will say this about the Zapatistas and the FARC-EP. At the end of the day, the difference between the two, aside from which is condoned or condemned by those outside the conflict, is that one is winning and one is losing…because one understands the iron logic of war, and the other does not.

Endnotes

1. Amnesty International. (1998). *The Acteal massacre.* Index AMR 41-43-98. **2.** International Commission of the FARC-EP. (2000). *FARC-EP: Historical outline.* $14.00 payable to "Historical Outline" to PO BOX 69051, Toronto, Ontario, M4T 3A1, Canada. In Canada this includes shipping. US orders in US dollars. **3.** Tse-tung, Mao. Report on an investigation of the peasant movement in Hunan. In *Selected works of Mao Tse-tung*, vol. I. (Peking: Foreign Languages Press, 1975), pp 23–9. **4.** *Ibid., FARC-EP: Historical Outline.* **5.** Vargas Meza, Ricardo. (1999). *The Revolutionary Armed Forces of Colombia (FARC) and the illicit drug trade.* Washington Office on Latin America. **6.** Giraldo, Javier. (1996). *Colombia: The genocidal democracy.* Monroe, Maine: Common Courage Press, p 68. **7.** Colombia Watch. (2002). Army, paramilitaries implicated in Bojaya tragedy. May. **8.** Cabral, Amilcar. (1979). *Unity and struggle.* New York: Monthly Review Press.

2002, 3 ISRAELI SOLDIERS ARE SHOT ON THE EGYPTIAN BORDER.

THESE SOLDIERS ARE NOT JEWS.

THEY ARE BEDOUIN.

BEDOUIN ARE A RACIALLY DIVERSE ETHNIC GROUP. THEY CAN BE DARK OR LIGHT.

THEY ARE UNITED BY A COMMON CULTURE.

BEDOUIN BLUES

BEDOUIN ARE THE INDIGENOUS PEOPLE OF THE NEGEV DESERT. IN THE PAST, THEY WERE SEMI-NOMADIC, MAKING SEASONAL MIGRATIONS BETWEEN THIER LANDS.

BY SETH TOBOCMAN, WRITTEN WITH THE HELP OF DEVORAH BROUS

You Are Still Being Lied To

THE BEDOUIN GRAZED SHEEP & GREW CROPS IN THE NEGEV FOR GENERATIONS. MANY HAVE DEEDS TO THIS LAND.

1948, ZIONISTS DECLARED THE STATE OF ISRAEL, BEDOUIN BECAME ISRAELI CITIZENS.

IN FACT, MANY BEDOUIN JOINED THE ISRAELI ARMY TO SHOW THEIR LOYALTY.

ISRAEL RESTRICTED BEDOUIN TO THE ZONE OF ENCLOSURE 20% OF BEDOUIN LAND.

1960s AFTER 18 YEARS, THE BEDOUIN WERE ALLOWED TO LEAVE THE ZONE.

ISRAEL TRIED TO PUSH THEM INTO

NEWLY BUILT TOWNS.

THE TOWNS ARE SLUMS WITH FEW JOBS.

SOME BEDOUIN STILL LIVE IN THE NEGEV, MAINTAINING HUMBLE VILLAGES IN THE DESERT.

Beduoin Blues

Seth Tobocman

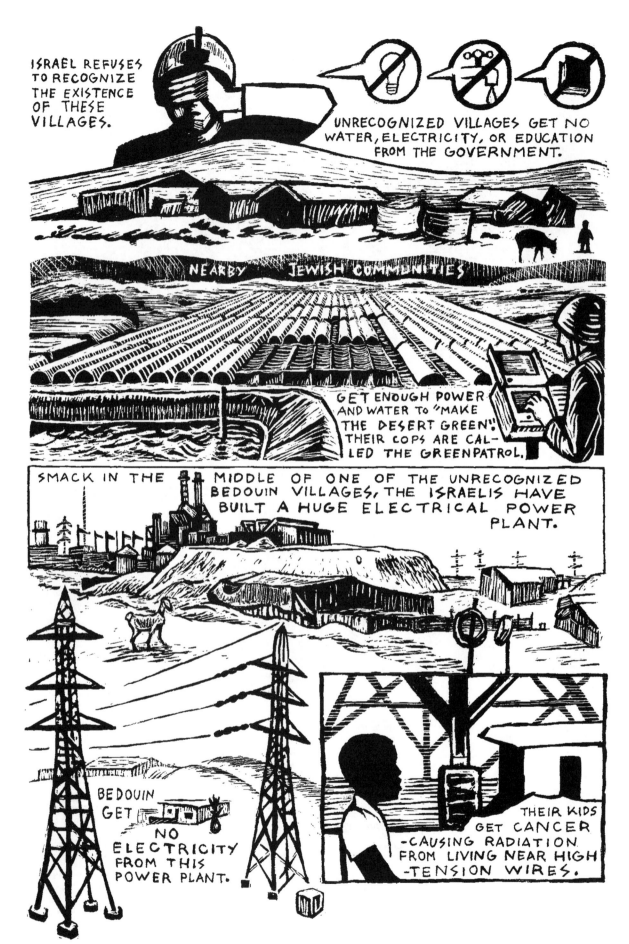

ISRAEL REFUSES TO RECOGNIZE THE EXISTENCE OF THESE VILLAGES.

UNRECOGNIZED VILLAGES GET NO WATER, ELECTRICITY, OR EDUCATION FROM THE GOVERNMENT.

NEARBY JEWISH COMMUNITIES

GET ENOUGH POWER AND WATER TO "MAKE THE DESERT GREEN" THEIR COPS ARE CALLED THE GREEN PATROL.

SMACK IN THE MIDDLE OF ONE OF THE UNRECOGNIZED BEDOUIN VILLAGES, THE ISRAELIS HAVE BUILT A HUGE ELECTRICAL POWER PLANT.

BEDOUIN GET NO ELECTRICITY FROM THIS POWER PLANT.

THEIR KIDS GET CANCER-CAUSING RADIATION FROM LIVING NEAR HIGH-TENSION WIRES.

NEARBY, ISRAELIS HAVE BUILT A TOXIC WASTE DUMP.

THE GREEN PATROL SPRAYS HERBICIDES TO KILL BEDOUIN CROPS. THE GAS ALSO CHOKES BEDOUIN CHILDREN.

IN SPITE OF ALL OF THIS, BEDOUIN REFUSE TO LEAVE THEIR LAND IN THE NEGEV.

SO THE ISRAELI GREEN PATROL BULLDOZES BEDOUIN HOMES.

THE LAND IS CLEARED AND GIVEN TO THE JEWISH NATIONAL FUND WHO "MAKE THE DESERT GREEN".

THIS NEW GREEN LAND IS THEN USED TO BUILD HOUSING FOR ISRAEL'S GROWING JEWISH POPULATON.

ISRAEL CLAIMS THAT ITS HUMAN-RIGHTS VIOLATIONS ARE DONE IN SELF DEFENSE AGAINST TERRORISM.

BUT WHAT ACTS OF VIOLENCE DO THE BEDOUIN COMMIT AGAINST ISRAEL?

Beduoin Blues

Seth Tobocman

OFFICIAL VERSIONS

How the People Seldom Catch Intelligence

(Or, How to Be a Successful Drug Dealer)

Preston Peet

For me, one could write about lies from morning till night, but this is the one most worth writing about, because the domestic consequences are so horrible; it's contributed to police brutality, police corruption, militarizations of police forces, and now, as we speak, it contributes to the pretext for another Vietnam War.

—Peter Dale Scott, July 24, 2000

This is a sordid history of lies and outright criminality by sections of the US government, mainly by its military and intelligence forces (ignoring the more common and mundane corruption amongst domestic law enforcement and their anti-narcotics operations), which is continuing right through today. Blatant business procedure for decades at the very least, the practice of working with drug traffickers, enabling their profitable business dealings to continue, is only picking up speed as the foreign invasions, entanglements, and covert operations by the US increase year by year since the September 11th terrorist attacks. While linking the War on Terror with the seemingly endless War on Some Drugs, the hypocrisy of our government propping up the cartels and narcotics warlords who support US foreign policies—as the US justice system simultaneously continues arresting, trying, and incarcerating Joe Citizenry for buying, selling, and using the very same drugs our "allies" and so-called protectors traffic into the country—is stark.

"I See Nothing!" Said the Man

On May 11, 2000, the US House Permanent Select Committee on Intelligence made public their "Report on the Central Intelligence Agency's Alleged Involvement in Crack Cocaine Trafficking in the Los Angeles Area."[1] The investigation by the

HPSCI focused solely on the "implications" of facts reported in investigative reporter Gary Webb's three-part exposé in the *San Jose Mercury News* titled "Dark Alliance." Published on August 18, 19, and 20, 1996, the series alleged that a core group of Nicaraguan Contra supporters formed an alliance with black dealers in South Central Los Angeles to sell cocaine to the Bloods and Crips street gangs, who turned it into crack. The drug profits were then funneled back to Contra coffers by the Contra supporters.

DEA agent Celerino Castillo in front of his major Operation Condor tool, a chopper.

One would have to intentionally ignore the copious amounts of evidence of drug trafficking sanctioned, protected, or simply ignored by the CIA, even in LA, that exists in the public record.

Approved for release in February 2000, the HPSCI report states the Committee "found no evidence" to support allegations that CIA agents or assets associated in any way with the Nicaraguan Contra movement were involved in the supply or sale of drugs in the Los Angeles area. Utilizing a not-so-

> "I've got them [CIA] personally involved in 18 counts of drugs trafficking. I've got them on three counts of murders of which they personally were aware, that were occurring, and to make a long story short, I [also] came out with money laundering, three or four counts."

subtle strategy of semantics and misdirection, the HPSCI report seeks to shore up the justifiably crumbling trust in government in the US and elsewhere. But the report is still a lie.

One would have to intentionally ignore the copious amounts of evidence of drug trafficking sanctioned, protected, or simply ignored by the CIA, even in LA, that exists in the public record. The HPSCI spent its entire "investigation" disregarding sworn testimony and government reports, even ignoring what agents on the ground at the scene have to say.

An Eyewitness Strongly Disagrees, Says: "It Is a Flat-Out Lie"

A Vietnam veteran, the DEA's lead agent in El Salvador and Guatemala from 1985 to 1990 was Celerino Castillo, who documented massive CIA-sanctioned and -protected drug trafficking, and illegal Contra-supply operations at Illapango Airbase in El Salvador. Asked what he thought of the HPSCI report, Castillo said, "It is a flat-out lie. It is a massive cover-up. They completely lied, and I'm going to prove that they are lying with the case file numbers. I was there during the whole thing."[2]

After participating in a historic CIA-Drugs Symposium held in Eugene, Oregon, June 11, 2000,[3] Castillo decided to go back through his notes, journals, and his DEA-6's—the biweekly reports he'd filled out at the time—to see just how many times his records didn't match the "not guilty" verdict of the HPSCI report. "I've got them [CIA] personally involved in 18 counts of drugs trafficking. I've got them on three counts of murders of which they personally were aware, that were occurring, and to make a long story short, I [also] came out with money laundering, three or four counts."[4]

Among the cases Castillo describes in his scathing written response to the HPSCI report—full of DEA case file numbers and Narcotics and Dangerous Drugs Information System (NADDIS) numbers—is that of drug trafficker Francisco Rodrigo

Guirola Beeche, who has two DEA NADDIS jackets, and is documented in DEA, CIA, and US Customs files. On February 6, 1985, Guirola flew out of Orange County, California, "in a private airplane with three Cuban-Americans. It made a stop in South Texas where US Customs seized $5.9 million in cash. It was alleged that it was drug money, but because of his ties to the Salvadoran death squads and the CIA he was released, and the airplane given back."[5] In other words, the government kept the money, and known drug trafficker Guirola got off with his airplane.

(As we shall later show, these incidents of CIA-connected, drug-laden planes getting busted as their occupants get off scot-free, are not limited to the Iran-Contra era. These sorts of happenings continued throughout the 1990s, right through to today, with connections to some of the major events of the past nearly eight years since this article was first published in 2001, including some extremely disturbing ties to the September 11th attacks.)

Celerino Castillo, DEA agent and anti-drug police, with General G.C. Walter Andrade of Peruvian anti-drug police, in 1984.

In May of 1984, Guirola had gone with Major Roberto D'Abuisson, head of the death squads in El Salvador at that time, to a highly secret, sensitive, and as it turns out, successful meeting with former Deputy Director of Central Intelligence Vernon Walters. "Walters was sent to stop the assassination of [then] US Ambassador to El Salvador, Thomas Pickering."[6] The CIA knew Guirola, and knew him well. The HPSCI report notes that John McCavitt, a senior CIA official in Guatemala and El Salvador at the time, "rejects forcefully" the idea that there was CIA involvement in trafficking in either country, and that he told the Committee that Illopango Airport in El Salvador hadn't been used as a narcotics trans-shipment point by Contra leaders.[7] But Castillo documented Guirola less than a year after the arrest in South Texas, flying drugs, cash, and weapons in and out of Illopango Airfield, out of hangers Four and Five, run respectively by Oliver North/Gen. Richard Secord's National Security Council (NSC) Contra-supply operation, and the CIA.[8] There's no sign of Guirola within the entire 44-page HPSCI report.

The CIA Practice of Recruiting Drug-Financed Armies

Prof. Peter Dale Scott also wrote a response to the HPSCI report, in which he says that "this latest deception cannot be written off as an academic or historical matter. The CIA's practice of recruiting drug-financed armies is an on-going matter."[9] He wasn't exaggerating then, and still isn't today, as we will later cover when discussing current operations in Afghanistan.

A Professor Emeritus at the University of California-Berkeley, a prolific author, and a Canadian diplomat from 1957 to 1961, Scott has spent years studying and reporting on drug-trafficking connections and activities on the part of the CIA and other US government agencies. Knowing that the HPSCI report is full of lies and misrepresentations, Scott is at a loss as to how this report could have been authorized for release by the Committee, voicing serious concerns about the staff of the HPSCI.

Professor Peter Dale Scott
PHOTO BY PRESTON PEET

"Well, they were headed by this guy who just committed suicide [Chief of Staff John Millis], who not only was ex-CIA, he'd actually been working with Gulbuddin Hekmatyer in Afghanistan [as part of CIA covert operations assisting in the fight against the Soviets in the late 1970s and early 1980s, while Hekmatyar moved tons of opium and smack]. He may not have known about the Contra-drug connections, but he certainly knew about some CIA-drugs ties. I don't think it was an accident that they picked someone from that area to sit over the staff either. I mean, this was one of the most sensitive political threats that the CIA had ever faced."[10] John Millis, a 19-year veteran of the CIA, was found dead of "suicide"

in a dingy hotel room in Vienna, Virginia, just outside of Washington, DC, June 3, 2000—less than a month after the release of the HPSCI report.

The CIA released its own report, the Hitz Report, in two parts—Volume 1 in January 1998 and Volume 2 in October 1998[11] (within hours of the vote by Congress to hold impeachment hearings over Clinton's lying about a blowjob). It examined the allegations of the CIA protecting, facilitating, and directly participating in drug trafficking. There were numerous examples contained therein, particularly in Vol. 2, of just how much the CIA really knew about the drug trafficking of its "assets" during the Contra support operations, and *admitted to knowing*. But by the time the report was released to the public, the major news outlets—"the regular villains," as Scott calls them—had already denigrated the story for two years, attacking and vilifying Gary Webb, instead of investigating the facts themselves.

"The *Washington Post*, the *New York Times*, and the *Los Angeles Times* all insisted that the Contra-cocaine was minor, and could not be blamed for the crack epidemic. As the government investigations [Hitz/CIA and DoJ] unfolded, however, it became clear that nearly every major cocaine-smuggling network used the Contras in some way, and that the Contras were connected—directly or indirectly—with possibly the bulk of cocaine that flooded the United States in the 1980s," wrote Robert Parry, one journalist who has covered this story extensively from the very start.[12]

"This has been the case since the beginning," says Scott.[13] "The strategy of how to refute Webb is to claim that he said something that in fact he didn't say. The Committee didn't invent this kind of deflection away from the truth; they just followed in the footsteps of the *New York Times* and the *Washington Post*, and they in turn may have been following in the footsteps of the CIA to begin with, but I don't know. The Committee was originally created to exert Congressional checks and restraints on the

There were numerous examples contained therein, particularly in Vol. 2, of just how much the CIA really knew about the drug trafficking of its "assets" during the Contra support operations, and *admitted to knowing*.

> Fred Hitz, then–Inspector General of the CIA, had already testified to US Representatives at the sole Congressional hearing on the first half of this report, Hitz Vol. 1, that the CIA had worked with companies and different individuals that it knew were involved in the drug trade.

intelligence community, in accordance with the spirit of the Constitution. For some time it has operated instead as a rubber-stamp, deflecting public concern rather than representing it."[14]

Allegedly as a result of the mainstream press' vilification of him, and the subsequent utter destruction of his career as an award-winning journalist, Webb committed "suicide" on December 11, 2004, by shooting himself in the face, twice. In the days leading up to Webb's suicide, as reported by Alex Jones and Paul Joseph Watson, "Credible sources who were close to Gary Webb have stated that he was receiving death threats, being regularly followed, and that he was concerned about strange individuals who were seen on multiple occasions breaking into and leaving his house before his apparent 'suicide' on Friday morning." "Freeway" Rick Ross, Webb's primary source for the "Dark Alliance" series, told Kevin Booth during a phone interview that during conversations just prior to his so-called suicide, that Webb told him "that he had seen men scaling down the pipes outside his home and that they were obviously not burglars but 'government people.'" Ross also told Booth that Webb said he'd been receiving death threats and was regularly being followed. Ross said Webb was working on a new story about the CIA and drug trafficking. Webb told Ross the men he saw around his home were "professionals," who "jumped from his balcony and ran away when Gary confronted them."[15]

CIA/DoJ Memorandum of Understanding

On Saturday, October 10, 1998, anyone watching CNN in the morning might have caught a brief mention of the release of the Hitz Report, Vol. 2. CNN reported that the CIA acknowledged it knew of at least 58 companies and individuals involved in bringing cocaine into the US and selling cocaine to US citizens to help fund the Contra war in Nicaragua, while they were working for the CIA in some capacity.

March 16, 1998. Fred Hitz, then–Inspector General of the CIA, had already testified to US Representatives at the sole Congressional hearing on the first half of this report, Hitz Vol. 1, that the CIA had worked with companies and different individuals that it knew were involved in the drug trade.[16] I.G. Hitz went on to say that the CIA knew that drugs were coming into the US along the same supply routes used by and for the Contras, and that the Agency did not attempt to report these traffickers in an expeditious manner, nor did the CIA sever its relationship with those Contra supporters who were also alleged traffickers.

One of the most important things Hitz testified to was that William Casey, Director of the CIA under President Ronald Reagan, and William F. Smith, US Attorney General at that time, in March 1982 signed a "Memorandum of Understanding" in which it was made clear that the CIA had no obligation to report the allegations of trafficking involving "non-employees." Casey sent a private message to A.G. Smith on March 2, 1982, in which he stated that he had signed the "procedures," saying that he believed the new regulations struck a "…proper balance between enforcement of the law and protection of intelligence sources and methods…."[17] This was in response to a letter from Smith to Casey on February 11, 1982, regarding President Reagan's new Executive Order that had recently been implemented (E.O. 12333, issued in 1981), which required the reporting of drug crimes by US employees.[18]

With the MOU in place, the CIA, in cooperation with the Department of Justice, changed the CIA's regulations in 1982, redefining the term "employee" to mean only full-time career

> Matta's SETCO airline was one of four companies that, although known by the US government to be engaged in drug trafficking, in 1986 were still awarded contracts by the US State Department with the Nicaraguan Humanitarian Assistance Organization (NHAO).

CIA officials. The result of this was that suddenly there were thousands of people, contract agents, until then "employees" of the CIA, who were no longer called employees. Now they were "employed by, assigned to, or acting for an agency within the intelligence community."[19] Non-employees, if you will.

According to a February 8, 1985, memo sent to Mark M. Richard, the Deputy Assistant Attorney General/Criminal Division of the US, on the subject of CIA reporting of drug offenses, this meant, as per the 1982 MOU, that the CIA really was under no obligation to report alleged drug violations by these "non-employees."[20]

Juan Matta Ballesteros and SETCO

It is pure disinformation for the HPSCI to print, "CIA reporting to DoJ of information on Contra involvement in narcotics trafficking was inconsistent but in compliance with then-current policies and regulations. There is no evidence however that CIA officers in the field or at headquarters ever concealed narcotics trafficking information or allegations involving the Contras."[21]

"On April 29, 1989, the DoJ requested that the Agency provide information regarding Juan Matta Ballesteros and six codefendants for use in prosecution. DoJ also requested information regarding SETCO, described as 'a Honduran corporation set up by Juan Matta Ballesteros.' The May 2 CIA memo to DoJ containing the results of Agency traces on Matta, his codefendants, and SETCO stated that following an 'extensive search of the files and indices of the directorate of Operations.... There are no records of a SETCO Air.'"[22]

Juan Ramón Matta Ballesteros.

Matta—whom *Newsweek* magazine described as being responsible for up to a third of all cocaine entering the US[23]— was wanted by the DEA in connection with the brutal 30-hour torture and murder of one of their agents, Enrique Camarena, in Mexico in February 1985. Obviously, Matta was a very well-known

> Noting a *New York Times* article dated November 20, 1993, she stated that "the CIA anti-drug program in Venezuela shipped a ton of nearly pure cocaine into the USA in 1990. The CIA acknowledged that the drugs were sold on the streets of the USA."

trafficker. It is ludicrous to suggest that the CIA hasn't covered up evidence of drug trafficking, and even murder of US anti-drug agents, by assets, even from their own investigators.

"I mean, this is different than the MOU, which said the CIA was under no obligation to volunteer information to the DoJ," said Scott. "It never said the CIA was allowed to withhold information from the DoJ. In the case of SETCO, they were asked for the information, and the CIA replied falsely that there was none. The Hitz people tried to find out how this could have happened, and one person said I just didn't know about SETCO, but that is impossible. If people like me knew about SETCO, how could they not? Because the SETCO thing was a big thing."[24]

Matta's SETCO airline was one of four companies that, although known by the US government to be engaged in drug trafficking, in 1986 were still awarded contracts by the US State Department with the Nicaraguan Humanitarian Assistance Organization (NHAO). These companies were flying weapons and supplies in to the Contras, then drugs back to the US on the same aircraft, with the knowledge of CIA officials. Matta was protected from prosecution until his usefulness to the Contra efforts came to an end. Then he was arrested, tried and convicted in 1989, the same year Manuel Noriega was indicted in US court, was removed from office in Panama by a bloody invasion by US troops, then arrested and imprisoned within the US for trafficking, where he still rots to this day.

The CIA Admits to Shipping a Ton of Cocaine to US Streets

The Contra-CIA drug trafficking was no anomaly, but rather normal operating procedure for US Intelligence, particularly the CIA and military, and for the US government, while they simultaneously and actively perpetuate their profitable War on Some Drugs.

Rep. Maxine Waters, (D-CA), in a speech in the House of Representatives on March 18, 1997, outlined various reports of CIA drug-trafficking complicity. Noting a *New York Times* article dated November 20, 1993, she stated that "the CIA anti-drug program in Venezuela shipped a ton of nearly pure cocaine into the USA in 1990. The CIA acknowledged that the drugs were sold on the streets of the USA.... Not one CIA official has ever been indicted or prosecuted for this abuse of authority."

Rep. Maxine Waters (D-CA).

Rep. Waters continued, calling it a "cockamamie scheme." She described how the CIA had approached the DEA, who has the authority over operations of this nature, and asked for their permission to go through with the operation, but the DEA said, "No." The CIA did it anyway, explaining later to investigators that this was the only way to get in good with the traffickers, so as to set them up for a bigger bust the next time.[25]

Keith Boone's excellent 2007 documentary, *American Drug War—the Last White Hope*, features a brief clip of former DEA head Richard Bonner admitting on film that indeed the CIA allowed this ton of cocaine to hit US streets with no oversight or follow-up whatsoever.

In late 1990, CIA Agent Mark McFarlin and General Ramon Guillen Davila of the Venezuelan National Guard, sent an 800-pound shipment of cocaine to Florida, where it was intercepted by US Customs at Miami International Airport, which lead to the eventual indictment of Guillen in 1996 in Miami for his involvement in trafficking up to 22 tons of cocaine into the city.[26] Gen. Guillen was the former chief Venezuelan anti-drug cop.

Researcher Dan Russell relates, "Speaking from his safe haven in Caracas, Guillen insisted that this was a joint CIA-Venezuelan operation aimed at the Cali cartel. Given that Guillen was a long-time CIA employee, and that the drugs were stored in a Venezuelan warehouse owned by the CIA, the joint part of

Guillen's statement is almost certainly true, although the 'aimed at' part is almost certainly false."[27]

"That is the case that has gone closest to the heart of the CIA, because the CIA actually admitted to the introduction of a ton [of cocaine onto US streets]. The man was indicted for 22 tons, and [some people said] that his defense was that the CIA approved all of it," Scott said, recalling the audacity of the case. For the very same *Times* article mentioned in Rep. Waters' speech, "the spin the CIA gave the *Times* was that it was trying to sting Haiti's National Intelligence Service (SIN)—which the CIA itself had created."[28]

Death Threats Against the Head of the DEA in Haiti

Which brings us to the case of Colonel Michel Francois, one of the Haitian coup leaders who overthrew democratically elected Jean-Bertrand Aristide in 1991, helping rule Haiti until 1994. In her impassioned speech, Rep. Waters mentioned a *Los Angeles Times* article (dated March 8, 1997) that reported, "Lt. Col. Michel Francois, one of the CIA's reported Haitian agents, a former Army officer and a key leader in the military regime that ran Haiti between 1991 and 1994, was indicted in Miami with smuggling 33 tons of cocaine into the USA."[29]

"When the DEA's Tony Greco tried to stop a massive cocaine shipment in May, 1991, four months before the coup, his family received death threats on their private number from 'the boss of the man arrested.' The only people in Haiti who had that number were the coup leaders, army commander Raoul Cedras and his partner, Port-au-Prince police chief Michel Francois, 'the boss of the man arrested.' A 1993 U.S. GAO [Government Accounting Office] report insisted that Cedras

"We have uncovered more than sufficient evidence that conclusively shows that the US State Department was overtly—there wasn't anything secret about it—overtly supporting the PRD, and that the PRD had as part of its structure a gang that was dedicated to selling drugs in the United States," said former US Congressman Don Bailey.

and Francois were running one of the largest cocaine export rings in the world."[30]

In January 2000, US Customs found five cocaine hauls welded deep within the steel hulls of "Haitian" freighters on the Miami River in Florida. (There have since been many more such shipments intercepted.) The mainstream press reported that the drugs had "passed through" Haiti from Colombia. What the mainstream press did not focus on was that the five freighters were registered in Honduras, where, coincidentally, Haitian expatriate Michel Francois lives. Francois, a graduate of the infamous US Army's School of the Americas, has an extradition request out for him from the DEA. During the subsequent DEA investigation of this freighter smuggling, two Haitians were arrested in Miami, suspected of masterminding the operation. One, Emmanuelle Thibaud, had been allowed to emigrate to Miami in 1996, two years after Aristide returned to power. When US police searched his Florida home in January 2000, "they found documents linking him to Michel Francois."[31] The *Los Angeles Times* quoted an FBI investigator, Hardrick Crawford, saying "it is not a big leap to assume that Francois is still directing the trafficking from Honduras."[32] Although the US requested extradition of Francois in 1997, the Honduran Supreme Court ruled against it. So the CIA-molded and nurtured Francois continues to surface in these international drug investigations.

> In one memorable raid, officers found $136,000 "wrapped and ready" to be shipped to Sea Crest Trading, a suspected CIA front company.

Explaining why they feel the US government recertified Haiti again that year (2002) as a cooperative partner in the War on Some Drugs, even with the abundance of evidence pointing to Haitian officials' continued involvement in the drug trade, *Haiti Progres*, the leftist Haitian weekly based in New York, wrote: "Because they need the 'drug war' to camouflage their real war, which is a war against any people which rejects US hegemony, neoliberal doctrine, and imperialism…. Like Frankenstein with his monster, the US often has to chase after the very criminals it creates. Just as in the case of Cuba and Nicaragua, the thugs trained and equipped by the Pentagon and CIA go on to form vicious mafias, involved in drug trafficking, assassinations, and money laundering.[33]

Most-Favored Traffickers Receive Overt Support

A case involving the CIA stepping in and crushing an investigation into drug trafficking by CIA assets and favored clients took place in Philadelphia from 1995 to 1996, and continues in the official harassment of the investigating officer in charge. John "Sparky" McLaughlin is a narcotics officer in the Philadelphia, Pennsylvania Bureau of Narcotics Investigations and Drug Control, Office of the Attorney General (OAG/BNI). On October 20, 1995, McLaughlin and two other officers approached Daniel Croussett, who was acting suspiciously. While questioning Croussett, the officers found documents in his car marked "Trifuno '96," which Croussett told McLaughlin's team belonged "to a political party back in the DR [Dominican Republic], and they are running Jose Francisco Pena-Gomez for President in May."[34] This political party was the Dominican Revolutionary Party (PRD).

McLaughlin, in a supplemental report filed January 29, 1996, wrote that "Trifuno '96" was basically a set of instructions on how to "organize the estimated 1.2 million Dominicans who currently reside outside the Dominican Republic to overthrow the present regime in the elections May, 1996."[35] Soon it was obvious that McLaughlin's team had uncovered an enormous drug-trafficking operation, run by a group associated with the PRD, the Dominican Federation, who were supporters of the man most favored to win the Dominican Presidency in 1996, and more ominously, most favored by the US government and the Clinton Administration. An informant for McLaughlin had told him that if Pena was elected, he was going to make sure that the price of heroin for Dominican supporters fell dramatically.

On October 26, 1995, former CIA operations officer and State Department field observer Wilson Prichett, hired as a security analyst by the BNI, wrote a memo to McLaughlin's boss, BNI supervisor John Sunderhauf, stating he felt it time to bring in the CIA as they may already have had a covert interest in the PRD. By December 7, 1995, the CIA was called in to give assistance and to advise the local officers in this case that had potential international ramifications. On January 27, 1996, Sunderhauf received a memo from Larry Leightley, the CIA Chief of Station in Santo Domingo, Dominican Republic.

"'It is important to note that Pena-Gomez and the PRD in 1995 are considered mainstream in the political spectrum,' Leightley wrote. 'Pena-Gomez currently leads in the polls and has a better than even chance of being elected the next President of the Dominican Republic in May, 1996 elections. He and his PRD ideology pose no specific problems for U.S. foreign policy and, in fact, Pena-Gomez was widely seen as the 'U.S. Embassy's candidate' in the 1994 elections given the embassy's strong role in pressuring for free and fair elections and Pena's role as opposition challenger.' Leightley went on to say that on Dec. 11, 1995, Undersecretary of State Alex Watson had a lengthy meeting with Pena-Gomez, whom Leightley stated 'is a well-respected political leader in the Caribbean.'"[36]

By this time, McLaughlin's team had hooked up with DEA investigators in Worcester, Massachusetts, who informed them that the PRD headquarters in Worcester was the main hub of the Dominican narcotics trafficking for all of New England. McLaughlin was able to get an informant wearing a wire inside some meetings of the PRD. He taped instructions being given by PRD officials on how to raise money for the Pena-Gomez candidacy by narcotics trafficking. Then the CIA turned ugly and wanted the name of McLaughlin's informant, and all memos they had written to the BNI on the matter.

McLaughlin and his team refused to turn the name over, fearing for the informant's life. On March 27, 1996, CIA Agent Dave Lawrence arrived for a meeting with McLaughlin and Sunderhauf at BNI headquarters. According to court documents filed in McLaughlin's civil suit against the CIA, the Pennsylvania Attorney General, the United States Attorney in Philadelphia, and the State Department, "CIA Agent Lawrence stated that he wanted the memo that he gave this agency on Jan. 31, 1996, and that BNI shouldn't have received it in the first place. CIA agent Lawrence went on to state that he wanted the identification of the C/I and what province he came from in the Dominican Republic, CIA agent Lawrence was adamant about getting this information and he was agitated when BNI personnel refused his request."[37] Because this was potentially a very damaging case for the US government, which seemed to be protecting a known group of traffickers, if the informant disappeared there'd be no more potential problem for the government.

Within two weeks of refusing to turn over the name of his informant to the CIA, all of McLaughlin's pending cases were dismissed as unprosecutable by the Philadelphia District Attorney, stories were leaked to the press alleging investigations into McLaughlin's team for corruption, and superiors ordered McLaughlin's team not to comment on charges publicly to the press, putting McLaughlin under a gag order.[38] McLaughlin's team broke up, and McLaughlin lost his initial civil suit against his employers and the CIA, although as reported by the National Whistleblowers Coalition, he did win a "retaliatory lawsuit," though he still remained off the streets through at least 2006, barred from working anti-narcotics investigations.

"We have uncovered more than sufficient evidence that conclusively shows that the US State Department was overtly—there wasn't anything secret about it—overtly supporting the PRD, and that the PRD had as part of its structure a gang that was dedicated to selling drugs in the United States," said former US Congressman Don Bailey, who represented McLaughlin in his original suit.[39] Bailey said that he suspects the government got the name of the informant anyway, as he cannot find the informant now.

> The CIA and the US government do not want anyone bringing Hitz Vol. 2 into a court room and giving it the public hearing that former CIA Director John Deutch promised.

A source close to the case confirms that photographs were taken of Al Gore attending a fundraising event at Coogan's Pub in Washington Heights in September 1996. The fundraiser was held by Dominicans associated with the PRD, some of whom—such as PRD officers Simon A. Diaz and Pablo Espinal—even having DEA NADDIS jackets, and several had "convictions for sales of pounds of cocaine, weapons violations and the laundering of millions of dollars in drug money."[40] Why was the Secret Service allowing Vice President Gore to meet with known traffickers and accept campaign contributions from them?

Sea Crest Trading and More Dominican Connections

Joe Occhipinti, a senior Immigration and Naturalization Service agent in New York City with 22 years service—one of the most decorated federal officers in history, with 78 commendations and awards to his credit—began investigating Dominican drug connections in 1989. Occhipinti developed evidence, while solving the murder of a NYC cop by Dominican drug lords, that one of the Dominican drug lords was "buying up Spanish grocery stores, called bodegas in Washington Heights to facilitate his drug trafficking and money laundering activities."[41] Occhipinti launched what began to turn into the very successful, multi-agency task-force Operation Bodega, netting 40 arrests and the seizure of more than $1 million cash from drug proceeds.

In one memorable raid, officers found $136,000 "wrapped and ready" to be shipped to Sea Crest Trading, a suspected CIA front company.[42] Then Occhipinti found himself set up, arrested, tried, and convicted for violating the rights of some members of the Dominican Federation he'd busted during the operation. Sentenced to 36 months in prison in 1991, Occhipinti was pardoned by the out-going President Bush in 1993.

Another investigator who tied Sea Crest Trading to the CIA was former NYPD detective Benjamin Jackobson, who began investigating the company for food-coupon fraud in 1994. "According to Justice Department documents obtained by Congressman James Trafficant (D-OH), the Drug Enforcement Administration (DEA) believes that Sea Crest is behind much of the money laundering in New York's Washington Heights area of Manhattan, but that attempts to prosecute the company 'have been hampered and legislatively fought by certain interest groups and not a single case has been initiated.' Jacobson's inquiry led him to conclude that one of those 'interest groups' was the CIA, which, the investigator believes, was using Sea Crest as a front for covert operations, including weapons shipments to *mujahideen* groups in Afghanistan."[43]

"All I can say is," said Occhipinti, "I find it very unusual that dozens of viable federal and state investigations into the Dominican Federation and the activities of Sea Crest Trading company were prematurely terminated…. I am not optimistic that this stuff is ever going to really break. They will just simply attempt to discredit the people bringing forward the evidence, and to try to selectively prosecute some to intimidate the rest."[44]

In sworn testimony entered into the Congressional Record by Representative James Trafficant, NYPD Internal Affairs officer William Acosta said, "My investigation confirmed that Sea Crest, as well as the Dominican Federation, are being politically protected by high ranking public officials who have received illegal political contributions which were drug proceeds. In addition, the operatives in Sea Crest were former CIA-Cuban operatives who were involved in the 'Bay of Pigs.' This is one of the reasons why the intelligence community has consistently protected and insulated Sea Crest and the Dominican Federation from criminal prosecution. I have evidence which can corroborate the drug cartel conspiracy against Mr. Occhipinti."[45]

It should also cause no undue concern among American citizens that the winner of the Dominican presidential race on May 18, 2000, was Hipolito Mejia, who was the vice-presidential running mate of the infamous Pena-Gomez in 1990 and who was the vice-president of his party, the PRD, for years before winning the race.[46] The inauguration took place August 16, 2000. Not to mention that Clinton Administration insider and former Chairman of the Democratic National Party, Charles Manatt, accepted the US Ambassadorship to the poverty-stricken Dominican Republic, presenting his credentials on December 9, 1999, to the Dominican government.[47]

The Ninth Circuit Court of Appeals Has Its Doubts About US Government Drug-Ties Denials

Bringing one of the minor players in Gary Webb's story back into the limelight, on July 26, 2000, the US Ninth Circuit Court of Appeals (the second-highest court in the US) ruled that asylum-seeking Nicaraguan Renato Pena Cabrera—a former cocaine dealer and Fuerza Democratica Nicaraguense (FDN)

> "If you ask: In the process of fighting a war against the Sandinistas, did people connected with the US government open channels which allowed drug traffickers to move drugs into the United States, did they know the drug traffickers were doing it, and did they protect them from law enforcement? The answer to all those questions is 'YES.'"
>
> —Jack Blum, former Chief Counsel to the Kerry Committee

Contra faction spokesman in Northern California during the early 1980s—should have a judge hear his story in court. Pena is fighting extradition from the US stemming from a 1985 conviction for cocaine trafficking. Pena alleges the drug dealing he was involved in had the express permission of the US government, and that he was told by the prosecutor soon after his 1984 arrest that he would not face deportation, due to his assisting the Contra efforts.

"Pena and his allies supporting the Contras became involved in selling cocaine in order to circumvent the congressional ban on non-humanitarian aid to the Contras. Pena states that he was told that leading Contra military commanders, with ties to the CIA, knew about the drug dealing," the three-judge panel wrote in its decision.[48] Efforts to find out the results of his asylum bid in 2008 have proven fruitless.

Pena's story seemed plausible to the judges, who decided that the charges were of such serious import they deserved to be heard and evaluated in court. It also means that they probably do not believe the HPSCI report. Perhaps they were remembering the entries in Oliver North's notebooks, dated July 9, 1984, concerning a conversation with CIA agent Duane "Dewey" Clarridge: "Wanted aircraft to go to Bolivia to pick up paste," and, "Want aircraft to pick up 1,500 kilos."[49]

The CIA-created FDN was the best-trained, best-equipped Contra faction, based in Honduras, and lead by former Nicaraguan dictator Anastasio Samoza's National Guardsman, Enrique Bermudez. Pena was selling drugs in San Francisco for Norwin Meneses, one of the main figures in Webb's story, another Nicaraguan who was in turn sending much of that money to the Contras. "It was during October, 1982, that FDN leaders met with Meneses in L.A. and San Francisco in an effort to set up local Contra support groups in those cities."[50] Pena was arrested along with Jairo Meneses, Norwin's nephew. Pena copped a guilty plea to one count of possession with intent to sell, in March 1985, getting a two-year sentence in exchange for informing on Jairo.

Choppers returning Contra troops to Ilopango from Nicaragua.
PHOTO: CELERINO CASTILLO

Dennis Ainsworth, an American Contra supporter in San Francisco, told the FBI in 1987 that he was told by Pena that "the FDN is involved in drug smuggling with the aid of Norwin Meneses." Ainsworth also told the FBI that the FDN "had become more involved in selling arms and cocaine for personal gain than in a military effort to overthrow the current Nicaraguan Sandinista government." He went so far as to tell them that he'd been contacted in 1985 by a US Customs Agent, who told him that "national security interests kept him from making good narcotics cases." When Jairo Meneses reached court for sentencing in 1985, in exchange for a three-year sentence he testified against his uncle, claiming to be a book keeper for Norwin, but nothing happened. Norwin Meneses continued to operate freely.[51]

Webb's attention was initially directed toward Norwin Meneses' partner, Danilo Blandon Reyes, who turned out to be the supplier for "Freeway" Ricky Ross, described by many as being instrumental in the spread of crack throughout South Central Los Angeles and beyond, beginning in late 1981. By 1983, Ross "was buying over 100 kilos of cocaine a week, and selling as much as $3 million worth of crack a day."[52] Pena, during this same time (1982 to1984)—according to information in the CIA's Hitz Report, Vol. 2—made six to eight trips "for Meneses' drug-trafficking organization. Each time, he says he carried anywhere from $600,000 to $1,000,000 to Los Angeles and returned to San Fransisco with 6 to 8 kilos of cocaine." Webb speculates that, "Even with the inflated cocaine prices of the early 1980s, the amount of money Pena was taking to LA was far more than was needed to pay for six to eight kilos of cocaine. It seems like that the excess—$300,000 to $500,000 per trip—was the Contra's cut of the drug proceeds."[53]

Whether Pena's appeal will eventually reach a court is not yet known. Most likely someone in Washington, DC—perhaps even former CIA officer and current Chairman of the HPSCI, Rep. Porter Goss himself, (R-FL)—is going to pick up the phone and call the Special Assistant US Attorney listed in the court filings, Robert Yeargin, tell him to drop the case, and allow Pena to remain in the US. The CIA and the US government do not want anyone bringing Hitz Vol. 2 into a court room and giving it the public hearing that former CIA Director John Deutch promised. As noted, attempts in June and July 2008 by this author to find out what happened to Pena's suit have been unsuccessful.

Older Reports, Irrefutable Evidence

The evidence of the CIA working with traffickers is irrefutable. Many Congressional inquiries and committees have gathered massive amounts of evidence of CIA drug connections. Senator John Kerry's (D-Mass) Senate Subcommittee on Narcotics and Terrorism, which released a report in December 1988,[54] explored many of the Contra/CIA-drug allegations. As Jack Blum, former Chief Counsel to the Kerry Committee, testified in Senate hearings October 23, 1996 (before the subcommittee of Arlen Specter, the inventor of the infamous "magic-bullet theory" for the Warren Commission's investigation of the Kennedy assassination): "If you ask: In the process of fighting a war against the Sandinistas, did people connected with the US government open channels which allowed drug traffickers to move drugs into the United States, did they know the drug traffickers were doing it, and did they protect them from law enforcement? The answer to all those questions is 'YES.'"[55]

The Kerry Report's main conclusions are directly opposite those of the latest HPSCI report: "It is clear that individuals who provided support for the Contras were involved in drug trafficking. The supply network of the Contras was used by drug trafficking organizations, and elements of the Contras themselves received financial and material assistance from drug traffickers.[56]

Webb's article also resulted in a Department of Justice investigation, lead by DoJ Inspector General Michael Bromwich. The Bromwich report found that that the CIA did indeed intervene to stop an investigation into Julio Zavala, a suspect in the "Frogman" case in San Francisco, in which swimmers in wetsuits were bringing cocaine to shore from Colombian freighters. When police arrested Zavala, they seized $36,000. The CIA got wind of depositions being planned and stepped in. "It is clear that the CIA believed that it had an interest in preventing the depositions, partly because it was concerned about an allegation that its funds were being diverted into the drug trade. The CIA discussed the matter with the US Attorney's Office, the depositions were canceled, and the money was returned."[57]

Since the release of the HPSCI report, there has been a noticeable silence emanating from the office of Rep. Maxine Waters, who after the release of Hitz Vol. 1, had called for open hearings, and who had still not authorized her staff to make any statements on the subject at the time of this writing (July 2008). Rep. Waters told the HPSCI in 1998 it was a shame that

after all the evidence of CIA assets being involved in drug trafficking gathered by Senate officials in the 1980s, that the CIA either absolutely knew, or turned its head, "at the same time we are spending millions of dollars talking about a war on drugs? Give me a break, Mr. Chairman, and Members. We can do better than this."[58]

There has yet to be a public hearing on Hitz Vol. 2. The HPSCI has released a report that blatantly lied to the American people, who have watched their rights and liberties chipped away a bit at a time in the name of the War on Some Drugs, while certain unscrupulous individuals within the CIA and other branches of US government, as well as the private sector, continue making themselves rich off the war. The investigations into the CIA-Contra-Cocaine connections serve only to focus attention upon one small part of the whole picture, while the HPSCI report narrows the field even further, by insisting on refuting—poorly, one might add—Webb's reporting yet again. "These guys have long ago become convinced that they can control what people believe and think entirely through power and that facts are irrelevant," said Catherine Austin Fitts, former Assistant Secretary of Housing and Federal Housing Commissioner under Bush.[59]

The HPSCI mentions the most prolific drug smuggler in US history—who used the Contra-supply operations to broaden his own smuggling operation—only in passing, relegating Barry Seal to a mere footnote. Mena, Arkansas—Seal's base of operations during the same time then-Arkansas Governor Clinton's good friend Dan Lasatar was linked by the FBI to a massive cocaine trafficking ring—isn't mentioned once. White House NSC members Oliver North, Admiral John Poindexter, and General Richard Secord were all barred for life from entering Costa Rica by the Costa Rican government in 1989 due to their Contra drug trafficking-connections, but you won't read that in the HPSCI report.

Then there are the drug-financed armies, such as the Kosovo Liberation Army (KLA), which in 1996 was being called a terrorist organization by the US State Department, while the European Interpol was compiling a report on their domination of the European heroin trade. US forces handed a country to the KLA/Albanian drug cartels, and just over one year later the US was facing a sharp increase in heroin seizures and addiction figures.

Back in the 1960s and 1970s it was the Hmong guerrilla army fighting a "secret" war completely run by the CIA in Laos.

Senator Frank Church's Committee hearings on CIA assassinations and covert operations in 1975 "accepted the results of the Agency's own internal investigation, which found, not surprisingly, that none of its operatives had ever been in any way involved in the drug trade. Although the CIA's report had expressed concern about opium dealing by its Southeast Asian allies, Congress did not question the Agency about is allegiances with leading drug lords—the key aspect, in my view, of CIA complicity in narcotics trafficking," Alfred McCoy, author of the seminal *The Politics of Heroin*, wrote in 1972.[60]

Sounds a bit familiar, doesn't it? Brit Snider, then–Inspector General of the CIA, testified before the HPSCI in a closed-door session, May 5, 1999. "While we found no evidence that any CIA employees involved in the Contra program had participated in drug-related activities or had conspired with others in such activities, we found that the Agency did not deal with Contra-related drug trafficking allegations and information in a consistent, reasoned or justifiable manner. In the end, the objective of unseating the Sandinistas appears to have taken precedence over dealing properly with potentially serious allegations against those whom the Agency was working."[61] Yet, somehow the HPSCI felt justified in releasing its utter sham of a report to the American people, assuring us that it "found no evidence to support allegations" that CIA-connected individuals were selling drugs in the Los Angeles area.

Are We About to Commit Another Vietnam, or Has It Already Begun?

US politicians continue hollering for stronger law enforcement tactics and tougher sentencing guidelines. They voted in 2000 to give the Colombian military $1.3 billion dollars—so it can turn around and buy 68 Blackhawk helicopters from US arms merchants—to assist Colombia in its War on Some Drugs. The lies have a personal effect on our lives. This is not a harmless

White House NSC members Oliver North, Admiral John Poindexter, and General Richard Secord were all barred for life from entering Costa Rica by the Costa Rican government in 1989 due to their Contra drug trafficking-connections, but you won't read that in the HPSCI report.

little white lie—this is costing thousands of undue, horrible deaths and ruined lives each year around the world, this sham of a war. For US politicians to continue to vote for increased Drug War funding—when the evidence is irrefutable that US intelligence agencies, federal law enforcement agencies, and even some government officials in elected office have actively worked to protect and cover up for the real, major drug lords—the analogies to Vietnam are not so far off the mark.

"When I came to America in 1961, the US was just beginning a program where they were sending advisors [to Vietnam], insisting that they would never be anything more," said Scott. "And [they had] a defoliation program, an extensive defoliation program, which is what we are doing now in Colombia. Only, I think we now have even more advisors in Colombia, and we've graduated to biowarfare in Colombia, which is something we are treaty-bound not to do. Yet we are doing it. The deeper in

Colombian paramilitary.

we get, the harder it will be to get out. So there may be still a chance to get out of this mess, or to change it to a political solution, but it is dangerously like Vietnam."[62]

Colombia is a perfect illustration of the hypocrisy of the War on some Drugs, when we consider the case of Colonel James Hiett, former head of the US anti-drug efforts in Colombia. Col. Hiett covered up for his wife, Laurie, who in 1998 came under investigation by the US Army for smuggling cocaine and heroin through the US Embassy postal service in Bogata. Laurie gave thousands of dollars of drug profits to her husband to launder for her. The US military put her under investigation, but they told Col. Hiett they did so, giving him time to cover his tracks. The Army performed a perfunctory investigation of the colonel, cleared him of any wrongdoing, then recommended he get probation. In May 1999, Laurie was sentenced to five years, and in July 2000 Col. Hiett was sentenced to five months of prison.

"In the Colombian drug war, denial goes far beyond the domesticated: Col. Hiett turned a blind eye not only to his wife's drug profiteering but to the paramilitaries, to the well-documented collusion of Colombian officers in those death squads and to the massive corruption of the whole drug-fighting enterprise."

Hopsicker has uncovered FBI cover-ups involving terrorist hijacker training at Huffman Aviation, and their connections to what appears to be a US-sanctioned drug-trafficking operation underway at the very same tiny airport where lead hijacker Mohammad Atta trained.

Hernan Aquila, the mule that Laurie hired to pick up the drugs in NYC and deliver them to the dealers, got a longer sentence than the two Hietts put together—five and a half years. He is Colombian; they are white Americans. He was simply a mule, while Col. Hiett was in charge of all US anti-drug efforts in Colombia, and his wife was one of the masterminds of the operation.

One aghast reporter wrote: "In the Colombian drug war, denial goes far beyond the domesticated: Col. Hiett turned a blind eye not only to his wife's drug profiteering but to the paramilitaries, to the well-documented collusion of Colombian officers in those death squads and to the massive corruption of the whole drug-fighting enterprise. [Col.] Hiett's sentencing revealed not an overprotective husband, but a military policy in which blindness is the operative strategy—a habit of mind so entrenched that neither Col. Hiett nor the Clinton administration nor the U.S. Congress can renounce it, even as the prison door is swinging shut."[63]

Former US Ambassador to Paraguay and El Salvador Robert White said, "Cocaine is now Colombia's leading export," laughing at "the idea that an operation of that magnitude can take place without the cooperation of the business, banking, transportation executives, and the government, civil as well as military."[64]

Which Brings Us to the New Millennium, the Post-9/11 Age

Researcher Daniel Hopsicker has reported: "A two-year investigation in Venice, Fl. into the flight school attended by Atta and his bodyguard Marwan Al-Shehhi and which provided them with their 'cover' while in the U.S. unearthed the amazing fact that during the same month the two men began flying lessons at Huffman Aviation, July of 2000, the flight school's owner's Lear jet was seized on the runway of Orlando Executive Airport by Federal Agents who found 43 pounds of heroin onboard."

Atta arrived at the Venice flight school at the same time that 43 pounds of heroin were seized from a plane owned by Walter Hilliard (co-owner, with Dutch national Rudi Dekkers, of Venice airport's terror flight school Huffman Aviation) by machine gun–wielding DEA agents who apparently were not in on the operation. Although authorities found Hilliard innocent of any knowledge of the heroin shipment, they still kept his plane under asset-forfeiture laws. The same plane made between 30 to 40 of the exact same runs before getting busted, yet the pilot was never charged, for "lack of evidence." The Orlando Sentinel (August 2, 2000) called this Florida's largest-ever seizure of heroin.

Hopsicker suspects that the entire episode was kept out of the public's eye to protect the US intelligence operation Able Danger, which had Mohammad Atta under surveillance for at least two years prior to the September 11th attacks, though the official US government 9-11 Report insists that no US intelligence service had any foreknowledge of Atta before the attacks. Hopsicker also raises the interesting point that only he and former FBI translator Sibel Edmonds made public other, numerous connections between the attacks and the international illicit drug trade. "FBI whistle-blower Sibel Edmonds, in the months after the attack, bumped into the arms for drugs deals. Edmonds alleged that the US State Department blocked investigations showing links between criminal drug trafficking networks and the terror attacks on 9/11 'Certain investigations were being quashed, let's say per State Department's request, because it would have affected certain foreign relations [or] affected certain business relations with foreign organizations,' she stated."[65]

In an interview, Daniel Ellsberg—who famously leaked the Pentagon Papers, proving the entire Vietnam fiasco was predicated on lies and greed by the military-industrial complex—summarized two interviews Edmonds gave to Antiwar.com:

Al Qaeda, she's been saying to Congress, according to these interviews, is financed 95 percent by drug money—drug traffic to which the US government shows a blind eye, has been ignoring, because it very heavily involves allies and assets of ours—such as Turkey, Kyrgyzstan, Tajikistan, Pakistan, Afghanistan—all the 'Stans—in a drug traffic where the opium originates in Afghanistan, is processed in Turkey, and delivered to Europe, where it furnishes 96 percent of Europe's heroin, by Albanians, either in Albania or Kosovo—Albanian Muslims in Kosovo—basically the KLA, the Kosovo Liberation Army which we backed heavily in that episode at the end of the century.

It was known at the time that the KLA consisted largely of drug dealers, and they still do. They're dominating the politics, pretty much, of Kosovo right now. Now, all of these people are, for various reasons, allies, or clients, of the US—and the fact that they get a large amount of their income from the heroin trade is something the US just regards as the price of doing business with them. That means that not only is the heroin coming into our markets where it furnishes, according to Sibel based on her FBI experience, some 14 percent of our heroin—up from four percent before the invasion of Afghanistan.

The major effect of that is that terrorist gangs are taking a cut of this, including Al Qaeda, which essentially taxes this traffic as it goes through the various lands where each 'band' pays a percentage as they hand it off. In other words, the US is in effect, endorsing—well, 'endorsing' is too strong a word—"permitting," definitely permitting, or "not acting against," a heroin trade—which not only corrupts our cities and our city politics, *and* our congress, as Sibel makes very specific—but is financing the terrorist organization that constitutes a genuine threat to us. And this seems to be a fact that is accepted by our top leaders, according to Sibel, for various geopolitical reasons, and for corrupt reasons as well. Sometimes things are simpler than they might appear—and they involve envelopes of cash. Sibel says that suitcases of cash have been delivered to the Speaker of the House, Dennis Hastert, at his home, near Chicago, from Turkish sources, knowing that a lot of that is drug money.[66]

"If You Don't Violate Someone's Human Rights, You're Probably Not Doing Your Job." —Anonymous US Official, US Torture Facility, Bagram Airbase, Afghanistan

And just how is it that there's so much heroin being produced in and exported from Afghanistan, a country which has been under US military occupation since 2003? Each year the US and coalition forces have been in-country, Afghanistan has produced ever-larger, record-sized poppy crops. In May 2001, the US awarded the Taliban $43 million in humanitarian aid, due to its having eradicated all poppy crops in areas it controlled. Only the 10 percent of the country controlled by the Northern Alliance was still producing poppies. Yet, it's the Northern Alliance now on the receiving end of US financial and military aid.

"The occupation forces in Afghanistan are supporting the drug trade, which brings between 120 and 194 billion dollars of revenues to organized crime, intelligence agencies and Western financial institutions," reports Professor Michael Chossudovsky. "The proceeds of this lucrative multibillion dollar contraband are deposited in Western banks. Almost the totality of revenues accrue to corporate interests and criminal syndicates *outside* Afghanistan. The Golden Crescent drug trade, launched by the CIA in the early 1980s, continues to be protected by US intelligence, in liason with NATO occupation forces and the British military. In recent developments, British occupation forces have promoted opium cultivation through paid radio advertisements…. Afghanistan and Colombia (together with Bolivia and Peru) constitute the largest drug producing economies in the world, which feed a flourishing criminal economy."[67]

"These countries are heavily militarized. The drug trade is protected. Amply documented the CIA has played a central role in the development of both the Latin American and Asian drug triangles," reporter Devlon Buckley wrote in another article.[68]

The aforementioned radio advertisements, aired in Afghanistan in 2007, put it bluntly: "Respected people of Helmand. The soldiers of ISAF and ANA do not destroy poppy fields. They know that many people of Afghanistan have no choice but to grow poppy. ISAF and the ANA do not want to stop people from earning their livelihoods."

Declan Walsh of the London *Guardian* reported from Kabul: "The advertisement, which was drafted by British officers and carried on two local stations, infuriated Afghan officials as high up as President Hamid Karzai, who demanded an explanation."[69]

Some reports state that as of 2008, 14 million Afghanistan people are dependent upon harvesting opium for their livlihoods. "For Afghanistan, narcotics and insurgency are intertwined and inseparable problems," reported Romesh Bhattacharji for the Indian magazine *Frontline*.[70] "Illicit cultivation of opium was used by the US to finance the insurrection against the Najibullah government. Many members of the Mujahideen, who were the Central Intelligence Agency's [pawns], are now holding powerful posts in the US-propped Hamid Karzai government. These collaborations have ensured the Karzai government's failure to contain opium production.

"In December 2005, the US Drug Enforcement Administration (DEA) seized nine tons of opium from the house of the then Governor of Helmand, Sher Muhammad Akhundzada—the DEA is the only US organization that seems sincere about reducing narcotics trafficking. But, American and British military intelligence forces ensured that he was made a Member of Parliament. Similar is the case of Izzatullah Wasifi, the Director of the General Independent Administration of Anti-Corruption (GIAAC). He was arrested in July 1987 with 600 grams of heroin in Caesar's Palace Hotel, Las Vegas.

"President Karzai's step-brother Ahmed Wali Karzai is reported to be the ablest protector of all drug traffickers. With such patronage given by US forces and some people in the Afghan government, it is no surprise that opium production does not decrease.

"The latest United Nations Rapid Survey for 2008 has projected that Afghanistan produced 8,200 tons of opium in 2007. During the days of the much-maligned Najibullah government in the 1980s, the average opium production was only around 300 tons annually."[71]

I interviewed a Blackwater Security employee, who wants to be identified only by his nickname, Rabbit. "Basically it's going to happen whether you are a part of it or not, and it's so much money or military money, or money that can be used by a military or paramilitary, if you don't get involved in it, you lose control of the distribution, the profits, and you also lose knowledge of what's going on, the ins and outs of the underworld. You lose the knowledge of who knows or has what, so if a $10-million deal happened in Fallujah, you know to keep an eye on Fallujah, rather than the next town over, so you will know where to concentrate your forces. It's going to happen,

so you may as well be a part of it or allow it to happen, because it's silly to waste that asset."

When I asked him if he himself felt this way, he replied, "Yeah. It's an asset that should be used, not wasted."

But "how would it be wasted by our not working with such criminal elements?" I asked him. "Doesn't that reflect on us as a society, that we are engaged at home and abroad in a massively expensive, not to mention destructive, War on Some Drugs and Users, yet are working hand in hand with the very same people smuggling the drugs we're arresting millions of our own citizens for using?"

His reply: "Sometimes to kill a pig you have to crawl into the pig pen."

What in the world does that mean, I asked him.

"If you want to complete your mission, your may have to engage in activities that may seem to some to be unethical or morally questionable."

Keeping in mind what was written above about Afghanistan President Hamid Karzai's brother-in-law being the head protector, I asked Rabbit what he believed his duties were. "To insure that the just-forming government of Hamid Karzai survived, and that the laws of this fledgling nation were being respected and adhered to by the common citizenry as well as the Taliban and other so-called bad guys."

"Were you at all involved in opium-eradication efforts while in Afghanistan?" I flat-out asked this killer for hire. "What were your observations on the effectiveness of such programs? Did you feel they were sincere or more theater for the public eye instead? In other words, were there actually effective eradication efforts ongoing, or were some in positions of power being selective as to whose fields were being uprooted and destroyed? What are your thoughts as to the fact that opium is the largest cash crop in Afghanistan since US and NATO forces have been in-country there? Do you feel that there are those in positions of power and responsibility making money by allowing the illegal trade to continue?"

"Well, yeah," he replied matter-of-factly, "someone is making money! Some of the things we did as a unit, such as taking care of a family, and kind of like in exchange for giving the kids something or replacing a windshield in the family truck, while being nice we'd ask questions. Often all we'd get was 'No, no, no,' but sometimes we'd get a lead. They'd tell us there'd been a couple of foreigners, Jordanians or Syrians, around, or about a cache of weapons nearby. Proper use of intelligence helped us determine whether they were resisting or fighting for the Taliban. There's the old rule, "The enemy of my enemy is now my friend," which came into play with the Taliban resistance. Though morally gray, to obtain the support of the resistance, we helped the resistance get their opium, smuggled people and fuel, ammunition, and whatever other contraband they would be trafficking, through Taliban-controlled checkpoints. The anti-Taliban resistance funded itself primarily through the opium trade."

So there you have it, right from the word of the mouth of one of those private soldiers paid for with US tax money and accountable to no one. We are enabling the trade without any qualms whatsoever.[72]

Who Are the Real "Bad Guys?"

Then there's the State Department's annual report listing those countries that are working against, or at least being uncooperative with the US, in waging the War on Some Drugs. Around 20 countries are on the initial list each year—including Colombia, Mexico, and Afghanistan—but when it comes time for the White House to make the final determination of the bad guys, President Bush always narrowed the list to just two or three countries—countries that the US doesn't like. Those nations helping the US in its War on Some Terror, like the three listed above, somehow never make the final list, no matter how much they're flooding the US with illegal drugs.[73]

Afghanistan—ruled by a US puppet government—produces 95 percent of the world's heroin. Up to 14 percent of that reaches US shores, but the British lieutenant-general in charge of coalition forces in Afghanistan told the London *Independent* in 2006: "Nato will not be involved in poppy eradication, because we are deeply cautious that if we get it wrong and create the wrong environment, we will tip otherwise perfectly law-abiding and co-operative people into the opposition camp."[74] Nonetheless, this is precisely what has happened, with all sides of the conflict making money on the production, trade, and taxing of the illicit poppy and hashish markets in Afghanistan.

Meanwhile, Venezuelan President Hugo Chavez has kicked US DEA agents out of his country, accusing them of engaging in efforts to infiltrate and undermine his country and government. Bush in turn has taken to calling the Venezuelan president the new Castro, a commie pinko narco-thug. With CIA-connected planes loaded with 5.5 tons of cocaine (some with more, some with less) falling out of the skies in Mexico from late 2007 into summer 2008, a concentrated effort was made by the US government to connect these flights to the Chavez government, until it was pointed out that some of these same planes had been spotted being used in "extraordinary rendition flights," where the CIA flies terrorist suspects to a variety of "secret" torture prisons around the world. Two American-owned flights loaded with cocaine actually crashed in Venezuala itself, within 45 days of one another, reports Daniel Hopsicker.[75]

To Be Continued, and Continued, and Continued...

Will the American people continue to accept the lies and cover-ups? Will the people allow Congress to continue refusing to address the officially sanctioned and CIA-assisted global trafficking, insisting that it cannot find any evidence that it exists, meanwhile voting ever-more cash to support the War on Some Drugs? Every American should feel personally insulted that regardless of the facts, their elected representatives again and again choose to foist more lies upon them, but they shouldn't feel surprised. This entire war is predicated upon the existence of the black market, so to ensure the existence of that black market, agencies such as the CIA and the US military actively promote and protect the power and wealth of the cartels, and themselves, by creating endless enemies, and now by coupling the War on Some Terror with their War on Some Drugs.

Perhaps the suitable way to stop their lies and cover-ups would be to sentence these men and women to ten years of addiction in the streets of America under current prohibition policies, to suffer the consequences of their actions, and give them a taste of their own medicine.

Endnotes

1. US Congress (106th, 2nd session), House Permanent Select Committee on Intelligence. (2000). *Report on the Central Intelligence Agency's alleged involvement in trafficking crack cocaine in the Los Angeles area.* Washington, DC: GPO. **2.** Interview with Celerino Castillo by Preston Peet, 23 Jul 2000. **3.** The "CIA-Drugs Symposium" was held in Eugene, Oregon, 11 Jun 2000. An all-day event, there were nine speakers and presenters with evidence of CIA and official US-sanctioned drug trafficking, including Catherine Austin Fitts, Mike Ruppert, Didon Kamathi, Kris Milligan, Rodney Stich, Cele Castillo, Dan Hopsicker, and Peter Dale Scott, plus a presentation by Bernadette Armand, an attorney working for teams of attorneys in the ongoing lawsuits against the CIA and others for their failure to offer equal protection under the law to everyone in South Central Los Angeles, Oakland, and elsewhere in California. Anita Belle, a Florida attorney, is handling various class-action suits filed in eight other states around the US along the same grounds as the California suits. None of these suits had accomplished anything as of 2008. **4.** *Op cit.*, Castillo interview. **5.** "Written Statement of Celerino Castillo 3rd, (former DEA Special Agent), July 2000, for the House Select Committee on Intelligence," p 16. **6.** *Ibid*, p 17. Also see: Webb, Gary. (1998). *Dark alliance: The CIA, the contras, and the crack cocaine explosion.* New York: Seven Stories Press, p 249. **7.** *Op cit.*, HPSCI report, p 18. **8.** *Op cit.*, "Written Statement of Castillo," p 17; *op cit.*, Webb, pp 249–50. **9.** Scott, Peter Dale, Ph.D. (2000). *Drug, Contras, and the CIA: Government policies and the cocaine economy. An analysis of media and government response to the Gary Webb stories in the "San Jose Mercury News," (1996–2000).* From The Wilderness Publications, p 47. **10.** Interview with Peter Dale Scott by Preston Peet, 24 Jul 2000. **11.** Office of the Inspector General, Central Intelligence Agency. (1998). *Allegations of connections between CIA and the Contras in cocaine trafficking to the United States, (96-0143-IG), Volume 1: The California story.* 29 Jan. (Classified and unclassified versions); Office of the Inspector General, Central Intelligence Agency. (1998). *Allegations of connections between CIA and the Contras in cocaine trafficking to the United States, (96-0143-IG), Volume II: The Contra story.* 8 Oct. (Classified and unclassified versions.) **12.** Parry, Robert. (1999). Congress puts Contra-coke secrets behind closed doors. *IF magazine*, Jul/Aug, p 19. Parry was instrumental in breaking the Contra-cocaine connections in the early 1980s. He won the George Polk Award for Journalism in 1984 for reporting on the CIA assassination/torture manual given to the Contras, and wrote, along with Brian Barger, the very first published article on Oliver North's connection to the secret Contra-supply operations on June 10, 1985, and the first story linking the Contras to drug running on Dec. 20, 1986, while working for the Associated Press. **13.** *Op cit.*, Scott interview. **14.** *Op cit.*, Scott (2000). (Emphasis added.) **15.** Jones, Alex, and Paul Joseph Watson. (2004). Evidence begins to mount that Gary Webb was murdered; Webb spoke of death threats, 'government' people around his home. Prison Planet website, 15 Dec. **16.** Testimony of CIA Inspector General Fredrick P. Hitz, before the House Permanent Select Committee on Intelligence, on the CIA OIG Report of Investigation, (Hitz) "Vol 1: The California Story," 16 Mar 1998. **17.** Memo to William French Smith, Attorney General, US Department of Justice, from William J. Casey, Director of Central Intelligence, dated 2 Mar 1982. Obtained at <www.copvcia.com>. **18.** Memo from William F. Smith, Attorney General, US Department of Justice, to William Casey, Director of Central Intelligence, dated 11 Feb 1982. Obtained at <www.copvcia.com>. **19.** As noted in the lawsuit *Lyons vs. CIA* (Class-Action Lawsuit on Behalf of Victims of the Crack Cocaine Epidemic), filed 15 Mar 1999, in Oakland and simultaneously in Los Angeles. **20.** Memo to Mark M. Richard, the US Deputy Assistant Attorney General, from A.R. Cinquegrana, Deputy Counsel for Intelligence Policy, dated 8 Feb 1985, subject: CIA Reporting of Drug Offenses. **21.** *Op cit.*, HPSCI report, p 42. **22.** Ruppert, Michael C. (1998). *Selected excerpts with commentary from "The Central Intelligence Agency Inspector General report of investigation, allegations of connections between CIA and the Contras in cocaine trafficking to the United States. Vol. 2: The Contra story" (declassified version).* From the Wilderness Publications. **23.** *Op cit.*, Scott (2000), p 7. **24.** *Op cit.*, Scott interview. SETCO was the airline owned by known drug trafficker Juan Mattas Ballestaros, whom *Newsweek*, on May 15, 1985, estimated was responsible for up to one third of all cocaine reaching the US at that time. SETCO was just one of the 58 companies and individuals mentioned in the Hitz report. **25.** Speech of Representative Maxine Waters in the US House of Representatives, 18 Mar 1997. Televised on C-Span. Also see: Adams, David. (1997). Anti-drug mission turns sour. *St. Petersburg Times*, 26 Jan, p A1. **26.** Cockburn, Alexander. (1998). *Whiteout: The CIA, drugs, and the press.* Verso, p 96. **27.** Russell, Dan. (1999). *Drug war. Covert money, power, and policy.* Kalyx.com, p 450. **28.** *Ibid.* 29. *Ibid*, p 451. **29.** *Op cit.*, speech of Rep. Maxine Waters; Also see: Scott, Peter Dale, and Jonathan Marshall. (1991, 1998). *Cocaine politics, drugs, armies, and the CIA in Central America.* University of California Press, p vii. **30.** Op cit., Russell, pp 451–2. **31.** *Haiti Progres*, 16–22 Feb 2000. **32.** Fineman, Mark. (2000). Haiti takes on major role in cocaine trade. *Los Angeles Times*, 29 Mar. **33.** *Op cit.*, *Haiti Progres*. **34.** Altman, Howard, and Jim Barry. (2000). The Dominican connection, part 1. *City Paper* (Philadelphia, Pennsylvania), 27 Jul-3 Aug, front page; Altman, Howard, and Jim Barry. (2000). The Dominican connection, part

2: Shafted. *City Paper*, 3–10 Aug, front page; see also: Ruppert, Michael C. (1999). Sparky: A case study in heroism and perseverance. *From the Wilderness*, 30 Aug, pp 7–11. **35.** *Op cit.*, Altman and Barry. **36.** *Ibid.* **37.** *Op cit.*, Ruppert (1999). **38.** Interview with Michael C. Ruppert by Preston Peet, 1 Aug 2000; *ibid*, p 9. **39.** Interview with Don Bailey by Preston Peet, 31 Jul 2000. **40.** *Op cit.*, Ruppert (1999), p 9. **41.** House Judiciary Committee, Subcommittee on Commercial and Administrative Law, Sworn Testimony by Joseph Occhipinti, 27 July 2000, testifying in support of H.R. 4105. "The Fair Justice Act of 2000," which would form an agency to investigate alleged misconduct within the Justice Department. **42.** Grigg, William Norman. (1997). Smuggler's dues. *New American* 13.9, 28 Apr. **43.** Unsigned. (1997). US grocery coupon fraud funds Middle Eastern terrorism. *New American* 13.5, 3 Mar. **44.** Interview with Joseph Occhipinti by Preston Peet, 31 Jul 2000. **45.** Sworn Affidavit of William Acosta, entered into the *Congressional Record* in the ongoing investigation of Joe Occhipinti, by Hon. James A Trafficant Jr, 26 Sep 1996, pp E1733–4; also see sworn affidavit of Manuel DeDios, former editor of *El Diario Le Prensa* newspaper, and the first US journalist killed by the Dominican Federation drug cartel, same pages of *Congressional Record*. **46.** Unsigned. (2000). Mejia wins in Dominican presidential race. Associated Press, 20 May. **47.** Ruppert, Michael. (2000). The Democratic National Party's presidential drug money pipeline. *From the wilderness*, 30 Apr, p 8. **48.** Egelco, Bob. (2000). Former Contra wins review of drug ties, fights deportation to Nicaragua, says CIA knew of drug trafficking . *San Francisco examiner and chronicle*, 27 Jul, p A4. **49.** *Op cit.*, Cockburn, p 35. **50.** *Op cit.*, Webb, p 166. **51.** *Ibid.*, pp 168–9. **52.** *Op cit.*, Cockburn, p 7. **53.** *Op cit.*, Webb, pp 166–7. **54.** US Senate, Subcommittee on Narcotic, Terrorism, and International Operations. (1998). *Drugs, law enforcement, and foreign policy*, Committee Staff Report, Dec. **55.** Testimony and prepared statement of Jack Blum, Chief Counsel for Senator John Kerry's Subcommittee on Narcotics, Terrorism, and International Relations, which released its own report in 1986, testifying before Sen. Arlen Specter's Subcommittee Hearings in 1996; see also: *op cit.*, Cockburn, p 304; *op cit.*, Scott (2000), p 6. **56.** *Op cit.*, Cockburn, p 303. **57.** US Department of Justice, Office of Inspector General (1997). *The CIA-Contra-crack cocaine controversy: A review of the Justice Department's investigations and prosecutions.* Dec, Executive Summary, Section VIII. **58.** Testimony of Rep. Maxine Waters Before the House Permanent Select Committee on Intelligence, On the CIA OIG Report of Investigation, "Vol 1: The California Story," 16 Mar 1998. **59.** Email correspondence of Catherine Austin Fitts with Preston Peet, 2 Aug 2000. **60.** McCoy, Alfred. (1972). *The politics of heroin in Southeast Asia.* Harper & Row. Reprinted in 1991 as *The politics of heroin: CIA complicity in the global drug trade.* Lawrence Hill Books, p xviii. **61.** *Op cit.*, HPSCI report, p 34. **62.** *Op cit.*, Scott interview; also see: Stevenson, Sharon, and Jeremy Bigwood (2000). Drug control or biowarfare. *Mother Jones* website, 3 May, updated 6 Jul, discussing the planned forcing of Colombia by US drug warriors to spray Fursarium Oxysporum, a hideous, mutating, killer fungicide on their coca fields, and hence their land and themselves, in exchange for the $1.3 billion in "anti-drug" aid. Florida has banned the spraying of Fusarmrium Oxysporum within its borders, yet the drug warriors will export it to Colombia. **63.** Shapiro, Bruce. (2000). Nobody questions the colonel. Salon.com, 15 Jul. **64.** Stein, Jeff. (2000). The unquiet death of Jennifer Odom. Salon.com, 5 Jul. **65.** Hopsicker, Daniel. (2005). Able Danger intel exposed protected heroin trafficking. <www.MadCowProd.com>, 17 Apr. **66.** Daniel Ellsberg interviewed by Kris Welch. *Living room* radio program. KPFA 94.1 (Berkeley, CA), 26 Aug 2005. Transcription by Kill the Messenger blog <sibeledmonds.blogspot.com>, 21 Oct 2006. **67.** Chossudovsky, Professor Michael. (2007). Heroin is 'good for your health': Occupation forces support Afghan narcotics trade: Multibillion dollar earnings for organized crime and Western financial institutions. Center for Research on Globalization <GlobalResearch.ca>, 29 Apr. **68.** Buckley, Devlin. Drug mafia, CIA blamed for sacking of Afghan governor. Center for Research on Globalization <GlobalResearch.ca>, 6 Jan. **69.** Walsh, Declan. (2007). Afghan fury over UK troops telling farmers they can grow poppies. *Guardian* (London), 28 Apr. **70.** Bhattacharji, Romesh. (2008). A losing war. *Frontline: India's national magazine* 25.14, 5–18 Jul. **71.** *Ibid.* **72.** Interview by Preston Peet with former Blackwater Security employee on the ground in both Iraq and Afghaistan, conducted 8 Jul 2008. **73.** Brinkley, Joel. (2008). Bush fails to flay world's obvious offenders. *San Francisco chronicle*, 15 Jun; Johnson, David T., Assistant Secretary of State for International Narcotics and Law Enforcement Affairs, US State Dept. (2008). Remarks on release of the annual report on the major illicit drug producing countries for fiscal year 2008. Washington, DC, 16 Sept. Aailable on <www.state.gov>. **74.** Coghlan, Tom. (2007). Afghanistan: Opium wars. *Independent* (London), 30 Apr. **75.** Hopsicker, Daniel. (2008). CIA ghost planes hidden in Cayman Isle trusts. <www.madcowprod.com>, 12 Jun.

Reassessing OKC
The Truck-bomb Hoax
Cletus Nelson

Overview

In the blink of an eye, the 1995 Oklahoma City bombing abruptly transformed the United States from an invulnerable superpower to a nation under siege. As grisly images of death and dismemberment invaded the capsular world of our television screens, Americans witnessed the true horror of a large-scale terrorist attack. However, within 48 hours of this senseless tragedy, the Justice Department had broken the case. A disaffected ex-soldier named Timothy McVeigh was the prime suspect and, five years later, after a rather anti-climactic day in court, the taciturn Gulf War veteran was found guilty on all counts and sentenced to death. He was executed in June

Was It ANFO?

According to federal prosecutors, McVeigh and co-conspirator Terry Nichols constructed a bomb containing 4,800 pounds of Ammonium Nitrate mixed with fuel oil to create a combustible "slurry" known as ANFO. The destructive device was then placed in a 24-foot Ryder truck and driven to the curb just outside the Alfred P. Murrah building on Fifth Street and detonated at 9:02 A.M., April 19, 1995.[1] With few exceptions, most trial-watchers and members of the establishment press have unquestioningly accepted this version of events. Yet from the outset, the government's conclusions have been called into question by a battery of esteemed experts, particularly those

> "To produce the resulting damage pattern in the building, there would have to have been an effort with demolition charges at column bases to complement or supplement the truck bomb damage," asserts Brigadier General Benton K. Partin (USAF ret.).

2001. Few will doubt that his conviction along with the life sentence meted out to his confederate, Terry Nichols, has provided an institutional palliative to the mass outrage that followed the homicidal attack. However, although the two appear guilty of attempting to destroy the Alfred P. Murrah federal building, the story is far from over.

From day one, a surfeit of scientific anomalies and inexplicable events has surrounded the allegedly airtight case against the two men. Indeed, despite widespread public belief that the crime has been solved, a number of looming questions remain unanswered. While many would prefer to ignore the shroud of mystery that still envelops this monumental tragedy, to do so would sacrifice perhaps our most valuable commodity: the historical record. In order to better understand why many people remain intractably opposed to the government's "lone bomber" scenario, one must begin by examining the alleged bomb itself.

with training and experience with explosives. To these researchers, accepting this dubious interpretation of the bomb's destructive capacity would require a physical and scientific leap of faith that openly contradicts accepted knowledge of the explosive capabilities of Ammonium Nitrate.

The first individual to point out the many glaring inconsistencies in the truck-bomb theory was someone with very little to gain by joining the embattled ranks of OKC conspiracy theorists: Brigadier General Benton K. Partin (USAF ret.). A world-renowned expert in the field of explosives and weapons systems, Partin is well-acquainted with the military capabilities of a variety of destructive charges. His immediate misgivings about the single-bomb theory compelled him to produce a highly technical assessment of the damage sustained by the Murrah building that remains a samizdat document to OKC researchers. His authoritative report certainly makes some startling observations.

"To produce the resulting damage pattern in the building, there would have to have been an effort with demolition charges at column bases to complement or supplement the truck bomb damage," he asserts in his lengthy "Bomb Damage Analysis of the Alfred P. Murrah Federal Building, Oklahoma City, Oklahoma." According to the detailed analysis, it would be physically impossible for an ANFO bomb to have destroyed the many steel-reinforced concrete columns which were situated far from the bomb site, as blast "pressure would have fallen off to about 375 pounds per square inch. That would be far below the 3,500 pound compressive yield strength of concrete."[2]

To substantiate his assertions, the military expert notes that building columns B-4 and B-5, which were in direct proximity to the blast, remained standing, while column A-7, which stood some 60 feet from the Ryder truck, was mysteriously demolished. "The much closer columns…are still standing, while the much larger column A-7 is down…These facts are sufficient reason to know that columns B-3 and A-7 had demolition charges on them," he states confidently.[3]

Partin's skepticism was echoed by Gary McClenny, an Army veteran with years of hands-on experience working with ANFO. In a May 16, 1995 letter to FBI Director Louis Freeh, McClenny adamantly disputed the Bureau's preliminary findings. "Ammonium Nitrate is a poor choice for breaching reinforced concrete…it is a low-level, low velocity (2,700 m/sec by itself, 3,400 m/sec when boosted by a 25% TNT charge) explosive primarily used to remove dirt from drilled holes," he notes.[4]

Sam Groning, a demolitions expert with three decades' worth of experience, also told researcher Jim Keith that after a lifetime spent "using everything from 100 percent Nitrogel to ANFO, I've never seen anything to support that story." In fact, Groning recalls setting off 16,000 pounds of ANFO and alleges he was "standing upright" a mere 300 yards from the blast site.[5]

bombing, *The Oklahoma City Bombing and the Politics of Terror*, investigative reporter David Hoffman cites a little-known August 1996 study published by the Federal Emergency Management Agency (FEMA), which concluded that "4,800 pounds of ANFO would have been virtually unable to have caused the so-called 30-foot crater in Oklahoma City."[6] Hoffman also discusses a leaked Pentagon study that originally appeared in *Strategic Investment Newsletter,* which reported that, "the destruction of the federal building last April was caused by five separate bombs."[7]

Hoping to counter this obvious threat to the state's case, in 1997 the Air Force conducted the "Eglin Blast Effects Study" in a last-ditch attempt to reconcile the ANFO theory with expert opinion. The plan backfired. The final report, which was never released to the general public, could not "ascribe the damage that occurred on April 19, 1995 to a single truck bomb containing 4,800 pounds of ANFO" and instead suggested that "other factors such as locally placed charges within the building itself" may have been responsible.[8]

Adding yet more weight to this determined opposition is Samuel Cohen, the legendary physicist credited with inventing the neutron bomb. "I believe that demolition charges in the building placed inside at certain key concrete columns did the primary damage to the Murrah Federal Building," he commented three years after the bombing. "It seems to me that the evidence has gotten much stronger in favor of internal charges, while the ammonium nitrate bomb theory has fallen apart." The observations of this scholar echo those of General Partin.[9]

Further imperiling the single-bomb theory are the findings of the Justice Department Inspector General's Office (IGO), which publicly questioned the shoddy practices and overt bias in favor of the prosecution that pervaded the Bureau's investigation of the bombing. Indeed, prior to McVeigh's 1997 trial, a draft report

The Inspector General's Office rebuked the FBI laboratory for engaging in "unsound science" and concluded that "officials…may not know for certain if ammonium nitrate was used for the main charge that killed 168 people and injured more than 850 others."

Few FBI experts have publicly contradicted these damaging observations. In fact, numerous internal government studies soundly debunk allegations that an ANFO bomb destroyed the Murrah building. In his exhaustively researched tome on the

issued by the IGO rebuked the FBI laboratory for engaging in "unsound science" and concluded that "officials…may not know for certain if ammonium nitrate was used for the main charge that killed 168 people and injured more than 850 others."[10]

These well-reasoned critiques of the evidence, steeped in the unambiguous language of hard science, leave little room for politicized or abstract argument. Indeed, the simplistic theory that a home-brewed fertilizer bomb nearly leveled a fortified federal installation becomes downright untenable, especially when considering US Government Technical Manual No. 9-1910, issued by both the Army and Air Force, which implies that ANFO couldn't possibly produce a shock wave capable of mangling the building's concrete supports.[11] This growing body of evidence seems to ominously point toward an alternative scenario involving additional explosives.

Bomb(s)?

Although given little coverage by the mainstream press, eyewitness testimony and other supporting evidence show that undetonated charges were located and defused once rescue efforts were underway. "We got lucky today, if you can consider anything about this tragedy lucky. It's actually a great stroke of luck, that we've got undefused bombs," noted terrorism expert Dr. Randall Heather on Oklahoma's Channel Four after the blast.[12]

At approximately 11:31 EST, on the day of the bombing, KFOR television broadcast the following announcement:

> The FBI has confirmed there is another bomb in the federal building. It's in the east side of the building... We're not sure what floor, what level, but there is definitely danger of a second explosion.[13]

Radio logs and other documentary materials provide transcripts of OKC police and fire department personnel discussing the removal of additional explosives. Reports of up to four bombs have surfaced.[14]

"As reported widely on CNN and TV stations across the nation, up to four primed bombs were found...inside what remained of the Murrah federal building on April 19, 1995," asserts investigative journalist Ian Williams Goddard.[15] Even more revealing: on the day of the bombing, KFOR television also broadcast that as many as two explosive charges had been located that were far more lethal than the *original* charge that nearly toppled the Murrah building.[16] The significance of

this statement cannot be ignored as it suggests that highly powerful non-ANFO explosive devices were detected *inside* the building.

Although press flacks for the Bureau of Alcohol, Tobacco, and Firearms (BATF) later claimed these devices were "training bombs," Goddard scoffs at this explanation. He notes that the allegedly non-explosive "practice bombs" were tracked down by dogs trained to sniff for explosives, and if they were indeed deactivated "dummies," as described by BATF spokesmen, there would be little need for the bomb squad to "defuse" them.[17]

There are also a number of witnesses who have testified to distinctly hearing or experiencing two separate blasts. Attorney Charles Watts was in the federal courtroom across the street at 9:02 that fateful morning. He told *Media Bypass* that he heard an explosion that knocked everyone to the floor and, as the Vietnam vet hit the deck, he alleges he felt a second detonation far more powerful than the first. "There were two explosions...the second blast made me think the whole building was coming in," he recalls.[18]

Adam Parfrey's influential essay on the subject, "Oklahoma City: Cui Bono," reveals that Dr. Charles Mankin of the University of Oklahoma Geological Survey found that there were two separate explosions based on his analysis of seismographic data from two facilities. Seismograms show two distinct "spikes" roughly ten seconds apart.[19] "The Norman seismogram clearly shows two shocks of equal magnitude... the Omniplex...depicts events so violent they sent the instruments off the scale for more than ten seconds," reports *New Dawn* magazine.[20]

This substantial body of evidence lends credence to the existence of additional (and deadlier) explosives inside the building, which creates the distinct possibility that other suspects were either ignored or successfully eluded federal law enforcement. This development openly contradicts Attorney General Janet Reno's claim that the bombing investigation would "leave no stone unturned."[21]

"Others Unknown"

Despite the indictment and later conviction of McVeigh and Nichols, many still maintain that other conspirators were selectively ignored by federal investigators. These allegations are not just being voiced in the underground press. In the months leading up to McVeigh's trial, the *Denver Post* also "found evidence that the Oklahoma City Bombing plot involved the assistance of at least one person the government hasn't charged in the case."[22]

This belief that a more far-reaching conspiracy helped facilitate the attack on the Murrah building was shared by the Grand Jury that indicted Timothy McVeigh. The official indictment cites "others unknown," a decision obviously intended by the jury to signify the existence of co-conspirators still not apprehended.[23] Unfortunately, the subsequent convictions of Nichols and McVeigh have led government sources to staunchly assert that the embittered veterans were the sole perpetrators behind the terrorist attack. However, if ANFO is physically incapable of causing the level of damage sustained by the Murrah building,

> In the months leading up to McVeigh's trial, the *Denver Post* "found evidence that the Oklahoma City Bombing plot involved the assistance of at least one person the government hasn't charged in the case."

and if evidence shows that more than one explosion occurred on April 19, 1995, one must at least consider the existence of a more far-reaching conspiracy than the one sanctified by the mainstream media.

Another disturbing development that has served to undermine the credibility of the prosecution is the discovery of evidence which seems to indicate that the federal government possessed prior knowledge of an imminent terrorist strike on the Murrah building.

Those Who Knew

In the wake of the blast, rumors immediately began circulating that members of law enforcement received warnings of the bombing which they failed to relay to the public. Edye Smith, whose sons, toddlers Chase and Colton, perished in the blast, brought this issue before the public in the aftermath of the deadly blast. "Where was ATF?" she asked. "Fifteen of seventeen employees survived…They were the target of the explosion…Did they have advance warning?…My two kids didn't get that option," Smith lamented. The distraught mother went

on to tell reporters that BATF investigators ordered her to "shut up…don't talk about it," when she demanded to know why only two employees of the embattled agency were in the building at the time of the blast.[24]

Soon others began to relate further insights into the possibility of prior government knowledge. Frustrated federal informants Gary Cagan and Carol Howe described their repeated attempts to alert federal authorities that various white supremacist groups were planning a major undertaking in the Oklahoma City area, and Judge Wayne Alley later told the *Oregonian* that he was advised to "take extra precautions" by security officials prior to the bombing.[25]

The allegations that various officials were forewarned of the imminent disaster became so widespread that on January 17, 1997, ABC's *20/20* broadcast a story discussing this controversial issue. The results were far from flattering to members of the Justice Department.

One man, his face hidden behind a shadow for fear of BATF reprisal, asserted that he was told by a BATF agent that, "we were tipped off by our pagers not to come into work [that day]." His employer, who overheard the conversation, willingly confirmed this controversial claim. The *20/20* reporters, who spent seven months investigating the "prior knowledge" issue, also located several eyewitnesses who vividly recalled seeing the county bomb-squad truck outside the Murrah building on the morning of the bombing. ABC investigators also provided substantial proof that local fire department officials were instructed by the FBI five days before the blast that "there were some people coming through town they should be on the lookout for."[26]

In perhaps the most startling revelation, the *20/20* investigation uncovered proof that the Executive Secretariat's Office at the Justice Department received a call 24 minutes before the explosion announcing that, "The Oklahoma federal building has just been bombed!" Unfortunately, in an unforgivable sin of omission, authorities failed to notify anyone of this strange call, much less demand the building in question be evacuated.[27] Thus, after numerous warnings of an impending catastrophe, the federal government not only squandered what might have been a last chance to avert this atrocity, but has been far from forthcoming about this knowledge ever since.

Aftermath

When taken together, these disclosures reveal gross negligence on the part of federal investigators and a strange indifference to the possibility of a wider conspiracy in this case. Indeed, the sins of omission committed during the course of everlasting truth of the matter, the victims of this immoral crime deserve nothing less than full explanations for the inconsistencies in the "official version" of events. The public has been offered an alternate reality that simply cannot be reconciled with science and the facts as we know them.

The Executive Secretariat's Office at the Justice Department received a call 24 minutes before the explosion announcing that, "The Oklahoma federal building has just been bombed!"

the bombing probe have inadvertently created a climate of suspicion and mistrust that has led the more vociferous anti-government activists to compare the Oklahoma City bombing to the Nazi Reichstag Fire of 1933, in which Nazi party activists set fire to the building housing the German legislature to pave the way for a brutal crackdown on communists and other political opponents.

What is perhaps most unsettling is that the latter conclusion is not entirely inconceivable in post-Waco America. Indeed, FBI informant Emad Ali Salem played a crucial and controversial role in the 1993 World Trade Center bombing,[28] and many believe OKC might have been yet another instance of a state-sanctioned operation that went fatally sour. Although this assertion remains speculative, the historical debate on this subject lingers, and one truth has emerged that few will deny: These two events have provided the impetus for a State-sanctioned war against "anti-government" dissent that has produced a chilling effect on certain forms of political activism in this country ever since.

"History tells us to pay attention to the aftermath," Adam Parfrey astutely observes in his essay on the bombing. One need only read the paper to trace the continuation of the OKC epic. Repressive anti-terrorism laws, Internet surveillance, crackdowns on politically suspect dissident groups, and the Clinton Administration's proposal to create a "Homelands Defense Force" that will allow the US military to police the citizenry are but a few manifestations of the growth of State power that has occurred in the wake of this singular tragedy.

Before we willingly cede our cherished civil liberties under the benign notion of "National Security," and the "lone bomber" theory is inscribed in American history books as the final and

Endnotes

1. Trial transcripts, *United States of America vs. Timothy James McVeigh* (see <www.apb.com>). **2.** Partin, Benton K. "Bomb damage analysis of Alfred P. Murrah Federal Building, Oklahoma City, Oklahoma", pp 1,3. **3.** *Ibid*, p 3. **4.** Keith, Jim. (1995). *OK bomb!: Conspiracy and cover-up*, p 94. IllumiNet Press. **5.** *Ibid*, p 93. **6.** Hoffman, David. (1998). *Oklahoma City Bombing and the Politics of Terror*, p 17. Feral House. **7.** *Ibid*, p 16. **8.** *Ibid*, p 17. **9.** Jasper, William. (1998). Proof of bombs and cover-up, *New American*, July 20. **10.** Serrano, Richard. (1997). Faulty testimony, practices found in FBI lab probe, *Los Angeles Times*, April 21. **11.** Parfrey, Adam. Oklahoma City: Cui bono, *Prevailing Winds Research* #2. **12.** Unattributed. Oklahoma City bombing evidence cover-up, World Internet News Distributary Source (WINDS), October 1997 (see <www.thewinds.org>). **13.** *Op cit.*, Keith, pp 14–15. **14.** Goddard, Ian Williams. "Conspiracy Fact vs. Government Fabrication" (see <www.imt.net/~mtpatriot/goddard.htm>). **15.** *Ibid*. Many of that day's news reports of additional explosives are available on YouTube. **16.** *Op cit.*, Hoffman, p 29. **17.** *Op cit.*, Goddard. **18.** *Media Bypass,* June 1995. **19.** *Op cit.*, Parfrey. **20.** Matthews, Clark. (1995). Behind the Oklahoma City bombing, *New Dawn*, July-August. **21.** *Op. cit.*, Hoffman, p 227. **22.** Wilmsen, Steve and Mark Eddy. (1996). Who bombed the Murrah building, *Denver Post*, December 15. **23.** *United States of America vs. Timothy James McVeigh and Terry Lynn Nichols* (filed August 10, 1995). **24.** Hoffman, David. (1997). A real fertilizer story, *Washington Weekly*, January 27. **25.** Goddard, Ian Williams. Federal government prior knowledge, *Prevailing Winds* #5 (see also <www.eros.com/igoddard/prior.htm>). **26.** Jasper, William. (1996). Evidence of prior knowledge, *New American*, May 13. **27.** *Op. cit.*, Goddard. **28.** DeRienzo, Paul, Frank Morales, and Chris Flash. (1995). Who bombed the World Trade Center?, *The Shadow,* January.

Postscript: The Past as Precedent—From OKC to DHS

It seems my well-founded concerns that Washington officials would raise the specter of terrorism to justify enhanced surveillance powers, "repressive anti-terrorism" measures, and the creation of an Orwellian "Homelands [*sic*] Defense Force" have fatefully come to pass. While the enemy may have changed, some of us can't help but feel a distinct sense of déjà vu. Again, there is talk of America's "lost innocence," and the ritual two-minute hate once reserved for so-called "militia sympathizers" and government critics is now directed at Islamic radicals and, by extension, the antiwar movement. As investigative journalist James Ridgeway has observed, "The Oklahoma City Bombing prefigured 9/11 in many ways."[1]

One cannot help but notice an unsettling continuum between the two atrocities: a lack of communication between competing federal agencies; warnings of an impending plot that were tragically ignored; a wealth of investigative data but few willing or able to connect the dots. Moreover, in the smoldering aftermath of both deadly attacks, Washington politicians in concert with the Department of Justice skillfully harnessed public fear and outrage to enact Constitutionally questionable measures allegedly designed to protect the public. Those who dared object to these opportunistic power grabs were charged with

Readers who may be curious as to how the PATRIOT ACT suddenly materialized within weeks of 9/11 need only look to the Anti-Terrorism and Effective Death Penalty Act of 1996 (AEDPA).

being tacitly complicit in the next terrorist attack—a crude rhetorical tactic that foreclosed any sort of open debate.

Readers who may be curious as to how the PATRIOT ACT suddenly materialized within weeks of 9/11 need only look to the Anti-Terrorism and Effective Death Penalty Act of 1996 (AEDPA). Enacted in the aftermath of the OKC blast when emotions were running high, the controversial measure can be seen as a sort of rough draft for the later bill. In an ominous preview of its Bush-era incarnation, the 1996 legislation limited the habeas protections of defendants, expedited the death penalty review process, and provided critical funding for government surveillance operations.

Are we any safer? Author John Robb, a renowned expert in counterterrorism and unconventional warfare, believes the existing top-down approach that defines US anti-terror policy has only made us that much more vulnerable. "Not only does the centralization of security result in a slide towards police state methods," he writes, "it also results in unresponsive systems and inefficiencies."[2] The limitations of vast, unaccountable bureaucracies like the Department of Homeland Security to address what probability theorists call "black swan" events can be seen in the systemic failures that characterized the vaunted agency's blundering response to the 2005 Hurricane Katrina disaster.

Sunlight, as is often said, is the best disinfectant. The first step

towards restoring a semblance of sanity to current counterterrorism policy is greater accountability. So long as self-serving political calculations, secrecy, and fear-mongering replace clear-headed analysis and forthright honesty with the public, we can expect more of the same.

The deadly 1995 attack on the Alfred P. Murrah Federal Building offers a disturbing case study of what happens when information is withheld from the public and questions go unanswered. While many believed that Timothy McVeigh's execution in June 2001 was the final chapter in the OKC story, the Justice Department's questionable "lone bomber" courtroom narrative continues to provide fertile ground for public speculation.

9/11 skeptics who believe that the federal government was complicit in the World Trade Center/Pentagon attacks cite OKC as evidence of a similar state-sponsored "false flag" operation. To bolster the case for preemptive war with Iraq, neoconservative propagandists repeatedly alleged in the run-up to war that Iraqi operatives working at the behest of Saddam Hussein were behind the blast.

Nevertheless, a wealth of compelling evidence continues to mount that there may have been additional co-conspirators behind the shadowy bombing conspiracy. While the Justice Department has worked tirelessly to airbrush these inconvenient facts from the historical record, the new revelations have bolstered arguments that federal law enforcement knew far more about the bombing conspiracy than they have publically admitted, and presents the very real possibility that there may be co-conspirators who have yet to be apprehended.

The new revelations shed light on the machinations of a group of bank robbers with ties to the far-right Aryan Republic Army (ARA). The criminal gang, who mainly targeted banks in the Midwest, has been linked to a white separatist compound in Oklahoma known as Elohim City.

According to a February 2003 Associated Press investigation, evidence gleaned from "hotel records, a speeding ticket, prisoner interviews, informant reports and phone records" indicates that OKC bomber Timothy McVeigh had repeated contact with both the ARA and Elohim City prior to the bombing. It seems this development did not go unnoticed by investigators. "It is suspected that members of Elohim City are involved [in OKC] either directly or indirectly through conspiracy," agents remarked in an FBI memo issued within days of the blast.[3] According to the AP investigation, none of these suspicions were brought to the attention of Danny Defenbaugh, the lead agent in the OKBOMB investigation.

The AP article also cited evidence that McVeigh contacted a home where "members of a violent Aryan National bank robbery gang were present" literally minutes after "calling the Ryder truck company where he rented the truck that carried the deadly bomb."[4]

Internal FBI memos also revealed that two members of the ARA "left Elohim City" on April 16—three days before the attack—and decamped to a location in Kansas that places them just a few short hours away from where "McVeigh was doing the final assembly of the bomb."[5]

We now know that Elohim City was also rife with federal informants. Carol Howe, a former Oklahoma beauty queen who once had ties to the far-right, was asked to infiltrate Elohim City in 1994 and '95 at the behest of the Bureau of Alcohol, Tobacco, and Firearms (ATF). Although her credibility was challenged by the Justice Department when she later told reporters of her warnings that a bombing conspiracy involving an Elohim City resident named Andreas Strassmeier and others was underway, a revealing 1997 courtroom exchange between her attorney, Clark Brewster, and her ATF handler, Angela Finley-Graham, seems to confirm her statements that she gave advance warning:

> Brewster: And Ms. Howe told you about Mr. Strassmeier's threats to blow up federal buildings, didn't she?
>
> Finley-Graham: In general. Yes.
>
> Brewster: And that was before the Oklahoma City bombing?
>
> Finley-Graham: Yes.[6]

FBI teletypes have also surfaced which provide evidence that the FBI was receiving information from an Elohim City informant linked to the Southern Poverty Law Center (SPLC), a nationally known civil rights organization with close ties to the Clinton Justice Department. Although an SPLC spokesman recently told James Ridgeway of *Mother Jones* that the information-gathering effort mainly consisted of "second or third hand reports,"[7] the fact that the informant was directly mentioned in internal FBI documents makes it hard to dismiss the charge that the FBI may have known about the unfolding bombing plot and the existing links between the ARA, Elohim City, and Timothy McVeigh.

Jesse Trentadue, a Utah-based attorney, can be credited with uncovering the multiple connections between the ARA, Elohim, and McVeigh. This tenacious investigator has spent over a decade probing the suspicious death of his brother Kenneth, who died while being held for a minor parole violation at the Federal Transfer Center in Oklahoma.

Although officially ruled a suicide by prison officials, Kenneth Trentadue's battered corpse seemed to indicate something far more sinister. Despite repeated stonewalling by both the Bureau of Prisons and the Justice Department, Jesse now contends that his brother may have perished during a vicious interrogation that went horribly awry. Trentadue believes that his brother was mistakenly thought to be Richard Lee Guthrie, an ARA associate and convicted bank robber whom many OKC researchers believe was the mysterious "John Doe #2" whom dozens of witnesses testified to seeing with McVeigh prior to the bombing.

Over the past few years, Trentadue has filed a number of successful Freedom of Information Act lawsuits pertaining to the Oklahoma City bombing, and his efforts have not gone unnoticed. In November 2005, former FBI Deputy Assistant Director Danny Coulson joined a chorus of voices calling for a new investigation of the blast. Coulson, who initially led evidence-gathering efforts during the OKC probe, now believes that there may have been additional co-conspirators. "For many years," he told reporter J.D. Cash, "I've believed Elohim City was important to this case, and I think we now know Tim McVeigh had contacts there." According to Coulson, "any future investigation should focus strictly on McVeigh's associates within that group."[8]

"It is suspected that members of Elohim City are involved [in OKC] either directly or indirectly through conspiracy," agents remarked in an FBI memo issued within days of the blast.

Whenever political institutions seek to withhold, destroy, or cover up evidence of a major historic occurrence, there is usually a reason why. Obviously the definitive history of the Oklahoma City bombing has yet to be written. Stay tuned.

Terry Nichols, the man considered McVeigh's chief accomplice—currently serving a life sentence for his role in the bombing—filed an affidavit in federal court in February 2007, alleging a wider conspiracy behind the OKC bombing. In his remarks to the court he asserts that "crucial parts of this terrorist act remain hidden from the American people—especially the identities of the 'Others Unknown' who collaborated with McVeigh in the bombing." Nichols also asserts that the bomb he helped McVeigh construct at Geary lake "did not resemble in any fashion" the bomb described in later accounts of the bombing, which "displayed a level of expertise and sophistication which neither McVeigh nor I had in building a bomb."[9] Whether these are the self-serving statements of a convict hoping to gain leniency from the court, a deranged man (he alleges that former FBI official Larry Potts was part of the conspiracy), or an honest accounting of the facts merits further investigation, but his statement should not be ignored.

Some thirteen years after the bombing, it seems incontestable that both the FBI and ATF had informants inside the Elohim City compound, were well aware of a possible bombing plot, and knew that McVeigh had connections to the ARA bank robbers. We also know that the FBI and ATF have repeatedly tried to keep this information from the public.

Was OKC a sting operation involving protected informants that went horribly wrong, or were federal officials pressured to adhere to the "lone bomber" scenario out of political considerations? Could additional bombs have been planted by McVeigh's alleged conspirators? These questions demand answers.

Regardless of intent, the failure to thoroughly investigate the bombing conspiracy has had far-reaching consequences. As James Ridgeway has written, "The government's refusal to disclose what it knew—and what it did not know—may also have forestalled the nation's best opportunity to address the problems in federal law enforcement and intelligence that would become tragically apparent on September 11, 2001."[10]

Endnotes

1. Ridgeway, James. (2007). In search of John Doe #2: The story the feds never told about the Oklahoma City bombing. *Mother Jones*, 31 Jul. **2.** Robb, John. (2007). *Brave new war: The next stage of terrorism and the end of globalization.* New Jersey: John Wiley and Sons, p 157. **3.** Solomon, John. (2003). FBI evidence linked McVeigh to white supremacists. Associated Press, 13 Feb. **4.** *Ibid.* **5.** *Ibid.* **6.** Cash, J.D. (2005). Agent: Feds told of threats to blow up buildings. *McCurtain Daily Gazette*, 10 Nov. **7.** *Op. cit.*, Ridgeway. **8.** Cash, J.D. (2005). Former high ranking FBI official calls for new OKC probe. *McCurtain Daily Gazette*, 28 Nov. [See the Oklahoma City Bombing Archive at <www.mccurtain.com>.] **9.** Terry Nichols Affidavit, filed February 2007. For full text see: <intelfiles.egoplex.com/trentadue-nichols-declaration-1.pdf>. **10.** *Op. cit.*, Ridgeway.

The Rabin Murder Cover-up

Barry Chamish

It took two years before Americans began to suspect that Lee Harvey Oswald did not shoot President Kennedy. It took large sections of the Israeli population less than a week to suspect that Yigal Amir did not shoot the fatal bullets at Prime Minister Yitzhak Rabin. It took me about two hours. Around midnight of November 4, 1995, I asked how Amir could possibly have broken through Rabin's bodyguards to take a clear shot at Rabin's back. My answer was that he couldn't have: unless someone wanted him to.

> There was a fourth person in the car waiting for Rabin.

The next day my suspicions were reinforced by eyewitness testimonies that appeared in the media. After Amir's first shot, one witness after another heard Rabin's bodyguards shout, "They're blanks," "They're not real," and the like. And then, instead of killing Amir on the spot, the same bodyguards let him get off two more rounds. It just didn't add up. The bodyguards are trained to shoot an assassin in less than a second; it would take longer to shout, "They're blanks, they're not real." Why would they think the bullets were duds? Why didn't they kill Amir to save Rabin?

And far more serious, why did they allow Amir into the so-called sterile security area where only authorized personnel were permitted entrance? The next day, Israel TV broadcast a film clip of Amir being taken away from an anti-Rabin demonstration just two weeks before. Amir was well-known to Rabin's security detail; he was a member of the most extreme anti-Rabin right-wing organization of all, Eyal (an acronym for Jewish Warriors), run by the most extreme right-wing radical of them all, the notorious Avishai Raviv.

Only on November 10, a public accusation was made by (now) Knesset Member Benny Elon that Avishai Raviv was in fact an agent for the General Security Services (Shabak), the very same Shabak charged with protecting Rabin. If people scoffed, it was only for a day. On November 11, respected left-wing journalist Amnon Abramovich broke the truth on Israel's Television One: Raviv was a Shabak officer code-named Champagne, whose duty was to infiltrate groups opposed to the government's peace process and incriminate them in crime. To make his task easier, he created a straw group called Eyal and hyper-radicalized young people, turning legitimate protest into illegitimate outrage. He was the Shabak's chief provocateur.

From that moment on, it was a matter of time before the conspiracy to assassinate Rabin was exposed. The assassin belonged to an organization created by the very Shabak which was charged with protecting Rabin. And that was not all. Amir had spent the spring and summer of 1992 in Riga, Latvia, working with a nest of spies called the Prime Minister's Liaison Office, or Nativ for short. There, the newspapers reported, he had received training from the Shabak.

Yigal Amir was not just a religious kid who got mad one night and shot a prime minister. He had an intelligence background.

Enter: The First Informer

At the time, I was the co-editor of Israel's only intelligence newsletter, *Inside Israel*. My partner was Joel Bainerman. We had both written books, recently published. My book, *The Fall of Israel* (Cannongate Publishers) was about political corruption; his book, *Crimes of a President* (SPI Books), was about the covert and illegal operations that took place during the first Bush administration. Combined, we were producing the most

> After Amir shoots, Rabin turns his head in the direction of the shot and keeps walking.

honest reporting of Israel's hidden political shenanigans anywhere. We had gained a strong reputation in numerous circles for the exposés of the criminal deceit that lay behind Israel's agreements with the Palestine Liberation Organization (PLO).

And that is why one Moshe Pavlov chose to call me on November 17. His first call was brief: "Watch Channel Two News tonight and you'll see me," he said. "Then I'll call back." He appeared on the news and was described as one of the country's "most dangerous right-wing leaders." Odd, I thought; why hadn't I heard of him before?

The next call wasn't from Pavlov but from my neighbor Joel Bainerman. Though Joel lived in a most obscure location, Pavlov had found his way to Joel's doorstep and appeared unannounced. Joel said, "I don't think we should meet here. I'll see you downtown in ten minutes."

Though he aggressively denies it, all—literally all—of my sources later told me Pavlov is a Shabak agent. In retrospect, there is no other way he could have had the information in his

He gave us the name and details of the bodyguard: Yoav Kuriel. A Yoav Kuriel was reported dead in the media the next day, but of a suicide. It would be another two years before I received his death certificate and spoke with the man who prepared his body for burial. He died of seven bullets to the chest. No one was allowed to identify his remains.

And then Pavlov gave us information that *no one* was allowed to know. To this day, only the man's initials can legally appear in the Israeli media. "The guy behind the operation is Eli Barak, a lunatic. He runs the Shabak's Jewish Department. He is Raviv's superior and set up Amir to take the fall."

He added a fact that was positively unknown at the time. "Barak takes his orders from the head of the Shabak. His first name is Carmi, he lives in Mevasseret Tzion, and that's all I want to say." It took over a year before the Israeli public was to learn the name of the Shabak Chief: Carmi Gillon.

Pavlov was insistent: "You have to publish this and my name. Otherwise I'm finished." Joel and I decided to publish the story

A researcher on one program told me the idea was to get me on the show to humiliate me, but after reviewing my evidence, she and her fellow researchers concluded that I was right.

possession if he wasn't an insider. Joel and I sat in a quiet corner of the town square of Bet Shemesh, as a terrified and agitated Moshe Pavlov spewed out reams of, what turned out to be, the truth.

"Amir was supposed to shoot blanks," he insisted. "That's why the bodyguards shouted that he did. He was supposed to. It was a fake assassination. Rabin was supposed to survive the blank bullets, dramatically go back on the podium, condemn the violence of his opponents and become a hero. That's how he was going to save the Oslo Accords. Raviv was supposed to give him the gun with the blanks, but Amir got wind of the plan and changed the bullets."

Pavlov was way off on this point. Later evidence proved beyond doubt that Amir did shoot blanks and that Rabin was shot elsewhere. Pavlov became nearly hysterical. "They're killing people to cover this up, and they're setting me up for a fall. Already one of Rabin's bodyguards is dead."

in *Inside Israel*. When it came out, I met Pavlov at the Holiday Inn lobby in Jerusalem. We were surrounded by policemen. Wherever he went, they followed. That was good enough proof for me that our faith in Pavlov's version of events was justified.

An Assassination Film Emerges

Just under two months after the assassination, to the total shock of the nation, an "amateur" videotape of the murder emerged and was broadcast over Channel Two. Joel taped the film from the television, and we scrutinized it closely. Though we are being petty, to this day we argue over who first noticed the mysterious closing car door.

The story of Rabin's last two hours of life is bizarre now, as it was then. The drive to the hospital should have taken less than a minute. But the driver, Menachem Damti, claimed he became confused, and that's why he got lost and took nine minutes to arrive. After seven minutes driving, he stopped the car and asked a cop, Pinchas Terem, to get in the car and direct him to the hospital. So, only three people were alleged to be in the car until then: Rabin, Menachem Damti (the driver), and Yoram Rubin (the personal bodyguard). In the film all three are clearly outside the vehicle when the right back passenger door was slammed shut from the inside. There was a fourth person in the car waiting for Rabin.

We saw two other shocking moments: The first occurs just before Amir makes his move towards Rabin's back. Rabin's rear bodyguard stops dead in his tracks, turns his head sideways, and allows the "killer" in. The act was deliberate, there was no doubting the film.

And then, after Amir shoots, Rabin turns his head in the direction of the shot and keeps walking. Just like eyewitnesses

Morrison proves that the Israeli media are in the hands of the Shabak.

claimed on the night of the assassination. Rabin was unhurt by Amir's shot to the back. It was a blank bullet after all.

A month later, the government-appointed Shamgar Commission of Inquiry into the Rabin Assassination issued its findings. It concluded that Amir shot twice at Rabin's back, once from 50 centimeters while Rabin was walking, then from about 20 to 30 centimeters after he fell. Very logical, except the film showed that Amir never got anywhere near such close range for the second shot. In fact, he was no closer than six feet away for the second shot.

The contradictions had reached and far surpassed the point of being utterly ridiculous.

The Trial

After the government had already declared him the murderer, Amir stood trial for murder…which lets you know how fair a trial he received. Before the trial began, there was a hearing. When Amir stepped into the courtroom, he shouted to reporters: "The whole system is rotten. If I open my mouth I can bring it all down. The people will forgive me when they know the truth. I didn't think they'd start killing anyone."

After this revealing outburst, he was taken away and never

allowed to address journalists again. After a month in Shabak custody, he appeared a different person for his trial: a grinning idiot determined to prove his own guilt. He had been transformed, we surmised, by a combination of threats, promises, sleep deprivation, and drugs.

The trial was barely covered by the media, but what emerged was astounding. Damti and Rubin lied through their teeth. Just for starters, Damti claimed he was opening the door for Leah Rabin (Yitzhak's wife) when the first shot rang out. Then he immediately sat in the driver's seat as he had been trained to do. The truth was that Leah Rabin was 24 feet away and nowhere in sight, and the film showed that Damti did not sit in the driver's seat until Rabin was placed in the car.

And if those statements were mere whoppers, Rubin's version of events was a lollapalooza. He testified that he lay on top of Rabin and that Rabin helped him get up. Then they both jumped headfirst into the car, Rabin landing on the seat, Rubin on the floor. Without elaborating on the depth of the lie, no witnesses saw Rabin jump and the film proves he didn't.

After the trial, I received my first prized secret document—the testimony of Chief Lieutenant Baruch Gladstein of the Israel Police Crime Laboratory, taken from the protocols of Amir's trial. After testing Rabin's clothes scientifically, Gladstein testified that the Prime Minister was shot at point-blank, with the gun's barrel on his skin. He insisted that his conclusion was certain and that the combination of massed gunpowder and an explosion tear on the clothing could only have occurred at zero distance. Even half a centimeter would have been too far.

Amir never, ever shot from point-blank range. He did not kill Rabin. That was enough for me. Gathering the film and the testimonies, I started giving lectures on the Rabin murder conspiracy in Jerusalem, and the crowds who came to hear me were always large.

Shutting Me Up

In October 1996, I received a phone call from the *Weekend Magazine* program on Channel Two. They had heard about my lectures and also believed there were inconsistencies between the evidence and the Shamgar Commission findings. They wanted to interview me.

The Rabin Murder Cover-up
Barry Chamish

What liars they were! They broadcast an eight-minute snow job which compared me to a Holocaust denier. And they rebroadcast the show the next night. At first it looked like a disaster for my life. The organizations which had sponsored my lectures were forced to cancel them, cabinet ministers condemned me as a "fascist," and a few threatening crank calls resulted.

However, the program did include the clip of Rabin's car door slamming shut when no one was supposed to be in the car. And a few of my strongest points slipped through loud and clear. Everywhere I went, people congratulated me on my courage. The show boomeranged and ended up encouraging me to carry on.

I was not the only one on the show. A Ramat Gan computer technician named Natan Gefen also appeared briefly with his own proofs. As a result of his appearance, the local Ramat Gan newspaper interviewed him at length about his evidence of a conspiracy behind the Rabin assassination.

One would not believe that Natan Gefen deserves to be recognized as one of the greatest investigators of all time. He doesn't look the part, and by day he operates a computer at a pharmaceutical firm. But Gefen uncovered the most sensitive documents of any political assassination, and here's how he did it.

He made a hundred copies of his interview in the Ramat Gan paper, added his fax number and a request for proof, and placed the package in every corner of the hospital Rabin was taken to, Ichilov. And someone faxed him Rabin's medical records.

What an incredible tale they told! The surgeon who operated on Rabin, Dr. Mordechai Gutman, and his surgical team recorded the following fact: Rabin arrived with two bullet holes in the back, was revived, was shot again, and left with a third bullet which passed through the upper lobe of his right lung from the front and finally shattered dorsal vertebrae five and six.

The conspiracy was broken. The State Pathologist's report had erased all the wounds the hospital staff reported because Amir never shot from the front and couldn't have. And Rabin could not have had his backbone shattered because the videotape of the murder clearly shows him walking after the only shot to the upper back. Gefen had provided the definitive proof that Amir did not shoot the deadly bullets into Rabin.

Three times, I was invited to appear on major TV programs—once I was even filmed beforehand—and all three times my appearances were cancelled at the last moment. A researcher on one program told me the idea was to get me on the show to humiliate me, but after reviewing my evidence, she and her fellow researchers concluded that I was right. So out I went. On another occasion a producer cancelled not just me, but two other researchers who had reached my conclusions. I was told that someone made a phone call two hours before airtime that turned the tide against us. The third time, the producer called me three hours before showtime with the excuse that he was canceling because no one was willing to debate me. I had no idea until then that a debate was planned.

I have a friend who is a producer for the Voice of Israel, which runs three radio stations. She called me with this message: "You won't believe this. They're distributing a memo at the station forbidding us to ever mention your name. It's from the top. Gotta go, someone's coming."

I have been interviewed by a long list of Israeli journalists who understood my case was right. One after another, their stories and filmed reports were cancelled or badly altered. A case in point: Matti Cohen of Television Two interviewed me for four hours, but his station forbade him to broadcast his findings. So he presented them to Rabin's daughter, now a Knesset member, and she publicly demanded a reinvestigation of her father's murder.

People can't believe it's so easy to control Israel's media. But they're wrong. Perhaps 85 percent of all media influence is in the hands of three families: Nimrodi, Mozes, and Shocken. All have deep intelligence and political ties to the Labor Party and its enforcement arm, the Shabak. News is manipulated on a daily basis. There may be *no* accurate reports about stories of import coming from the Israeli media.

I had to get the true information out, but my lectures were cancelled. Then Joel had a brilliant idea: If your lectures are cancelled, let's rent a hotel auditorium and do one ourselves. On a stormy January night in 1997, over 70 people braved the wet and arrived for the lecture. And Channel One television covered it.

I was back.

Attending the lecture was Brian Bunn, who sat on the Foreign

Student's council of the Hebrew University of Jerusalem. He was impressed and booked me to speak at the country's most respected educational institution. This the Shabak could not tolerate, so they organized a violent riot against me. And I must thank them for that because I was front page news for a week in Israel, and the riot was covered worldwide.

Next, a smear campaign was organized against me in the Israeli media, but a few reporters listened to me, read the evidence I had gathered, and wrote long, favorable pieces. And over 300 people contacted me within a week, *all* to congratulate me and some 20 to pass along invaluable information. I was invited to give the same lecture in New York, where I met Jay Sidman, who set up a brilliant Rabin Website for me. It turned into a meeting place for an international exchange of ideas and information about the assassination.

A Toronto talk was videotaped and later sold commercially. I was really on that night, and the videotape convinced tens of thousands of people that I was right. And best of all, the publicity led to book contracts, first in America, then in Israel and France. I took care with the book (*Who Murdered Yitzhak Rabin?*), reviews have been excellent, and hundreds of thousands have been swayed by the facts.

Further Vindication

In June 2000, a new book called *Lies: Israel's Secret Service and the Rabin Murder* by David Morrison (Gefen Books) lifted the lid off the coffin, and the Israeli media were exposed.

Morrison proves that the Israeli media are in the hands of the Shabak. He does so by referring back to the Bus 300 scandal of 1987. To hide its role in the murder of two shackled terrorists, the Shabak persuaded then-Prime Minister Shimon Peres to call a meeting of the Media Forum—a shadowy organization of media owners—and ordered them to ban release of information about the scandal. All immediately complied. However, a new newspaper, *Chadashot*, was not a member of this cabal and released details of Bus 300. The government ordered the paper shut until its policy changed.

The same tactics and the same personalities are shutting down Rabin murder evidence but are going much further this

time around. They are also viciously attacking the advocates of "the conspiracy theory" and deliberately promulgating a fake alternative scenario, one which blames the religious community and its leaders for the murder. Morrison traces and proves this media sub-conspiracy convincingly. And it's about time someone did.

He begins by reviewing the only three Rabin conspiracy books available at the time: mine, *Fatal Sting* by Natan Gefen, and *Murder in the Name of God: The Plot To Kill Yitzhak Rabin* by Michael Karpin and Ina Friedman, which was paid for by Peace Now financier David Moshovitz. Of *Fatal Sting*, Morrison regrets that it hasn't been given the notice it deserves. But he has many nice words to say about me:

> When this author first heard about Chamish's thesis that Rabin was not killed by Amir, but was killed after he got into the car, he dismissed it out of hand as ridiculous. Who in his right mind would want to believe such a thing? After one examines the data Chamish cites, and verifies that it is, with minor exceptions, accurate, one still does not want to believe it but confronts "difficulties in thought…"
>
> Karpin and Friedman cite Chamish's "convoluted theories" about "the angle of trajectory, the composition of explosives," and those things sound very technical and not very interesting. One could posit that they want to discourage the reader from reading Chamish's book. They do not grapple with the abundance of data cited by Chamish that raises serious questions about the official version of Yitzhak Rabin's murder….
>
> So where is the "plot to kill Yitzhak Rabin?" Karpin and Fiedman do not mention that Carmi Gillon's Shabak agents tortured army officer Oren Edri and a number of other religious settlers and still were unable to uncover any evidence of a religious, right-wing underground….
>
> If we have the whole truth, we may also have proof that Karpin and Friedman and other left-wing, secular elements participated in the cover-up, possibly in an obstruction of justice.

And Morrison is just as good at exposing the lies of a variety of Israeli journalists like Dan Margalit, Yoel Marcus, Hirsh Goodman, and others. The *Jerusalem Report* comes in for special treatment because it actually published a whole cover-up book. *Lies* exposes some of the more blatant falsehoods that the *Jerusalem Report*'s staff must have known about but included anyway, and concludes that only the book's amateurish writing saved it from being accepted as a legitimate account of the Rabin murder.

Morrison's own feeling about the Shabak-orchestrated campaign of lies in the Israeli media is:

> The Israeli media will stand exposed as a willing agent of the power structure, or participant in the power structure that has something to hide.

When it does,

> Each element of society, each in its own way, will have an opportunity to purge themselves of the corrupt elements in their leadership and choose new leaders to represent them….
>
> One could argue that full disclosure of the truth would only increase the schisms in Israeli society. Another view is that it could have exactly the opposite effect. Instead of exacerbating the splits in Israeli society, it may bring together the many components of the culture. It may unite them together against the common enemy—the elite of all the groups, those with the most to lose if the full truth emerges.

It is hard to say if Morrison's book will lead to media reform, but recently there was an indication of some change. The far-left newsmagazine *Kol Ha'ir* published a three-page article on the phenomenon of an anti-media media determined to get the truth about the Rabin murder out to the nation. It noted that since my book was published, four others reaching similar conclusions have hit the Israeli market. The article noted that lately my work has "become legitimized" by a public seeking new media.

It's small, maybe a one-time fluke, but it's a start. Perhaps the Israeli people, after all, won't permit their mass media to perpetrate a not-believable coverup of the true circumstances of Yitzhak Rabin's murder.

What's Missing from This Picture?

Jim Marrs

Through the years, controversies have continually raged over some of the most painful and traumatic events in United States history.

There have been ongoing arguments over who was behind the assassinations of Abraham Lincoln, John Kennedy, and Robert Kennedy, as well as the truth of what really happened in Waco and Oklahoma City and many more recent events.

The poor public has been buffeted by a barrage of neatly-packaged government pronouncements and by ever-broadening conspiracy theories.

What's missing from this picture?

Only the proof, the hard evidence.

Yes, the information which could prove the truth behind these events has gone missing, and the corporate-controlled news media do not seem overly interested. They appear strangely unable or unwilling to dig into these issues or report them with any clarity. So the public has been left at the mercy of private researchers, many diligent and objective, others less so.

Lincoln

Take the assassination of President Abraham Lincoln, for example. It is an historical fact that Lincoln's death was the result of a large conspiracy involving actor John Wilkes Booth, Confederate agents, a secret society called the Knights of the Golden Circle, and, according to a credible mass of evidence, even persons within Lincoln's own administration.

The facts of this conspiracy may never be fully known since much of the vital evidence in the case went missing. This included the body of the man—identified as Booth—killed in a Virginia barn, as well as eighteen critical pages of Booth's diary.

The body of the man thought to be Booth was hustled to Washington and quickly buried after a physician who had briefly lanced a boil on Booth's neck more than a year earlier first denied the body was Booth but later tentatively made an identification. The body was quickly buried in a prison yard and later sunk in the Potomac River to prevent any possible review.

Booth's diary was taken by Lincoln's Secretary of War, Edwin Stanton, and later released as evidence.

> The body was quickly buried in a prison yard and later sunk in the Potomac River to prevent any possible review.

But eighteen pages were missing!

Years later, the missing pages, which incriminated not only Northern Radical Republicans and speculator Jay Gould but Stanton himself, were discovered among Stanton's possessions.

Unfortunately, though, most missing evidence is never found.

Nixon

During the Watergate scandal, it was not eighteen pages but eighteen minutes of recording tape that proved the downfall of President Richard M. Nixon.

"Tricky Dick," as he was being called by his enemies, told a national TV audience, "I am not a crook!" But, after his Oval Office tapes were released, the swear words, racial epithets, and political scheming proved unacceptable to his mainstream supporters. One critical conversation dealing with his fore-knowledge of the Watergate break-in was of particular interest to the special prosecutor assigned to this case.

But eighteen minutes on the tape are missing!

Nixon, under threat of impeachment, resigned in disgrace.

Johnson

Missing evidence has become a hallmark of American politics. Apparently the idea is that, circumstances notwithstanding, if there's no proof then there can be no guilt.

An example of this tactic came early in the career of Lyndon B. Johnson, whose entire political life was surrounded by controversy and allegations of criminal behavior.

From the infamous stolen election of 1948 to the murder-for-hire death of a golf pro despised by Johnson for courting his sister, Johnson had come under investigation by several Texas authorities including Frank L. Scofield, then Austin District Collector for the IRS.

"I am unable to conceive of any manner in which the casket could have an evidentiary value nor can I conceive of any reason why the national interest would require its preservation."

Scofield was accused of forcing political contributions from his employees (a minor infraction of the law) just as he had amassed a quantity of evidence against Johnson. Scofield was eventually cleared of this charge, but in the meantime, his replacement placed all of Johnson's files in a Quonset hut in South Austin. Within days, the prefab structure mysteriously caught fire and burned to the ground.

The incriminating evidence became missing!

Johnson, of course, went on to become President upon the assassination of John F. Kennedy.

JFK

The Kennedy assassination, too, is replete with missing data. Not just a few government or intelligence files, but even some

of the most vital evidence, including a critical part of Kennedy, is gone.

Although Naval Technician Paul O'Connor said Kennedy's cranial cavity was empty when the body arrived at Bethesda Naval Hospital in Washington, autopsy records indicate his brain was routinely sectioned and fixed in formaldehyde. Today, any competent forensic pathologist would be able to determine how many shots penetrated the brain and from which direction they came.

But Kennedy's brain is missing!

Tissue samples from Kennedy's body and color slides of his autopsy, all evidence vital to determining the number and trajectory of the bullets, are also missing. Many files on accused assassin Lee Harvey Oswald and his connection to US intelligence, as well his Civil Air Patrol youth leader and Mafia/CIA pilot David Ferrie, turned up missing. Even a half-dozen frames from the famed Zapruder film of Kennedy's assassination are missing, thus altering the time frame of the film, making it useless as a true timetable of the shooting.

At the time of Kennedy's assassination, nearly his entire Cabinet was high over the Pacific on a flight to Japan. When word came of the Dallas shooting, the powerful passengers onboard dithered for more than an hour while searching for the code book which would have allowed them encrypted communication with Washington.

But the code book was missing!

The Cabinet members finally radioed in using standard open frequencies and were told the situation was under control in Washington.

Newly released documents from the National Archives, missed by researchers for years, have given the public even further revelations about Kennedy's death.

One of the revelations involved missing words which may have changed the verdict of history. The initial Warren Commission Report stated, "A bullet entered his back at a point slightly below the shoulder to the right of the spine." This statement conformed to both the medical and eyewitness evidence. However, then-Representative Gerald Ford, the only US President appointed to office, directed that the wording be changed to, "A bullet had entered the back of his neck slightly to the right of the spine." This subtle change of wording has allowed champions of the government version of the assassination to argue that a single bullet caused all of Kennedy's body wounds and thus supports the idea that all shots were fired by a lone assassin. This conclusion is untenable when the basic facts behind the report are studied.

In 1999 the National Archives released documents that showed the expensive bronze casket used to transport Kennedy's body from Dallas to Bethesda was unceremoniously and secretly dumped in the Atlantic Ocean in 9,000 feet of water off the Maryland-Delaware coast in early 1966.

The casket had been missing since 1964, and General Services Administration (GSA) officials claimed as late as 1998 that they didn't know what happened to it.

This destruction of evidence reportedly was at the request of the President's brother, Robert. However, the dumping was authorized by then-Attorney General Nicholas Katzenbach, the same person mentioned in an FBI memo from Director J. Edgar Hoover issued just two days after JFK's assassination. The memo read, "The thing I am most concerned about, and so is Mr. Katzenbach, is having something issued so we can convince the public that Oswald is the real assassin." Never mind about a true investigation.

Katzenbach, in a February 11, 1966, letter to the GSA ordering the casket's disposal, stated, "I am unable to conceive of any manner in which the casket could have an evidentiary value nor can I conceive of any reason why the national interest would require its preservation."

One reason might have been that the documents stated the bronze coffin was replaced by a mahogany one because it was damaged.

Damaged? This was a brand-new casket ordered from the Vernon O'Neal Funeral Home in Dallas upon Kennedy's death. After placing the President's body in it at Parkland Hospital, it was loaded into an O'Neal ambulance and taken to Dallas Love Field, where it was carefully loaded onto Air Force One. Upon

landing at Dulles Airport, it was lowered to a waiting ambulance by a mechanical lift. When did it become damaged and why?

Another most pertinent reason becomes clear in considering the arguments by many assassination researchers who point to glaring discrepancies in the accounts of JFK's wounds and the disposition of the body between Parkland Hospital in Dallas and the naval hospital where his autopsy was performed by inexperienced military doctors under the close direction of senior military officers.

Parkland witnesses said Kennedy's nude body was wrapped in a sheet and carefully placed in the bronze casket. Several medical technicians at Bethesda said JFK's body arrived there wrapped in a rubber body bag inside a slate-gray military shipping casket.

Through the years, a strong argument has been made for the alteration of Kennedy's wounds while in transit, and the casket could possibly have settled the issue.

But by 1966, the casket, as well as any public discourse on this matter, was missing!

Such missing evidence allowed Ford to state repeatedly, "We could find no evidence of conspiracy." It has also allowed various authors, untroubled by this obvious destruction and suppression of evidence, to present a reasonable argument that Oswald acted alone and that any idea to the contrary is simply "conspiracy theory."

RFK

The same pattern of missing evidence was seen in the June 4, 1968, assassination of Robert F. Kennedy, gunned down in the kitchen of Los Angeles' Ambassador Hotel minutes after he had received the California Democratic Primary presidential nomination, which most pundits declared would have cinched his place on the national ticket.

Unlike his brother's assassination, in which no one actually saw Oswald firing a gun, RFK's death was immediately attributed to a nondescript Palestinian named Sirhan Sirhan. Sirhan was in the kitchen firing a .22-caliber pistol and was quickly wrestled to the floor by bystanders including pro football players.

It appeared to be an open and shut case. But then Dr. Thomas T. Noguchi, the world-class county coroner who autopsied

RFK, testified under oath that the fatal shot, which entered behind his right ear at a steep upward angle, came from a distance of less than one inch. Sirhan was never closer than about six feet *in front* of the senator.

However, a private security guard named Thane Cesar was walking by Kennedy's right side. Cesar also was carrying a .22-caliber pistol and according to witness Don Schulman, drew his weapon during the shooting. Cesar's clip-on black necktie apparently was pulled from his shirt as Kennedy fell to the floor and can be seen lying beside the stricken senator in photos.

Cesar, who has admitted drawing his pistol that night but denied shooting RFK, initially said he had sold the .22 pistol shortly before the assassination but later decided he had sold it after the assassination. When the weapon was traced to its new owner, the Arkansas man said it had been stolen in a burglary shortly after Cesar was finally questioned by authorities.

This key piece of evidence is missing!

Other evidence indicated that more than one gunman was involved in the RFK shooting. Sirhan carried an eight-shot revolver. Two slugs were recovered from Kennedy's body, and another five from other victims. An eighth slug passed through ceiling panels. Two additional shots were found in the kitchen's door frame and were actually identified as bullet holes in official LAPD and FBI photos. But LAPD officials, after some foot-dragging, finally admitted they destroyed the door and ceiling panels, and no one could locate records of tests conducted on these extraneous bullet holes.

The evidence is missing!

One news photographer who was in the kitchen had his photos, which might have clarified the matter, confiscated by the LAPD. He fought in court for years to have them returned, fearing they might join an estimated 2,500 RFK-assassination photographs unaccountably destroyed just three months after the event. But when a court ordered his pictures returned, a courier was sent to the state capitol at Sacramento to retrieve them from state archives. They were stolen from his car.

These photos are now missing!

In 1988 Professor Philip H. Melanson surveyed released LAPD files on RFK's assassination and concluded that much of the material, especially that suggesting a conspiracy, had disappeared.

Vietnam

Soon after the assassination of RFK and Johnson's escalation of the Vietnam conflict, the anti-war movement began to gain strength. Its youthful leaders made many attempts to discover from government documents which persons were responsible for the debacle in Vietnam. But, to their chagrin, they found many of the government files detailing our involvement in Southeast Asia, as well as the killing of students by the Ohio National Guard at Kent State, were not available.

They're missing!

Only after Daniel Ellsberg made the Pentagon Papers public did some of the historical holes begin to be filled.

Military Scandals

One stumbling block to investigating military-related issues and scandals was a fire which in 1973 swept through a portion

> When the weapon was traced to its new owner, the Arkansas man said it had been stolen in a burglary.

of the National Personnel Records Center in St. Louis, destroying many personnel records. This one fire impeded investigations for years for, while it only affected certain Air Force records, it permitted the federal authorities to plead ignorance of several military whistleblowers.

Their records are missing!

MK-ULTRA

The tactic of disappearing evidence has proved even better than foot-dragging during investigations into government wrongdoing. Former CIA Director William Colby explained that during inquiries into assassination plots during the 1970s, CIA officers warned him that "…Congress could not be trusted with intelligence secrets, that release to it was the equivalent to release to the world at large. And still others…asserted that each item that the investigators requested should be fought over tenaciously and turned over only when there was no alternative."

This "defend the bunker" mentality continued during investigations into the CIA's fatal experiments with mind control.

Carrying forward the work of Nazi psychologists in concentration camps, the CIA's mind control experiments, collectively coded MK-ULTRA, began as far back as 1953. According to author Walter H. Bowart, its purpose was "to devise operational techniques to disturb the memory, to discredit people through aberrant behavior, to alter sex patterns, to elicit information and to create emotional dependence."

Many researchers contend that Sirhan Sirhan is an assassin created by mind control, since he has repeatedly said he cannot remember what happened in the Ambassador Hotel and wrote strange words, including mention of the "Illuminati," in a repetitive manner in his personal notebook. When a horrified public finally learned of the mind-control experiments, some of them fatal to people involved, standard government methodology came into play. Memories faded and filing cabinets were emptied.

Former CIA Director Richard Helms, who admitted not revealing CIA assassination plots to the Warren Commission because he was not asked the right questions, also suffered a lapse of memory regarding mind control. He did recall, however, that a majority of MK-ULTRA documents were destroyed on his orders in an effort to solve a "burgeoning paper problem."

So the crucial documents are missing!

With little paper trail and faulty memories, no one was ever jailed over these criminally harmful experiments.

Pan Am 103

Space does not permit the detailed enumeration of evidence and documentation missing from federal government filing cabinets, safes, and archives.

But one further example would have to be the materials, including a briefcase, recovered by CIA agents following the crash of Pan Am Flight 103 near Lockerbie, Scotland, in December 1988. The agents reportedly were on the crash scene before many rescue workers and firefighters.

Barron's, the mainstream business publication, ran a story in 1990 stating that the flight carried CIA officers and that terrorists had substituted a suitcase-bomb for an identical suitcase containing a CIA-approved heroin shipment. By several reports, as many as eight CIA agents, some of whom reportedly were making an unauthorized return to the United States to blow the whistle on the drug smuggling, were killed in the crash. The story remains in controversy due to lack of evidence.

Of course, the briefcase, reportedly containing proof of the plot, was missing!

TWA 800

In another plane disaster—the crash of TWA Flight 800, which killed 230 people when the Boeing 747 crashed off Long Island on July 17, 1996—missing evidence again became the rule rather than the exception.

Many witnesses said they saw strange lights in the sky and a fiery trail reaching upward from the ground to the plane just prior to the crash. Within 24 hours, Congressman Michael P. Forbes of New York told CNN that the craft's flight data recorder, popularly known as the black box, had been recovered. Federal authorities quickly denied this.

So, during the first critical days, the black box was missing!

Six days later, federal officials acknowledged obtaining the box. But even then, there were signs that data on the device had been altered, according to Kelly O'Meara, a former congressional chief of staff turned journalist.

O'Meara also doggedly sought radar logs for the time of the TWA 800 crash.

Officials of the National Transportation Safety Board (NTSB) said the radar data were unavailable—missing!

When the missing data finally turned up, they showed a large number of ships concentrated in the area of the crash, a fact totally contrary to initial government pronouncements that only two military vessels were in the area at the time.

Other evidence went missing when FBI agents took pieces of the plane's wreckage to Washington rather than to the National Transportation Safety Board (NTSB), which was charged with investigating the crash.

Other evidence went missing when FBI agents took pieces of the plane's wreckage to Washington rather than to the National Transportation Safety Board (NTSB), which was charged with investigating the crash. The families of French passengers killed in the crash hired a lawyer, who argued their belief that US government officials lied about significant facts of the case and were withholding critical documents. Senior NTSB Investigator Henry F. Hughes testified to the Senate Judiciary Committee in 1999 that federal agents and officials tampered with the wreckage, destroyed and altered evidence, mishandled forensic evidence, and failed to establish a chain of evidence in connection with passenger autopsies.

The transcripts containing his statements are missing!

The Senate committee was still withholding transcripts of their hearings as of mid-2000, prompting charges of a cover-up. Even Admiral Thomas H. Moorer, former chairman of the Joint Chiefs of Staff, called for a new investigation, stating, "It absolutely deserves more investigation—a lot more. This time, I wouldn't let the FBI do it. I'd have the NTSB do it. I think Congress certainly should get more answers from the FBI."

Space Photos

Even issues not involving deaths include missing evidence. In May 1963, US astronaut Gordon Cooper became the first human to orbit the Earth an astounding 22 times. In a recent book, he detailed how these early spacecraft carried cameras with telephoto lenses of such high resolution they were capable of taking "some unbelievable close-ups of car license plates." Yet today the low-resolution photos of the notorious "Face on Mars" and anomalies on the moon presented to the public by NASA were made by cameras which cannot seem to focus on anything smaller than the size of a football stadium.

The high-resolution photos are missing!

■ ■ ■ ■ ■ ■ ■ ■ ■ ■

Two events of the 1990s most traumatic to the American public were the 1993 deaths at the Branch Davidian home in Waco and the 1995 deaths caused by the explosion of the Murrah Federal Building in Oklahoma City.

In both instances, the primary evidence should have been the remaining structures, which could have been studied for years by both official and unofficial investigators to determine the truth of those tragedies. But both structures were bulldozed and covered with earth by federal government personnel before any independent probe could be launched. And within hours of the Oklahoma City explosion, work crews were filling in the bomb crater.

The primary evidence became missing!

Waco

The tragically fatal events in Waco began with the February 28, 1993, assault by federal agents on the church home of the Branch Davidian sect near Waco, Texas, and ended with the deaths of 84 persons, including four agents and about 21 children.

The fiery end of a 51-day siege on April 19 followed a full-scale attack, complete with special forces snipers, helicopters, and tanks. Despite repeated claims by the government that the Davidians, under the charismatic leadership of David Koresh, committed suicide and torched their own home, troubling questions continued to be raised for years afterward.

For example, someone—no one seems to know exactly who—ordered the refrigeration unit shut off on the truck containing the burnt corpses of the Davidians. The Texas heat quickly caused such decomposition that it was difficult, if not impossible, for autopsy doctors to determine if bullets, rather than the fire, caused their deaths.

Once again, the best evidence is missing!

The Davidians adamantly charged the federal officers with firing the first shots, while the feds claimed just the opposite. If the feds fired first, then any action taken by the Davidians to protect themselves was permissible under existing law. If the Davidians fired first, then they are guilty of firing on law enforcement personnel in the performance of their duties and arguably brought ruin on themselves. The debate continues to this day, despite the year 2000 seeing a civil court decision and a Justice Department special counsel report absolving the federal government of any responsibility in the deaths.

One item of evidence might have brought out the truth of this issue—one of the bullet-riddled front doors to the Davidian home and church.

But the door is missing!

According to the testimony of a Texas state trooper, the door may have been taken by federal agents. Testifying in the wrongful death civil suit brought against the US government by surviving Davidians, Sergeant David Keys testified that he saw an object the size of a door being loaded into a U-Haul truck by federal agents just prior to the crime scene being turned over for security to the Texas Department of Public Safety. The seventeen-year law enforcement veteran also said he saw what appeared to be a body spirited away in a government vehicle and overheard FBI agents telling of a "firefight" at the rear of the home at the time of the fatal fire.

Federal agents have always claimed that no shots were fired at the Davidians after the initial February 28 assault. But then they also claimed that no incendiary devices were used at the time of the fiery destruction of the building. However, after Texas authorities in 1999 announced the presence of pyrotechnic devices in the Waco evidence they were holding for the federal government, the FBI finally acknowledged that "a limited number" of military M651 incendiary rounds were fired during the final assault.

Lead Davidian attorney Michael Caddell argued that photographs, some taken by Texas troopers and turned over the FBI, as well as others, could have established who started the fatal fire in the Davidian home.

But the photographs are missing!

"The pattern of the photographs produced [in the civil trial] by the FBI suggests only one thing," said Caddell: "The FBI has turned over only those photographs to the court and the press that the FBI wants the court and the public to see."

Two experts in infrared photography who might have settled the question of whether or not federal agents caused the deaths of the Davidians by pinning them inside the burning home with gunfire were missing from the civil court trial—one stricken by a stroke and the other found dead.

Dr. Edward Allard, who, as a holder of three patents on FLIR (Forward Looking Infrared) technology, had been considered one of the world's leading experts on infrared imaging systems, nearly died from a stroke before he could testify in the Waco civil suit. Allard had analyzed FLIR tapes made by the British Special Air Service (SAS), who taped the final assault while working for the FBI during the 1993 siege. He concluded that the video clearly showed persons firing into the Davidian home/church. He was quoted as saying, "This type of behavior, men running up and down the building, firing automatic weapons into a church is disgusting."

With Dr. Allard out of the picture, the Davidians turned to Carlos Ghigliotti, another infrared expert who had been retained by the US House Government Reform Committee investigating the Waco case.

But both structures were bulldozed and covered with earth by federal government personnel before any independent probe could be launched.

According to friend and attorney David T. Hardy, Ghigliotti owned Infrared Technologies Corporation and had spent months studying the infrared tapes made by the SAS. Hardy said Ghigliotti had verified nearly 200 gunshots from federal agents on the tape and had said the Waco FLIR would probably be the next Zapruder film.

Furthermore, a Texas Rangers report released in 1999 stated that three-dozen spent rifle shell casings were found in an outpost used by federal agents during the siege. Although a government spokesman claimed the casings were left over from the initial assault, others saw the late arrival of this report as suppression of evidence.

But before the Waco civil case began, Ghigliotti turned up missing!

Someone—no one seems to know exactly who—ordered the refrigeration unit shut off on the truck containing the burnt corpses of the Davidians.

Not for long, though. A building manager, concerned that Ghigliotti had not been seen in weeks, notified police in Laurel, Maryland, who discovered Ghigliotti's badly decomposed body in his home, which doubled as his office.

Laurel Police spokesman Jim Collins initially said, "We're investigating it as a homicide." But later, with no signs of a break-in or a struggle, investigators concluded that no foul play had been involved.

There was no apparent foul play either in the sudden death of longtime Waco Sheriff Jack Harwell, one of the only authorities involved in the Davidian siege who offered any sympathy for the religious group. Even while the siege was underway, Harwell consistently stated that he had experienced no problems with David Koresh and his followers in the past. He said whenever he wanted to speak with Koresh, he would call him on the phone and Koresh would come to his office.

According to Clive Doyle, the last Davidian to escape the blazing home, Harwell had called him just prior to the civil trial and said that the death of the Davidian children was starting to weigh on him and asked for a meeting with Doyle to talk about the case and "some other things."

There was no meeting, and the sheriff never testified at the trial. Harwell died of a sudden heart attack.

Whatever he, Ghigliotti, and Allard had to say is now missing!

Washington Times columnist Michelle Malkin summed up the federal government's actions in this case by writing, "They lodged bogus charges of child abuse against Branch Davidians. They denied using incendiary devices during the raid—only to acknowledge having fired at least two flammable tear-gas canisters into the compound. They 'misplaced' audio recordings from infrared footage that demonstrated official government orders to use pyrotechnics. They confiscated—then 'lost'—vital autopsy evidence from the Tarrant County, Texas, coroner's office.

"And now they want us to believe that what Mr. Ghigliotti and Mr. Allard separately concluded were gunshots were merely flashes of sunlight and reflections of broken window glass." The major news media dutifully reported the government's version, not realizing that infrared technology measures heat, not light, and that reflected light gives off little heat.

Needless to say, with witnesses dead and hospitalized, as well as documents and some photos and audio recordings missing, it came as no surprise when Federal District Judge Walter Smith in mid-2000 found that while "there may be some indication of mishandling and/or mislabeling by the FBI, there is nothing to indicate that this was the result of anything more than mere negligence."

Judge Smith, after hearing testimony from FBI agents in charge of the infrared taping that clearly indicated tampering with the tapes, decided that an expert hired by the government who disputed this account "was more persuasive."

He also declined to punish the Bureau for failing to hand over documents and other evidence in a timely manner and generally absolved the government of any responsibility in the deaths.

This opinion was echoed about a week later with the release of a preliminary report from John Danforth, who was appointed as a special counsel by Attorney General Janet Reno to investigate the Waco tragedy. While critical of a 1993 Justice Department review of the case stating investigators "went into the project with the assumption that the FBI had done nothing wrong," Danforth nevertheless "fully exonerated" his boss Reno of any wrongdoing in the matter.

Unreported to the public was the fact that Danforth's investigation suffered from the same problem as the others. For example, when a ballistics expert returned to the Tarrant County Medical Examiner's Office to retrieve subpoenaed ballistic records on the Davidians for the Danforth probe, the computer has been emptied.

"The FBI has turned over only those photographs to the court and the press that the FBI wants the court and the public to see."

This crucial evidence is missing!

Nevertheless, at a news conference announcing his preliminary report, Danforth said, "I hope that it lays these questions, the darkest questions relating to Waco, to rest."

There was no meeting, and the sheriff never testified at the trial. Harwell died of a sudden heart attack.

But undoubtedly, the many questions raised in this and other cases will not be put to rest by further pronouncements from a government consistently caught in lies and unwilling to take notice of the missing evidence and witnesses.

Oklahoma City

On April 19, 1995, shortly after 9:00 AM a tremendous blast ripped through the Alfred P. Murrah Federal Building, killing 168 people, including many children in the building's day care center, and demolishing one whole side of the structure.

Just 34 days later, over the objections of many people, including Oklahoma Representative Charles Key, Senator James Inhofe, and explosives experts who were already voicing disagreement with the federal government's version of the explosion, the Murrah building was demolished and the rubble hauled away to a guarded, barbwire-enclosed landfill. According to federal officials, it was a "health hazard."

Questions over the destruction of the federal building in Oklahoma City have never been satisfactorily answered.

This is because the best evidence, the building, is missing!

Also missing are the additional bombs reportedly removed from the building just after the initial explosions. In the minutes following the first reports from Oklahoma City, KFOR reported, "The FBI has confirmed there is another bomb in the Federal Building. It's in the east side of the building. They've moved everybody back several blocks, obviously to, uh, unplug it so it won't go off. They're moving everybody back." KWTV also reported another bomb was found in the building and added that a bomb disposal unit had moved into

the building. Even Oklahoma Governor Frank Keating told newsmen, "The reports I have is that one device was deactivated and there's another device, and obviously whatever did the damage to the Murrah Building was a tremendous, very sophisticated explosive device."

Keating later would reverse himself, supporting the federal government's contention that one man, Timothy McVeigh, destroyed the building with 4,800 pounds of ammonium nitrate fertilizer and characterizing those who questioned this version as "howling at the moon."

Oklahoma City FBI chief Bob Ricks, who spearheaded the official publicity effort at Waco and was later named head of the Oklahoma State Police by Governor Keating, told the media, "We never did find another device...we confirmed that no other device existed."

Several witnesses, including firemen at the scene, reported two military ambulances were loaded with stretchers containing boxes during the time that spectators and rescue workers were pulled back because, they were told, additional bombs had been found.

Once again, the chief evidence of conspiracy is missing!

Early on, media members talked about the possibility that the bomber or bombers may have been caught on tape by surveillance cameras in the parking lot of a Southwestern Bell office across the street from the Murrah Building. David Hall, manager of TV station KPOC, reported that two Bell employees stated that the tapes showed the Murrah Building shaking before the truck bomb exploded, strong evidence that more than one explosion took place.

The Bell surveillance tapes have never been made available to the public, so are missing from public debate!

The idea that more than one explosion occurred was voiced by several survivors and corroborated by a tape recording made during a conference of the Water Resources Board across from the Murrah Building and by a seismograph at the Oklahoma Geological Survey at the University of Oklahoma. Both recordings indicated large explosions ten seconds apart.

But today this evidence is missing!

The United States Geological Survey released a report stating USGS geologist Dr. Thomas Holzer concluded that the second spike on the seismograph was simply the building's side collapsing. However, Professor Raymond Brown, senior geophysicist at the University of California who studied the seismograph data as well as interviewing victims, argued against the one-bomb theory, saying, "[T]his was a demolition job. Somebody who went in there with equipment tried to take that building down."

Like so many other cases in recent history, foot-dragging and obstructionism on the part of federal authorities prevented any truthful investigation. Representative Key reported that a subsequent federal grand jury was prevented from hearing even one of more than 20 witnesses who saw persons other than McVeigh at the scene of the bombing. "Indeed, the best witnesses who can positively place McVeigh in downtown Oklahoma City that morning, saw him with one or more individuals and are able to describe to some degree what that person or persons looked like. These witnesses were not even allowed to testify at McVeigh's trial," said Key, who added, "… the Federal Grand Jury wanted to interview both the eyewitnesses and the sketch artist who drew John Doe [unknown accomplices] composites but were flatly refused by the federal 'authorities.' Clearly, they were blatantly deprived of their basic constitutional rights as grand jurors. Why?"

The congressman answered his own rhetorical question by stating, "[S]ome in our federal law enforcement agencies (i.e. ATF and FBI) had prior knowledge that certain individuals were planning to bomb the Murrah Federal Building!"

In 1999 Republican Key was defeated by another Republican, and his voice advocating a truthful investigation is now missing.

Danny Casolaro

In the early 1990s one intrepid investigator was on the trail of the conspirators behind many of this nation's recent scandals.

A 44-year-old freelance journalist named Danny Casolaro had been digging into the interlocking nexus of intelligence agencies, arms and drug dealers of the Iran-Contra scandal, the financial criminals of the BCCI bank, Justice Department officials involved in the PROMIS software theft, and connected issues like the October Surprise scandal, covert biological warfare testing, and Area 51. He called this sprawling conspiracy "The Octopus." He told friends that he was close to identifying an international cabal of just a handful of men who were the masterminds behind "The Octopus."

According to close friends, Casolaro kept his "Octopus" files in a large accordion-style file case, which he carried with him at all times. He began growing anxious about his safety, telling his physician brother, "I have been getting some very threatening phone calls. If anything happens to me, don't believe it was accidental."

On the afternoon of August 10, 1991, a cleaning woman found Casolaro's nude body in the bathtub of his Martinsburg, West Virginia, motel room. His wrists had been slashed more than a dozen times. Nearby a scrawled note stated, "Please forgive me for the worst possible thing I could have done."

His death was quickly ruled a suicide, and his body was released to a local mortician, who promptly embalmed the body before contacting the next of kin, an action not only hasty but illegal.

Casolaro's file box, which he took with him to his motel, remains missing!

Vince Foster

On July 20, 1993, the body of President Clinton's friend and attorney Vincent Foster was discovered in Fort Macy Park near Washington, DC. His body was stretched out in a serene posture on a gentle slope. A pistol was still gripped in one hand. He had been shot in the head. Most thought it was a classic suicide pose, although veteran investigators knew that a suicide's muscles flinch with gunshot trauma, and the gun never remains in the victim's hands. However, within days his death was ruled a suicide. But serious questions began to surface until the controversy over Foster's death reached national proportions.

Although his death was attributed to a gunshot wound to the head, an official crime-scene Polaroid seemed to show a small bullet wound in his neck. This was corroborated by Fairfax County EMT Richard Arthur, who worked on Foster's body and claimed to have seen such a hole. Obviously, X-rays of Foster's body would have cleared up this issue.

But X-rays of the body are missing!

Then, perhaps a careful examination of the fatal bullet might shed some light on this case. Investigators and park police conducted an exhaustive search of the park but failed to find any trace of the fatal projectile at the scene or elsewhere.

The bullet is missing!

> "Freak things can happen in any violent death. But the laws of nature cannot be suspended and inconsistencies don't range into the dozens, as in this case."

Investigators turned to the official crime scene photographs, which originally reportedly numbered 30 Polaroids and one roll of 35mm film. Police later listed only thirteen Polaroid photos, only one of which—a close-up of Foster's hand—was later leaked to the public.

The photos are missing!

Park police searched Foster's body and clothing, but his car keys were missing. But in a later search in the morgue, his keys turned up in his pants pocket. In another peculiar circumstance, six days after the death, Associate White House Counsel Stephen Neuwirth discovered a shredded, handwritten "suicide" note in Foster's office briefcase. (His briefcase had already been checked twice before, but no note had been found during those searches.) The FBI lab found no fingerprints on the note despite the fact that it was torn into 27 pieces. Toward the bottom right-hand corner, where one would expect to find a signature, there was a gap.

The critical piece was missing!

Although the FBI concluded the note was genuine, three separate first-class forensic handwriting experts—Reginald E. Alton, Vincent Scalice, and Ronald Rice—all reported that it was a clever forgery.

Scalice, formerly a veteran NYPD homicide detective, stated, "Freak things can happen in any violent death. But the laws of nature cannot be suspended and inconsistencies don't range into the dozens, as in this case."

Foster's death was only the beginning of the scandals and improprieties of the Clinton Administration.

Ron Brown

On April 3, 1996, Commerce Secretary Ron Brown and 34 other passengers onboard a T-43 military transport plane died when the craft crashed into the rocky hills of Croatia. With Brown were other government officials, twelve corporate chiefs, a CIA analyst, and a New York Times bureau chief.

The major media reported that Brown's plane went down in the Adriatic Sea during "the worst storm in a decade." Yet the Dubrounik Airport, less than two miles from the actual inland crash site, reported only light scattered rain with five miles visibility. Several other planes landed safely immediately before and after Brown's plane crashed.

Brown, at the time of his death, was the object of an investigation by an independent counsel appointed by a three-judge panel in the wake of a lawsuit by Judicial Watch. This case had already uncovered the illegal campaign contributions of John Huang, prompting a minor scandal. According to Judicial Watch head Larry Klayman, "...Brown had told President Clinton days before he was asked unexpectedly to travel to Croatia that he would negotiate a plea agreement with the independent counsel, which would entail telling the independent counsel what he knew about alleged illegalities in the Clinton-Gore administration."

The suspicions over the crash could have been ended by studying the cockpit voice and flight data recorders, the black box. When Prime Minister Zlatko Matesa of Croatia said a voice recorder had been recovered from the tail of Brown's plane and offered to turn it over to US officials, Air Force officials declined, saying that the converted training plane had not carried such equipment.

The black box remains missing!

The White House and the mass media reported that Brown died in the plane crash, but two members of the Armed Forces Institute of Pathology reported that he had a large hole in his head. Air Force Lieutenant Colonel Steve

Brown, at the time of his death, was the object of an investigation by an independent counsel appointed by a three-judge panel in the wake of a lawsuit by Judicial Watch.

Cogswell and Army Lieutenant Colonel David Hause both said the hole was consistent with a bullet wound. Their conclusion was supported by veteran pathologist Dr. Cyril Wecht. This question of homicide could be resolved by simply checking the photos and X-rays of the body.

But they're all missing!

White House Email

Illegal campaign finances, Whitewater, Travelgate, Chinagate, Filegate…the list of Clinton Administration scandals goes on and on. How could the investigators of the various ongoing probes get to the truth?

One such probe, the Justice Department's campaign-finance task force, decided to look at White House email for clues and evidence. Congress also wanted the emails. Imagine their surprise when they found that a mysterious malfunction of a critical White House Office email server caused some emails not be to archived.

Robert Haas, a computer contractor from Northrop Grumman assigned to audit the missing email, was among the technicians who discovered that the White House automated archiving system had failed to scan and store email sent to the server by the Executive Office.

Almost a million West Wing emails are missing!

These missing emails, initially reported to number only about 100,000, include messages to prominent White House officials, including President Clinton himself, according to reporter Paul Sperry of WorldNetDaily. Other missing messages came from the Democratic National Committee. Recipients of the lost email include Clinton's secretary Betty Currie, whose email reportedly included 400 to 500 messages from Monica Lewinsky in just one file.

"When I heard the number, I couldn't believe they talked that much," said one of the computer contractors involved. "They must have been busy typing all day long. I don't know if they did any work."

Other investigators were more concerned about serious scandals. Sheryl Hall, a former manager in the White House's Information Systems and Technology Division, said she learned that within the missing email were "smoking guns" to many contentious issues. Hall told WorldNetDaily that "different people…would go to jail. And that there was a lot of stuff out there." This "stuff" involved illegal campaign finances, as well as the involvement of Vice President Al Gore in some of the controversies.

"Every White House aide whose name has popped up during the parade of scandals was on that server," noted one investigator. "And those that helped them do their jobs."

Technicians learned that of the 526 persons whose email went missing, 464 of them worked in the White House Office. Someone suggested that perhaps a study of Gore's email might provide a clue as to why so much information had been lost.

But all of Gore's office email from that period is missing!

The Final Missing Piece

There is enough information available today regarding missing information and evidence to fill an entire book, a sad commentary on justice in America.

The public must summon the will to demand truth and honesty from their elected leaders and from federal authorities who seem to feel they are above the laws and ethics imposed on the rest of us.

But that will seems to be missing!

THE SOCIAL FABRICATION

Don't Blame Your Parents

An Interview with Judith Rich Harris

When *The Nurture Assumption: Why Children Turn Out the Way They Do* was published in 1998, a lot of heads turned quickly. Seemingly out of nowhere, Judith Rich Harris—a former author of psychology textbooks on child development—unleashed a theory that has the potential to change not only the way we view parents and children but also the way we view ourselves. Hers is not an abstract theory. It hits us where we live, because each of us is the child of two parents, and some of us were raised by step-parents, adoptive parents, or grandparents in addition to two, one, or no biological parents. People who are themselves parents get hit with a double whammy, since Harris' revolutionary idea alters their beliefs not only about their own parents but also about their own children.

Psychologists, reporters, and other people couldn't believe that this theorist—who doesn't even have a Ph.D. behind her name—strolled up and told us that almost everything we think we know about parents' effects on their children is wrong. To top it off, she had a lot of evidence to back her up, which she presented with fierce intelligence and a witty writing style. The insular world of child development studies was rocked. The mainstream media caught on, and lots of articles and interviews followed. The *New York Times* listed *The Nurture Assumption* as a notable book. It was nominated for the Pulitzer Prize in nonfiction.

By the time I interviewed Harris via email in August 2000, most of the furor had died down, but the deeper effects of her theory hadn't. No developmental psychologist can legitimately continue researching and theorizing without taking into account her thesis. More importantly to the rest of us, we can no longer whine about how our parents raised us, blaming them for our faults, nor can the parents among us worry themselves sick about whether they're doing everything possible to create the next Florence Nightingale and Albert Einstein rolled into one. No wonder *The Nurture Assumption* shook everybody up!

Russ Kick: I think the best way to start out is by asking you to summarize your groundbreaking thesis (or, judging by the reactions it's triggered, earthquaking thesis) at the heart of your book, *The Nurture Assumption.*

Judith Rich Harris: Most people believe that children's psychological characteristics are formed by a combination of "nature"—meaning their genes—and "nurture"—meaning the way their parents bring them up. The "nature" part of that statement is unquestionably true. It's the "nurture" part I disagree with. The evidence I've put together in my book indicates that parents have little or no long-term effect on their children's personality, intelligence, or mental health. The *environment* definitely has an effect on how children turn out, but it's not the *home* environment. It's not the nurture they do or don't get from their parents.

That's the first half of my thesis—what you called the "earthquaking" part. The second half—I call it group socialization theory—is my answer to the question, Well, if it isn't the home environment, what environment is it? My answer: the environment children share with their peers.

Oddly enough, it's the controversial part of my thesis that is well-supported by evidence. The second part, group socialization theory, is much more speculative. It's consistent with the existing evidence but as yet largely untested. It will take new research, using better research techniques, to test it.

RK: So the evidence indicates that parents have no important effects, in the long run, on the way their children turn out? If that's true, why hasn't anyone noticed it before? Why does almost everyone believe that parents do have important effects?

JRH: Several reasons. The primary one is that most children are reared by their biological parents—the same people who gave them their genes. About 50 percent of the variation in personality traits is genetic, which means that for genetic reasons alone, children have many of the same faults and virtues as their parents. Heredity can explain why "dysfunctional" parents tend to have "dysfunctional" kids. But the effects of heredity are generally underestimated, and children's successes and failures are assumed to be due to the way they are treated by their parents.

To test that assumption, you have to use research methods that provide a way to control for the effects of genes. When researchers do that, the similarities between parents and children disappear. Adopted children, for example, do not resemble their adoptive parents in personality or intelligence. On the average, once you control for genetic effects, the children of sociable parents are no more (or less) sociable than the children of introverts, and the children of tidy parents are no more (or less) tidy than the children of slobs.

Another reason for the belief in the efficacy of parenting has do with what I call "context effects." According to my theory, children learn separately how to behave in each of their environments. Children don't blindly generalize from one context to another—their behavior is a function of what they've experienced in *that particular context*. If the behavior they learned at home turns out to be inappropriate outside the home—and this is often the case—they drop the home behavior and learn something new.

The evidence I've put together in my book indicates that parents have little or no long-term effect on their children's personality, intelligence, or mental health.

I've never questioned the fact that parents influence how their children behave at home—what I question is that the children take these behaviors with them to school or the day-care center or the playground. In fact, there is very little correlation between how children behave with their parents and how they behave with their peers—a child may be obnoxious with his parents, pleasant and cooperative with his peers, or vice versa. Even more surprising, there is very little correlation between how children behave with their *siblings* and how they behave with their peers.

RK: Let's take an extreme example based on your thesis. Assuming that we could magically control for factors like genetics, time, and location, you're saying that children of Eva Braun, Mother Teresa, Madonna (the pop star), and the Madonna (the Virgin Mary) would all turn out pretty much the same if they had basically the same set of peers?

JRH: Actually, we *can* control for factors like genetics, time, and location, though not, alas, with Madonna (either one). Nature has allowed us to perform exactly the experiment you've suggested, by providing us with identical twins. Identical twins have the same genes; usually they are reared in the same home at the same time; and they have basically the same set of peers (identical twins often belong to the same peer group). And yet there are noticeable differences between them in personality. This is one of the mysteries that inspired me to think up a new theory: not the fact that twins separated at birth and reared in separate homes are so similar, but the fact that twins reared in the *same* home are much less similar than you would expect!

There are personality differences, not due to genes, between twins or siblings reared in the same home, and group socialization theory can explain them. According to my theory, the things that happen within peer groups not only create or increase similarities among the members—they also create or widen certain kinds of differences. The kids become more alike in some ways (due to a process called assimilation) and *less* alike in others (due to differentiation).

Assimilation is the way children are socialized—how they acquire the behaviors and attitudes that are appropriate for their culture. But personality development, I believe, is more a function of differentiation. Groups sort people out. The members of groups differ in status and in the way they are typecast or labeled by the others. This is true even for identical twins who belong to the same peer group: One might be characterized as the bold one, the other as the shy one, for instance. Or the other members might address their comments and questions to one twin rather than the other—a sign that they regard that twin as the dominant one. If such differences in status or typecasting are persistent, I believe they can leave permanent marks on the personality.

So the answer to your question is no. If we could clone the people you named and give them the same set of peers and so on, according to my theory they probably wouldn't turn out the same.

RK: The theory seems so incredibly counterintuitive. Looking at parents and children around me, and thinking back on my own childhood, it seems to go without saying that parents have drastic effects on who children become. Some of this impression is, as you've pointed out, due to genetics and to context effects, but you've also described other factors that contribute to the impression that parents mold their children. An example is what you've called "child-to-parent effects"—the overlooked fact that often it's the children who mold their parents' behavior, rather than vice versa. Please discuss how these effects work.

JRH: Yes, you're right—child-to-parent effects are another reason why the parents are held responsible for the way the child turns out. People notice that children who are treated nicely by their parents tend to turn out better than children who are treated harshly, and they jump to the conclusion that the good treatment caused the good outcome. But it could be the other way around. An amiable, cooperative child is likely to receive affectionate parenting—it's easy to be nice to a child like this. A surly or defiant child, on the other hand, is likely to

RK: When a friend of mine first told me about your book, I have to say that it basically fried my brain circuits. It was very tough to wrap my head around, although now that I've read the book, I have to admit that I'm quite convinced of your theory. However, after reading your previous responses, there are undoubtedly some readers who are having the same reaction I originally had. Please lay out one or two of the most convincing pieces of evidence that support your theory.

JRH: I think the most convincing evidence comes from the study of language and accents. Most of the behaviors that people observe in children are influenced both by their genes and their experiences, so it's very difficult, without using special methodology, to figure out what's going on. But children don't inherit a tendency to speak English or Russian or Korean, and they don't inherit their accents. So looking at language gives us an easy way to eliminate the effects of genes.

The nurture assumption is a creation of the twentieth century.

be treated harshly. The parents find that reasoning with this child doesn't work and end up losing their tempers.

The failure to take account of child-to-parent effects is particularly flagrant among researchers who study adolescents. They've found, for example, that teenagers whose parents monitor their activities get into less trouble than teenagers whose parents fail to keep track of them. Therefore, the researchers conclude, it must be the parents' fault if the teenager gets into trouble—the parents didn't monitor the kid carefully enough. But did you ever try keeping track of the whereabouts of a kid who is determined to outwit your efforts to do so? A kid who wants to do things he knows his parents wouldn't approve of can always find ways to evade parental supervision. The parents of well-behaved teenagers don't realize how much their ability to monitor their kids' activities depends on the kids' willingness to cooperate with them.

The same error is made by the people who advise parents to talk to their kids about drugs and sex, because kids whose parents don't do this—or, more accurately, kids who *tell* researchers that their parents don't do it—are more likely to use drugs and have sex. Aside from the fact that it's always risky to take what respondents tell you at face value, have you ever tried talking to a sullen or contemptuous teenager about the hazards of drugs or sex?

The first thing we notice is that most children speak the same language as their parents, which turns out to be another of those misleading observations. It's misleading because most children are reared by parents who speak the same language as everyone else in their community. The children's two environments are in harmony, so you can't tell which one is having the effect. You have to look for cases in which the environment of the home conflicts with the environment outside the home. What happens when children are reared by parents who speak a *different* language from the one that's used outside the home?

What happens is that children learn their parents' language first. Then, when they go outside and encounter other children who are using a different language, they quickly pick up that second language as well. Usually they go through a period where they'll switch back and forth between the two languages, using their parents' language at home and their peers' language outside the home. The interesting thing is that there's no carryover from the home language to the outside-the-home language, no blurring together of contexts. Unless they were past elementary-school age when they encountered their second language, they will speak it without a foreign accent.

What happens next is that the outside-the-home language will gradually supplant the home language. Pretty soon these children will be trying to talk to their parents in English, even if their parents continue to address them in Russian or Korean.

English will become their "native" language—the language they'll think in, the language they'll speak as adults.

The example of language shows that parents have a powerful effect on the children's *early* behavior, but in the long run it's what the children experience outside the home—in particular, what they experience in the company of their peers—that determines the ultimate outcome. (I know it's the peers' language that matters, rather than the language of the adults in their community, because there are cases in which the children of a community speak a language that is different from the adults'.)

RK: I think it's important to note that you say parents can and, indeed, do affect their children's behavior and personality when the children are with their parents. But you maintain that how they act with their parents not only doesn't generalize to the rest of the world but it also doesn't affect who they are when they grow up. How can this be?

JRH: I think this is how children were designed by evolution. After all, what's childhood for? It's preparation for the future. Parents aren't the future—parents are the past! In order to be successful as an adult, a child has to figure out what works best in the world that he or she is destined to inhabit in adulthood. They will share that world with their peers, not (at least under the conditions in which our species evolved) with their parents.

RK: It's interesting to note that not all time periods and cultures have held the belief that parents are crucial in determining their children's course in life. In fact, most didn't/don't believe that, including America up to the 1930s. What does this tell us about the nurture assumption?

JRH: Quite true: The nurture assumption is a creation of the twentieth century. Freud has a lot to answer for. In other cultures, and in previous generations of our own culture, parents were given condolences, not blame, if their children didn't turn out as hoped.

Consider the changes in child-rearing styles that have occurred just within the past century. I was born in 1938, and when I was growing up it was considered perfectly all right for a parent to strike a child with a weapon such as a belt or a ruler—some parents even kept a suitable object specifically for that purpose! Kisses and hugs were administered sparingly in those days, and declarations of parental love were made only on the deathbed.

A generation later, when I was rearing my children, it was no longer considered all right to strike a child with a belt or a ruler, but it was still okay to give them an occasional swat on the seat of the pants. Hugs, kisses, and declarations of parental love were more common.

Now, another generation later, it's no longer considered okay to hit children at all—my 4-year-old granddaughter has never experienced any kind of physical punishment—and the words "I love you" have become as common as "please" and "thank you."

If the experts were right, wouldn't you think that such drastic changes in child-rearing methods would produce a better product? But there are no signs that children are happier or less aggressive today than they were when I was growing up; there are no signs that they have higher self-esteem. Rates of childhood depression and suicide have gone up, not down, over this period. And yet the experts continue to claim that if parents would only follow their instructions to the letter, their children will turn into happy, well-adjusted people. Happy, well-adjusted, and *smart*!

RK: In your research, you've also studied other factors that are supposed to influence children's development and mold who they become. In particular, can you briefly comment on birth order?

JRH: Birth order is an interesting question, because most people believe that it has important effects on personality. The idea is that firstborns, because of their special place in the family—the fact that they've had their parents all to themselves for a while, the fact that they can dominate their younger siblings—have personality characteristics that differ, on the average, from laterborns. But objective evidence does not support this widespread belief. Studies in which personality tests are given to large numbers of subjects do not show consistent differences in personality as a function of birth order. Similarly, if you look at educational achievement, you find that (contra the usual stereotypes) laterborns are not more likely to be underachievers or dropouts, and firstborns are not more likely to graduate from high school and go to college.

On the other hand, there is no question that birth order influences the way people behave with, and feel about, their siblings and their parents. But this is a context effect—these behaviors and feelings are left behind when people leave home. This is true even in childhood. Research has shown that laterborns who are dominated at home by older siblings are no more likely than firstborns to allow themselves to be dominated by their peers. Which makes sense, from an evolutionary point

They seemed to feel that if people believed my message, it would be the end of civilization as we know it.

of view. Why should a child who is dominated by his siblings be handicapped by the notion that he's going to be dominated everywhere he goes? This child might turn out to be the largest and strongest in his age group!

The reason why the belief in birth order effects is so prevalent is that we don't know the birth orders of most of the people we meet—we know the birth orders only of relatives and close friends, and of the children of our friends and neighbors. These are the people we are most likely to see in the presence of their parents and siblings. We see the way they behave with their parents and siblings and assume that they behave that way in other contexts, too. But they don't! Outside of the context of the family they grew up in, firstborns and laterborns are indistinguishable.

RK: Tell me about the reactions your book has caused. What were some of the immediate and longer-term reactions?

JRH: There was quite a lot of response to the book—from the media, from members of the academic world, and from ordinary people who wrote to me in email or postal mail. The mail from the public was overwhelmingly favorable; many people told me that I had made parenting seem less burdensome—less fraught with anxiety—or that I had explained some mystery about their own childhood.

The media response was vigorous but mixed. There were many published essays by writers who absolutely hated what I was saying. They seemed to feel that if people believed my message, it would be the end of civilization as we know it. Parents, once they learned that trying hard wouldn't necessarily make their children turn out better, would surely let them die of neglect! Another criticism—usually made by journalists who hadn't actually read the book—was that my theory was an oversimplification and things were really much more complicated than I had made them out to be. But there were also plenty of open-minded journalists who felt that my book was interesting and enlightening, and who approved of my criticisms of the research methods commonly used in the field of child development.

The reception from the academic world was also mixed. In general, social psychologists, evolutionary psychologists, and behavioral geneticists tended to be favorable; clinical psychologists tended to be unfavorable. Developmental psychologists, by and large, were outraged. Not surprising, since I was saying that the entire careers of many of them were built upon a falsehood and that they'd have to start all over from square one. This, coming from a nobody like me, who doesn't even have a Ph.D. or an academic appointment! (I do have some graduate training in psychology, but Harvard kicked me out without a Ph.D. Before I had the idea that led to *The Nurture Assumption*, I spent many years as a writer of textbooks for college courses in child development.)

But aside from their efforts to discredit me by pointing out my lack of credentials, the developmental psychologists have been remarkably ineffectual. Journalists kept interviewing prominent members of the field and asking them what they thought of my book, and they'd say things like, "There are lots and lots of studies that Harris has ignored and that prove she's wrong!" But generally they didn't name specific studies. When specific studies have been named, I've examined them and found them to be full of holes.

Let me give you a couple of examples. Here's a quote from an article in *Newsweek* (September 7, 1998):

> [M]any of the nation's leading scholars of child development accuse Harris of screwy logic, of misunderstanding behavioral genetics and of ignoring studies that do not fit her thesis. Exhibit A: the work of Harvard's [Jerome] Kagan. He has shown how different parenting styles can shape a timid, shy child who perceives the world as a threat. Kagan measured babies at 4 months and at school age. The fearful children whose parents (over)protected them were still timid. Those whose parents pushed them to try new things—"get into that sandbox and play with the other kids, dammit!" lost their shyness. (Begley, 1998, p 56)

What Kagan is evidently referring to here is a study by one of his students, Doreen Arcus. Arcus reported her results in 1991, in her doctoral dissertation. She followed 24 timid babies (that is, babies whose test results at the age of four months indicated that they might turn out to be timid) to the age of 21 months—not to school age, as reported in *Newsweek*. The mothers who were less indulgent—who held their babies less and who used firmer methods of discipline—had babies who were less likely to be timid at 21 months.

This study has never been published in a peer-reviewed journal. Kagan described it in a 1994 book—a book in which he summarized his fifteen years of research on timid children—but he didn't give the details. It was, by the way, the only evidence he offered in that book to support his belief that the right kind of child-rearing style can prevent a nervous infant from turning into a timid child.

If there have been any follow-ups of these 24 children, to check on whether the results found at age 21 months held up when the children were retested at school age, they haven't been reported in the child-development literature. This is not, by the way, the only case I have found in which evidence used against me turned out to be nonexistent or at least unpublished.

Here's my second example—another quote from the same *Newsweek* article:

> "Intervention" studies—where a scientist gets a parent to act differently—also undercut Harris. "These show that if you change the behavior of the parents you change the behavior of the kids, with effects outside the home," says John Gottman of the University of Washington. (Begley, 1998, p 56–57)

Well, that worried me, because if it were true it would indeed be very good evidence against my theory. My theory predicts that if you change the behavior of the parents, you can change the way the children behave *at home*, but it won't affect the way the children behave outside the home—in school, for example.

So I did a thorough review of published intervention studies. The conclusion I came to was the same as that expressed by Michelle Wierson and Rex Forehand in an article in a psychology journal. Wierson and Forehand (Forehand is a leading figure in the field of intervention studies) reported that parent training interventions, in which parents are taught better ways of getting their children to listen to them, can improve the way the child behaves in the presence of the parents. "However," the researchers admitted, "research has been unable to show that child behavior is modified at school." Which is exactly what

my theory predicts, and quite different from the claim made in the *Newsweek* article.

RK: What's next for you? Are you still concentrating on this theory, or are you tackling something else?

JRH: I've been writing articles for psychology journals—mostly critiques of the work of traditional developmental psychologists. In my next article, I plan to illuminate the defects in developmental research by comparing it to medical research. Over the years, medical researchers have developed elaborate procedures to guard against experimenter bias and other sources of spurious results. These procedures are seldom used in psychology; most developmentalists have never heard of them, and consequently their studies are riddled with methodological errors.

The problem is that no one bothers to question the methodology if the results turn out the way they're expected to. That's why it's so important, in science, to put aside prior assumptions and ideology. There are important questions that require answers based on solid science—for example, if parent training interventions don't make children behave better in school, what kind of interventions do make children behave better in school? One reason there has been so little progress in answering such questions is that most of the research time and money has been spent on futile efforts to confirm the researchers' assumptions.

Worse still, some developmentalists seem to have the idea that, even if what I'm saying is true, the public shouldn't be told about it, because it would be bad for parents to think that what they do for their kids doesn't matter. Well, that's not what I'm saying—I've never said that parents don't matter, only that they don't have long-term effects on their children's personalities. But let's not split hairs. If what I'm saying is true, do the developmentalists have the right to say that people shouldn't be told about it? Do they have the right, or even the knowledge, to decide what's best for people?

References

Begley, S. (1998, Sept. 7). The parent trap. *Newsweek*, pp 52–59.

Wierson, M., & R. Forehand. (1994). Parent behavioral training for child noncompliance: Rationale, concepts, and effectiveness. *Current Directions in Psychological Science*, 5, pp 146–150.

The Unkindest Cut
Circumcision: Health-conscious Procedure or Unnecessary Sexual Amputation?
Tristan Taormino

A father-to-be recently sent me a letter asking for advice: He and his wife are expecting a baby boy and debating whether to have him circumcised. He wrote, "I'm uncircumcised and I kind of want him to 'match' me in the plumbing department, just to avoid any psychological problems with proper sexual identification, but my greatest fear is that he might be missing out sexually as a result of the procedure. Also, I kind of felt this should be his choice to make, since it's his body." He became conflicted, though, when he read a report on new research in Africa that shows circumcision reduces the risk of HIV infection. "Our son is going to be getting comprehensive sex ed as he grows up, but condoms do sometimes break and this added level of protection certainly wouldn't be a bad thing. But if he goes under the knife, will he be 'missing' anything sexually?"

While the cultural contexts surrounding the practice are different, male circumcision is the equivalent of female circumcision (removal of the clitoral hood that protects the clit's glans). As a society, we vehemently oppose this when it's done to women and see it as a way of mutilating their bodies, controlling their sexuality, and limiting their sexual pleasure. Why, then, don't we view male circumcision the same way?

The procedure is not just the "little snip" it's often referred to as—there's nothing minor about cutting away the fold of skin that surrounds and protects the head of the penis. The practice began in English-speaking countries in the mid-1800s as a way to prevent masturbation, which was believed to cause many diseases. By the 1900s, infant circumcision had become widespread thanks to the shift in control over the birthing process from female midwives to male obstetricians, the rise of medical experts, who began recommending it, and the increase of advertising aimed at convincing people they were dirty in order to sell hygiene products. Today, about 60 percent of men in this country are circumcised.

I recently browsed the parenting section of Borders and found dozens of books that cover every aspect of child rearing, from the moment of conception through each trimester to the birthing process, infancy, and beyond. Yet of everything a new parent needs to consider, circumcision is notably absent or glossed over in a few sentences that basically say, Talk to your doctor. But rarely—if ever—does a doctor ask a parent, "Do you want to lessen your son's penile sensitivity and erotic enjoyment?" And when the majority of doctors (and fathers) in a country are circumcised, they are invested in perpetuating the practice. Interestingly, one study found that parents who have the opportunity to discuss the procedure decide against it.

Pro-circumcision literature focuses on hygiene and disease-transmission as the primary reasons to circumcise. Proponents argue that the foreskin of an intact penis traps bacteria, making it harder to clean and more likely to cause infections. One pamphlet from the Gilgal Society in England claims that circumcision significantly decreases the risk of contracting urinary-tract infections in infancy, as well as prostate cancer, penile cancer, some STDs, and HIV through vaginal intercourse with an infected woman. In addition, those in favor of circumcision emphasize that a boy with an intact penis may feel alienated from his circumcised father and be ridiculed by his peers for being different.

Eighty percent of the world's men have intact penises, and no medical association recommends infant circumcision. Anti-

> As a society, we vehemently oppose this when it's done to women and see it as a way of mutilating their bodies, controlling their sexuality, and limiting their sexual pleasure.

The procedure is not just the "little snip" it's often referred to as—there's nothing minor about cutting away the fold of skin that surrounds and protects the head of the penis.

circumcision advocates believe that the procedure is risky, unnecessary, and equivalent to genital amputation, since it removes a vital part of the penis. They contend that by removing the foreskin, you take away the part of the penis with the most nerve endings, which serves to lubricate and protect the glans and enhance sexual sensitivity. As a result, the unprotected head of the circumcised penis becomes thick, leathery, and desensitized. In his book *Circumcision: The Hidden Trauma*, Ronald Goldman, Ph.D., asserts that the practice is physically and emotionally traumatic for any infant, and he attempts to link it to a variety of future problems, including abnormalities in neurological development, low self-esteem, anger-management problems, rape, violence, intimacy issues, and sexual anxiety and dysfunction.

Complicating matters for parents are the recent findings of two separate studies conducted by the National Institutes of Health in Africa, which found that uncircumcised men in the study were becoming infected with HIV at twice the rate of circumcised men. The theory is that the delicate inside fold of the foreskin contains a particular kind of white blood cell vulnerable to the virus; furthermore, uncircumcised men are more likely to have another STD that can lead to open sores on the penis, giving the HIV virus direct access to the bloodstream. Notably, both studies were halted before they could be completed, which some researchers argue has skewed the results.

Using these results to inform the decision to circumcise an American child does not take into account the significant differences that exist between the two countries with respect to AIDS. Uncircumcised penises are not the only element driving the high infection rates in Africa. Poor genital hygiene, lack of safer-sex education, little knowledge about or access to condoms, non-monogamous sexual practices, and cultural practices like dry sex and wife inheritance all contribute to the AIDS pandemic, which is why mass circumcision alone will not solve the problem. Furthermore, circumcision as a prophylactic measure does not translate in the United States, where the rates and methods of transmission are much different. In fact, according to NOCIRC—the National Organization of Circumcision Information Resource Centers (nocirc.org)—the

US has the highest rate of infant circumcision and the highest rate of HIV/AIDS among industrialized nations.

After reading Goldman's exhaustive, passionate book and seeing graphic diagrams and photos of circumcision, I am convinced that if people were well-informed about the foreskin's important functions and actually witnessed a circumcision, they would never subject anyone to it.

Art and the Eroticism of Puberty

David Steinberg

*The following talk was part of a plenary panel on this subject at the Western Regional meeting of the Society for the Scientific Study of Sexuality (SSSS), April 24, 1999. SSSS is the principal organization of professional sex educators, counselors, and therapists in the US. Other panel members were photographer Jock Sturges (*Radiant Identities*; The Last Day of Summer*) and author Judith Levine *(My Enemy, My Love: Women, Men, and the Dilemmas of Gender; Harmful to Minors: How Sexual Protectionism Hurts Children).*

I want to use my portion of this panel to examine some current sex-cultural dynamics that help explain the tremendous emotional charge behind the debate about nude photography of children and adolescents.

What's in need of explanation is not simply the fact that nude photographs of children are considered controversial. This in itself, while a sad commentary on the sexual state of the nation, is hardly surprising. Nudity is still controversial in this country, and nude photography, while accepted as legitimate in the world of fine art, still raises eyebrows in the general population. In addition, we know all too well that any artistic work that treats eroticism or sexuality in a friendly, let alone explicit, way is itself decidedly suspect.

What is surprising about the current controversy is why these predictable aesthetic and ethical disagreements have taken on such intensely loaded meaning and significance over the past several years. By looking at the dynamics behind this particular controversy, we stand to learn a great deal not only about nude photography, but also about how a variety of cultural attitudes relating to both sex and children affect us more generally.

Let me start with a basic observation that I think just about everyone in this room would embrace: That our particular culture still sees sex fundamentally as a dangerous, demonic, potentially chaotic force, a force that requires constant vigilance lest it tear apart otherwise sensible individuals, their primary relationships and, indeed, the very fabric of society. This in contrast, say, to the possibility of relating to sex primarily as a blessing, as a positive, joyous, wholesome, or spiritual part of life, as a way of connecting with other human beings in loving, intimate, creative, and enriching ways.

Because our basic cultural fear and suspicion of sex sets social order in opposition to many forms of natural and common sexual expression, elaborate institutions of social indoctrination and control are required to suppress those forms of sexual behavior and desire that are considered unacceptable. I want to look at two institutions of enforced sexual control that I think animate the extreme reactions we are seeing around the issue of nude photography of children and adolescents.

> While the particular groups assigned these archetypal roles of sexual innocents and sexual deviants has varied, the perception of an ongoing battle between sexual innocence and sexual perversion has been continuous.

The first of these is the creation and maintenance of a mythical, idealized class of innocent, supposedly non-sexual, individuals onto which society can project its yearning to escape the conflicts generated by overly repressed sexual desire. I'm going to call these the "designated innocents."

The second is the creation and maintenance of a parallel mythical, demonized class of subhuman sexual deviants onto which individuals can project their transgressive sexual desires as a way of keeping those desires under control. I'm going to call these the "designated perverts."

If we look back historically, we can see that, while the particular groups assigned these archetypal roles of sexual innocents and sexual deviants has varied, the perception of an ongoing battle between sexual innocence and sexual perversion has been continuous. It is a battle that is represented as being the eternal struggle between good and evil, between God and Satan. Sadly, it is also defined as the battle between asexual purity and the sexual contamination of that purity.

In its current incarnation, this drama pits the imagined asexual innocence of children and adolescents against the imagined perversion of anyone who dares acknowledge and respect, let alone appreciate or celebrate, the eroticism or sexuality of anyone who has not crossed the socially defined threshold into adulthood.

Designated Innocents

The role of designated innocents in the social drama of asexuality and perversion has well-defined requirements. The social function of this group is to posit the existence of a class of people so pure of heart and spirit that they have not been sullied by sex in any form. Traditionally, this role has been filled not only by children but also by women.

As late as the mid-nineteenth century, American women were still presumed to have no natural sexual desire of their own. Indeed, an entire culture developed to enforce asexuality on women, whether they liked it or not. Historian Barbara Goldsmith details one aspect of this culture of asexuality in her book, *Other Powers*. "In 1868," she writes, "American gynecological surgeons began performing clitoridectomies to quell sexual desire in women, which was considered a form of derangement. Upper- and middle-class white women who had been taught that any sexual urges were sinful, willingly surrendered their bodies to these male doctors, who tested them for abnormal arousal by stimulating the breast and clitoris; if there was a response, they surgically removed the clitoris."

Along with the creation of women as an asexual class came

the need to protect women from sexual contamination of any form—whether this be from sexual predators (men) or from the corrupting influence of sexual awareness and

It has thus become more important than ever, among those who see sex as a form of impurity, to insist that children are entirely non-sexual beings.

information—even as we now assume that society must protect its asexual children both from predators and from sexual information.

As women gained social and political power in the twentieth century, they have not surprisingly demanded recognition and respect for the reality of their sexual desires, and for their right to fulfill those desires without being denigrated as insane or immoral. While women's right to sexual expression equal to that of men's is still far from complete, the notion that women are naturally asexual, or that asexuality can be forced on them by social commandments and expectations, is certainly a thing of the past. As a result, the group of innocents presumed to be asexual has been reduced to the children alone. It has thus become more important than ever, among those who see sex as a form of impurity, to insist that children are entirely non-sexual beings.

Since, as we know, children are in fact far from asexual, maintaining this myth—and with it, to some extent, an exaggerated sense of the sexual innocence of adolescent girls—requires both a significant denial system and an elaborate program of societal enforcement. Pat Califia describes this well in her book *Public Sex*. Children, she notes, "are not innocent; they are ignorant, and that ignorance is deliberately created and maintained by parents who won't answer questions about sex and often punish their children for being bold enough to ask. This does not make sex disappear.... Sex becomes the thing not seen, the word not spoken, the forbidden impulse, the action that must be denied."

Designated Perverts

The second role in the drama of innocence and violation is that of the deviant or, more precisely, the pervert. As with the role of designated innocent, requirements for the role of designated pervert are both specific and extreme.

Art and the Eroticism of Puberty
David Steinberg

To fulfill the function of the designated pervert it is not sufficient for a form of sexual deviance to simply be disapproved of by those in the sexual mainstream. Nor is it sufficient for the designated pervert to be seen as merely a misguided soul in need of understanding or therapeutic help. The designated pervert must be so loathsome to the general population that the social outrage he generates (designated perverts are usually male) is extreme enough to serve as a warning to all who would deviate from sexual normalcy as to what will happen to them if they do. Designated perverts must be seen as so vile, so subhuman really, that the full venom of social punishment—social ostracism, legal confinement, even violent personal attack—can be visited upon them without any sense of guilt, mercy, or compromise.

As with the designated innocents, the specific incarnation of the designated pervert has varied with changing historical circumstances. In general, the designated pervert of any given era will be whoever most threatens to overturn the prevailing myth of asexual innocence.

In the late nineteenth century, for example, all that was required to be branded a "Satanic Free Loveist" was believing that women had sexual appetites of their own, and that they should have equal rights with men to choose their sexual partners, in and out of marriage, and equal rights to end their

> Designated perverts must be seen as so vile, so subhuman really, that the full venom of social punishment—social ostracism, legal confinement, even violent personal attack—can be visited upon them without any sense of guilt, mercy, or compromise.

marriages if those marriages were unsatisfactory to them, sexually or otherwise. Those who acknowledged and validated women's sexuality were deemed loathsome perverts because they threatened to desecrate women—the mythical "asexuals" of the day—with the scourge of sex.

The leading "Free Love" spokesperson of the time was Victoria Woodhull, the first woman to run for the office of President of the United States (in 1872). On the issue of women' sexual desire, she was outspoken and uncompromising. "Some women," she declared, "seem to glory over the fact that they never had any sexual desire and to think that desire is vulgar. What? Vulgar?… Vulgar rather must be the mind that can conceive such blasphemy. No sexual passion, say you. Say, rather, a sexual idiot, and confess your life is a failure…. The possession of strong sexual powers [is] a necessary part of human character, the foundation upon which civilization rests."

Predictably, Woodhull was subjected to the harshest attacks of the church, the press, and those in political power. Because of her sexual beliefs, she was driven out of the Suffragist movement (where she had until that time played a leading role), vilified in the major newspapers of the day, and driven into poverty. She was the first person prosecuted under the then-new Comstock Act, the Federal law that to this day prohibits sending obscene material through the mails.

As it became impossible to maintain the myth of women's asexual nature, it also became impossible to brand as a Satanic act the affirmation of women's sexual desire. As respect for women's sexuality grew in the early twentieth century, the issue lost the absolutist edge required for a true antisexual crusade. A new class of designated perverts was needed, and a new class was found.

The new targets of antisexual hatred and vilification were gays and lesbians. Once again, the full symphony of social loathing was called out to define the new designated perverts as truly subhuman, evil-minded threats to decency and social order. Once again, attacks on the designated perversion were justified by the supposed threat these perverts posed to the sexually innocent. Being a gay man was equated with being a vicious molester of young boys. Being a lesbian was equated with slyly seducing decent women out of their heterosexuality. Once again, the Devil was at the door, and the men and women of the sexual mainstream created a vivid image of vile perversion they could use to keep their own straying desires in check.

The Search for a New Designated Pervert

Recently, however, the horror of homosexuality has also begun to lose its punch. This is not to say that American society has truly embraced or accepted homosexuality, as it obviously has not. But the successes of the Gay Rights movement and the increased visibility of gays and lesbians have diluted the subhuman characterization required of true designated perverts. As more and more heterosexual Americans become aware of homosexuals as human beings instead of archetypes of evil, antisexual society once again needs to find a new class of perverts loathsome enough to serve as the vehicles for the general suppression of sexual deviance.

For a while it seemed that sadomasochists would fill the role quite nicely. S/M was just weird and disgusting enough to mainstream American consciousness to justify full vilification and violent suppression. But just as that wheel began to turn, S/M rather unexpectedly slipped into mainstream American culture as an intriguing, even chic, sexual variation, something altogether different from full-on perversion. Madonna's flawed book, *Sex*, was a significant factor in this rather instantaneous social turnaround, as was the widespread experience with S/M of many media celebrities themselves.

For a while it seemed that transsexuals might arouse sufficient scorn and revulsion to take on the designated pervert mantle but, like S/M, transsexuals have been surprisingly embraced in the past few years both by the mass media and by popular culture—perhaps, as James Green (a leading transgender advocate) points out, because the issue that transsexuals challenge is not sex at all, but gender.

While the precise definition of the new designated perverts is still evolving, it seems clear that it will center on those who acknowledge and affirm the sexuality of young people. The work of photographers like Jock Sturges, David Hamilton, and even Sally Mann happens to fall in the line of fire of this need to find new villains in the ongoing battle against sex itself. I believe this is why the objections to nude photographs of children have been so vicious and impassioned.

The continuing pattern of these attacks suggests that it will not be necessary to be a child molester, or even a pedophile, to be seen as the new pervert. The social need to enforce the non-sexuality of children and the exaggerated sexual innocence of adolescents is so great that the simple act of photographically addressing the eroticism of adolescents in an honest, respectful, and appreciative way has become sufficient to draw the full venom familiar to designated perverts.

Photographic Content

While, in this climate, all nude photographs of young people have become suspect, it is worth noting that some photographs seem to generate more reactive heat than others, and not always in predictable ways. A photograph by Czech photographer Jan Saudek, for example, included in a recent book of his work widely distributed in the US, depicts a young girl passively having intercourse with Saudek himself. Yet, to my knowledge, neither the book nor the photograph have drawn any criticism whatsoever.

On the other hand, two photographs by Robert Mapplethorpe, showing nothing more than a nude and partially nude young boy and girl, sitting and standing alone, were considered so objectionable that they helped bring the curtain down on Mapplethorpe's scheduled exhibition at the Corcoran Museum and were then seized from the Cincinnati museum that went ahead and exhibited the show.

The art photographs that current antisexual critics are finding most objectionable seem to fall into three categories. First there are the photos that portray the eroticism of their subjects so clearly that they force the viewer to acknowledge this eroticism as well. These portraits are threatening because they so clearly challenge the mythical belief in the complete asexuality of young people. The more successful the portrait—the more deeply and compellingly it captures the full personhood of its subject—the more threatening it becomes.

Second are photographs that generate some level of sexual response, and therefore extreme discomfort, in the people who look at them. These photos are threatening because they force viewers to acknowledge their own attraction, or potential attraction, however mild, to the sexuality and eroticism of young people.

In general, the designated pervert of any given era will be whoever most threatens to overturn the prevailing myth of asexual innocence.

Art and the Eroticism of Puberty
David Steinberg

225

"It is important to realize that sexual fantasies about one's children are normal," therapist and author Lonnie Barbach wrote in 1975, appealing to reason at a time when it was more safe to talk publicly about these things. "Many mothers report having some such fantasies at least occasionally. Children are sexual, warm, cuddly human beings—we can feel turned on and have the fantasies but we don't have to act them out." Yet, despite reassurance from therapists and media professionals that simply having sexual feelings for one's children is natural and almost always harmless, most people still feel intense distress at having any such feelings, and intense anger at any visual stimulus that forces them to acknowledge what they feel, or might potentially feel.

combination of denying the sexual existence of young people and vilifying those who acknowledge and affirm their sexuality only creates an impossibly conflicted social climate, divorced from sexual reality, that does nothing to support the emotional well-being of children. Indeed, it is the refusal to deal realistically with the sexuality of young people that lies at the heart of our failure to address this social problem effectively. If people like Christian fundamentalist Randall Terry and Operation Rescue truly want to protect children from sexual abuse, they might begin by taking a good, long look at the images of photographers like Jock Sturges and Sally Mann, and take to heart what the faces and bodies looking out at them have to say.

While the precise definition of the new designated perverts is still evolving, it seems clear that it will center on those who acknowledge and affirm the sexuality of young people.

Third are photos that are seen as affronts to innocence whether or not they have anything to do with sexuality, such as the inclusion of the photos of nude children in the Mapplethorpe retrospective. In this case, the mere proximity of photos of childhood innocence to photos of radical sexuality was considered an attack on innocence itself.

In closing, let me emphasize that I strongly believe that protection of the sexual integrity of children and adolescents from the intrusion of adults is a crucial issue of social concern. National attention to the genuine sexual abuse of children is something that has been long overdue. Photography critic A.D. Coleman is correct when he appreciates that our culture is now "in a climate of deep terror over child abuse, and deep concern over the difficulty of catching child abusers. The system and the culture are understandably frustrated about this." But, as Coleman goes on to say, "the problem is that people are taking this frustration out on photographers who have absolutely no intention of contributing to that problem in any way, and whose work, as I read it, does not in any way contribute to that problem."

The current definition of children as a class of non-sexual innocents, and the attack on photographers whose work contradicts that notion, is the latest version of the false dichotomy between asexuality and sexual perversion that has been a long-standing characteristic of American sexual culture. The

"A World That Hates Gays"
Is There Really a Gay Teen Suicide Epidemic?
Philip Jenkins

Though official statistics can seem dull, some figures emerge with such power that they can achieve something like scriptural status in public debate, and these memorable numbers can even have the power to drive social policy. The 1980s was

> Through the 1990s, it was common to claim that gay victims represented perhaps a third of the teen suicide "epidemic," and this figure became simply a social fact, something that "everybody knows."

a golden age of factoids and nifty numbers. That was for instance the era of "one and a half million missing children," which either meant that a million and a half children were missing in all, or else, that was the number that went missing each year. Agencies reported claims that serial killers claimed 5,000 American lives each year, and the media reported it until it became a social fact.[1] Such awe-inspiring numbers presented a knock-down case for the urgency of finding an official response to these obvious menaces, respectively child abduction and repeat homicide. The difficulty is that in each of these cases, the memorable numbers offered were simply bogus, a fact which must raise devastating questions about the legitimacy of the political campaigns which they inspired. The figures were deliberately chosen in order to attract people's attention to the particular issue at hand, to make it seem as serious as possible.

Such instances of misleading statistics are quite well-known in the social science literature, but other glaring examples of wholly false numbers continue to be cited as undeniably correct. Over the past quarter-century, mythical numbers have dominated discussions of the prevalence of "gay teen suicide," that is, the statistics for suicide by young homosexual people. Not surprisingly, suicide by teenagers and young adults has been regarded for some years as a particularly grave form of

social pathology, and it has given rise to numerous official investigations as well as preventive programs by schools and social service agencies. And from the 1980s onwards, gay social and political groups began to draw attention to a particular aspect of this perceived crisis, namely the high over-representation of young gay men and lesbians as victims of these tragic acts. By the 1990s, these claims were reaching hysterical proportions. To quote the gay newspaper the *Advocate*:

> Gay and lesbian teenagers are killing themselves in staggering numbers. They are hanging themselves in high school classrooms, jumping from bridges, shooting themselves on church altars, cutting themselves with razor blades and downing lethal numbers of pills. A conservatively estimated 1500 young gay and lesbian lives are terminated every year because these troubled youths have nowhere to turn.[2]

Through the 1990s, it was common to claim that gay victims represented perhaps a third of the teen suicide "epidemic," and this figure became simply a social fact, something that "everybody knows." And although later studies have challenged this kind of universal knowledge, the ideas remain very much at large. Today, Googling "gay teen suicide" rapidly brings you to the White Ribbon Gay Teen Suicide Awareness Campaign, designed to fight this "epidemic of GLBT teen suicide. It is estimated that a teen in the United States takes his or her own life every 5 hours because he or she is gay, lesbian, bisexual, or transgender, and can not deal with the added stresses that society puts upon them." The site informs us that some 30 percent of teen suicides involve GLBT youngsters.[3] Google also soon takes you to Ciara Torres' essay "Searching for a Way Out," written in the mid-1990s but still circulating time-lessly on the Internet. Torres states from the outset, "For a number of years, researchers have known that one-third of all teenagers who commit suicide are gay."[4] Yet although the numbers may seem high, Torres thinks: "In another sense, it is predictable that gay teens kill themselves more often than other young people simply because their life chances are so limited by social and legal discrimination. Only when this discrimination is eliminated will these shocking statistics change."

The teen suicide phenomenon predictably led to protests about the hostile social environment which caused such emotional turmoil for so many young people. "Each year an estimated fifteen hundred gay youth kill themselves because they cannot continue to live in a world that hates gays."[5] Gay rights activists continue to use the teen suicide issue as one of their most effective rhetorical weapons, chiefly because of its appeal to audiences who might not normally be sympathetic to liberal views in this area. The theme easily lends itself to moving illustration by stories of specific young people who had killed themselves, the presumption being that homosexuality had been a determining factor in their decisions. Rhetorical lessons drawn from such incidents were invaluable in debates over the coverage of homosexual issues in the schools, one of the most controversial political issues of the last twenty years.

So mainstream has the alleged problem become that it became a standard part of the social ills on which political candidates were expected to comment. During the 2008 presidential campaign, Hillary Clinton was asked what she would do, "considering the extraordinarily high incidence of depression and suicide among gay teenagers." And of course, she had a pat answer:

It's such a serious problem, and I've done a lot of work on this in New York because I'm well aware of the depression and anxiety and frankly the high rate of suicide comparatively among gay teens.… There need to be more services. Sometimes it's difficult in school, and there's not a lot of understanding or sensitivity. We've got to do more to help prepare school officials and frankly your peers in school. Just because somebody doesn't understand doesn't mean that they should be a bully.… There's even a school in

New York that I have supported that is just for gay teens because it is very difficult in many areas for people to find any acceptance whatsoever. We need more health services. We need more mentoring and assistance so that you don't feel so alone.[6]

But how real was, or is, the problem? In fact, estimates for the level of gay teen suicide are quite misleading and wildly inflated.[7] Advocates citing the very high figure ignore grave methodological flaws both in the definition and prevalence of homosexuality, and the statistical shortcomings should certainly have been evident to the groups and individuals citing the numbers. Believers in a "crisis" of gay teen suicide employ definitions of the term "gay" that are malleable, dubious, and self-contradictory, while estimates of the gay population, however defined, rely on statistics that are hopelessly discredited. If we have no idea how many "gay teens" there are, we can conclude nothing about the proportion of suicide victims who meet this criterion.

In fact, estimates for the level of gay teen suicide are quite misleading and wildly inflated.

The claims were based on data and assumptions so profoundly flawed that they can tell us little about the objective realities of suicide. However, the appearance and popularization of these claims is valuable in its own right as evidence for the development of a social problem, and the means by which an interest group has been able to formulate and publicize claims until they achieved the status of unchallenged social fact. Crucially, the suicide issue permitted gay rights campaigners to transform the common stereotype of homosexuals from victimizers of the young to young victims themselves: Gays in fact were the victims of official neglect, persecution, and even conspiracy. The locus of victimization was thus fundamentally altered, and with it the whole rhetorical direction of the suicide problem.

The phenomenon also offers yet another illustration of a rhetorical tactic that has long distinguished the gay rights movement, namely the use of very high estimates of the incidence of homosexuality to portray as mainstream problems that might otherwise be considered specifically gay issues. Thus redefined and mainstreamed, issues like gay teen suicide and gay-bashing can successfully seek the attention and sympathy of a substantial majority of the population.

Teen Suicide: Formulating a Crisis

From the late 1970s, the issue of suicides by teenagers and young adults attained general recognition as a serious social problem. (Though standard federal categories studied individuals aged 15 through 24, the problem was generally defined as one of "teen suicide," and that term will be employed here.) This perception was founded on the straightforward observation that suicide rates in this age group had indeed been increasing steadily since the 1950s, and growth in the 1960s and 1970s was quite explosive. Suicide rates for persons aged 15 to 24 stood at 4.5 per hundred thousand in 1950, and 5 per hundred thousand in 1960, but subsequently grew to 8.8 in 1970, and 12.4 by 1978–79. Though the rate stabilized somewhat, the

killed themselves. Was it, at least in part, a change in recording practices? In bygone days, the public stigma attached to suicide often led to undercounting, while correct identification of such an act depends on the conduct of investigators no less than the skill of medical examiners. Particularly where a juvenile is concerned, police and doctors would be likely to exercise discretion in ways intended to ease the emotional suffering of a family, even to the point of concealing suicide notes. For statistical purposes, this behavior would not be significant if it could be assumed to be constant, but some have suggested, controversially, that the dramatic increases in youth suicide rates since the 1950s were mainly due to changes in the behavior of medical examiners, who reversed the older trend towards undercounting. While admitting a rise in suicide rates between about 1964 and 1972, Michael Males views the "epidemic" terminology as quite misleading. In fact, he argues, juvenile rates have not increased much more than those for adults, while rates for both categories have remained relatively constant since the early 1970s.[8]

Youth suicide was used to illustrate the social harm caused by divorce and broken families, by child abuse, by drugs and substance abuse, by schoolyard bullying, by rock music, or by young people dabbling in the occult and fantasy role-playing games.

1990 figure was approaching 13 per hundred thousand. This was also a problem affecting young men: Males outnumbered females by three to one in 1970, five to one by 1980.

Between 1975 and 1990, the average annual total for teen suicides amounted to 5,000 fatalities each year, and this age group was heavily over-represented in overall suicide statistics. By the early 1980s, suicide even briefly overtook homicide as the second largest killer of teens and young adults, following accidents. Moreover, completed or "successful" suicides were well known to constitute only a small fraction of suicidal behavior, and estimates for the number of suicide attempts by young people each year ranged from 400,000 to two million. There is also speculation that the 5,000 known cases of teen suicide might understate the scale of the issue, in that other deaths recorded as "accidents," especially in automobile crashes, might in reality have involved suicidal intent.

One obvious question is whether higher suicide statistics reflected a real growth in the number of people who actually

But even if an authentic rise in suicide rates is acknowledged, what does it actually mean? Only a tiny proportion of episodes involving self-directed violence result in an event officially recorded as suicide, perhaps less than one percent of the total, with the outcome dependent on a complex array of factors. These include the lethality of the particular means of violence chosen, firearms usually being the most deadly weapon of choice, and also the likelihood of early and effective medical intervention. Put crudely, imagine two men both equally determined to kill themselves. One man shoots himself in rural Wyoming, and is likely to die before reaching a hospital; another person who takes pills in a Manhattan apartment may well wake up in intensive care. For both reasons— availability of guns and remoteness of medical facilities— Western states have been marked by the highest youth suicide rates, with rural regions often exceeding urban. We should never assume that the individuals who actually commit suicide constitute a truly representative sample of the youth population at large.

But such statistical caveats were rarely noted in the growing concern of these years, in which youth suicide rates were repeatedly employed as an index of juvenile alienation and despair. Few denied that there was a "teen suicide problem" or even a national epidemic. The plight of "kids on the brink" had a potent ability to attract public and media attention.[9] Suicides were distributed across all social categories, and some of the most notorious incidents affected better-off or even elite families; the popular media often had occasion to report incidents affecting celebrities. In addition, whites were over-represented among the victims, constituting 93 percent of completed suicides.

Throughout the 1980s, teen suicide was the subject of a steady outpouring of books and magazine articles, most of which aimed to provide advice for parents seeking to detect warning signs of suicide within their families and for schools wishing to implement prevention programs. The theme also appeared regularly in the visual media, in TV movies and after-school specials aimed at teenagers.

This emerging problem offered rich rhetorical opportunities for numerous interest groups and activists, who were not shy about offering explanations of just what social dysfunctions and injustices had led to such a tragic loss of young people. Depending on the literature you read, you found that youth suicide reflected the social harm caused by divorce and bro-

ures to win support from multiple constituencies, and inevitably there were calls for action at federal level. In 1984, Health and Human Services Secretary Margaret Heckler commissioned a prestigious "Task Force on Youth Suicide" to determine means by which the number of deaths might be substantially reduced, with an initial target of reducing the rate to 11 per hundred thousand by 1990.

Suicide and Homosexuality

In deciding appropriate areas for study, there was no question that the Task Force would allocate at least some attention to sexual issues, particularly homosexuality. At least from the mid-nineteenth century, observers had frequently suggested that homosexuals were at greater risk of suicidal behavior, a stereotype epitomized by the title of the 1983 book *I Thought People Like That Killed Themselves*. The late-Victorian English writer John Addington Symonds expressed the opinion that "I do not think it far from wrong when I mention that at least half of the suicides of young men are due to this one circumstance." "It is not difficult for anyone familiar with gay literature to name dozens of novels and stories that climax with the suicide of a homosexual."[10] In the cinema, portrayals of gay characters prior to the 1980s almost inevitably concluded with their violent deaths, usually by murder but often by suicide.[11]

By the mid-1980s, cumulative evidence from these and other studies did indeed indicate a higher incidence of suicidal behavior or attempts among the homosexual population, especially among younger men and women.

Most gay activists radically disliked the clichéd association between homosexuality and suicide, which reflected the common assumption that homosexuals were emotionally disturbed, "that the inherent psychopathology of gay people makes them suicidal."[12] Eric Rofes attacked the "dual myth of homosexual suicide. This myth asserts that lesbians and gay men not only commit suicide at a rate considerably higher than society-at-large, but that somehow a person's homosexuality is itself the source of self-destructiveness."[13] In fact, the belief that homosexuality increased one's self-destructive tendencies was repeatedly cited in the anti-gay literature produced by religious activists like Tim LaHaye and Anita Bryant. Both claimed that approximately half of all American suicides were the direct consequence of homosexuality, while LaHaye suggested that gays tended to kill themselves at a rate

ken families, by child abuse or rape, by drugs and substance abuse, by schoolyard bullying, by rock music, or by young people dabbling in the occult and fantasy role-playing games. Some of these rhetorical lessons were conservative or traditionalist in nature, but the issue also lent itself to liberal or radical interpretation, for example in a critique of youth unemployment and shrinking economic opportunities, or of the evils of the traditional patriarchal family.

From both liberal and traditionalist standpoints, public rhetoric and claims-making about youth suicide reached new heights in the mid-1980s, when the theme was often linked to wider concerns about the state of the nation's "threatened children." Responding to this concern was a natural way for political fig-

twelve to fourteen times higher than for non-homosexuals. Combating such theories had played a crucial role in the struggle during the 1970s to have homosexuality removed from the list of "diseases" acknowledged by the American psychiatric profession.

The suicide issue attracted a substantial scholarly literature, although many of the quantitative studies had serious methodological problems. Some studies concentrated on suicidal

The Federal Task Force

Research on the gay aspect of the teen suicide problem attained national visibility through the work of Margaret Heckler's federal Task Force, and especially through a number of conferences convened in association with that investigation. In 1986, two important meetings were held, and both heard papers directly positing a major link between homosexuality and teen suicide. One of the papers, by Professor Joseph

Several influential studies in the early 1990s necessitated a further revision of the estimated homosexuality rate for men, down to between 1 and 3 percent.

behavior among groups of homosexuals without attempting to use a control group, while designs that did involve controls were often of limited scale and relied too heavily on institutionalized populations. Prior to the late 1980s, only a handful of studies used large and well-chosen samples both for homosexual subjects and non-homosexual controls, and only in more recent times do we have reliable research that seriously debunks most of the key myths about gay suicide. In 2001, Ritch Savin-Williams published a critical study that exposed the flaws of older work. In fact, as he demonstrated, gay youths were somewhat more likely to kill themselves than heterosexuals, but only by a small margin. Findings to the contrary relied on very atypical populations, such as inmates of urban youth shelters.[14]

But such critical work was still far in the future in the mid-1980s, when available evidence seemed to indicate a high incidence of suicidal behavior or attempts among the gay population, especially among younger men and women.[15] Observers were swift to explore this trend. In 1983, Rofes' book on suicide and homosexuality included a groundbreaking chapter on "lesbians and gay youth and suicide," in which he remarks that hitherto "the relationship between homosexuality and youth suicide has virtually been ignored," and cites examples in which television presentations on the suicide issue were forced to omit reference to sexual orientation. However, the coming years would more than compensate for this gap, and most of the themes discussed in his work would soon become commonplace in the mainstream literature.

Harry, examined the literature relating suicide to "sexual identity issues," a term which included pregnancy, sexual abuse, and venereal disease, but which also presented several pages on homosexuality. Reviewing the admittedly flawed literature, Harry argued plausibly that homosexual youth attempted or committed suicide at a rate from two to six times that of non-homosexuals. The author was careful to emphasize that his conclusions affected individuals of definitely homosexual orientation, as opposed to bisexuals, or those with some same-sex experience in their pasts.

This restrained finding was in marked contrast in tone and methodology to a paper presented at the other conference by Paul Gibson, a clinical social worker based at San Francisco's Huckleberry House shelter. This paper deserves special attention because, in short, it created what would for over twenty years be the dominant model of teen suicide. Gibson argued at length that "gay youth are two or three times more likely to attempt suicide than other people. They may comprise up to 30 percent of completed youth suicides annually."[16] Gibson therefore took a reasonably well-accepted figure for the high prevalence of suicidal behavior among homosexual youth and added a crucial but dubious statistical extrapolation, which tried to estimate the "gay element" in the overall figures for teen suicides. Though Gibson repeatedly presents anecdotal and survey evidence to show that young homosexuals are likely to contemplate suicide, he never explicitly states how the "thirty percent" statistic is derived. The logical process by which this second stage is established seems to develop as follows:

1. Every year, some 5,000 young people commit suicide.

2. Assuming that one-tenth of the population is homosexual, we would expect about 500 of these cases to involve gay teenagers and young adults, *if* homosexuals had a "normal" rate of suicidal behavior.

3. However, homosexuals are approximately three times as likely as heterosexuals to commit suicide, so that the actual number of homosexual suicides in a given year would be closer to 1,500.

4. Therefore, the proportion of teen and young adult suicide cases involving homosexuals is about 30 percent of the whole, or approximately one-third.

Gibson's argument, especially in step two, depends on his estimate of the proportion of the total population that is homosexual, and it is here that we encounter serious difficulties. He evidently accepts a higher figure for the prevalence of homosexuality than would commonly be accepted, in order to reach the conclusion: "There are far more gay youth than you are presently aware of." This is substantiated by Kinsey's account "of homosexual behavior among adolescents surveyed with 28

Evidence based strictly on homosexual subjects has been illegitimately extended to cover a poorly-defined "gay" population.

percent of the males and 17 percent of the females reporting at least one homosexual experience. He also found that that approximately 13 percent of adult males and 7 percent of adult females had engaged in predominantly homosexual behavior for at least three years prior to his survey. That is where that figure that 10 percent of the homosexual comes from…a substantial minority of youth—perhaps one in ten as one book suggests—have a primary gay male, lesbian or bisexual orientation."

Though not explicitly named, the "one book" probably refers to Ann Heron's 1983 selection of writings by young gay people, entitled *One Teenager in Ten*.

Given gay tendencies towards suicidal behavior, "this means that 20–30 percent of all youth suicides may involve gay youth."[17] He feels that this is a minimum figure, and notes another study which suggests that gay teen suicides might amount to 3,000 each year, or 60 percent of the whole. If the proportion of gay victims is extended to the problem of suicide

attempts rather than completed acts, then each year the number of homosexual youths who try to kill themselves would run into the hundreds of thousands.

Gibson's argument makes some dubious assumptions, but the figures for gay suicidal behavior are quite of a piece with other estimates in the paper, which suggest for example that "gay male, lesbian, bisexual and transsexual youth comprise as many as 25 percent of all youth living on the streets in this country." This surprising statistic, unsupported by any citation, relies on anecdotal evidence of the sort found throughout the paper, which largely derives from grass-roots and mutual-assistance organizations and shelters concentrated in major urban centers like San Francisco. The paper achieves its very high estimates for homosexual behavior by extrapolating such atypical characteristics of an urban underclass to the nation at large. In addition, the paper repeatedly refers with little distinction to "gay male, lesbian, bisexual and transsexual youth," which raises serious difficulties of definition.

It is worth remembering here just what Gibson's paper was: a contribution to a discussion that had not been subject to peer review or fact-checking. It thus remains one man's opinion. Yet the paper gained immense prestige from the context, appearing as it did in a document produced under the imprimatur of the federal government, and a conservative Republican administration at that. The Task Force Report was widely cited. For years afterwards, it was the chief source for the claims that lesbian and gay youth may constitute "up to thirty percent of completed suicides annually," and that "homosexuals of both sexes are two to six times more likely to attempt suicide than are heterosexuals."[18]

"One in Ten"

Though Gibson's argument achieved immediate recognition from many researchers and activist groups, its conclusions are suspect, and so are those of the many other articles which rely upon it. His assumptions involve two chief areas of difficulty: firstly, that cases of youth suicide represent a cross-section of the young adult population; second, that about 10 percent of the population can be characterized as gay or homosexual. The first argument is questionable for the reasons noted above, that a suicide attempt is far more likely to result in death in some circumstances rather than others, and the social categories likely to kill themselves don't necessarily correlate with those groups likely to have a high incidence of homosexuality. Notably, homosexual populations are likely to be found disproportionately in urban areas, where guns might be less available to teenagers but where emergency medical facilities are more abundant. Though this is controversial, it can be argued that areas marked by high youth suicide rates are less likely to have substantial homosexual populations.

Much more serious, however, is Gibson's estimate of the gay element of the population at large. Both for Gibson and his many successors, the main cited source for estimating the homosexual population is Kinsey, rather than any of the later

Finally, the whole "gay teen" hypothesis provides no explanation for the sharp rise of youth suicide since the 1950s, and in fact is counterintuitive.

revisions of that much-challenged study, or one of the more recent surveys that rely on far superior data-gathering techniques.[19] As is common in gay activist writing on other social issues, the prevalence of homosexuality was estimated at a round but very dubious "one in ten" of the population.

Though Kinsey himself rejected a simplistic "one in ten" rate, his study had argued that about 10 percent of men were chiefly or exclusively homosexual for at least three years between the ages of 16 and 55. The original methodology was, however, so flawed as to create grave concern. The study relied chiefly on volunteer subjects disproportionately drawn from metropolitan areas, and active homosexuals were overrepresented in the sample, as were college-educated individuals. In addition, a substantial number of subjects had institutional backgrounds, generally in jails or prisons. In sum, the study was likely to produce a sizable over-representation of subjects who reported same-sex contacts both on a sporadic basis and as a continuing lifestyle. Later scholars were divided over whether the data might usefully be reinterpreted, or if indeed the whole project was beyond salvage.[20]

The numerical issue was sensitive because of its political connotations. For the gay rights movement of the 1970s and 1980s, the "one in ten" figure became a powerful slogan, suggesting as it did that homosexual legal and political rights were a crucial matter for a large portion of the population, and that a very large number of individuals were suppressing their authentic sexual nature for fear of the consequences. The National Gay and Lesbian Task Force claimed to represent "23 million gay and lesbian persons," while some activists even viewed the 10 percent estimate as excessively conservative. Conversely, moral conservatives minimized the number of homosexuals in order to present the condition as "a behavioral oddity, certainly not entitled to special protective status," in the words of Lou Sheldon of the Traditional Values Coalition.

Already by the early 1970s, studies employing methodologies superior to Kinsey's found the number of active homosexuals to be far less than the popular commonplace. In 1972, Gebhard's re-evaluation of the Kinsey figures suggested a revised estimate of around 4 percent of men, which long remained the most convincing figure, and which *should* have been the source employed by the suicide studies of the 1980s.[21] The scale of the gay population became an urgent issue during these years because of the need to determine accurately the population at special risk from AIDS. New estimates were far more conservative than the Kinsey figures, and in 1988, the estimated number of gay males in New York city alone was revised downward by some 80 percent.

Several influential studies in the early 1990s demanded a further revision of the estimated homosexuality rate for men, down to between 1 and 3 percent. In 1993, the Alan Guttmacher Institute reported that between 1.8 and 2.8 percent of men surveyed reported at least one sexual contact with another man in the previous decade, while only about 1 percent had been exclusively homosexual in the previous year. This was in accord with the findings of a national survey recently undertaken in France.[22] In 1994, a University of Chicago study found that 2.8 percent of men and 1.4 percent of women surveyed identified themselves as homosexual or bisexual, with respondents in urban areas reporting same-sex contacts at far higher rates than their counterparts in suburban or rural regions.[23] However, of all the groups sampled, only one reported recent homosexual contacts at the 10 percent level, and that figure was attained by men living in the largest cities.

Contrary to Kinsey's "one in ten," a figure of one in thirty would offer a more accurate assessment of the male population that can be described as homosexual or bisexual, and one in sixty would best represent the exclusively homosexual. The corresponding figures for women reporting sexual contacts with other women are somewhat lower.

Counting Gay Suicides

The gay teen suicide problem also depended upon a highly expansive interpretation of the term *gay*. Research had shown that "homosexuals" had a greater tendency to attempt suicide, meaning individuals whose sexual orientation is predominantly towards the same sex. However, the *suicide* figures of Gibson and others concern that "one in ten" element of the population who have "a primary gay male, lesbian or bisexual orientation." This is a substantial leap, even if we set aside the quandary of whether one can in fact refer to a "primary…bisexual orientation." Evidence based strictly on homosexual subjects has been illegitimately extended to cover a poorly defined "gay" population. This extrapolation may derive from Kinsey's suggestion of a spectrum of sexual preference in which individuals are located in terms of their degree of homosexual or heterosexual orientation. If this model is correct, then terms like *homosexual* and *bisexual* are strictly relative, and the general term *gay* could appropriately be applied to those individuals towards one end of the spectrum, as opposed to a discrete population. However, criticisms of the Kinsey material also raise grave doubts about the accuracy of the whole "spectrum" idea, and thus the use of the term *gay*.

For the gay suicide statistics, the difficulty lies not in the original Kinsey research but in its misapplication. In the original studies, homosexual subjects were located by quite proper techniques, requesting volunteers from homosexual activist or self-help groups, or through gay-oriented newspapers. This produced a sample of self-identified and (usually) overt homosexuals, and we can reasonably assume that findings will reflect the conditions and behavior of a wider population of active homosexuals whose sexual orientation is more or less exclusively focused on others of the same sex. However, Gibson and others imply that the studies are applicable to "gay and bisexual" individuals, the criterion being that a person had had one or more same-sex contacts within the past number of years, even though he or she would not define themselves as actively homosexual.

While similar emotional problems and suicidal tendencies *might* be found among this larger population, the available research findings don't allow us to assume that. Perhaps, for instance, the higher suicide rates recorded for overt homosexuals reflect social ostracism and legal discrimination, which would not apply to a "closeted" homosexual, and still less to someone with an isolated same-sex experience some years in his past. Does one same-sex contact predispose one to suicide? No basis was offered for the link repeatedly drawn between same-sex experience and suicide, still less an established causal relationship. As Erwin notes, "The distinction between behavior and identity raises important questions with respect to the impact of heterosexism on mental health."[24]

And there were other difficulties, such as the inclusion of lesbians in the statistics, with the suggestion that homosexual women also represented "one in ten" of the female population. Even Kinsey claimed to find only seven percent of the female population meeting his definition of lesbianism, a rate that no subsequent study has ever approached. Given that girls and women compose a small minority of completed suicides, the number of additional cases supplied by lesbian victims is tiny.

Finally, the whole "gay teen" hypothesis provides no explanation for the sharp rise of youth suicide since the 1950s, and in fact is counterintuitive. According to the "one in ten" theory, the frequency of homosexual tendencies should be more or less constant over time and should not have changed significantly since the 1950s. What has unquestionably changed since the 1950s is the social environment, which uniformly has altered in directions favoring the overt expression of homosexuality, whether this is measured through the reform or repeal of criminal statutes, hate crime laws penalizing anti-gay violence, or media depictions of homosexuality. Logically, we should expect this to have resulted in a massive decline in the suicide rates of homosexuals, yet this is not suggested in the literature. All in all, the evidentiary foundations of the "gay teen suicide" problem appear fragile in the extreme.

"Death By Denial": The Rhetoric of Gay Teen Suicide

Despite difficulties of evidence, the inflated scale of the issue soon achieved national visibility, a process accelerated by the publication of other research confirming that homosexual teens did indeed appear at high risk of attempting or completing suicide. In 1991, especially, an influential article by Gary Remafedi *et al* in the journal *Pediatrics* was reported under dramatic headlines claiming : "Nearly One-Third of Young Gay Men May Attempt Suicide, Study Suggests." Incredibly, the study did not employ a control group, presumably on the basis that the relative vulnerability of gay youth (however defined) could be taken as a given; why argue with the obvious?[25] But this omission did not prevent the "one-third" figure from becoming a public commonplace. Accidental transposition or misunderstanding of the figures during the course of reporting may also have reinforced the popular notion that "one-third of teen suicides involve homosexuals."

Accumulating testimony from the behavioral sciences now provided the basis for a popularization of the issue and the construction of "gay teen suicide" as a pressing social problem. Initially, the figures were presented in the gay activist press in late 1991 and early 1992, when the suicide issue was prominently stressed in gay publications like the *Advocate* and

view, the document was simply too incendiary for the administration, and the failure to take account of the Gibson paper thus reflected not methodological concerns but a craven submission to conservative protests.

There was a systematic and perhaps ingenuous misunderstanding of Gibson's original argument, which has repeatedly been cited as the considered findings of the Task Force as a whole rather than merely the opinion of one participant and which made little impact on the final report. One article in *Education Digest* claimed: "*The U.S. Department of Health and Human Services reported* in 1989 that 30 percent of all teens who commit suicide are gay" (my emphasis). One collection of essays quotes the Task Force findings on gay suicide in its blurb, and continues, "The report was swept aside by the Bush administration, yet the problem didn't go away."[26] The book, *Death by Denial,* reprinted the "alarming and hotly contested" Gibson paper in its entirety, presumably as a definitive statement on the dimensions of the perceived crisis.

By 1992, the construction of the gay teen suicide problem had become so well-established that the issue could be used as a multifaceted weapon in numerous struggles over gay issues, and not merely in schools and churches.

Christopher Street. The theme was used to attack the Republican administration of the first President Bush, then under liberal assault for adopting extremist positions on social issues including abortion and homosexuality in order to appease religious conservatives.

These articles viewed the muted official reaction to the 1989 Task Force as part of a deliberate strategy of anti-gay persecution, or at least "denial." The sequence of events ran as follows: Conservatives such as California Republican Congressman William Dannemeyer hated the Task Force report, which they viewed as pseudoscience with a gay rights slant. They therefore fought any action based upon it. But the more the report was attacked, the easier it was to present it as an inconvenient truth, which was suppressed entirely due to "pressure from conservative religious and family groups," with Dannemeyer as the prominent villain. In Massachusetts, a state commission on gay and lesbian issues made the incorrect assertion that "Pressure from anti-gay forces…led to suppression not only of the controversial chapter, but also of the entire report." In this

Themes of conspiracy, cover-up, and official denial pervaded the activist press. The *Advocate*, for example, examined "The Government's Cover-Up and America's Lost Children." Examining a "conservatively estimated" total of 1,500 gay teen suicides each year, the author argued that the problem arose from cynical neglect by a bureaucracy that had fallen under the influence of right-wing religious fundamentalists. According to Robert Bray of the National Gay and Lesbian Task Force, gay youth suicide was "an unconscionable tragedy that has been ignored by health officials in Washington because of homophobia."[27] Teen suicide was thus but another aspect of official abuse that was also reflected in the lack of progress in stemming the AIDS epidemic. Federal inaction aggravated an already dangerous situation and literally cost many young lives.

Christopher Street similarly traced a pattern of malign neglect, arguing that "government officials, scientists, writers, commentators and activists have been criminally silent on the issue" of gay youth suicide, despite its "epidemic proportions." The suicide statistics indicated the "plain fact that…thousands of gay and lesbian youth all over the United States are calling out for help in the face of bigotry, ignorance and hatred." In the *New York Native*, David Lafontaine of the Coalition for Lesbian and Gay Civil Rights estimated "that about one third of the estimated one million teen suicide attempts are committed by gay youth." According to such claims, the pervasive social, political, and emotional crisis afflicting young homosexuals drove hundreds of thousands each year to attempt violence against themselves. Urgent action was demanded to stop the "hidden holocaust."

In these months, the gay suicide issue won an audience outside the activist press, as it received attention in the national news media. In 1992, the ABC news program *20/20* showed a report on the problem of suicide among gay and lesbian teens, an item criticized as "overheated" for its acceptance of the most extreme claims about the perceived menace. The ideas now permeated the self-help literature directed at young people and parents concerned about suicide prevention. One book characteristically notes that "researchers who study gay youth and suicide estimate that about one-third of the young people who attempt or commit suicide are gay or lesbian," but the only citation is to a reprint from the Gibson paper.[28]

Homosexuality and the Young

By this point, the magnitude of the "epidemic" seemed to have been established quantitatively, so that authors could proceed to a wide-ranging social and political analysis of the roots of the problem, and to proposing solutions. The common assumption was that gay teens are killing themselves in very large numbers because of the anti-homosexual attitudes pervading society. These difficulties would certainly include overt violence in the form of gay-bashing, but homophobia was also reflected in social ostracism, derision, and hostile media stereotypes. Suicide could only be prevented by curing the social climate of homophobia, by providing legal, physical, and emotional protection for homosexuals. To adapt the common slogan of AIDS activists, this is an instance where "Silence = Death," and lives would be saved only by forthright militancy. As Remafedi writes, "[T]o ignore the problem now is a missed opportunity to save thousands of young lives, tantamount to sanctioning death by denial."

Claims-makers in this affair had a number of agendas. In general terms, they were seeking to illustrate the sufferings of the homosexual population and the necessity for official action in the form of protective laws or proactive government policies. Valerie Jenness has shown how the perceived threat of gay-bashing was employed for exactly these ends in this same time period.[29] But the activist perspective on teen suicide now suggested that the protection of homosexuals as a category directly benefited young people and might actually preserve them from harm or violence. Gay rights, in short, would save young lives. We can realize how significant this linkage was only when we appreciate the long historical association of homosexuality with the exploitation or injury of the young, for many years one of the most powerful weapons in the rhetorical arsenal of homophobia.

Campaigns against pedophiles and sex offenders often have at least a covert anti-homosexual agenda, on the grounds that individuals who might tolerate consensual sexual acts between adults would not be prepared to extend this acquiescence to the exploitation of children. The gay/pedophile association appeared regularly in gay rights referenda since the 1970s, when a notorious slogan alleged that "homosexuals aren't born—they recruit." Pedophilia was central to anti-gay rhetoric until the mid-1980s, when it was largely replaced by the still more effective terror weapon of AIDS. However, the pedophile issue has since reemerged in recent attempts to weaken or abolish gay rights legislation, especially in numerous state referenda through the 1990s.

A perceived homosexual threat against the young gave rise to countless local battles of the early 1990s, for example over attempts to permit gay couples to adopt children, but public education was the most common arena of conflict. Battles often developed when school boards sought to introduce curricular materials depicting gay relationships in a favorable light, books like *Heather Has Two Mommies* and *Daddy's Roommate*. Such texts and materials were widely denounced and their sponsors accused of promoting homosexuality among underage children. Also at issue were programs which used homosexual speakers in order to address gay issues and schemes to provide support and counseling services for gay and lesbian students. Resistance to gay-oriented curricula was a major issue in mobilizing conservative activism on school boards, often providing a vehicle for candidates of the Christian Right.

The new focus on gay teen suicide offered an ideal opportunity to counter such linkages, showing that the introduction of homosexual themes in the classroom or other youth contexts might actually protect young people from physical and emotional harm and even an untimely death. Gay activists thus adopted children's rights rhetoric, placing themselves in the position of defending the best interests of the young. Conversely, they sought to show that—to quote the *Advocate*—"the government does not have the best interest of children at heart."

The response demanded by the suicide problem would certainly focus on educational issues. Gibson's pioneering paper had argued:

> We need to make a conscious effort to promote a positive image of homosexuals at all levels of society that provide gay youth with a diversity of Lesbian and gay adult role models. We each need to take personal responsibility for revising homophobic attitudes and conduct. Families should be educated about the development and positive nature of homosexuality. They must be able to accept their child as gay or lesbian. Schools need to include information about homosexuality in their curriculum and protect gay youth from abuse by their peers to ensure they receive an equal education.[30]

Though the Task Force called forth no federal response, gay teen suicide proved a powerful issue at state level. In Massachusetts, notably, the discovery of a gay suicide problem led several school districts in 1991 to initiate programs involving support groups for gay and lesbian pupils. Later that year, the socially liberal Republican Governor William Weld proposed an advisory body with the goal of developing strategies to stem the "epidemic." This scheme was challenged by legislators who felt that the commission's mandate should extend to all vulnerable students, but the gay focus was retained after activists emphasized the "stunning" fact "revealed" by the Task Force that 30 percent of all youth suicides involved homosexuals. Weld himself asserted: "Half a million young people attempt suicide every year. Nearly 30 percent of youth suicides are committed by gays and lesbians." In 1993, a state Commission on Gay and Lesbian Youth envisaged far-reaching reforms that would train teachers and families, promote anti-harassment and anti-discrimination policies, and generally "guarantee gay and lesbian students equal rights to an education and equal access to school activities."[31]

A public crusade against gay youth suicide would also have to combat homophobic attitudes in the churches. This was a significant theme, in view of the central role played by religious groups in movements against homosexual rights and the related controversies within churches about the toleration or ordination of gay clergy. For Gibson and others, religious denominations were primary villains in the production of the hostile rhetoric which drove so many teens to their deaths, with Catholics, Baptists, and Protestant fundamentalists singled out for special blame. Gibson explicitly demanded that "faiths that condemn homosexuality should recognize how they contribute to the rejection of gay youth by their families, and suicide among gay and lesbian youth."

I have suggested that the "gay teen suicide" myth was closely linked to the politics of a specific historical moment, namely the intense cultural politics of the early 1990s, but the underlying idea did not simply fade away when that environment changed. Throughout the 1990s, the notion that "one third of teen suicides are gay" continued to be recycled and cited every time young people or teenagers featured in gay rights debates. And as we have seen, the bogus idea was still firmly part of social knowledge by the time of Hillary Clinton's presidential run in 2008. The prolonged life of the mythology suggests how very valuable it is to its proponents.[32]

Building the Problem

In establishing a problem as serious and worthy of public concern, claims-makers inevitably employ the terminology that will carry the greatest conviction in a given society. Though in earlier periods this might involve using scriptural or Classical references, modern audiences are more generally impressed by the rhetoric of social and behavioral science, so quantitative measures are given great prominence. Statements about a given issue thus tend to begin with estimates about the scale or prevalence of a given behavior, claiming that x thousand children are abused or abducted each year, or that y million Americans have been harmed by a particular drug. These statistics are intended to impress, both by their very large scale and by the suggestion of rapid and uncontrollable growth and ubiquitous threat. In the case of gay teen suicide, the awful (and easily memorable) statistics provided a powerful warrant for the case that activists were making so passionately. One-third of all suicides! Fifteen hundred teenagers a year!

"A World That Hates Gays"
Is There Really a Gay Teen Suicide Epidemic?   Philip Jenkins

237

Claiming a vast scale for the gay suicide problem was closely related to other themes emphasized by gay activists in these years, above all the transformation of homosexuality from a deviant or pathological state to a condition that attracted unmerited persecution. It was all part of a process of constructing gays as victims of social injustice. In the United States especially, modern movements claiming rights for a particular segment of the population have all been influenced to a greater or lesser degree by the rhetoric of the African-American civil rights movement and its emphasis on structural oppression and group victimization. Other groups who viewed themselves as historically oppressed have claimed a parallel victim status, so that feminists stressed the systematic violence inflicted on women in the form of rape and domestic abuse. A claim to collective victim status implied that the group was "unjustly harmed or damaged by forces beyond their control" and that victimization occurred chiefly or solely due to the essential characteristics of that group.[33] On the analogy of civil rights legislation, government had the right and duty to seek to prevent this victimization.

For the gay rights movement, which emerged alongside modern feminism, oppression and persecution manifested themselves most visibly in the form of anti-gay violence, but the same themes were also applied to other dysfunctions where a victimization theme was not initially evident. In the matter of AIDS, notably, it was by no means apparent that blame for the epidemic could be attached to anti-homosexual prejudice, still less to any particular institution or administration. During the 1980s, however, activism over the issue successfully cast the problem as an issue of homophobia, in the sense that anti-gay prejudice prevented the allocation of sufficient resources to find a cure for the disease, while prudery prevented the establishment of public education programs to limit the spread of AIDS.

Teen suicide followed on similar lines, taking a matter that had previously been viewed as one of personal misfortune or dysfunction and presenting it as the consequence of structural bias and victimization, and even of official conspiracy. The teen suicide issue benefited from a cumulative process, in that AIDS campaigners had already established notions of official neglect and suppression of evidence, which could easily be transferred to the sensitive issue of teen suicide. If so many teenagers killed themselves because they lived in "a world that hate gays," the

obvious rhetorical message was that this world should be changed and that reform would have to begin with those institutions and laws which most directly affected the young.

Debates over homosexuality have often revolved around the issue of the victimization of the young. In rhetorical terms, the gay suicide issue succeeded in retaining concerns about exploitation but transferring the stereotypical role of the homosexual from abuser and molester to victim—from defiler of the young, to young victim. The political benefits for gay activism have been substantial. The whole affair amply demonstrates the real-world consequences of the recasting of a social problem in a particular ideological direction. And once again, we see the immense value of potent-sounding statistics—whether or not they contain a grain of truth.

> In establishing a problem as serious and worthy of public concern, claims-makers inevitably employ the terminology likely to carry the greatest conviction in a given society.

Endnotes

1. Jenkins, Philip. (2006). *Decade of Nightmares.* New York: Oxford University Press. **2.** Maguen, Shira. (1991). Teen suicide. *Advocate*, September 24, p 40. **3.** White Ribbon Campaign [w-ribbon.tripod.com]. **4.** Torres, Ciara. Searching for a way out, [www.healthyplace.com/Communities/gender/gayisok/stopping_suicide.html]. **5.** Galas, Judith C. (1994). *Teen suicide.* San Diego, CA: Lucent Overview, p 60. **6.** Hillary speaks for the unspoken; addresses gay teen suicide. [www.mydd.com/story/2008/1/26/0409/69649]. **7.** Shaffer, David. (1993). Political science. *New yorker*, May 3; Knight, Al. (2000). Gay suicide studies flawed. *Denver post*, April 9. **8.** Males, Mike. (1991). Teen suicide and changing cause of death certification 1953–1987. *Suicide and life-threatening behavior* 21(3), pp 245–59. **9.** Bergman, David B. (1990). *Kids on the brink.* Washington DC: PIA Press. **10.** Symonds is quoted in Tremblay, Pierre J. (1995). The homosexuality factor in the youth suicide problem. Paper presented at the Sixth Annual Conference of the Canadian Association for Suicide Prevention, Banff, Alberta, October 11–14; Rofes, Eric E. (1983). *"I thought people like that killed themselves": Lesbians, gay men and suicide.* San Francisco, CA: Grey Fox, pp 11. **11.** Russo, Vito. (1981). *The celluloid closet.* New York: Harper and Row, pp 261–2. **12.** Erwin, Kathleen. (1993). Interpreting the evidence: Competing paradigms and the emergence of lesbian and gay suicide as a social fact. *International journal of health services*, 23(3), pp 437–53. **13.** *Op cit.*, Rofes. **14.** Savin-Williams, R.C. (2001). Suicide attempts among sexual-minority youths: Population and measurement issues. *Journal of consulting and clinical psychology*, 69(6), pp 983–91. **15.** Saunders, Judith M., and S.M. Valente (1987). Suicide risk among gay men and lesbians. *Death studies*, 11, pp 1–23; Kourany, R.F. (1987). Suicide among homosexual adolescents. *Journal of homosexuality*, 13, pp 111–7. **16.** Gibson, Paul. (1989). Gay male and lesbian teen suicide. In *Report of the secretary's task force on youth suicide*, pp iii: 110. **17.** *Ibid.*, Gibson, pp iii, 115. **18.** Adams, Jane Meredith. (1989). For many gay teenagers, torment leads to suicide tries. *Boston globe*, Jan 3. **19.** Kinsey, A., W. Pomeroy, and C. Martin. (1948). *Sexual behavior in the human male.* Philadelphia: W. B. Saunders. Compare Heron, Ann, ed. (1983). *One teenager in ten.* Boston: Alyson Publications; Heron, Ann, ed. (1994). *Two teenagers in twenty.* Boston: Alyson Publications. **20.** Reisman, Judith, and Edward Eichel. (1990). *Kinsey, sex and fraud.* Lafayette, LA: Lochinvar/Huntington House. **21.** Rogers, Susan M., and Charles F. Turner. (1991). Male-male sexual contact in the USA. *Journal*

Even Kinsey claimed to find only 7 percent of the female population meeting his definition of lesbianism, a rate that has never been approached by any subsequent study.

of sex research, 28(4), pp 491–519. **22.** Dunlap, David W. (2994). Gay survey raises a new question. New York times, October 18; Barringer, Felicity. Sex survey of American men finds one percent are gay. New York times, April 15; Fumento, Michael. (1993). How many gays? National review, April 26, pp 28–9. **23.** Laumann, Edward O., et al. (1994). The social organization of sexuality. Chicago: University of Chicago Press. **24.** Op cit., Erwin, p 447. **25.** Remafedi, Gary, James A. Farrow, and Robert W. Deisher (1991). Risk factors for attempted suicide in gay and bisexual youth. Pediatrics, 87(6), pp 869–75; Flax, Ellen (1991). Nearly one-third of young gay men may attempt suicide, study suggests. Education week, June 12, p 12.; compare Proctor, Curtis D. (1994). Risk factors for suicide among gay, lesbian and bisexual youths. Social work, 39(5), pp 504–13. See also the special supplementary issue of the journal Suicide and life-threatening behavior (1995) on "Research Issues in Suicide and Sexual Orientation," vol. 25. **26.** Remafedi, Gary. (1994). Death by denial. Boston: Alyson. **27.** Op cit., Maguen. **28.** Nelson, Richard E., and Judith C. Galas. (1994). The power to prevent suicide. Minneapolis: Free Spirit, p 45. **29.** Jenness, Valerie. (1995). Hate crimes in the United States. In Images of issues, 2nd edition. Joel Best, ed. Hawthorne, NY: Aldine de Gruyter, pp 213–37. **30.** Op cit., Gibson, iii, p 110. **31.** "Making schools safe for gay and lesbian youth." In op cit., Remafedi, pp 151–205, at p 156. **32.** The whole issue of "gay teens" continues to thrive in the media: See for instance Woog, Dan. (1995). School's out : The impact of gay and lesbian issues on America's schools. Boston: Alyson; Ryan, Caitlin, and Donna Futterman. (1998). Lesbian and gay youth. New York: Columbia University Press. **33.** Jenness, Valerie, and Kendal Broad. (1997). Hate crime. Hawthorne, NY: Aldine De Gruyter.

Media Violence Studies Put Reason on a Rack

Paul McMasters

For more than eight decades, dating to the Payne Fund studies on movie violence in 1933, experts have produced study after study and political leaders have conducted hearing after hearing, all in an effort to prove—by repetition, if not by hard evidence—that media violence causes real violence.

Despite those efforts, drawing a straight line from violence in the media to violence in reality remains difficult, if not impossible.

> Although there has been a steady—and to some, an alarming—increase in fictional violence in electronic media over recent decades, that has been accompanied by a steady decline in the violent-crime rates.

The cause-and-effect relationship cannot be produced reliably in the lab nor demonstrated plausibly in real life. Common experience, common sense, and logic also get in the way.

In fact, hard evidence in the form of crime statistics points us in the opposite direction.

For example, while young people and adults have been exposed to larger and larger doses of fictional violence in more kinds of media, a dramatic increase in violent crime that exposure would supposedly create has not materialized.

Although there has been a steady—and to some, an alarming—increase in fictional violence in electronic media over recent decades, that has been accompanied by a steady decline in the violent-crime rates. The number of violent crimes per 100,000 people has gone from a high of 730 in 1990 to 469 in 2005.

Statistics for juveniles are even more dramatic. Juvenile arrest rates for all crimes decreased by 31 percent between 1996 and 2004. According to the Violent Crime Index maintained by the FBI, the violent-crime arrest rate among 10- to 17-year-olds for 2004 was lower than in any year since 1980—and 49 percent below the peak year of 1994.

An interesting adjunct to these statistics is the finding by economists Gordon Dahl and Stefano DellaVigna in a study released early in 2008. The researchers concluded that violent movies actually reduced assaults by 1,000 a weekend because potential criminals were in theaters instead of out on the streets.

In the face of all that, powerful forces in our society continue to insist that media violence does cause real violence and, therefore, must be regulated, i.e., censored. But delegating the job of policing our media to legislators, judges, and would-be censors driven by fear and hunches not only defies common sense and logic, it flouts science, the law, and the Constitution.

Yet the idea persists and seduces some very powerful and otherwise credible organizations.

For example, in 2000 the American Bar Association's Division for Public Education announced the publication of a new guide to help teachers address violence in television programs, movies, video games, and on the Internet. The division quoted Mary A. Hepburn, professor emeritus of social science at the University of Georgia in Athens, as saying that media violence is "a powerful ingredient" in violent youth behavior. The ABA group went on to cite "an increasing number of studies linking media violence" and "violence in the classroom."

It is not the only prestigious professional group to put reason on the rack and offer censorship of media content as a way to prevent actual violence.

Four major health groups issued a joint statement in 2000 endorsing the scientifically tortuous claim of a link between media and actual violence. Later, a spokesman for the American Medical Association conceded that 1) the groups issued their joint statement at the request of a US Senator championing the idea that media violence promotes real violence, 2) members of the AMA board had not read any of the studies they were citing, and 3) an AMA report on the issue actually hadn't been written at the time.

Yet the statement proclaimed: "At this time, well over 1,000 studies…point overwhelmingly to a causal connection between media violence and aggressive behavior in some children."

It would be most difficult for these groups to produce a list of more than 1,000 studies on media violence. It would be even more difficult to produce a list of 1,000 studies that focus primarily on children and violence. It would be impossible to produce a list of 1,000 studies that demonstrate an unequivocal causal link between media and "aggressive behavior" in children, let alone actual violence committed by children.

No one has yet persuaded courts—where the rule of law, the force of logic, and the presentation of hard evidence hold sway—that there is a cause-and-effect relationship between media violence and real violence.

To be fair, these groups are not the only ones who have arrived at a similar conclusion. They have in common an impatience with parental responsibility, a disregard for free-speech principles, and an unrequited infatuation with "studies" that flirt with causal connections instead of proving them.

Such studies—and there have been many, both publicly and privately funded—attempt to make up in mass what they lack in hard evidence of causation.

Yet the "fact" of causation has been tossed about so often by politicians and activists that even professionals and scholars feel safe in using it. Thus the loopy nature of the public dialogue: Academics produce highly nuanced studies. Political leaders exaggerate and distort their findings and write their own rhetoric into legislation as reality. Advocates adopt and cite the "official" position, and in turn are quoted by political leaders in proposing yet more legislation to solve the problem by regulating expression containing violence.

That is the sort of circular routine at work in more than twenty states and local jurisdictions, as well as Congress, launching legislative efforts to regulate the sale of video games. But none has gotten very far because courts have made it clear that video games are forms of expression deserving the same First Amendment protection as television, movies, and books.

More important, no one has yet persuaded courts—where the rule of law, the force of logic, and the presentation of hard evidence hold sway—that there is a cause-and-effect relationship between media violence and real violence.

In 2001, the Supreme Court let stand a ruling by the Seventh US Circuit Court of Appeals that struck down an Indianapolis ordinance regulating access to video games. In 2003, the Eighth Circuit also ruled that such a law was unconstitutional, noting that "the government cannot silence protected speech by wrapping itself in the cloak of parental authority."

Despite all of this, the assertion persists, partly because the dialogue takes place in an environment where terms are ambiguous and agenda are numerous. Definitions of "violence" as depicted in entertainment media frequently are broad and vary from one pronouncement to another. They conflate all so-called "violent acts" into one negative or harmful category, with little or no regard given to content or context or whether the depiction is fact or fiction, virtual or real.

A few studies do suggest a connection between television violence and "aggressive behavior" in a small percentage of the individuals studied (the causal link for other types of media is often assumed since few non-TV studies exist). The reality is that there are significant scientific hurdles to overcome in demonstrating that media violence actually causes violence, no matter whether the research takes place in a laboratory study, a field study, a longitudinal study, or a combination or variation of those approaches.

The methodological challenges are nearly insurmountable. Researchers are bound ethically not to produce actual violence among their subjects, so they must rely instead on measuring "arousal" or monitoring for "aggressive behavior"—responses that often are modeled or sanctioned by the studies or researchers themselves and sometime cannot be distinguished from the emotional reactions to the medium itself rather than the content of the programming.

Those who cite these carefully qualified studies suggesting a connection between media and violence ignore the reality that there is absolutely no way of predicting with certainty whether a so-called violent depiction will produce a positive, negative, or neutral result in a given individual—or no result at all.

They also ignore the expertise of criminologists, sociologists, biologists, and others who insist that media is not even a significant factor in determining the causes and interventions for violence. The real causes of violence, in fact, are well-known and carefully documented: poverty, drugs, gangs, guns, broken families, neglect and abuse, harsh and inconsistent discipline, and peer association.

These problems, however, don't lend themselves to easy solutions or political posturing.

But policy-makers are not the only ones who bear the blame for diverting the nation's attention from the real causes of violence and wasting time, energy, and resources on false solutions.

There is plenty of blame to go around: Health professionals for lending their authority and credibility to this delay and denial. Child advocacy groups for letting others hijack their campaigns for addressing children's real needs. Scholars for failing to set the record straight when their studies are misrepresented, exaggerated, or harnessed to a political agenda. And the rest of us for allowing all of that to go on while our children wait for real answers.

Some public officials as well as academics have even endorsed the idea that violence can be treated as obscenity and banned accordingly. There is a reason, of course, that the concept of violence as obscenity has not taken hold in the courts, where evidence and reason trump assertions and wishfulness, and where freedom of expression is a constitutional

mandate rather than a political inconvenience.

To argue that violence in media causes actual violence is to argue that the cleansing of movies, television, radio, video games, comic books, the Internet, and even books will remove crime and other unpleasantness from our midst.

Those who push for laws based on exaggerated science and a low opinion of the moral and emotional fiber of young people and their parents' judgment should think through the logic of their efforts. If they can harness the law to punish any form of expression based on the claim that it might cause bad acts, or

> The real causes of violence, in fact, are well-known and carefully documented: poverty, drugs, gangs, guns, broken families, neglect and abuse, harsh and inconsistent discipline, and peer association.

disfavored attitudes, then what is left but a dismayingly homogenized and narrow range of expression, reflecting only the dominant passions and prejudices of the moment?

There should be no surprise that human beings gravitate toward entertainment that reflects life, stimulates the senses, sparks a laugh, or offers an excuse to waste a bit of time. But it should be a surprise, even a shock, to realize that so many of us would embrace governmental regulation of media as a substitute for the individual's ability, and right, to distinguish between life and fantasy, reality and fiction—or cause and effect.

The Man in the Bushes

Mythkiller Philip Jenkins Deconstructs Serial Killers, Child Molesters, and Other Scary People

Interview with Philip Jenkins

> "Although a phenomenon may remain more or less unchanged over time, it can be seen as a problem or social fact in one era but not another."
>
> —from Moral Panic by Philip Jenkins

Russ Kick: I was hoping you'd briefly discuss your approach to studying social problems (or, perhaps more accurately, phenomena correctly or incorrectly regarded as problems). You employ social constructionism. Please tell me about that approach.

Philip Jenkins: Any society faces a range of problems and crises, and there are two ways of looking at them. One is to assume that the problem really is there, it is what people believe it to be, and then you have to decide how to combat it. Put in extreme terms, if people are worried about interracial couples having sex, or about witches causing bad weather, then as an expert, your job is to come up with ways of solving these terrible problems. Perhaps you should go out and draw up personality profiles of witches, or find what dreadful mental diseases cause people to have sex across the color line.

> In many cases, "no known suspect or motive" just meant the local police could not be bothered to fill in the forms.

A constructionist would ask totally different questions, namely why people are concerned about these particular issues. They would also note that some phenomena are around for a very long time before suddenly being recognized as problems. So what is it about a particular time or place that leads people to imagine that X is a problem? One basic assumption is that there is no necessary link between the objective threat posed by a particular issue and how seriously people take it at any given time.

How Many Serial Killers?

RK: In your book *Using Murder*, you look at the serial killer phenomenon, showing that the danger was blown way out of proportion. For example, the government came up with the oft-quoted statistic that 4,000 people are murdered by serial killers every year. You believe that the number is much lower. What do you think the real number is, and how did you arrive at it?

PJ: How the FBI got to the 4,000 figure was this. They looked at homicide statistics and counted the number of murders without an immediate and obvious suspect, and assumed that this was the number of serial murders. That's ludicrous, especially since in many cases the actual killers were turning up a week or month after the stats were recorded, and were obviously not serial killers.

In many cases, "no known suspect or motive" just meant the local police could not be bothered to fill in the forms—guess what, the NYPD has a vast number of such crimes, because they have such a low opinion of the feds, and don't want to do their paperwork for them. But the figures were very useful for the FBI, which suddenly declared a serial killer menace, and used this to argue for new resources.

I used a couple of different tactics, partly taking all the known serial killers for particular periods, and estimating the number of their victims. Also, I found how many recorded cases could not be explained any other way. That leaves us with between 100 and 300 serial-murder victims each year, which in the

1980s meant around 1 percent of total homicides, really a minuscule fraction of the whole. So the problem was vastly exaggerated and distorted, and any fool should have been able to see that. I am still amazed that the media gave the FBI a free ride on this one.

Oh—and the FBI also stressed that all their imagined killers wandered around to commit their crimes, killed in various cities and states, which the vast majority do not do: Most are homebodies, killing in the same town or even street. But wandering killers fall under federal jurisdiction.

Not Just White Males

RK: You also note that stereotypes of serial killers are highly inaccurate. There's the idea that serial killers are almost always male; there may be a female serial killer or two, but they're basically statistical flukes. Then there's the popular idea that serial killers are white.

PJ: The best breakdown of known American serial-killer cases is by Eric Hickey, who finds substantial numbers of women and minorities as serial killers. Also, even his figures are likely to be underestimates, since women kill in ways that are less likely to be detected. If a body is found nude and disemboweled, a police officer does not need to be a genius to deduce that a sex killer is on the loose, and the police will start looking for other unsolved cases. On the other hand, if an old man turns up without obvious signs of violence, police and doctors will not spend too much time looking for foul play, especially in a nursing home or hospital. Women tend to smother, strangle, or poison, so there are likely far more women serial killers than we ever know. I would suggest anywhere between a third and a half of all serial killers are women.

The same is true of black serial killers. Hickey's records show that about 15 percent of known serial cases are black, but again, that's a minimum figure, due to discriminatory police attitudes. Put simply, poor people living in certain high-crime neighborhoods appear to inspire less concern when they die or vanish.

The case of Calvin Jackson is interesting here. When he was arrested in 1974 for a murder committed in a New York apartment building, he confessed with little prompting to a series of other homicides committed in the same building over a six-month period. Before this confession, there had been no suggestion that any of the crimes were linked, or indeed that most of the deaths were caused by anything other than natural causes. The police had not been too concerned, in large part a consequence of the nature of the victims and of the environment in which they died: The building was a single-occupancy hotel, where most of the guests were poor, isolated, and often elderly. In the case of Jackson's victims, foul play was only recorded in cases where victims were killed with conspicuous signs of violence; autopsies were rare. Deaths resulting from smothering were customarily dismissed as the result of natural causes. Where foul play was noted, the police saw no reason to suspect a serial killer, and naturally viewed the crime as part of the interpersonal violence that was endemic in such a transient community.

In other words, whether we are talking about blacks or women, police naturally approach a suspicious death with certain preconceptions that depend both on the nature of the victim and the social environment in which the incident occurs. In some contexts, a sudden death can be explained in many ways without the need to assume the existence of a random or repeat killer, and serial murder activity is thus less likely to be noted. Then we get a cyclical effect: Police and media do not record many serial killers who are blacks or women, so they begin to believe that not many exist; so when a new case does show up involving a black or a woman, there is no conceptual model to fit it into, no convenient profile; and so these cases remain unstudied. In contrast, serial killers who target people for obviously sexual reasons, "rippers" if you like, are easy to spot, and make up a wholly disproportionate amount of the writing on the subject. And to cut a long story short, that's why we think all serial killers are rippers.

Changing Concepts of Child Molestation

RK: Please explain the basic premise—the overarching theme—of your book *Moral Panic: Changing Concepts of the Child Molester in America*.

PJ: The idea of child abuse is so deeply ingrained in our society that it seems absolutely obvious that all sensible people, everywhere, will think likewise unless they are deeply sick. To the contrary, even this absolute orthodoxy is in fact very new in historic terms: Even within the US, anti-child abuse movements can be overwhelmingly strong in one year, and nonexistent 20 or 30 years later. My book is both about the history of child abuse as a concept and how society forms its orthodoxies. It is as much about mass amnesia as social learning (i.e. how problems are forgotten and then relearned).

In England and America prior to the 1880s, the age of sexual consent was *ten*.

RK: You note that words and phrases such as "pervert," "pedophile," "child molester," and "sex offender" have had different meanings and have been used in different ways at different times. Please elaborate.

PJ: There is a long record of people trying to get neutral, objective, nonjudgmental words for different types of conduct that are seen as pathological but not necessarily evil. Through the years, each of these medical words has been annexed by media and law enforcement as a demon word, usually distorting its original meaning. "Molestation" originally meant mild bothering, and people invented it to refer to acts which were trivial compared with rape—yet a "molester" today is the worst thing in the world.

The inflation process is under way right now with "pedophile," which just refers to people sexually interested in kids under the age of puberty. It does not imply violence, and more to the point, it does not refer to sex with older teenagers, "jailbait."

RK: Let's break down the phrase "child molestation" into its two parts and examine each one. First of all, you have "child." Obviously, the notion of what constitutes a child is very fluid. This topic could fill an entire book of its own, but could you briefly discuss how the concept of "child" has been constructed?

PJ: All societies are likely to limit the sexual activity of kids under the age of puberty, and most do—yet in England and America prior to the 1880s, the age of sexual consent was *ten*, and only gradually did it creep up to fourteen, fifteen. As time has gone by and people have tried to expand the borders of childhood, the age has grown, so that in American child porn legislation makes any sexual depiction of a person under *eighteen* pornographic and illegal, even if taken with his/her own consent. At the same time, the age of puberty has fallen, so we have an ever-wider gap between girls being physically ready

for sex, and what the law permits. The scope of criminal law grows proportionately.

RK: Turning to the second part of the phrase "child molestation," the concept of molestation is also up for grabs in various times, locations, and arenas. How has this concept changed? What are some accepted behaviors of the past (or of other current cultures) that most Americans would now define as molestation?

PJ: As I said, molestation originally meant milder acts short of rape—often mutual masturbation. As time has gone by, the concept has extended to acts of voyeurism and fondling, and even taking pornographic pictures. It always pays to ask just what a "molester" is supposed to have done—and what was the age of the "victim." This lack of definition is a basic problem with much sex-offender legislation, since many "sex predators" are in fact guilty of fairly trivial acts, and with willing victims little short of the age of consent.

RK: You've pointed out a double standard regarding the perception and treatment of men who molest girls versus women who molest boys. In fact, it's almost as if child molestation automatically refers to men molesting children of either gender, while the phenomenon of women who molest children of either gender is almost entirely swept under the rug. Please comment on this.

I would say that when we have moved to fifteen or sixteen, we should not be speaking of molestation.

PJ: Well, this does raise the issue of whether we can speak of "molestation" when a 25-year-old woman sleeps with a 15-year-old boy—or vice versa. I honestly don't know. I would say that when we have moved to fifteen or sixteen, we should not be speaking of molestation. Such intergenerational affairs might be ill-advised or destructive, but should they be criminal? Obviously, I am drawing a distinction here with encounters involving pubescent youngsters, or even prepubescent kids: There, we all agree the law has a legitimate protective role to play. But can we really call youngsters of sixteen or so "victims"?

Going in Cycles

I think that threats to children serve as stealth justifications for policies that advocates would be afraid to avow openly.

RK: You've noted that like many other panics, the molestation panic in America has gone in cycles from approximately 1894 to today. Please give a broad overview of this timetable, explaining what may have caused the upsurges and—just as importantly—the lulls. (Also, according to the cycles, the 1990s should've seen a lull, but saw just the opposite. What happened to explain this?)

PJ: There are "booms" of concern roughly in the mid-1890s, again from 1908–22, 1936–58, and 1977–present. Real peak panic years have occurred in 1915, 1950, and 1985. I think the variables that matter are demographic and gender-related. Gender, because in a society in which women are establishing their own set of issues, they draw attention to sex crime as a particular threat to them, and stress male violence. Demography, because of booms and slumps in the proportion of children in a society: The baby boom of the 1950s was by no means the first of its kind.

Equally, there are troughs of concern, when gender politics lie low and sex crime is seen as trivial, and these too are cyclical. The cycle seems to have come to an end in the 1980s-90s, because the voices of gender politics were no longer struggling to be heard but had now established themselves as a firm part of social orthodoxy, based on women getting firmly ensconced in the workplace and the economic order.

RK: On the question of who represents the gravest danger to children, the pendulum has swung many times from family members to strangers, and back again. Please elaborate.

PJ: Societies with intense gender politics focus on the incest problem because it illustrates problems within the family and gender roles; societies with more of a law enforcement emphasis stress the threat from stranger pedophiles. We have gone back and forth on this issue quite as much as the overall cycle of concern about abuse. In the 1910s, the issue was incest, and again in the 1980s; in the 1940s and 1990s, the focus shifted to stranger pedophiles.

Current Problems

RK: What ill effects have come from these child molestation panics? What ill effects are we currently seeing?

PJ: I think that threats to children serve as stealth justifications for policies that advocates would be afraid to avow openly, including hostility to fringe religions (see the ritual abuse panic of the 1980s), homosexuality (witness every anti-gay referendum), and sexual experimentation by the young. Also, they justify a vast and self-sustaining bureaucracy of social workers and psychologists, whose whole careers and (let's be frank) bank accounts depend entirely on maintaining a level of panic about threats to children.

RK: Your book *Priests and Pedophiles* looked at the 1990s brouhaha over men of the cloth molesting children. You found that things were not really as they seemed. Please tell me more.

PJ: The received idea was that Catholic priests were abusing children in large numbers because of frustration resulting from their forced celibacy. In reality, there is no evidence that priests were abusing at a greater or lesser rate than any other religious professionals, or indeed than people in any walk of life. The charges resulted from rhetoric thrown around by rival Catholic factions.

Also, the Catholic church was the easiest and most attractive target of litigation, so we just heard more about Catholic cases. Finally, most priests involved in sex cases were not active with children, but with older teenagers, and should more properly be described as homosexuals.

RK: The murder of a child—especially coupled with that child being sexually attacked by a stranger—is tied to the whole concept of child molestation. You wrote that although we can never know how many children are molested, we can know

The Catholic church was the easiest and most attractive target of litigation, so we just heard more about Catholic cases.

pretty accurately how many children are murdered by strangers. What are these figures, and what do they tell us?

PJ: The problem here is that any attempt to minimize child murder has to sound callous, because you have to use phrases like "only" x children were murdered. But the picture is very different from what most people think. If we take children below the age of twelve (the age-group of interest to pedophiles), then between 1980 and 1994, 13,600 individuals were murdered in the US, about 900 each year. Of these, over 400 were babies or infants below the age of one, usually killed by parents. Family members killed 54 percent of all child victims.

We have a lot of evidence on this now, and there is no accurate predictor of who will become a sex killer.

In contrast, strangers accounted for just 6 percent of the annual total, or about 54 children each year. Only about *five* victims per year involved the murder of a child by a stranger in a sexual assault, the classic sort of crime people imagine when they think about homicidal pedophiles.

Questioning Assumptions

RK: There are a lot of people—mainly feminists and Christian conservatives (those odd bedfellows)—who *still* believe that there is a multi-billion dollar child pornography "industry" that spans the globe. Please explain how we know that this is a myth and why it refuses to die.

PJ: In the late 1970s, there were claims about child porn being a billion dollar industry, and estimates just swelled over the years. In reality, the last real child porn entrepreneur was jailed in the early 1980s, and she (it was a woman, incidentally) never made more than a million or two. The Internet has revolutionized matters, and most people trade child porn for free, with money never changing hands.

RK: I'd like to look at some of the currently accepted ideas about child molestation and see what your research has uncovered about them. First up: Abuse is cyclical in nature. An abused child grows up to abuse children.

PJ: The argument is often stated, but it rests on very weak evidence: Of course abusers claim they were abused, since like everyone else who watches TV, they know the "right" answers to give to courts and psychologists.

RK: Sexual contact with adults always scars a child for life.

PJ: Answer as above. There is a good deal of contrary evidence, which publishers are terrified to put out for fear of the backlash.

RK: Child molesters cannot be helped. They will always abuse children, usually lots of them.

PJ: Define "molesters;" define "children;" define "abused;" define "helped."

RK: You can identify potential child molesters (and other potential sex offenders) early, before they do any serious harm.

PJ: Define "molesters;" define "children." How to identify them? Most sex killers begin their careers by minor sex acts (e.g. voyeurism and exhibitionism). However, if we identify and incarcerate every person guilty of such acts, we had better set up our own Gulag Archipelago for the millions involved—the vast majority of whom will never progress to violent or predatory behavior. We have a lot of evidence on this now, and there is *no* accurate predictor of who will become a sex killer.

RK: There are millions of active pedophiles.

PJ: Define "pedophiles."

RK: One-fourth to one-half of all girls are victims of incest.

PJ: Not according to any survey done by a competent scholar without a major feminist agenda to establish.

The Crystal Ball

RK: What do you see regarding the future of attitudes towards child molestation?

PJ: The shift in gender politics and the role of women in the economy means that in the foreseeable future at least, we can never go back to the old idea about child abuse not mattering or not harming people: Sex crime will remain in the forefront of moral politics. I wonder, though, as a new baby boomlet comes of age in the next decade, whether they will insist on greater sexual rights like the original boomers did in the 1960s and 1970s.

Panic Inoculation

RK: Finally, what can the reader of this book do to spot panics? In other words, how can we inoculate ourselves against hyped-up dangers? What are some of the telltale signs of a hysteria?

PJ: I always look for anyone claiming an "epidemic" or using impressively round numbers—five million attacks, 50,000 incidents. Also pseudoscientific words like "addict." As you know, 94.5 percent of all social statistics are made up on the spot, without any supporting evidence. And yes, that is a joke.

From Untouchables to Conscientious Objectors
Lessons From Students at Alternative Schools
Daniel Grego

As the sun rose, I saw Nick in a new light. Away from the classroom, he was relaxed and amiable. On the pier extending into Lake Michigan from the McKinley Marina, he was in his element. He was an accomplished fisherman. I was a novice. So now our roles were reversed. He was the teacher. I was the student. We met that morning so he could show me how to cast with spoons and spinners in an attempt to catch lake or rainbow or brown trout or coho salmon—and so I could mull over a decision I had to make.

> When Shalom's personnel committee discovered I enjoyed working with joukers, jiggers, kippers, tickers, mitchers, plunkers, scivers, school skippers, attendance spoilers, excusers, and dirty dodgers, I was hired on the spot.

I do not remember catching any fish that day. But I do remember enjoying the sunrise, the quiet, the vastness of the lake, and getting to know a little better a fellow traveler on this earth.

Nick and I were first introduced the year before (in 1980), when I began teaching math at Shalom High School. Shalom had been founded seven years before as an alternative school for what were then called "marginal students," those students who were not succeeding in traditional high schools and who were potential dropouts. The school survived on a shoestring budget and depended on volunteers and people willing to work for low wages and no benefits. Not surprisingly, there was high staff turnover. When my wife and I moved to Milwaukee so she could pursue graduate studies at the University of Wisconsin, Shalom had an opening for a math teacher. On our first day in town, I applied for the job. I had previous experience teaching "marginal students" in the Chicago area, and when Shalom's personnel committee discovered I enjoyed working with joukers, jiggers, kippers, tickers, mitchers, plunkers, scivers,

school skippers, attendance spoilers, excusers, and dirty dodgers, I was hired on the spot.[1]

My first day in the classroom that fall was right out of a Hollywood movie, something like *Stand and Deliver* or *Dangerous Minds*. About 80 students were enrolled at that time. They had all started ninth grade in one of the large public high schools but had stopped attending for one reason or another. Some were bored. Some were lost. Some felt unsafe. Some just could not tolerate it any longer.

On a given day, about three-quarters of the students enrolled at Shalom dropped by the school. Most of them were African Americans, but there were Latinos, Native Americans, and some students from the German families who had hung on in the neighborhood. Nick was from this latter group.

I had been hired to teach algebra and geometry, but many of the students had not mastered basic arithmetic. Nick had already taken algebra at his former high school and although he understood it, he had failed the class because he had refused, as he put it, "to kiss the teacher's ass." That first day, he sauntered into my room, found a desk by the window, and slouched so low in his chair, he was more lying down than sitting.

I gave the students a diagnostic test to find out what they knew. They interpreted it as an attempt to expose their ignorance and to embarrass them. Nick wrote his name on the test paper and that was all. During those first weeks his main contributions to my class, on those occasions when he was present, were obnoxious remarks. The thought crossed my mind that the best way to deal with him would be to hang him out the second story window by his ankles. But being a disciple of Mahatma Gandhi, I decided against it.

One day, after he had been particularly disagreeable, I asked Nick to stay after class. I inquired about his behavior. At first, he was reluctant to say anything. Finally, he told me about his previous algebra class and some of his feelings about school. He hated it. He hated being cooped up inside all day. At the age of sixteen, he had "waived out" of public school. (In Wisconsin at that time, children were required to attend school until they were eighteen unless they had earned their diplomas or had formally "waived out," which they could do at sixteen.) Nick was one of dozens of students in those days who told me that on their sixteenth birthday, they had been met at the door

"I'll think about it," he said and left.

Following the Hollywood script, Nick decided to run for president and won. He started to come to my class more often and helped his classmates with their math. He even made the honor roll once or twice. I do not remember him ever sitting up straight in a chair, however.

After my first year of teaching at Shalom, I was asked to become the school's director—a combination of principal, spokesperson, fundraiser, bookkeeper, personnel manager, teacher, counselor, and janitor. I hesitated. In the school's first eight years, there had been six directors. Sustaining alternative schools for "marginal stu-

I gave the students a diagnostic test to find out what they knew. They interpreted it as an attempt to expose their ignorance and to embarrass them.

of their high school by an administrator who explained to them that if they signed a waiver form, one of which the administrator just happened to have with him, they could legally drop out of school. Nick signed.

He had enrolled at Shalom under pressure from his family who knew about the school because one of his older siblings had attended. Repeating the conventional wisdom, they told him he would need some kind of credential to get a good job. He was just biding his time there until he figured out what he wanted to do.

I asked him if he understood the material we were covering in class. He said he did, so I tried to enlist his help in explaining it to some of the other students who did not.

"I'll think about it," he said and started for the door.

As he was leaving, an inspiration came to me.

"Nick," I called after him, "student government elections are coming up. Why don't you run for president?"

He was startled by my suggestion. Later, I learned that, in all his years of schooling, no one had ever asked him to do anything like that before. Most of the attention he had received from teachers and other school personnel had been in the form of punishment. His *modus operandi* in school had been to disrupt class and then affect indifference. This made him look doubly cool in the eyes of his friends.

dents" was not easy, then or now. I was not sure I wanted the responsibility or the stress. I was not sure my wife and I would stay in Milwaukee after she finished graduate school. I was not sure it was what I was called to do.

I sought the advice of family and friends, board members and staff. I also asked Nick if he thought I should take the job. He wondered if I liked to fish. I told him I had never been fishing but that I would be interested in trying.

"I always do my best thinking when I'm fishing," he explained.

So we agreed to rendezvous the next morning on the pier at the McKinley Marina. Nick lent me a rod and reel, showed me how to cast and how to set the hook if I got a bite. After a while, we started talking. He told me about himself. He said he enjoyed working with his hands. He enjoyed taking things apart and putting them back together. He loved being outdoors. He loved to hunt and to fish. He dreamed someday of owning a cabin in northern Wisconsin, a part of the world he referred to simply as "up north."

When we grew quiet again, I thought about Nick and his classmates. Each one of them had special gifts and interests, hopes and fears, joys and sorrows. And all of them had been tossed aside by the System as uneducable failures or troublemakers. Shalom's 80 students were like thousands more in Milwaukee in the same circumstances, the young men and women who today are labeled "at risk."

In Milwaukee, as in other large cities in the United States, for every ten bright, curious, enthusiastic children who enter the System, only about five graduate.[2] As I thought more about this plight, I was haunted by the following questions: Are the children (and their families) who do not make it through the System still part of the "public"? If they are, why are educational resources not made available to them in some other way? What happens to those other five kids?

As the sun rose, the lake began sparkling. I looked at Nick, whose face glowed in the early light.

"I might be crazy," I said. "But I think I'm going to take the job."

"You won't get an argument from me," my friend grinned. "Not about that first part anyway."

asking the wrong question. Given what high school is, the question you should ask is why anyone bothers to stay." After further reflection, he added, "I guess some students tolerate school better than others."

Schools have never served poor and minority children well. As Colin Greer noted in *The Great School Legend*:

> The rate of school failure among the urban poor, in fact, has been consistently and remarkably high since before 1900. The truth is that the immigrant children dropped out in great numbers—to fall back on the customs and skills their families brought with them to America. It was in spite of, and *not* because of, compulsory public education that some eventually made their way.[3]

In the school's first eight years, there had been six directors.

2

A few years after I began my tenure as director of Shalom High School, I attended a conference about "at-risk" children in Madison, Wisconsin. The keynote speaker was Gary Wehlage, who was at the time the Associate Director of the Center on Organization and Restructuring of Schools at the University of Wisconsin. Wehlage told his audience that the basic question that had to be asked about "at-risk" students was why so many of them dropped out of school. He suggested two possible answers: Either something was wrong with the students or something was wrong with the schools.

For many years, I assumed the problem was the schools. They were too big and impersonal. The curriculum was arbitrary and irrelevant to the students' lives. The pedagogy favored students with certain intelligences and learning styles and frustrated others. There was little opportunity for students to do real work and have it recognized in their communities.

One of Shalom's students was once asked by a prominent politician why so many young people drop out of school. He thought for a moment and then responded: "I think you're

For many years, I used Wehlage's question as a way to introduce the work we were doing at Shalom. The schools were the problem, and we were part of a movement to create alternatives to them.

It never occurred to me that Wehlage had omitted a third possibility. Perhaps the reason the schools fail so many students is that they are doing exactly what they were designed to do: sort people into winners and losers, perpetuate an elite group to run the world, and maintain a class of "untouchables" to complete the shitwork, the dirty work, the work Wendell Berry has called "fundamental and inescapable" that no one else wants to do. And since we persist in our desire "to rise above the sweat and bother of taking care of anything—of ourselves, of each other, or of our country," some method for assigning these tasks had to be invented.[4]

One of the "at-risk" students Murray Levin interviewed at Greater Egleston Community High School in Boston understood the sorting function of schools:

> What do we do when we finish here? Slap hamburgers at McDonald's or Burger King? Clean up shit at hospitals? Drive buses? Janitor? Handyman? Dealer? They gotta get this shit done. Who going to do it? We're at the bottom of the pyramid so we do this. And for them to stay at the top, we got to stay at the bottom.[5]

Whether compulsory schooling was *intended* to divide students into winners and losers or not, that has been its inevitable effect, as has been pointed out by Ivan Illich and Everett Reimer, among others. Twenty years after he published *Deschooling Society*, Ivan Illich summarized his findings:

> In the minds of the people who financed and engineered them, schools were established to increase equality. I discovered that they really acted as a lottery system in which those who didn't make it didn't just lose what they had paid in but were also stigmatized as inferior for the rest of their lives.[6]

Illich's critique was continued by John Holt and more recently by Madhu Suri Prakash and Gustavo Esteva. The latter expose the duplicity of those of us engaged in schooling:

> Educators continue espousing radical democracy, justice, equality, and excellence as the goal of their project, while enjoying the privileges of the global educational system, designed to spew and vomit out millions of Ds, dropouts, and failures while providing to a few a socially recognized certificate—a patente de corso. This legitimizes the As and other "successes" in their disposition to impose, control, and oppress, for consuming at the expense of the majorities they doom to the life of failures.[7]

John Holt concluded his book *Instead of Education* with his characteristic directness:

> Education—compulsory schooling, compulsory learning—is a tyranny and a crime against the human mind and spirit. Let all those escape it who can, any way they can.[8]

3

After 30 years of working with "at-risk" teenagers in Chicago and Milwaukee, I have come to the conclusion that Holt was right. Compulsory schooling is a tyranny. I understand now that the educational alternatives and alternative schools to which I have given so much time and energy "cover up the fact that the project of education is fundamentally flawed and indecent."[9] In spite of the best intentions of reformers, schooling will continue to be "a worldwide soul-shredder that junks the majority and burdens an elite to govern it."[10]

But I am terribly conflicted about these conclusions, for I have looked into the eyes of hundreds of young men and women like Nick who are stuck in *this* society and who have been designated "untouchables." And as long as children are still compelled by law to attend school and can be harassed by the police (and their parents fined) if they fail to do so; as long as economic opportunities are divvied up according to school credentials (even though there is no evidence linking successful job performance with school performance); as long as people are taxed to pay for a System that many of them cannot use because it continues "to spew and vomit out millions" of children, places like Shalom can be justified.

I have attempted to escape my own cognitive dissonance by challenging the definitions of "education" employed by both its defenders and its critics. The philosophy of Mahatma Gandhi and the writings of Wendell Berry have led me to consider "education" not as an individual accomplishment, not as some *thing* that a person "gets" (nor as something done to someone for his or her own good), but as a community practice.

Perhaps the reason the schools fail so many students is that they are doing exactly what they were designed to do.

A more benign conception of "education" is to think of it as the process by which people become responsibly mature members of their communities. In non-industrial cultures, this educational process is inseparable from the life of the community. Children are "educated" by the example of their elders, by stories, by initiation rituals, and by performing the daily tasks required for subsistence. Schools are not necessary for education defined in this way, although communities might decide to use them as tools. *Compulsory schooling*, which is inextricably connected to what Esteva and Prakash call "The Global Project," the blight that is devastating communities around the world, clearly thwarts the educational process.[11]

"What do we do when we finish here? Slap hamburgers at McDonald's or Burger King? Clean up shit at hospitals? Drive buses? Janitor? Handyman? Dealer? They gotta get this shit done."

The schools I administer in Milwaukee—Shalom, the Northwest Opportunities Vocational Academy (NOVA), El Puente High School, and The CITIES Project High School—attempt to embed their activities as much as possible in their communities. In addition to academic work, the students plant gardens in vacant lots and share their produce with the hungry, organize food and clothing donations for the homeless, visit the incarcerated, document the stories of elders in nursing homes, tutor younger children at nearby elementary schools, write and produce plays, create art exhibits for the public, initiate neighborhood clean-ups and recycling programs, conduct voter-registration drives, and advocate for educational opportunities for other "at-risk" children. Elders from the community are invited into the schools to share their knowledge, to mentor the students, and to guide their rites of passage into adulthood.

In the mid-1980s, I convened a philosophy seminar at Shalom in which I asked the students to analyze "The Global Project." (Back then, we spoke of the monstrous abstraction called "The Economy.") By the end of the course, my young friends concluded they had three choices: They could resign themselves to the status of "untouchables" and endure, if they could, the crushing weight of "The Global Project" on their backs; they could learn "to play the game" of schooling and make their way into the exploiter class and pay (or force) someone else to do their shitwork for them; or they could rebel and become conscientious objectors to the System, using it if and when they chose for their own purposes.

Of course, the authorities who monitor schools like Shalom consider only students who make the second choice as "positive outcomes." And Shalom has had many of those. But I have taken greater personal satisfaction from knowing those young people who decided to redefine themselves from "untouchables" to conscientious objectors whether they graduated or not.

Nick's story did not have a Hollywood ending. After a couple of years, he dropped out of Shalom. He cannot be counted, therefore, as one of the school's "successes." But I think he made the third choice. Nick used Shalom to avoid the truant officers and the police and to placate his parents until he was ready to leave home. He made some good friends. He thought deeply about what he wanted out of life. When he quit, he may not have known what he was called to do, but he knew he had tolerated school long enough.

A few years ago, Nick stopped by to see me. He told me he is married with two children. He has a job he loves: building motorcycles for Harley-Davidson. He is saving money to buy his cabin "up north." And, on his days off, he takes his kids fishing.

Endnotes

1. For various names for truants, see: Opie, Iona and Peter. (2001). *The lore and language of schoolchildren.* New York: New York Review of Books, pp 371–2. **2.** Dropout data are difficult to analyze and compare because school officials are so adept at fudging the numbers, and nebulously and variously defining "dropout." A more accurate way to capture the problem of school failure is to look at what is being called "the cohort survival rate." Pick a given year's ninth-grade class and check to see how many graduated four years later. For example, in the 1992–93 school year, the Milwaukee Public Schools reported 6,874 students were enrolled in ninth grade. Four years later, in 1996, 2,434 students, or 35 percent of the original number, graduated. According to *City Kids Count*, a 1997 publication of the Annie E. Casey Foundation, Milwaukee's dropout rate was seventeenth among the 50 major cities in the United States. There were 33 cities where the dropout problem was worse than in Milwaukee. **3.** Greer, Colin. (1972). *The great school legend.* New York: Basic Books, p 4. Italics in the original. **4.** Berry, Wendell. (1989). The hidden wound. San Francisco: North Point Press, p 112. **5.** Levin, Murray. (2001). *Teach me!: Kids will learn when oppression is the lesson* (expanded edition). Lanham, MD: Rowman & Littlefield, p 28. **6.** Cayley, David. (1992). Ivan Illich in conversation. Concord, Ontario: Anansi, p 63. **7.** Prakash, Madhu Suri, and Gustavo Esteva. (1998). *Escaping education: Living as learning within grassroots cultures.* New York: Peter Lang, p 104. **8.** Holt, John. (1976). *Instead of Education.* New York: Dutton, p 222. **9.** *Op cit.*, Prakash and Esteva, p 97. **10.** Illich quoted in Prakash and Esteva, p 97. **11.** Esteva, Gustavo, and Madhu Suri Prakash. (1998). *Grassroots postmodernism: Remaking the soil of cultures.* London: Zed Books.

CONDEMNED TO REPEAT IT

The Constitution, War, and the Draft
from *The Revolution: A Manifesto*

Ron Paul

Ron Paul is a multiple-term US Congressman from Texas. Officially a Republican, he holds very strong libertarian principles.

During my public life I have earned the nickname Dr. No, a reference to my previous occupation as a physician combined with my willingness to stand against the entire Congress if necessary to vote no on some proposed measure. (I am told I have been the sole "no" vote in Congress more often than all other members of Congress put together.) As a matter of fact, I don't especially care for this nickname, since it may give people the impression that I am a contrarian for its own sake, and that for some reason I simply relish saying no. In those no votes, as in all my congressional votes, I have thought of myself as saying yes to the Constitution and to freedom.

The Constitution has much to say to us regarding foreign policy, if we will only listen. For over half a century the two major parties have done their best to ignore what it has to say, especially when it comes to the initiation of hostilities. Both parties have allowed the president to exercise powers of which the Framers of the Constitution thought they had deprived him. And since both parties have been contemptuous of the Constitution's allocation of war powers between the president and Congress, neither one—with very rare exceptions—ever calls the other out on it.

The Framers did not want the American president to resemble the British king, from whom they had separated just a few years earlier. Even Alexander Hamilton, who was known to be sympathetic toward the British model, was at pains in the *Federalist Papers* to point out a critical difference between the king and the president as envisioned by the Constitution:

> The President is to be commander-in-chief of the army and navy of the United States. In this respect his authority would be nominally the same with that of the king of Great Britain, but in substance much inferior to it. It would amount to nothing more than the supreme command and direction of the military and naval forces, as first General and admiral of the Confederacy; while that of the British king extends to the *declaring* of war and to the *raising* and *regulating* of fleets and armies—all of which, by the Constitution under consideration, would appertain to the legislature.

Whatever kind of evidence you want to examine, whether constitutional or historical, the verdict is clear: Congress was supposed to declare war, and the president in turn was to direct the war once it was declared. This rule was scrupulously observed throughout American history until 1950 and the Korean War. Short of a full-fledged declaration of war, in lesser conflicts Congress nevertheless authorized hostilities by statute. Any exceptions to this general rule involved military activities so minor and on such a small scale as hardly to be worth mentioning.

Whatever kind of evidence you want to examine, whether constitutional or historical, the verdict is clear: Congress was supposed to declare war, and the president in turn was to direct the war once it was declared.

The Korean War was the great watershed in the modern presidential power grab in war-making. President Harry Truman sent Americans halfway around the world without so much as a nod in the direction of Congress. According to Truman, authorization from the United Nations to use force was quite sufficient, and rendered congressional consent unnecessary. (Apart from being dangerous, that idea is simply false: Article 43 of the United Nations Charter states that any United Nations authorization to use force must be subsequently referred to the governments of each nation "in accordance with their respective constitutional processes"; this principle was reaffirmed in the United States in the debates over the United Nations Participation Act of 1945.) Truman also claimed that the Constitution's commander-in-chief clause gave him the authority to plunge America into war on his own initiative.

Truman's interpretation of the Constitution was completely untenable. Nothing in American history supports it: not the Constitutional Convention, the state ratifying conventions, the *Federalist Papers*, early Court decisions, or the actual practice of war-making throughout most of American history. Even the early examples that are typically cited as evidence of presidential war-making—John Adams' actions during the Quasi War with France, and Thomas Jefferson's confrontation with the Barbary pirates of North Africa—show no such thing. Both of these minor incidents were carried out according to congressional statute, with the Supreme Court ruling that a presidential directive contrary to such statutes was of no force.

In spite of its complete lack of constitutional foundation, this belief that the president may take the country to war on his own authority, without consulting anyone, has become the conventional wisdom in both major parties, although there has been a modest backlash against it since the Iraq war. Neoconservatives have been particularly eager to promote this deviation from the Constitution. This, it seems, is their version of the "living" Constitution.

Interestingly enough, one of the chief critics of Truman's exercise of power was Senator Robert A. Taft, one of the most conservative Republicans of his day (and who was in fact known as "Mr. Republican"). Speaking on the Senate floor, Taft denounced Truman's arguments and behavior in no uncertain terms:

I desire this afternoon to discuss only the question of the power claimed by the President to send troops anywhere in the world and involve us in any war in the world and involve us in any war in which he chooses to involve us. I wish to assert the powers of Congress, and to point out that Congress has the power to prevent any such action by the President; that he has no such power under the Constitution; and that it is incumbent upon the Congress to assert clearly its own constitutional powers unless it desires to lose them.

"In the long run," Taft went on,

the question we must decide involves vitally, I think, not only the freedom of the people of the United States, but the peace of the people of the United States…. If in the great field of foreign policy the President has arbitrary and unlimited power, as he now claims, then there is an end to freedom in the United States in a great realm of domestic activity which affects, in the long run, every person in the United States…. If the President has unlimited power to involve us in war, war is more likely. History shows that…arbitrary rulers are more inclined to favor war than are the people, at any time.

Responding to various defenses offered by the president and administration officials, Taft declared: "I deny the conclusions of the documents presented by the President or by the executive department, and I would say that if the doctrines therein proclaimed prevailed, they would bring an end to government by the people, because our foreign interests are going gradually to predominate and require a larger and larger place in the field of the activities of our people."

In 2002, as war with Iraq loomed, I proposed that Congress officially declare war against Iraq, making clear that I intended to oppose my own measure. The point was to underscore our

The Korean War was the great watershed in the modern presidential power grab in war-making.

Military conscription, said Ronald Reagan in 1979, "rests on the assumption that your kids belong to the state…. That assumption isn't a new one. The Nazis thought it was a great idea."

constitutional responsibility to declare war before commencing major military operations, rather than leaving the decision to the president or passing resolutions that delegate to the president the decision-making power over war. The chairman of the International Relations Committee responded by saying, "There are things in the Constitution that have been overtaken by events, by time. Declaration of war is one of them. There are things no longer relevant to a modern society. We are saying to the president, use your judgment. [What you have proposed is] inappropriate, anachronistic; it isn't done any more."

What a relief that we have people in our government who will keep us posted on which constitutional provisions they have decided are no longer "relevant"!

Now, didn't Congress authorize the war in Iraq after all? No, and certainly not in a manner consistent with the Constitution. Congress has no constitutional authority to delegate to the president the decision regarding whether to use military force. That power was consciously and for good reason put in the hands of the people's elected representatives in the legislature.

Louis Fisher, one of the nation's experts on the subject of presidential war powers, described what happened this way: "The resolution helped bring pressure on the Security Council to send inspectors into Iraq to search for weapons of mass destruction. They found nothing. As to whether war should or should not occur, the committee washed its hands. By passing legislation that allowed the president to make that decision, Congress transferred a primary constitutional duty from the legislative branch to the executive branch. That is precisely what the Framers fought against."

Meanwhile, all these wars have to be fought by someone, and that is why the military draft is being spoken about more and more. Given the overseas ambitions of so much of our political class, a return of the draft may actually be closer than we realize. (As a matter of fact we have something like a de facto draft already, what with all the extensions being imposed on our troops.) Having stretched our military to the breaking point, where do they expect to find the troops for the next conflict?

The draft is a totalitarian institution that is based on the idea that the government owns you and can dispose of your life as it wishes. Republican Senator Robert Taft said that the draft was "far more typical of totalitarian nations than of democratic nations. It is absolutely opposed to the principles of individual

Nowhere in the Constitution is the federal government given the power to conscript citizens. The power to raise armies is not a power to force people into the army.

liberty, which have always been considered a part of American democracy." Conservative thinker Russell Kirk referred to the draft as "slavery." Military conscription, said Ronald Reagan in 1979, "rests on the assumption that your kids belong to the state…. That assumption isn't a new one. The Nazis thought it was a great idea." The following year, in a speech at Louisiana State University, Reagan added:

I oppose registration for the draft…because I believe the security of freedom can best be achieved by security through freedom. The all-voluntary force is based on the sound and historic American principle of voluntary commitment to defense of freedom…. The United States of America believes a free people do not have to be coerced in defending their country or their values and that the principle of freedom is the best and only foundation upon which a defense of freedom can be made. My vision of a secure America is based on my belief that freedom calls forth the best in the human spirit and that the defense of freedom can and will best be made out of love of country, a love that needs no coercion. Out of such a love, a real security will develop, because in the final analysis, the free human heart and spirit are the best and most reliable defense.

The Constitution, War, and the Draft
from *The Revolution: A Manifesto*   Ron Paul

Young people are not raw material to be employed by the political class on behalf of whatever fashionable political, military, or social cause catches its fancy.

In late 1814, fearing that conscription was about to come to America, Daniel Webster delivered a stirring speech against it on the House floor. (Webster served for many years in both the House and the Senate, and he held the office of secretary of state in both the early 1840s and early 1850s.) Webster's belief in a strong central government made his words against the draft all the more striking. "Where is it written in the Constitution," he demanded, "in what article or section is it contained, that you may take children from their parents, and parents from their children, and compel them to fight the battles of any war, in which the folly or the wickedness of Government may engage it?" The draft was irreconcilable with both the principles of a free society and the provisions of the Constitution. "In granting Congress the power to raise armies," Webster explained, "the people have granted all the means which are ordinary and usual, and which are consistent with the liberties and security of the people themselves, and they have granted no others…. A free government with arbitrary means to administer it is a contradiction; a free government without adequate provisions for personal security is an absurdity; a free government, with an uncontrolled power of military conscription, is a solecism, at once the most ridiculous and abominable that ever entered into the head of man."

Webster was right both morally and constitutionally. Nowhere in the Constitution is the federal government given the power to conscript citizens. The power to raise armies is not a power to force people into the army. As Webster put it,

> I almost disdain to go to quotations and references to prove that such an abominable doctrine has no foundation in the Constitution of the country. It is enough to know that that instrument was intended as the basis of a free government, and that the power contended for is incompatible with any notion of personal liberty. An attempt to maintain this doctrine upon the provisions of the Constitution is an exercise of perverse ingenuity to extract slavery from substance of a free government.

He continued:

> Congress having, by the Constitution, a power to raise armies, the Secretary [of War] contends that no restraint is to be imposed on the exercise of this power, except such as is expressly stated in the written letter of the instrument. In other words, that Congress may execute its powers, by any means it chooses, unless such means are particularly prohibited. But the general nature and object of the Constitution impose as rigid a restriction on the means of exercising power as could be done by the most explicit injunctions. It is the first principle applicable to such a case, that no construction shall be admitted which impairs the general nature and character of the instrument. A free constitution of government is to be construed upon free principles, and every branch of its provisions is to receive such an interpretation as is full of its general spirit. No means are to be taken by implication which would strike us absurdly if expressed. And what would have been more absurd than for this Constitution to have said that to secure the great blessings of liberty it gave to government uncontrolled power of military conscription? Yet such is the absurdity which it is made to exhibit, under the commentary of the Secretary of War.

Lesser forms of the draft, such as compulsory "national service," are based on the same unacceptable premise. Young people are not raw material to be employed by the political class on behalf of whatever fashionable political, military, or social cause catches its fancy. In a free society, their lives are not the playthings of government.

Amnesia in America
Or, The Sociology of Forgetting
James W. Loewen

In colonial times, everyone knew about the great Indian plagues just past. Many citizens were aware that even before *Mayflower* sailed, King James of England gave thanks to "Almighty God in his great goodness and bounty towards us," for sending "this wonderful plague among the salvages [*sic*]." Two hundred years later J. W. Barber's *Interesting Events in the History of the United States*, published in 1829, supplied this treatment on its second prose page:

> A few years before the arrival of the Plymouth settlers, a very mortal sickness raged with great violence among the indians inhabiting the eastern parts of New England. "Whole towns were depopulated. The living were not able to bury the dead; and their bodies were found lying above ground, many years after. The Massachusetts Indians are said to have been reduced from 30,000 to 300 fighting men. In 1633, the small pox swept off great numbers."

Today, however, not one in a hundred of my college students has ever heard of these plagues or any of the other pandemics that swept Native Americans, because most American history textbooks leave them out.

Could this be because they are not important? Because they have been swept aside by developments in American history since 1829 that must be attended to?

Consider their importance: Europeans were never able to "settle" China, India, Indonesia, Japan, or most of Africa, because too many people already lived there. The crucial role played by the plagues in the Americas (and Hawaii and Australia) can be inferred from two historical population estimates: William McNeill reckons the population of the Americas at 100 million in 1492, while William Langer suggests that Europe had only about 70 million people when Columbus set forth. The advantages Europeans enjoyed in military and social technology would have enabled them to dominate the Americas, as they eventually dominated China, India, Indonesia, and Africa, but not to "settle" the hemisphere. For that, the plagues were required. Thus, after the European (and African) invasion itself, the pestilence is surely the most important event in the history of America.

Nevertheless, our history books leave it out.

Or consider our "knowledge" of the voyages of Christopher Columbus. In 1828 novelist Washington Irving wrote a three-volume biography of Columbus in which he described Columbus' supposed defense of his round-earth theory before the flat-earth savants at Salamanca University. Actually, in 1491 most Europeans knew the world was round. The Catholic Church held it to be round. In eclipses of the moon, it casts a round shadow on the moon. On this side of the Atlantic, most Native Americans saw it that way, too. It looks round. Sailors in particular see its roundness when ships disappear over the horizon, hull first. Nevertheless, *The American Pageant*, a bestselling American history textbook that has stayed in print since 1956 despite the death of its author, still proclaimed as late as 1986, "The superstitious sailors, fearful of sailing over the edge of the world, grew increasingly mutinous." (In the current edition, this sentence has been softened to "fearful of sailing into the oceanic unknown," thus allowing the publisher deniability while still implying the false flat-earth story.)

> Today, however, not one in a hundred of my college students has ever heard of these plagues or any of the other pandemics that swept Native Americans, because most American history textbooks leave them out.

In reality, Columbus never had to contend with a crew worried about falling off the end of the earth. His crew was no more superstitious than he was, and quite likely less. Again, histories written before 1828 got this right.

Something happens to our historical understanding over time, and it isn't pretty. Moving closer to our own time, consider John Brown, whose brief seizure of Harpers Ferry in 1859 helped lead to the Civil War. The great abolitionist has undergone his own transformation in American history textbooks. From 1890 to about 1970, John Brown was insane. Before 1890 he was perfectly sane, and after 1970 he has slowly been regaining his sanity in most of our textbooks.

Several history books still linger in the former era. *The American Pageant* is perhaps the worst offender: It calls him "deranged," "gaunt," "grim," "terrible," "crackbrained," and "probably of unsound mind," and claims that "thirteen of his near relatives were regarded as insane, including his mother and grandmother." In an unusual retro-action, the newest *Pageant* adds his mother to the list to make Brown even crazier than earlier editions. Still other books finesse the sanity issue by merely calling him "fanatical." No textbook among twelve I studied has any sympathy for the man or takes any pleasure in his ideals and actions.

For the benefit of readers who, like me, grew up reading that Brown was at least fanatic if not crazed, let's consider the evidence. To be sure, some of his lawyers and relatives, hoping to save his neck, suggested an insanity defense. But no one who knew Brown thought him crazy. He impressed people who spoke with him after his capture, including his jailer and even reporters writing for Democratic newspapers, which favored slavery. Governor Wise of Virginia called him "a man of clear head" after Brown got the better of him in an informal interview.

Textbook authors in the period after 1890 didn't rest their judgment of insanity on primary sources. They inferred Brown's madness from his plan for the Harpers Ferry raid, which admittedly was farfetched. Never mind that John Brown himself told Frederick Douglass presciently that the venture would make a stunning impact even if it failed. Nor that his twenty-odd followers can hardly be considered crazed, too. As Brown pointed out in his last speech in court, each "joined me of his own accord." This was true even of his sons.

No new evidence of insanity caused authors to withdraw sympathy from John Brown. Rather, we must recognize that the insanity with which historians have charged John Brown was never psychological. It was ideological. Brown's actions made no sense to textbook writers between 1890 and about 1965. To make no sense is to be crazy. Since Brown himself did not change after his death, his sanity provides an inadvertent index of the level of white racism in our society.

After 1890, as Southern and border states disfranchised African Americans, as lynchings increased, as blackface minstrel shows dominated American popular culture, white America abandoned the last shards of its racial idealism. White historians lost their ability to empathize with whites who might genuinely believe in equal rights for blacks. John Spencer Bassett's *A Short History of the United States*, published in 1923, makes plain the connection: "The farther we get away from the excitement of 1859 the more we are disposed to consider this extraordinary man the victim of mental delusions."

Thus as white supremacy increasingly pervaded American culture during this era, more even than during slavery, Brown's actions became less and less intelligible. Not until the civil rights movement of the 1960s was white America freed from enough of its racism to accept that a white person did not have to be crazy to die for black equality. In a sense, the murders of Mickey Schwerner and Andrew Goodman in Mississippi, James Reeb and Viola Liuzzo in Alabama, and various other whites in various other Southern states during the civil rights movement liberated textbook writers to see sanity again in John Brown. Observe their impact on the bestselling high-school American history textbook of the period: *Rise of the American Nation*, written in 1961, calls the Harpers Ferry plan "a wild idea, certain to fail," while in 1986 in *Triumph of the American Nation* (the same book, retitled after we lost the Vietnam War) it becomes "a bold idea, but almost certain to fail."

Not just textbooks change over time. So do historical markers and monuments. Consider this comparison of two Civil War memorials, early and late. A sphinx in Mount Auburn Cemetery in Cambridge, Massachusetts, proclaims, "American Union preserved, African slavery destroyed, by the uprising of a great people, by the blood of fallen heroes." The first two phrases constitute a reasonable statement of the war's immediate outcome. The last two have become cryptic—what uprising? Surely not white Unionists—they hardly "uprose." This seems to be a representation on the landscape of black historian W.E.B. DuBois' claim of a general strike by slaves during the

You Are Still Being Lied To

260

Civil War. Certainly it was true that after mid-1863 slaves across the South bargained for better living conditions, escaped to US lines when possible, and on some plantations stopped work altogether except for their own gardens. Early on, white historians mislaid any understanding of this action, especially as a general phenomenon, and have never rediscovered it.

In contrast, South Carolina's monument at Gettysburg, dedicated in 1965, gives a very different version of what the Civil War was about:

> ### South Carolina
> That men of honor might forever know the responsibilities of freedom, dedicated South Carolinians stood and were counted for their heritage and convictions. Abiding faith in the sacredness of states rights provided their creed here. Many earned eternal glory.

If this monument were in remembrance of South Carolina's 5,500 volunteers to the Union cause, the first sentence might make sense. Those men, almost all African American, took up arms precisely to obtain "the responsibilities of freedom" for themselves and for their friends and relatives who still languished in slavery. Unionist South Carolinians never fought at Gettysburg, however. Nor in 1965, at the height of its white supremacist reaction to the Supreme Court's 1954 school desegregation decree, would South Carolina have erected a monument to black South Carolinians or white Unionists. This monument is an attempt to do the impossible: to convert the Confederate cause—a war to guarantee that 3,950,000 people might never know the responsibilities of freedom—into a crusade on behalf of states' rights.

declared the South Carolina Ordinance of Secession, approvingly. "But an increasing hostility on the part of the non-slave-holding States to the institution of slavery, has led to a disregard of their obligations…The States of Maine, New Hampshire, Vermont, Massachusetts, Connecticut, Rhode Island, New York, Pennsylvania, Illinois, Indiana, Michigan, Wisconsin and Iowa, have enacted laws which either nullify the Acts of Congress or render useless any attempt to execute them."

Thus abiding opposition to states' rights when claimed by free states provided South Carolinians' creed here. Since the pro-slavery wing of the Democratic party had controlled the federal government throughout the 1850s, slaveowners favored a strong central power and opposed states' rights. And the delegates went on to condemn Northern states for allowing blacks to vote, refusing to let slaveowners transport slaves through their borders, and even for allowing their residents the freedom of speech to "denounce as sinful the institution of slavery."

South Carolinians in 1965 knew perfectly well that slavery, not states' rights, prompted their state to leave the United States. But in 1965 white supremacists still controlled South Carolina and strove mightily to keep African Americans in separate and unequal institutions. Controlling the past, including how that past is told across the American landscape, helped white supremacists control the future. "States' rights" was just a subterfuge for those who wanted to take away individual rights. Converting the Confederate cause after the fact into a struggle for states' rights in the 1860s helped transmogrify the segregationist cause of the 1960s into a similar struggle for states' rights against an intrusive federal gov-

The ideology of progress lets historians sequester repugnant people and events, from racists to robber barons, in the distant past, so we don't have to worry about them now.

Again, the original record was clear and the misunderstanding is recent. On Christmas Eve, 1860, South Carolinian leaders signed a document to justify leaving the United States. Their first grievance: "that fourteen of the States have deliberately refused, for years past, to fulfill their constitutional obligations," under Article Four of the United States Constitution. Article Four (Section 2, Paragraph 3) is the fugitive slave clause.

"The General Government, as the common agent, passed laws to carry into effect these stipulations of the States,"

ernment. Glorifying the Confederacy in Pennsylvania thus had ideological consequences in South Carolina in 1965.

Amazingly, historians do not often admit that history often grows less accurate over time. Instead, they preach just the reverse: that historians today know better than persons in the past who were "too close" to an event to have "historical perspective." On the landscape, historians enforce this notion by requiring petitioners who want to celebrate historical characters to wait "a sufficient length of time" (50 years in Georgia, whose regulations I am quoting) "for their ideas, services, and accomplishments to be placed in accurate historical perspective" so we can phrase a historical marker to do them justice.

It is true that one can sometimes view a building better by stepping back from it, but this is merely an analogy when applied to the past. No such animal as historical perspective exists—not as an outcome of the simple passage of time, at any rate. To claim that it does is itself an example of limited historical vision that we might call chronological ethnocentrism or the myth of progress. It assumes without evidence that we today are more tolerant, more advanced, wiser than the dimwits who preceded us. Actually, as time passes we know less and less about more and more. The ideology of progress lets historians sequester repugnant people and events, from racists to robber barons, in the distant past, so we don't have to worry about them now.

Are Americans more tolerant today of personal idiosyncrasies? Surely we have reached an arresting state of intolerance when the huge Disney organization, founded by a man with a mustache, will not allow one now even on a janitor. Are we more empirical in our health practice, to avoid such noto-

Our most prudent course is to be suspicious whenever every authority agrees that x happened in the past.

rious practices as bloodletting, that probably killed more people than the maladies for which they were used? Well, yes, but consider our anti-empirical, anti-gravity birthing system, which makes giving birth analogous to a medical operation instead of to an enormous bowel movement, with many unfortunate consequences.

Instead of assuming that the present is so advanced, we need to think about the characteristics of our present society, better to assess its effects on our reconstructions of past events. It follows that we should never take for granted the aphorisms that our schoolbooks and memorials use to sum up the past. Did people get to the Americas across the Bering Land Bridge? We really don't have a clue. Were the Dark Ages "dark?" Maybe not. Why did Europe "win?" The usual answers make no sense. Is the United States a classless society compared to more ossified British and French societies? Not at all.

Our most prudent course is to be suspicious whenever every authority agrees that x happened in the past. Precisely then, x is likely to be a myth for which no one has recently examined the evidence.

Columbus and Western Civilization

Howard Zinn

INTRODUCTORY NOTE FROM THE AUTHOR:

In the year 1992, the celebration of Columbus Day was different from previous ones in two ways. First, this was the quincentennial, 500 years after Columbus' landing in this hemisphere. Second, it was a celebration challenged all over the country by people—many of them native Americans but also others—who had "discovered" a Columbus not worth celebrating, and who were rethinking the traditional glorification of "Western civilization." I gave this talk at the University of Wisconsin in Madison in October 1991. It was published the following year by the Open Magazine Pamphlet Series with the title "Christopher Columbus & the Myth of Human Progress."

George Orwell, who was a very wise man, wrote: "Who controls the past controls the future. And who controls the present controls the past." In other words, those who dominate our society are in a position to write our histories. And if they can do that, they can decide our futures. That is why the telling of the Columbus story is important.

Let me make a confession. I knew very little about Columbus until about twelve years ago, when I began writing my book *A People's History of the United States*. I had a Ph.D. in history from Columbia University—that is, I had the proper training of a historian, and what I knew about Columbus was pretty much what I had learned in elementary school.

But when I began to write my *People's History*, I decided I must learn about Columbus. I had already concluded that I did not want to write just another overview of American history—I knew my point of view would be different. I was going to write about the United States from the point of view of those people who had been largely neglected in the history books: the indigenous Americans, the black slaves, the women, the working people, whether native or immigrant.

I wanted to tell the story of the nation's industrial progress from the standpoint, not of Rockefeller and Carnegie and Vanderbilt, but of the people who worked in their mines, their oil fields, who lost their limbs or their lives building the railroads.

I wanted to tell the story of wars, not from the standpoint of generals and presidents, not from the standpoint of those military heroes whose statues you see all over this country, but through the eyes of the G.I.s, or through the eyes of "the enemy." Yes, why not look at the Mexican War, that great military triumph of the United States, from the viewpoint of the Mexicans?

And so, how must I tell the story of Columbus? I concluded, I must see him through the eyes of the people who were here when he arrived, the people he called "Indians" because he thought he was in Asia.

Well, they left no memoirs, no histories. Their culture was an oral culture, not a written one. Besides, they had been wiped out in a few decades after Columbus' arrival. So I was compelled to turn to the next best thing: the Spaniards who were on the scene at the time. First, Columbus himself. He had kept a journal.

His journal was revealing. He described the people who greeted him when he landed in the Bahamas—they were Arawak Indians, sometimes called Tainos—and told how they waded out into the sea to greet him and his men, who must have looked and sounded like people from another world, and brought them gifts of various kinds. He described them as peaceable, gentle, and said: "They do not bear arms, and do not know them for I showed them a sword—they took it by the edge and cut themselves."

Throughout his journal, over the next months, Columbus spoke of the native Americans with what seemed like admiring awe: "They are the best people in the world and above all the gentlest—without knowledge of what is evil—nor do they murder or steal…they love their neighbors as themselves and they have the sweetest talk in the world…always laughing."

And in a letter he wrote to one of his Spanish patrons, Columbus said: "They are very simple and honest and exceedingly liberal with all they have, none of them refusing anything he may possess when he is asked for it. They exhibit great love toward all others in preference to themselves." But then, in the midst of all this, in his journal, Columbus writes: "They would make fine servants. With fifty men we could subjugate them all and make them do whatever we want."

Yes, this was how Columbus saw the Indians—not as hospitable hosts, but as "servants," to "do whatever we want."

And what did Columbus want? This is not hard to determine. In the first two weeks of journal entries, there is one word that recurs 75 times: GOLD.

In the standard accounts of Columbus what is emphasized again and again is his religious feeling, his desire to convert the natives to Christianity, his reverence for the Bible. Yes, he was concerned about God. But more about Gold. Just one additional letter. His was a limited alphabet. Yes, all over the island of Hispaniola, where he, his brothers, his men, spent most of their time, he erected crosses. But also, all over the island, they built gallows—340 of them by the year 1500. Crosses and gallows—that deadly historic juxtaposition.

In his quest for gold, Columbus, seeing bits of gold among the Indians, concluded there were huge amounts of it. He ordered the natives to find a certain amount of gold within a certain period of time. And if they did not meet their quota, their arms were hacked off. The others were to learn from this and deliver the gold.

Samuel Eliot Morison, the Harvard historian who was Columbus' admiring biographer, acknowledged this. He wrote: "Whoever thought up this ghastly system, Columbus was responsible for it, as the only means of producing gold for export…. Those who fled to the mountains were hunted with hounds, and of those who escaped, starvation and disease took toll, while thousands of the poor creatures in desperation took cassava poison to end their miseries."

Morison continues: "So the policy and acts of Columbus for which he alone was responsible began the depopulation of the terrestrial paradise that was Hispaniola in 1492. Of the original natives, estimated by a modern ethnologist at 300,000 in number, one-third were killed off between 1494 and 1496. By 1508, an enumeration showed only 60,000 alive…. in 1548 Oviedo [Morison is referring to Fernandez de Oviedo, the official Spanish historian of the conquest] doubted whether 500 Indians remained."

But Columbus could not obtain enough gold to send home to impress the King and Queen and his Spanish financiers, so he decided to send back to Spain another kind of loot: slaves. They rounded up about 1,200 natives, selected 500, and these were sent, jammed together, on the voyage across the Atlantic. Two hundred died on the way, of cold, of sickness.

In Columbus' journal, an entry of September 1498 reads: "From here one might send, in the name of the Holy Trinity, as many slaves as could be sold…"

What the Spaniards did to the Indians is told in horrifying detail by Bartolomé de las Casas, whose writings give the most thorough account of the Spanish-Indian encounter. Las Casas was a Dominican priest who came to the New World a few years after Columbus, spent 40 years on Hispaniola and nearby islands, and became the leading advocate in Spain for the rights of the natives. Las Casas, in his book *The Devastation of the Indies,* writes of the Arawaks: "…of all the infinite universe of humanity, these people are the most guileless, the most devoid of wickedness and duplicity…yet into this sheepfold…there came some Spaniards who immediately behaved like ravening beasts…. Their reason for killing and destroying…is that the Christians have an ultimate aim which is to acquire gold…"

The cruelties multiplied. Las Casas saw soldiers stabbing Indians for sport, dashing babies' heads on rocks. And when the Indians resisted, the Spaniards hunted them down, equipped for killing with horses, armor plate, lances, pikes, rifles, crossbows, and vicious dogs. Indians who took things belonging to the Spaniards—they were not accustomed to the concept of private ownership and gave freely of their own possessions—were beheaded or burned at the stake.

Las Casas' testimony was corroborated by other eyewitnesses. A group of Dominican friars, addressing the Spanish monarchy in 1519, hoping for the Spanish government to intercede, told about unspeakable atrocities, children thrown to dogs to be devoured, newborn babies born to women prisoners flung into the jungle to die.

Las Casas saw soldiers stabbing Indians for sport, dashing babies' heads on rocks.

Forced labor in the mines and on the land led to much sickness and death. Many children died because their mothers, overworked and starved, had no milk for them. Las Casas, in Cuba, estimated that 7,000 children died in *three months*.

The greatest toll was taken by sickness, because the Europeans brought with them diseases against which the natives had no immunity: typhoid, typhus, diphtheria, smallpox.

As in any military conquest, women came in for especially brutal treatment. One Italian nobleman named Cuneo recorded an early sexual encounter. The "Admiral" he refers to is Columbus, who, as part of his agreement with the Spanish monarchy, insisted he be made an Admiral. Cuneo wrote:

> ...I captured a very beautiful Carib woman, whom the said Lord Admiral gave to me and with whom...I conceived desire to take pleasure. I wanted to put my desire into execution but she did not want it and treated me with her finger nails in such a manner that I wished I had never begun. But seeing that, I took a rope and thrashed her well.... Finally we came to an agreement.

There is other evidence which adds up to a picture of widespread rape of native women. Samuel Eliot Morison wrote: "In the Bahamas, Cuba and Hispaniola they found young and beautiful women, who everywhere were naked, in most places accessible, and presumably complaisant." Who presumes this? Morison, and so many others.

Morison saw the conquest as so many writers after him have done, as one of the great romantic adventures of world history. He seemed to get carried away by what appeared to him as a *masculine* conquest. He wrote:

> Never again may mortal men hope to recapture the amazement, the wonder, the delight of those October days in 1492, when the new world gracefully yielded her virginity to the conquering Castilians.

The language of Cuneo ("we came to an agreement"), and of Morison ("gracefully yielded") written almost 500 years apart, surely suggests how persistent through modern history has been the mythology that rationalizes sexual brutality by seeing it as "complaisant."

So, I read Columbus' journal, I read las Casas. I also read Hans Koning's pioneering work of our time—*Columbus: His Enterprise*, which, at the time I wrote my *People's History*, was the only contemporary account I could find which departed from the standard treatment.

When my book appeared, I began to get letters from all over the country about it. Here was a book of 600 pages, starting with Columbus, ending with the 1970s, but most of the letters I got from readers were about one subject: Columbus. I could have interpreted this to mean that, since this was the very beginning of the book, that's all these people had read. But no, it seemed that the Columbus story was simply the part of my book that readers found most startling. Because every American, from elementary school on, learns the Columbus story, and learns it the same way: "In Fourteen Hundred and Ninety-Two, Columbus Sailed the Ocean Blue."

How many of you have heard of Tigard, Oregon? Well, I didn't until, about seven years ago, I began receiving, every semester, a bunch of letters, 20 or 30, from students at one high school in Tigard. It seems that their teacher was having them (knowing high schools, I almost said "forcing them") read my *People's History*. He was photocopying a number of chapters and giving them to the students. And then he had them write letters to me, with comments and questions. Roughly half of them thanked me for giving them data which they had never seen before. The others were angry, or wondered how I got such information, and how I had arrived at such outrageous conclusions.

One high school student named Bethany wrote: "Out of all the articles that I've read of yours I found 'Columbus, The Indians, and Human Progress' the most shocking." Another student named Brian, seventeen years old, wrote: "An example of the confusion I feel after reading your article concerns Columbus coming to America.... According to you, it seems he came for women, slaves, and gold. You say that Columbus physically abused the Indians that didn't help him find gold. You've said you have gained a lot of this information from Columbus' own journal. I am wondering if there is such a journal, and if so, why isn't it

In Columbus' journal, an entry of September 1498 reads: "From here one might send, in the name of the Holy Trinity, as many slaves as could be sold..."

Some of the teachers made suggestions on how the truth could be told in a way that would not frighten children unnecessarily, but that would avoid the falsification of history now taking place.

part of our history. Why isn't any of what you say in my history book, or in history books people have access to each day?"

I pondered this letter. It could be interpreted to mean that the writer was indignant that no other history books had told him what I did. Or, as was more likely, he was saying: "I don't believe a word of what you wrote! You made this up!"

I am not surprised at such reactions. It tells something about the claims of pluralism and diversity in American culture, the pride in our "free society," that generation after generation has learned exactly the same set of facts about Columbus, and finished their education with the same glaring omissions.

A school teacher in Portland, Oregon, named Bill Bigelow has undertaken a crusade to change the way the Columbus story is taught all over America. He tells of how he sometimes starts a new class. He goes over to a girl sitting in the front row, and takes her purse. She says: "You took my purse!" Bigelow responds: "No, I discovered it."

Bill Bigelow did a study of recent children's books on Columbus. He found them remarkably alike in their repetition of the traditional point of view. A typical fifth-grade biography of Columbus begins: "There once was a boy who loved the salty sea." Well! I can imagine a children's biography of Attila the Hun beginning with the sentence: "There once was a boy who loved horses."

Another children's book in Bigelow's study, this time for second-graders: "The King and Queen looked at the gold and the Indians. They listened in wonder to Columbus' stories of adventure. Then they all went to church to pray and sing. Tears of joy filled Columbus' eyes."

I once spoke about Columbus to a workshop of school teachers, and one of them suggested that school children were too young to hear of the horrors recounted by las Casas and others. Other teachers disagreed, said children's stories include plenty of violence, but the perpetrators are witches and monsters and "bad people," not national heroes who have holidays named after them.

The argument about children "not being ready to hear the truth" does not account for the fact that in American society, when the children grow up, they *still* are not told the truth. As I said earlier, right up through graduate school I was not presented with the information that would counter the myths told to me in the early grades. And it is clear that my experience is typical, judging from the shocked reactions to my book that I have received from readers of all ages.

If you look in an *adult* book, the *Columbia Encyclopedia* (my edition was put together in 1950, but all the relevant information was available then, including Morison's biography), there is a long entry on Columbus (about 1,000 words), but you will find no mention of the atrocities committed by him and his men.

In the 1986 edition of the *Columbia History of the World* there are several mentions of Columbus, but nothing about what he did to the natives. Several pages are devoted to "Spain and Portugal in America," in which the treatment of the native population is presented as a matter of controversy, among theologians at that time, and among historians today. You can get the flavor of this "balanced approach," containing a nugget of reality, by the following passage from that *History*:

> The determination of the Crown and the Church to Christianize the Indians, the need for labor to exploit the new lands, and the attempts of some Spaniards to protect the Indians, resulted in a very remarkable complex of customs, laws, and institutions which even today leads historians to contradictory conclusions about Spanish rule in America.... Academic disputes flourish on this debatable and in a sense insoluble question, but there is no doubt that cruelty, overwork and disease resulted in an appalling depopulation. There were, according to recent estimates, about 25 million Indians in Mexico in 1519, slightly more than 1 million in 1605.

Despite this scholarly language—"contradictory conclusions... academic disputes...insoluble question"—there is no real dispute about the facts of enslavement, forced labor, rape, murder, the taking of hostages, the ravages of diseases carried

I can imagine a children's biography of Attila the Hun beginning with the sentence: "There once was a boy who loved horses."

from Europe, and the wiping out of huge numbers of native people. The only dispute is over how much emphasis is to be placed on these facts, and how they carry over into the issues of our time.

For instance, Samuel Eliot Morison does spend some time detailing the treatment of the natives by Columbus and his men, and uses the word "genocide" to describe the overall effect of the "discovery." But he buries this in the midst of a long, admiring treatment of Columbus, and sums up his view in the concluding paragraph of his popular book *Christopher Columbus, Mariner*, as follows:

> He had his faults and his defects, but they were largely the defects of the qualities that made him great—his indomitable will, his superb faith in God and in his own mission as the Christ-bearer to lands beyond the seas, his stubborn persistence despite neglect, poverty and discouragement. But there was no flaw, no dark side to the most outstanding and essential of all his qualities—his seamanship.

Yes, his seamanship!

Let me make myself clear. I am not interested in either denouncing or exalting Columbus. It is too late for that. We are not writing a letter of recommendation for him to decide his qualifications for undertaking another voyage to another part of the universe. To me, the Columbus story is important for what it tells us about ourselves, about our time, about the decisions we have to make for our century, for the next century.

Why this great controversy today about Columbus and the celebration of the quincentennial? Why the indignation of native Americans and others about the glorification of that conqueror? Why the heated defense of Columbus by others?

The intensity of the debate can only be because it is not about 1492, it is about 1992.

We can get a clue to this if we look back a hundred years to 1892, the year of the quadricentennial. There were great celebrations in Chicago and New York. In New York there were five days of parades, fireworks, military marches, naval pageants, a million visitors to the city, a memorial statue unveiled at a corner of Central Park, now to be known as Columbus Circle. A celebratory meeting took place at Carnegie Hall, addressed by Chauncey DePew.

You might not know the name of Chauncey DePew, unless you recently looked at Gustavus Myers' classic work, *A History of the Great American Fortunes*. In that book, Chauncey DePew is described as the front man for Cornelius Vanderbilt and his New York Central railroad. DePew traveled to Albany, the capital of New York State, with satchels of money and free railroad passes for members of the New York State legislature, and came away with subsidies and land grants for the New York Central.

DePew saw the Columbus festivities as a celebration of wealth and prosperity—you might say, as a self-celebration. He said that the quadricentennial event "marks the wealth and the civilization of a great people...it marks the things that belong to their comfort and their ease, their pleasure and their luxuries...and their power."

We might note that at the time he said this, there was much suffering among the working poor of America, huddled in city slums, their children sick and undernourished. The plight of people who worked on the land—which at this time was a considerable part of the population—was desperate, leading to the anger of the Farmers' Alliances and the rise of the People's (Populist) Party. And the following year, 1893, was a year of economic crisis and widespread misery.

The argument about children "not being ready to hear the truth" does not account for the fact that in American society, when the children grow up, they *still* are not told the truth.

Columbus and Western Civilization
Howard Zinn

DePew must have sensed, as he stood on the platform at Carnegie Hall, some murmurings of discontent at the smugness that accompanied the Columbus celebrations, for he said: "If there is anything I detest…it is that spirit of historical inquiry which doubts everything; that modern spirit which destroys all the illusions and all the heroes which have been the inspiration of patriotism through all the centuries."

So, to celebrate Columbus was to be patriotic. To doubt was to be unpatriotic. And what did "patriotism" mean to DePew? It meant the glorification of expansion and conquest—which Columbus represented, and which America represented. It was just six years after his speech that the United States, expelling Spain from Cuba, began its own long occupation (sporadically military, continuously political and economic) of Cuba, took Puerto Rico and Hawaii, and began its bloody war against the Filipinos to take over their country.

That "patriotism" which was tied to the celebration of Columbus, and the celebration of conquest, was reinforced in the second World War by the emergence of the United States as the superpower, all the old European empires now in decline. At that time, Henry Luce, the powerful president-maker and multimillion-aire, owner of *Time, Life,* and *Fortune* (not just the publications, but the *things*!) wrote that the twentieth century was turning into the "American Century," in which the United States would have its way in the world.

George Bush, accepting the presidential nomination in 1988, said: "This has been called the American Century because in it we were the dominant force for good in the world…. Now we are on the verge of a new century, and what country's name will it bear? I say it will be another American Century."

What arrogance! That the twenty-first century, when we should be getting away from the murderous jingoism of this century, should already be anticipated as an *American* century, or as any one nation's century. Bush must think of himself as a new Columbus, "discovering" and planting his nation's flag on new worlds, because he called for a US colony on the moon early in the next century. And forecast a mission to Mars in the year 2019.

The "patriotism" that Chauncey Depew invoked in celebrat-

ing Columbus was profoundly tied to the notion of the inferiority of the conquered peoples. Columbus' attacks on the Indians were justified by their status as subhumans. The taking of Texas and much of Mexico by the United States just before the Civil War was done with the same racist rationale. Sam Houston, the first governor of Texas, proclaimed: "The Anglo-Saxon race must pervade the whole southern extremity of this vast continent. The Mexicans are no better than the Indians and I see no reason why we should not take their land."

At the start of the twentieth century, the violence of the new American expansionism into the Caribbean and the Pacific was accepted because we were dealing with lesser beings.

In the year 1900, Chauncey DePew, now a US senator, spoke again in Carnegie Hall, this time to support Theodore Roosevelt's candidacy for vice president. Celebrating the conquest of the Philippines as a beginning of the American penetration of China and more, he proclaimed: "The guns of Dewey in Manila Bay were heard across Asia and Africa, they echoed through the palace at Peking and brought to the Oriental mind

> "The Mexicans are no better than the Indians and I see no reason why we should not take their land."

a new and potent force among western nations. We, in common with the countries of Europe, are striving to enter the limitless markets of the east…. These people respect nothing but power. I believe the Philippines will be enormous markets and sources of wealth."

Theodore Roosevelt, who appears endlessly on lists of our "great presidents," and whose face is one of the four colossal sculptures of American presidents (along with Washington, Jefferson, Lincoln) carved into Mount Rushmore in South Dakota, was the quintessential racist-imperialist. He was furious, back in 1893, when President Cleveland failed to annex Hawaii, telling the Naval War College it was "a crime against white civilization." In his book *The Strenuous Life,* Roosevelt wrote:

> Of course our whole national history has been one of expansion…that the barbarians recede or are conquered…is due solely to the power of the mighty civilized races which have not lost the fighting instinct.

An Army officer in the Philippines put it even more bluntly: "There is no use mincing words…. We exterminated the American Indians and I guess most of us are proud of it…and we must have no scruples about exterminating this other race standing in the way of progress and enlightenment, if it is necessary…"

The official historian of the Indies in the early sixteenth century, Fernandez de Oviedo, did not deny what was done to natives by the *conquistadores.* He described "innumerable cruel deaths as countless as the stars." But this was acceptable, because "to use gunpowder against pagans is to offer incense to the Lord."

(One is reminded of President McKinley's decision to send the army and navy to take the Philippines, saying it was the duty of the United States to "Christianize and civilize" the Filipinos.)

Against las Casas' pleas for mercy to the Indians, the theologian Juan Gines de Sepulveda declared: "How can we doubt that these people, so uncivilized, so barbaric, so contaminated with so many sins and obscenities, have been justly conquered."

Sepulveda in the year 1531 visited his former college in Spain and was outraged by seeing the students there protesting Spain's war against Turkey. The students were saying: "All war…is contrary to the Catholic religion."

This led him to write a philosophical defense of the Spanish treatment of the Indians. He quoted Aristotle, who wrote in his *Politics* that some people were "slaves by nature," who "should be hunted down like wild beasts in order to bring them to the correct way of life."

Las Casas responded: "Let us send Aristotle packing, for we have in our favor the command of Christ: Thou shalt love thy neighbor as thyself."

The dehumanization of the "enemy" has been a necessary accompaniment to wars of conquest. It is easier to explain atrocities if they are committed against infidels or people of an inferior race. Slavery and racial segregation in the United States, and European imperialism in Asia and Africa, were justified in this way.

The bombing of Vietnamese villages by the United States, the search and destroy missions, the My Lai massacre, were all made palatable to their perpetrators by the idea that the victims were not human. They were "gooks" or "communists," and deserved what they received.

In the Gulf War, the dehumanization of the Iraqis consisted of not recognizing their existence. We were not bombing women, children, not bombing and shelling ordinary Iraqi young men in the act of flight and surrender. We were acting against a Hitler-like monster, Saddam Hussein, although the people we were

"To use gunpowder against pagans is to offer incense to the Lord."

killing were the Iraqi victims of this monster. When General Colin Powell was asked about Iraqi casualties he said that was "really not a matter I am terribly interested in."

The American people were led to accept the violence of the war in Iraq because the Iraqis were made invisible—because the United States only used "smart bombs." The major media ignored the enormous death toll in Iraq, ignored the report of the Harvard medical team that visited Iraq shortly after the war and found that tens of thousands of Iraqi children were dying because of the bombing of the water supply and the resultant epidemics of disease.

The celebrations of Columbus are declared to be celebrations not just of his maritime exploits but of "progress," of his arrival in the Bahamas as the beginning of that much-praised 500 years of "Western civilization." But those concepts need to be reexamined. When Gandhi was once asked what he thought about Western civilization, he replied: "It's a good idea."

The point is not to deny the benefits of "progress" and "civilization"—advances in technology, knowledge, science, health, education, and standards of living. But there is a question to be asked: Progress, yes, but at what human cost?

Would we accept a Russian justification of Stalin's rule, including the enormous toll in human suffering, on the ground that he made Russia a great industrial power?

I recall that in my high school classes in American history when we came to the period after the Civil War, roughly the years between that war and World War I, it was looked on as the Gilded Age, the period of the great Industrial Revolution, when the United States became an economic giant. I remember how thrilled we were to learn of the dramatic growth of the steel and oil industries, of the building of the great fortunes, of the crisscrossing of the country by the railroads.

We were not told of the human cost of this great industrial progress: how the huge production of cotton came from the labor of black slaves; how the textile industry was built up by the labor of young girls who went into the mills at twelve and died at 25; how the railroads were constructed by Irish and Chinese immigrants who were literally worked to death, in the heat of summer and cold of winter; how working people, immigrants and native-born, had to go out on strike and be beaten by police and jailed by National Guardsmen before they could win the eight-hour day; how the children of the working class, in the slums of the city, had to drink polluted water, and how they died early of malnutrition and disease. All this in the name of "progress."

And yes, there are huge benefits from industrialization, science, technology, medicine. But so far, in these 500 years of Western civilization, of Western domination of the rest of the world, most of those benefits have gone to a small part of the human race. For billions of people in the Third World, they still face starvation, homelessness, disease, the early deaths of their children.

Did the Columbus expeditions mark the transition from savagery to civilization? What of the Indian civilizations which had been built up over thousands of years before Columbus came? Las Casas and others marveled at the spirit of sharing and generosity which marked the Indian societies, the communal buildings in which they lived, their aesthetic sensibilities, the egalitarianism among men and women.

The British colonists in North America were startled at the democracy of the Iroquois—the tribes who occupied much of New York and Pennsylvania. The American historian Gary Nash describes Iroquois culture: "No laws and ordinances,

The British colonists in North America were startled at the democracy of the Iroquois.

sheriffs and constables, judges and juries, or courts or jails— the apparatus of authority in European societies—were to be found in the northeast woodlands prior to European arrival. Yet boundaries of acceptable behavior were firmly set...Though priding themselves on the autonomous individual, the Iroquois maintained a strict sense of right and wrong..."

In the course of westward expansion, the new nation, the United States, stole the Indians' land, killed them when they resisted, destroyed their sources of food and shelter, pushed them into smaller and smaller sections of the country, went about the systematic destruction of Indian society. At the time of the Black Hawk War in the 1830s—one of hundreds of wars waged against the Indians of North America—Lewis Cass, the governor of the Michigan territory, referred to his taking of millions of acres from the Indians as "the progress of civilization." He said: "A barbarous people cannot live in contact with a civilized community."

We get a sense of how "barbarous" these Indians were when, in the 1880s, Congress prepared legislation to break up the communal lands in which Indians still lived, into small private possessions, what today some people would call, admiringly, "privatization." Senator Henry Dawes, author of this legislation, visited the Cherokee Nation and described what he found: "… there was not a family in that whole nation that had not a home of its own. There was not a pauper in that nation, and the nation did not owe a dollar…it built its own schools and its hospitals. Yet the defect of the system was apparent. They have got as far as they can go, because they own their land in common…there is not enterprise to make your home any better than that of your neighbors. There is no selfishness, which is at the bottom of civilization."

That selfishness at the bottom of "civilization" is connected with what drove Columbus on, and what is much-praised today, as American political leaders and the media speak about how the West will do a great favor to the Soviet Union and Eastern Europe by introducing "the profit motive."

Granted, there may be certain ways in which the incentive of profit may be helpful in economic development, but that incentive, in the history of the "free market" in the West, has had horrendous consequences. It led, throughout the centuries of "Western Civilization," to a ruthless imperialism.

In Joseph Conrad's novel *Heart of Darkness,* written in the 1890s, after some time spent in the Upper Congo of Africa, he describes the work done by black men in chains on behalf of white men who were interested only in ivory. He writes: "The word 'ivory' rang in the air, was whispered, was sighed. You would think they were praying to it…. To tear treasure out of the bowels of the land was their desire, with no more moral purpose at the back of it than there is in burglars breaking into a safe." The uncontrolled drive for profit has led to enormous human suffering, exploitation, slavery, cruelty in the workplace, dangerous working conditions, child labor, the destruction of land and forests, the poisoning of the air we breathe, the water we drink, the food we eat.

In his 1933 autobiography, Chief Luther Standing Bear wrote: "True the white man brought great change. But the varied fruits of his civilization, though highly colored and inviting, are sickening and deadening. And if it be the part of civilization to maim, rob, and thwart, then what is progress? I am going to venture that the man who sat on the ground in his tipi meditating on life and its meaning, accepting the kinship of all creatures, and acknowledging unity with the universe of things, was infusing into his being the true essence of civilization."

The present threats to the environment have caused a reconsideration among scientists and other scholars of the value of "progress" as it has been so far defined. In December 1991, there was a two-day conference at MIT, in which 50 scientists and historians discussed the idea of progress in Western thought. Here is part of the report on that conference in the *Boston Globe*:

> In a world where resources are being squandered and the environment poisoned, participants in an MIT conference said yesterday, it is time for people to start thinking in terms of sustainability and stability rather than growth and progress.... Verbal fireworks and heated exchanges that sometimes grew into shouting matches punctuated the discussions among scholars of economics, religion, medicine, history and the sciences.

One of the participants, historian Leo Marx, said that working toward a more harmonious coexistence with nature is itself a kind of progress, but different than the traditional one in which people try to overpower nature.

So, to look back at Columbus in a critical way is to raise all these questions about progress, civilization, our relations with one another, our relationship to the natural world.

You probably have heard—as I have, quite often—that it is wrong for us to treat the Columbus story the way we do. What they say is: "You are taking Columbus out of context, looking at him with the eyes of the twentieth century. You must not superimpose the values of our time on events that took place 500 years ago. That is ahistorical."

I find this argument strange. Does it mean that cruelty, exploitation, greed, enslavement, violence against helpless people, are values peculiar to the fifteenth and sixteenth centuries? And that we in the twentieth century are beyond that? Are there not certain human values which are common to the age of Columbus and to our own? Proof of that is that both in his time and in ours there were enslavers and exploiters; in both his

> "What does it matter who discovered America, really?… But the thought that I've been lied to all my life about this, and who knows what else, really makes me angry."

time and ours there were those who protested against that, on behalf of human rights.

It is encouraging that, in this year of the quincentennial, there is a wave of protest, unprecedented in all the years of celebration of Columbus, all over the United States, and throughout the Americas. Much of this protest is being led by Indians, who are organizing conferences and meetings, who are engaging in acts of civil disobedience, who are trying to educate the American public about what really happened 500 years ago, and what it tells us about the issues of our time.

There is a new generation of teachers in our schools, and many of them are insisting that the Columbus story be told from the point of view of the native Americans. In the fall of 1990 I was telephoned from Los Angeles by a talk-show host who wanted to discuss Columbus. Also on the line was a high school student in that city, named Blake Lindsey, who had insisted on addressing the Los Angeles City Council to oppose the traditional Columbus Day celebration. She told them of the genocide committed by the Spaniards against the Arawak Indians. The City Council did not respond.

Someone called in on that talk show, introducing herself as a woman who had emigrated from Haiti. She said: "The girl is right—we have no Indians left. In our last uprising against the government, the people knocked down the statue of Columbus and now it is in the basement of the city hall in Port-au-Prince." The caller finished by saying: "Why don't we build statues for the aborigines?"

Despite the textbooks still in use, more teachers are questioning, more students are questioning. Bill Bigelow reports on the reactions of his students after he introduces them to reading material which contradicts the traditional histories. One student wrote: "In 1492, Columbus sailed the ocean blue…. That story is about as complete as Swiss cheese."

Another wrote a critique of her American history textbook to the publisher, Allyn and Bacon, pointing to many important omissions in that text. She said: "I'll just pick one topic to keep it simple. How about Columbus?"

It is the guardians of the old stories, the orthodox histories, who refuse to widen the spectrum of ideas, to take in new books, new approaches, new information, new views of history.

Another student: "It seemed to me as if the publishers had just printed up some glory story that was supposed to make us feel more patriotic about our country…. They want us to look at our country as great and powerful and forever right…. We're being fed lies."

When students discover that in the very first history they learn—the story of Columbus—they have not been told the whole truth, it leads to a healthy skepticism about all of their historical education. One of Bigelow's students, named Rebecca, wrote: "What does it matter who discovered America, really?… But the thought that I've been lied to all my life about this, and who knows what else, really makes me angry."

This new critical thinking in the schools and in the colleges seems to frighten those who have glorified what is called "Western civilization." Reagan's Secretary of Education, William Bennett, in his 1984 "Report on the Humanities in Higher Education," writes of Western civilization as "our common culture…its highest ideas and aspirations."

One of the most ferocious defenders of Western civilization is philosopher Allan Bloom, who wrote *The Closing of the American Mind* in a spirit of panic at what the social movements of the 1960s had done to change the educational atmosphere of American universities. He was frightened by the student demonstrations he saw at Cornell, which he saw as a terrible interference with education.

Bloom's idea of education was a small group of very smart students, in an elite university, studying Plato and Aristotle, and refusing to be disturbed in their contemplation by the noise outside their windows of students rallying against racism or protesting against the war in Vietnam.

As I read him, I was reminded of some of my colleagues, when I was teaching in a black college in Atlanta, Georgia, at the time of the civil rights movement, who shook their heads in disapproval when our students left their classes to sit-in, to be arrested, in protest against racial segregation. These students were neglecting their education, they said. In fact, these students were learning more in a few weeks of participation in social struggle than they could learn in a year of going to class.

What a narrow, stunted understanding of education! It corresponds perfectly to the view of history which insists that Western civilization is the summit of human achievement. As Bloom wrote in his book: "…only in the Western nations, i.e. those influenced by Greek philosophy, is there some willingness to doubt the identification of the good with one's own way." Well, if this willingness to doubt is the hallmark of Greek philosophy, then Bloom and his fellow idolizers of Western civilization are ignorant of that philosophy.

If Western civilization is considered the high point of human progress, the United States is the best representative of this civilization. Here is Allan Bloom again: "This is the American moment in world history…. America tells one story: the unbroken, ineluctable progress of freedom and equality. From its first settlers and its political foundings on, there has been no dispute that freedom and equality are the essence of justice for us…"

Yes, tell black people and native Americans and the homeless and those without health insurance, and all the victims abroad of American foreign policy that America "tells one story…freedom and equality."

In rethinking our history, we are not just looking at the past, but at the present, and trying to look at it from the point of view of those who have been left out of the benefits of so-called civilization.

Western civilization is complex. It represents many things, some decent, some horrifying. We would have to pause before celebrating it uncritically when we note that David Duke, the Louisiana Ku Klux Klan member and ex-Nazi, says that people have got him wrong. "The common strain in my thinking," he told a reporter, "is my love for Western civilization."

We who insist on looking critically at the Columbus story, and indeed at everything in our traditional histories, are often accused of insisting on political correctness, to the detriment of free speech. I find this odd. It is the guardians of the old stories, the orthodox histories, who refuse to widen the spectrum of ideas, to take in new books, new approaches, new information, new views of history. They, who claim to believe in "free markets," do not believe in a free marketplace of ideas, any more than they believe in a free marketplace of goods and services. In both material goods and in ideas, they want the market dominated by those who have always held power and wealth. They worry that if new ideas enter the marketplace, people may begin to rethink the social arrangements that have given us so much suffering, so much violence, so much war these last 500 years of "civilization."

Of course we had all that before Columbus arrived in this hemisphere, but resources were puny, people were isolated from one another, and the possibilities were narrow. In recent centuries, however, the world has become amazingly small, our possibilities for creating a decent society have enormously magnified, and so the excuses for hunger, ignorance, violence, and racism no longer exist.

In rethinking our history, we are not just looking at the past, but at the present, and trying to look at it from the point of view of those who have been left out of the benefits of so-called civilization. It is a simple but profoundly important thing we are trying to accomplish, to look at the world from other points of view. We need to do that, as we come into the next century, if we want this coming century to be different, if we want it to be, not an American century, or a Western century, or a white century, or a male century, or any nation's, any group's century, but a century for the human race.

Saving Private Power
The Hidden History of "The Good War"
excerpts from a book by Michael Zezima (aka Mickey Z)

Was World War II a just war? Is the "Good War" fable rooted in reality, false hope, or propaganda? This enduring myth goes well beyond Memorial Day barbecues and flickering black-and-white movies on late-night TV. According to the accepted history, WWII was an inevitable war forced upon a peaceful people thanks to a surprise attack by a sneaky enemy. This war, then and now, has been carefully and consciously sold to us as a life-and-death battle against pure evil. For most Americans, WWII was nothing less than good and bad going toe-to-toe in khaki fatigues.

But, Hollywood aside, John Wayne never set foot on Iwo Jima. Despite the former President's dim recollections, Ronald Reagan did not liberate any concentration camps. And, con-

and denial was the order of the day. For example, the publicity arm of the American Motion Picture Industry put out a full-page ad in several magazines in 1942. Entitled "Our Morale is Mightier than the Sword," the ad declared that in order to win the war, "[o]ur minds must be as keen as our swords, our hearts as strong as our tanks, our spirits as buoyant as our planes. For morale is a mighty force—as vital as the materials of war themselves...so it is the job of the Motion Picture Industry to *keep 'em smiling*." (Emphasis in original.)

Indeed, if the folks back home had any idea of what was really going on, few of them would have been *smiling*. That was the true genius of "Good War" propaganda: lies of omission.

WWII was about territory, power, control, money, and imperialism.

trary to popular belief, FDR never actually got around to sending American troops "over there" to take on Hitler's Germany until after the Nazis had already declared war on the US.

American lives weren't sacrificed in a holy war to avenge Pearl Harbor nor to end the Nazi Holocaust, just as the Civil War wasn't fought to end slavery. WWII was about territory, power, control, money, and imperialism. Sure, the Allies won and ultimately, that's a very good thing—but it doesn't mean they did it fair and square. Precisely how unfairly they behaved will be explored in detail herein but, for now, the words of US General Curtis LeMay, commander of the 1945 Tokyo fire-bombing operation, will suffice: "I suppose if I had lost the war, I would have been tried as a war criminal. Fortunately, we were on the winning side."

Myth #1: WWII Was "Good"

When the US entered WWII, patriotism was the watchword

Celebrated author John Steinbeck served as a wartime correspondent. "We were all part of the war effort," he later remarked. "We went along with it, and not only that, we abetted it…. I don't mean that the correspondents were liars…. It is in the things not mentioned that the untruth lies." Steinbeck went on to explain that "the foolish reporter who broke the rules would not be printed at home and in addition would be put out of the theater by the command."

"By not mentioning a lot of things," adds author Paul Fussell, "a correspondent could give the audience at home the impression that there were no cowards in the service, no thieves and rapists and looters, no cruel or stupid commanders."

Let's take a look at some of what we weren't told about the "greatest generation," as we just keep *smiling*.

With few exceptions, the Hollywood version of war evokes images of the noble everyman, fighting for freedom and honor without asking any questions. Watching John Wayne or Tom

Hanks perform their patriotic duty helps obscure many battle-field realities that would put the "Good War" label in doubt. Some of those realities:

- At least 50 percent of US combat soldiers soiled themselves during battle.
- Ten percent or more of American troops took amphetamines at some time.
- By the war's end, there were roughly 75,000 US MIAs, most of whom, thanks to modern weaponry, "had been blown into vapor."
- Only 18 percent of combat veterans in the Pacific said they were "usually in good spirits."
- The psychological breakdown rate of men consistently in action for 28 days ran as high as 90 percent.
- As of 1994, roughly 25 percent of the WWII veterans still in the hospital were psychiatric cases.
- About 25 to 30 percent of wartime casualties were psychological cases (under severe conditions, that number could reach 70 to 80 percent).
- Mental problems accounted for 54 percent of total casualties in Italy.
- During the battle for Okinawa, 7,613 Americans died and 31,807 sustained physical wounds, while an astounding 26,221 were mental casualties.

■ ■ ■ ■ ■ ■ ■ ■ ■ ■

For those on the homefront, the good old days don't exactly pan out either. Part of the more recent "Good War" facade is the "greatest generation" hype. This fiction enables the family-values crowd to claim that generation as their own despite the fact that those who lived during the Depression and WWII were no more or less human than the rest of us. There were a record-high 600,000 divorces in 1946. In addition, the divorce rate in 1940 was 16 percent; by 1944, it had jumped to 27 percent. Between 1939 and 1945, illegitimate births in the US rose by 42 percent. The venereal disease rate for girls 15- to 18-years-old in New York City increased 204 percent between 1941 and 1944, while truancy in Detroit jumped 24 percent between 1938 and 1943.

As for the legendary efficiency of homefront war production, the results are mixed. Despite the fable of unquestioned unity, the forces of labor remained focused on the issue of workplace reform. There were some 14,000 strikes involving nearly seven million workers during the war years. "In 1944 alone," says historian Howard Zinn, "a million workers were on strike, in the mines, in the steel mills, in the auto and transportation equipment industries."

As ubiquitous as labor unrest in those days was WWII poster art. Distributed by the US Office of War Information, these colorful single-sheet posters demonized the enemy, canonized "our boys," and helped restore the tattered image of corporate America—all in the name of increasing production, erasing the Depression, and selling the war to a decidedly suspicious public. Representatives from the major advertising firm Young & Rubicam, Inc. argued that the "most effective war posters appealed to the emotions," and must be understood by the "lower third" of the population. Battlefield casualty images were banned, and any labor-management tensions were glossed over. Thus, the consciously fabricated—but effectively unifying—patriotism of the war effort made it harder for labor to mobilize public support for actions against corporations.

WWII poster art also served to define the role of American women in the war effort. "We Can Do It!" said Rosie the Riveter, with "it" meaning following orders on the factory floor until the war was over and then returning to the kitchen.

> About 25 to 30 percent of wartime casualties were psychological cases.

"This image," says historian Maureen Honey, "both idealized women as a strong, capable fighter infused with a holy spirit and undercut the notion that women deserved and wanted a larger role in public life."

Myth #2: WWII Was Inevitable

To believe this myth, one must accept the rise of fascism as practically a force of nature. By taking a closer look at the decisions made by many of the "good guys," however, one comes away with a new perspective.

When William E. Dodd, US Ambassador to Germany during the 1930s, declared that "a clique of U.S. industrialists is… working closely with the fascist regime[s] in Germany and Italy," he wasn't kidding.

"Many leaders of Wall Street and of the US foreign policy establishment had maintained close ties with their German counterparts since the 1920s, some having intermarried or shared investments," says investigative reporter Christopher Simpson. "This went so far in the 1930s as the sale in New York of bonds whose proceeds helped finance the Aryanization of companies and real estate looted from German Jews…. US investment in Germany accelerated rapidly after Hitler came to power." Such investment, says Simpson, increased "by some 48.5 percent between 1929 and 1940, while declining sharply everywhere else in continental Europe."

Indeed, when a resolution was introduced in January 1934 asking the Senate and the President to express "surprise and pain" at the German treatment of the Jews, the resolution never got out of committee.

One benefactor of Corporate America's largesse was German banker Hermann Abs, who was close enough to *der Führer* to receive advance notice that Germany was planning to seize Austria. Tellingly, upon his death, Abs was judiciously eulogized by the *New York Times* as an "art collector" whose financial career "took off after 1945." The *Times* piece cryptically quoted David Rockefeller as calling Abs "the most important banker of our time."

■ ■ ■ ■ ■ ■ ■ ■ ■ ■

It wasn't just the Rockefellers who admired Nazi ingenuity. Among the major US corporations who invested in Germany during the 1920s were Ford, General Motors, General Electric, Standard Oil, Texaco, International Harvester, ITT, and IBM—all of whom were more than happy to see the German labor movement and working-class parties smashed. For many of these companies, operations in Germany continued during the war (even if it meant the use of concentration-camp slave labor) with overt US government support.

"Pilots were given instructions not to hit factories in Germany that were owned by US firms," says author Michael Parenti. "Thus Cologne was almost leveled by Allied bombing but its Ford plant, providing military equipment for the Nazi army, was untouched; indeed, German civilians began using the plant as an air raid shelter."

These pre-war business liaisons carried over into the post-war tribunals. "The dominant faction of America's establishment had always opposed bringing Germany's elite to trial," Simpson explained.

Myth #3: The Allies Fought to Liberate the Death Camps

Apologists can pretend that the details of the Holocaust were not known and that if they had been, the US would have intervened, but as Kenneth C. Davis explains, "Prior to the American entry into the war, the Nazi treatment of Jews evoked little more than a weak diplomatic condemnation. It is clear that Roosevelt knew about the treatment of the Jews in Germany and elsewhere in Europe, and about the methodical, systematic destruction of the Jews during the Holocaust. Clearly, saving the Jews and other groups that Hitler was destroying *en masse* was not a critical issue for American war planners."

Indeed, when a resolution was introduced in January 1934 asking the Senate and the President to express "surprise and pain" at the German treatment of the Jews, the resolution never got out of committee.

Such inaction was not reversed even as more specific details began to reach the average American. On October 30, 1939, the *New York Times* wrote of "freight cars…full of people" heading eastward and broached the subject of the "complete elimination of the Jews from European life," which, according to the *Times*, appeared to be "a fixed German policy."

As for the particulars on the Nazi final solution, as early as July 1941, the New York Yiddish dailies offered stories of Jews massacred by Germans in Russia. Three months later, the *New York Times* wrote of eyewitness accounts of 10,000 to 15,000 Jews slaughtered in Galicia. On December 7, 1942, the *London Times* joined the chorus with this observation:

> The question now arises whether the Allied Governments, even now, can do anything to prevent Hitler's threat of extermination from being literally carried out.

The German persecution and mass murder of Eastern European Jews was indeed a poorly kept secret, and the United States and its Allies cannot honestly nor realistically hide behind the excuse of ignorance.

Even when the Nazis themselves initiated proposals to ship Jews from both Germany and Czechoslovakia to Western countries or even Palestine, the Allied nations could never get beyond negotiations, and the rescue plans never materialized.

One particularly egregious example was the 1939 journey of the *St. Louis*. Carrying 1,128 German Jewish refugees from Europe, the ocean liner was turned back by US officials because the German immigration quota had been met. The *St. Louis* then returned to Europe where the refugees found temporary sanctuary in France, Great Britain, Belgium, and the Netherlands. "Most of the émigrés were eventually captured by the Nazis after their invasion of the Low Countries in the spring of 1940 and were shipped to death camps," wrote Jerome Agel and Walter D. Glanze.

Myth #4: The Attack on Pearl Harbor Was a Surprise

Especially after the attack on Pearl Harbor, Japan had a reputation of being "treacherous," a tag that justified many war crimes and lasted well past the bombing of Hiroshima and Nagasaki. However, before accepting such a racist stereotype someone should have at least provided some evidence of treachery.

As historian Thomas A. Bailey has written: "Franklin Roosevelt repeatedly deceived the American people during the period before Pearl Harbor…. He was like the physician who must tell the patient lies for the patient's own good."

The diplomatic record reveals some of what Dr. Roosevelt neglected to tell his easily-deluded patients in that now-mythical "Date of Infamy" speech:

December 14, 1940: Joseph Grew, US Ambassador to Japan, sends a letter to FDR, announcing that, "It seems to me increasingly clear that we are bound to have a showdown [with Japan] some day."

December 30, 1940: Pearl Harbor is considered so likely a target of Japanese attack that Rear Admiral Claude C. Bloch, Commander of the Fourteenth Naval District, authors a memorandum entitled, "Situation Concerning the Security of the Fleet and the Present Ability of the Local Defense Forces to Meet Surprise Attacks."

January 27, 1941: Grew (in Tokyo) sends a dispatch to the State Department: "My Peruvian Colleague told a member of my staff that the Japanese military forces planned, in the event of trouble with the United States, to attempt a surprise mass attack on Pearl Harbor using all of their military facilities."

February 5, 1941: Bloch's December 30, 1940, memorandum leads to much discussion and eventually a letter from Rear Admiral Richmond Kelly Turner to Secretary of War Henry Stimson in which Turner warns, "The security of the US Pacific Fleet while in Pearl Harbor, and of the Pearl Harbor Naval Base itself, has been under renewed study by the Navy Department and forces afloat for the past several weeks…. If war eventuates with Japan, it is believed easily possible that hostilities would be initiated by a surprise attack upon the Fleet or the Naval Base at Pearl Harbor…. In my opinion, the inherent possibilities of a major disaster to the fleet or naval base warrant taking every step, as rapidly as can be done, that will increase the joint readiness of the Army and Navy to withstand a raid of the character mentioned above."

February 18, 1941: Commander in Chief of the US Pacific Fleet, Admiral Husband E. Kimmel, says, "I feel that a surprise attack on Pearl Harbor is a possibility."

September 11, 1941: Kimmel says, "A strong Pacific Fleet is unquestionably a deterrent to Japan—a weaker one may be an invitation."

November 25, 1941: Secretary of War Henry L. Stimson writes in his diary that, "The President…brought up entirely the relations with the Japanese. He brought up the event that we're likely to be attacked [as soon as] next Monday for the Japanese are notorious for making an attack without warning."

November 27, 1941: US Army Chief of Staff George C. Marshall issues a memorandum cautioning that, "Japanese future action unpredictable but hostile action possible at any moment. If hostilities cannot…be avoided, the United States desires that Japan commit the first overt action."

November 29, 1941: Secretary of State Cordell Hull, responding to a speech by Japanese General Hideki Tojo one week before the attack, phones FDR at Warm Springs, Georgia, to warn of "the imminent danger of a Japanese attack," and urge him to return to Washington sooner than planned.

Regardless of this record, there were still racists within the US military and government who never imagined that Japan could orchestrate such a successful offensive. Few Westerners took the Japanese seriously, with journalists regularly referring to them as "apes in khaki" during the early months of their con-

Shortly after the attack, with the image of a uniquely treacherous enemy spread throughout America, Admiral William Halsey—soon to become Commander of the South Pacific Force—vowed that by the end of the war, "Japanese would be spoken only in hell." His favorite slogan, "Kill Japs, kill Japs, kill more Japs," echoed the sentiments of Admiral William D. Leahy, Chair of the Joint Chiefs of Staff, who wrote that, "in fighting with Japanese savages, all previously accepted rules of warfare must be abandoned."

Myth #5: Only the Axis Nations Committed War Crimes

In the Pacific theater, the aforementioned General Curtis LeMay was head of the Twenty-first Bomber Command. Acting upon Marshall's 1941 idea of torching the poorer areas of Japan's cities, on the night of March 9–10, 1945, LeMay's bombers laid siege on Tokyo, where tightly-packed wooden buildings were assaulted by 1,665 tons of incendiaries. LeMay later recalled that a few explosives had been mixed in with the

It is believed that more people died from fire in a six-hour time period than ever before in the history of mankind.

quest of Southeast Asia. The simian metaphor was maintained thereafter. This racist attitude continued as the two sides approached war—with unexpected consequences

"Most American military minds expected a Japanese attack to come in the Philippines, America's major base in the Pacific," writes Kenneth C. Davis. "Many Americans, including Roosevelt, dismissed the Japanese as combat pilots because they were all presumed to be 'near-sighted.'… There was also a sense that any attack on Pearl Harbor would be easily repulsed." Such an attitude appears even more ludicrous in light of the pre-Pearl Harbor record of the Japanese fighter pilots flying the world's most advanced fighter plane, the Mitsubishi Zero. "The first actual combat test of the Zero occurred in September 1940," reports historian John W. Dower, "when thirteen of the planes downed twenty-seven Chinese aircraft in ten minutes." By August 31, 1941, thirty Japanese Zeros "accounted for 266 confirmed kills in China." Still, the American military planners were somehow shocked by the skill displayed by the Japanese at Pearl Harbor.

incendiaries to demoralize firefighters (96 fire engines burned to ashes and 88 firemen died).

One Japanese doctor recalled "countless bodies" floating in the Sumida River. These bodies were "as black as charcoal" and indistinguishable as men or women. The total dead for one night was an estimated 85,000, with 40,000 injured and one million left homeless. This was only the first strike in a fire-bombing campaign that dropped 250 tons of bombs per square mile, destroying 40 percent of the surface area in 66 death-list cities (including Hiroshima and Nagasaki). The attack area was 87.4 percent residential.

It is believed that more people died from fire in a six-hour time period than ever before in the history of mankind. At ground zero, the temperature reached 1800° Fahrenheit. Flames from the ensuing inferno were visible for 200 miles. Due to the intense heat, canals boiled over, metals melted, and human beings burst spontaneously into flames.

By May 1945, 75 percent of the bombs being dropped on

About a dozen or more American POWs were killed in Hiroshima, a truth that remained hidden for some 30 years.

Japan were incendiaries. Cheered on by the likes of *Time* magazine—which explained that "properly kindled, Japanese cities will burn like autumn leaves"—LeMay's campaign took an estimated 672,000 lives.

Radio Tokyo termed LeMay's tactics "slaughter bombing" and the Japanese press declared that through the fire raids:

> America has revealed her barbaric character... It was an attempt at mass murder of women and children.... The action of the Americans is all the more despicable because of the noisy pretensions they constantly make about their humanity and idealism.... No one expects war to be anything but a brutal business, but it remains for the Americans to make it systematically and unnecessarily a wholesale horror for innocent victims.

Rather than denying this, a spokesman for the Fifth Air Force categorized "the entire population of Japan [as] a proper military target." Colonel Harry F. Cunningham explained the US policy in no uncertain terms:

> We military men do not pull punches or put on Sunday School picnics. We are making War and making it in the all-out fashion which saves American lives, shortens the agony which War is and seeks to bring about an enduring Peace. We intend to seek out and destroy the enemy wherever he or she is, in the greatest possible numbers, in the shortest possible time. For us, THERE ARE NO CIVILIANS IN JAPAN.

On the morning of August 6, 1945, before the Hiroshima story broke, a page-one headline in the *Atlanta Constitution* read: "580 B-29s RAIN FIRE ON 4 MORE DEATH-LIST CITIES." Ironically, the success of LeMay's firebombing raids had effectively eliminated Tokyo from the list of possible A-bomb targets—as there was nothing left to bomb.

Myth #6: The Atomic Bombs Dropped on Japan Were Necessary

Although hundreds of thousands of Japanese lives were lost in Hiroshima and Nagasaki, the bombings are often explained away as a lifesaving measure—American lives. Exactly how many lives saved is, however, up for grabs. (We do know of a few US soldiers who fell between the cracks. About a dozen or more American POWs were killed in Hiroshima, a truth that remained hidden for some 30 years.)

In an August 9, 1945, statement to "the men and women of the Manhattan Project," President Truman declared the hope that "this new weapon will result in saving thousands of American lives" by aborting a planned US invasion of the Japanese islands.

"The president's initial formulation of 'thousands,' however, was clearly not his final statement on the matter to say the least," remarks historian Gar Alperovitz. In fact, Alperovitz documents but a few of Truman's public estimates throughout the years:

December 15, 1945: "It occurred to me that a quarter of a million of the flower of our young manhood was worth a couple of Japanese cities..."

Late 1946: "A year less of war will mean life for three hundred thousand—maybe half a million—of America's finest youth."

October 1948: "...in the long run we could save a quarter of a million young Americans from being killed, and would save an equal number of Japanese young men from being killed."

April 6, 1949: "...I thought 200,000 of our young men would be saved..."

November 1949: Truman quotes Army Chief of Staff George S. Marshall as estimating the cost of an Allied invasion of Japan to be "half a million casualties."

January 12, 1953: Still quoting Marshall, Truman raises the estimate to "a minimum one quarter of a million" and maybe "as much as a million, on the American side alone, with an equal number of the enemy."

It was widely known at the time that Japan had been trying to surrender for months prior to the atomic bombing.

Finally, on April 28, 1959, Truman concluded: "the dropping of the bombs...saved millions of lives."

Winston Churchill proclaimed that the Allies "now had something in [their] hands which would redress the balance with the Russians." He topped Truman's ceiling by exclaiming how those A-bombs spared well over 1.2 million Allied lives.

Fortunately, we are not operating without the benefit of official estimates.

In June 1945, President Truman ordered the US military to calculate the cost in American lives for a planned assault on Japan. Consequently, the Joint War Plans Committee prepared a report for the Chiefs of Staff, dated June 15, 1945, thus providing the closest thing anyone has to "accurate": 40,000 US soldiers killed, 150,000 wounded, and 3,500 missing.

■ ■ ■ ■ ■ ■ ■ ■ ■ ■

While the actual casualty count remains unknowable, it was widely known at the time that Japan had been trying to surrender for months prior to the atomic bombing. A May 5, 1945, cable, intercepted and decoded by the US, "dispelled any possible doubt that the Japanese were eager to sue for peace." In fact, the United States Strategic Bombing Survey reported, shortly after the war, that Japan "in all probability" would have surrendered *before* the much-discussed November 1, 1945, Allied invasion of the homeland, thereby saving all kinds of lives.

Truman himself eloquently noted in his diary that Stalin would "be in the Jap War on August 15th. Fini [*sic*] Japs when that comes about."

Clearly, Truman saw the bombs as way to end the war before the Soviet Union could claim a major role in Japan's terms of surrender. However, one year after Hiroshima and Nagasaki, a top-secret US study concluded that the Japanese surrender was based more upon Stalin's declaration of war than either of the atomic bombs.

Myth #7: WWII Was Fought to End Fascism

Even before the CIA was the CIA, it was acting an awful lot like the CIA. According to Christopher Simpson—the journalist who has perhaps done more work than any other in the area of US recruitment of ex-Nazis—an August 16, 1983, Justice Department report "acknowledged that a US intelligence agency known as the Army Counterintelligence Corps (CIC) had recruited Schutzstaffel (SS) and Gestapo officer Klaus Barbie for espionage work in early 1947; that the CIC had hidden him from French war crimes investigators; and that it had then spirited him out of Europe through a clandestine 'ratline'—escape route—run by a priest who was himself a fugitive from war crimes charges."

The report went on to state that the CIC agents had no idea at the time what Barbie had done during the war (apparently, having to hide him from French war crimes investigators didn't set off any alarms), and that Barbie was the only such war criminal that the US had protected.

Let's examine the specious claim that the Butcher of Lyon was the only former Nazi welcomed into the American espionage fold.

"The pattern was set," writes Noam Chomsky, "in the first area liberated by US forces, North Africa, where in 1942 the US placed in power Admiral Jean Darlan, a leading Nazi collaborator who was the author of the Vichy regime's anti-Semitic laws." Even WWII's official historian, Stephen Ambrose, has admitted:

> The result was that in its first major foreign-policy venture in World War II, the United States gave its support to a man who stood for everything Roosevelt and Churchill had spoken out against in the Atlantic Charter. As much as Goering or Goebbels, Darlan was the antithesis of the principles the Allies said they were struggling to establish.

Darlan was merely the first step in a premeditated program of collaboration with notorious war criminals.

■ ■ ■ ■ ■ ■ ■ ■ ■ ■

"I am a general and chief of the intelligence department of the High Command of the German Army. I have information of the highest importance for your Supreme Commander and the American government, and I must be taken immediately to your senior commander."

It was with these words that General Reinhard Gehlen, Hitler's notorious eastern front espionage chief, began his relationship with the Office of Strategic Services (OSS) and the budding US intelligence community. As the OSS was transformed into the Central Intelligence Agency (CIA), yet another of many dark alliances emerged.

After surrendering on May 22, 1945, Gehlen, or "Reinhard the Fox," was eventually interviewed by OSS founders "Wild" Bill Donovon and Allen Dulles after flying to Washington in the uniform of a US general. According to his biographer, Leonard Mosley, Dulles recommended that the Nazi superspy be given a budget of $3.5 million and "set up in business as the supplier of Russian and east European intelligence." But the shrewd Gehlen had some conditions:

1. His organization would not be regarded as part of the American intelligence services but as an autonomous apparatus under his exclusive management. Liaison with American intelligence would be maintained by a US officer whose selection Gehlen would approve.

2. The Gehlen Organization would be used solely to procure intelligence on the Soviet Union and the satellite countries of the communist bloc.

3. Upon the establishment of a German government, the organization would be transferred to it and all previous agreements and arrangements cancelled, subject to discussions between the new sovereign authority and the United States.

4. Nothing detrimental or contrary to German interests must be required or expected from the organization, nor must it be called upon for security activities against Germans in West Germany.

Considering that Gehlen was essentially a prisoner of war who could have been brought up on war crimes, these demands were remarkable. Even more remarkable, at first blush, is the fact that the US complied. However, when viewed through the prism of the rapidly escalating Cold War, a Nazi-CIA alliance becomes rather predictable.

With German defeat imminent, Gehlen instructed several members of his staff to microfilm intelligence on the USSR beginning in March 1945. After secretly burying this material throughout the Austrian Alps, Gehlen and his men sought a deal.

Upon his surrender, Gehlen was taken to Fort Hunt, Virginia, where he convinced his US counterparts that the Soviets were

"A US intelligence agency known as the Army Counterintelligence Corps (CIC) had recruited Schutzstaffel (SS) and Gestapo officer Klaus Barbie for espionage work in early 1947."

planning a westward expansion. Before the end of 1945, Gehlen and most of his high command were freed from POW camps and ready to supply what rabid American cold warriors were dying to hear.

"Gehlen had to make his money by creating a threat that we were afraid of, so we would give him more money to tell us about it," explains Victor Marchetti, formerly the CIA's chief analyst of Soviet strategic war plans and capabilities.

When Allen Dulles became CIA Director in 1953 (brother John was already Eisenhower's Secretary of State by that time), his response to the claim that Gehlen, a known Nazi war criminal, was purposely intensifying the Cold War and influencing American public opinion was:

> I don't know if he's a rascal. There are few archbishops in espionage.... Besides, one needn't ask him to one's club.

Myth #8: The Legacy of WWII Is "Good"

The "Good War" had been won. Now what? Well, besides actively recruiting Nazis and bringing humanity to the brink of nuclear Armageddon, the winners did have a plan. An internal document, written in 1948 by George Kennan, head of the State Department planning staff in the early post-war period, highlights the philosophy behind the US strategy:

…we have about 50% of the world's wealth, but only 6.3% of its population…. In this situation, we cannot fail to be the object of envy and resentment. Our real task in the coming period is to devise a pattern of relationships which will permit us to maintain this position of disparity without positive detriment to our national security. To do so, we will have to dispense with all sentimentality and day-dreaming; and our attention will have to be concentrated everywhere on our immediate national objectives. We need not deceive ourselves that we can afford today the luxury of altruism and world-benefaction…. We should cease to talk about vague and—for the Far East—unreal objectives [such] as human rights, the raising of living standards, and democratization. The day is not far off when we are going to have to deal in straight power concepts. The less we are then hampered by idealistic slogans, the better.

Thus the post-war era and the age of Cold War propaganda commenced—driven by corporate globalism and virulent anti-communism. The few years spent fighting fascism during WWII were essentially nothing more than a subtle diversion from a larger war to control resources and smash any ideology deemed incompatible with that control. When the dust had cleared, fascism had survived the saturation bombings, the genocide, and the atomic weapons to rise again in a new, more insidious form. The development of the highly unaccountable multinational corporation is one of the saddest legacies of WWII.

so it becomes necessary to create the false arguments discussed earlier. This helps explain how the Department of War was reborn as the Defense Department after WWII.

■ ■ ■ ■ ■ ■ ■ ■ ■ ■

Much of this is possible because the "Good War" myth granted the US the freedom to intervene practically at will across the globe. After all, who could question Uncle Sam's motives when his boys had just saved the world from Hitler? Upon the end of the Cold War and the defeat of yet another evil empire, the Soviet deterrent essentially vanished. This development provided further latitude for the US to frame its military actions as humanitarian, as part of a democratic new world order forged on the battlefields of WWII and affirmed during the Cold War. America is simply defending freedom, we're told, and who could possibly be against freedom?

Saving Private Ryan and *The Greatest Generation* can only serve to reinforce this form of denial by preying upon a citizenry wishing to believe the best about its country. Such books, films, and other forms of pop culture help provide cover for the rich and powerful who seek global dominion through imperialism and warfare while simultaneously keeping much of the general public fragmented and uninformed about alternatives.

However, those who view such manipulation as inescapable, insurmountable, and perhaps even necessary are yet again ignoring the historical record by underestimating the inspirational power of collective human action.

These excerpts represent a fraction of the information exposed in Saving Private Power: The Hidden History of "The Good War" *(published by Soft Skull Press). The book also includes over 300 endnotes and an extensive bibliography.*

The development of the highly unaccountable multinational corporation is one of the saddest legacies of WWII.

Accordingly, Australian scholar Alex Carey has noted the three developments of great political importance that characterize the twentieth century: "…the growth of democracy, the growth of corporate power, and the growth of corporate propaganda as a means of protecting corporate power against democracy." Simply, democratic institutions can hinder the pursuit of capital,

What I Didn't Know About the Communist Conspiracy
Jim Martin

After fifteen years of selling conspiracy books, I took a year off from Flatland in 1999 and concentrated on completing my own book, *Wilhelm Reich and the Cold War*. I had been researching the topic ever since I became aware of the suppressed biography of Reich in 1983. Reich, who died in a US prison in 1957, believed that he was the victim of a communist conspiracy. Little credence was given to this suspicion of Reich's even by his most sympathetic biographers.[1]

After the collapse of the Soviet Union, new evidence about the extent of its espionage apparatus and wide-ranging conspiratorial activities came to light. It will take some years to sort out the data—for a brief time the internal files of the KGB were opened to Western scholars, and everyone is hoping they will become available again, just as we hope for new documents from the US government. In the last few years, a small bookcase of new history books was published in rapid succession, and a picture emerged that requires us to rethink Cold War history. I was certainly surprised by the developments, having known next to nothing about the Cambridge Five, the Silvermaster Ring, the Ware Group, and many other conspirators prior to research for my book.

To make the long story of my book short, Wilhelm Reich underestimated the importance of the role of Soviet intelligence in the suppression of his work, the burning of his books, and his death in prison.

I was predisposed, admittedly, to hear bad things about the Soviet Union. But I was shocked to see exactly what's been going on. After making a survey of about 20 new books on the Cold War, I reached a fundamentally new understanding of post-war history.

Here are a few of the highlights of what I learned:

I have in my hand a list of 349 Americans and US residents who had a covert relationship with Soviet Intelligence agencies during World War II and beyond. No, I didn't find this list rummaging through old "Tailgunner" Joe McCarthy's laundry basket. It's right here in John Earl Haynes and Harvey Klehr's *Venona*, published in 1999 and examining for the first time in detail a set of decoded Soviet cable traffic during the 1940s that reveals hundreds of average citizens, soldiers, government officials, and courtiers to the White House. Each one actively engaged in two jobs: one for the public, and one for a vast, international communist conspiracy directed from Moscow. One recurring phrase in the discussions of the intelligence officers when criticizing agents in the field: "politically incorrect."

The body count. Being politically incorrect in Russia did not earn you a radio show, but only a bullet in the neck. In France, *The Black Book of Communism* appeared in 1997; in 1999 it

> They tabulate the number of people killed by communist regimes around the world at just under 100 million.

was translated into English. It's a gut-wrenching book, and it provoked a deep public controversy in France, where many communist politicians were freely elected. The authors, who at one time or another considered themselves as partisans of some variant of communism, make an incredibly detailed survey of the "crimes, terror and repression" of the world communist movement. They tabulate the number of people killed by communist regimes around the world at just under 100 million.[2] Well-researched and tightly documented, *The Black Book of Communism* is worth reading and begs an ongoing question debated today, throughout the world: What are the basic differences between Soviet and Nazi totalitarianism, if any?

Was Stalinism different than Leninism? The historians say, "No." Stalin's reign was a continuation of Lenin's aggressive policies. It's too simplistic to portray Stalin as a madman who corrupted the essentially socialist policies of Lenin. What's more interesting is the overwhelming appeal of the authoritarian program. This appeal wasn't limited to Russia, but gained millions of adherents across the globe.

"I've got a sock full of shit and I know how to use it." So said Senator Joe McCarthy, who never exposed a single Soviet spy during his tenure in Congress. By the time McCarthy was elected to the Senate in 1948, the Army's Signal

These messages revealed an extensive Soviet espionage apparatus operating in Washington, New York, and San Francisco throughout the war years.

Intelligence Special Branch had already decoded significant portions of Soviet wartime cable traffic. These messages revealed an extensive Soviet espionage apparatus operating in Washington, New York, and San Francisco throughout the war years. The FBI, working in cooperation with cryptoanalysts at the National Security Agency, had identified many US government officials at a wide range of federal agencies. Most were quietly removed from their positions, and were not prosecuted because the evidence against them was entirely based on the decrypted cable traffic—and the Army intelligence command was loath to reveal its sources. President Truman, along with the American public, was initially unaware of the information from the Army's VENONA Project, but the Soviets knew that their codes had been broken and discontinued many of the spy rings as a result.

The entire McCarthyite spymania was pointless, and could have been cleared up by 1952 if only the results of the decoded VENONA messages had been revealed. The subtext of McCarthy's rant, however, had a large kernel of truth: All Communist Party USA (CPUSA) members were potential spies, insofar as they submitted to "party discipline." Liberal New Deal Democrats were quite supportive of the "Soviet experiment" and protected pro-Soviet conspirators within the Roosevelt Administration. These agents stole sensitive government documents and worked hard at influencing US foreign policy in favor of the USSR. Yet even as McCarthy belatedly railed against the communist conspiracy, the USSR had long since rolled up many of its agents in the US government after the defection of Elizabeth Bentley in 1945. After that time,

there was a steep incline in the severity with which the US dealt with the traitors, culminating with the execution of the Rosenbergs. Still, to protect the VENONA secret, they avoided bringing charges against known spies where the decrypts were the only proof.

First, the basics. Alger Hiss was a paid, ideologically-committed agent of Soviet intelligence. Whittaker Chambers was a reliable witness. Ethel and Julius Rosenberg were deeply involved with atomic espionage and certainly knew what kinds of risks they had taken. The Manhattan Project was rife with Soviet agents, sources, and sympathizers who designed, built, and deployed a $2 billion superweapon to fight "black" fascism, gave the plans for the atom bomb to the "red" fascists, and then handed the American taxpayer the tab. Aside from the Rosenbergs, most dangerous espionage agents in the US received little retribution or punishment beyond losing high-paying jobs as government bureaucrats.

The Consumers Union: A front group? During the 1930s, the International Communist Movement, as embodied by the Comintern, and directed from the Soviet Union, abruptly changed policy and endorsed cooperation with other social-change organizations after many years of attacking everybody else on the left. The hitch was that Party members should only "work with" organizations insofar as they secretly directed them from within. Thus many "Popular Front Organizations" became home to liberals, socialists, and fellow travelers, many of whom were unaware of the secret leadership.

When I was younger, one of the examples for the McCarthyite excess our history teachers gave us was that the Consumers Union, publisher of the highly popular *Consumers Reports* magazine, had been placed on an official blacklist of organizations with ties to the Communist Party back in the McCarthy Era. We all laughed—imagine that, the stodgy consumers advocate group linked to the communist conspiracy. Well, imagine no more—Consumers Union formed in 1936 as a CPUSA splinter-group after a violent strike against the original group, Consumers' Research, Inc. Enraged by the tactics used by the strikers, the leadership devoted the rest of their organizational lives charting the subversive links of Consumers Union and its leading lights. Much of the documentation was later used by the House Un-American Activities Committee, where former Consumers' Research board member J. B. Matthews served as an advisor and investigator. Matthews, a liberal with a long history in left politics, coined the term "fellow traveler" to describe the non-Party supporters of the Stalinist regime.

The Consumers Union developed into a massive fundraising nonprofit, with enormous influence as a lobby with the FDA and other federal agencies. One employee at the Consumers Union served as an operation-courier in the Soviet assassination of Trotsky in Mexico. Today, an amazing archival trove resides at Rutgers University's special collections library, including detailed files on Ralph Nader. I have yet to see Nader's files, and can't comment on whether Ralph was personally allied with the CPUSA. Without doubt, at least some of the people he worked for in his early career with Consumers Union were covert operators.[3]

The House Un-American Activities Committee—brought to us by an agent of Soviet Intelligence. Samuel Dickstein, who served as US Congressman from New York from 1923 until 1944, was a paid informant and "agent of influence" whose code-name was "Crook" in view of his incessant

after testifying before Congress, where he denied charges of "disloyalty." While functioning as a paid Soviet agent within the Department of Treasury, White wrote much of the Bretton Woods Agreement which formed the International Monetary Fund and the World Bank. (How many of our young anti-globalism protesters are aware of this? Most establishment historians have yet to factor in the recent revelations regarding the Soviet conspiracy with postwar internationalist institutions such as the UN, whose first General Secretary was none other than Alger Hiss.)

White's proposal to lend the USSR $10 billion at an annual rate of 2 percent was rejected by the State Department, but no matter; White was able to provide the Russians with the plates, ink, and paper samples for post-war German occupation currency.[7] Cost to the American taxpayer is unknown, but estimated to be in the millions of dollars.

The Al Gores and Armand Hammer. Al Gore, Sr. served as the political bagman for millionaire communist Armand Hammer for a large part of his career. Hammer's father, Dr. Julius Hammer, was one of the earliest American supporters of the Bolshevik regime and a personal friend of Lenin's. Armand Hammer learned how to launder money at the feet of his father, who

Liberal New Deal Democrats were quite supportive of the "Soviet experiment" and protected pro-Soviet conspirators within the Roosevelt Administration.

demands for money from his Soviet handlers.[4] In 1934 he drafted a proposal for Congressional inquiries into subversive activities, and became the vice chairman of what became known as "The Committee" investigating pro-Nazi elements, rather than communist subversion, in America. It was Dickstein who introduced the concept of ongoing congressional investigations into what he called "slanderous or libelous un-American propaganda."[5]

It almost happened here. Had President Franklin Roosevelt died one year earlier than he did, or had he not chosen Harry Truman as his running mate in 1944, the pro-Soviet Vice President Henry A. Wallace would have become President in 1945. Wallace told reporters at the time that he would consider Harry Dexter White and Laurance Duggan for appointment to Cabinet positions. Both men spent the war providing Soviet agents with sensitive government documents.[6]

Belly up to the beerhall, comrades, this putsch is on the Americans. Harry Dexter White died of a heart attack shortly

was the first conduit between Moscow and the CPUSA. Edward Jay Epstein's exposé about Hammer, titled *Dossier*, examines the ingenious techniques of money laundering, and one example remains enshrined in my mind: Armand toured the entire country throughout the 1920s and sold Tsarist collectibles, including vast numbers of Fabergé Eggs, at bargain prices, in every major city's department stores. Of course, many of them were fake. The money went straight to Lenin, whose young dictatorship suffered for hard currency.

Armand went on to develop a career as a go-get-'em American capitalist with an uncanny ability to extract complicated yet profitable venture capital deals with the Soviet Union. As the leading proponent of doing business with the USSR, Armand Hammer advised many American Presidents, including Richard Nixon. As time went on, Hammer came to relish his role as a wheeler-dealer and worked more or less independently of his former collectivist masters. It wasn't so much that he was greedy, but his whole life was devoted to covert chicanery, and old habits are hard to break.

Had President Franklin Roosevelt died one year earlier than he did, the pro-Soviet Vice President Henry A. Wallace would have become President in 1945.

Al Gore, Sr. was still on the board of directors of Hammer's Occidental Petroleum in 1997 at the age of 88. Al Gore the younger appeared publicly with his father's patron, Armand Hammer, up until Hammer's death.[8]

Only the poor die young. In 1990 the only surviving member of the original Bolshevik Party, the one that took over Russia in 1917, besides Armand Hammer, was the Russian physicist and musician who, like Prince and Madonna, went by a single name. Theremin invented the first electronic instrument, the one which bears his name and can still be heard in the opening bars of the Beach Boy's "Good Vibrations" and also in bad Cold-War-era sci-fi movies. After a long term in the gulags, Theremin emerged as a darling in the West, and died in his nineties after his apartment was ransacked by thugs in Moscow. All the other old members of the Party who seized the state apparatus in 1918 were dead by then. Both survivors, Hammer and Theremin, died millionaires.[9]

Don't touch that dial. There are uncounted caches of radios and arms protected by booby traps hidden around the US and the rest of the world, placed there decades ago by Soviet agents in anticipation of world revolution.[10]

I have a nightmare. Yuri Modin, former controller of the Cambridge Five spy ring (Philby, Burgess, Blunt, Maclean, and Cairncross), was assigned to conduct "active measures" against Martin Luther King in August 1967, to discredit him in the eyes of the public and bolster the support of pro-Soviet black radicals such as Stokely Carmichael.[11] King was the only American to be the victim of KGB *and* FBI special operations.

Messin' with our heads. Mark Lane, author of the best-selling Kennedy assassination conspiracy book, *Rush to Judgment*, received money and information from the KGB—probably without Lane realizing the true source—while researching his book. The KGB had spent a great deal of money on American conspiracy theorists to promote the idea that Kennedy was assassinated by the CIA and right-wing

elements. (The 1970 "Torbitt Document"[12] is undoubtedly one fruit of such efforts.)

In 1975, at the time of the Watergate investigations, the KGB produced a forged letter, purportedly written by Lee Harvey Oswald the night before the assassination, to a "Mr. Hunt"—the KGB intended to implicate E. Howard Hunt, one of the Watergate conspirators. They sent the letter to three "conspiracy buffs"—who, significantly, did not rise to the bait and didn't publish the document. A while later the *New York Times* published the forgery announcing that handwriting experts had confirmed its authenticity. (Conspiracy Buffs: 3, *New York Times*: 0.)

The Soviets spent millions of dollars on these kinds of "active measures." The highly popular anti-CIA magazine published in the late 1970s and 1980s, *Covert Action Intelligence Bulletin*, was founded by a defector from the CIA, Philip Agee, and bankrolled by the KGB. I myself was a regular reader of *Covert Action* during the Reagan years, and indeed I wondered where they were getting their information. We know now that V. N. Kosterin from the KGB's Service A (propaganda and disinformation section) had been assigned to keep the journal supplied with material. You can read all about it in Christopher Andrew's *The Sword and the Shield: The Mitrokhin Archive*.[13] Philip Agee's popular book, *Inside the Company*, was written with the support and assistance of both Soviet and Cuban intelligence agencies.

AIDS and biowarfare. Up until 1987, the Soviet press promulgated the theory that AIDS was a bioweapon developed at Fort Detrick. When Mikhail Gorbachev announced that, as a part of *glasnost* and *perestroika*, the Soviets would renounce disinformation tactics, the Soviet officials quietly notified US diplomats in Moscow that they had disowned the AIDS story, and the press campaign abruptly ceased.[14] Of course, this fact doesn't rule out the possibility of some type of relationship between

While functioning as a paid Soviet agent within the Department of Treasury, White wrote much of the Bretton Woods Agreement which formed the International Monetary Fund and the World Bank.

AIDS and biowarfare, as practiced around the globe.

Sandinistas invaded California. As early as 1966, the Sandinista National Liberation Front (FSLN) provided guerrillas for elaborate KGB sabotage teams along the US-Mexico border in cities like Ensenada and Tijuana. The targets of the sab-teams included California oil pipelines and radar installations; they set up networks for smuggling agents and munitions through infiltration of migrant laborers. Recon teams staffed by Sandinistas and coordinated by the KGB crossed the border and identified landing sites and large ammo-dumps along the coast in anticipation of war between the US and the USSR in Europe.[15] Other KGB sabotage and intelligence teams were arrayed along the Canadian border; in 1967 they scouted border crossings and identified targets including Montana's Flathead Dam and hydroelectric systems in New York and Pennsylvania.

> The targets of the KGB sab-teams included California oil pipelines and radar installations.

■ ■ ■ ■ ■ ■ ■ ■ ■ ■

I should stress that the information presented here is based on the best evidence I could find, and that new information is coming in all the time. One of the most time-consuming aspects of the process will be sorting out the river of data and coordinating it with old references published long ago and now forgotten. Even the best historians with the latest information can't foresee the future impact of this incredible material, released from both sides of the former Iron Curtain to a bewildered public.

Let's take one example from the 1930s.

Most books on the Cambridge Five place a man named Arnold Deutsch at the center of the conspiracy to recruit young University students at Cambridge—generally regarded as the most profitable long-term espionage effort in recorded history. Deutsch recruited at least 25 spies in London in the 1930s. Among his pupils: Kim Philby, Guy Burgess, Donald Maclean, Michael Straight, Anthony Blunt, Elizabeth Tudor Hart, Litzi Friedman, and other unnamed agents. Not only did Deutsch originate the plan of seducing well-connected sons of the British establishment for careers in the NKVD, but he accomplished it using Wilhelm Reich's techniques of character analysis, and a promise of a Soviet reality that coincided with

Reich's own hopes for a "sexual revolution." Deutsch and several other Viennese radicals played a significant role with USSR intelligence as well as in Reich's "sex-pol" clinics—first organized in 1927 for the education and psychoanalytic treatment of working people at little or no fees. Deutsch was killed in the early 1940s, but serious discrepancies between several stories of his death remain, variants with multiple "witness statements."

Reich repudiated communism between 1931 and 1936. Nobody so far has come clean about the Reich-Deutsch connection. The historians of the "West and East" are silent about these contradictions, for now. I see the story of Wilhelm Reich's relationship—friend, tutor, and coworker—with Arnold Deutsch as a linchpin of any understanding of the Cold War era.

Finally, it's remarkable that so much information has been coming out of the Russian archives, while the US President's Executive Order that the CIA, FBI, and NSA release all documents older than 30 years has largely been ignored.

New Books on Soviet Espionage

Albright, Joseph & Marcia Kunstel. (1997). *Bombshell: The secret story of America's unknown atomic spy conspiracy*. New York: Times Books, 1st edition.
The story of Ted Hall, teenage atom spy.

Andrew, Christopher & Vasili Mitrokhin. (1999). *The sword and the shield: The Mitrokhin archive and the secret history of the KGB*. New York: Basic Books.
Retired KGB officer and archivist Mitrokhin defected from the former Soviet Union, with trunkloads of secret KGB documents dating back to 1918. His notes and copied documents have been verified by independent sources. Andrew is the chair of the History Department at Cambridge University.

Haynes, John Earl & Harvey Klehr. (1999). *Venona: Decoding Soviet espionage in America*. New Haven, CT: Yale University Press.
The VENONA decrypts were released by the National Security Agency and verified by comparison to the Russian originals; a crucial study.

Klehr, Harvey, John Earl Haynes & Fridrikh Igorevich Firsov. (1995). *The secret world of American communism*. New Haven, CT: Yale University Press.
Based on files released in Russia, a detailed account of the Soviet funding for the CPUSA and its role in recruiting spies among Party members.

What I Didn't Know About the Communist Conspiracy
Jim Martin

Klehr, Harvey & Ronald Radosh. (1996). *The Amerasia case: Prelude to McCarthyism*. Chapel Hill, NC: University of North Carolina Press.
First Soviet espionage case predates the end of WWII, sets off the Cold War in 1945.

Schwartz, Stephen. (1998). *From East to West: California and the making of the American mind*. New York: The Free Press.
A quirky and important history of California with special emphasis on the role of California CPUSA members in atomic espionage.

Sudoplatov, Pavel & Anatoli; with Jerrold L. and Leona Schecter. (1994). *Special tasks: The memoirs of an unwanted witness—a Soviet spymaster*. New York: Little, Brown.
How to keep your nose clean when you're up to your eyeballs in blood, by a former Soviet intelligence officer who plotted to kill Trotsky.

Tannenhaus, Sam. (1997). *Whittaker Chambers*. New York: Random House.
They used to say Whittaker Chambers was crazy, queer, and built a typewriter to frame Alger Hiss.

Weinstein, Allen & Alexander Vassiliev. (1999). *The haunted wood: Soviet espionage in America—the Stalin era*. New York: Random House, 1st edition.
Incorporates much of the VENONA documentation, takes an overview of the influence of the USSR's espionage on American history. Probably the most enjoyable read of the bunch.

Endnotes

1. See Sharaf, Myron. (1983). *Fury on earth*. New York: St. Martin's; Greenfield, Jerome. (1974). *Wilhelm Reich vs the USA*. New York: Norton. **2.** Courtois, Stéphan, et al. (1999). *The black book of communism*. Cambridge: Harvard University Press. **3.** Martin, Jim. (2000). *Wilhelm Reich and the Cold War*. Fort Bragg, CA: Flatland, p 279ff. **4.** Weinstein, Allen & Alexander Vassiliev. (1999). *The haunted wood: Soviet espionage in America—the Stalin era*. New York: Random House, p 142. **5.** Goodman, Walter. (1964). *The Committee*. New York: Farrar, Straus and Giroux, p 14. **6.** Haynes, John Earl & Harvey Klehr. (1999). *Venona: Decoding Soviet espionage in America*. New Haven, CT: Yale University Press, p 139. **7.** Andrew, Christopher & Oleg Gordievsky. (1990). *KGB: The inside story*. New York: HarperCollins, p 336. **8.** Epstein, Edward Jay. (1999). *Dossier*. New York: Carroll & Graf. **9.** Radzhinsky, Edvard. (1997). *Stalin*. New York: Anchor. **10.** Andrew, Christopher & Vasili Mitrokhin. (1999). *The sword and the shield: The Mitrokhin archive and the secret history of the KGB*. New York: Basic Books, chapter 22. **11.** *Ibid.*, p 237. **12.** see Thomas, Kenn (Ed.). (1996). *NASA, Nazis & JFK: The Torbitt document & the JFK assassination*. Kempton, IL: Adventures Unlimited Press. **13.** *Op cit.*, Andrew & Vasili, p 233. **14.** *Ibid.*, p 245. **15.** *Ibid.*, p 363.

Dreaming Up America, Reel One
The Earliest Signs of an American Sensibility
Russell Banks

In Dreaming Up America *(Seven Stories Press, 2008), international-prize-winning writer Russell Banks—known primarily for his novels, including* Cloudsplitter, Affliction, *and* The Sweet Hereafter—*discusses the United States' sense of self, its purpose, and how various forces have shaped what the country has been and has become. The book grew from a French documentary in which Banks offered a "corrective" to the image of America that comes through in its films;* Dreaming Up America *is an edited transcript of Banks' answers to the director's off-camera questions.*

Banks pays particular attention to the so-called American Dream, noting that "the path to the American Dream has become a tortured path. It has led to our building an empire. The small engine of one person's dream of starting over has somehow morphed into the mighty engine of Manifest Destiny, of empire. From that point of view, it may be a psychotic dream, no less powerful for that—more powerful, rather, but unhealthy, an expression of dysfunction and disease. It is psychotic, in a way, to think that you can start your life over, that there's no such thing as the past. It's a kind of madness to think that you can always improve your life, financially, economically, generation after generation, with each generation succeeding further, and not recognize that this is simply an impossibility, one that ultimately, inevitably, like any Ponzi scheme, will lead to failure. And the economic demands and expectations that back this distorted dream are always going to be in conflict with the ideals of democracy. They demand and expect one person to trample on another. This conflicts with the democratic ideals in our sacred documents and in our hearts." In chapter one, below, he ruminates on how the Dream started.

Before we start to think or talk seriously about our American values, there are a few things I want to say about the first colonists, the first Europeans residing in North America. We have to remember that they came from different parts of Europe and that they came to North America with very different ideas about what they wanted to do here. The English colonists came to New England in search of religious freedom, with a fundamentalist Protestant vision of their own mission and with their own religious and political agenda. The Dutch came to the area where I live— New York, Manhattan, the Hudson Valley—strictly for commercial reasons, to fish and to trade for beaver and lumber, not for reasons of religion or freedom or politics. The Spanish sailed into the Caribbean, to Florida, to the coast of the Gulf of Mexico, and into Mexico for gold, and had no particular ambitions to make a community or colony.

There were all these different motives and very different values associated with each of them. At the very beginning of the colonization of America—which we'll do well to remember wasn't the same as the beginning of America, since the place these Europeans "discovered" was inhabited already—these differences between the English, the Dutch, and the Spanish established at the start a world of potential conflict between the spiritual intentions of those fleeing inhospitable European societies on the one hand, and the commercial ambitions of those seeking profitable opportunities on the other. Was America going to be a haven, a miraculous place where you could build a Protestant City on a Hill? Or was it a vast continent ripe for pillage and exploitation, a bottomless storehouse to loot for the enrichment of Europe—Spain, Holland, France, and England?

> We have to remember that they came from different parts of Europe and that they came to North America with very different ideas about what they wanted to do here.

So when we speak of the values of the first colonists, we cannot lump them together. It depends on who we're talking about. *Which* colonists? And since for various reasons they grouped themselves together geographically, it also depends on where we're talking about. Is it the southern United States, the coastal regions along the Gulf of Mexico and the Caribbean? If so, the dominant values driving early settlement were coldly materialistic and exploitative. If we're talking about the middle colonies like Virginia, Maryland, New York, and Pennsylvania, then the dominant interests were more narrowly commercial: trading, fishing, lumber, tapping the region for its products. And in New England from the time of the earliest colonists, issues of religion and of creating a new spiritual haven were front and center, not simply the accouterments of commerce or exploitation.

> In Quebec and in the French colonies, for instance, and even in Maryland, which existed briefly as a French colony, and in Louisiana, when the French ruled, they ruled from home, as if their colonies were branch offices, whereas the English decentralized authority to a much greater extent, as if their colonies were franchises.

Gradually, of course, those ambitions began to merge. In the South you saw materialist ambitions justified by religious and spiritual aspirations and principles. In New England you saw spiritual and religious ambitions begin to fade as the colonists seized the opportunity to exploit the region's natural resources economically. So that by the early eighteenth century enough blending had occurred for Americans, the colonists, to no longer think of themselves as Europeans. By then the braiding together of the two strands had begun to form a national culture, a shared sense of national values. But at bottom these were still conflicting values. And I think that as we move forward in this discussion we'll see the inherent conflict between those two sets of values come up again and again and again.

I spoke of the point at which the pioneers stopped feeling European. But I don't know that they ever felt European as such. When they first arrived on our shores, their separate national identities were stronger than any single overarching European sense of identity. In the sixteenth and seventeenth centuries, the Spanish colonists felt Spanish more than they felt European. The French felt French more than European.

And the English felt English, not at all European. So we have to make that distinction at the beginning. The question is, at what point did the English colonists stop feeling English? At what point did the Spanish colonists stop feeling Spanish, and the French stop feeling French? It didn't all happen at the same time. And what's interesting is that the types of governance that were established for each country's colonies helped determine how they identified themselves initially and the pace at which their new American identities evolved.

The English managed to set up administrative structures that provided a great deal of local autonomy, in New England particularly. And in Virginia and throughout all the English colonies, there were local legislative bodies, local governors and public officials who operated rather independently from the mother country, whereas the Spanish and the French still ruled much more closely from home. In Quebec and in the French colonies, for instance, and even in Maryland, which existed briefly as a French colony, and in Louisiana, when the French ruled, they ruled from home, as if their colonies were branch offices, whereas the English decentralized authority to a much greater extent, as if their colonies were franchises.

Therefore most New Englanders by the mid- to late seventeenth century, the 1680s and '90s, felt more American than English. They stopped feeling English much earlier than the French and Spanish stopped feeling French and Spanish. In Quebec, for instance, where even today they feel more French than Canadian, there's still that pull from the mother country, and I think this was also true at the time for the Spanish and the Dutch. It's an interesting question, but once again it shows us that you can't generalize about the early colonists unless you acknowledge their multiple places of origin. We don't just have one mother country. We have many dueling mothers who all play a significant role in creating us.

And of course African origins were very important in this period. There were vast numbers of Africans present from the start, in the South particularly, but throughout the colonies. After all, until the 1830s there were slaves in New England, slaves in New York and New Jersey. It wasn't just in the South that Americans owned slaves. So we have to consider the influence of African values, African culture. It's just below the surface at the start, necessarily so, but it's there. The African factor was profoundly operative, and it was influential to an extreme degree on the dominant white culture, especially in the South, so we have to acknowledge that strand, too. The very same culture that would have its flourishing in the twentieth century with the blues, with jazz, and in the visual and language arts, was already a force in the eighteenth century and especially throughout the nineteenth century when Africans made up a significant portion of the American population.

Was there an early form of the American Dream? I can't say there was one American Dream. There were several dreams to begin with. There was El Dorado, the City of Gold that Cortez and Pizarro dreamed of finding. And then there was Ponce de León's dream of the Fountain of Youth, where you could start life over again, and the New England Puritan dream of God's Protestant utopian City on a Hill, the New Jerusalem. There were at least three distinct dreams in the beginning.

The religious dream of the City on the Hill, where you could live a life that was pure and uninfected by European cosmopolitanism, was almost a pastoral dream, one in which you could become a natural human being living a holy life under the eye of God. And you could only do it here, in the New Jerusalem. You couldn't do it in corrupt old Europe. It was only possible in the New World.

The dream of the City of Gold, where you discovered untold wealth, was a dream of glory in the service of the Old World. You melted down the gold, poured it into bullion, and shipped it back to enrich the crowned heads of Europe. It was a powerful material dream, and it was this dream that became the model for the exploitation of the New World, although it was the least transformative of the three.

The dream of the Fountain of Youth may yet prove to be the strongest of the three, since it carries within it the sense of the new, the dream of starting over, of having a New Life. It's essentially the dream of being a child again, and it's the dream that persists more strongly than the other two and is today perhaps the most vivid of the three.

We can think of there being three braided strands, or perhaps three mutually reinforcing dreams: one is of a place where a sinner can become virtuous, free from the decadence of the secular cosmopolitanism of old Europe; another is of a place where a poor man can become wealthy; and a third is of a place where a person can be born again.

The three together are much more powerful than any one of them alone. And they are there at the inception, at the very beginning of colonial America, side by side at first, specific to

> We don't just have one mother country. We have many dueling mothers who all play a significant role in creating us.

the three separate regions, but gradually merging. By the late seventeenth and early eighteenth centuries they come together, just as the colonies themselves begin to come together. As the northern colonies in New England begin to attach themselves to the middle colonies—New York, Pennsylvania, Maryland, Virginia—and then the southern colonies—South Carolina, North Carolina, Georgia—begin to draw together, and as the English more or less achieve military and economic control and establish a kind of cultural hegemony across the eastern seaboard, you see the three dreams merge.

Forging America's Idea of Itself

As Americans from New England moved west into Ohio and Wisconsin and into the far northwestern territories, the first building they put up in every newly settled village was a white church with a steeple. The second building was the town hall, where everyone voted. In other words, the two pillars they carried with them were their form of representative government and along with that the notion that God was central to the community. The third building was the schoolhouse. The fourth was probably the bank. No brothels or saloons till much later, of course.

Religious fundamentalism and the idea of God are as central to our social and political organization as our vaunted democratic institutions. It has to do with the particular Protestant sects that settled in New England in the seventeenth century and made God central to the political organization there. It was not made central anywhere else—not by the French in Quebec and the north of New England, and not by the Spanish in Florida and the Caribbean. Catholic priests accompanied the Spanish and French colonists, yes, but they were not central to the political life in the same way as the Protestant ministers were in New England. So that's where I think it begins, the notion that God is an American. It begins in New England. And the degree to which the seventeenth- and eighteenth-century New England village is the primary source and model for our American social democracy and provides the template for representative government in America, the degree to which that form of democracy came to be practiced across all the thirteen colonies, is the degree to which God is central to American political thinking and American political and social discourse. It's the main mark of the ascendancy of the New England form of political comity.

Which brings us to the question of taxes. Why did the issue elicit such a strong response, such a violent reaction, in 1776? I don't think it was a simple matter of taxes per se. It was taxation without representation. That's how it was phrased. They weren't simply rebelling against taxes. They were rebelling

Was there an early form of the American Dream? I can't say there was one American Dream. There were several dreams to begin with.

against control from abroad by the English Parliament and Crown. By the late eighteenth century—the 1750s, '60s, '70s—New Englanders had gotten used to representing themselves in their own towns, their own counties, their own colonies. They elected their own officials, passed their own regulations, and taxed themselves. In other words, they had already by then cut the umbilical cord between the mother country and the colonial child, and in this they were far ahead of the other colonies.

Remember, politically speaking, the American Revolution has its ideological and intellectual roots mainly in New England. But in economic terms, it finds its energy and roots in the South, in Virginia and Maryland and the Carolinas. There, to the landed gentry and the slave holders, given the size and scale and wealth of the plantation system in the South, it made economic sense to become a distinct nation independent of the mother country. As inevitably happens, when the wealth produced by a colony seems to be returning from the source to the mother country, the colonials feel cheated. To no small degree, they were right to feel cheated.

So again there was a mixed set of motives—more idealistic, ideological, and political motives in the North, and more commercial and economic in the South. But they served each

other's needs. The North gave the South the ideological, intellectual, and political rationale for independence. The South gave the North the economic means and justification, and the belief that, should the colonies unite, they could survive independently without the mother country. That's why they pulled together. Simply, the South couldn't survive independence without the North; the North couldn't survive without the South. So these thirteen separate and disparate colonies managed to unite out of both practical and ideological reasons. From there they managed to pull off an extraordinary war of independence and successfully separate themselves from what was, at the time, the most powerful nation on earth.

Was our War of Independence a revolt or a revolution? I think it was a true revolution, because it articulated, for the first time and for all to use, the most radical concept of democracy then on the planet: the idea of representative government—governance obtained without a monarchy of any sort, without a nobility, without any rank of nobility; governance by and for the governed.

Though it took a decade before the French managed to apply that radical concept to their own situation, it should be noted that the vocabulary and ideals for the American Revolution come straight out of the European Enlightenment. America's so-called founding fathers, Thomas Paine, Thomas Jefferson, Ben Franklin, James Madison, and so on, took their vocabulary from European Enlightenment thinking. They articulated it on the ground and institutionalized it in Philadelphia in 1776 and again in 1787 in our founding and guiding documents: the Declaration of Independence and the United States Constitution. It was a revolutionary concept at that time, a radical break with the European notion of comity and authority. Yes, it was to some degree, by today's standards, an elitist movement. Most successful political movements are. The ideas and the expression of those ideas came from the top down. And yes, only white men with property were qualified to vote. Several million slaves were excluded from this process. Women were excluded. And in the dispensation of proportional representation in Congress, each slave was to count as three-fifths of a person, which gave the South a numerical bulge sufficient to balance against the more populous North. So by definition it was elitist many times over. But at the same time it was established that there would be no nobility and no monarchy, giving life to what was essentially a populist notion. Imbedded in the words chosen carefully by those white men were concepts of freedom and inclusion that would in time carry weight and intentions far beyond anything the founding fathers may have intended. If we go back to that moment in time, to 1787 when the Constitution was ratified, we have to admit that those early Americans produced some very radical documents. We have to wait until a decade later, in France, to see anything as radical as that again. The French gave the Americans the vocabulary, the Americans created the institutions to express that vocabulary, and then the French took the institutions back a decade later. The Americans took the theory, made it pragmatic and applied it, and then the French brought the applications back home and, in a more radical form, put them to use there—a cycle that's characteristic of both cultures, one we've seen over and over in many different fields of human endeavor. And today, two and a quarter centuries later, we are still waiting for the inspiring words in those radical documents to have their full effect.

Americans have tended to misread and understate how difficult and long was the war against the British army, because the Civil War, when it was over, quickly became a great distorting screen or scrim for us. When you read documents, including

were able to prevail. It was extraordinary. And it was not at all inevitable or even likely. It wasn't something that you could have predicted at the time. And right up to the very end of the war it looked as though the Americans would not prevail.

Speaking of the Marquis de Lafayette, he lived a very long life, and in 1824, about ten years before he died, he returned to the United States for a triumphal tour to all the places he had been during the war, starting in New York and making his way to the South, the middle Atlantic states, north to Boston, and all the way up the Hudson River to Saratoga, where I live for much of the year. In each place he was greeted like a conquering hero. No foreigner at that time, and perhaps no foreigner since, has ever come to America and been received with such jubilation and excitement and vast crowds as when Lafayette returned. What that shows us is that a whole generation later he was still seen as a grand hero, a hero of the first order. That's how powerful the memory of the war and the image of Lafayette's role in it were in the American imagination in the years leading up to the Civil War. But if Lafayette had lived long enough to show up today in New York, or at any time after 1861, he wouldn't draw a very big crowd. Only a couple of curiosity

Americans have tended to misread and understate how difficult and long was the war against the British army, because the Civil War, when it was over, quickly became a great distorting screen or scrim for us.

letters and so forth, written by Americans before the Civil War, where they're looking back towards the Revolution barely half a century earlier, Americans viewed the Revolutionary War with greater clarity of thought and with greater understanding of its costs and sacrifices, its duration and difficulty, than they did after the Civil War. The Civil War threw such a huge shadow across America and the American imagination that it was difficult, after the war, to look back and imagine what it must have been like to conduct and finally win that Revolution, that seven-year war against the British.

Our War of Independence was fought by untrained soldiers, laymen, farmers, and mechanics, led by young men in their twenties and thirties, with very few supplies and arms, against the largest, best-trained, most professional army in the world. Through the tactical brilliance of George Washington and several others—and the support of the French, and the Marquis de Lafayette, and other Continental Europeans as well—they

seekers and history buffs would turn out to see him. He'd be disappointed. The role of Lafayette, and with it the memory and true meaning of the Revolutionary War, have diminished to the point where they are lost now, mostly forgotten, part of a past to which we're no longer connected.

TRIPPING

Drug War Mythology
Paul Armentano

It's been said that the first casualty of war is truth; the aptly titled US "War on Drugs" is no different. America's Drug War is a $50 billion-per-year[1] boondoggle which thrives on federal lies and distortions, media complicity, and an ill-informed public. Over the course of this battle, bureaucrats and prohibitionists—including the country's top-ranking anti-drug official, Drug Czar Barry McCaffrey—have popularized countless myths to justify and support their endeavor. More often than not these lies go unchallenged and become accepted by the public as truth. Those that are exposed are quickly replaced by even grander sophistry. Let's explore some of the more pervasive myths of America's longest war.

Myth: Law enforcement rarely arrest or jail drug offenders.

"Very few drug-use offenders ever see the inside of a prison cell. It's simply a myth that our prison cells are filled with people who don't belong there."
—Rep. John Mica (R-FL), speaking before Congress, July 1999

Fact: Approximately 25 percent of American inmates are imprisoned on drug charges.
—US Department of Justice, Bureau of Justice Statistics

Drug offenders, often low-level users, comprise the fastest-rising percentage of today's inmates. According to statistics compiled by the Washington, DC Justice Policy Institute, 76 percent of the increase in admissions to US prisons from 1978 to 1996 was attributable to nonviolent offenders.[2] The majority of these were drug violators. Since 1989, the number of drug offenders sent to prison has exceeded the number of violent commitments every year.[3]

Over the past 20 years, the total number of inmates incarcer-ated on drug charges in federal and state prisons and local jails has grown over 1,000 percent. There are now more than 450,000 drug offenders behind bars, a total nearly equal to the *entire* US prison population of 1980.[4] Put another way, there are presently 100,000 more Americans imprisoned for drug offenses than total prisoners in the European Union, even though the EU has 100 million more citizens than the US. As a result, nearly one out of every four Americans behind bars is incarcerated for drugs.[5]

The ratio for federal prisoners is even more apalling; drug offenders comprise approximately two out of every three federal inmates.[6] Punishment for first-time federal drug offenders averages 82.4 months, a sentence longer than those for manslaughter, assault, and sexual abuse.[7]

State prosecutors are sending drug offenders to jail in greater and greater numbers. One recent study found that approximately half of all California prisoners are there on drug charges.[8] A review of 1999 New York State sentencing data revealed that 91 percent of all drug offenders sentenced to prison that year were incarcerated for either drug possession or violating one of the state's three lowest level drug offenses.[9]

The federal drug control budget has escalated at a similarly alarming rate. Today, the federal government spends over $13 billion annually on domestic anti-drug law enforcement alone, a figure that is 800 times larger than the entire federal drug control budget of 1981.[10] Predictably, this increase has led to an unprecedented explosion of drug arrests. Police today annually arrest three times as many individuals on drug charges than they did in 1980. According to FBI crime report figures, approximately 1.6 million Americans were arrested on drug charges in 1998, one of the highest totals ever recorded.[11]

Contrary to prohibitionist rhetoric, the majority of those arrested are low-level offenders charged with drug possession, not sale.

Seventy-nine percent of all drug arrests in 1998 were for possession only.[12] Overwhelmingly, those arrested are marijuana smokers. In 1998 police arrested 682,885 Americans for marijuana offenses, more than the total number of arrestees for all violent crimes combined, including murder, rape, robbery, and aggravated assault.[13] Eighty-eight percent of these arrests were for marijuana possession only. This translates into one out of every 25 criminal arrests in the United States.[14] Believe it or not, one in seven drug prisoners is now behind bars for pot![15]

Those drug offenders arrested and sent to prison, typically for lengthy sentences, are citizens not much different than you or I. They are mothers, fathers, and grandparents.[16] They are families like Joane, Gary, and Steve Tucker, together serving 26 years for selling legal hydroponics gardening equipment from their family-owned store. Prosecutors charged and convicted them with conspiracy to manufacture marijuana based on the offenses of a handful of their customers, and the Tuckers' failure to allow DEA agents to install surveillance cameras in their store.

They are patients like Will Foster, sentenced to 93 years by an Oklahoma jury for cultivating marijuana for the purpose of alleviating pain associated with rheumatoid arthritis.

There are now more than 450,000 drug offenders behind bars, a total nearly equal to the *entire* US prison population of 1980.

They are grandfathers like Loren Pogue, age 64, presently serving 22 years for conspiracy to import drugs and money laundering. Pogue helped a paid government informant sell a plot of land to undercover agents posing as "investors." The investors, whom Pogue met only once, allegedly were to use the land to build an airstrip for the purpose of smuggling drugs. The fact that there were no actual drugs involved, that Pogue was an upstanding citizen with no prior drug history, and that the airstrip was never built failed to mitigate his virtual life sentence.

These are the faces of America's snowballing drug inmate population, nonviolent offenders that law enforcement and prosecutors are now targeting with frightening regularity. To Drug War hawks, these individuals are simply collateral damage; to the rest of us, they are the unfortunate victims of more than 80 years of lies, propaganda, and political posturing.

Myth: Relaxing anti-drug laws will significantly increase drug use and crime.

"The murder rate in Holland is double that in the United States. The per capita crime rates are much higher than the United States…. That's drugs!"
—US Drug Czar Barry McCaffrey, July 23, 1998

Fact: Jurisdictions that have decriminalized the possession of marijuana and other drugs experience drug use and crime rates equal to or lower than those that have maintained strict criminal penalties.

The Dutch murder rate is 440 percent lower (1.8 per 100,000) than the US murder rate (8.2 per 100,000).
—Dutch Central Planning Bureau of Statistics, 1996, and FBI Uniform Crime Report data, 1998

Drug War proponents argue that any relaxation of anti-drug laws will result in a sharp increase in drug use and associated crime. This assertion is unsupported by epidemiological and survey evidence in America and abroad. In many cases, drug liberalization policies are associated with a reduction in drug use and crime.

Beginning with Oregon in 1973, ten US states removed criminal penalties for the possession of small amounts of marijuana.[17] To date, more than a dozen federal and independent commissions have examined the social and criminal impact of this legislative reform.[18] In short, the available evidence indicates that the decriminalization of marijuana possession has little or no impact on use patterns or individuals' attitudes toward the drug.[19] According to a 1981 US government study investigating the issue, "Overall, the preponderance of the evidence which we have gathered and examined points to the conclusion that decriminalization has had virtually no effect either on the marijuana use or on related attitudes and beliefs about marijuana use among American young people in this age group…. In fact,…states showed a small, cumulative net decline in lifetime prevalence, as well as in annual and monthly prevalence, after decriminalization."[20] A 1999 study by the National Academy of Sciences Institute of Medicine affirmed these conclusions.[21]

There also exists no evidence that decriminalization encourages more prevalent use of other drugs. A 1993 study published in the *Social Sciences Journal* determined: "There is no strong evidence that decriminalization affects either the choice or frequency of use of drugs, either legal (alcohol) or illegal (marijuana and cocaine)."[22] A 1993 examination of drug-related emergency room (ER) cases suggested that decriminalization may reduce recreational demand for hard drugs. It found that incidents of marijuana use among patients were equal in decriminalized states versus non-decriminalized areas, but noted that rates of other illicit drug use among ER patients were substantially higher in states that retained criminal penalties for marijuana.[23]

Research further indicates that decriminalization fails to increase crime, and even reduces criminal justice costs. For example, California saved $958,305,499 from 1976 to 1985 by decriminalizing the personal possession of one ounce of marijuana, according to a study of the state justice department budget.[24] An investigation of the impact of marijuana decriminalization in Maine found that the policy reduced court costs and increased revenue.[25]

International studies of marijuana decriminalization in Australia and elsewhere demonstrate similar results. A 1994 study by the Australian National Drug Research Center reported: "Those jurisdictions which have decriminalized personal cannabis use have

> ## Since the Dutch government liberalized its marijuana policies, the number of problem hard drug users has fallen steadily.

not experienced any dramatic increase in prevalence of use."[26] At the same time, those jurisdictions raised significant revenue by issuing instant, non-criminal fines to marijuana users.

In recent years, most Western nations have significantly liberalized their cannabis laws with no ill effects; Germany, Holland, and Switzerland have ceased enforcing criminal penalties against the drug altogether. Spain, Italy, and Portugal have decriminalized the possession of all drugs. Clearly, American drug policy is moving in the opposite direction of the rest of the world.

Unfortunately, American prohibitionists have chosen to malign rather than learn from these examples. They have launched the bulk of their attacks on the Dutch, who have allowed for the public consumption of small amounts of marijuana since the mid-1970s. While on a purported "fact-finding" mission regarding European drug policy in July 1998, Drug Czar Barry

McCaffrey publicly charged that the Dutch murder rate is more than twice America's rate.[27] He further purported that three times as many Dutch youth admit trying marijuana than do their US counterparts.[28] McCaffrey said that liberal drug policies were to blame for the higher Dutch figures. As one might expect from the loose-lipped Czar, both charges were absolutely false. Dutch homicide rates and pot use remain far lower than those in America. Official data released by the Dutch government's Central Planning Bureau immediately after McCaffrey's allegations put the country's murder rate for 1996 at 1.8 per 100,000 people, a figure substantially lower than the US murder rate. McCaffrey had falsely claimed that the Dutch murder rate was 17.58 per 100,000.[29]

McCaffrey's charges concerning adolescent marijuana use also proved fallacious. 1996 data recorded by the University of Michigan's Monitoring the Future project determined that 45 percent of America's high school seniors admit having tried marijuana.[30] By comparison, research compiled by the National Institute of Medicine, Health and Addiction in the Netherlands found that only 30 percent of Dutch adolescents have experimented with the drug.[31] McCaffrey falsely stated that only 9.1 percent of American teens had ever experimented with marijuana.

If any cause and effect relationship exists between Dutch drug policy and drug use, it is associated with reducing substance use. Fewer than half as many Dutch adults have tried marijuana as have Americans.[32] Dutch adults also use hard drugs like cocaine and heroin at rates dramatically lower than US citizens.[33] Since the Dutch government liberalized its marijuana policies, the number of problem hard drug users has fallen steadily.[34] Dutch Ambassador to the US Joris M. Vos publicly denounced McCaffey's false allegations. Nevertheless, McCaffrey never apologized or retracted his remarks, and continues to bash Dutch drug policy. Diplomacy has never been his strong suit.

Myth: Marijuana is a "gateway" to the use of hard drugs.

"Statistically speaking, marijuana stands convicted as a gateway drug. Twelve to seventeen year olds who smoke marijuana are 85 times more likely to use cocaine than those who do not."
—Joseph Califano, Executive Director, The Center for Alcohol and Substance Abuse, July 13, 1997

Drug War Mythology
Paul Armentano

Fact: For every 104 people who have used marijuana, there is only one regular user of cocaine and less than one heroin addict.
—Department of Health and Human Services, National Household Survey on Drug Abuse, 1997.

Since the dawn of drug prohibition, proponents have alleged that experimenting with pot inevitably leads to the use of other illicit substances. Known as the "gateway theory," this notion remains one of the staples of Drug War rhetoric. However, like most prohibitionist arguments, there exist no sound scientific data to support it.

One of the first major studies to explore this issue was commissioned by New York City Mayor Fiorello LaGuardia in 1938. The five-year fact-finding mission was the most comprehensive marijuana study of its era. Released in 1944, the LaGuardia Report concluded: "The use of marijuana does not lead to morphine or heroin or cocaine addiction.... The instances are extremely rare where the habit of marijuana smoking is associated with addiction to these narcotics."[35]

Despite this sound rebuttal, prohibitionists resurrected their hypothesis in the 1960s under a new moniker: "the stepping stone theory." Fortunately, federally-contracted researchers from the National Institute of Mental Health were quick to set the record straight by releasing their pioneering study: *Ganja in Jamaica: A medical anthropological study of chronic marijuana use*.[36] Summarizing its findings in the July 4, 1975, issue of *Science* magazine, Dr. Erich Goode of the State University of New York at Stony Brook wrote: "One of the more interesting findings to emerge from the study relates to the 'stepping stone hypothesis.'... Nothing like that occurs among heavy, chronic, ganja smokers of Jamaica. No other drugs were used, aside from aspirin, tea, alcohol and tobacco. The only hard drug use known on the island is indulged by North American tourists."[37]

Yet another federally commissioned study rejected the gateway premise in 1982. This study, authored by the National Academy of Sciences Institute of Medicine, determined that: "There is no evidence to support the belief that the use of one drug will inevitably lead to the use of any other drug."[38] A follow-up study released by the IOM in 1999 affirmed this conclusion.[39]

Federal drug use statistics compiled by the US Department of Health and Human Services (HHS) further expose the gateway theory as fraudulent. As self-reported marijuana use increased in the 1960s and 1970s, heroin use declined; while cocaine use rose in the early 1980s, pot use dropped sharply. Conversely, marijuana's rising popularity in the 1990s has not spawned a corresponding increase in the use of cocaine.[40] According to the findings of the 1998 US Government Annual Household Survey on Drug Abuse, although more than 72 million Americans have tried marijuana, only 23 million have ever experimented with cocaine.[41] Less than 4.5 million have ever used crack, and less than 2.4 million have ever tried heroin.[42]

Nevertheless, prohibitionists—most notably the National Center on Addiction and Substance Abuse (CASA) and Drug Czar Barry McCaffrey—continue to tout the gateway theory as fact, and frequently charge that marijuana users are 85 times more likely than nonusers to try cocaine.[43] CASA's misleading calculation is based on cannabis and cocaine prevalence data from 1991.[44] To obtain the 85 times "risk factor," CASA divided the proportion of cannabis users who had ever tried cocaine (17 percent) by the proportion of cocaine users who had never used cannabis (0.2 percent). The "risk factor" is not large because so many cannabis users experimented with cocaine—indeed 83 percent did not—but because very few people try cocaine without trying cannabis first. According to 1998 data, only 21 percent of the 13.6 million estimated current marijuana users also used another illicit substance.[45] For the majority of marijuana users, cannabis is a terminus rather than a "gateway" drug.

Some evidence exists supporting the notion that cannabis may serve as a doorway to the world of illegal drugs, in which adolescents have a greater opportunity and are under greater social pressure to experiment with additional substances. This theory may explain why a minority of cannabis users graduate to other illicit drugs such as cocaine.[46] However, if this is the case, then it is cannabis prohibition which forces users to associate with the illicit drug black market, and not cannabis use alone that influences this pattern of behavior.

Myth: Cannabis has no medical or therapeutic value.

"There is not a shred of scientific evidence that shows that smoked marijuana is useful or needed. This is not science. This is not medical. This is a cruel hoax."
—US Drug Czar Barry McCaffrey, August 16, 1996

Fact: Available scientific research indicates that medical cannabis provides symptomatic relief for a number of serious ailments, and is less toxic and costly than many conventional medicines for which it may be substituted.

"Scientific data indicate the potential therapeutic value of cannabinoid drugs, primarily THC, for pain relief, control of nausea and vomiting, and appetite stimulation…. Except for the harms associated with smoking, the adverse effects of marijuana use are within the range tolerated for other medications."
—Final conclusions of US Institute of Medicine, March 1999

Written references to medical marijuana date back more than 2,000 years. The world's oldest surviving text on medical drugs, the Chinese *Shen-nung Pen-tshao Ching*, specifically cites cannabis' value for reducing the pain of rheumatism and for treating digestive disorders.[47] Western medicine embraced pot's medical properties in the mid-1800s, and by the beginning of the twentieth century, physicians had published more than 100 papers in the Western medical literature recommending its use for a variety of disorders.[48]

Cannabis remained in the United States' pharmacopoeia until the late 1930s when Congress passed the Marijuana Tax Act prohibiting physicians from prescribing it. The American Medical Association was one of the most vocal organizations to testify against the ban, arguing that it would deprive patients of a safe and effective medicine.[49]

Modern research suggests that cannabis is a valuable aid in the treatment of a wide range of clinical applications.[50] These include

Written references to medical marijuana date back more than 2,000 years.

pain relief—particularly neuropathic pain associated with cancer, arthritis, and spinal cord damage—nausea, spasticity, glaucoma, movement disorders, and hypertension.[51] Marijuana is also a powerful appetite stimulant, specifically in patients suffering from HIV, the AIDS wasting syndrome, or dementia. Emerging research suggests that pot's medicinal constituents (known as cannabinoids) may protect the body against some types of malignant tumors and are neuroprotective.

Despite overwhelming evidence of marijuana's therapeutic value, it remains classified as a Schedule I substance, the most stringent drug classification available under US law. By definition, Schedule I substances have "no accepted medical use in treatment," and physicians may not legally prescribe them. Federal officials have rejected legal challenges ordering pot to be rescheduled—including a 1988 ruling from the Drug Enforcement Administration's own administrative law judge[52]—and ignored pleas from dozens of esteemed medical organizations[53] to lift the ban on medical cannabis. As a result, physicians often recommend pot to their patients clandestinely. A 1991 Harvard study found that 44 percent of oncologists had previously advised marijuana therapy to their patients.[54] Fifty percent admitted that they would do so if marijuana were legal.

Virtually every government-appointed commission to investigate marijuana's medical potential has issued favorable findings. These include the US Institute of Medicine in 1982,[55] the Australian National Task Force on Cannabis in 1994,[56] and the US National Institutes of Health Workshop on Medical Marijuana in 1997.[57]

After a one-year scientific inquiry, members of the United Kingdom's House of Lords Science and Technology Committee found in 1998 that the available evidence supported the legal use of medical cannabis.[58] MPs determined: "The government should allow doctors to prescribe cannabis for medical use…. Cannabis can be effective in some patients to relieve symptoms of multiple sclerosis, and against certain forms of pain…. This evidence is enough to justify a change in the law."[59]

Five months later, US investigators reached a similar conclusion. After conducting a nearly two-year review of the medical literature—at the request of Drug Czar Barry McCaffrey—investigators at the National Academy of Sciences Institute of Medicine affirmed, "Marijuana's active components are potentially effective in treating pain, nausea, anorexia of AIDS wasting syndrome, and other symptoms [including the involuntary spasticity associated with multiple sclerosis]."[60] The authors added that inhaling cannabis "would be advantageous" in the treatment of some diseases, and that the herb's short-term medical benefits outweigh any smoking-related harms for some patients. Nevertheless, McCaffrey and other Washington bureaucrats—none of whom is a doctor—rejected the findings of their own hand-picked expert commission, and continue to publicly assail medical cannabis as "a crock."[61]

Myth: We can attain a drug-free America by 2003.

"We must continue our commitment to deter the demand inside our country, stop the supply on and beyond our borders and increase the accountability within drug fighting programs. We must win the War on Drugs by 2003."
—House Speaker Dennis Hastert (R-Il), February 25, 1999

Fact: We will never become drug-free, only less free.

"For more than a quarter century the United States has been on a rampage, kicking in doors and locking people up in the name of protecting its citizens from illegal drugs. Hundreds of billions of dollars into the Drug War, nobody claims victory. Yet we continue, devoted to a policy as expensive, ineffective, delusional, and destructive as government policy gets."
—Dan Baum, author of *Smoke and Mirrors: The War on Drugs and the Politics of Failure* (Little, Brown & Company, 1996)

The "War on Drugs" has become America's longest and most costly battle. Though casualties remain high, its leaders show no indication of retreating.

Congress passed the first federal law authorizing law enforcement to control individuals' use of specific substances in

On a per capita basis, more people use cocaine today than when its use was legal.

1914.[62] It outlawed marijuana in 1937. It introduced mandatory sentences for drug offenders in the 1950s and again in the 1980s. Yet despite Congress' best efforts, Americans continue to use illicit drugs in greater and greater numbers. In 1937, an estimated 60,000 Americans had tried pot;[63] this total rose to 100,000 in 1945,[64] and tops 72 million today.[65] On a per capita basis, more people use cocaine today than when its use was legal.[66] More Americans die today from illicit drug overdoses, often as a result of administering tainted narcotics, than at any time in our nation's history.[67]

The prohibitionists' response to this stark reality is unthinking and predictable: tougher laws, stricter enforcement, longer jail terms, and greater intrusions into the lives of suspected drug offenders, a category that includes all of us! This latter approach threatens to shred the US Constitution in its wake. In many instances it already has. High school students are now urine-tested without probable cause; law enforcement seize individuals' property and cash based on little or no suspicion; police conduct warrantless searches of people's trash and infrared scans of citizens' homes to look for clues of drug activity; passengers in motor vehicles are frequently stopped and searched; warrants are procured based solely upon the testimony of confidential informants and are executed in "no-knock" raids;[68] drug roadblocks are common. In one shocking Supreme Court decision, Justices "approved a prolonged and humiliating detention of an incomer who was held by customs agents to determine, through her natural bodily processes, whether or not she was carrying narcotics internally," even though probable cause was lacking.[69] In other words, law enforcement forced a woman to defecate even though there was no probable cause to believe she was carrying drugs.

"Zero tolerance" abandons our nation's traditional sense of justice. Judges are forced to sentence drug offenders to lengthy prison terms without considering mitigating factors. Students are expelled for possessing small amounts of pot or, in some cases, legal over-the-counter medications. Tenants are evicted from public housing because of drug offenses committed without their knowledge by friends and family members. College applicants are denied student aid if they have a prior drug conviction. Former House Speaker Newt Gingrich (R-Ga.) supported legislation in the mid-1990s that would have imposed the death penalty for people convicted of importing two ounces or more of marijuana.[70] A 1999 bill introduced by Congress threatened to impose a ten-year felony sentence on anyone who disseminated—by any means—information relating to the manufacture of a controlled substance if that person should have somehow known that a recepient of the information would use it to commit a federal crime.[71]

And so it goes. Politicians continue to beat the Drug War drum and propagandize the enemy in order to justify their failing policies. All the while, it remains prohibition itself that creates the very problems their extreme measures are meant to target. As a result, "victory" in the "War on Drugs" remains unachievable regardless of our leaders' hollow promises and tall tales. Wake up and listen, America: You are being lied to!

Endnotes

1. Congress is requesting $19.2 billion to fight drugs for fiscal year 2001. State and local governments annually spend $33 billion to fund anti-drug activities. McCaffrey, B. "Fight drugs as you would a disease." *Chicago Tribune*, March 31, 1996. **2.** Irwin, J, V Schiraldi, & J Ziedenberg (1999). America's one million nonviolent prisoners. Washington, DC: Justice Policy Institute. **3.** Annual data compiled by the US Department of Justice, Bureau of Justice Statistics. Washington, DC. **4.** Schiraldi, V & J Ziedenberg. (2000). Poor prescription: The cost of imprisoning drug offenders in the United States. Washington, DC: Justice Policy Institute. **5.** DOJ, Bureau of Justice Statistics. Profile of jail inmates, 1996. Washington, DC: US Government Printing Office. **6.** US Federal Bureau of Prisons. (1998). United States federal prisoners profile, 1998. Washington, DC: US Government Printing Office. **7.** US Federal

of other illicit drugs, it is indeed a gateway drug. However, it does not appear to be a gateway drug to the extent that it is the cause or even that it is the most significant predictor of serious drug abuse; that is, care must be taken not to attribute cause to association. The most consistent predictors of serious drug use appear to be the intensity of marijuana use and co-occuring psychiatric disorders or a family history of psychopathology (including alcoholism)." Joy, J, S Watson, & J Benson. (1999). *Marijuana and medicine: Assessing the science base.* Washington, DC: National Academy Press. **40.** Summary of annual findings of the Substance Abuse and Mental Health Services Administration's (SAMHSA) National Household Survey on Drug Abuse, as cited by Zimmer, L & J Morgan. (1997). *Marijuana myths, marijuana facts: A review of the scientific evidence.* New York: The Lindesmith Center. **41.** SAMHSA Office of Applied Studies. (1999). Table 3A: Estimated Number (in Thousands) of Lifetime Users of Illicit Drugs, Alcohol and Tobacco in the US

The federal government spends over $13 billion annually on domestic anti-drug law enforcement alone, a figure that is 800 times larger than the entire federal drug control budget of 1981.

Bureau of Prisons. (1996). Quick facts. Washington, DC: US Government Printing Office. **8.** *Op cit.*, Schiraldi & Ziedenberg. **9.** *Ibid.* **10.** Based on proposed FY 2001 drug control budget data. Congress appropriated $1.5 billion for drug control in 1981. **11.** Federal Bureau of Investigation. (1999). Table 29: Total estimated arrests United States, 1998. **12.** *Ibid.* **13.** *Ibid.* **14.** *Ibid.* **15.** DOJ, Bureau of Justice Statistics. (1999). Substance abuse and treatment, state and federal prisoners. Washington DC: US Government Printing Office. **16.** The following profiles were initially summarized in Norris, M, C Conrad, & V Resner. (2000). *Shattered lives: Portraits from America's Drug War.* El Cerrito, CA: Creative Xpressions. **17.** Alaska, California, Colorado, Maine, Mississippi, Nebraska, New York, North Carolina, Ohio, and Oregon decriminalized the possession of personal-use amounts of cannabis between 1973 and 1977. To date, not one state legislature has reimposed criminal penalties. (Alaska, the only arguable exception, amended their law via ballot initiative.) The fact that these states have stood by their policy despite pressure from federal anti-drug advocates illustrates the real-world success of this policy as an alternative to criminal penalties and incarceration. .**18.** Commissions include: Australian Institute of Criminology; California State Office of Narcotics and Drug Abuse; Connecticut Law Review Commission; National Academy of Sciences Institute of Medicine; National Drug and Alcohol Resource Centre (Australia); University of Michigan Institute of Social Research; etc. **19.** Conclusions from these commissions are available online at <www.norml.org/recreational/decrim.shtml>. **20.** Johnson, L, P O'Malley, & J Bachman. (1981). Marijuana decriminalization: The impact on youth 1975–1980. Monitoring the Future, Occasional Paper series, paper 13. Ann Arbor: Institute for Social Research, University of Michigan. **21.** Joy, J, S Watson, & J Bensen. (1999). *Marijuana and medicine: Assessing the science base.* Washington, DC: National Academy Press. **22.** Theis, C & C Register. (1993). Decriminalization of marijuana and the demand for alcohol, marijuana and cocaine. *The Social Sciences Journal*, 30. **23.** Model K. (1993). The effect of marijuana on hospital emergency room drug episodes: 1975–1978. *Journal of the American Statistical Association*, 88: 737–747. **24.** Aldrich, M & T Mikuriya. (1988). Savings in California marijuana law enforcement costs attributable to the Moscone Act of 1976. *Journal of Psychoactive Drugs*, 20: 75–81. **25.** Kopel, D. (1991). Marijuana jail terms. Independence Institute Issue Paper. Golden CO, as cited by Conrad, C. (1994). *Hemp: Lifeline to the future.* Los Angeles: Creative Xpressions. **26.** National Drug and Alcohol Research Centre. (1994). Patterns of cannabis use in Australia. Monograph Series No. 27. Canberra: Australian Government Publishing Service. **27.** He also charged that the Dutch crime rate is 40 percent higher than America's. "US Drug Czar bashes Dutch policy on eve of visit." Reuters News Wire. July 13, 1998. **28.** "McCaffrey takes his charge to officials in the Netherlands." *Washington Times*. July 15, 1998. **29.** Lucassen, C. "Dutch rebuke US drug advisor." Reuters News Wire. July 14, 1998. **30.** Johnston, L, P O'Malley, & J Bachman. (2000). Table 1A: Trends in Lifetime Prevalence of Use of Various Drugs for 8th, 10th, 12th Graders, 1991–1999. Ann Arbor: Institute for Social Research, University of Michigan. **31.** Letter from Dutch Ambassador to the United States Joris Vos to the *Washington Times*, July 20, 1998. **32.** 32.9 percent of Americans have tried marijuana versus 15.6 percent of Dutch citizens. Center for Drug Research. (1999). Drug use in the population of 12 years and older in the USA and the Netherlands. University of Amsterdam. **33.** 10.5 percent of Americans have tried cocaine versus 2.1 percent of Dutch citizens. 0.9 percent of Americans have tried heroin versus 0.3 percent of Dutch citizens. *Ibid.* **34.** Drucker, E. (1995). Harm reduction: a public health strategy. *Current Issues in Public Health*, 1: 64–70. **35.** Mayor's Committee on Marihuana. (1944). The marihuana problem in the City of New York: Sociological, medical, psychological, and pharmacological studies (aka The LaGuardia Report). Lancaster, PA: Jacques Cattel Press. **36.** Rubin, V & L Comitas. (Eds.). (1975). *Ganja in Jamaica: A medical anthropoligical study of chronic marijuana use.* The Hague: Netherlands: Moulton & Company. **37.** Goode, E. (1975). Effects of cannabis in another culture. *Science*, July: 41–42. **38.** Institute of Medicine. (1982). *Marijuana and health.* Washington, DC: National Academy Press. **39.** "In the sense that marijuana use typically precedes rather than follows initiation into the use

Population Aged 12 and Older: 1979–1998. Rockville, MD: US Department of Health and Human Services. **42.** *Ibid.* **43.** National Center on Addiction and Substance Abuse at Columbia University. (1994). *Cigarettes, alcohol, and marijuana: Gateways to illicit drugs.* New York: CASA. **44.** As compiled by the US Department of Health and Human Services. **45.** SAMHSA Office of Applied Studies. (1999). Summary Findings from the 1998 National Household Survey on Drug Abuse. Rockville, MD: US Department of Health and Human Services. **46.** Researchers at the Netherlands Institute of Medicine, Health and Addiction maintain that separating cannabis from the illicit drug market is an essential step in preventing marijuana users from experimenting with hard drugs. "As for a possible switch from cannabis to hard drugs, it is clear that the pharmacological properties of cannabis are irrelevant in this respect. There is no physically determined tendency towards switching from marijuana to harder substances. Social factors, however, do appear to play a role. The more users become integrated in an environment ('subculture') where, apart from cannabis, hard drugs can also be obtained, the greater the chance that they may switch to hard drugs. Separation of the drug markets is therefore essential." The Trimbos Institute. (1997). Netherlands alcohol and drug report: Fact sheet 7: Cannabis policy: Update. Utrecht: Netherlands. **47.** Zimmerman B, N Crumpaker, & R Bayer. (1998). *Is marijuana the right medicine for you?: A factual guide to medical uses of marijuana.* New Canaan, CT: Keats Publishing. **48.** Mikuriya, T. (Ed.) (1973). *Marijuana: Medical papers 1839–1972.* Oakland: Medi-Comp Press. **49.** AMA Legislative Counsel William C. Woodword testified before Congress on July 12, 1937, against the Marihuana Tax Act. He said: "We cannot understand…why this bill should have been prepared in secret for two years without any initiative, even to the profession, that it was being prepared…. The obvious purpose of and effect of this bill is to impose so many restrictions on the medicinal use [of cannabis] as to prevent such use altogether…. It may serve to deprive the public of the benefits of a drug that on further research may prove to be of substantial benefit. **50.** Several books explore this issue in further detail. These include: Grinspoon, L, & J Bakalar. (1999). *Marihuana: The forbidden medicine* (second edition). New Haven: Yale University Press; Zimmerman, B, N Crumpacker, & R Bayer. (1998). *Is marijuana the right medicine for you?: A factual guide to medical uses of marijuana.* Keats Publishing; Conrad, C. (1997). *Hemp for health: The medicinal and nutritional uses of Cannabis Sativa.* Rochester VT: Healing Arts Press; and Mechoulam, R. (Ed.). (1986). *Cannabinoids as therapeutic agents.* Boca Raton: CRC Press. **51.** A comprehensive literature review by the author on the use of medical cannabis to mitigate these and other indications is available online from the GW Pharmaceuticals Website <www.medicinal-cannabis.org>. Indications explored are: AIDS wasting syndrome, Alzheimer's disease, arthritis, asthma, brain injury/stroke, Crohn's disease, depression and other mental illnesses, eating disorders, epilepsy, fibromyalgia, glaucoma, gliomas, hypertension, migraine, Multiple Sclerosis, nausea, neuropathic pain, schizophrenia, spinal cord injury, Tourette's syndrome and other movement disorders, and ulcerative colitis. **52.** After conducting two years of hearings, DEA Administrative Law Judge Francis Young ruled on September 6, 1988, that cannabis met the legal requirements of a Schedule II drug. He affirmed: "Based upon the facts established in this record and set out above, one must reasonably conclude that there is accepted safety for the use of marijuana under medical supervision. To conclude otherwise, on this record, would be unreasonable, arbitrary and capricious." The DEA refused to implement Young's decision. **53.** These include the AIDS Action Counsel, the American Public Health Association, and *The New England Journal of Medicine*. The author recently compiled a list of these organizations and their supporting statements for the National Organization for the Reform of Marijuana Laws (NORML). It may be accessed online at <www.norml.org/medical/mjorgs.shtml>. **54.** Doblin, R & M Kleiman. (1991). Marijuana as anti-emetic medicine: A survey of oncologists attitudes and experiences. *Journal of Clinical Oncology*, 9: 1275–1280. **55.** "Cannabis and its derivatives have shown promise in a varieties of disorders. The evidence is most impressive in glaucoma,…asthma,…and in [combating] the nausea and vomiting of cancer chemotherapy…. Smaller trials have suggested cannabis might also be useful in seizures,

Drug War Mythology
Paul Armentano

spasticity, and other nervous system disorders." Conclusion of the National Academy of Sciences Institute of Medicine. (1982). *Marijuana and health*. Washington, DC: National Academy Press. **56.** "First, there is good evidence that THC is an effective anti-emetic agent for patients undergoing cancer chemotherapy.... Second, there is reasonable evidence for the potential efficacy of THC and marijuana in the treatment of glaucoma, especially in cases which have proved resistant to existing anti-glaucoma agents. Further research is...required, but this should not prevent its use under medical supervision.... Third, there is sufficient suggestive evidence of the potential usefulness of various cannabinoids as analgesic, anti-asthmatic, anti-spasmodic, and anti-convulsant agents." Hall, W, N Solowij, & J Lemon. (1994). The health and psychological consequences of cannabis use: Monograph prepared for the National Task for on Cannabis. Canberra: Australian Government Publishing Service. **57.** "Marijuana looks promising enough to recommend that there be new controlled studies done. The indications in which varying levels of interest was expressed are the following: appetite stimulation/cachexia, nausea and vomiting following anti-cancer therapy, neurological and movement disorders, analgesia [and] glaucoma." Conclusions of the National Institutes of Health. (1997). Workshop on the medical utility of marijuana: Report to the director. Bethesda: National Institutes of Health. **58.** House of Lords Select Committee on Science and Technology. (1998). Ninth report: Cannabis: The scientific and medical evidence. London: The Stationary Office. **59.** "Lords say, legalise cannabis for medical use." (1998). House of Lords Select Committee on Science and Technology Press Office. **60.** Joy, J, S Watson, & J Benson. (1999). *Marijuana and medicine: Assessing the science base*. Washington, DC: National Academy Press. **61.** Speaking at a national conference on addictions on March 3, 2000, Drug Czar Barry McCaffrey told reporters: "Ask a doctor if he really wants a big blunt stuck in a patient's face as treatment. A lot of this is a crock." **62.** The Harrison Narcotics Act. **63.** Herer, J. (1991). *The emperor wears no clothes*. Van Nuys, CA: HEMP Publishing. **64.** "Army study of marijuana smokers." *Newsweek*. January 15, 1945. **65.** See footnote 41. **66.** Ostrowski, J. (1989.) *Thinking about drug legalization*. (CATO Policy Analysis No. 121). Washington, DC: The CATO Institute. **67.** Less than 2,500 deaths were attributable to illicit drugs in 1985. By 1995, total deaths rose to almost 10,000. Drucker, E. (1999). Drug prohibition and public health: 25 years of evidence. *Public Health Reports*, 114: 14–27. **68.** Often with deadly results. See Armentano, P. "A man's home once was his castle." *Ideas on Liberty*, October 2000. **69.** *People v. Luna*, 1989 WL 13231 (N.Y. Court of Appeals, 1989), discussing, *US v. de Hernandez*. 473 US 531 in Ostrowski. **70.** Gingrich introduced H.R. 4170, "The Drug Importer Death Penalty Act of 1996," on September 25, 1996. The bill failed to gain majority support in Congress. **71.** This language was included in the Senate's "1999 Anti-Methamphetamine Proliferation Act" (S.R. 486), but was later removed by the House.

Postscript

Despite continued political debates regarding the legality of medicinal marijuana—debates that, frustratingly, have advanced little in the nearly ten years since my initial writing—clinical investigations of the therapeutic use of cannabis and cannabinoids are now more prevalent than at any other time in history. A search of the National Library of Medicine's PubMed website quantifies this fact. A keyword search using the terms "cannabinoids, 1996" reveals just 258 scientific journal articles published on the subject for that year. Perform this same search for the year 2007, and one will find over 3,400 published scientific studies.

While much of the renewed interest in cannabinoid therapeutics is a result of the discovery of the endocannabinoid regulatory system, some of this increased attention is also due to the growing body of testimonials from medicinal cannabis patients and their physicians. Nevertheless, despite this influx of anecdotal reports, much of the modern investigation of medicinal cannabis remains limited to preclinical (animal) studies of individual cannabinoids (e.g., THC or cannabidiol) and/or synthetic cannabinoid agonists (e.g. dronabinol or WIN 55, 212-2) rather than clinical trial investigations involving whole plant material. Predictably, because of the US government's strong public policy stance against any use of cannabis, the bulk of this modern marijuana research is taking place outside the United States.

As clinical research into the therapeutic value of marijuana has proliferated exponentially, so too has investigators' understanding of cannabis' remarkable ability to combat disease. Whereas researchers in the 1970s, '80s, and '90s primarily assessed cannabis' ability to temporarily alleviate various disease symptoms—such as the nausea associated with cancer chemotherapy—scientists today are exploring the potential role of cannabis to alter disease progression. Of particular interest, scientists are investigating cannabinoids' capacity to moderate autoimmune disorders such as multiple sclerosis, rheumatoid arthritis, and inflammatory bowel disease, as well as their role in the treatment of neurological disorders such as Alzheimer's disease and amyotrophic lateral sclerosis (a.k.a. Lou Gehrig's disease).

Investigators are also studying the anti-cancer activities of cannabis, as a growing body of preclinical and clinical data concludes that cannabinoids can reduce the spread of specific cancer cells via apoptosis (programmed cell death) and by the inhibition of angiogenesis (the formation of new blood vessels). Arguably, these latter trends represent far broader and more significant applications for cannabinoid therapeutics than researchers could have imagined some thirty or even twenty years ago. In 2007, I reviewed more than 150 published preclinical and clinical studies assessing the therapeutic potential of marijuana and its active compounds. Virtually all of these studies had been published within the past eight years. I summarized the findings of these studies in a book, now in its third edition, entitled *Emerging Clinical Applications for Cannabis and Cannabinoids: A Review of the Scientific Literature* (NORML Foundation, 2008; an online version is available at <www.norml.org>).

In many cases, this modern science is now affirming longtime anecdotal reports of medicinal marijuana users (e.g., the use of cannabis to alleviate gastrointestinal disorders). In other cases, this research is highlighting entirely new potential clinical utilities for cannabis (e.g., the use of cannabinoids to modify the progression of diabetes). In every case, this research illustrates the moral and intellectual bankruptcy of the US government's prevailing ban on medical cannabis—a policy that is as malicious as it is inept, and that has led to immeasurable human suffering.

Crushing Butterflies With Iron Boots
The 10 Longest Prison Sentences Being Served in the US for Cannabis
Peter Gorman

Since 1961, when the Single Convention Treaty on Psychotropic Drugs was signed by all member states of the United Nations at the urging of the United States, 26 million people have been arrested for marijuana throughout the world. Thirteen million of those were charged in the US. What started as a trickle of cannabis "offenders'" in 1961 rose to over 150,000 arrests in 1969; 380,000 in 1979; between 300,000 and 400,000 each year up to 1993, when arrests soared upwards every year under Bill Clinton and the Newt Gingrich Congress. There were 704,812 arrests in 1999.

Under George W. Bush, numbers rose virtually every year to reach a staggering 771,608 in 2004. Sentences being imposed in 2006 for cannabis offenses were longer than ever before. Of the 771,000-plus arrested in 2004, over 100,000 will serve some jail time, and tens of thousands will serve long, hard time for growing, selling, and even possessing (buying) cannabis. Any time in jail is heartbreaking for those imprisoned, their families, and those who love them. It is a crime against humankind that millions have been made to suffer pernicious punishment for living a peaceful and honest lifestyle with cannabis.

While we celebrate the incredible powers of cannabis, it is easy to forget the tens of thousands doing long, hard time. We're about to remember them.

■ ■ ■ ■ ■ ■ ■ ■ ■

Weldon Angelos was an aspiring rap producer from Salt Lake City who made a few bucks selling marijuana. His label, Extravagant Records, boasted Snoop Dogg among its initial clients. That they'll ever make a record together is unlikely, however, because Angelos—a/k/a #10053-081—has recently begun serving a 55-year sentence for a pot bust. His new home is the federal penitentiary at Lompoc, about 175 miles northwest of Los Angeles. His projected release date is November 18, 2051.

Angelos' crimes were that during 2002 he made three half-pound pot sales to an informant working as an undercover narc. According to the informant (whom even the prosecution painted as an unsavory character), during one of the sales Angelos had a gun in his car's front seat console, and during the other two he wore a gun in an ankle holster. Angelos has consistently denied that, saying he never took his guns from the safe in his apartment. Even the informant admitted that at no time were the alleged guns brandished. At no time was he threatened. In 2003, a year after the third buy, Angelos was arrested. When police searched his apartment they found several guns locked in a safe, money, and a small amount of marijuana.

> In all, Assistant US Attorney Robert Lund managed to blow the small pot deals into 20 separate felonies.

The Assistant US Attorney in the case, Robert Lund, offered Angelos a plea bargain that would have given him fifteen years. Angelos turned it down and went to trial. Lund, who had it in his discretion to charge Angelos with just the pot sales—as the guns never were alleged to have been used in the commission of them—instead charged Angelos with three separate offences of using a firearm during the commission of a drug felony, three drug sales, several drug possessions, and money-laundering. In all, Lund managed to blow the small pot deals into 20 separate felonies. Angelos was found guilty on sixteen. At sentencing, Lund insisted that the gun charges be stacked, and their sentences served consecutively, rather than concurrently, which gave Angelos five years mandatory on the first and 25 years mandatory on each of the others. He was given one additional day on the thirteen money-laundering and drug counts.

Crushing Butterflies With Iron Boots
The 10 Longest Prison Sentences Being Served in the US for Cannabis
Peter Gorman

303

US District Judge Paul Cassell reluctantly meted out the 55-years-plus-one-day mandatory sentence, calling it "unjust, cruel, and even irrational." He also called on President Bush to intervene and commute the sentence down to what he thought would be a reasonable eighteen years. In January 2006, the Tenth Circuit Court in Denver upheld the sentence after Angelos' attorneys appealed it on the grounds that it was cruel and unusual. They are now considering their legal options but have vowed to continue the appeal process. Technically, Angelos is serving time for guns. In fact, without the small cannabis sales, there would have been no federal case against him at all: A pound and a half in pot sales by a person with no criminal record isn't what they go after...normally. But it does happen, and Angelos is the proof.

With that in mind, and as a reminder of just how brutal our government can be, we present ten of the worst pot sentences currently being served.

■ ■ ■ ■ ■ ■ ■ ■ ■

1) Douglas Lamar Gray

#115332—Alabama State Penitentiary, St. Clair Correctional Facility. Life without parole. Sentence begun on July 1, 1992. No date of release.

Fifty-two-year-old roofing contractor Douglas Lamar Gray had a good business going in Moulton, Alabama, during the 1980s. As many as a dozen men were on his payroll during peak season. He had a young wife and baby boy. They owned their own house and had nothing but a good life to look forward to. Gray had no vices to speak of, and a history that was marred only by a burglary he'd committed at seventeen—for which he'd done a couple of months—and two more burglaries committed when he was twenty-one. Convictions so old they were not in the Alabama state computer system when he was arrested.

To relax, Gray liked to smoke marijuana. In 1989, a guy he knew offered to sell him a pound (the state claims it was a kilo) of weed for a good price. Gray said okay and agreed to meet at a local motel. They met, he paid the man $900, took his reefer, and left. What Gray didn't know was that the guy was working for the Morgan County Task Force. Gray would later discover that the snitch was a felon with more than two-dozen convictions who had been released specifically to work as a narc—and that he'd been paid $100 for the deal.

According to sketchy reports, Gray's car was followed from the motel meeting by several police cars. He managed to ditch the weed before he was caught. Gray imagined he'd get off because the police didn't find any marijuana; at the worst, he thought he'd have to do a little time for the pot, so when the prosecutor offered him a plea deal he turned it down and decided to go to trial.

Gray was found guilty, not of possession or attempted possession, but of trafficking. That still shouldn't have brought too much time. But horribly, he was sentenced to life without parole under Alabama's Habitual Offender Act, a sentence meted out because of the burglary convictions fifteen and nineteen years earlier. During his imprisonment his wife tried to commit suicide. All of Gray's appeals have been turned down. He'll grow old and die in prison. "Life behind bars is a lot of punishment for being set up on a pound of pot," he told the November Coalition in a letter in 2000.

2) Vernon C. McElroy

#102606—Alabama State Penitentiary, St. Clair Correctional Facility. Life with possibility of parole. Sentence begun on Nov. 5, 1981. No date of release.

Little is known about 58-year-old Vernon Cleve McElroy. In 1981 he was caught with 20 hemp stalks. He had a prior too old to be looked up in the Alabama computer system. He might never have been known to exist at all except that in 1991, when NORML's Executive Director, Allen St. Pierre, was

> "Life behind bars is a lot of punishment for being set up on a pound of pot."

brand-new to the organization, he received a letter from McElroy. A short correspondence ensued, during which McElroy claimed to be incarcerated at a maximum-security state prison in Alabama with several other men who were all serving life sentences for pot.

Using that as a lead, I tracked down McElroy at the maximum facility at St. Clair and spoke with the Alabama prison system's media representative, Brian Corbett, about him. Corbett confirmed that McElroy has been in since 1981. "But don't say it was just for pot," Corbett cautioned, reading a list of offenses for which McElroy had been sentenced. They included possession of marijuana, marijuana trafficking, receiving stolen property, and defacing the identification of a motor vehicle. The several convictions, coupled with McElroy's earlier conviction that the state cannot identify, led to the life sentence.

All of the crimes for which McElroy was sentenced occurred on the same day, during the same bust. What looks like happened was this: Someone approached McElroy and asked if McElroy could get him some weed. McElroy couldn't, but thinking the fellow an idiot instead of a snitch, he went out and cut 20 eight-foot ditch weed stalks. He brought them to the fellow, who said he had no money to pay for the dope but could give McElroy the stolen car he'd just heisted. McElroy accepted and blacked out the vehicle identification number (VIN) on the car door, at which point he was arrested and all of the charges followed.

Because he was not sentenced to life without parole, McElroy has a chance to one day be free.

3) George Martorano

#12973-004—Federal Bureau of Prisons, Coleman Penitentiary, central Florida. Life without parole. Entered prison in 1984. No release date.

George Martorano entered the federal prison system in 1984 when he was 34 years old. He's 56 now. Tall, good-looking, rugged, he has not let the years, the cells, or the injustice break him. If anything, they've made him stronger. Martorano was born to Raymond (Long John) Martorano, a Philadelphia mobster, in 1950. His godfather was the Philly mob-boss Angelo Bruno.

But rather than growing up Mafia, both his dad and Bruno insisted that Martorano would never be dirty. Unfortunately, Martorano found that being clean in business didn't really pay the bills, and when a chance to run shipments of marijuana from Florida up to Philly came his way, Martorano took it. "I ran pot for three years," he told *City Paper*, the Philadelphia alternative weekly, in March 2005.

In 1980, when Martorano was beginning to run truckloads of pot, his godfather Bruno died, leading to a mob war that stretched from Philly to South Jersey. It was bloody. Within two years more than a dozen mobsters had been killed, and the feds thought that George's father was in the thick of it. But he was untouchable at that time, so they turned their attention to the son. In 1982 he was arrested in a Holiday Inn in North Miami and charged with running an international narcotics-smuggling ring that moved marijuana and cocaine and manufactured meth and heroin.

Martorano's attorney advised him to plead guilty to the marijuana charge—there were 2,000 pounds of evidence—with the idea that he'd get 40 months, the length of time a parole board recommended he serve. Unexpectedly, the judge sentenced him to life and had him shipped off to the super-maximum pen

> Prior to her 25-year sentence, her record was spotless. She'd never gotten even a traffic ticket.

at Marion, Illinois, where he served two years in solitary before being moved to the general population in a New York facility. During that time there were hints that if he gave up what he knew about the Philly mob things might change for him, but he claimed—and still claims (according to people he's been in touch with)—that he had nothing to share, as he was never part of the mob.

During the past 22+ years, Martorano has become an accomplished writer, penning more than 20 books. He teaches yoga, counsels suicidal inmates, and is an officer of the Coleman chapter of the National Association for the Advancement of Colored People (NAACP).

4) Shirley Womble

#09330-017—Federal Bureau of Prisons, Marianna Penitentiary, Marianna, Florida. Twenty-five years for Conspiracy to Distribute Marijuana. Began serving on February 25, 1992. Release date: September 20, 2013.

Shirley Tucker Womble was 44 years old when she began serving her sentence for Conspiracy to Distribute Marijuana, and she won't be out until she's 65. That's if she completes only 85 percent of her mandatory 25 years. Her husband, Willard, convicted of trafficking marijuana, won't get out until six years after that. Of course, she might want the distance, as it was his pot sales that brought them both down. The Wombles owned an auto-sales business that brought in money, but Willard liked extra cash. According to a profile of Womble from

Crushing Butterflies With Iron Boots
The 10 Longest Prison Sentences Being Served in the US for Cannabis
Peter Gorman

305

the Human Rights 95 organization, she regularly tried to get her husband to stop putting their business and family in jeopardy, but he wouldn't quit.

"The extent of Shirley's involvement in the 'conspiracy' consisted of counting some money that Willard had earned from marijuana sales and being present on a few occasions when Willard met with co-conspirators," notes HR95. Nonetheless, the government charged her with being the marijuana organization's bookkeeper. Since being jailed, Womble has undergone several serious operations, and her health is not good. Prior to her 25-year sentence, her record was spotless. She'd never gotten even a traffic ticket.

5) Irma Estella Calderon Alred

#03436-017—Tallahassee Penitentiary, Tallahassee, Florida. Thirty years and four months for Marijuana Conspiracy. Began serving on December 12, 1994. Release date: September 28, 2020.

According to court records:

From 1984 until 1994, a group of individuals, known as the Alred Organization in Holmes County, Florida, engaged in an extensive marijuana distribution conspiracy involving thousands of pounds of marijuana. They primarily purchased the marijuana in the Texas/ Mexico area and transported it by vehicles to Holmes County, where it was sold. The principal source for obtaining Mexican marijuana was defendant-appellant Irma Alred, who was Irma Calderon in the mid-1980s when the conspiracy began. After delivering approximately 300 pounds of marijuana to co-conspirator Charles Douglas Mixon in Holmes County and remaining there until it was sold, she became an active participant in the organization.

In early 1994 the Alred Organization was busted, and nine people were subsequently indicted. Two served two years, one served seven, one served nine, and the rest got no jail time. In all, the court held Irma Alred responsible for a total of 2,899 pounds of marijuana—lousy Mexican brick—over a ten-year period. Irma got the time because the others, including her husband, made deals with the government, leaving her holding the bag.

6) Calvin John Treiber

#03999-046—Florence Federal Penitentiary, Florence, Colorado. Twenty-nine years for Conspiracy to Distribute Marijuana and other marijuana counts. Began serving on February 4, 1994. Release date: September 2, 2017. (Treiber served nearly eighteen months in a local jail prior to his federal sentencing.)

In an operation the FBI dubbed "Operation Reggae North," Calvin Treiber, a Rastafarian, his wife, Jodie Israel-Treiber, and 24 others were indicted in November 1992 and charged with possession of marijuana, possession with intent to distribute, conspiracy to distribute, money-laundering, and a host of other

These sentences were handed down in a case that involved little marijuana, no money, and three witnesses who should've been doing jail time.

counts. The government alleged that the group had moved hundreds of pounds of Mexican marijuana to Billings, Montana, over a ten-year period. Found guilty on several charges, Treiber was sentenced to 29 years, while his wife—who played a very minor role, if any—was sentenced to eleven. She was fortunate enough to be granted clemency by then-President Bill Clinton in his final days in office, but Treiber didn't have the same luck.

In 1996, Treiber (who is now 46), along with two others from the conspiracy, appealed on the grounds that they should have been allowed to present a religious-use defense, as cannabis use is sacramental to Rastafarians. On February 2, 1996, the Ninth Circuit Court of Appeals responded that subsequent to the Religious Freedom Restoration Act of 1993, Rastafarians had the right to present such a defense. However, in writing for the court, Judge John T. Noonan, Jr., noted that while a religious defense might protect against simple possession, the RFRA could not be applied to charges of conspiracy to distribute, possession, or money-laundering. "Nothing before us suggests that Rastafarianism would require that conduct," Noonan wrote.

7) Clyde Edward Young

#03933-003—Yazoo City Federal Penitentiary, Yazoo, Mississippi. Twenty-six years for Possession and Conspiracy to Distribute Marijuana and Career Criminal Enterprise. Began serving on February 1, 1991. Release date: June 23, 2013.

In a true horror story from the old South, Clyde Edward Young, his wife Patricia, their son Clyde Young, Jr., and three of their other children were given sentences of twenty-six years, twenty-four years and eight months, fifteen years, ten years, five years, and three years, respectively. These sentences were handed down in a case that involved little marijuana, no money, and three witnesses who should've been doing jail time.

The Young family, Clyde and Patricia with their eight kids, lived on the border of Mississippi and Alabama. Their property was surrounded by the property of local wealthy businessman J.P. Altmire. Altmire tried to buy the Young place. They didn't want to sell. Altmire didn't like that and began a campaign of harassment against them that included writing letters to "lawyers, prosecutors and the local sheriff branding the family a bunch of troublemakers," according to Mikki Norris and Human Rights 95, who profiled them on the HR95.org website.

The harassment led to an August 1988 bust of Clyde Jr., who was charged with growing marijuana on Altmire's land. But in a thorough and apparently brutal search of the Young home following the bust, no drugs were found. Nonetheless, a year later the Young house was again raided, and several members of the family were arrested. At their indictment it was revealed that drug residue, a scale, and a notebook containing names were found in an earlier 1986 raid at a hunt club owned by Clyde Young's mother.

Though there was apparently little or no marijuana found that could be tied to the Youngs, at trial several witnesses testified that the Youngs were marijuana dealers. Among them was the local police chief's son, then facing serious time for several drug convictions, and a witness facing 40 years for trafficking and who is now serving time for perjury. The Youngs were convicted. Patricia was paroled on April 22, 2005, after serving more than fourteen years. Their children have all been released. Only Clyde Sr. remains inside.

8) Olen Maffett Pound

#09064-042—Montgomery Federal Penitentiary, Montgomery, Alabama. Twenty years for Continuing Criminal Enterprise. Started serving on February 27, 1990. Released 2006.

It's nearly incomprehensible that people get put in prisons for drug offenses in which there are little or no actual drugs. But to be convicted of a Continuing Criminal Enterprise in that sort of case—particularly when the charge is brought against someone with no priors—is beyond the beyond. Yet that's what happened to Olen Pound.

Pound and his friends used to buy pot for each other. It went on for years. No large amounts, nobody really making any-

> They ransacked his home and came up with one-tenth of a gram of pot, on the strength of which they arrested Pound and his wife.

thing, just an excuse for friends to get together. Whoever could make the score would. But in 1989 one of the friends was popped in Memphis, Tennessee, turned snitch, and set up one of the others. The rest tumbled like dominos, each one ratting out as many as they could, and each time they bleated, Pound's name came up as one of their crew. Police tried and failed to set up a buy from him, and resorted to raiding his home in rural Mississippi. They ransacked it and came up with one-tenth of a gram of pot, on the strength of which they arrested Pound and his wife.

Based on the word of the snitches, the police charged them with involvement with a total of 300 pounds of cannabis, for which a first-timer would normally get five years—the sentence meted out to his wife. But the prosecutor decided not to go for attempted possession or possession with intent to distribute. Instead he went for the jugular: Continuing Criminal Enterprise. Pound was hit with the automatic 20 years. Incidentally, the government got to seize the Pound's property—on which he'd built a recreational park business worth $1,000,000, and another $250,000 in general assets: cars, house, personal property, and so forth. Oh, and none of the others were ever prosecuted.

Crushing Butterflies With Iron Boots
The 10 Longest Prison Sentences Being Served in the US for Cannabis
Peter Gorman

307

9) Charles Fred Cundiff

#09400-017—Coleman Federal Penitentiary, Coleman, Florida. Life without parole for Marijuana Conspiracy and Career Criminal. Started serving on January 8, 1992. Release date: Never.

In 1976, as a 30-year-old, Charles Cundiff was busted for possession of a pound and a half of weed and paraphernalia. Eight months later, while out on bail, he was busted again, this

As in many of the other cases, no marijuana was connected with him physically, or even via ledger, telephone, or any other way—it was just plain snitching.

time for selling a half-pound. He was subsequently convicted of felonies on both busts and got two years on each, served concurrently. He served seven months and stayed clean for nine years. But in 1985, he was busted again, his third felony. This time it was for growing 100 marijuana plants. He served 47 days and got three years probation.

Then, in the early 1990s, he and some friends were convicted of a conspiracy to traffic in marijuana, and Cundiff was held responsible for 2,273 kilograms. Worse, there were two guns found in his car shortly after his arrest, and the prosecutor decided to ask for, and subsequently received, a Career Criminal Enhancement to the sentence, which would otherwise have been about 22 years. The enhancement was granted and Cundiff got life.

10) Steven Roger Treleaven

#08656-023—Florence Federal Penitentiary, Florence, Colorado. Twenty years for Conspiracy to Manufacture Marijuana. Started serving on November 30, 1992. Release date: September 1, 2009.

Mandatory minimums and a prior felony cost Steven Treleaven an extra ten years. During the late 1980s, Treleaven began growing marijuana, primarily to provide his brother, who suffered from AIDS, with a medical supply.

Unfortunately he didn't do it alone; he had two partners, and not all of the marijuana was being used for medicinal purposes. When busted, the three were charged with conspiracy to manufacture a total of 3,698 plants, each of which was assigned a weight of 1,000 grams. Under mandatory mini-

mums, Treleaven, found guilty of possessing more than 3,000 kilos of marijuana, was given a mandatory ten years. A prior conviction for cocaine possession doubled that. His brother died during Treleaven's first year in prison.

■ ■ ■ ■ ■ ■ ■ ■ ■

These ten snapshots aren't nearly enough. Scott Howard Walt is just over halfway into 24 years at the Tucson Federal Pen for possession of marijuana and intent to distribute, in a case where the only marijuana was found on an acquaintance who claimed Walt was a pot boss and he was just a courier. It worked out for the government, as they were able to seize Walt's assets, and it worked out for the busted fellow, as he wound up with only one year.

Then there's Steve Williams, also a little over midway through 24 years for conspiracy to distribute marijuana. Like most of the others, the case against him began when someone came looking for pot and wound up getting busted and turning informant. As in many of the other cases, no marijuana was connected with him physically, or even via ledger, telephone, or any other way—it was just plain snitching.

And there's the Avery family, headed by John Paul Avery, who were found to be growing 1,250 plants in an underground grow room in Kentucky in 1994. Story is, when Avery's son-in-law and a friend were busted by the DEA for the grow room, they took the heat off themselves and pointed fingers at John's family. Avery got 20 years for an ongoing criminal enterprise and is expected to see daylight again in 2012.

Perhaps the topper of them all, though it isn't strictly related to marijuana, is the case of Tyrone Dwayne Brown, sentenced to life in Texas. Known on the street as T-Baby, Brown was a hell-raiser and a thug as a young teen. Regularly sent to special schools and juvenile jails for car-theft and a host of other crimes, at seventeen he was busted for aggravated robbery. He got ten years deferred, one of the conditions of which was peeing in a cup for drug tests. Two months into the program he failed and had his probation revoked. At his court date on the probation violation, the judge decided he'd had enough and sentenced him to aggravated-life. Though it wasn't marijuana that caused his initial problems, Brown may well be the only guy in the whole country sentenced to life for failing a urine test. He was given a conditional release by Texas Governor Rick Perry in early 2007.

The list goes on. If it weren't for public outcry, some of the people who've been given the worst sentences would be sitting until their children's children had children. Will Foster got 93 years in Oklahoma for a small pot grow that came from an informant's tip that he was a big-time meth manufacturer. There was no meth, of course, and media light forced the state to release him after four years.

Jimmy Montgomery, also of Oklahoma, got 110 years for less than two ounces on a first-time bust. A paraplegic, he had a gun—one he'd inherited from his father, a former cop—under his wheelchair seat when he was busted at home. The issue of his medical problems forced Oklahoma's governor to shorten the sentence to ten years and have him serve it at home rather than force the state to care for a paraplegic for 110 years.

meth, crack, cocaine, LSD, and every other substance the US government has felt it has a right to ban, all in the name of protecting us from ourselves.

Don't forget them. Don't ignore them. No one deserves this kind of time for nonviolent offences.

■ ■ ■ ■ ■ ■ ■ ■ ■

For more information on prisoners with excessive sentences, please visit:

www.Famm.org
www.November.com
www.HR95.org
www.Candoclemency.com

Read the book *Busted: Drug War Survival Skills* by M. Chris Fabricant to help mitigate any charges or difficulties that you may encounter while being involved with the cannabis culture.

Though it wasn't marijuana that caused his initial problems, Brown may well be the only guy in the whole country sentenced to life for failing a urine test.

Don Clark was nailed with a life sentence as "the man who taught people to grow pot in the Florida swamps." The government charged him with responsibility for *one million* plants, but he got real lucky and was released in just under ten years when Bill Clinton gave him clemency, due partly to public outcry.

James Geddes also got lucky when enough people pointed out the injustice of his case. Geddes was busted with a friend and charged with cultivation of five plants. He refused a plea, took it to trial, and lost. Geddes was sentenced to 150 years: 75 for the cultivation and 75 for possession of the same plants. That was also in Oklahoma, home of marijuana hell. He served more than eleven years before the state decided that perhaps 150 years was excessive for five plants and let him out on early release.

These are just a few of many horror stories, and they don't even begin to touch the sentences people are serving for

Crushing Butterflies With Iron Boots
The 10 Longest Prison Sentences Being Served in the US for Cannabis
Peter Gorman

309

Toad-Licking Blues
Thomas Lyttle

"Toad licking" or "toad smoking" are the terms that newspaper reporters attached to the ingestion of *Bufo* venom by users of illicit drugs. This was (and is) done with the intent purpose of getting stoned or high, or going into a trance in a shamanic manner. (It is important to note that bufotenine—a minor constituent of all *Bufo* toad venoms—is *not* hallucinogenic.) In light of this, politicians and the courts stepped in to attempt to control this perceived drug-misuse problem.

It is important to note that bufotenine— a minor constituent of all *Bufo* toad venoms—is *not* hallucinogenic.

In 1967 the Food and Drug Administration placed bufotenine in Schedule 1 of the Controlled Substances Act. Schedule 1 maintains that a drug (or plant or substance) shows no redeeming medical value, is too dangerous for human research, and has a high potential for abuse.

Bufo toads are well-known as part of shamanic rituals. No mention of the oral ingestion of toad venom exists in classic shamanic literature, however, because the bufotenine present in the venom does not cause trance or mystical experiences, and both bufotenine and the hallucinogenic 5-MeO-DMT are inactive orally.[1] Also, 5-MeO-DMT is present in only one species of *Bufo* toad, *Bufo alvarius*.

Toxic reactions in human and lower animals are common, however, and include death (in animals) from oral toad venom ingestion.[2] Toad smoking and toad licking should be profiled and studied as two distinct activities. This is an important consideration, especially when studying media reports about toad licking, which involves the oral ingestion of the venom only.

The subject of these clandestine or cult-like uses of *Bufo* toads presents an interesting dilemma for researchers. The very nature of such activity makes open data-gathering troublesome. Anecdotal or word-of-mouth descriptions often prove invaluable for building a tentative profile of any illegal drug activity or a legal but persecuted drug activity. This case involves alleged illegal bufotenine use and misuse, and legal but persecuted 5-MeO-DMT misuse.

From all this (but usually with little concern for scientific facts), the media continue to print "psychedelic toad" articles, thus continuing and sensationalizing age-old *Bufo* toad mythologies, including the myth that bufotenine is hallucinogenic. The focus of these many popular articles is on *Bufo* toads and getting high from bufotenine and its analogs. This is confusing, as only one of the analogs (not bufotenine) causes hallucination.

Bufo Toad Smoking

In the late 1960s, LSD evangelist Art Kleps founded a psychedelic church called the Neo-American Church. The church's newsletter was called "Divine Toad Sweat."[3] In 1984, *Bufo* toad evangelist Albert Most revealed his Church of the Toad of Light with his publication of the book *Bufo Alvarius: Psychedelic Toad of the Sonoran Desert*. (The Sonoran Desert covers parts of Arizona, California, and Mexico.) This small booklet details how to use the *Bufo* toad for ritual and pleasure, as well as how to catch the *Bufo alvarius* toad, extract or "milk" the glandular secretions, dry them, and "enjoy the smoked venom." Most's book claims that 5-MeO-DMT (5-methoxy-N, N-dimethyltryptamine) is the active hallucinogen, not bufotenine. He is correct, as 5-MeO-DMT is the O-methylated version of bufotenine.[4] Again, it is important to mention that 5-Me0-DMT is present in only one of the more than 200 types of *Bufo* toads.

Bufotenine is illegal to possess in the United States because it is a Schedule 1 drug, even though it is not psychoactive; 5-MeO-DMT is unscheduled and legal to possess, even though it is psychoactive. This makes 5-MeO-DMT potentially illegal in the US as an analog of bufotenine or DMT, by application of the 1987 drug analog act. Possession of only one type of *Bufo* toad (the type that contains both substances in endogenous forms) for the purpose of getting "stoned or high" or for sacramental use remains in legal limbo, pending legislative debate, which is ongoing at the time of this writing. Although seemingly far-fetched, conspiracy to possess a (certain type of) *Bufo* toad may someday be a civil violation or a crime in the United States.

In contrast, a letter to the author talks about the introduction of "hallucinatory toad venom" to well-known American Indian artist Christobal. This letter details Christobal's "yarn art" (a stylized shamanic art form, based loosely in traditional Huichol yarn art). One of Christobal's artworks was based on his ritually taking *Bufo* toad venom. Letter writer Jacaeber Kastor stated that "the colors are very subdued in the Polaroid. They are vibrant and fluorescent in the yarn painting, etc. This piece has to do with Leo [Mercado] turning Christobal on to the *Bufo* toad secretions and Christobal incorporating the desert toad into his technology-iconography, etc….a very interesting mixology."[5] Kastor is the owner of an art gallery in New York City called Psychedelic Solution. Leo Mercado, at the time, was a deacon in the Peyote Way Church of God in Arizona. In a note to author Bartlett J. Ridge, Kastor stated that "the *Bufo* toad is in their [Huichol] cosmology, but I don't think any of the elders have tried smoking it."[6]

Christobal's actual description of the *Bufo* toad-venom "visions" is as follows:

> The symbol of brother toad and the mushroom, which are Gods…to give wisdom of the shamanism, and how to study; how to be able to communicate and be able to receive direction. And encounter the sacred spaces that exist. Because not all (places) serve for that which one wants to know.
>
> For the Gods say in which place, one can ask for that; which a person "living in reality" wants to know. To be able to learn here, is when the shaman are in the sacred places with their candles, praying to wait for the

> hour when God arrives…to be able to communicate for their powers and ask for luck for their shamanism. And when that hour arrives, they see the candles surge… the life-force appears, as if it explodes…. And from the sparks, the force which comes out is seen, and that is the way it is, where the transformation occurs. It is power which the brother toad and the mushrooms have. Because in this way…the Gods speak.[7]

A more recent anecdotal account showing *Bufo* toad-venom use comes from the *Village Voice* in July 1990. Author G. Trebay described art critic Carlo McCormick's sojourn with the hallucinogenic *Bufo* toad: "the group drank tincture of Peyote, chewed dried Peyote buttons and smoked the dried secretions of a desert toad whose toxins produce…'an effect'"[8]

There is anthropological literature to support *Bufo* toad smoking among New World tribes and shamans. Part of this literature is riddled with confusion, based on hearsay and poor research. The excellent paper "Identity of a New World

5-MeO-DMT is present in only one of the more than 200 types of *Bufo* toads.

Psychoactive Toad"[9] sums up parts of the research problems: "When Dobkin de Rios asserts that 'Bufotenine' is an hallucinogenic drug which has dangerous cardiovascular effects in man and is usable only in low doses (1974:149) she not only ignores pharmacological evidence (Holmstedt & Lindren 1967; Turner & Merfis 1959) but she also appears to be confusing the physiological effects of the cardioactive steroid in the venom, with the purported activity of bufotenine on the central nervous system…."

The paper goes on to dispel research myths "created by experts": "When LaBarre (1970:146) refers to bufotenine as a 'violently hallucinogenic drug' he mistakenly attributes the psychoactivity of the South American vegetable snuffs to bufotenine (5-OH-DMT) when it has already been well established that the compound responsible was not bufotenine but rather 5-MeO-DMT (Holmstedt & Lindgren 1967)." These authors also clearly understand the many confusions. They have shown that it may be a mistake to cite secondary as opposed to primary sources when establishing a profile of the pharmacological action of a little-known drug like bufotenine or 5-MeO-DMT.

Bufo Toad Licking

The first wave of news reports regarding toad licking occurred in the early 1980s in the popular press, and have continued to the present.[10] Although highly sensationalized in the media, this story is developing still, and holds implications for serious social

Although seemingly farfetched, conspiracy to possess a (certain type of) *Bufo* toad may someday be a civil violation or a crime in the United States.

pharmacologists, sociologists, and legal experts, not to mention animal-rights activists.

These toad-licking stories are usually reported in English-speaking regions (South America and Central America, Canada, the United States, and Australia) where the *Bufo* toad is either indigenous or where it has been introduced from its indigenous environment and bred. Reports have also appeared where the *Bufo* toad has been artificially introduced into an ecosystem for reasons of "pest control."[11]

The practice of toad licking seems to have developed out of the legendary and mythological uses of *Bufo* toads throughout history. For example, Christopher Columbus carried *Bufo* toads aboard his ships on his return trip from "discovering" America.[12] And both *Lancet* and *Discover* magazines reported that "classic German violinists used to handle [*Bufo*] toads before their performances because the toxins reduced the sweat on their palm."[13]

In the mid-1980s, *Discover* reported that Australian "hippies" were forsaking "traditional illegal drugs for *Cane* toads, which they boil for a slimy, potentially lethal cocktail."[14] A later corresponding report described "the drug squad in Brisbane (Australia) as having...a Heinz Baby-Food jar which carried the label 'Venom Cane Toad: Hallucinogenic; Bufotenine'."[15]

In 1986 a report by Hitt and Ettinger[16] described a five-year-old boy licking (by accident) a live *Bufo* toad. Profuse salivation and seizures were reported, and the boy was admitted to the University of Arizona Medical Center. Within fifteen minutes of licking the toad, severe complications developed; the child survived.

A few months later, a "Dr. Inaga" gave a lecture in Baltimore in which he "comically" mentioned the Australian report, and the "phenomena [of toad licking]."[17] Almost simultaneously Dr. Alex Stalcup, then of the Haight-Ashbury Free Medical Clinics, gave this statement to reporters: "[I]t is amazing the lengths that people will go to, to get high."[18] He was referring to the many recent toad-licking articles starting to circulate in the media.

The media interest regarding *Bufo* toads was the topic of discussion at a 1989 conference on crack cocaine misuse in San Francisco.[19] Police Chief R. Nelson of Berkeley, California, was there, and commented that "[toad-licking]...is a problem that comes up from time to time," legitimizing the rumors. Pressed at a news conference, Robert Sager, head of the Drug Enforcement Administration's (DEA) Western regional laboratory, said "[*Bufo* toad venom/bufotenine]...is in the same legal category as LSD and heroin."[20] This further confused the issue through incomplete comparisons. While all three are in the same legal category, only LSD and heroin are widely misused drugs; and bufotenine is not psychoactive, regardless of the DEA's beliefs.

A New York City DEA spokesman also stated to the press that "we have heard of it [toad licking or smoking]...but have yet to make an arrest," implying that there was some sort of an active problem.[21] The rumors now circled back to the Haight-Ashbury Free Medical Clinics. In response to the *Bufo* toad press releases, the Clinic stated that "ironically...the DEA's actions have inspired a few people to try licking live toads."[22]

Reporters now pressed anyone they could find to investigate these fantastic but apparently "legitimate" stories. In Australia, Glen Ingram—a herpetologist at Queensland Museum—told the press "it [*Bufo* toad venom] gives them a kick like alcohol." This and other wire-service stories led some Australians to react with "panic" according to *Scientific American*.[23] Alarmed at the latest "drug craze" and the infestation of *Cane* toads (which also occasionally poison pets, especially dogs that cannot leave them alone), people in Australia formed "toad eradication leagues."[24] Back in California a probation officer stated to the media that "we hear of youngsters who do this frequently [lick live *Bufo* toads]...it's not as strong as LSD, but it's free."[25]

At this point little in the way of actual names, precise locations, witnesses to events, hospital reports, or deaths appeared in the legitimate press surrounding these stories. The press had repeatedly quoted "experts" in related drug-misuse fields. These quotes fueled rumors, hyperbole, and a lot of fantastic misinformation. As well, most of the press reports surrounding *Bufo* toad misuse lacked the solid primary sources needed for tracing facts.

Later in 1990, after a bulk of fantastic literature had been created, this started to change. The press grew even bolder. Reports naming "P. Cherrie and R. Murphy" appeared in the *Albany Times Union*. These stories reported that "Paul Cherrie saw a TV show about 'toad-licking' and decided to experiment. They scraped some [*Bufo*] toad secretions from the back of the *Cane* toads in Cherrie's collection and spread it on a cracker."[26] Murphy, 21, said that after an hour of "deep hallucinations" that he "awoke…'bam!'…in the hospital. Both men suffered from severe vomiting." This story was amended a few days later in the tabloids, which reported that "Murphy had killed himself after being prematurely released from the hospital."[27]

Stanton Geer was named next, awaiting trial in Columbia after being arrested on "toad licking" charges. He faced a sentence of "two years and a $10,000 fine, if convicted of drug misuse."[28] Other names also started appealing in press releases.

During all of this, Dr. Alex Stalcup of the Haight-Ashbury Free Medical Clinics in San Francisco complained that "we were getting calls from all over the world—Germany, England, South America, etc.—from reporters wondering about this new high."[29] According to Dr. Sager of the DEA, Australian journalists were now studying the situation in the US "to see if there was a *Cane* toad problem in California."[30]

According to *Scientific American*, the main problem with substantiating these original and then these later reports was "that they are all based in other reports…and that there is no evidence to support them."[31] Journalist Edeen Uzelac said "that this is a case of media feeding on media."[32] Words like "urban legend," a term coined by professor and author Jan Brunvand (*The Choking Doberman*, etc.), were now being used along with other explanations for this media circus. Around this time, the popular television show *LA Law* even did a segment about a man charged with using *Bufo* toads to illegally get high.

In all this confusion, a number of legislators were convinced that where there was smoke there must be fire. Not to be beaten to the punch so far as solutions to this new so-called drug epidemic, Georgia State Representative Beverly Langford (D–Calhoun) introduced legislation to the State General Assembly regarding toad licking: "In a resolution introduced Monday, apparently with a straight face, Rep. Beverly Langford…called on the General Assembly to look into the 'extreme dangers of toad licking becoming the designer drug of choice in today's sophisticated society…The [Assembly] has been very diligent in finding and proposing a legitimate solution to every conceivable type of drug problem….'"[33] South Carolina Representative Patrick P. Harris also introduced similar legislation that same year (1990), finding the practice of toad licking "repulsive but amusing" and suggested sentencing offenders to "60 hours of public service in a local zoo."[34]

The next legislative attempt to curb this new drug menace appeared in Vancouver, British Columbia (Canada). This report stated that "…Vancouver police today said that they want the Canadian government to ban imports of the potentially lethal giant toad blamed on the deaths of several Australian drug users…. Cpl. John Dragoni said the city police force is applying to Ottowa to prohibit ownership of…the toads…by outlawing them under the Federal Narcotics Control Act."[35] Amid this hysteria, legislators in New South Wales, Australia, also passed laws against psychoactive toad use, making bufotenine a Schedule 2 Controlled Substance under the Queensland Drug Misuse Act of 1986,[36] which again is ironic as bufotenine is not hallucinogenic.

> "In a resolution introduced Monday, apparently with a straight face, Rep. Beverly Langford…called on the General Assembly to look into the 'extreme dangers of toad licking becoming the designer drug of choice in today's sophisticated society…'"

Trying to lend credibility to what was becoming an embarrassing flurry of misinformation, medical anthropologist George Root—a former administrator at SP Labs in Miami, Florida—had this to say: "[T]here has been much speculation in the anthropological literature regarding the possible hallucinogenic uses of *Bufo*. This debate is largely based on the fact that *Bufo* is a common representation in the art of some Meso American peoples…and the fact that *Bufo* skeletal remains have been

Toad-Licking Blues
Thomas Lyttle

discovered at archaeological sites…. Speculations aside… there is a very good reason why licking toads will not get you high. The toxic compounds are likely to kill you before you could possibly consume enough bufotenine to have any hallucinogenic effect (if there is an hallucinogenic effect)."[37] The author's academic article "Misuse and Legend in the Toad Licking Phenomena"[38] also capsulized a lot of this data, as well as the media "comedy of errors" created in part by quotes from legitimate but misinformed scholars.

Calavaras County, California, has also been the site of a highly publicized *Bufo* toad seizure and arrest. In early 1994, Bob and Connie Shepard were arrested for breeding *Bufo* toads for psychoactive uses. Four toads were impounded and the couple was charged with possession of bufotenine, called "toad missionaries," and Bob Shepard was placed on a special form of probation called PC-1000 (of the California Drug Diversion Act for first-time, nonviolent offenders) after a highly publicized media circus.[39]

James Kent's short article "The Truth About Toad Licking"[40] talked about "smoking the chopped skins" of the toad and "coming on almost instantly…you will feel a buzzing head-rush, and notice a profound change in light and color perception. Acute closed-eye visual hallucinations…and heart palpitations…are commonly reported." Kent also mentioned a graduate thesis by David Spoerke, M.S., R.Ph., in this area. This thesis gives a lot of detailed information regarding emergency-room treatments of humans and animals poisoned by toad venom.

High Times magazine also ran a brief review of the psychedelic toad myths, mentioning that the MTV show *Beavis and Butt-Head* was touting toad licking in one episode, although a bullfrog, not an actual toad, was shown.[41] "The show reflects what is going on in the youth culture" said a spokesman for the TV show.[42] *High Times* has periodically run articles following the *Bufo* story, with seven articles appearing between 1974 and 1995.

■ ■ ■ ■ ■ ■ ■ ■ ■ ■

Science often supports myth, but sometimes science is overtaken, creating or re-creating newer and more complex myths. There is no doubt that the *Bufo* toad has been and is central to humankind's medicines, mythologies, and religions since ancient times. Part of this connection is based in psychology, part in pharmacology, and a good part remains a mystery. Future researchers must recognize that there is a considerable confusion regarding this subject, but that it is possible to turn a toad into a prince with correct and accurate information.

Endnotes

1. Root, G. (1990). "First, the bad news, toad licking will not get you high." [Letter]. *New Times* (Miami, Florida); Horgan, J. (1990). "*Bufo* abuse—A toxic toad gets licked, boiled, tee'd up and tanned." *Scientific American* 263 (2), pp 26–7; McKim, W. (1986). *Drugs and behavior: An introduction to behavioral pharmacology.* New Jersey: Prentice Hall. **2.** Chem, M.S., C.Y. Ray, & D.L. Wu. (1991). "Biologic intoxication due to digitalis-like substance after ingestion of cooked toad soup." *American Journal of Cardiology* 67 (5), pp 443–4; Uzelac, E. (1990). (Reprinted from the *Baltimore Sun*). "A desperation high: Crack? Coke? Croak!" *Seattle Times*, Jan. 30; Anonymous (1986). "It could have been an extremely grim fairy tale." *Discover* 7 (8), p 12; McLeod, W.R. & B.R. Sitaram. (1985). "Bufotenine reconsidered." *Acta Psychiatrica Scandinavica* 72, pp 447–50. **3.** Kleps, A. (1971). *The boo-hoo bible.* San Cristobal, New Mexico: Toad Books. **4.** Shulgin, A.T. (1988). *The Controlled Substances Act.* Lafayette, California: privately published; Marki, F., J. Axelrod, & B. Witkop. (1962). "Catecholeamines and methyl transferases in the South American toad, *Bufo marinus*." *Biochimica et Biophysica Acta* 58, pp 367–9; Gessner, P.K., P.A. Khairallah, & W.M. McIsaac. (1961). "Pharmacological actions of some methoxy-indolealkylamines." *Nature* 190, pp 179–80. **5.** Lyttle, T. (1989a). Letter from Jacaeber Kastor. Personal communication. **6.** Lyttle, T. (1989b). "Drug-based religions and contemporary drug taking." *Journal of Drug Issues* 18 (2), pp 271–84. **7.** Christobal. (1989). One-page handwritten note describing *Bufo* visions. (From the collection of Thomas Lyttle.) **8.** Trebay, G. (1990). "Mexican standoff: Carlo McComick's bad trip." *Village Voice*, July 10, pp 19. **9.** Davis, W. & A.T. Weil. (1992). "Identity of a New World psychoactive toad." *Ancient Mesoamerica* 3 (1), pp 51–9. **10.** Chamakura, R.P. (1994). "Bufotenine—a hallucinogen in ancient snuff powders of South America and a drug of abuse on the streets of New York City." *Forensic Science Review* 6 (1), pp 1–18; *Op cit.*, Davis & Weil. **11.** Anonymous. (1990). "Australia's investment in cane toads." *Chicago Tribune*, April 19, section 1, p 14a; Lewis, S. & M. Lewis. (1989). *Cane toads: An unnatural history.* (Based on a film by Mark Lewis.) New York: Dolphin, Doubleday; Ebert, R. (1988). "Hungry toads raising cane." (Review of Lewis & Lewis, *Cane toads*.) *New York Post*, October 1, p 2. **12.** Davis, W. (1985). *The serpent and the rainbow.* New York: Simon & Schuster. **13.** *Op cit.*, Anonymous (1986). **14.** *Ibid.* **15.** *Op cit.*, Lewis & Lewis. **16.** Hitt, M. & D.D. Ettinger. (1986). "Toad toxicity." *New England Journal of Medicine* 314, p 1517. **17.** *Op cit.*, Lewis & Lewis. **18.** Carillo, C. (1990). "Toads take a licking from desperate druggies." *New York Post*, Jan. 31, p 4. **19.** Presley, D. (1990). "Toad licking poses threat to youth of America." *Weekly World News*, July 11, p 5; Seligman, K. (1989). "The latest high—warts and all—thrill seekers risk death to lick toads." *San Francisco Examiner*, May 29, pp A1, A10. **20.** *Op cit.*, Seligman. **21.** *Op cit.*, Carillo. **22.** *Ibid.* **23.** *Op cit.*, Horgan. **24.** *Ibid.* **25.** Montgomery, C. (1990). "Druggies find new way to get high: They lick toads." *Weekly World News*, Oct. 28, p 6. **26.** Anonymous. (1990b). "Toad lickers gamble with death." *Sea Frontiers* 36 (May/June), p 5–6. **27.** Alexander, J. (1990). "Toad licker kills himself." *Weekly World News*, Oct. 2, p 21. **28.** Street, M. (1990). "Toad licker busted." *Weekly World News*, March 13, p 9. **29.** Dorgan, M. (1990). "Nobody, but nobody licks toads in California." *Albany Sunday Times Union*, February 18, p A24. **30.** *Ibid.* **31.** *Ibid.* **32.** *Ibid.* **33.** Secrest, D.K. (1990). "Bill gets hopping on way to lick toad drug problem." *Atlanta Journal and Constitution*, Feb 13, p D1f. **34.** Richards, B. (1994). "Toad smoking gains on toad licking among drug users." *Wall Street Journal*, March 7, pp A1, A8. **35.** Anonymous. (1991). [Reuters News Service.] "Drug addicts licking giant toads to get high." *Palm Beach Post*, July 31, p 9a. **36.** *Op cit.*, Chamakura. **37.** *Op cit.*, Root. **38.** Lyttle, T. (1993). "Misuse and legend in the 'toad licking' phenomena." *International Journal of the Addictions* 28 (6), pp 521–38. **39.** Bancroft, A. (1994). "Couple who smoked toad venom avoid jail." *San Francisco Chronicle*, April 29, p B5; Boire, R.G. (1994). "Criminalizing nature and knowledge." *The Entheogen Law Reporter* 2, pp 1–3; De Korne, J. (1994). "Toadal confusion." *The Entheogen Review*, Summer, pp 10–1; Reed, D. (1994). "Man gets high on toad, narcotics agents are not amused." *San Francisco Chronicle*, Jan. 29, pp A17, 122. **40.** Kent, J. (1994). "The truth about toad licking." *Psychedelic Illuminations*, Winter. **41.** Wishnia. (1995). "Dances with toads." *High Times*, January, pp 21, 34. **42.** *Op cit.*, Richards.

You Are Still Being Lied To

The War on Consciousness
Graham Hancock

We are told that the "War on Drugs" is being waged, on our behalf, by our governments and their armed bureaucracies and police forces, to save us from ourselves. "Potential for abuse and harm" are supposed to be the criteria by which the use of drugs is suppressed—the greater a drug's potential for abuse and harm, the greater and more vigorous the degree of suppression, and the more draconian the penalties applied against its users.

In line with this scheme drugs are typically ranked into a hierarchy: Schedules I, II, and III in the US, Classes A, B, and C in the UK, and so on and so forth all around the world. Thus, to be arrested for possession of a Schedule I or Class A drug results in heavier penalties than possession of a Schedule III or Class C drug. Generally if a drug is deemed to have some currently accepted medical use it is likely to be placed in a lower schedule than if it has none, notwithstanding the fact that it may have potential for abuse or harm. In the absence of any recognized therapeutic effects, drugs that are highly addictive,

The Failed War

When we look at the history of the "War on Drugs" over approximately the last 40 years, it must be asked whether the criminalization of the use of any of the prohibited substances has in any way been effective in terms of the stated goals that this "war" was supposedly mounted to achieve. Specifically, has there been a marked reduction in the use of illegal drugs over the past 40 years—as one would expect with billions of dollars of taxpayers' money having been spent over such a long period on their suppression—and has there been a reduction in the harms that these drugs supposedly cause to the individual and to society?

It is unnecessary here to set down screeds of statistics, facts, and figures readily available from published sources to assert that in terms of its own stated objectives the "War on Drugs" has been an abject failure and a shameful and scandalous waste of public money. Indeed, it is well known, and not dis-

> When we look at the history of the "War on Drugs" over approximately the last 40 years, it must be asked whether the criminalization of the use of any of the prohibited substances has in any way been effective in terms of the stated goals that this "war" was supposedly mounted to achieve.

such as heroin or crack cocaine, or drugs that are profoundly psychotropic, including hallucinogens such as LSD, psilocybin, or DMT, are almost universally placed in the highest schedules and their use attracts the heaviest penalties.

The notable exceptions to this system of ranking according to perceived "harms" are, of course, alcohol and tobacco, both highly addictive and harmful drugs—far more so than cannabis or psilocybin, for example—but yet socially accepted on the grounds of long customary use and thus not placed in any schedule at all.

puted, that the very societies that attempt most vigorously to suppress various drugs, and in which users are subject to the most stringent penalties, have seen a vast and continuous *increase* in the per capita consumption of these drugs. This is tacitly admitted by the vast armed bureaucracies set up to persecute drug users in our societies, which every year demand more and more public money to fund their suppressive activities; if the suppression were working, one would expect their budgets to go down, not up.

Meanwhile the social harms caused by the "War on Drugs" itself are manifest and everywhere evident. In the United States, for example, there have been more than 20 million arrests for the possession of the Schedule I drug marijuana since 1965 and 11 million since 1990. The pace of arrests is increasing year on year, bringing us to the astonishing situation where, today, a marijuana smoker is arrested every 38 seconds.[1] The result, as Rob Kampia, executive director of the Marijuana Policy Project, recently observed, is that marijuana arrests outnumber arrests for "all violent crimes combined," meaning police are spending inordinate amounts of time chasing nonviolent criminals.[2] And it goes without saying that those who are arrested for the use of marijuana and other illegal drugs do suffer immense harm as a result of the punishments inflicted on them—including, but not limited to, personal trauma, loss of freedom, loss of reputation, loss of employment prospects, and serious, long-lasting financial damage.

Inventory of Harm

Such matters are only the beginning of the long inventory of harm caused by the "War on Drugs."

Western industrial societies, and all those cultures around the globe that increasingly seek to emulate them, teach us to venerate above all else the alert, problem-solving state of consciousness that is particularly appropriate to the conduct of science, business, war, and logical inquiry, and to such activities as driving cars, operating machinery, performing surgery, doing accounts, drawing up plans, accumulating wealth, etc., etc., etc. But there are many other states of consciousness that the amazing and mysterious human brain is capable of embracing, and it appears to be a natural human urge, as deep-rooted as our urges for food, sex, and nurturing relationships, to seek out and explore such "altered states of consciousness." A surprisingly wide range of methods and techniques (from breathing exercises, to meditation, to fasting, to hypnosis, to rhythmic music, to extended periods of vigorous dancing, etc.) is available to help us to achieve this goal, but there is no doubt that the consumption of those plants and substances called "drugs" in our societies is amongst the most effective and efficient means available to mankind to explore these profoundly altered states of consciousness.

The result is that people naturally seek out drugs and the temporary alterations in consciousness that they produce. Not all people in every society will do this, perhaps not even a majority, but certainly a very substantial minority—for example the 2 million Britons who are known to take illegal drugs each month[3] or those 20 million people in the US who have been arrested for marijuana possession since 1965. And these of course are only the tip of the iceberg of the much larger population of American marijuana users, running into many more tens of millions, who have, by luck or care, not yet fallen foul of the law and are thus not reflected in the arrest statistics.

Needless to say, it is of course exactly the same urge to alter consciousness that also impels even larger numbers of people to use legal (and often extremely harmful) drugs such as alcohol and tobacco—which, though they may not alter consciousness as dramatically as, say, LSD, are nevertheless undoubtedly used and sought out for the limited alterations of consciousness that they do produce.

For the hundreds of millions of people around the world whose need to experience altered states is not and cannot be satisfied by drunken oblivion or the stimulant effects of tobacco, it is therefore completely natural to turn to "drugs"—and, since the "War on Drugs" means that there is no legal source of supply of these substances, the inevitable result is that those who wish to use them *must* resort to illegal sources of supply.

Herein lies great and enduring harm. For it is obvious, and we may all see the effects everywhere, that the criminalization of drug use has empowered and enriched a vast and truly horrible global criminal underworld by guaranteeing that it is the *only* source of supply of these drugs. We have, in effect, delivered our youth—the sector within our societies that most strongly feels the need to experience altered states of consciousness—into the hands of the very worst mobsters and sleazeballs on the planet. To buy drugs our sons and daughters have no choice but to approach and associate with violent and greedy criminals. And because the proceeds from illegal drug sales are so enormous, we are all caught up in the inevitable consequences of turf wars and murders amongst the gangs and cartels competing in this blackest of black markets.

It should be completely obvious to our governments, after more than 40 years of dismal failure to suppress illegal drug use, that their policies in this area do not work and will never work. It should be completely obvious, a simple logical step, to realize that by decriminalizing drug use, and making the supply of all drugs available to those adults who wish to use them through legal and properly regulated channels, we could, at a stroke, put out of business the vast criminal enterprise that presently flourishes on the supply of illegal drugs.

It ought to be obvious, but somehow it is not.

Instead the powers that be continue to pursue the same harsh and cruel policies that they have been wedded to from the outset, ever seeking to strengthen and reinforce them rather than to replace them with something better. Indeed the *only* "change" that the large, armed bureaucracies that enforce these policies has ever sought since the "War on Drugs" began has, year on year, been to demand even more money, even more arms, and even more draconian legislative powers to break into homes, to confiscate property, and to deprive otherwise law-abiding citizens of liberty and wreck their lives. In the process we have seen our once free and upstanding societies—which used to respect individual choice and freedom of

Enforcement Administration agent or a prison guard, you naturally have a deeply vested interest in maintaining the miserable status quo, justified by the "War on Drugs," that keeps you in your job, that ensures your monthly paychecks continue to come in, and that continuously expands your budgets.

The second main category of beneficiaries is—of course!—the criminal gangs and cartels that the present misguided official policies have empowered as the sole source of drugs in our societies. Over the past 40-plus years they have earned countless billions of dollars from the sale of illegal drugs which, had they only been legal, would not have earned them a single penny.

Who are the losers? First and most directly those millions upon millions of good, nonviolent people in our societies who have been jailed or otherwise punished for the possession and use of drugs. And second (regardless of whether or not they use illegal drugs themselves), virtually everyone else in our societ-

It appears to be a natural human urge, as deep-rooted as our urges for food, sex, and nurturing relationships, to seek out and explore such "altered states of consciousness."

conscience above all else—slide remorselessly down the slippery slope that leads to the police state. And all this is being done in our name, with our money, by our own governments, to "save us from ourselves"!

Winners and Losers

Who benefits from this colossal stupidity and systematic wickedness? And who loses?

The beneficiaries are easy to spot.

First, the large and ever-expanding armed bureaucracies, funded with large and ever-growing sums of public money to suppress the use of drugs, have benefited enormously. Everyone who works for them, including the PR people and spin merchants who concoct the propaganda used to sell their policies to us, including their subcontractors both public and private, and including the (often privately run) prisons stuffed to bursting point with their victims, are the beneficiaries of this catastrophic failure on the part of our governments to think laterally, generously, and creatively. Whether you are a Drug

ies as well. For the quality of life of all of us has been diminished by the growth of the police state and by the murderous activities of the criminal gangs enfranchised, and kept in business, by the blind and mindless perpetuation of this failed and bankrupt "War on Drugs."

So, in summary, the criminalization of drug use has brought no positive effects, only negative ones, and it has not stopped or even reduced the use of dangerous and harmful drugs. On the contrary, we have been so little "saved from ourselves" by this phony war that the use of almost all illegal drugs, far from decreasing, has dramatically increased during the past 40 years.

Learning from Tobacco

A contrary example, but one that is most instructive, concerns the use of tobacco in our societies.

Tobacco has never been illegal; far from that, its use has been actively encouraged by clever advertising campaigns mounted by the multibillion-dollar tobacco industry. But the use of tobacco does undoubtedly lead to great harms, both for the health of the individual and the health of society at large, and facts about these harms have been widely and successfully disseminated without a single tobacco user ever being arrested or persecuted.

It's interesting in this connection to compare the success of public information campaigns about the dangers of tobacco use with the utter failure of public information campaigns about the dangers of marijuana use. The reason the anti-marijuana campaigns have failed is that millions of users know from their own direct, long-term experience that marijuana does *not* do them any great harm and (with reference to the most recent anti-marijuana propaganda) most definitely does *not* drive them mad. It may well be true that very small numbers of fragile teenagers whose mental health was already compromised have had their latent schizophrenia or other similar conditions worsened by the use of marijuana—but the vast majority of marijuana users are not at all affected in this way. Likewise efforts by government agencies to persuade us that new, stronger strains of marijuana presently available on the market (e.g., "skunk") are more dangerous to our health than traditional strains of marijuana because they deliver much more of the active ingredient THC to our systems, have not persuaded anyone. Regular marijuana users presented with a stronger strain simply adjust their consumption, consuming far less of it than they would of a weaker strain in order to achieve the same effect, and feel intuitively that smoking less of any substance has got to be better for their lungs and general health than smoking more.

The consequence of this disconnect between personal experience and "facts" purveyed by official public information campaigns is that huge numbers of people no longer believe anything that our governments have to say to us about drugs. There is an increasingly widespread recognition that tainted, unreliable, and tendentious information is being passed on—information that cannot be trusted. And this distrust of official sources of information is, of course, only worsened by the propagandistic character, witch hunts, and scare tactics of the "War on Drugs" and by the realization that the health information purveyed in anti-drug campaigns is not underwritten by caring and nurturing official policies but instead by draconian criminal sanctions and punitive authoritarian attitudes.

Where the health hazards of tobacco use are concerned, on the other hand, since there are no criminal sanctions against tobacco users, no large, armed bureaucracies to enforce them, and no special interests to serve by the dissemination of misleading information, the evidence has been accepted and believed by most rational adults freely making up their own minds, precisely as one would expect.

The result? While the use of illegal drugs has everywhere skyrocketed over the past 40 years, regardless of the violent persecution of the users of these drugs, the use of tobacco, in a climate of free choice and reliable information, has plummeted to an all-time low. The consumption of tobacco, once seen as a socially approved, even desirable, and, indeed, "stylish" habit, has come to be regarded as a pariah-creating activity that only idiots would indulge themselves in. Although there are, of course, still many tobacco users—because nicotine is intensely addictive—their numbers continue to fall dramatically year on year as more and more of us make the free choice to give up the habit for the sake of our health.

Is it not obvious that the "tobacco model" could be applied with equal success to all illegal drugs? In other words, is it not obvious, if our governments really wish us to stop using drugs, that immediate legalization of adult personal use must follow, that the giant, armed bureaucracies that persecute drug users must be closed down, and that the whole matter must be thrown open, in the way that tobacco use has been thrown open, to the effects of good, reliable information and the sound common-

We have, in effect, delivered our youth—the sector within our societies that most strongly feels the need to experience altered states of consciousness—into the hands of the very worst mobsters and sleazeballs on the planet.

sense of the vast majority of the population? If that happens then we can be certain that drugs that are genuinely harmful to health and wellbeing (in the way that tobacco certainly is) will fall out of favor with their users in exactly the way that tobacco has done. And if it turns out that some of these drugs are in fact not so harmful, then it should not concern us at all if some adults make the free choice to continue to use them.

Of course, even against a backdrop of legalization and good information, some adults will make the free choice to continue to use genuinely harmful drugs as well, just as some adults today do continue to make the free choice to continue to use tobacco. But that, too, is as it should be in a truly free society. Republican Congressman Barney Frank was spot on the truth of what a free society really means when he announced a proposal in August 2008 to end federal penalties for Americans carrying fewer than 100 grams (almost a quarter of a pound) of marijuana. "The vast amount of human activity ought to be none of the government's business," Frank said on Capitol Hill. "I don't think it is the government's business to tell you how to spend your leisure time."

It goes without saying that Frank's proposal is unlikely to succeed in the hysterical climate of disinformation that presently surrounds this subject, and we must ask ourselves why this should be so. Why are commonsense proposals for the legalization of drugs never adopted, or even seriously considered by our governments? Why, on the contrary, are such proposals dogmatically opposed with even more propaganda and tainted information emanating from the big, armed anti-drug bureaucracies?

That legalization of drugs would shrink the budgets of those selfsame bureaucracies, and ultimately put them out of business, is part of the answer. But to find the real engine that perpetuates the "War on Drugs" we need to look deeper and ask fundamental questions about the relationship between the individual and the state in modern Western democracies.

Freedom of Consciousness

What is Western civilization all about? What are its greatest achievements and highest aspirations?

It's my guess that most people's replies to these questions would touch—before all the other splendid achievements of science, literature, technology, and the economy—on the nurture and growth of freedom.

Individual freedom.

Including, but not limited to freedom from the unruly power of monarchs, freedom from the unwarranted intrusions of the state and its agents into our personal lives, freedom from the tyranny of the Church and its Inquisition, freedom from hunger and want, freedom from slavery and servitude, freedom of conscience, freedom of religion, freedom of thought and speech, freedom of assembly, freedom to elect our own leaders, freedom to be homosexual—and so on and so forth.

The list of freedoms we enjoy today that were not enjoyed by our ancestors is indeed a long and impressive one. It is therefore exceedingly strange that Western civilization in the twenty-first century enjoys no real **freedom of consciousness.**

There can be no more intimate and elemental part of the individual than his or her own consciousness. At the deepest level, our consciousness *is* what we are—to the extent that if we are not sovereign over our own consciousness then we cannot in any meaningful sense be sovereign over anything else either. So it has to be highly significant that, far from encouraging freedom of consciousness, our societies in fact violently deny our right to sovereignty in this intensely personal area, and

> The reason the anti-marijuana campaigns have failed is that millions of users know from their own direct, long-term experience that marijuana does *not* do them any great harm and (with reference to the most recent anti-marijuana propaganda) most definitely does *not* drive them mad.

have effectively outlawed all states of consciousness other than those on a very narrowly defined and officially approved list. The "War on Drugs" has thus unexpectedly succeeded in engineering a stark reversal of the true direction of Western history by empowering faceless bureaucratic authorities to send armed agents to break into our homes, arrest us, throw us into prison, and deprive us of our income and reputation simply because we wish to explore the sometimes radical, though always temporary, alterations in **our own consciousness** that drugs facilitate.

Other than being against arbitrary rules that the state has imposed on us, personal drug use by adults is not a "crime" in any true moral or ethical sense and usually takes place in the privacy of our own homes, where it cannot possibly do any harm to others. For some it is a simple lifestyle choice. For others, particularly where the hallucinogens such as LSD, psilocybin, and DMT are concerned, it is a means to make contact with alternate realms and parallel dimensions, and perhaps even with the divine. For some, drugs are an aid to creativity and focussed mental effort. For others they are a means to tune out for a while from everyday cares and worries. But in all cases it seems probable that the drive to alter consciousness, from which all drug use stems, has deep genetic roots.

Other adult lifestyle choices with deep genetic roots also used to be violently persecuted by our societies.

A notable example is homosexuality, once punishable by death or long periods of imprisonment, which is now entirely legal between consenting adults—and fully recognized as being none of the state's business—in all Western cultures. (Although approximately thirteen US states have "anti-sodomy" laws outlawing homosexuality, these statutes have rarely been enforced in recent years, and in 2003 the US Supreme Court invalidated those laws.) The legalization of homosexuality lifted a huge burden of human misery, secretiveness, paranoia, and genuine fear from our societies, and at the same time not a single one of the homophobic lobby's fire-and-brimstone predictions about the end of Western civilization came true.

Likewise, it was not so long ago that natural seers, mediums, and healers who felt the calling to become "witches" were burned at the stake for "crimes" that we now look back on as harmless eccentricities at worst.

Perhaps it will be the same with drugs? Perhaps in a century or two, if we have not destroyed human civilization by then, our descendants will look back with disgust on the barbaric laws of our time that punished a minority so harshly (with imprisonment, financial ruin, and worse) for responsibly, quietly, and in the privacy of their own homes seeking alterations in their own consciousness through the use of drugs. Perhaps we will even end up looking back on the persecution of drug users with the same sense of shame and horror that we now view the persecution of gays and lesbians, the burning of "witches," and the imposition of slavery on others.

Meanwhile it's no accident that the "War on Drugs" has been accompanied by an unprecedented expansion of governmental power into the previously inviolable inner sanctum of individual consciousness. On the contrary, it seems to me that the state's urge to power has all along been the real reason for this "war"—not an honest desire on the part of the authorities to rescue society and the individual from the harms caused by drugs, but the thin of a wedge intended to legitimize increasing bureaucratic control and intervention in almost every other area of our lives as well.

This is the way freedom is hijacked—not all at once, out in the open, but stealthily, little by little, behind closed doors, *and with our own agreement.* How will we be able to resist when so many of us have already willingly handed over the keys to our own consciousness to the state and accepted without protest that it is OK to be told what we may and may not do, what we may and may not explore, even what we may and may not *experience,* with this most precious, sapient, unique, and individual part of ourselves?

If we are willing to accept that then we can be persuaded to accept anything.

Endnotes

1. Uncredited. (2008). Legislators aim to snuff out penalties for pot use. CNN, 30 July. **2.** Cited in *ibid*. **3.** *Independent*, London, 15 August 2008, page 1, citing Department of Health research.

At the deepest level, our consciousness *is* what we are—to the extent that if we are not sovereign over our own consciousness then we cannot in any meaningful sense be sovereign over anything else either.

AA Lies
Charles Bufe

There are probably more myths and misconceptions about Alcoholics Anonymous, America's most sacrosanct institution, than there are about any other mass organization in our country. Neglecting how this came to be,[1] the primary misconceptions regarding AA are that:

1. **AA is the most effective (or the only) way to deal with an alcohol problem.**
2. **AA existed from the start as an independent organization.**
3. **AA's co-founder, Bill Wilson, independently devised AA's "program," its 12 steps.**
4. **AA is "spiritual, not religious."**
5. **AA is a completely voluntary organization—AA works by "attraction, not promotion."**
6. **AA has nothing to do with "outside enterprises" or "related facilities."**
7. **AA takes no position on matters of "public controversy."**

AA's Effectiveness

AA's supporters commonly trumpet AA as the best, if not the only, way to deal with alcohol problems. To back their claims, they cite anecdotal evidence and uncontrolled studies, but they ignore the best scientific evidence—the only available controlled studies of AA's effectiveness, as well as the results of AA's own triennial surveys of its membership.

There have been only two controlled studies (with no-treatment comparison groups) of AA's effectiveness. Both of these studies indicated that AA attendance is no better than no treatment at all.

The first of these studies was conducted in San Diego in 1964 and 1965, and its subjects were 301 "chronic drunk offenders."[2] These individuals were assigned as a condition of probation to attend AA, to treatment at a clinic (type of treatment not specified), or to a no-treatment control group. All of the subjects were followed for at least a year after conviction, and the primary outcome measure was the number of rearrests during the year following conviction. The results were that 69 percent of the group assigned to AA was rearrested within a year; 68 percent of the clinic-treatment group was rearrested; but only 56 percent of the no-treatment control group was rearrested. Based on these results, the authors concluded: "No statistically significant differences between the three groups were discovered in recidivism rate, in number of subsequent rearrests, or in time elapsed prior to rearrest."[3]

The second controlled study of AA's effectiveness was carried out in Kentucky in the mid-1970s, and its subjects were 260 clients "representative of the 'revolving door' alcoholic court cases in our cities."[4] These subjects were divided into five groups: one was assigned to AA; a second was assigned to nonprofessionally-led Rational Behavior Therapy; a third was assigned to professionally-led Rational Behavior Therapy; a fourth was assigned to professionally-led traditional insight (Freudian) therapy; and the fifth group was the no-treatment control group. The individuals in these groups were given an outcome assessment following completion of treatment, and were then reinterviewed three, six, nine, and twelve months later.

The results of this study were revealing: AA had by far the highest dropout rate of any of the treatment groups—68 percent. In contrast, the lay RBT group had a 40 percent dropout rate; the professionally-led RBT group had a 42 percent dropout rate; and the professionally-led insight group had a 46 percent dropout rate.

In terms of drinking behavior, 100 percent of the lay RBT group reported decreased drinking at the outcome assessment; 92 percent of the insight group reported decreased drinking; 80

percent of the professionally-led RBT group reported decreased drinking; and 67 percent of the AA attendees reported decreased drinking, whereas only 50 percent of the no-treatment control group reported decreased drinking.

But in regard to bingeing behavior, the group assigned to AA did far worse than any of the other groups, including the no-treatment control group. The study's authors reported: "The mean number of binges was significantly greater (p = .004)[5] for the AA group (2.37 in the past 3 months) in contrast to both the control (0.56) and lay-RBT group (0.26). In this analysis, AA was [over 4] times [more] likely to binge than the control [group] and nine times more likely than the lay-RBT [group]. The AA average was 2.4 binges in the last 3 months since outcome."[6]

It seems likely that the reason for this dismal outcome for the AA group was a direct result of AA's "one drink, one drunk" dogma, which is drummed into the heads of members at virtually every AA meeting. It seems very likely that this belief all too often becomes a self-fulfilling prophecy, as it apparently did with the AA attendees in this study.

The third significant piece of evidence regarding AA's effectiveness is that provided by AA's triennial membership surveys. In 1990 or 1991, AA produced an analysis of the previous five membership surveys, "Comments on A.A.'s Triennial Surveys."[7] This document revealed that 95 percent of those coming to AA drop out during their first year of attendance.[8] Even if all those who remain in AA stay sober (which often is not the case), this is still a poor success rate, even in comparison with the rate of spontaneous remission.

There have been many studies of spontaneous remission (sometimes called spontaneous recovery), and one meta-analysis of such studies indicates that between 3.7 percent and 7.4 percent of individuals with alcohol problems "spontaneously" recover in any given year.[9] In comparison with this, AA's 5 percent retention rate is not impressive. And that 5 percent rate might be optimistic—it was derived from surveys conducted during a period of very high growth in AA membership. In contrast, since the mid-1990s—a time when over one million Americans per year were, and still are, being coerced into AA attendance—AA's US membership has been essentially flat, hovering around 1.16 to 1.17 million persons for the last few years.[10] Even taking into account dropouts with "time" (from this "program for life"), this means that AA's current new-member retention rate could well be *under* 5 percent.

As for AA being the *only* way to beat an alcohol problem, it has been known for decades that alcoholism (alcohol *dependence*—as contrasted with mere alcohol abuse) disappears faster than can be explained by mortality after the age of 40.[11] Also, a very large Census Bureau-conducted study in the early 1990s found that over 70 percent of the formerly alcohol-dependent individuals surveyed (over 4,500 in all) had recovered without participating in AA or attending treatment of any kind, and that those who had not participated in AA or attended treatment had a *higher* rate of recovery than those who had.[12]

As well, in contrast to AA and treatment derived from it (the dominant mode in the US), there are several types of treatment that are well-supported by the best available scientific evidence (studies with random assignment of subjects and no-treatment control groups, and/or comparison groups using standard 12-step treatment). Among the best-supported therapies are those known as the community reinforcement approach, social skills training, motivational enhancement, and brief intervention.[13] All of these well-supported therapies are low-cost, cognitive-behavioral approaches in which alcohol abusers are reinforced in the belief that they have power over their own actions, and are responsible for them. (This is in direct contrast to the 12-step approach, which teaches alcohol abusers that they are "powerless.") Unfortunately, none of these effective, low-cost therapies is in common use in the United States, in which the 12-step approach dominates.

Finally, over the last quarter-century a number of "alternative" (non-12-step) recovery groups have arisen in the US, and many, many individuals have recovered through them. The four largest are SMART Recovery, Women for Sobriety, Moderation Management, and Secular Organizations for Sobriety.[14] Between them, they have hundreds of meetings scattered across the country, and all are easy to contact via the Internet.[15]

In sum, those who trumpet AA as the best (or only) way to deal with an alcohol problem do so only by ignoring well-supported alternative therapies, the widespread "alternative" self-help groups, the best available scientific evidence, and the evidence generated by AA itself.

AA as an Independent Organization

One of the most widespread myths concerning AA is that it has existed as an independent organization from day one, from the day in 1935 that Bill Wilson met AA's other co-founder, Bob Smith, in Akron, Ohio. When they met, Smith and Wilson were both members of a Protestant evangelical group called the Oxford Group Movement (OGM). Convinced that Oxford Group principles were the key to overcoming alcohol abuse (and all other problems in life), they devoted themselves to carrying the Oxford Group message to other alcoholics.[16] What they called "the alcoholic squadron of the Akron Oxford Group" remained as part of the Oxford Group Movement until 1939, and the group Bill Wilson founded in New York remained as part of the Oxford Group Movement until late 1937.

The reasons that AA parted ways with the Oxford Group Movement had nothing to do with differences over ideology; rather, they had to do with personality conflicts, the fear that Catholics would be forbidden to join what was to become AA as long as it was part of a Protestant organization, and, quite possibly, embarrassment over OGM founder Frank Buchman's statements in a 1936 *New York World Telegram* interview, in which he said, "Thank heaven for a man like Adolf Hitler," and in which he pined for "a God-controlled Fascist dictatorship."[17]

One reason that this link between AA and the Oxford Group Movement is not more widely known is that during the years following the adoption of the name Alcoholics Anonymous, AA never credited the Oxford Group Movement for anything—even though AA took its central beliefs, program, and practices almost unaltered from the OGM. For instance, there is not a single acknowledgment of the Oxford Groups in *Alcoholics Anonymous*, AA's "Big Book." It wasn't until the late 1950s, in *Alcoholics Anonymous Comes of Age*, that Bill Wilson and AA (partially) acknowledged AA's debt to the Oxford Groups. Even today, most AA members know little if anything about the AA/OGM connection—and the few who are well-acquainted with it tend not to talk much about it.[18]

The Origin of the 12 Steps

A common myth—even within AA—is that AA co-founder Bill Wilson wrote the 12 steps entirely independently, that they were completely his own invention. A closely-related myth common in AA is that Bill Wilson wrote the 12 steps directly under divine guidance. Neither myth has any but the scantiest relation to reality.

The author of AA's 12 steps and the text portion of AA's bible,

the "Big Book" (though not the personal stories in it), Bill Wilson, was a dedicated Oxford Group member who was convinced that the principles of the Oxford Group Movement were the only route to recovery for alcoholics, and the 12 steps he included in the "Big Book" are a direct codification of those principles. Indeed, in *Alcoholics Anonymous Comes of Age*, Wilson directly credits the OGM as the source of the teachings codified in the 12 steps.[19] In a letter to former OGM American leader Sam Shoemaker, Wilson stated:

> The Twelve Steps of A.A. simply represented an attempt to state in more detail, breadth, and depth, what we had been taught—primarily by you [Rev. Shoemaker]. Without this, there could have been nothing—nothing at all.[20]

Wilson also stated publicly:

> Where did early AA's…learn about moral inventory, amends for harm done, turning our wills and lives over to God? Where did we learn about meditation and prayer and all the rest of it?… [S]traight from Dr. Bob's and my own early association with the Oxford Groups….[21]

To be more specific, the Oxford Group principles of *personal powerlessness* and the necessity of *divine guidance* are codified in steps 1, 2, 3, 6, 7, and 11. The principle of *confession* is embodied in steps 4, 5, and 10. The principle of *restitution* to those one has harmed is embodied in steps 8 and 9. And the principle of *continuance* is embodied in steps 10 and 12.

There is not a single original concept in the 12 steps. They all came directly from the Oxford Group Movement.[22]

AA as a Religious, Not Spiritual, Organization

Members of AA routinely assert that AA is "spiritual, not religious," though even a cursory glance at AA's practices and official ("conference approved") publications reveals just the opposite to be true.

As for AA's practices, most meetings open with a prayer to God—the Serenity Prayer ("God grant us the serenity to accept the things we cannot change, the courage to change the things we can, and the wisdom to know the difference"). Most also feature reading (and often discussion) of the 12 steps, with their exhortations to pray and to turn one's life and will over to God. And almost all AA meetings close with a reading of a specifically Christian prayer, the Lord's Prayer.

AA's 12 steps, the backbone of its "program," are even more revealing:

1. We admitted we were powerless over alcohol—that our lives had become unmanageable.
2. Came to believe that a Power greater than ourselves could restore us to sanity.
3. Made a decision to turn our will and our lives over to the care of God *as we understood Him.*
4. Made a searching and fearless moral inventory of ourselves.
5. Admitted to God, to ourselves, and to another human being the exact nature of our wrongs.
6. Were entirely ready to have God remove all these defects of character.
7. Humbly asked Him to remove our shortcomings.
8. Made a list of all persons we had harmed, and became willing to make amends to them all.
9. Made direct amends to such people wherever possible, except when to do so would injure them or others.
10. Continued to take personal inventory and when we were wrong promptly admitted it.
11. Sought through prayer and meditation to improve our conscious contact with God *as we understood Him,* praying only for knowledge of His will for us and the power to carry that out.
12. Having had a spiritual awakening as the result of these steps, we tried to carry this message to alcoholics, and to practice these principles in all our affairs.

It's noteworthy that alcohol is mentioned only in the first step, which strongly implies that alcoholics *cannot* overcome their problems on their own. The remainder of the steps implore alcohol abusers to engage in religious activities (prayer, confession) and to "turn [their] will[s] and [their] lives over to the care of God."

Much of the rest of the "Big Book" is just as religious, if not more so, than the 12 steps. In his comments immediately preceding the 12 steps, Bill Wilson exhorts the reader: "Remember that we deal with alcohol—cunning, baffling, powerful! Without help it is too much for us. But there is One who has all power—that one is God. May you find Him now!"[23] Wilson also devotes an entire chapter in the book (chapter 4, "We Agnostics") to attacking atheists and agnostics as "prejudice[d]" or crazy, and to presenting belief in God as the only way to restore "sanity." Wilson also recommends that AA members "work" the seventh step through prayer, and even provides the wording for a prayer to "My Creator."[24] It's also worthy of note that the "Big Book" is saturated with religious terms. There are well over 200 references to God, capitalized masculine pronouns ("He," "Him"), or synonyms for God ("Creator," "Father," etc.) in its 164 pages of text—and this doesn't even take into account such terms in the personal stories that make up the bulk of the book.

AA's second—and second-most important—book, *Twelve Steps and Twelve Traditions*, also written by Wilson, is just as religious as the "Big Book." For instance, the nine pages devoted to "working" step 2 contain at least 30 references to God, synonyms for it, or capitalized masculine pronouns referring to it. Wilson also repeatedly exhorts the reader to pray, noting in one place that, "Those of us who have come to make regular use of prayer would no more do without it than we would refuse air, food, or sunshine."[25] And in his discussion of step 4, making "a searching and fearless moral inventory," Wilson makes a truly extraordinary recommendation: that the list of one's "moral defects" be based on "a universally recognized list of major human failings—the Seven Deadly Sins[!] of pride, greed, lust, anger, gluttony, envy, and sloth."[26] Contrary to Wilson's assertion, these are *not* "a universally recognized list of major human failings," rather, they are a specifically Christian list of sins as enumerated by Pope Gregory the Great in the sixth century. (Even ignoring their origin, one wonders why this "universally recognized list" would omit such obvious "defects" as cruelty, intrusiveness, dishonesty, hypocrisy, and sanctimoniousness.) That Wilson would make such an extraordinary recommendation underlines the Christian origins of AA and its program.

Indeed, the religious nature of AA and its "program" is so obvious that in the late 1990s four appeal-level courts (the Second and Seventh Federal Circuit Courts of Appeal and the state high courts in New York and Tennessee) ruled that government-coerced attendance at AA and NA (Narcotics

> AA is a very anti-intellectual organization, in which questioning and skeptical attitudes are viewed as "disease symptoms."

Anonymous—a clone of AA) is unconstitutional in that it violates the "Establishment Clause" of the First Amendment because AA is obviously religious in nature.[27] There have been no contrary rulings on the appeal level, but there is as yet no national precedent because the Supreme Court has not ruled on the issue.

Given all this, it seems amazing that AA members routinely and vehemently assert that AA is "spiritual, not religious." There are two primary reasons that they do this. The first is that AA is a very anti-intellectual organization, in which questioning and skeptical attitudes are viewed as "disease symptoms," and in which great emphasis is placed upon unquestioning acceptance of revealed wisdom. Three of the most common AA slogans embody this anti-intellectualism: "Utilize, don't analyze;" "Let go and let God;" and "Your best thinking got you here." So, in a milieu which demands blind acceptance and denigrates critical thought, AA members hear that AA is "spiritual, not religious" and repeat it in parrot-like fashion.

AA members who own treatment facilities and/or work in them have an additional incentive to repeat the "spiritual, not religious" assertion: money. Over 93 percent of treatment facilities in the United States are 12-step facilities,[28] and treatment is a $10 billion-a-year industry.[29] If 12-step members who work in and own treatment facilities would honestly admit that their approach is religious in nature, that river of government and insurance-industry cash would dry up in short order.

AA as a "Voluntary" Organization

AA apologists routinely paint AA as a lily-white, all-volunteer group offering its "spiritual" program on a take-it-or-leave-it basis, and that AA operates on the principle of "attraction, not promotion." This is about as far from the truth as maintaining that people "voluntarily" pay taxes.

That AA depends heavily upon coercion for "attracting" new members can be seen even in AA's promotional "Alcoholics Anonymous [insert year] Membership Survey" brochure. The brochure describing the 1996 survey, for instance, reveals that 16 percent of AA members were originally "introduced" to AA by the courts or penal system. Taking other avenues of coercion into account, such as threats of job loss and coercion by treatment centers,[30] the statistics published in AA's "Membership Survey" brochures strongly suggest that the total percentage of AA's active members who were originally coerced into attendance exceeds 40 percent.[31]

When one considers that these figures apply only to those *currently attending* AA, it becomes clear that in all likelihood a significant majority of newcomers to AA are coerced into attendance—and then leave as quickly as they can through AA's "revolving door." To cite but one example, in a great many jurisdictions throughout the United States it is routine for the courts to sentence DUI defendants to attend AA (and often 12-step treatment as well).

That most such coerced persons leave AA as quickly as they can, can be seen in AA's sky-high dropout rate (discussed above), and in the fact that AA's membership has been flat for the past several years[32] (which means that either experienced members from this "program for life," or the at least one million coerced newcomers per year—who are routinely threatened with "jails, institutions, or death," should they leave AA—are dropping out in droves).

Further confirmation of AA's dependence upon coercion for recruitment of new members can be seen in the vast numbers of individuals who are coerced annually into 12-step (AA-based) treatment. There are approximately 15,000 treatment centers in this country treating approximately 2,000,000 persons annually (with "alcohol only" and "alcohol with secondary drug" clients making up 48 percent of the total),[33] and a recent national survey indicates that 93 percent of treatment facilities are 12-step facilities.[34] Given that virtually all 12-step facilities require that clients attend AA (or its clone, NA) and "work the steps," and that discharge before completion of treatment

> The statistics published in AA's "Membership Survey" brochures strongly suggest that the total percentage of AA's active members who were originally coerced into attendance exceeds 40 percent.

often means imprisonment, loss of employment, loss of professional certification (for doctors, nurses, and lawyers), loss of child custody, loss of organ transplant candidacy, etc., etc., for the majority of the clients in such treatment centers (that is, coerced clients),[35] this means that the vast majority of newcomers to AA are coerced into attending not only 12-step treatment, but also AA, the program which allegedly works through "attraction, not promotion."

AA and "Outside Enterprises"

Yet another common myth is that AA, the ultra-independent "voluntary" organization, has no connection with "outside enterprises" or "related facilities."

AA's sixth tradition (the traditions are to AA groups and AA as a whole as the 12 steps are to individual AA members) states that, "An AA group ought never endorse, finance, or lend the AA name to any related facility or outside enterprise, lest problems of money, property, and prestige divert us from our primary purpose." Thus AA members keep to the letter (though not the spirit) of this tradition by endorsing, organizing, financing, and staffing "related facilit[ies]" and "outside enterprise[s]" as individual AA members or groups of individual AA members, not as self-declared AA groups.

This is most obvious in the case of 12-step treatment facilities, which as we saw above constitute 93 percent of the total. The percentage for inpatient facilities reported by the National Treatment Center Study investigators is even higher: 96 percent.[36] A great many of these facilities were founded by AA members, are owned by AA members, are staffed (often entirely—down to cooks and janitors) by AA members, have the 12 steps as the centerpiece of their "treatment," force clients to "work" the first three to five steps (depending on the facility and length of stay), and the primary purpose of these programs is to expose clients to AA and to induce them to attend AA meetings for the rest of their lives. Indeed, one pro-AA MD states in a professional journal that a primary goal of 12-step treatment is that, "The patient is indoctrinated into the AA program and instructed as to the content and application of the 12 steps of the program."[37] He then goes on to note that, "followup usually consists of ongoing support by the treatment

facility as well as participation in community self-help groups such as AA, NA, OA, and the like."[38, 39]

Yet AA members routinely claim that 12-step treatment has "nothing to do with AA."

AA and "Matters of Public Controversy"

Groups of AA members have set up "educational" and "medical" front groups to promote AA and its core beliefs (especially the disease concept of alcoholism and the absolute necessity of abstinence for anyone who has ever abused alcohol). This allows AA to maintain its pristine, above-the-fray image, while its hidden members and allies do its dirty work. (AA members in these front groups and in other media hide behind AA's tradition of "anonymity" while they promote AA, the disease concept, and the abstinence-only approach, and attack critics of AA and those who promote, study, or practice non-12-step approaches to addictions, many of which are much better supported scientifically than AA and 12-step treatment).[40] Indeed, the hidden members in AA's front groups have moved beyond merely attacking those they disagree with, and have worked actively to suppress alternative modes of treatment.[41]

The two prime examples here are the National Council on Alcoholism and Drug Dependence (NCADD, AA's educational front group—formerly the National Council on Alcoholism [NCA]) and the American Society of Addiction Medicine (AA's medical front group, which was a part of the NCADD for over a decade—like NCADD it promotes the disease model of addiction, preaches the necessity of abstinence, and promotes AA).[42] The connection between AA and the NCADD was obvious from the first, as the group was founded by PR flack Marty Mann, the first female AA member who maintained sobriety for any length of time, and as the full names of AA's co-founders, Bill Wilson and Bob Smith appeared on the group's letterhead. (This caused a great deal of controversy in AA, not because AA members saw anything wrong in the setting up of front groups, but because Wilson and Smith had "broken anonymity" by allowing their full names to be used.)

The primary purpose of the NCADD, in addition to promoting AA and its core beliefs, is to act as AA's spokesman (indeed,

Groups of AA members have set up "educational" and "medical" front groups to promote AA and its core beliefs.

enforcer) on "outside issues" and "matters of public controversy;" and the NCADD has indeed been instrumental in helping to maintain adherence to 12-step orthodoxy. This is most obvious in the matter of treatment approaches. There's good evidence that controlled-drinking approaches work at least as well as abstinence approaches in the treatment of problem drinkers,[43] yet the NCADD has virulently attacked controlled-drinking researchers and clinicians over the years in an attempt to limit treatment options in the United States to abstinence-only approaches. To cite but one example, the Rand Report on controlled drinking, Don Cahalan, a well-known alcoholism researcher, reports that, "After valiant year-long attempts by prominent NCA members to have the report suppressed altogether or drastically revised in its findings, it was finally released by Rand in June 1976."[44]

Those who had not participated in AA or attended treatment had a *higher* rate of recovery than those who had.

When the report was released, 12-step spokespersons denounced it with dire warnings that "some alcoholics have resumed drinking as a result of [the report],"[45] and admonitions that, "After all, people's right to know does not mean the people's right to be confused—especially when it is a matter of life and death."[46]

To cite a more recent example of NCADD attempts to vilify controlled-drinking advocates, on March 25, 2000, Audrey Kishline, founder of the group Moderation Management (MM—a controlled-drinking self-help group), drank herself blind (to a blood-alcohol level of .26—roughly three times the legal limit), climbed into her truck, drove the wrong way on a freeway, and got in a head-on crash with another pickup, killing its driver and his 12-year-old daughter.

The NCADD's response? In late June, after the incident was reported first in the *Seattle Times* and later in the national media, the NCADD, under the signature of its president, Stacia Murphy, issued a press release which strongly implied that the crash was one of the "consequences of 'moderation management'." The NCADD went on to piously implore that, "As a society we must finally accept that abstinence offers the safest and most predictable course for the treatment of alcohol and other drug-related problems and we must do everything we can to break through the denial of those who are actively addicted."

AA's supporters in the media were also quick to exploit the Kishline tragedy. The *San Francisco Chronicle, Indianapolis Star,* and other newspapers ran editorials decrying the moderation approach, while making no mention of Kishline's AA involvement either before or after her involvement with MM. *Time* magazine and Scripps-Howard news service each ran a story on the incident which also failed to mention Kishline's AA involvement. One strongly suspects, but cannot prove, that many of the stories and editorials attacking MM and the moderation approach were written by AA members hiding behind AA's "anonymity" stricture.

What the NCADD and AA's media supporters (with almost no exceptions) didn't mention—and this was something that they almost certainly knew—was that on January 20, Audrey Kishline had announced on the MM email list that she was abandoning her attempt to drink moderately, and was instead returning to AA and the abstinence approach! (One self-proclaimed AA member, Caroline Knapp, wrote a lengthy story for Salon <salon.com>, which was very pro-AA and very condemnatory of the moderation approach; deep in the story Knapp included a short, dismissive mention of Kishline's AA involvement immediately prior to the crash. Her piece was later reproduced in the *Los Angeles Times*.)

As well, the NCADD and literally *all* of AA's media supporters did not mention that Audrey Kishline had learned to binge drink during years of AA membership and following participation in an intensive, 28-day, 12-step inpatient program. In her book, *Moderate Drinking: The New Option for Problem Drinkers*, Kishline noted that she had "attended literally hundreds of AA meetings in 10 different states…. The result of all this 'treatment'? At first my drinking became far worse. Hospital staff members had told me that I had a physical disease that I had no control over…I kept hearing 'one drink, one drunk'…In possibly the most defenseless and dependent stage of my entire life, I began to fulfill some of these prophecies. I became a binge drinker…"[47]

Given this, it seems entirely possible that Kishline's 12-step-induced binge drinking had more to do with her criminal actions than the moderation program she was no longer even attempting to follow. But AA's front group, the NCADD, and AA's supporters in the media, saw fit not to mention this. Their only interest was in attributing the fatal crash to the moderation approach which Kishline had abandoned.

AA Lies
Charles Bufe

Summary

In contrast to what you've heard over and over again in the media (and from AA's often-hidden spokespersons) this is the truth about AA:

1. AA is not only far from the only way to deal with an alcohol problem, but the best available scientific evidence indicates that it is ineffective.

2. AA began its life—for its first several years—as part of the Protestant evangelical group, the Oxford Group Movement, not as an independent organization.

3. AA's co-founder, Bill Wilson, did not independently devise AA's "program," its 12 steps; instead, he merely codified the central Oxford Group Movement beliefs.

4. AA is religious, not spiritual; this is so obvious that even several appeal-level courts have ruled that this is so.

5. AA relies upon coercion to bring it a majority of its new members, and AA members take an active part in much of that coercion.

6. 12-step treatment is essentially institutionalized AA.

7. AA employs front groups and hidden members in the media to do its dirty work for it on matters of "public controversy."

Endnotes

1. See *Alcoholics Anonymous: Cult or cure? (second edition)*, Chapter 8 ("AA's Influence on Society"), pp 105–124. Tucson, AZ: See Sharp Press, 1998. **2.** Ditman, KS, GC Crawford, WE Forgy, H Moskowitz, & C MacAndrew. (1967). A controlled experiment on the use of court probation for drunk arrests. *American Journal of Psychiatry*, 124(2), pp 64–67. **3.** *Ibid.*, p 64. **4.** Brandsma, JM, MC Maultsby, & RJ Welsh. (1980). *Outpatient treatment of alcoholism: A review and comparative study*. Baltimore: University Park Press. **5.** Meaning that the possibility of this outcome being due to random chance was only 1 in 250. **6.** *Op cit.*, Brandsma et al., p 105. **7.** "Comments on A.A.'s Triennial Surveys." New York: Alcoholics Anonymous World Services, n.d. (This document was apparently produced for internal use, as it's very crudely produced—typewritten xeroxed pages bound in one corner with a staple—and is not part of AA's "conference-approved" literature. Other researchers and I obtained copies of it shortly after it was produced by writing to AA's General Service Office and asking for it.) **8.** *Ibid.*, p 12, Figure C-1. **9.** Smart, RG. (1975/76). Spontaneous recovery in alcoholics: A review and analysis of the available research. *Drug and Alcohol Dependence*, (1), pp 277–285. **10.** Membership information taken from AA's official Website <www.alcoholics-anonymous.org>. **11.** Drew, RH. (1968). Alcoholism as a self-limiting disease. *Quarterly Journal of Studies on Alcohol*, 29, pp 956–967. **12.** Dawson, Deborah. (1996). Correlates of past-year status among treated and untreated persons with form alcohol dependence: United States, 1992. *Alcoholism: Clinical and Experimental Research*, Vol. 20, pp 771–779. **13.** See Hester, Reid & William Miller (Eds.). (1995). *Handbook of alcoholism treatment approaches: Effective alternatives (second edition)*. Boston: Allyn & Bacon, for discussion of these and other effective approaches. For a discussion of the evidence supporting various approaches, see Hester & Miller and see also Peele, Stanton, et al. (2000). *Resisting 12-Step coercion: How to fight forced participation in AA, NA, or 12-step treatment*, Chapter 2. Tucson, AZ: See Sharp Press. **14.** I do not include Rational Recovery (RR) here, because at the turn of the year 2000 RR founder Jack Trimpey directed all RR self-help groups to disband. While a significant number of RR groups apparently ignored Trimpey's order, they cannot be considered a part of a national organization. **15.** Their Website addresses are: SMART Recovery <www.smartrecovery.org>, Women for Sobriety <www.womenforsobriety.org>, Moderation Management <www.moderation.org>, and Secular Organizations for Sobriety <www.unhooked.com>. **16.** That message was that individuals are powerless in themselves, that the only route to "sanity" is to turn one's life and will over to God, and that God will remove your shortcomings and direct your life if only asked properly. **17.** The entire text of this August 26, 1936, interview is reproduced in Tom Driberg's *The Mystery of Moral Re-Armament*. New York: Alfred A. Knopf, 1965, pp 68–69. For additional treatment of this matter (and the extremely dishonest manner in which AA treats in its "conference-approved" Wilson biography, *Pass It On*), see *Alcoholics Anonymous: Cult or cure? (second edition)*, *op cit.*, pp 21–23. **18.** There are some exceptions to this rule, notably AA historian Dick B. who has written several scholarly and reliable books on AA's debt to the Oxford Group Movement. One relevant title is *The Oxford Group & Alcoholics Anonymous: A design for living that works (revised edition)*. Kihei, HI: Paradise Research Publications, 1998. See also <www.dickb.com>. **19.** Wilson, W. (1957). *Alcoholics Anonymous comes of age*. New York: Alcoholics Anonymous World Services, pp 58–63, 160–167. **20.** Quoted by Dick B. in *Design for living: The Oxford Group's contribution to early A.A.* Kihei, HI: Paradise Research Publications, 1992, p 10. **21.** Quoted in *The Language of the Heart: Bill W.'s grapevine writings*. New York: A.A. Grapevine, Inc., 1988, p 198. **22.** For further discussion of the 12 steps and AA's debt to the Oxford Groups, see *Alcoholics Anonymous: Cult or cure? (second edition)*, *op cit.*, Chapters 4 and 5, pp 57–76. **23.** Wilson, William. (1939, 1976). *Alcoholics Anonymous*. New York: Alcoholics Anonymous World Services, p 58. **24.** *Ibid.*, p 76. **25.** Wilson, William. (1953). *Twelve Steps and Twelve Traditions*. New York: Alcoholics Anonymous World Services, p 97. **26.** *Ibid.*, p 48. **27.** The cases are *Griffin v. Coughlin* (1996); *Kerr v. Farrey* (1996); *Evans v. Tennessee Department of Paroles* (1997); and *Warner v. Orange County Department of Probation* (1999). **28.** *National Treatment Center summary report*, Paul Blum and Terry Roman principal investigators. Athens, GA: Institute for Behavioral Research, 1997, p 24. **29.** Institute of Medicine. (1990). *Broadening the base of treatment for alcohol problems*. Washington, DC: National Academy Press. **30.** For a fuller discussion of avenues of coercion into AA, other 12-step groups, and 12-step treatment, see *Resisting 12-Step Coercion*, *op cit.*, pp 25–30. **31.** For a fuller discussion of these statistics, see *Resisting 12-Step Coercion*, *op cit.*, p 27, or see *Alcoholics Anonymous: Cult or cure? (second edition)*, *op cit.*, pp 101f–102f. **32.** According to statistics posted on AA's official Website <www.alcoholics-anonymous.org>, AA membership as of January 1, 1998, was 1,166,000; as of January 1, 1999, it was 1,167,000; and as of January 2000, it was 1,161,000. **33.** *The treatment episode data set (TEDS): 1992–1997 national admissions to substance abuse treatment services*. Rockville, MD: Substance Abuse and Mental Health Services Administration, 1999, p 67, Table 3.4. **34.** *National Treatment Center summary report*, *op cit.*, p 24. **35.** For a discussion of the percentage of coerced clients in 12-step treatment, see *Resisting 12-Step Coercion*, *op cit.*, pp 28–30. The percentage cited in that work (at least 50 percent) is derived from data gathered and published by the Substance Abuse and Mental Health Services Administration. **36.** Email message to this author from J.A. Johnson, Research Coordinator, Center for Research on Behavioral Health and Health Services Delivery, University of Georgia, November 4, 1998. **37.** Collins, Gregory B, MD. Contemporary issues in the treatment of alcohol dependence. *Psychiatric Clinics of North America*, Vol. 16, No. 1, March 1993, p 35. In the quotation, Collins is paraphrasing G.A. Mann. **38.** *Ibid.* **39.** Note that all three of these are 12-step groups, and that NA and OA borrowed their 12 steps directly from AA, virtually unaltered. **40.** See *Handbook of alcoholism treatment approaches*, *op cit.* See also *Resisting 12-Step coercion*, *op cit.*, and *Alcoholics Anonymous: Cult or cure? (second edition)*, *op cit.* **41.** See *Alcoholics Anonymous: Cult or cure? (second edition)*, Chapter 8, "Suppression of Dissent" subsection, *op cit.*, pp 120–123. See also, Peele, Stanton. (1986). Denial—of reality and freedom—in addiction research and treatment. *Bulletin of the Society of Psychologists in Addictive Behaviors*, Vol. 5, No. 4, 1986, pp 149–166. **42.** To appreciate just how disease-model-, abstinence-, and 12-step-oriented these organizations are, see their Websites: <www.ncadd.org> and <www.asam.org>. The NCADD site, for example, contains a page specifically advocating coercive "interventions," probably the single most invasive practice in the addictions field. **43.** See *Handbook of alcoholism treatment approaches*, *op cit.* See also *Resisting 12-Step coercion*, *op cit.* **44.** Cahalan, Don. (1987). *Understanding America's drinking problem*. San Francisco: Jossey-Bass, p 135. **45.** Dr. Luther Cloud, quoted by Stanton Peele (1986), *op cit.* **46.** An unnamed "director of the community services department of a large labor union" quoted by Cahalan, *op cit.*, p 135. **47.** Kishline, Audrey. (1994). *Moderate drinking: The new option for problem drinkers*. Tucson, Arizona: See Sharp Press, p 6.

The Unconscious Roots of the Drug War

Excerpts from *Shamanism and the Drug Propaganda:*
The Birth of Patriarchy and the Drug War

Dan Russell

Author of *Shamanism and the Drug Propaganda*
and *Drug War: Covert Money, Power & Policy* <www.drugwar.com>

The central sacrament of all Paleolithic, Neolithic and Bronze Age cultures known is an inebriative herb, a plant totem, which became metaphoric of the communal epiphany. These herbs, herbal concoctions and herbal metaphors are at the heart of all mythologies. They include such familiar images as the Burning Bush, the Tree of Life, the Cross, the Golden Bough, the Forbidden Fruit, the Blood of Christ, the Blood of Dionysos, the Holy Grail (or rather its contents), the Chalice (*Kalyx*: 'flower cup'), the Golden Flower (*Chrysanthemon*), Ambrosia (*Ambrotos*: 'immortal'), Nectar (*Nektar*: 'overcomes death'), the Sacred Lotus, the Golden Apples, the Mystic Mandrake, the Mystic Rose, the Divine Mushroom (*teonana-*

catl), the Divine Water Lily, Soma, Ayahuasca ('Vine of the Soul'), Kava, Iboga, Mama Coca and Peyote Woman.

They are the archetypal—the emotionally, the instantaneously understood—symbols at the center of the drug propaganda. A sexually attractive man or woman is an archetypal image, the basis of most advertising. A loaf of bread is an archetypal

image. The emotional impact of the sacramental herbal images, or, rather, the historical confusion of their natural function, is central to the successful manipulation of mass emotion and individual self-image.

Inebriation—ritual, social, alimentary and medical —is basic to all cultures, ancient and modern.

Jung: "An image which frequently appears among the archetypal configurations of the unconscious is that of the tree or the wonder-working plant." When people reproduce these dream images they often take the form of a mandala. Jung calls the mandala "a symbol of the self in cross section," comparing it to the tree, which represents the evolving self, the self as a process of growth.[1]

"Like all archetypal symbols, the symbol of the tree has undergone a development of meaning in the course of the centuries. It is far removed from the original meaning of the shamanistic tree, even though certain basic features prove to be unalterable."[2]

"…it is the decisive factors in the unconscious psyche, the archetypes, which constitute the structure of the collective unconscious. The latter represents a psyche that is identical in all individuals…. The archetypes are formal factors responsible for the organization of unconscious psychic processes: they are 'patterns of behaviour.'"[3]

Those patterns of behavior are rooted in our evolutionary biology as surely as is the shape of our body. Inebriative behavior

I doubt there is a solvent culture on earth in which breakfast isn't accompanied by a traditional herbal stimulant, or in which some herbal inebriant isn't wildly popular.

The Unconscious Roots of the Drug War
Dan Russell
Excerpts from *Shamanism and the Drug Propaganda:*
The Birth of Patriarchy and the Drug War

329

is an oral behavior, related, physiologically and psychologically, to eating and sex. It is as instinctive in people as socializing or music making. I doubt there is a solvent culture on earth in which breakfast isn't accompanied by a traditional herbal stimulant, or in which some herbal inebriant isn't wildly popular.

Inebriation—ritual, social, alimentary and medical—is basic to all cultures, ancient and modern. Traditional cultures don't separate inebriative herbalism from any of the other 'archaic techniques of ecstacy'—dancing, musicalizing, socializing, ritualizing, fasting, curing, ordeal—which are part of the same shamanic behavior complex; nor do they separate medicine from food.

Rome, the last of the great ancient slave states, institutionalized the conquistador ethos of industrial conformity in Western culture. That ethos translates itself

We will cease to live in the world of the ancients only when sex, birth, hunger and death become different for us than they were for them.

today as irrational fear of the shamanic experience; fear, that is, of the unconscious itself and of primitivity in general.

We don't escape the thrall of our dreams. The *psychology* of contemporary politics, 'history,' moves much more slowly than technology, which is a mechanical, not a biological process. We will cease to live in the world of the ancients only when sex, birth, hunger and death become different for us than they were for them. Our dream language, our spectacular automatic creativity, is, of course, archetypal imagery, the evolutionarily-determined picture-language that is the same for all peoples, regardless of culture, just as the human body and emotions are the same.

The artistic level achieved by many Neolithic cultures is extraordinary. The graphite- and gold-painted pottery produced by the Karanovo civilization of central Bulgaria in 4700 BC proves the existence of very sophisticated firing techniques. The Karanovo and Cucuteni cultures traded copper and gold artifacts and precious stones as well as their extraordinary pottery with each other. The largest Cucuteni town in western

Ukraine, dating to about 3700 BC, contained 2,000 houses, about 16,000 people.

Ceramic workshops were found there in two-story buildings, the top floors of which were apparently temples. The many clay temple models recovered show only women producing pottery in the downstairs temple workshops. Cucuteni pottery, employing the wheel, rivals anything the world produced for the next thousand years. Wheeled vehicles are depicted in both Cucuteni and Karanovo layers from about 4500 BC. A basic element of Cucuteni pottery design was the caduceus, or at least two s-shaped snakes creating an 'energy field,' drawn as floating lines, where their heads met.[4]

The snake, archetypal symbol of earthly regeneration and herbal healing, was a major motif of Neolithic art, both sacred and secular. An 8,000-year-old cult vessel from Yugoslavia has two bird-headed snakes guarding the contents of a ritual bowl.[5] A 6,500-year-old vase from Romania shows snakes encircling the concentric circles of the world, "making the world roll" as Gimbutas says.

Horned snakes, or horned animals in association with snakes, or bird-headed Goddesses wrapped in snakes, or Goddesses with snakes for hair, or schematic snakes, are reproduced on sacred drinking vessels, shrine Goddesses and pottery more frequently than any other imagery, from the Ukraine to Crete, from 8000 to 1500 BC. "The pregnant figurines of the seventh and sixth millennia BC are nude, while the pregnant ladies of the fifth and fourth millennia are exquisitely clothed except for the abdomen, which is exposed and on which lies a sacred snake."[6] At right, a sacramental vase from late Neolithic Greece.

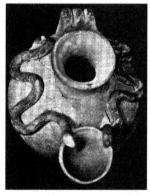

Female Neolithic images, many with the head of a snake or bird, outnumber male images thirty to one.[7] Like the bison-men of the Upper Paleolithic caves, the male god's principal Neolithic manifestation was in the form of a bull or bull-man, the Son of His Mother. The Snake-Bird Goddess, a figure of cthonic transformation and ecstatic resurrection, was the original Creatrix.

Evans: "The Gournia...relics dedicated to the snake cult are associated with small clay figures of doves and a relief showing the Double Axe. These conjunctions are singularly illuminating since they reveal the fact that the Snake Goddess herself represents only another aspect of the Minoan Lady of the Dove, while the Double Axe itself was connected with both. Just as the celestial inspiration descends in bird form either on the image of the divinity itself or on that of its votary...so the spirit of the Nether World, in serpent form, makes its ascent to a similar position from the earth itself."[8] The Double Axe, then, cuts both ways.[9]

Jung: "Archetypes are systems of readiness for action, and at the same time images and emotions. They are inherited with the brain structure—indeed, they are its psychic aspect. They represent, on the one hand, a very strong instinctive conservatism, while on the other hand they are the most effective means conceivable of instinctive adaptation. They are thus, essentially, the cthonic portion of the psyche, if we may use such an expression—that portion through which the psyche is attached to nature, or in which its link with the earth and the world appears at its most tangible. The psychic influence of the earth and its laws is seen most clearly in these primordial images."[10]

Primary among them, the snake, archetypal image of ecstatic creativity and the life force, of herbal magic and evolutionary adaptation, in all Neolithic cultures known. Gimbutas: "The snake is a transfunctional symbol; it permeates all themes of Old European symbolism. Its vital influence was felt not only in life creation, but also in fertility and increase, and particularly in the regeneration of dying life energy. Combined with magical plants, the snake's powers were potent in healing and creating life anew. A vertically winding snake symbolized ascending life force, viewed as a column of life rising from caves and tombs, and was an interchangeable symbol with the tree of life and spinal cord."[11]

The snake, the phallus, the mushroom and the bull, of course, aren't really separable images, as both Neolithic art and contemporary dreams suggest. Gimbutas: "The whole group of interconnected symbols—phallus (or cylinder, mushroom and conical cap), ithyphallic animal-masked man, goat-man and the bull-man—represents a male stimulating principle in nature without whose influence nothing would grow and thrive.... The 'bisexualism' of the water-bird divinity is apparent in the emphasis on the long neck of the bird symbolically linked with the phallus or the snake from Upper Paleolithic times and onwards through many millennia.... The image of a phallic Bird Goddess dominates during the seventh and sixth millennia in the Aegean and the Balkans. Sometimes she is a life-like erect phallus with small wings and a posterior of a woman, which, if seen in profile, is readily identifiable as a bird's body and tail.... 'Bisexualism' is reflected in bird-shaped vases with cylindrical necks and...in representations of hermaphroditic figurines of the Vinca culture having male genital organs and female breasts." (Parenthesis hers.)

"The 'Fertility Goddess' or 'Mother Goddess' is a more complex image than most people think. She was not only the Mother Goddess who commands fertility, or the Lady of the Beasts who governs the fecundity of animals and all wild nature, or the frightening Mother Terrible, but a composite image with traits accumulated from both the pre-agricultural and agricultural eras.... Throughout the Neolithic period her head is phallus-shaped suggesting her androgynous nature, and its derivation from Paleolithic times...divine bisexuality stresses her absolute power."[12]

Marshack reproduces a 20,000-year-old lunar counting bone which is simply a phallic head with two pendulous breasts. A 16,000-year-old lunar counting baton from France is a phallic bone with a vulva. A Goddess figure from Hungary, c.5400 BC, is shaped like a penis and testicles.[13] Just as it was obvious that life came from the womb or egg, so it was obvious that the conjunction of the sexes produced a numinous power. Respect for the power of the Bull was in no way contrary to respect for the Goddess, who bore the Bull.

Many of the magical signs found on Old European pottery from 6000 to 4000 BC are direct descendants of Upper Paleolithic symbols, such as the V sign, used to indicate the Goddess' pubic triangle on 19,000-year-old ivory figurines from the Ukraine. The inverted V sign was used to indicate the cap of sacred mushrooms. Snakes, flowers, eyes, ears, waves,

The Unconscious Roots of the Drug War
Dan Russell
Excerpts from *Shamanism and the Drug Propaganda:*
The Birth of Patriarchy and the Drug War

331

chevrons and x's are equally ancient. These signs evolved into linguistic magical signs, consistently found in all Old European cultures. They include moon-counting lines and circles, triangles, meanders, v's, m's, n's, squares, s's, diamonds, arcs, y's, +'s, tridents, bidents, swastikas, bird's feet, concentric circles, houses and numerous other geometric and schematic patterns.[14]

The 'sacral' ivy-leaf, a standard device of Cretan potters for millennia, became a letter in both Linear A and B.[15] Gimbutas, organizing linguistic work that began with Evans, has graphed 68 Old European signs that can be shown to be identical to either Cretan Linear A or Classical Cypriot syllabic phonemes, the two great island survivals of this Old European, pre-Indo-European, language.[16] This script, which predates the earliest evolved temple-palace script of Old Sumer by 2,000 years, isn't a bureaucratic device designed to manage the tax rolls, as in Sumer, but magical script, produced only on religious items. The Near Eastern scripts, of course, also originated in their predecessor Neolithic communities, thus the evolution is contemporaneous.

The Egyptian name for their hieroglyphs, originally used only for sacral purposes, was 'speech of the gods.'[17] We have 8,000-year-old stamp seals from Macedonia designed to leave their geometric impressions in wet clay, that is, moveable type. We also have Macedonian cylinder seals, designed to be rolled over the wet clay. This script is found only on figurines, thrones, temple models, altars, communion vases, sacred bread models, pendants, plaques and spindle whorls found in temples. Its purpose was to trigger magical communication, automatic speech, not accounting. Spindle whorls were often used as temple ornaments since the Goddess,

like the Spider, the Wasp and the Bee, was a weaver of, and carried the sting of, magical plants. At left is a Queen's pendant, Knossos, c.2000 BC.

The Cretan Queens of Knossos were consistently portrayed, for thousands of years, as winged wasps or bee-headed women surrounded by floating eyes and snakes. They were also depicted as bare-breasted shamans,

in a flounced skirt, with a flower crown and outstretched arms holding a cobra in each hand.[18] They cast spells. Their flower crowns were sometimes capped by the image of a panther, the premier transformation beast.[19] At right, the image from a Cretan signet seal, worn as a ring by a royal woman.

The throne of the Queen of Knossos was found in its original position against the north wall of the Throne Room. It was flanked by intensely colorful frescoes of huge eagle-headed lions, wingless griffins sprouting peacock plumes to indicate their benevolent character. They are couchant amongst the sacramental papyrus reeds. At their heart, near their lion's shoulder blade, are spiraliform rosettes, symbolic entheogens.[20]

In most ancient cultures, including Mesoamerican and Hellenic, the butterfly represents the soul; a common Greek word for butterfly is *psyche*, soul.[21] Many contemporary Mazatecs and Cretans alike still regard butterflies as the souls of the departed. Some clay seal impressions from Knossos show the dots in the wings of a butterfly actually transformed into floating eyes.[22]

In both cultures the butterfly is equated with the bee. Like the wasp, the power of the bee's sting came from the power of the plants it pollinated. A Mycenaean gem of Minoan workmanship, below right, c.1400 BC, pictures a large sacred plant growing from horns of consecration, supported by a chalice. The plant is ceremonially flanked by two lion-headed satyrs in bee skins, that is two shamans, each holding aloft, directly over the plant, a jug of sacramental drink.[23] The bees not only made honey for the honey-beer, but pollinated the magical flowers the mead was spiked with, thus transforming the shamans themselves into buzzing lion-headed bees.

The horse, the tarpan, was first tamed as an engine of war and high-speed travel by fierce nomadic pastoralists from the Ukraine and Kazakhstan about 5300 BC, using antler-tine bridles. Their economy was based on very large horse herds used for milk, meat, hide and sinew, which they didn't hesitate to drive into new territory. Since they relied on conquest, their mobile society was militarized and hierarchical, and their mythology stressed the role of the warrior as Creator. They carried bows and arrows, spears, long daggers and, later, short metal swords.

Since they left barrow or tumulus graves, individual pits covered by a low cairn or mound, *kurgan* in Russian, Gimbutas adopted this as the general name for the various steppe peoples sharing this culture. Kurgan hordes flooded Old Europe in three successive waves, c.4400 BC, c.3500 BC and c.3000 BC. These are the 'Proto-Indo-European' speakers whose language became the basis of the Greek, Celtic, Germanic, Italic, Albanian, Slavic, Armenian, Iranian and Indic language groups.[24]

Kurgan warriors could travel at least five times faster than the sedentary competition, and soon controlled the trade routes over vast areas of Southeastern Europe. For the first time, rich male graves, replete with weapons and horse-head sceptres, appear in Europe, indicating chieftancy and patriarchal organization. Over the centuries Europe's Neolithic villages became socially stratified, with the bulk of the Mediterranean-type population ruled by a warrior-elite of Kurgan, proto-Europid type. Hilltop forts appear, along with a pastoral economy, signs of violence, and patriarchal religious symbols emphasizing the sun. For the first time, throughout the Alpine valleys, Bulgaria, Romania, the Black Sea region and the Caucasus, heavily-armed male gods appear on stone stelae along with their solar symbolism.

By 3500 BC the official solar symbolism replaced the beautifully executed sacred script on Cucuteni pottery. The building of Cucuteni temples, the making of graceful communion vessels and the writing of the Old European script came to an end. Trade in metals and metal weaponry burgeoned. Daggers, shaft-hole axes and flat axes of arsenic bronze are found throughout the Pontic region, along with metal workshops containing clay bivalve molds. Northwest Yugoslavia, southwest Hungary, Slovenia and Slovakia yield an impressive chain of hill forts, where most of the metallurgy took place.[25]

The well-established Neolithic cultures of Old Europe didn't just die out overnight; those that remained unconquered adapted to the new environment. Sacred monarchy, a military institution,

was born. As the ecology militarized, the loving Mother-Queen found herself managing constant warfare. She became a Mother-Terrible, a *SHE* Who Must Be Obeyed, as H. Ryder Haggard put it. As the Bull's blood once was, so the Warrior's blood became—the source of life for the tribe. More and more authority devolved to the war shamans, as their responsibility for the survival of the tribe increased. They still ruled by deputizing for the Queen, for the Mother remained the Source of life. It was She, and her Priestesses, who sacrificed the Bull, or the Warrior-Bull, at the solstices.

The evolution, then, was from tribal to theacratic, to theocratic, to militaristic.

Since initiation is mock death and resurrection, and since plants became 'plant-man' and bulls became 'bull-man,' the 'sacrifice' would have been symbolic or entheogenic in most cases, since, most often, the Queen and her entourage would be 'killing' the old year and bringing in the new, as in the Bull sacrifice on the Cretan Hagia Triada sarcophagus, c. 1500 BC, below.

Island Crete, however, until the Mycenaean-Dorian age, was militarily secure. Times of terror came to mainland Europe much earlier. And in such times, extreme unction was demanded, one way or the other, of the war shaman, as it was among Paleolithic tribes. The first conception of a 'king' was as the sacrificial servant of the people, the war shaman who would lay down his life. Like the ritual Bull and the *pharmakon* which were traditionally consumed together, the king would sacrifice himself for the common good. The *pharmakos*, the sacrificial king, replaced the *pharmakon* more and more often as competition for the land increased. The Paleolithic Bull became a Warrior sacrificed to an emerging ethos of warfare, to an ecology of territorial competition and functional specialization—to a glorification of servitude and sacrifice that would have been alien to most Neolithic communities, except in extreme circumstances. The evolution, then, was from tribal to theacratic, to theocratic, to militaristic.

The Unconscious Roots of the Drug War
Dan Russell
Excerpts from *Shamanism and the Drug Propaganda:
The Birth of Patriarchy and the Drug War*

333

All the great originary city-states of Mesopotamia, China, Mesoamerica, Peru, Africa, India and Europe ended up 'militaristic,' that is, completely absorbed in internecine warfare. Cultural anthropologists classify the stages in the development of early civilizations as Incipient Farming, Formative, Florescent, Theocratic Irrigation-Trade State, and Militaristic State. Although there are regional and sub-regional differences—irrigation, for instance, was less important in some areas than in others—the pattern of creative, matristic, tribal, egalitiarian Neolithic villages enslaved by warrior tribes, or transfixed by internecine warfare, holds throughout. 'Militaristic' is used as a *synonym* for 'historical' by cultural anthropologists. This is not merely a function of the nastiness of those darn men, since increased agricultural efficiency itself produces intense population pressures and competition for resources. The resultant internecine warfare automatically produces the need for an effective defense.

Braidwood and Reed estimate 0.125 people per square mile in Late Paleolithic Iraq, c.10,000 BC.[26] Flannery estimates zero to one person per square kilometre in southwestern Iran, bordering Iraq, in the Late Paleolithic, growing to more than six people after large-scale irrigation appears, c.3000 BC—a sixty-fold increase.[27] Agriculture, then, is a cybernetic engine, creating its own pressure for increased production and territorial expansion. This was the exact opposite of the Neolithic process, which stressed the powerful hearth skills of women. The Bronze Age process stressed the confrontational skills of the warrior.

Furthermore, humans have an inherently carnivorous psychology. Even the tribal Neolithic communities lived by hunting and practicing animal sacrifice, which they uniformly associated with religious epiphany. Animal sacrifice, as the Cretan rite illustrates, was a major function of Neolithic priestesses. Blood was considered nourishing, entheogenic, and the entheogenic or curative sap of plants was regarded as their 'blood.' Wealth-managing bureaucracies, of course, which the Neolithic communities lacked, were careful to generate reasons for acquiring more wealth. In this sense, Early Bronze Age city-states can be seen as military institutions.

Iahu, the Sumerian Exalted Dove, was the daughter of Tiamat, the primeval waters. As the renowned linguist Professor John Allegro, Secretary of the Dead Sea Scrolls Fund and one of the original translators of the Scrolls, teaches, IA, in Sumerian, means 'juice' or 'strong water.' The root idea of U, according to its usage in words like 'copulate,' 'mount,' 'create,' and 'vegeta-

tion,' is 'fertility,' thus 'Iahu' means 'juice of fertility.'[28] That is the name of an entheogen, the fruit of 'the menses of Eileithyia.' The Sumerian Goddess was also called Inanna. 'Ishtar,' the Akkadian-Babylonian name, is derived from the Sumerian USh-TAR, 'uterus' in Latin. 'Dove,' *peristera* in Greek, also means 'womb,' as does its Semitic cognate *yonah*, Jonah.

The Akkadian era of Lower Mesopotamia (southern Iraq) was founded by Sargon of Agade or Akkad, c.2360 BC. Bab-ilu, 'the Gate of God,' Hammurabi's capitol city, inherited the political ascendancy about 600 years later. In Hammurabi's Babylon, the Exalted Dove was cut in two by Marduk. "You, Marduk, are the most revered of the awesome gods. Your fiat is unequalled, your dictate is Anu. From this day forward your pronouncements shall be unalterable. Your hands shall have the power to raise up or bring down. Your word shall be prophetic, your command shall be unrivalled. None of the gods shall be above you!"

"Let any downtrodden man with a cause present himself to my statue, for I am the king of justice. Let him read my inscribed words carefully, and ponder their meaning, for these will make his case clear to him, and give peace to his troubled mind! 'He is Hammurabi, the King, a father to all the people. He has heard the word of Marduk, his lord, and thus has guaranteed the prosperity of the people forever, leading the land into righteousness'—let my supplicant proclaim this, praying with his whole heart and soul for me!"[29]

Enuma Elish, 'When on High,' has the unrivalled Marduk creating order out of the corpse of Tiamat (above center), the Primordial Ocean-Woman, specifically called a woman in the myth and portrayed as an enraged shaman, like Hera, creating poisonous monsters for self-protection. Marduk, Tiamat's son, volunteers to rescue the rest of her rebellious progeny from the enraged Goddess: "He looked toward the enraged Tiamat, with a spell on his lips. He carried a magical plant to ward off her poison…. After slaying Tiamat the lord rested, pondering what to do with her dead body. He resolved to undo this abortion by creating ingenious things with it. Like a clam, he split her in two, setting half of her to form the sky as a roof for our earthly house."[30]

Tiamat became the *Tehom* of Genesis. 'Firmament' means 'what is spread out,' and is a reference to the body of Tiamat. Marduk is Yahweh to Tiamat's Tehom.[31] Marduk, or his hero Gilgamesh, was craftily portrayed as a winged shaman bringing the herb of immortality from heaven to earth, thus usurping

the function of Tiamat's daughter Iahu, the original Yahweh, the Exalted Dove. At left, Gilgamesh brings magical opium poppies to earth from the palace of Ashurnasirpal II, c. 875 BC. Marduk's rite involved ceremoniously cutting a dove in two at the Spring Equinox, an enormously powerful image for a culture that understood the meaning of the dove. Henceforth the wings belonged to Marduk, who proved as useful to Nebuchadnezzar in 600 BC as to Hammurabi in 1700 BC.[32]

Like the Mycenaeans before them, the Dorians, mounted pastoralists, entered the Peloponnese as conquerors. Their three main tribes were divided into 27 phratries, patrilinear brotherhoods, some of the names of which were found at Argos inscribed on water-pipes.[33] The native population of 'Helots' were enslaved as hereditary community property by the pipe-smoking brothers. Their military hierarchy tolerated no social dissent. By 800 BC Sparta controlled all Laconia, and, along with Argos, Corinth and Megara, all the Peloponnese except the mountains of Arcadia. Attica went through the same process of military consolidation under the Ionians, as did the northern regions under the Aeolians, Boeotians and Thessalians.

The demand for metal, and slaves to work the mines, played a major role in the founding of overseas trading colonies. Archaic Greek states, 800–500 BC, founded hundreds of colonies throughout Europe and North Africa.[34] The enslavement of the locals was standard colonization procedure. Slaves were at a premium since most children never saw fifteen; rare was the woman who lived past 30 or the man who lived past 40.

The canonical Boeotian Hesiod dated the ages of man by the

precious metals mined by the slaves: the original golden race of the orchard garden, whose spirits "roam everywhere over the earth, clothed in mist and keep watch on judgements and cruel deeds, givers of wealth"; the matriarchal silver race destroyed by Zeus for refusing to recognize him; the flesh-eating bronze race "sprung from ash trees…terrible and strong," who destroyed themselves in warfare; the founding fathers of Mycenae and Troy who dwell "untouched by sorrow in the islands of the blessed"; and their descendants of iron, who "never rest from labor and sorrow."[35]

In the *Works and Days*, when Pandora "lifts the great lid of the *pithos*" all the misfortunes of mortality fly out. Hesiod, the official mythologer of the Greek warrior class, thus equates the Mystery of the Spring Resurrection with death itself, as the Israelis did in their complex Passover legend. The winged 'All-giver,' Pandora, originally, on Crete, from whence the festival comes, instigated the rebirth of the world, not its woes.[36]

Life comes from Eleusis, 'the place of happy arrival,' from Delphi, 'the womb,' but to acknowledge that would be to acknowledge the primacy of *Thea*. Not Zeus, or his Only Begotten Son Apollon, nor Elohim or his Only Begotten Son *Moshiy'a*/*Yehoshu'a*/Jesus, but the Saviour Persephone, as she was called, the *Arrhetos Koura*, 'the ineffable maiden,' the Only Begotten Daughter, as she was called, first.

Persephone, the winged Snake Nymph Korykia, was inseparable from her herbal magic. Apollonius: "Thereupon the handmaids were making ready the chariot; and Medea meanwhile took from the hollow casket a charm which men say is called the charm of Prometheus. If a man should anoint his body therewithal, having first appeased the Maiden, the only-begot-

ten, with sacrifice by night, surely that man could not be wounded by the stroke of bronze nor would he flinch from blazing fire; but for that day he would prove superior both in prowess and in might. It shot up first-born when the ravening eagle on the rugged flanks of Caucasus let drip to the earth the blood-like ichor of tortured Prometheus. And its flower appeared a cubit above ground in color like the

The Unconscious Roots of the Drug War
Dan Russell
Excerpts from *Shamanism and the Drug Propaganda:*
The Birth of Patriarchy and the Drug War

Korykian crocus, rising on twin stalks; but in the earth the root was like newly-cut flesh. The dark juice of it, like the sap of a mountain-oak, she had gathered in a Caspian shell to make the charm withal, when she had first bathed in seven ever-flowing streams, and had called seven times on Brimo, nurse of youth, night-wandering Brimo, of the underworld, queen among the dead,—in the gloom of night, clad in dusky garments. And beneath, the dark earth shook and bellowed when the Titanian root was cut; and the son of Iapetos himself groaned, his soul distraught with pain. And she brought the charm forth and placed it in the fragrant band which engirdled her, just beneath her bosom, divinely fair. And going forth she mounted the swift chariot…"[37]

Pandora-Korykia-Persephone is the Greek equivalent of Eve, and is similarly manipulated. Eve is the Hebrew equivalent of Ishtar, whose Babylonian legend is a virtual duplicate of the legend of Persephone, as is the legend of Ishtar's Sumerian mother Inanna or Iahu, dug up at ancient Nippur. Ishtar is smitten in the underworld with 60 diseases, stopping all reproductive life on earth. Ea, the Babylonian Prometheus, extracts a magical flagon from Ereshkigal, the Babylonian Hecate, the water from which enables Ishtar to rise to the surface. Reunited with Tammuz (Dionysos), they perform the sacred rites for the dead, who restore life to the upper world as the two make love.

During 'cups,' through entheogenic and erotic ecstacy, the dead earth was brought back to life. By dancing with the ghosts, ancient Eros, the fructifying power, was reborn. After 'cups' came *Chytroi*, 'pots for the food of the dead'—gifts to encourage the ghosts to return once again to their homes underground.[38]

'Death' was a state that could be visited, one could be 'abducted' to the realm of the dead, hence the sacramental identity of Greek women with Persephone; they regularly *became* Persephone. Explains Ishtar: "On the day when Tammuz comes up to me,/When with him the lapis flute and the carnelian ring come up to me,/When with him the wailing men and the wailing women come up to me,/May the dead rise and smell the incense."[39] (Nippur, c.1800 BC.)

Eliade: "It certainly seems that the chief function of the dead in the granting of shamanic powers is less a matter of taking 'possession' of the subject than of helping him to become a 'dead man'—in short, of helping him to become a 'spirit' too."[40]

But shamanic spirituality becomes a threat to slavers bent on conquest. Almost every significant government from the Late Bronze Age to the nineteenth century has been a theocratic slave state in which the official rituals of the culture reinforced mass servitude. The sacred fire of the Mother City which the colonists so treasured on their arduous voyage of conquest was meant to replace that of their hosts. "Conquering gods their titles take/From the foes they captive make."

Propaganda works by way of true myth, imagery which instantly affects our emotions. This archetypal imagery is brought to life by pharmaco-shamanic rites in tribal cultures, and those rites are criminalized and co-opted by their industrial conquerors. The solar monotheism, the Aten of Akhenaten, served the same purpose as the Apollo of the Delphian powers, or the Juppiter Maximus of Caesar, or the Jesus Invictus of Constantine and Charles V. The Imperial Icon facilitated the efficient management of the conquered by requiring the replacement of their culture with the Imperial syncretism. This cultural genocide effectively turned once independent people into farm animals—*andrapoda*, as the Greeks put it, 'human-footed stock.'

The archetypal matristic imagery remained an organic if diminished part of classical Olympian mythology because the Greeks remained more decentralized than either the Israelis or the Romans. King David organized all the women of royal blood into a royal harem, thus making the 'matrilineal' throne of Israel the exclusive province of the King and his line. This device was adopted in Rome on the founding of the Vestal College, but, because there was no central Greek government, and because the canonical Hesiod, early on, had, as Herodotus put it, "given the deities their titles and distinguished their several provinces and special powers,"[41] absolute theological patriarchy never reached Greece, although Olympian tradition is certainly warrior-based.

As Graves puts it, "The institution of patriarchy ends the period of true myth; historical legend then begins and fades into the light of common history."[42] That is, true myth, the archetypes of consciousness evoking evolutionary, that is behavioral, realities, instinct, the stuff of dreams, is more easily discerned through the fog of Greek legend than Israeli or the much later

> But shamanic spirituality becomes a threat to slavers bent on conquest.

Roman. As Homer put it, "Two gates for ghostly dreams there are: one gateway/of honest horn, and one of ivory./Issuing by the ivory gate are dreams/of glimmering illusion, fantasies,/but those that come through solid polished horn/may be borne out, if mortals only know them."[43]

Graves says that all true poetry celebrates the thirteen lunar months of the ancient year, the birth, life, death and resurrection of the God of the Waxing year, who is the son, lover and victim of the threefold Goddess, the Muse of all true poets. "Her names and titles are innumerable. In ghost stories she often figures as 'The White Lady,' and in ancient religions, from the British Isles to the Caucasus, as the 'White Goddess.' I cannot think of any true poet, from Homer onwards who has not independently recorded his experience of her. The test of a poet's vision, one might say, is the accuracy of his portrayal of the White Goddess and of the island over which she rules. The reason why the hairs stand on end, the eyes water, the throat is constricted, the skin crawls and a shiver runs down the spine when one writes or reads a true poem is that a true poem is necessarily an invocation of the White Goddess, or Muse, the Mother of All Living, the ancient power of fright and lust—the female spider or the queen-bee whose embrace is death."[44]

Human industry is to the ecosphere what individual consciousness is to the collective unconscious. Just as sensitivity to the ineffable ecosphere must be our teacher if we are to survive the effects of our own technology, so must sensitivity to our own ineffable logosphere, our collective unconscious, be our teacher if we are to survive the politics that technology has generated.

Jung: "Just as the day-star rises out of the nocturnal sea, so, ontogenetically and phylogenetically, consciousness is born of unconsciousness and sinks back every night to this primal condition. This duality of our psychic life is the prototype and archetype of the Sol-Luna symbolism."[45] "Luna is really the mother of the sun, which means, psychologically, that the unconscious is pregnant with consciousness and gives birth to it."[46] "The foundation of consciousness, the psyche *per se*, is unconscious, and its structure, like that of the body, is common to all, its individual features being only insignificant variants."[47]

The loss of connection to the ecstatic processes, the loss of an easy bridge between the conscious and the unconscious, is the beginning of neurosis, the loss of connection to the Holy Mother, the irrational voice of our emotions, the fountainhead of our genius. The last thing Greek slaves needed was genuine inspiration, so, for them, the contents of the Jug became taboo. We have all become Greek slaves. The Mycenaeans, conquerors and transmitters of Cretan culture, were themselves absorbed by the southerly march of the Dorians and Ionians. Their Classical Greek imagery was then transformed by the Romans into the Orthodox Christianity which became the mandatory religion of the late Roman slave states, of all the medieval European slave states, and the theological underpinning of the Euro-American industrial theocracy.

Kannabis, as the Greeks called it, sacred mushrooms, coca leaf, Peyote and the other ancient herbal sacraments are among the most easily accessible doorways to the proprioceptive and oracular available. They are fountainheads of creativity and earth-consciousness industrial culture desperately needs. Without institutionalized, or at least legalized shamanism, a Paleolithic adaptive technique, human political culture risks domination by the suicidally robotic, as our repeated acts of genocide and our virtually institutionalized ecocide tend to indicate. It is the tribal, the mammalian, the creative part of our psyche that is sensitive to our biological relationship to the earth. Is global political culture successfully dealing with the industrial destabilization of the ecosphere? Unmitigated industrial values are a path to evolutionary suicide.

The ancient shamanic bridges need to be rebuilt; the familial tribal cultures need to be listened to very carefully. Humanizing the evolved industrial polity will be every bit as difficult as healing the damaged ecosphere and rendering human industry ecological. "The Teleut shaman calls back the soul of a sick child in these words: 'Come back to your country!… to the yurt, by the bright fire!… Come back to your father…to your mother!…' …It is only if the soul refuses or is unable to return to its place in the body that the shaman goes to look for it and finally descends to the realm of the dead to bring it back."[48] Hence historiography.

This archetypal imagery is brought to life by pharmaco-shamanic rites in tribal cultures, and those rites are criminalized and co-opted by their industrial conquerors.

The Unconscious Roots of the Drug War
Dan Russell
Excerpts from *Shamanism and the Drug Propaganda:
The Birth of Patriarchy and the Drug War*

The central sacrament of Incan culture, coca leaf, a medicinal chew and tea leaf, was determined to be *un delusio del demonio* by Pizarro's priests, who proceeded to save Incan souls by working them to death as beasts of burden under the lash.

There is nothing whatever dangerous about whole coca leaves; they are as harmless as orange pekoe tea. Cocaine, which wasn't isolated until 1860, comprises about one-half of 1 percent of the weight of a coca leaf. It takes a ton of coca leaves to make 5 to 20 pounds of cocaine. There are far more dangerous compounds in potatoes, tomatoes, celery and fava beans, all of which are perfectly safe to eat.

Traditional sacramental plant-foods can't be equated with poisons, and poisons can't be equated with naturally-occurring plant isolates. Some plants are poisonous, and some plant isolates are as safe to use as corn. This Drug War is largely the political history of that intentional confusion, a confusion rooted in the *unconscious* contents of our political culture. That is, in the planted axiom that "the drug problem" can be discussed in terms of modern politics.

The Drug War can't be separated from the cultural compulsion of our conquistador history. Nor can it be separated from the evolutionary function of inebriative behavior. The industrial process has been as successful in burying conscious knowledge of the archaic techniques of ecstacy as it has been in burying the wolf, and those that understood it. Unconscious knowledge, on the other hand, is a tad more difficult to manipulate, as the neurotic lurching of so many of our public figures demonstrates; "just say no," after all, was promulgated by an alcoholic.

We are no longer overtly racist, in our public laws at least, but we are still brutally anti-tribal, in many ways institutionally unloving, structurally violent, to millions of our children, our tribal primitives, and to our shamanic adults. This is a *psychological* inheritance from our conquistador past, as well as a legal one.

This internalized industrial fascism, this proscription, *causes* drug problems, in the same way that violent sexual puritanism causes sexual problems. The ancient tribal wisdom prevents them. There are many cultures, both tribal and industrial, the Vicosinos of Peru and the Dutch, for instance, that don't have anything like our current disaster, and they all apply prescription rather than proscription.

Endnotes

1. Jung, Carl. (1956). *The collected works, volume 13: Alchemical studies*, p 253. Princeton University Press. **2.** *Ibid.*, p 272 **3.** Jung, Carl. (1956). *The collected works, volume 8: The structure and dynamics of the psyche*, p 436. Princeton University Press. **4.** Gimbutas, Marija. (1982). *The goddesses and gods of old Europe*, p 95. University of California Press. Gimbutas, Marija. (1989). *The language of Goddess*, pp 282, 293. HarperCollins Publishers. **5.** *Op cit.*, Gimbutas (1982), p 101. **6.** *Ibid*, p 201. **7.** *Op cit.*, Gimbutas (1989), p 175. **8.** Evans, Sir Arthur. (1921). *The palace of Minos at Knossos, volume 3*, p 508. Macmillan & Company. **9.** *Ibid.*, pp 438–440. **10.** Jung, C. (1956). *The collected works, volume 10: Civilization in transition*, p 31. Princeton University Press. **11.** *Op cit.*, Gimbutas (1989), p 121. **12.** *Op cit.*, Gimbutas (1982), pp 216, 135, 152, 196. **13.** *Op cit.*, Gimbutas (1989), pp 231, M-292 **14.** Gimbutas, Marija. (1991). *The civilization of the Goddess*, p 308. HarperCollins Publishers. **15.** Evans, Sir Arthur. (1921). *The palace of Minos at Knossos, volume 2*, p 284. Macmillan & Company. **16.** *Op cit.*, Gimbutas (1991), p 320. evans, 1-134, 1:2:641 **17.** Hawkes, Jacquetta (1993). *The atlas of early man*, p 62. St. Martin's Press. **18.** Palmer, Leonard R. (1965). *Mycenaeans and Minoans*, plate 14. Alfred A. Knopf. **19.** Evans, Sir Arthur. (1921). *The palace of Minos at Knossos, volume 1*, pp 501–507. *Op cit.*, Evans, Vol 2, p 748. **20.** Evans, Sir Arthur. (1921). *The palace of Minos at Knossos, volume 4*, pp 910ff. *Op cit.*, Palmer, plate 11. **21.** Wasson, R. Gordon, with Stella Kramrisch, Jonathan Ott & Carl A.P. Ruck. (1989). *Persephone's quest*, p 189. Yale University Press. **22.** *Op cit.*, Evans, Vol 2, p 789. **23.** *Op cit.*, Evans, vol 4, p 453. *Op cit.*, Gimbutas (1982), p 184. **24.** Crystal, David. (1987). *The Cambridge encyclopedia of language*, p 299. Cambridge University Press. **25.** *Op cit.*, Gimbutas (1991), pp 352–400. **26.** Struever, Stuart (Ed.). (1971). *Prehistoric agriculture*, p 304. The Natural History Press. **27.** *Ibid.*, p 75. **28.** Allegro, John. (1970). *The sacred mushroom and the cross*, pp 20, 91. Doubleday & Company. **29.** Finegan, Jack. (1959). *Light from the ancient past*, p 59. Princeton University Press. **30.** Pritchard, James B. (Ed.). (1971). *The ancient Near East*, pp 33–35. Princeton University Press. *Op cit.*, Finegan, p 64. **31.** Gordon, Cyrus H. (1965). *The common background of Greek and Hebrew civilization*, p 91. W.W. Norton & Company. **32.** *Op cit.*, Finegan, p 224. **33.** *The Cambridge ancient vistory, vol 3:1: The prehistory of the Balkans, the Middle East, and the Aegean*, p 714. Cambridge University Press. **34.** *The Cambridge ancient history, Vol 3:3: Expansion of the Greek world, eighth to sixth centuries BC*, p 160. Cambridge University Press. **35.** Hesiod. Hugh G. Evelin-White, translator. (1914). *The collected works, the Homeric hymns and Homerica*, pp 110–200. G.P. Putnam's Sons. **36.** *Op cit.*, Palmer, p 137 **37.** Apollonius Rhodius. R.C. Seaton, translator. (1921). *The Argonautica*, p 843. G.P. Putnam's Sons. **38.** Kerenyi, Karl. (1976). *Dionysos*, p 304. Princeton University Press. **39.** *Op cit.*, Pritchard, p 85. *Op cit.*, Gordon, p 90. **40.** Eliade, Mircea. (1974). *Shamanism*, p 85. Princeton University Press. **41.** Herodotus. David Grene, translator. (1987). *The history*, p 53. University of Chicago Press. **42.** Graves, Robert. (1959). *The Greek myths*, p 20. George Braziller, Inc. **43.** Homer. Robert Fitzgerald, translator. (1963). *The odyssey*, p 560. Doubleday & Company. **44.** Graves, Robert. (1959). *The white goddess*, p 11. Vintage Books. **45.** Jung, C. (1956). *The collected works, volume 14: Mysterium coniunctionis*, p 97. Princeton University Press. **46.** *Ibid.*, p 177. **47.** *Op cit.*, Jung, vol 13, p 347. **48.** *Op cit.*, Eliade, p 217.

You Are Still Being Lied To

HOLY ROLLING

The Eurabian Revolution

Gregory M. Davis

We have today, in the opening years of the twenty-first century, front-row seats to what is surely one of the most astonishing revolutions ever to transpire on the face of the earth. Like the spectacular upheavals of 1789, 1848, and 1917, this one has been simmering for decades but is still in its progressive rather than explosive stage (though the latter may not be far off). The revolutions of the past each professed a glorious future just beyond the horizon, and while those utopian visions differed, the intent and consequence of those revolutions were primarily destructive. They destroyed rather than created; they left behind not shining cities on a hill, but valleys of woe, carnage, and landscapes of unprecedented material and spiritual wreckage. As it was then, so it is today.

> The temperate, tolerant Western European republics are handing themselves over to what has proven the leading progenitor of war, slavery, and civilizational disaster of the past fourteen centuries: Islam.

What is happening in Europe is that in the heartland of the leading civilization of the past 500 years, the dominant political culture is being supplanted by an alien invader, hitherto inferior in every dimension. Western Europe, whose influence on the course of modern world history is second to none, is today unmistakably and deliberately welcoming into its midst a civilizational force that strove, unsuccessfully, for a thousand years to destroy it. What that force was unable to accomplish through force of arms is now being accomplished through Europe's own suicidal policies. The temperate, tolerant Western European republics are handing themselves over to what has proven the leading progenitor of war, slavery, and civilizational disaster of the past fourteen centuries: Islam.

While analysts of recent years have observed the social difficulties facing Europe by its growing Muslim population, few have been willing or able to grasp the bigger picture. In 1945, there were perhaps a few hundred-thousand Muslims in Western Europe; today there are 25 million. If one includes Russia in the calculation, the figure is 50 million. The societal shift underway in Europe today is nothing short of seismic. While Muslims press into Europe in huge numbers and continue to have children at levels far above the European average, the native European populations are collapsing. While Western Europe's Muslim population is expected to double during the decade 2005–15, the native population will actually decline by several percent. Perhaps most significant, it appears that Islamic identity is actually stronger among second- and third-generation Muslims, a fact that contradicts all of the sanguine hopes about assimilation. And these tendencies are no mere blips on the screen but have shown themselves to be transgenerationally robust, dating back roughly forty years, and they only seem to be accelerating.

Europe and the Religion of Peace

Major demographic shifts have occurred before, of course, but in the case of Islam growing in a non-Islamic society, it is more than just a matter of "there goes the neighborhood." While there have been major shifts of power in Europe before (the Spanish being supplanted by the Dutch being supplanted by the French, the English, the Germans, the Americans, etc.), the major players have all been grounded, at least loosely, in a Greco-Roman-Christian universe. Not so with Islam, whose inspiration lies not in Athens and Jerusalem but in Mecca and Medina. Thanks to the indiscriminateness of contemporary academic and political assumptions, Islam was casually tossed into that garbage-can rubric, "religion," and enough said. But far from being merely a religion in the personal sense, Islam is a political ideology that has never recognized a distinction between the

> In a century's time, the Muslim Arab armies had crushed Christian North Africa, the Holy Land, overrun Spain and Portugal, and were hammering at the gates of Paris.

secular and the spiritual. Islam is in fact a system of government ordained by Allah to comprehend the planet; any individual or society that does not submit ("Islam" translates best as "submission") to Allah's governance (Islamic law or *Sharia*) places itself in an ipso facto state of rebellion.

While many Muslims (like many Christians, Jews, etc.) are slack in the practice of their faith, *orthodox* Islam—*Sharia* and all—is once again asserting itself around the globe and, now, in Europe. From the terrorism that struck London and Madrid to the brazen demonstrations of European Muslims calling for the deaths of European statesmen during the Muhammad-cartoon and Koran-commode crises, to the increasing number of "honor" killings against wayward Muslim girls, to the expanding no-go areas off-limits to non-Muslim police and government authority, the violent calling cards of Islam, seen previously only in the Third World, are now *internal* phenomena. Yet, whenever a bus or a plane and its occupants are blown to smithereens by a devotee of the "religion of peace," we hear repeated in ever-patient, reasonable tones that Islam has nothing to do with violence and that "extremism" is to be found in every religion. While it is not really so remarkable that there are people who would engage in such transparent sophistry, what astonishes is that so many seem to listen to them.

What has been forgotten is that Europe's fight against Islamic imperialism is its salient, perhaps defining, historical achievement. It has been only in the post-war, post-revolutionary, post-Christian era that Europe lowered its guard to let in the ancient enemy. For a thousand years (roughly the seventh through seventeenth centuries), Europe existed on the knife-edge of destruction at the hands of Islamic jihad.

A quick historical refresher is in order. Following the death of Muhammad in 632 CE, Islam burst out of Arabia with unprecedented violence. In a century's time, the Muslim Arab armies had crushed Christian North Africa, the Holy Land, overrun Spain and Portugal, and were hammering at the gates of Paris. It was at Poitiers-Tours, in 732 CE, that Charles, King of the Franks, turned back the tsunami—and earned the sobriquet, *Martel*, "the Hammer." Following the Islamic destruction of the most holy site in Christendom, the Church of the Holy

Sepulchre, and the defeat of the Byzantine Empire at Manzikert by the Muslim Turks, the Vatican in 1095 commissioned the First Crusade, the first serious counter-offensive against Islamic predations during 450 years of jihadi aggression. Unhappily, the Crusades were as much about Rome's desire to wrest Jerusalem from the Byzantines (following Rome's split from the Eastern Church in 1054, the Great Schism) as it was about preserving Europe from the jihad. The Fourth Crusade of 1204, far from helping the Eastern Christians to stop the tide of Islam, culminated in the Latins' sacking of Constantinople, thus rendering the split between Eastern and Western Christianity permanent, and fatally crippling the principal bulwark against Islamic aggression, the Byzantine Empire. In 1453, Constantinople, the jewel of Eastern Christendom, having held out against Muslim attacks since the eighth century, finally succumbed. In less than a hundred years, the Muslims would be at the walls of Vienna. They were decisively turned back on their second attempt to take the city by the King of Poland, John Sobieski, on a date that ought to be among the most famous in history: September 11, 1683. Still, Muslim raiders would be abducting Europeans into slavery from as far away as Ireland into the nineteenth century.

But the high priests of multiculturalism today would have us believe that Europe's thousand-year struggle for survival against Islamic jihad was just a bad dream. When presented with contemporary instances of the Muslim penchant for violence, they tell us that, you see, the situation is very complex, one mustn't jump to conclusions, etc. The world is a complex place, of course, but there is no need to complicate something that is actually fairly straightforward. Let us propose, as a competing hypothesis to the convoluted platitudes about how Muslim terrorists are "disenfranchised" or "undervalued," about how Europe mistreated them for all those years, about the problems of the inner city, lack of health care, feelings of "isolation," etc., etc. (all of which possess their grains of truth), the following simple, limpid idea: Islam, as a creed and ideology, is violent.

Ask yourself this: If terrorism is a function of poverty, why have so many Muslim terrorists—from 9/11 to 7/7 to the archjihadi himself, bin Laden—been from wealthy, educated backgrounds? Why so few impoverished Hindu suicide bombers or

The Eurabian Revolution
Gregory M. Davis

shamanist jihadis? Where are all those poor, disenfranchised Appalachian Baptist martyrs' brigades? Why no air piracy waged by radical Christianists? A continent that has in living memory experienced the horrors of Communism and National Socialism should not have so much difficulty appreciating that certain ideas are fully capable of motivating large numbers of people to do very ugly things. If the French salons produced the ideological underpinnings of the Terror, and the most cultured Western nation could hatch National Socialism, what do we expect from a religion forged in seventh-century desert Araby, not exactly the most genteel environment? We have become so domesticated by "experts" and men in white coats as to what to eat, drink, and whom to vote for that we can no longer discern the elephant in the room, even when it's wearing a suicide belt.

The dominant Islam-is-peaceful crowd would have us reject the plain evidence of our eyes. Of the myriad post–Cold War conflicts in the world, the overwhelming majority of them are Islamic in nature. Of course, we are usually not told what is the common element of the terrorism in the Philippines, the "unrest" in Thailand, the low-grade strife in Western China, Kashmir, Chechnya, Bosnia, Kosovo, Algeria, Nigeria, the Ivory Coast, Sudan, Mauritania, as well as of course Lebanon, Israel, Iraq, and global terrorism from Bali to New York, Washington, London, Madrid, Moscow, Luxor, etc., etc.: It is Islam. Indeed, it is easier to enumerate the wars of today which do *not* involve Islam than the other way around. Should this tell us something?

The violent nature of Islam is not some recent innovation that distorted an otherwise peaceful religion; rather it is confirmed throughout the life of Muhammad and the Koran. We have not

> Then they [the Jewish tribe of Qurayza] surrendered, and the Apostle confined them in Medina in the quarter of d. al-Harith, a woman of Bani al-Najjar. Then the Apostle went out to the market of Medina and dug trenches in it. Then he sent for them and struck off their heads in those trenches as they were brought out to him in batches. Among them was the enemy of Allah Huyayy bin Akhtab and Ka'b bin Asad their chief. There were 600 or 700 in all, though some put the figure as high as 800 or 900. As they were being taken out in batches to the Apostle they asked Ka'b what he thought would be done with them. He replied, "Will you never understand? Don't you see that the summoner never stops and those who are taken away do not return? By Allah it is death!" This went on until the Apostle made an end of them. (Ishaq 463–4, *The Life of Muhammad*, trans by A. Guillaume)

A single example cannot be said to establish a general rule. But it is worth bearing in mind, next time one hears about the similarities between Islam and Christianity, that Jesus Christ and the Apostles never cut off anybody's head.

The only reasonable objection to the idea that Islam as a rule is violent is the fact that so many of its adherents are peaceful (there are now, apparently, more Muslims than Roman Catholics worldwide); but then because there were urbane Communists and pleasant Nazis hardly meant that their ideologies were benign. The question remains as to whether peaceful Muslims are that way *because* of their religion or *in spite* of it. In any religion or ideology there are some very faithful adherents who will go to great lengths to fulfill its precepts—the Christian ascetics, for example—while others make greater compromise with the world. Some Muslims with the zeal and opportunity become mujahideen, others encourage jihad with word and checkbook, others are tacitly sympathetic, and still others indulge in hot dogs and beer, attend mosque once in a blue crescent moon, and guffaw at Jewish comedians. Just as not all Christians love their neighbor, so not all Muslims have the inner fortitude to kill the infidel while screaming, "God is great!" ("Allah Ahkbar!")—but this hardly means that Islam is therefore peaceful. Indeed, as the Muslim populations in Europe have grown, we have seen a corresponding increase of their violent minorities. What do

Of the myriad post–Cold War conflicts in the world, the overwhelming majority of them are Islamic in nature.

here the space to attempt a full-fledged discussion of the textual origins of Islamic violence, so we shall just mention one illustrative example in the life of *al insan al kamil*, the "ideal man," Muhammad, excerpted from the Sira, the canonical biography of the Prophet. The episode is taken from the last ten years of Muhammad's life, after he set up shop in Medina and had waged several successful battles against his Mecca rivals.

we make of the creed of Hamas, that leading social-services and terrorist organization of the Gaza strip, that "the Koran is our constitution, Muhammad is our example, jihad is our path"? Do all those martyrs-in-waiting, reciting the Koran and siting their Kalashnikovs, misunderstand their own religion, or—utterly removed from Islamic culture—do we? Do the Western politicians who insist on Islam's peacefulness do so because they are so knowledgeable of the origins, history, and doctrines of Islam, or because the alternative (now that Islam is inside the walls) is too terrible a reality to accept?

Islam and the Euro-Mediterranean Dream

Having attempted to bring some clarity to the issue of Islamic violence, we come to our next question: If Islam is such bad news, how on earth was it let into the European heartland? A question of paramount importance but one that has only recently received any serious attention. It took Bat Ye'or's seminal *Eurabia: The Euro-Arab Axis* to explain in cogent fashion the actual process of bringing Islam into Europe. While many observed only the outward movements of the

the gigantic task of political geology required to figure out what has actually been going on.

The upshot is that the opening of the EC and later EU countries to Islam was no accident or natural development; rather it was—and continues to be—a deliberate policy of the EU, shared to varying degrees by its member governments. Significantly, Bat Ye'or did not coin the term "Eurabia." It was the title of a journal of the mid-1970s that had the political union of Europe and the Arab world as its theme. "Eurabia," in other words, was not originally the term of alarm that Bat Ye'or has made it; instead, it was a positive reference to a new era of Euro-Islamic integration. This fact in itself is enough to lend credibility to the idea that the creation of a Euro-Muslim bloc has been very much intentional and is seen by some as a positive good.

The EU's principal instrument for building Eurabia has been the Euro-Arab Dialogue (EAD), a group of European and Arab-Muslim officials that guides integration at the highest levels, but the proliferation of organizations and bodies devoted to the "Euro-Med" project (as it is now openly referred to) are too

The question remains as to whether peaceful Muslims are that way *because* of their religion or *in spite* of it.

Eurabian organism—the increasing commingling of the European and Muslim-Arab polities—yet remained largely oblivious to its internal workings, Bat Ye'or dived in with her scalpel and forceps.

What she revealed was the tangled web of European official-dom in its full mind-bending madness. *Eurabia* documents the imbroglio of conferences, position papers, cultural exchanges, official declarations, partnerships, etc. that are effecting a quiet revolution that is slowly but surely removing Western Europe as a distinct political region. The picture *Eurabia* paints is one of officials who took it upon themselves to recast Europe's destiny without much consulting those they govern (hardly the first time). The policy-making nexus of individual national governments, the European Parliament, the Council of Ministers, the European Commission, etc. along with the vertiginous layers of international finance, nongovernmental organizations, academia, etc., etc., is effectively unaccountable to the European public by virtue of its own impenetrable complexity. It took someone of Bat Ye'or's scholarly patience to undertake

many to name. Some of the more significant ones are the Parliamentary Association for Euro-Arab Co-operation (PAEAC), the European Institute for Research on Mediterranean and Euro-Arab Co-operation (MEDA), the Facility for Euro-Mediterranean Investment and Partnership (FEMIP), and the European Committee and Coordination of Friendship Associations with the Arab World (EURABIA—I kid you not). Normal people, of course, have difficulty imagining that obscure bodies composed of career bureaucrats would have the wherewithal to accomplish much of anything. But, like a slowly expanding glacier, one day, after generations of incre-mental movement, one awakes to a landscape utterly trans-formed. And now that some are awakening to the burgeoning Eurabian catastrophe, the labyrinthine Eurabian infrastructure effectively forestalls any remedial action.

But the hypothesis that the opening of Europe to Islam has somehow been *deliberate* runs afoul of many. To them, it seems impossible that the transformation of Europe into Eurabia could wind up somehow being intentional—how on earth could any sane European mind actually *want* to see Europe absorbed into Eurabia? But the alternative, conventional wisdom—that the ongoing Islamization of Europe is the result of some big accident, that it was the unforeseen consequence of wholly well-intentioned policy—is a non-explanation that provides no insight into the phenomenon itself. Bat Ye'or's scholarship, like all serious inquiry, takes as its point of departure the assumption that things happen for a reason. While there certainly are coincidences and accidents, it does violence to the spirit of serious inquiry to suppose that an entire continent can, in the course of several decades, be set on its way from a collection of republics with Christian overtones to

entailed two principle points: 1) dump Israel and her patron, the United States, and 2) open Europe economically and culturally to the Arab-Muslim states. Right or wrong, shrewd or foolish, this was the calculation the European governments made.

The oil-driven decision of the early 1970s was reinforced by numerous jihadist terror attacks on European interests in the succeeding years. The Europeans chose the well-worn path of greater appeasement in the form of support for the PLO, hostility to Israel and the US, and ever-greater openness to penetration by Muslim-Arab finance and culture. The jihadist attacks ceased. Little in the way of Islamic terrorism occurred in pre-9/11 Europe.

> While there certainly are coincidences and accidents, it does violence to the spirit of serious inquiry to suppose that an entire continent can, in the course of several decades, be set on its way from a collection of republics with Christian overtones to an Islamic superstate all by accident.

an Islamic superstate all by accident. Perhaps the reason that people recoil from that idea that Islamizing Europe has been a *choice* is because the implication is that *it didn't have to happen*. It is always tempting after the fact to imagine that it was all "inevitable"—then there is no one to blame and we can all lament the grim inevitability of fate over our espresso. But if there is nothing "natural" or "inevitable" about replacing Europe with Eurabia, the implication is that someone, somewhere is to blame for having brought it about and the rest of us for having lacked the vision and resolution to forestall the disaster.

A criticism of the deliberate theory is that it smacks of "conspiracy," which for some reason is a distasteful word. Of course, "conspiracy" is a widely recognized legal concept, a crime regularly prosecuted by governments all over the world, yet it is supposedly impossible for government officials themselves to engage in it. But if the Eurabian thesis attests to a "conspiracy" of some kind, it is one that lacks methodical surreptitiousness. Like many of the revolutions beforehand, the Eurabian revolution is occurring, for the most part, out in the open. Thanks to Bat Ye'or, we can see quite plainly that the policies leading to Europe's ongoing Islamization stem from rational—if highly questionable—perceptions of self-interest. The seminal event appears to have been the oil embargo following the 1973 Israeli-Arab war. It became vividly apparent to Europe at that point that it would be more expedient to play nice with the Arabs if it meant more oil. It did. And playing nice

The Eurabian project has in fact been underway for some time, albeit in different forms. Since Napoleon landed in Egypt in 1798, France has dreamed of a broad Mediterranean empire, which it pursued pre-WWII with some success. With the loss of Algeria in 1962, France has attempted to recover its influence in North Africa and throughout the Arab-Muslim world by less imperious means. Germany also has had Eurabian dreams. German penetration into the Balkans in WWII developed contacts with Muslims for whom Nazi fascism meshed nicely with Islam, the oldest global fascist movement in history. Nazi Germany was an obvious ally for Muslims throughout the Middle East longing to put *dhimmis* (Jews and Christians, relegated by the Koran [9:29] to semi-slavery status and required to pay the *jizya*, the special protection tax) back in their place.

The assumption in Europe, of course, has been that in any political accommodation with the Islamic world, Europe will remain the senior partner. Thus, an emergent "Euro-Med" bloc will serve as a magnified platform for European voices to counter American, Russian, and Chinese ascendancy. But the foundations of that assumption have been steadily eroding since WWII. While the Eurabian project proceeds apace, increasingly it is less a matter of Europeanizing the Arabs than in Arabizing Europe—indeed, Islamizing it. For it is with Islam that Europe has failed to reckon. It is one thing to secularize (Western) Christians, as was done successfully in Europe following the wars of religion, but it is another thing to secularize

Muslims. Whereas Christianity seeks a kingdom "not of this world" and is thus compatible with many forms of government, Islamic politics are explicitly *prescribed* by the Islamic holy texts. Christianity recognizes Caesar as the earthly law-giver; Islam only Allah. Europe was able to pacify Christianity because Christianity is naturally pacific, its violent manifestations a distortion of its doctrines. Islam is another matter entirely. The Eurabian institutional framework is serving—knowingly or not—as the new vehicle for jihad in Europe. What the irreligious, champagne-sniffing Eurocrats have not counted on is having to blunt the religious feelings of millions of Muslims accustomed to having their political religion central in their lives.

Yugoslavia: Nation of the Future

The form the new European jihad is taking and the complicity of Western institutions in their own destruction is nowhere more visible than in the wars of the Yugoslav succession of the 1990s, which continue into the present day in the imposed breakup of Serbia-Kosovo. The conventional wisdom of these wars is that blood-thirsty Serbs (regularly equated with Nazis during the 1990s war—in fact the Serbs had fought the Nazis tooth and nail while suffering a genuine genocide at the hands of an Axis power, Croatia, to the tune of a million dead), seizing the opportunity of the breakdown of Communism, unleashed their designs for a "greater Serbia" that involved the destruction of the Croat and Bosnian ethnic groups. Serb aggression was halted, so the story goes, only by the overdue involvement of NATO.

This fiction serves a variety on interests (not least of all NATO, looking for something to do in the wake of the Soviet Collapse), but neatly inverts much of what really happened. In fact, Western Europe had long wanted to bring the historically independent Yugoslavia to heel. The Germans in particular wanted to pull Croatia (their WWII ally) into the EU system and isolate Serbia (their WWI and WWII enemy). The Americans, ever-eager to appear the friends of Islam to their Saudi petro-benefactors, egged on the Muslim president of Bosnia to reject a settlement with the Serbs in Bosnia that would have prevented the ensuing civil war. The Bosnian declaration of independence in April 1992 and Muslim attacks on Serb civilians left the Bosnian Serbs little choice but to defend themselves. What they never learned during the years of war, however, was that the real battlefront lay on American and European television

sets, and here the Bosnian Muslims, with multiple star-studded Western PR firms in their arsenal, proved themselves superior. Despite committing just about every sort of war crime imaginable—from rape to ethnic cleansing to wholesale murder, all the while enriching themselves personally through almost unbelievable levels of corruption—the Muslims in Bosnia, like the Albanian Muslims in Kosovo (now a world leader in drug and human trafficking), came out as the "good guys."

Like the throwaway line parroted by nearly every Western leader since 9/11 that "Islam is a religion of peace," a similar mantra was promoted to explain the war in Bosnia: As Richard Holbrooke put it, "The Serbs started this war, the Serbs are the original cause of the war." A similar story is being told today about the amputation of Kosovo from Serbia. Those interested in a serious critique of the standard, vicious oversimplification should see John Schindler's *Unholy Terror*. In it, Schindler details how the two leading jihad-exporting countries, Iran and Saudi Arabia, vied for position in the Balkans under the conniving eye of the American and European governments, who, in short, wanted the Muslims to win. What has been quietly forgotten (like so much) is that, prior to 9/11, the West pursued basically pro-jihadist policies not only abroad but in Europe proper. Thanks to the thousands of mujahideen imported into

> What the irreligious, champagne-sniffing Eurocrats have not counted on is having to blunt the religious feelings of millions of Muslims accustomed to having their political religion central in their lives.

Bosnia to fight the infidel Serbs during the 90s, major terrorist attacks against domestic Western interests became possible. In fact, every major Muslim terrorist attack since the time of the Bosnian war—from World Trade Center One (1993), to the "millennium plot" against Los Angeles airport, to 9/11, to Madrid, to 7/7—may be traced to the mujahideen brought in to wage the Bosnian jihad with the connivance of the Western powers. The shape of things to come.

The smashing up of the independent nation-state of Yugoslavia was the logical result of policies currently at work throughout Western Europe. During the Sarajevo Olympic games of 1984, no one imagined that, less than a decade hence, the whole place would come apart with tens of thousands killed in a civil war; just as it seems unimaginable today that London, Paris,

Rotterdam, or Malmö could disintegrate into urban warfare. Setting off a Muslim jihad in Bosnia was made easier thanks to the relatively large Muslim population and the contradictions of Yugoslav Communism, but the circumstances that fed the Yugoslav breakup—a growing Muslim minority at odds with the secular government and a decomposing welfare state—are fast taking hold in France, Holland, Britain, and elsewhere.

Why Eurabia?

But, like the victim in some horror movie pleading with the monster-villain, we are compelled to ask—*why?* Why support

tradition-minded European populations—unrepresented, disorganized, and increasingly terrorized by their Muslim minorities—have been rendered politically helpless, which suits the integrationists just fine. Indeed, the logical result of their policies, civil war, would leave a handful of crippled nation-states utterly dependent on the emerging supranational Euro-Med authority—just what they want. The European people have always been suspicious of programs to unite Europe (see Napoleon, Hitler, Stalin), which is why they had to be taken out of the political picture. The growing numbers of Europeans leaving Europe for good (usually well-to-do and educated), the decline of native European birth rates to below replacement levels, and the rising number of suicides in an age of unprec-

Despite committing just about every sort of war crime imaginable—from rape to ethnic cleansing to wholesale murder, all the while enriching themselves personally through almost unbelievable levels of corruption—the Muslims in Bosnia, like the Albanian Muslims in Kosovo (now a world leader in drug and human trafficking), came out as the "good guys."

Muslim terrorism against Christians in Bosnia and Kosovo? Why permit Islam to grow with geometric speed within Europe's borders and set the stage for civil war? Why go to such lengths to wreck Europe when it didn't have to be this way? Answer: Because the millennial project of integrating Europe—a project agreed on by all mainstream parties on both sides of the Atlantic—and the larger project of globalization of which it is a part, cannot proceed as long as political opposition, centered on individual national identities, persists. As long as France is French, Germany German, Spain Spanish, Britain British, and as long as there are independent countries such as Yugoslavia who resist falling into the Western orbit, the dream of an integrated Europe will be impossible. Ergo, national identities must be dissolved, and Islam is the solvent.

edented prosperity testify to the integrationists' efficacy in effacing the European national identities.

The modern age is the age of revolution, and the Eurabian Revolution is but a continuation of a process, harkening back to before the French Revolution of 1789, to eradicate the old ways of doing things in Europe. Today's Eurocrats are on the verge of accomplishing what previous generations of revolutionaries, with all their evil genius, failed to bring about: the destruction of Europe as a distinct civilization. Perhaps the most remarkable aspect of the Eurabian Revolution is that it is being effected so completely from *within* the halls of power, which is perhaps why so few seem to be aware that a revolution is afoot at all. But a genuine revolution it is, which, like its predecessors, can only

National identities must be dissolved, and Islam is the solvent.

The integrationists' object is possible only if the old nation-states are rendered too weak to resist their progressive destruction. The ever-growing millions of alienated Muslims in Europe, deliberately encouraged by EU policy to retain a Muslim identity across borders, thus serve as a means of smashing up the old social and political identities based in territorial nationhood. The

culminate in a similar spiritual and material oblivion. Whatever the complexities and subtleties of today's Eurabian Revolution, on that point there should be no mistake.

The Bible Code
Scientific, Statistical Proof of God? Or Just Another Lie?
David Thomas

We've all seen the tabloid headlines...for example, "Code in Bible Predicts Date of Christ's Return," or, "Bible Predicts Killer Storms This Winter." But there is, in fact, a serious effort by several mathematicians and scientists to show that the Bible actually *does* contain a hidden code which can be substantiated with advanced statistical methods. Code proponents point with pride to an article by Doron Witztum, Eliyahu Rips, and Yoav Rosenberg of Hebrew University in Israel, entitled "Equidistant Letter Sequences in the Book of Genesis." This article was published in the respected journal *Statistical Science* in 1994, and is claimed to provide compelling proof that details of modern people and events are indeed encoded in the ancient symbols of the Torah. A key claim of the code proponents is that, using the exact same methods, the secret codes found in the Bible can *not* be found in mundane texts such as Tolstoy's *War and Peace*.

However, there is a problem with the Bible code claims—they are lies.

In the Beginning

The Bible code has been under development in various forms for a few decades. It didn't really attract serious attention until Witztum and Rips' 1994 paper. In June of 1997, a sensational book entitled *The Bible Code*, by journalist and Howard Hughes' biographer Michael Drosnin, appeared. It occupied the best-seller lists for months, and was enthusiastically pumped on the talk-show circuit. Drosnin appeared on Oprah Winfrey's show in June, and his Bible code prediction of a possible California earthquake in 2008 was enough to prompt Oprah to swear she would move away from California before then. (She didn't.)

Drosnin's technique is heavily based on that of the Israeli mathematicians Witztum and Rips (Rosenberg did the computer programming for the work). Like them, Drosnin arranges the 304,805 Hebrew letters of the Bible into a large array. Spaces and punctuation marks are omitted, and words are run together one after another. A computer looks for matches to selected names or words by stepping to every nth letter in the array. One can go forward or backward, and for each value of "step distance," *n*, there are *n* different starting letters.

> McKay found assassination "predictions" in *Moby-Dick* for Indira Gandhi, Rene Moawad, Leon Trotsky, Rev. Martin Luther King, and Robert F. Kennedy.

Drosnin's "assassination prediction" match for "Yitzhak Rabin" had a step value *n* equal to 4,772. In other words, there were *4,771* letters between each letter in Rabin's name.

Both Rips and Drosnin work with the original Hebrew characters, which are said to have been given by God to Moses one character at a time, with no spaces or punctuation, just as they appear in "the code." The code is considered to exist *only* in the Hebrew Bible, not in translations or any other books. The code concept, however, can be easily demonstrated with English characters. Consider the following single verse from the King James Version (KJV) of the Book of Genesis:

31: 28 And hast not suffered me to kiss my sons and my daughters? thou hast now done foolishly in so doing.

If you start at the R in "daughters," and skip over three letters to the O in "thou," and three more to the S in "hast," and so on, the hidden message "Roswell" is revealed! This message has a step value of four, as shown below.

```
daughteRsthOuhaStnoWdonEfooLishLyinsodoing.
```

Once a name or word match is located for a given step value *n*, a common practice is to rearrange the letters into a huge matrix (which Drosnin calls a "crossword puzzle"). The matrix is typically *n* letters wide, and inside this puzzle, the letters for the "hidden message" line up together vertically. (Sometimes, a slightly different value of *n* is used to make the hidden word run diagonally, every other row, and so forth.) The analyst or the computer can then look for more keyword-related "hits" around the given hidden word. Secondary matches can be picked off vertically, horizontally, or diagonally. Drosnin found the word "Dallas" (connected with keywords "President Kennedy") in one of his puzzles by starting at a D, and then picking the next letters by moving one space over to the right and three spaces down several times.

An example of such a matrix, or "crossword puzzle," for the "Roswell" mentioned in KJV Genesis appears below. The letters of "Roswell" now appear vertically at the center of the puzzle. The actual matrix of unique letters is only four characters wide here (dashed box), but I took the liberty of showing extra letters for context. A companion hidden message— "UFO"—is indicated within circle symbols. This "UFO" is itself a hidden message with a step value of twelve. Drosnin accepts *any* such messages, even words running horizontally (i.e., the actual words of the Bible strung together). If either "Roswell" or "UFO" had been found encoded in the Hebrew Bible, Drosnin would not have hesitated to use words from the direct text as a "match" (for example, the words "thou hast now done foolishly.")

```
S A N D M Y D A U G H T E R S T H O U H
M Y D A U G H T E R S T H O U H A S T N
U G H T E R S T H O U H A S T N O W D O
E R S T H O U H A S T N O W D O N E F O
H O U H A S T N O W D O N E F O O L I S
A S T N O W D O N E F O O L I S H L Y I
O W D O N E F O O L I S H L Y I N S O D
N E F O O L I S H L Y I N S O D O I N G
O L I S H L Y I N S O D O I N G I T I S
H L Y I N S O D O I N G I T I S I N T H
```

The unusual pairing of "Roswell" and "UFO" is as stunning as any described in Drosnin's book—yet no one claims that the Bible code would have translated gracefully over to the KJV Genesis.

Drosnin claims mathematical proof that "no human could have encoded the Bible in this way." He says, "I do not know if it is God," but adds that the code proves "we are not alone."[1]

Some believe that these "messages" in the Hebrew Bible are not just coincidence—God put them there deliberately. But if someone finds a hidden message in a book, a song played backwards, funny-looking Martian mesas, or some other

I found *thousands* of hidden occurrences of these names in both Genesis and *Edwards*.

object or thing, does that prove someone else put the message there intentionally? Or might the message exist only in the eyes of the beholder (and in those of his or her followers)? Does perception of meaning prove the message was deliberately created?

Or is this phenomenon related mainly to the determination and skill of the person looking for a special message? *Any* special message?

For example, there are dozens of books about Nostradamus. In one, the authors find hidden predictions by scrambling the seer's quatrains (in French, no less), and then decoding according to an extremely complicated and mysterious formula.[2] The back cover prominently displays one such unscrambled prediction: "1992—George Bush re-elected." (Wrong.) The authors should have known that it's much safer to find hidden predictions of events that have already happened.

Some critics of Drosnin say the journalist is just "data mining." Mathematician Brendan McKay of Australian National University and his colleagues searched Hebrew texts besides the Bible. They found 59 words related to Chanukah in the Hebrew translation of *War and Peace*. But McKay doesn't think someone engineered this remarkable feat for his or anyone's benefit. Since then, McKay has responded to the following challenge Drosnin made in *Newsweek*: "When my critics find a message about the assassination of a prime minister encrypted in *Moby-Dick*, I'll believe them."[3]

McKay found assassination "predictions" in *Moby-Dick* for Indira Gandhi, Rene Moawad, Leon Trotsky, Rev. Martin Luther King, and Robert F. Kennedy.

Hidden Names in KJV Genesis and *Edwards v. Aguillard*

In one of my first investigations of the Bible code in 1996, I carried out a study on finding hidden names in both the KJV Genesis and the US Supreme Court's 1987 ruling on *Edwards v. Aguillard* (a well-known ruling on creationism, hereafter referred to as simply *Edwards*). I used the same set of rules for both the KJV Genesis (about 150,000 characters) and *Edwards* (about 100,000 characters). I loaded a list of preselected names and let the computer search for each one in turn, for equidistant letter sequences with step distances from two to 1000, and for every possible starting letter. I searched forward only.

One would expect that special biblical messages hidden in the Hebrew Bible would simply not make it into the King James Version (translated), much less into *Edwards*. And since the Hebrew alphabet doesn't include vowels, it should be *much* harder to find matches in the English texts, because an additional character match is required for each vowel. Drosnin's control was the Hebrew text of *War and Peace*. Drosnin claims that when they searched for words (such as "comet," "Jupiter," etc.) in the Bible, they often found them there, but not in *War and Peace*.

I picked my set of names carefully. The list contained five names of four letters, five of five letters, five of six letters, five of seven letters, and five of either eight or nine letters. I was more whimsical in my choice of subjects, and chose talk show hosts, scientists, and just plain folks as well as political or historical figures.

I found *thousands* of hidden occurrences of these names in both Genesis and *Edwards*. It was amazing that so many hidden occurrences were found for the 25 names submitted, for both Genesis and *Edwards*. More matches were found in the former, but it does have 50,000 more letters to work with.

Another important observation was immediately apparent— short names like "Leno" or "Reed" were found much more frequently than long names like "Gingrich" or "Matsumura" ("Matsumura" is, of course, Molleen Matsumura of the National Center for Science Education, in Berkeley). "Martin Gardner" was found hidden in *Edwards*, much as Gardner anticipated could happen in his discussion of gematria and the work of Rips and his colleagues.[4]

The results are clear and compelling, and certainly not surprising. It is much easier to find short names than long names. There might be thousands of occurrences of the four-letter name "Rich," for example. But matching "Gingrich" is much harder, since few or none of the thousands of instances of "Rich" will be preceded by "Ging" at exactly the right step locations. But there are 2,554 hidden occurrences of "Newt" in KJV Genesis, so one could imagine that the former Speaker of the House is certainly mentioned copiously.

There is, of course, another factor in the success of hidden-word searches. Simply put, some letters are more common than others. If one considers the relative frequencies for the letters in Genesis and *Edwards*, it is apparent that certain letters (such as A, D, E, H, I, N, O, R, S, and T) appear more often than others. Obviously, words made with these "hot" letters (such as "Reed," "Deer," "Stalin," or "Hitler") have a better chance of being found than words containing any "cool" letters like J or Q. "Rosie" had 202 Genesis matches, more than the 49 for "Oprah"—but "Oprah" contains a cool P. (I also searched for "Harpo," which is just "Oprah" backwards, and found 62 hits).

"Deion pins nude Oprah."

I then derived a formula for how many occurrences of given words you would expect to find in a text of a given number of random letters. One must calculate the probability of selection for each letter, which depends on the particular text being examined. This is just the number of occurrences of the letter divided by the total number of letters. Typically, the probability for getting an E is above 0.1 (better than 10 percent, or 1 chance in 10), while that for a Q can be just 0.005. For a given word like "Roswell," you multiply the chances for an R with that for an O, then an S, and so on. The final product is multiplied by the total possible number of equidistant letter sequences for the word, which is roughly the square of the number of letters in the entire text divided by one less than the number of letters in the candidate hidden word.

This formula works very well. I estimated that I would find 18.7 occurrences of "Clinton" in *War and Peace*, Book 1 (212,000 characters, 7.5 billion possible seven-letter equidistant sequences); the actual number was 21. I estimated I would find 128.1 matches for the name "Apollo"—and got 129. With each additional letter in candidate words, the chance for a match on a single try falls, because you must multiply your product by another number invariably less than one. And rare letters reduce the expected matches greatly. But the sheer number of possible skip sequences is so large as to often make the overall chances of obtaining matches very reasonable.

How well does this estimation work in the Torah itself? Very well indeed! I had to adapt my English-based code problems to Hebrew, which I did by using the Michigan-Claremont transliteration scheme for converting Hebrew into English and vice versa. I also developed a method for showing my new puzzles in the Hebrew characters. I calculated the expected number of matches for "Clinton" in the Torah.

In Modern Hebrew, "Clinton" appears as follows, reading from right to left: Quf, Lamed, Yod, Nun, Tet, Vav, and Nun:

Just as in English, some characters are more common than others. Lamed is popular (7 percent of the Torah's characters are Lameds), as is Yod (10 percent) and Vav (10 percent), but Tet is rare in the Torah (only half of a percent). The odds

How Unusual Are Paired Messages?

Drosnin and others sometimes admit that finding isolated hidden names or messages can be the product of random chance. But they claim that finding linked pairs or triples of names or words is so improbable that doing so proves the supernatural, divine, or alien origin of the "message." In Drosnin's words,

> Consistently, the Bible code brings together interlocking words that reveal related information. With Bill Clinton, President. With the Moon landing, spaceship and Apollo 11. With Hitler, Nazi. With Kennedy, Dallas. In experiment after experiment, the crossword puzzles were found only in the Bible. Not in *War and Peace*, not in any other book, and not in ten million computer-generated test cases.[5]

Perhaps there was a bug in Drosnin's computer program. Or perhaps he didn't really want to find hidden message pairs outside of the Hebrew Bible. I don't know if Drosnin was lying on purpose, but I do know the above statement is a lie. I was able to easily produce complex hidden messages in all the texts I worked with. I developed a computer program that takes various words already located as hidden

While there are just over 300,000 characters to work with in the entire Torah, the number of valid seven-letter equidistant sequences is over 15 *billion*.

of finding an exact match for "Clinton," for a single pick of seven equidistant letters in the Torah, is incredibly small: It works out to less than one in a billion. But there are a great many ways of selecting valid seven-letter equidistant sequences from a text. In fact, the number of possible seven-letter sequences in the Torah vastly outnumbers the count of letters in the Torah itself. While there are just over 300,000 characters to work with in the entire Torah, the number of valid seven-letter equidistant sequences is over 15 *billion*. And the computer lets the Bible code researcher look at each and every one of these sequences. Even though the chances for any given sequence to be a match are small (less than one in a billion), there are so many sequences to look at that the expected number of matches turns out to be reasonable. Thus, I expected to find around two "Clinton" matches in the Torah; the actual number is four (i.e. very close to what I expected).

codes (such as "Hitler" and "Nazi") and plays them against each other to find the best-linked pairs. The starting letters and equidistant steps provide all the necessary information, provided one learns how to manipulate it.

I then used this approach to develop many puzzles in many texts having direct coded linkages of "Hitler" and "Nazi." These puzzles are striking counterexamples of Drosnin's claims.

I found an English translation of Tolstoy's epic novel *War and Peace* on the Internet and downloaded the first 24 chapters of Book 1, giving me about 167,000 characters. By the time I got to steps of just 750, I already had found more than half a dozen excellent puzzle linkages of "Hitler" and "Nazi." The best of these appears below: This entire puzzle text spans just five paragraphs (or just 244 words, using 1083 characters) of the second chapter of Book 1 of Tolstoy's novel.

```
       PLOT L=11792,N=69,W=2
W O R D S A W H E R B R I G H T S M I L E A N D T H E C
Y W E R E I N A S P E C I A L L Y A M I A B L E M O O D
W I T H Q U I C K S H O R T S W A Y I N G S T E P S H E
E S S S A T D O W Ⓝ O N A S O F A N E A R T H E S I L V
H E R S E L F A N D T O A L L A R O U N D H E R I H A V
R B A G A N D A D D R E S S I N G A L L P R E S E N T M
C K O N M E S H E Ⓐ D D E D T U R N I N G T O H E R H O
P T I O N A N D J U S T S E E H O W B A D L Y I A M D R
W A I S T E D L A C E T R I M M E D D A I N T Y G R A Y
R E A S T S O Y E Ⓩ T R A N Q U I L L E L I S E Y O U W
N N A P A V L O V N A Y O U K N O W S A I D T H E P R I
T U R N I N G T O A G E N E R A L M Y H U S B A N D I S
L M E W H A T T H Ⓘ S W R E T C H E D W A R I S F O R S
I T I N G F O R A N A N S W E R S H E T U R N E D T O S
E L I G H T F U L W O M A N T H I S L I T T L E P R I N
T H E N E X T A R R I V A L S W A S A S T O U T H E A V
A C L E S T Ⓗ E L Ⓘ G H Ⓣ C O Ⓛ O R Ⓔ D Ⓑ R E E C H E S
R O W N D R E S S C O A T T H I S S T O U T Y O U N G M
```

Of special interest is that the match for "Hitler" occurs at the very small step of three, crossing just four words: t**H**e l**I**gh**T** co**L**or**E**d **B**Reeches. The word "Nazi" appears at the larger step of 207. Codes with small steps are much more impervious to slight changes in exact transcriptions than are large-step codes. To alter the "Hitler" above, one would have to change one of the four words involved: "the," "light," "colored," or "breeches." But a change to even *one* of the tens of thousands of characters in Drosnin's "Rabin" match (4,772 per letter, over eight letters) would destroy this match.

Drosnin uses many methods to improve the odds of "impossible-by-chance" linkages. For one, he uses horizontal words taken directly from the original text. For example, when Drosnin found "Clinton" linked to "president," the word "president" was just the Hebrew word for "chief," taken from its actual context in the original Bible. Secondly, Drosnin found some hidden dates referring to the Hebrew calendar; for example, Gulf War activity on January 18, 1991, was found in the words "3rd Shevat." But he found other dates referring to the Gregorian calendar, such as that of the Oklahoma City bombing, which was linked in the Bible by the hidden date "Day 19," and interpreted as a reference to both April 19, 1995, the date of the bombing, and April 19, 1993 (Waco). And finally, Drosnin takes full advantage of the eccentricities of the Hebrew language, in which words can be condensed and letters occasionally dropped.

My study generated several other examples that are just as spectacular and just as unlikely (if not more so) than most of Drosnin's matches. Now, Drosnin and his colleagues would probably say that the "Roswell/UFO" connection in KJV Genesis was just a lucky break and couldn't happen again. But I found 5,812 hidden "UFO"s in Genesis, and dozens of these happen to be flying right around and through the hidden word "Roswell." As the puzzle step is changed, linked matches appear and disappear with astonishing frequency. All that is really happening here is that codes can be engineered—*made* to happen. You just have to know how to harvest the field of possibilities.

Here is another striking linkage I found in KJV Genesis, 42: 18 through 45: 21. Here, the name "Regis" appears at a step distance of 808, but also at a step of 810, which makes a nice "X" pattern if the puzzle step is 809. (Perhaps someone should notify Regis Philbin and agents Mulder and Scully).

```
U S A L I T T L E F O O D A N D J U D A H S P A K
E R E D S U R E L Y N O W W E H A D R E T U R N E
N D T H E M E N W E Ⓡ E A F Ⓡ A I D B E C A U S E
R A N D T H E Y M A D Ⓔ Ⓡ Ⓔ A D Y T H E P R E S E
E E G Y P T I A N S M I Ⓖ H T N O T E A T B R E A
B Y I N D E E D H E D Ⓘ Ⓥ Ⓘ N E T H Y E H A V E D
R O U N D A N D J O Ⓢ E P H Ⓢ A I D U N T O T H E
E S A I D U N T O M Y L O R D T H E L A D C A N N
A N T S S H A L L B R I N G D O W N T H E G R A Y
```

If you work at any given puzzle for a while, large numbers of unexpected names and words invariably turn up. Consider the large puzzle below. This text is a contiguous rendition of Genesis 41: 38–46. This particular puzzle is easy for the reader to verify manually, since it has a relatively small step of 40. The puzzle itself is 41 characters wide, so the rightmost column is a repetition of the leftmost. I used the computer to find several diagonal messages here: "Deer," "Regis," "Nazi," "Leno," "Dole." Many vertical messages were simple enough to be found just by poring over the puzzle: for example, "Oprah," "here," "Leia," "Hale," "sent," "nude," "pure," "hate," "data," "Roe," "Reed," "Meg," "hood," "pins (snip)," "Deion," and "Ione." "Newt" is in there too, but at an offbeat step that makes for a jilted arrangement. And then, there are all those horizontal words, too!

```
S SERVANTSCANWEFINDSUCHAONEASTHISISAMANINW
WHOMTHESPIRITOFGODISANDPHARAOHSAIDUNTOJOS
SEPHFORASMUCHASGODHATHSHEWEDTHEEALLTHISTH
EREISNONESODISCREETANDWISEASTHOUARTTHOUS
SHALTBEOVERMYHOUSEANDACCORDINGUNTOTHYWORD
DSHALLALLMYPEOPLEBERULEDONLYINTHETHRONEWI
ILLIBEGREATERTHANTHOUANDPHARAOHSAIDUNTOJO
OSEPHSEEIHAVESETTHEEOVERALLTHELANDOFEGYPT
TANDPHARAOHTOOKOFFHISRINGFROMHISHANDANDPU
UTITUPONJOSEPHSHANDANDARRAYEDHIMINVESTURE
ESOFFINELINENANDPUTAGOLDCHAINABOUTHISNECK
KANDHEMADEHIMTORIDEINTHESECONDCHARIOTWHIC
CHHEHADANDTHEYCRIEDBEFOREHIMBOWTHEKNEEAND
DHEMADEHIMRULEROVERALLTHELANDOFEGYPTANDPH
HARAOHSAIDUNTOJOSEPHIAMPHARAOHANDWITHOUTT
THEESHALLNOMANLIFTUPHISHANDORFOOTINALLTHE
ELANDOFEGYPTANDPHARAOHCALLEDJOSEPHSNAMEZA
APHNATHPAANEAHANDHEGAVEHIMTOWIFEASENATHTH
HEDAUGHTEROFPOTIPHERAHPRIESTOFONANDJOSEPH
HWENTOUTOVERALLTHELANDOFEGYPTANDJOSEPHWAS
STHIRTYYEARSOLDWHENHESTOODBEFOREPHARAOHK
```

Genesis 41: 38–46, Multiple Matches, Step = 40

I suspect that with diligence, one could find enough matches to make almost all of the characters in the puzzle into parts of hidden words. The puzzle above is literally dripping with additional hidden surprises. Rips himself appears in "spirit" read backwards. "Pour," "Alan," and "sash" run vertically. And diagonal messages of varying complexity lurk everywhere. Can you find the "apes" swinging between "data" and "Reed"? "Love" intersecting with "nude"? How about "Ares," "reel," "deft," "lion," "dogs," "pony," "hard," "diet," "trace," "card," "Poe," and "wart"? They are all in there—and more.

There are dozens of linked messages in the puzzle above. But how are we to know which words are linked by the secretive author? Is the "real" message "Nazi sent pure hate here," or is it, "Deion pins nude Oprah?" All of these hits are authentic, encoded names and words that have lurked inside the text of the King James Version of Genesis for hundreds of years. But the whimsical combinations they appear in show that these surprises are simply lucky breaks, and not authentic messages from above.

What Are the Odds, Really?

Drosnin and his colleagues say that getting linked matches by coincidence is statistically impossible and cite the odds against such coincidences as more than 3,000 to one (and sometimes much more). Using numbers like these, the Bible code promoters try to convince their readers that the existence of God is now proven statistically beyond the shadow of a doubt, simply because they can find linked pairs like "Clinton" and "chief" in the same general area of the Bible.

But their core conclusions are based on severely flawed probability arguments. Drosnin's formulation of the improbability of the occurrence of linked pairs is implicitly based on the assumption that you have only one opportunity to get the match. But, with the help of the computer, Drosnin gets to take advantage of billions of opportunities.

Let's look at Drosnin's approach with a lottery analogy. The probability of winning a lottery with a single ticket is very small, and Drosnin says the probability of getting an improbable match (such as "Clinton" and "president") is also very small. But what happens if you buy more than one ticket?

In the "Powerball" lottery, the odds of winning the $10 million minimum jackpot with just one ticket are about eighty million to one against. With two tickets, the odds plummet, to about forty million to one. If you buy one million tickets, your odds drop to only about eighty to one against. And if you invest $80 million

> I was able to easily produce complex hidden messages in all the texts I worked with.

in tickets, the odds become approximately two to one in your favor! Most people can't afford to buy millions of tickets. Those who do have that kind of money usually don't dump it on the lottery, because you almost always end up losing.

But in Drosnin's game, you don't have to win more than you lose. You don't even have to break even. All you need for success is to win every once in a while. And you can have what amounts to millions of "free lottery tickets" simply by running a computer program or poring over crossword-puzzle printouts. Drosnin routinely tests billions of letter sequences for matches to selected words or names, and goes to steps of many thousands. By using only steps lower than 1,000, I limited myself to using only about 3 percent of the potential of Genesis or *Edwards*.

Australian mathematician Brendan McKay (in personal communication) showed me how to find hidden words much more efficiently, and a search of KJV Genesis at *all* possible steps for my list of 25 names came up with over **one million** additional matches. These include six hits for "Clinton," fifteen for "Gardner," three for "Hillary" and "Einstein," and two for "Kennedy." McKay's algorithm allows for much faster searches, and I quickly incorporated it into my own code programs. By being tens of times faster, it allows me to search for all possible step sequences. It is faster than my brute-force approach (checking all possible equidistant letter sequences) because it's more like the way you can find short words by inspection of the puzzles. You focus on those letters of the text that match the first letter of the desired

I found 5,812 hidden "UFO"s in Genesis, and dozens of these happen to be flying right around and through the hidden word "Roswell."

hidden word, and then find letters matching the second letter of the desired word. For each two-letter pair, check the location of the third letter in the pattern; if it matches your desired word, keep going, otherwise move on to the next pair.

Further Developments

Much has happened since the heyday of the Bible code. I predicted a sporting event's outcome in advance, using codes in War and Peace. McKay and colleagues published a devastating rebuttal to the Statistical Science article that got the whole thing rolling. Drosnin wrote a second book, to much less fanfare than the first. And new promoters of Bible codes continued to ply their wares on websites, books, and television. Here is a summary of recent developments.

The End of the Bible Code, Part I

As my wife and I were driving through New Mexico on Sunday, June 14, 1998, we listened to game six of the Chicago Bulls/ Utah Jazz National Basketball Association (NBA) playoffs. As the game drew to a close, we heard the Utah crowd groan as Michael Jordan sank the winning basket. And then and there, a chill went down my spine. "Oh my God," I thought to myself. "The Tolstoy code is real."

Fifty days (more than seven weeks) earlier, on April 27, I had undertaken a search for NBA teams and players using the Bible code technique of equidistant letter sequences. (One of Drosnin's strongest claims in support of the Bible code was that his code-based prediction of the assassination of Israeli Prime Minister Yitzhak Rabin was made a year before the

event took place.) Unlike Drosnin, however, I wasn't searching in the Hebrew Torah—instead, I was looking in Book 1 of an English translation of War and Peace.

I had wondered if the NBA playoff winner could actually be predicted in advance. What did my April search reveal? While "Chicago" was found encoded just once in War and Peace, "Jazz" was not encoded at all. "Bulls" was also encoded 32 times in Book 1 of War and Peace, and "Chicago" and one of the "Bulls" even appeared close to each other in a classic Bible code crossword puzzle. I also found fourteen hidden occurrences of "Jordan," and one of these nestled next to one of the hidden "Bulls."

With these Bible code indicators flashing (matching of long words, proximity of paired matches), I sent my prediction to several reporters and scientists. I thought about trying to warn Karl "the Mailman" Malone of the Jazz—but I decided to let history run its course. When I made my prediction, there were sixteen teams in the playoffs. And the Bulls, while favored, almost lost it all on more than one occasion. In fact, the Indiana Pacers came very close to defeating them, but Tolstoy's Bulls clung to their destiny.

And on June 14, my prediction came to pass. Not only had Tolstoy predicted the victors would be the Chicago Bulls, but Jordan's key role in the victory had been forecast—almost two months in advance.

Now we are left to ponder the somber truth. Either the Bible code nonsense is just a general, arcane mathematical technique that can be employed to find any desired messages or predictions hidden in any book or text…or Leo Tolstoy is the Supreme Being who created the Universe.

The End of the Bible Code, Part II

One of the chief arguments employed by proponents of the Bible code is to mention that the original code proponents— Witztum, Rips, and Rosenberg—published a paper supporting the phenomenon in the journal Statistical Science in 1994, and that, to date, no rebuttal has ever been published there.

But just such a paper, authored by Brendan McKay, Dror Bar-Natan, Maya Bar-Hillel, and Gil Kalai, was indeed published in the May 1999 issue of *Statistical Science*. The authors show definitively that the secret of the codes lies not in any special properties of Genesis, but rather in methods by which the lists of modern names and dates were chosen. In other words, even when the data (the text of Genesis) are not altered or modified, the choice of the experiments (e.g., the list of famous rabbis and

I predicted a sporting event's outcome in advance, using codes in *War and Peace*.

measures of closeness) completely determines the results. Drosnin's claims are so sensational that they can be dismissed rather easily. The claims of the original Israeli mathematicians are much more difficult to understand, and also to disprove. We are indeed fortunate that McKay and colleagues have published their extensive and devastating research on the codes of Rips and Witztum.

Drosnin Publishes a Second Book

Has Drosnin paid attention to his critics? Not at all. He has been far too busy trying to convince Yasser Arafat and Shimon Peres of the reality of the code, and analyzing new events like the terror attacks of September 11, 2001. Drosnin described his more recent efforts in a sequel, *The Bible Code II*, released in November 2002. The first chapter tells how Drosnin witnessed the attacks on the World Trade Center, and how he quickly found the event predicted as hidden messages in the Torah (the first five books of the Bible in the original Hebrew). Subsequent chapters discuss Drosnin's meetings with Arafat and Peres, his attempts to meet with Ariel Sharon and President Bush, his search for hidden Torah messages about Monica Lewinsky and Clinton and the Bush/Gore 2000 election debacle, and his ongoing search for a mysterious "obelisk" (the "key" to the Bible code, and to humanity's origin, which he feels is still buried in a valley near the Dead Sea). Drosnin's obsession with his own role as a major Bible code player is nowhere more obvious than in his introduction to the chapter on DNA, the genetic code: "Early in my search for the key to the Bible code, I may have also stumbled onto the key for the code of life…According to the Bible code, our 'DNA was brought in a vehicle.'" Drosnin has a whole chapter on the "aliens" he feels may be responsible for placing humans on

Earth. His words might offer comfort to "Intelligent Design" supporters like the Raelians of Clonaid, but surely will disturb most evangelical Christians.

In the appendix of Drosnin's second book, he finally gets around to discussing critics like McKay. Drosnin supplies a surprising revisionist history of the codes, often contradicting what he wrote in his first book. And he takes a number of cheap shots, for example, criticizing the rebuttal by McKay and his three Hebrew coauthors as "written by a team of mathematicians led by an Australian who did not read the language of the Bible code." On the next page, Drosnin extols the code-supporting findings of Harold Gans, but neglects to mention that Gans doesn't read Hebrew either. Drosnin unfairly labels McKay's open, public demonstration of what can be achieved by manipulation of data as a "hoax." And Drosnin even accuses McKay of initially finding a positive result, then hiding it. McKay responded to my query about this, saying: "This is an absolute lie. Nothing like this ever happened and we did not even see this claim before now."

Drosnin again claims: "No one has found in *War and Peace* or *Moby-Dick* a correct prediction, in advance, of a world event." Had he bothered to actually read what his critics are saying, he would have learned about my prediction of the Chicago Bulls victory in the 1998 NBA playoffs. Indeed, Drosnin has failed to learn the single most important fact about so-called Bible codes: This arcane technique allows one to find virtually any desired message hidden in any desired text.

New Bible Code Promoters Evolve

Ed Sherman, one of the more vigorous promoters of Bible codes, is the founder of *Bible Code Digest* (BCD), which offers "Stunning Proof of the Codes!" at its website <www.biblecode-digest.com>. Sherman's site is extensive, and he's got a book out, too: *The Bible Code Bombshell*. He claims to have found many clusters of long words in the Bible (for example, 89 matches of words seven letters or more in length near Ezekiel 37, 55 more near Isaiah 53, etc.). He also claims to have found valid codes that are complete Hebrew sentences, grammatically correct, that extend for scores of letters. Both claims are plagued by severe problems.

In regard to the first claim, clusters of long words, Sherman has introduced the "*Bible Code Digest* (BCD) Code Cluster Rating System" on his website. He writes:

> Here is our simple, yet reasonably accurate, approach to comparing different code clusters in terms of their improbability. For each code with a skip of more than one letter, we subtract six from the number of letters it has, so that any code with six or fewer letters counts for zero points. We then add up all the points for all of the codes in the cluster. The more lengthy codes in a cluster, the higher the score. The higher the score, the more improbable the cluster.... Clearly, the skeptics' best example of a code cluster from a book other than the Bible is severely outclassed....

When the now-defunct religious network PAX TV asked me to debate Sherman for Lee Strobel's series *Faith Under Fire* in 2005, I decided to take him up on his challenge to skeptics. Sherman claimed that skeptics had found only one seven-letter word in *War and Peace*, and another in *Moby-Dick*, and that even Drosnin had found only two in the Torah. Now, I knew this was flat wrong—I'd already published finding seven-letter hidden words like KENNEDY in *War and Peace*, TRINITY in a Supreme Court decision, and I'd even found eight-letter match-

"Do you really think that the God of Abraham and Moses needs a remedial Hebrew lesson?"

es like HARRISON and nine-letter matches for GREGHINES in *War and Peace*. Thus, I began searching in earnest for Thematic Clusters in *War and Peace*. I picked a particular two-page section because I'd found HARRISON there previously. I chose the late Beatle George Harrison as my "theme," although I could have picked William Henry Harrison, Harrison Ford, or Rex Harrison, and so on. Then I ran my home-brewed Bible code program and searched for words, selecting those having some relevance to the theme. My results: 254 Words (220 seven-letter, 33 eight-letter, 1 nine-letter), for an official BCD Score of 289, good enough to rank right in the middle of Sherman's all-time best clusters (such as Isaiah 53 with a score of 396, or Psalm 22 with a score of 237).

Here are a few of the 254 interesting matches I found for the "George Harrison Cluster in *War and Peace*":

HARRISON, FRANCAISE, ARTISTE, CHEERED, CHORIST, COMPOSE, DEAREST, DREAMER, DUETTIST, ELEANOR, FARTHER, FEVERED, GOATEED, ONENESS, ONSTAGE, ORDAINS, OUTRATE, PANACEA, PASSION, STERILE, SURGEON, TEACHER, TEATIME, THEATER, THROATS, TOURIST, TSUNAMI, WAKEFUL, WEAKEST, WITTIEST, and many, many more.

Of course, Sherman didn't agree that the Harrison Cluster rivaled his own findings. His first objection was that "the Rules were Wrong." He wrote: "Had I realized that some day an astute opponent like yourself would stretch the borderline situation of seven letter ELSs in the simplified rating system to produce a counter-example in the way that you have done, I definitely would have left out seven-letter ELSs from being worth anything."

He then added that I had looked for "Too Many Search Terms," complaining that "the rating of a cluster will almost certainly increase with the number of terms for which a search is conducted. So, no, there is no limit on the allowed number of search terms, but the score is directly affected by the amount of searching."

Sherman also criticized my "Unrelated & Missing Matches." He wrote "I failed in several instances to see what connection many of your terms had to George Harrison in particular, so I'd suggest that you explain why you included the less obvious ones. I also felt that there were many seven or eight letter words I could quickly think of that were very strong candidates for George Harrison terms that weren't shown on your list—so the fact that these terms weren't there left me unimpressed with the notion that the whole thing was about him."

In other words, Sherman dismissed my example of significant clusters in mundane texts by making a host of subjective rule changes to his "*Bible Code Digest* (BCD) Code Cluster Rating System," which was originally intended to "remove the evaluation of Bible codes from the realm of the subjective." I believe the proper description of this activity is "moving the goalposts."

The second major BCD claim involves "Mega Codes" that are many tens of letters long. While the Bible code can be used to find pairs of seven- or eight-letter words, the chances of finding exact ELS strings of tens of letters (50 or 70, say) are infinitesimal—they are as close to zero as one could wish for. But

Sherman declares that his very long skip sequences indeed spell out valid and grammatically correct Hebrew sentences, according to his Hebraic expert, Dr. Nathan Jacobi. When confronted with questions on the validity of these codes, Sherman just says Jacobi is an expert, and that's all there is to it. I consulted two respected Hebrew scholars in Albuquerque, Professor Shlomo Karni of the University of New Mexico, and Rabbi Joseph Black of Congregation Albert. When I showed Prof. Karni some of Sherman's alleged "Codes in Good Hebrew," he retorted: "Good? Not by any stretch of the imagination!" Rabbi Black also pointed out numerous missing letters and grammatical problems. "These are not Hebrew sentences, archaic or not," he said, adding that numerous grammatical errors made the messages so convoluted that they don't mean anything.

But I really didn't need to go to the Rabbi to see how ridiculous Sherman's claims are. Sherman himself admits his codes contain errors. While he lists several "Codes in Good Hebrew" on his site (these are the ones my experts found incoherent), Sherman also lists more codes in "Acceptable" and "Marginal" Hebrew. The very fact that Sherman feels the need to list "Marginal" sentences raises the question I asked him in the debate: "Do you really think that the God of Abraham and Moses needs a remedial Hebrew lesson?"

Sherman also complained that my search for codes in a mere two-page snippet of War and Peace was not anything like what he is doing at BCD. And, he was right! I was actually doing a much *harder* search over just a few thousand letters of text. That's because I naïvely believed Sherman when he made claims about "searching just two pages of text" for codes.

What Sherman was actually doing—searching the *entire Bible* for codes (over a million letters—1,196,921 to be exact), and counting those that happen to touch down in a two-page section of the text, comprising a few thousand letters—is much easier than what I was doing, which was restricting my entire searches to just the two pages of text.

When I got around to employing the BCD method as it is used, I was astonished at the new, "compelling" codes that turned up. It was like playing T-ball after trying to get hits off Major League pitchers.

Here are some of the truly amazing new "Harrison Cluster" codes I've since found in War and Peace:

Let It Be, Fab Four, Beatles, View Beatles, Sweet Lord, Yoko Ono, Sixties, Satsang, I Me Mine, Soloist, Rock God, Mop Tops, Magical, Clapton, Shankar, Piggies, and many more!

These were found by searching two books of *War and Peace* (just under 400,000 letters), and counting those that touch down (at least one letter) in the two-page section for the "Harrison Cluster."

Conclusion

The promoters of hidden-message claims say, "How could such amazing coincidences be the product of random chance?" I think the real question should be, "How could such coincidences not be the inevitable product of a huge sequence of trials on a large, essentially random database?" Once I learned how to navigate in puzzle-space, finding "incredible" predictions became a routine affair. One of my more elaborate puzzles to date is this one, from Tolstoy's *War and Peace*: "Guilty Lee Oswald shot Kennedy, Both Died." This is easily topped, however, by this hidden jewel I found in a single chapter of Drosnin's second Bible code book: "The Bible code is a silly, dumb, fake, false, evil, nasty, dismal fraud and snake-oil hoax."

The source of the mysterious "Bible code" has been revealed— it's *homo sapiens*.

Now somebody go tell Oprah.

Endnotes

1. Drosnin, Michael. (1997). *The Bible code*. New York: Simon and Schuster, pp 50–51. **2.** Hewitt, VJ, & Peter Lorie. (1991). *Nostradamus: The end of the millennium*. New York: Simon and Schuster. **3.** Begley, Sharon. (1997). Seek and ye shall find. *Newsweek*, June 9, pp 66–67. **4.** Gardner, Martin. (1997). Farrakhan, Cabala, Baha'i, and 19. *Skeptical Inquirer* 21 (2), pp 16–18, 57. **5.** *Op cit.*, Drosin, p 26.

Further References

McKay, Brendan, Dror Bar-Natan, Maya Bar-Hillel & Gil Kalai. (1999). Solving the Bible code puzzle. *Statistical Science* 14 (5), May.

Thomas, David E. (1997.) Hidden messages and the Bible code. *Skeptical Inquirer*, November/December.

Thomas, David E. (1998.) Bible code developments. *Skeptical Inquirer*, March/April.

Van Biema, David. (1997). Deciphering God's plan. *Time*, June 9, p 56.

Witztum, Doron, Eliyahu Rips, & Yoav Rosenberg. (1994). Equidistant letter sequences in the Book of Genesis. *Statistical Science* 9 (3).

Fear and Lying in 2012-Land

John Major Jenkins

The term "2012"—that is, the year 2012—is going to become commonplace in the next few years. If you haven't heard of it yet, here's your chance. It's already the centerpiece of alarmist apocalyptic fantasies, new-fangled philosophies of time, and forthcoming Hollywood movies about the cataclysmic end of the world.

These 2012 manifestations have their basis in a calendar system developed over 2,000 years ago by the early Maya people of southern Mexico, in which a cycle of 5,125 years will close on December 21, 2012. As a result of recent breakthroughs in deciphering ancient Maya cosmology, we can now understand what the ancient Maya were intending with their cycle-ending date. On one hand, these new discoveries should shake the superiority complex of Western science and philosophy down to its foundations. On the other hand, the average person on the street is going to want to know what all this 2012 hoopla is about, and we now have clear answers.

> These 2012 manifestations have their basis in a calendar system developed over 2,000 years ago by the early Maya people of southern Mexico, in which a cycle of 5,125 years will close on December 21, 2012.

Unfortunately, the 2012 discussion is riddled with misinformation, distortions, and exploitation. Here's a sober guide to the topic and the smorgasbord of disinformation that threatens to smother what, at its heart, is a profound insight into why modern civilization is experiencing a fundamental crisis of sustainability and so many urgent challenges.

The topic of 2012 is rife with lies. Lies that distract us from seeing the thing-in-itself, lies that trick us into thinking that there is no real core of the subject. It wouldn't be fair to characterize most of these as overt lies, since that implies an intentional subversion of truth in order to propagate a known falsehood. Most of it is misinformation and misconception, resulting from poor research, incomplete understanding of the Maya calendar, and, most unfortunately, the proffering of simplistic stereotypes in the marketplace.

There are a few cases in which certain writers, as truths have come to light, have continued to assert their exposed falsehoods, so in the absence of rescinding their revealed misapprehensions they become liars. And should we let a sleeping liar lie? If we choose not to, it's a bit of a fool's errand, for when pressed these grandstanders dig themselves in deeper and spin-doctor their lies into qualified, provisional beliefs. And continue to pollute the discussion with their distortions.

It is difficult to navigate this quagmire, and to the newcomer it can be hard to separate the wheat from the chaff. As my friend Jonathan Zap warns, "Welcome to Carnival 2012!"[1] You must choose from varieties of snake oil being foisted upon you by a plethora of charismatic silver-tongued carnival barkers. To the newcomer, a glance at the nauseating 2012 menu gives the impression that the whole discussion is a free-for-all, a mess of confusion, and nobody really seems to know what the truth is. This is a mistaken impression. As someone who has been intensely engaged in the study of these things for many years, I hope to provide some guidance through the fears and lies that spike the ideological soil of 2012-land.

I have been studying the Maya calendar since the mid-1980s. While frequently traveling to Central America to live and work with the traditional Quiché Maya in the highlands, I engaged in some pointed research and fact-finding that resulted in a series of articles and self-published books between 1989 and 1994, when Borderlands published my book *Tzolkin*. This was only the first phase of my research. One cannot get a university degree in Maya Calendar Studies, but I pursued a course of self-study and by the early 1990s was venturing beyond the cutting edge of where scholars themselves had tread. My work is grounded in good scholarship, and my working hypothesis has always been that it would be possible, and worthwhile, to reconstruct the forgotten Maya beliefs and cosmo-conceptions connected with their 2012 calendar.

Early on I studied the basics of Maya time philosophy and internalized the facts of how the calendar operates. Consequently, for many years now most of the popular books on the Maya calendar have seemed to me to be riddled with elementary errors, mistaken notions, and even willful deceptions, a.k.a., lies. For example, in 1992 I published a review of the calendar game-system created by José Argüelles called Dreamspell. The system was very different in structure, operation, and placement in real time from the surviving 260-day calendar in

problematic.[3] The main author went on to write a series of books on the Maya and related subjects, based largely on the clever idea that funny faces could be found in Maya hieroglyphs if you cut them up and reassembled them in different ways.

All new ideas and theories should be assessed with discernment. This is a time when much new information about the ancient Maya is coming to light. It just so happens that they had a calendar that points to a date in our near future—a date that the Maya believed to signal a shift in World Ages—and so a lot of attention is being generated. And an avalanche of speculation and disinformation is smothering what, at its heart, is really a very interesting story that can be apprehended with great clarity.

Here 2012ology reaches a fork in the road. In one direction, we try to reconstruct the authentic but lost cosmovision associated with the Maya calendar and the 2012 cycle ending date; in the other direction we disregard this concern and try to create trendy models and systems perhaps loosely based on

To the newcomer, a glance at the nauseating 2012 menu gives the impression that the whole discussion is a free-for-all, a mess of confusion, and nobody really seems to know what the truth is.

Guatemala. Yet it identified itself as "the Mayan calendar." It was over 50 days out of synchronization with the authentic day-count and also skipped counting February 29th—something Maya calendar priests would never do.[2]

My critique of these and other issues with Dreamspell are well-documented; between 1992 and 1996 I responded to hundreds of letters, often handling venomous attacks from those who had joined the Dreamspell clique and saw my truth-telling as threatening. Others had noticed the discrepancies and were grateful for my clear exposé. To this day I still occasionally receive emails from newcomers who enter the Maya calendar discussion through Dreamspell and then realize they have been misled. Although this experience is by nature "disillusioning," systems like Dreamspell provide a pit-stop where one can rev up their faculty of conscious discrimination—a valuable skill on any spiritual path.

On another front, the much-hailed book called *The Mayan Prophecies* came out in 1995. I interviewed one of the authors, wrote a lengthy review essay, and identified dozens of factual errors as well as many instances of internal contradictions within the book, rendering the theory it put forward extremely

Maya ideas, but for the most part we are willing to play fast and loose with the Maya tradition and propagate our own imaginative systems. To my mind, it goes without saying that the latter pursuit is problematic. It has given rise to the plethora of systems, assertions, and models one finds in the marketplace today.

If we pursue the former path with clarity and discernment, we eventually will uncover the facts of the matter and find the one, true cosmology at the heart of the 2012 calendar. This caveat should be enough to point newcomers in the right direction, but the clever new systems can be very seductive and it will be worth exposing the major misconceptions that clog the discussion. First, a brief sketch of the fundamental facts of the 2012 calendar.

The Maya Calendar in a Nutshell

The Long Count calendar is a system of timekeeping that first appears on carved monuments in the first century BCE. It is thus believed to have been invented around that time. It uses five place values, and scholars write a typical Long Count date like this: 7.16.4.1.1. The place values proceed left to right as follows: *baktuns*, *katuns*, *tuns*, *uinals*, and *kin*. *Baktuns* contain

144,000 days (roughly 394 years); *katuns* contain 7,200 days (just under 20 years); *tuns* contain 360 days; *uinals* contain 20 days; and a *kin* is one day. Some of the monuments dated in the Long Count do not record local historical events—they are what are referred to as Creation Monuments. They are sacred texts expressing Maya theology and philosophy, because they

From this we can gather that the end of a 13-*baktun* cycle (written 13.0.0.0.0) was very important in ancient Maya cosmology.

describe the creation and renewal events that happen when thirteen *baktuns* are completed. From this we can gather that the end of a 13-*baktun* cycle (written 13.0.0.0.0) was very important in ancient Maya cosmology.

Scholars have figured out how the Maya calendar correlates with our own. From this work we know that 13.0.0.0.0 falls on December 21, 2012, in our Gregorian calendar. My third book, *Tzolkin: Visionary Perspectives and Calendar Studies* (1992), thoroughly researched, examined, tested, and reported on this issue, known as the correlation question. I've studied, debated, and written thousands of pages on the correlation question issue. It is an important first step in any study of the Maya calendar. The facts, arguments, tests, and counterarguments have been addressed and filed away, and there is no doubt about it: The 13-*baktun* cycle ending date falls on December 21, 2012.

I emphasize this because a big lie in the 2012 discussion is that no one really knows when the "real" end date occurs. Such a deception opens the door for underinformed writers to invent their own end dates, or propose that this or that date is more significant than the established, authentic end date. In the limited space of a brief article, I can only encourage readers to look into it for themselves if they feel the need. As one who has already done so, I can report that all of the other propositions are chimeras and red herrings, either blindly asserted misconceptions or self-serving lies.

This introductory sketch is much like helping all art critics to agree that red is a color before we go any further. It is necessary for moving forward on the same page. Without it, splinter groups start setting up camp on the side of the road, digging in while clinging to misconceptions, proceeding to construct empires built on lies.

So, we have this big cycle ending on December 21, 2012. What of it? How can we understand it? Well, by now it's clear that the date comes to us from Maya tradition. (This is self-evident but needs to be emphasized because many writers on 2012 barely mention the Maya!) If we study the Maya traditions that relate to this 2012 date, we discover two things very quickly. First, it is the end of a 13-*baktun* cycle—a period of 5,125.36 years—and this was considered to be one World Age in Maya thought. Second, World Ages are described in the Maya Creation myth, known as the Hero Twin myth or the *Popol Vuh.*

Generally, the *Popol Vuh* states that the world moves through chapters or Ages of change, and at the end of each Age humanity passes through a transition during which transformation and renewal occur. In the *Popol Vuh*, humanity has already gone through several of these transformations. I repeat: The emphasis in the Creation myth is on transformation and renewal, then a new Age begins—a new 13-*baktun* cycle begins.

Two Big Lies

These are the absolute minimal basic facts of the 2012 calendar, what one would learn in Maya calendar kindergarten, but notice that with these facts, drawn directly from the primary document one needs to study in order to understand 2012, we've already challenged two of the biggest lies about 2012— the lies which many assume to be fundamental truisms and that are ubiquitous on book jackets, conference summaries, and catalog copy of 2012 books. These are: "The Maya calendar stops in 2012," and, "The Maya predicted the end of the world in 2012." On the first point, in the cyclical time philosophy of the Maya, 13.0.0.0.0 is followed by 0.0.0.0.1 in the next cycle. On the second point, the Creation Myth itself emphasizes transformation and renewal, not "the end of the world." If we could eradicate these basic misconceptions, the whole 2012 discussion would instantly become a lot less silly.

When these illusions about 2012 are shattered, we are then free to engage with the *ding an sich*, the thing-in-itself. It could be the beginning of really understanding what it is—and there's a lot of amazing ideas and knowledge to talk about. However, for some, when the bubble bursts it's the end of the discussion.

In 1999, I was interviewed by a popular radio-show host. Thirty minutes in we came to this issue, and I clarified that such a notion was absurd on several fronts. He was somewhat surprised, as this false notion is the perfect launching off point for all kinds of entertaining speculative fantasies, all of which had been duly flailed on his program by a smorgasbord of eager book writers. Unfortunately, after this disillusioning, I think the whole topic of 2012 then became uninteresting to him. The baby was thrown out with the bathwater, as if the entire discussion hinges on a tacit agreement that 2012 is about the end of the calendar, or the world, or time.

Maya (That Is, Illusion) and the Mass Media

So, where did this notion come from? It's hard to trace the specific origin, but it's easy to imagine. It is the perfect bumper sticker soundbite. It packs a bevy of inviting fearful scenarios. For someone to point out the patent falseness and absurdity of the notion is like the child saying the emperor is wearing no clothes. Some don't want the charade to come crashing down—hey, there's money to be made. You're an unwelcome guest in the House of Lies if you try to be a system-buster and truth-teller. On a personal level, individuals don't like their long-cherished beliefs to be exposed as B.S.—the messenger then gets criticized as being negative or otherwise undesirable.

We live in a world of materialism and appearances, superficial surface characteristics that are worshipped and slavered over as if they represented the epitome of truth and the heart of reality. We mistake illusion, *maya* as the Hindus call it, for reality, and the media is complicit in reinforcing this delusion. That is perhaps the biggest lie of the modern world. The fact is that we are trying to pull back the veil of appearances to see the essence underneath, the heart of reality, the thing in itself. We need to see and connect with the essential truth at the heart of things rather than continue to be distracted by glitz, talking points, drama, scandal, clever designer systems, and the cult of personality.

Another idea that has great currency is that "the Maya calendar was super accurate," and then four or six decimal places are mentioned. Yes, the Maya astronomers and mathematicians were capable of a high degree of accuracy, but more important, their cosmovision strove to embrace many dimensions of reality. Their worldview perceived a comprehensive grasp of the unifying threads running through plants, animals, ancestors, human beings, rock, water, air, planets, gods, and stars. That is where the real story is. To celebrate the Maya only for their accuracy is misleading and disingenuous, like celebrating Einstein for being a decent patent clerk.

The notion that the Maya were super-precision fanatics is compelling to modern people, because our own scientific paradigm values precision. It's a recognizable achievement that we apparently need to project onto the Maya in order to think they were great. Notice, however, that this takes ethnocentrism to a new level, to what we might call ethnonarcissism. We want to make them more like ourselves in order to respect them. We need to see our own values reflected in Maya culture before we can acknowledge any value in it.

Or, conversely, we need to demonize them so we can banish them forever from our considerations. This is the standard method for dealing with the Maya and their annoyingly baffling genius. Enter the screenwriters, directors, and movie-makers. With gazillion-dollar budgets at their disposal, all the clichés and stereotypes of anti-Indio nineteenth-century Manifest Destiny genocide are trotted out to be rendered in CGI and Dolby Sound, turning the Maya into pitiable savages or atavistic purveyors of Doom who couldn't possibly have anything

> Generally, the *Popol Vuh* states that the world moves through chapters or Ages of change, and at the end of each Age humanity passes through a transition during which transformation and renewal occur.

positive to contribute to our civilized world. We might think that the entertainment biz is harmless, but analysts of Hollywood like Jack Sheehan, in his insightful book *Reel Bad Arabs: How Hollywood Vilifies a People*, have exposed the churning machinations of a racist, politically biased, and ethnocentric propaganda machine. Likewise, the silver screen treatment of the Maya and 2012 looks like it will be a macabre, fear-mongering bloodbath.

Scholarly Coincidentalists and 2012

We may wish to take refuge from this mine field of media messiness in the safe harbor of cool, rational scholarship. Certainly, Maya specialists, archaeologists, and anthropologists will treat 2012 with discernment and respect. Where do the Maya scholars stand on the topic? This is perhaps the most surprising and disappointing aspect of the entire 2012 discussion. An assumed lie in academia has been the working hypothesis of scholars for many years, and only recently has a more open-minded attitude begun to emerge. That lie is this: There is no intention behind the 2012 date. In other words, the

which is agreed to be just another hyped millenarian charade, rather than examining, like they should, the 2012 artifact itself and how it plays a role in Maya iconography, calendrics, and eschatology. These circumstances place me in the position of being the annoying outsider-trailblazer.

Here I'll briefly summarize my pioneering reconstruction work. This is not the place for a detailed introduction, but an overview will locate my work within the larger themes addressed in this article. My work is intended to be a well-documented and carefully argued reconstruction of the lost cosmology associated with the Long Count calendar's 2012 cycle ending date. My approach was guided by asking questions like, "Where was the Long Count cosmology invented?" Realizing that astronomy was central to the Mayan World Age doctrine, I asked, "Is

To celebrate the Maya only for their accuracy is misleading and disingenuous, like celebrating Einstein for being a decent patent clerk.

fact that the end of the cycle falls on December 21, 2012—an accurate solstice date—is just a random happenstance, a mere mathematical consequence of the *beginning date* in 3114 BCE (whose placement is assumed by scholars to have greater bearing, even though Maya time philosophy is teleological—oriented toward *the ends* of processes).

This belief that the Maya never had any interest in the cycle ending has been the default assumption in academia for decades; little if any attention therefore has ever been paid to 2012; it's been a non-topic. Scholars never dropped the ball on leading the 2012 discussion because they never picked it up.

While exercising critical thinking in the mid-1980s, it occurred to me that, since the cycle ending falls on a winter solstice, some kind of intentionality may be present in its placement. I approached scholars with this observation, and for virtually two decades the response has been, "It's a coincidence." The subsequent implications, research, and findings that it pointed me to have therefore been waved aside.

More recently, scholars have deigned to talk about 2012; that is to say, they are more willing to say something about it. However, almost all of their commentary is directed to the popular effects happening in the culture—the predictable doomsday products and the silly things said in the murky deep end of the New Age movement. In other words, Maya scholars have deputized themselves as honorary 2012 sociologists, interested in commenting on the social phenomenon of 2012,

there something unusual happening astronomically in the years around 2012?" I was led to what emerged as the key to understanding the Maya's intention in pointing to 2012—a rare alignment within the cycle of the precession of equinoxes, a "galactic alignment" that can be defined as "the alignment of the December solstice sun with the dark-rift in the Milky Way" (or, as astronomers prefer it, with the "galactic equator").

When I studied the Maya Creation Mythology, their ballgame's symbolism, and the carved monuments of Izapa (the place that invented the Long Count), I found previously unrecognized evidence that the ancient Maya became aware of this future galactic alignment some 2,100 years ago. Furthermore, an entire galactic cosmology was embedded in these Maya institutions, involving astronomy as well as prophecy and spiritual teachings. So, the keys to my work are the galactic alignment, the Creation Myth's symbolization of the galactic alignment, and the underappreciated site of Izapa. Although my work has proceeded rationally with careful documentation, no one else asked the right questions, and so my findings are unprecedented.

Although this is the unavoidable approach to 2012 that any rational investigator would take, scholars have been barred from the path by the limiting dictates of their professed Coincidentalism. While often refusing to actually examine my work, scholars have unfairly tended to see me as belonging to the irrelevant arena of New Age speculation. Thomas Kuhn wrote that most major breakthroughs in an evolving field of study are made by self-taught outsiders—precisely because they are not in bed with the biases and assumptions that keep progress from happening. Goodman, Teeple, Knorosov, Proskouriakoff—Maya studies is in fact filled with these independent pioneers. Recently, new discoveries regarding the astronomical knowledge of the Maya have been made by scholars, notably by epigrapher Barbara MacLeod, effectively mitigating previous criticisms of my work.

The Maya on Their 2012 Date

One open-minded scholar who has addressed 2012 from an engaged viewpoint is Robert Sitler, who provided a survey of what the Maya themselves have documented about 2012 in the past and what they say today.[4] He suspends judgment on the evidence I identified in the Creation Myth and at Izapa and has stated that there were no documents that relate to 2012. However, in mid-2006 Sitler was instrumental, along with researcher Geoff Stray and myself, in shedding light on a neglected Maya carving from Tortuguero that points right at the end of the current 13-*baktun* cycle in 2012. Epigrapher David Stuart congenially translated the text. Now, scholars can no

always had a problem with this aspect of my work. They presumed that birth should happen at the start of the cycle (a Western scientific bias) rather than at the end of the process (a Maya idea). Now, with the creation deity Bolon Yok-te dancing around on a 2012 carving, my prescient hunch that was dismissed by scholars as absurd has been affirmed by new evidence.

So, what do the modern Maya say about 2012? Sitler observes that since the Long Count was lost, the modern Maya are influenced by outside authors. Disinformation has been generated, however, by dabblers who only wish to assemble new designer systems and models—models about consciousness or history or change that are only distantly reminiscent of authentic Maya tradition. This is the problem. What is at stake is the resuscitation, survival, and continuity of an ancient galactic paradigm whose heirs are still with us today. It's a complicated situation in which the cultural and genetic descendants of those who invented the 2012 calendar and its associated galactic eschatology may or may not decide to embrace what, for them, must seem like a truly strange and alien artifact from a long-lost past. It would be much like modern Egyptians taking up mummification and astral funerary rites as practiced by their ancient ancestors.

I was led to what emerged as the key to understanding the Maya's intention in pointing to 2012—a rare alignment within the cycle of the precession of equinoxes, a "galactic alignment" that can be defined as "the alignment of the December solstice sun with the dark-rift in the Milky Way" (or, as astronomers prefer it, with the "galactic equator").

longer say that the ancient Maya were never interested in 2012. In fact, I pointed out that the text mentions a Maya deity called Bolon Yok-te, a usual suspect in Maya creation narratives.[5] This reinforces the idea that the ancient Maya thought of 2012 as a creation, or re-creation, which of course makes sense in terms of the emphasis on transformation and renewal in the *Popol Vuh*'s World Age doctrine.

I titled my breakthrough book of 1998 *Maya Cosmogenesis 2012*. With "Maya," "Cosmogenesis," and "2012" being the operative words, the title presented an idea that, at the time, was radical—that 2012 was thought of by the Maya as a cosmo-genesis (a birth or rebirth of the world). Scholars have

It's true: The 2012 Long Count calendar stopped being followed. It must be recovered or reconstructed. However, teachings about cycle endings, fire ceremony, the *temizcal* (sweat bath), and the spiritual meaning of sacrifice do survive among the contemporary Maya and other indigenous groups. They are still doing ceremonies, and Maya shamans and leaders should be respected. The 2012 information, however, is being filtered through a quagmire of competing interests. Various comments by the Maya on 2012 were reported by Sitler in his essay "The 2012 Phenomenon," and almost all are echoes of modern research.[6] In lieu of university-approved academic reconstruction work, all of this comes from independent researchers and writers.

Often, the motive of writers in engaging with Maya elders is self-serving—like hijacking a handy elder to approve of your own theory.

For example, author Carl Calleman manipulated the words of a Maya elder and calendar priest named don Alejandro in a press release of early 2006, giving the impression that don Alejandro rejected the 2012 date (contrary to his former statements), and thus Calleman's own invented date, October 28, 2011, could by default step in and take over. Despite this transparent power ploy, other writers such as Barbara Clow have jumped on the Calleman bandwagon without apparently understanding how his approach sullies authentic Maya tradition in the interest of furthering his own idiosyncratic agenda. It's a lie to think we have any right to weave new apostate systems cobbled together piecemeal from selected fragments of Maya traditions.

Another writer has insinuated himself into the goings-on with don Alejandro and the Indigenous Council of Elders, asserting in his new book that "according to the Maya" the end date is February 19, 2013, not December 21, 2012.[7] A glance at the premise of the argument reveals a standard misconception. The new, improved end date, (the newly revealed elder-approved "real" end date) is stated as being the end of a 13-year cycle followed by the Maya. The 13-year cycle is indeed used by the highland Maya today, and is one-fourth of the 52-year Calendar Round period. This method of timekeeping is different than the one used in the Long Count system. Long Count and Calendar Round dates are usually found side by side on carved monuments, so they have a consistent relationship to each other, but

It would be much like modern Egyptians taking up mummification and astral funerary rites as practiced by their ancient ancestors.

they are two completely different methods of counting time, analogous to how the 7-day weekday names run separately but alongside the day numbers and months of the year.

The problem here is that the Calendar Round does not schedule the 2012 end date, nor should it be expected to. So, to use the 13-year period of the Calendar Round to adjust or correct the Long Count's end date is like trying to play a waltz in 4/4 time, or eat a sandwich with your ear, or use a canvas to paint a picture on a brush. It has no basis in the way that the calen-

dars work and interface, and betrays a fundamental misunderstanding. Writers who do not understand this should be very cautious with how they frame their rejection, or demoting, of the established solstice 2012 date.

According to the purveyor of the February 19, 2013 "real" end date, the Indigenous Council of Elders are preparing to assess and pass judgment on the work of non-Maya outsiders. My own work, for example, which was inspired by a love of Maya culture and stands alone in offering a carefully documented interdisciplinary synthesis/reconstruction based on the Creation Myth and Izapa, will come before the court of judgment. The Council of Elders could very easily decide that they just don't buy it. This is their prerogative, but such an "official" denouncement generates unusual problems if my pioneering work is indeed on target. And since my work on 2012 is unavailable in Spanish, let alone Mayan, one wonders how the assessment will proceed.

Ethnic Maya philosophers such as Victor Montejo and Gaspar Gonzalez are languaging the 2012 situation as a time when the limits of globalized self-serving greed and egoism come to a head and must be transformed, and a Maya renaissance is at hand.[8] My own emphasis on the archetypal dynamic of the ego-Self axis in the Maya Creation Myth, as an opportunity for transformation and renewal culminating in 2012, shares the viewpoints and insights of these Maya teachers.

As for the popular writers who play fast and loose with the Maya calendar's cycle ending date, there are two problems. One is simply not doing your homework. The other is trumping the facts with another assumption—that we really are trying to identify the moment, or day, or wave, of change, and thus if our historical graphs or crystal-gazing dictates a different date to us, we are justified in correcting the established Maya date. This position assumes that a definitive change is predetermined and fixed into the architecture of time and, worse, that we are robots fated to respond to the appointed hour like the blind forces of Newton's clockwork universe. Odd logic is brought to bear on the argument to reject 2012 as the authentic cycle-ending date, arguments that are much like saying we should reorder the days of the week alphabetically and—here's where it gets truly hilarious—that we've had it wrong all along! A serious demerit of rational processing occurs in these models.

The Rhapsodic Bloviations of New Age Fantasts

The oddest case of all is found in the rhapsodic bloviations that comprise a book enticingly titled *Apocalypse 2012*. The author flew to Guatemala to receive the Maya "prophecy" about 2012 directly from Maya teachers, the Barrios brothers, learning that: "On 12/21/12 our Solar System, with the Sun at its center, will, as the Maya have for millennia maintained, eclipse the view from Earth of the center of the Milky Way. This happens only once every 26,000 years. Ancient Maya astronomers considered this spot to be the Milky Way's womb."[9] Except for the fact that the Maya have not retained a continuity of this knowledge "for millennia," this is a fairly accurate paraphrase of my theory, including my breakthrough discovery that the galactic center was mythologized by the ancient Maya as a cosmic womb, a creation place.

If the reader is unclear whether the chicken or the egg came first, the back-story to this reporting of my pioneering theory through these Maya spokesmen can be traced to an interview they did with Steven McFadden six years ago that utilized material virtually cut-and-pasted from an article I wrote and posted online in 1995.[10] Whether intended or not, the impression was that the galactic alignment information came directly from the elders.

Armed with the Maya prophecy for 2012, handed to him by Real Maya Teachers, the author of *Apocalypse 2012* then proceeds to concur with said Teachers to excoriate clueless outsiders, who don't know how to read the symbols. I am mentioned by name as a "cultural imperialist,"[11] and while my breakthrough book *Maya Cosmogenesis 2012* was mentioned and wanly dismissed, its primary thesis (that the ancient Maya intended 2012 to target the rare alignment of the solstice sun and the galactic center—sound familiar?) was left unsaid. Obviously, to mention it would have created a conflict of interest, as the author wished to give the impression that the goods were delivered to him by a Maya teacher. This *contretemps* reveals either shoddy rational processing or outright intellectual dishonesty in a book that presumes to be "a scientific investigation." Pretty interesting. This was a real neat trick, and the author can certainly lay claim to inventing a new form of literary criticism—plagio-excoriation. I've now had the dubious honor of being plagiarized and excoriated in the same chapter.

A slightly less annoying situation is found in the insta-experts. They are come-latelies to the 2012 topic, who have never written about it before, have never apparently studied the topic, but have garnered status by writing popular books on ancient wisdom, human potential, and healing, or other topics seemingly similar to the 2012 meme. Asked to write something about 2012, they take their already polished rap and insert "2012" and "Maya calendar" in strategic places and, *voila!*— they are instant 2012 experts. 2012 is simply hijacked as a synonym for change or growth or consciousness, useful on the marquee for whatever it was they were previously doing. These examples merely illustrate the level of opportunistic behavior that is occurring in 2012-land, and how the topic attracts exploiters, posers, and self-promoters.

To many in the study of the Maya calendar, this is old news. Geoff Stray, for example, the author of *Beyond 2012*, has been tireless in his insightful critiquing of the endless barrage of 2012 products.[12] Author Jonathan Zap has pointed out the archetypal psychology behind the reactions of scholars and New Agers to 2012.[13] With the growing interest in 2012, waves

> According to the Maya World Age doctrine, 2012, like all cycle endings, signals a time of renewal and transformation, the promise of taking a good long look at the world and making some very deeply considered, appropriate, and lasting changes.

of newcomers are arriving on the scene, trying to make sense of the various threads, books, and ideas. False ideas continue to have currency because they resonate with a certain level of misapprehension as newcomers filter in and self-sort into their respective domains of understanding.

One hopes that this is a continuing process for newbies in which previously held notions get revised as deeper understanding and insights occur. Newcomers should be issued a B.S.-meter with a Lie Gauge attachment as they come in the door. Unfortunately, such a progression in one's path requires time and commitment, and 2012 fits all too easily into the disposable marketplace bins of a world gone trendy. Few who dabble with 2012 and Maya cosmovision will tarry long enough to internalize more than the most superficial distortions. The path is tricky, especially since the B.S. is sold with such alluring packaging, and all kinds of signals and distractions discourage people from going deep into anything. Too dangerous—might lead to real knowledge. There's a Mayan proverb that says, "The path to Hell is a garden stroll lined with butterflies, whereas the path to Paradise is a steep and rocky upward climb."

False Framings and the Expected Anti-Truth

Yes, this is a topic that requires some study and the careful sorting of bad information from good information. And this is not to say that we shouldn't expand the discussion into areas of metaphysics and spiritual teachings—in fact, that's where the discussion ultimately leads. But we have to start by getting our facts right. We need to come together on the basics, and the correct correlation of Maya time is Step 1. Sure, we can all agree that it's about love, or oneness, or peace, but this is a matter of being clear with an ancient tradition that we are all wanting to appreciate and respect. I am amazed that, time and time again in the marketplace, people feel it is justified, even desirable, to oust the established date. This highly questionable agenda exploits the fact that newcomers really don't know this from that, and then your own date becomes a valid choice on the menu of disinformation, the End Date of the Week.

Critics will often frame the ongoing debate as "Jenkins's date versus X's date" (add your favorite alternative). This is a false framing. *My* date is the established Maya date, the date that is proven—if you understand the subject—by an interdisciplinary set of criteria, including the 260-day sacred count still followed by the traditional Maya in Highland Guatemala. What more do you want? Announcement to 2012 writers: Stop inventing new end dates and day-counts! Let's just look at the thing-in-itself, and go deeper into it.

All of this is to be expected. At cycle endings, false authorities and false prophets (pocketing real profits) flood into the world. They manifest spontaneously and are created by the promise of power, status, and money. Why? Because at cycle endings we have a special opportunity to reconnect with Truth, with an empowering self-awareness of who we really are, an awareness of a higher perspective and wisdom. The revolutionary new idea in all of this is the way that the galactic alignment is the key to why the Maya chose 2012, why we are at a big cycle ending, and why we are living in an era in which we can open up to our essential unity, open to the heart and source of ourselves and the world.

This is a threat to the darkness, to ignorance, and to the control systems of deception installed by narcissistic egoism—by Seven Macaw as the *Popol Vuh* says. Thus, the Lords of Xibalba (the forces of limitation) deputize countless minions through which noise and disinformation can be spread. Ignorance will be maintained at the speed of dark. It is this net of lies that the intrepid seeker of truth must pierce and pass through in order to see the essence of the matter. Meditation is your best friend if you want to really understand 2012.

The root lie in all of this is the Big Lie, that we must be kept containerized, atomized, and separated, self-absorbed monads of conspicuous consumption. The French perennial philosopher Réne Guénon nailed this crisis of modernity to the wall over 60 years ago.[14] It is the lie of a world divorced from the bigger picture, a world whose basic premise is that all truth is relative, that *there is no absolute truth*. The perennial wisdom teachings of the world disagree, and the statement itself is a logical conundrum, as it states absolutely that there are no absolutes. The modern world is alone in harboring this belief; it is not the product of a superior and more sophisticated civilization, but of a debased and desacralized one.

According to the Maya World Age doctrine, 2012, like all cycle endings, signals a time of renewal and transformation, the promise of taking a good long look at the world and making some very deeply considered, appropriate, and lasting changes. In my study of not only the Maya but philosophies and religions from around the globe, this idea strikes me as a perennial wisdom, a universal insight, rather than an anomalous belief of one cultural group. But there's a problem. We are all spies in the house of lies, spying on…each other (but not on ourselves). We can and should see our complicity in maintaining the net of illusion—we just don't want to. Sadly, we are trapped in a designer reality-matrix that comes with a set of assumptions, an operating system that was scripted upon an Ur-level of dominator-style nihilism, something like Inevitable Apocalypse 1.0. In the face of this, the 2012 promise of renewal threatens to tear this Evil Disneyland of cards down to its foundations. Ego perceives transformation as certain death. Maya wisdom is therefore a threat that must be containerized, marginalized, or co-opted, its transformational power rendered impotent.

The modern world cannot even see the transformative power of the Maya teachings for cycle endings; instead we see the possibility of proactive, creative, conscious, engaged, renewal through fatalism-colored glasses. It must not be allowed. A good way to not allow it is to amp up the propaganda machine through the popular mass media—trendy movies, video games, salacious books, and so on—to infect the collective consciousness with images of horror, violence, death, and destruction. Emotion-laced imagery can be a very powerful evocative tool in the hands of those who wish to keep people frightened and controlled, cogs in the wheels of an impossible agenda—a voracious world that can only thrive on an endlessly accelerating Gross National Product.

So, in conclusion, here's the Cliff Notes guide to the lies and confusion that are found frolicking all over 2012-land: The Maya disappeared; 2012 is the creation of New Age writers; December 21, 2012, is not "the real" cycle ending date; there are no ancient Maya statements about 2012; the Maya calendar stops in 2012; it's OK to disregard the fundamental facts of the authentic Maya calendar tradition and promulgate one's own clever calendar system.

Finally, let me state something I believe to be true, just one more time for the record: It's *NOT all over on December 21, 2012*. Now let's just hope that a cabal of elected lunatics with their fingers on the Rapture button doesn't try to prove me wrong.

Endnotes

1. Writings at <www.zaporacle.com>. **2.** Jenkins, John Major. (1994). *Tzolkin*. Borderland Sciences Research Foundation. Also <Alignment2012.com/following.html>. **3.** See my review at <www.alignment2012.com/mproph.htm>. **4.** Sitler, Robert. (2007). 2012 and the Maya world. *The mystery of 2012* (Sounds True). **5.** Jenkins, John Major. (2006). In the roots of the Milky Way Tree: The Mayan Lord of Creation and 2012. *New dawn* 97 (Jul-Aug); <www.alignment2012.com/bolon-yokte.html>. **6.** Sitler, Robert. (2006). The 2012 phenomenon. *Nova religio* 9.3, pp 24–38. **7.** Melchezidek, Drunvalo. (2008). *Serpent of light: Beyond 2012*. Weiser Books. **8.** Gonzalez, Gaspar Pedro. (2005). *El 13 b'aktun: La nueva era, 2012, El fin del ciclo, Desde la Óptica Maya contemporánea*; Montejo, Victor. (2005). *Maya intellectual renaissance*. University of Texas Press. **9.** Joseph, Lawrence. (2007). *Apocalypse 2012*. Morgan Road Books, pp 32–3. **10.** The origin of all this in my 1995 online article "Thesis (From The Center of Mayan Time)" <www.alignment2012.com/fap2.html> is well-documented and confirmed by McFadden. His original 2002 interview did not specify the correct source of the alignment information, but in 2007 he graciously updated the online version <www.chiron-communications.com/communique%20 7-10.html>. Barrios published the book *The Maya Cholqij: Gateway to Aligning with the Energies of the Earth* in 2004, which Joseph apparently paraphrased in summarizing my pioneering work, possibly without understanding its true source. **11.** *Op cit.*, Joseph, p 40. **12.** See Geoff Stray's <www.diagnosis2012.co.uk>. **13.** Zap's writings: <www.zaporacle.com/textpattern/article/82/on-dreamspell-jenkinszap>; <www.alignment2012.com/zap-on-tonkins-error.html>; <www.famsi.org/pipermail/aztlan/2008-January/004027.html>. **14.** Guénon, René. (2000). *Reign of quantity and signs of the times*. New Delhi: Munshiram Manoharlal Publishers; Guénon, René. (1999). *Crisis of the modern world*. Varanasi, India: Indica Books. Also, see my discussion of Guénon and Coomaraswamy in my 2002 book *Galactic Alignment*.

Mystics and Messiahs
Mythkiller Philip Jenkins Unravels the Gospel about "Cults"
Interview with Philip Jenkins

> *"Extreme and bizzare religious ideas are so commonplace in American history that it is difficult to speak of them as fringe at all."*
> —*from* Mystics and Messiahs: Cults and New Religions in American History

Russ Kick: Since your book *Mystics and Messiahs* is about new religious groups in America, I thought it would be a good idea to start out by asking what a new religious group is, what features it typically has, etc. Also, what are your feelings of the words/phrases "new religious group" vs. "cult" vs. "sect"?

Philip Jenkins: Originally there were churches and sects, a division which developed in early twentieth-century European sociology. It's not terribly applicable to the US anyway, because in Europe "churches" were established and state-supported, and we don't have that here. Basically, churches are large and respectable and you're born into them; sects are small, fiercely active, and people join by conversion. In Europe today, what we call "cults" are called "sects," so there is a lot of confusion.

"New religious group," or "new religious movement" (NRM), is intended as a nice neutral term, partly to replace the word "cult," which had become almost unusable because of its cultural baggage. I use the word "cult" always in quotes, just to indicate a small, unpopular religious group, with no necessary reason for it to be unpopular. Having said this, some groups certainly do look more "cultish" than others. There is a nice definition of some small religious groups as "highly authoritarian, charismatically led, puritanical, and intolerant." This is

useful because it avoids the need to accept all the mythology about brainwashing, mind control, etc.

An excellent criterion is how easy it is to leave the group. If you can walk out without recriminations, it's not a cult. I'd also add that if they can laugh at themselves, you're not dealing with a terribly pernicious group.

New Religious Groups Aren't Very New

RK: In *Mystics and Messiahs*, one of your themes—probably the overarching theme—is that new religious groups are not a creation of the 1960s and 1970s but have been in the US throughout its entire history, even in colonial times. What were some of these sects from the early days of America and what became of them?

PJ: Think of it in market terms. Two people set up businesses. One is (say) Pam's Candle Store, and it lasts six months; the other is Microsoft, and it rules the world. The colonial groups are like this. The Methodists are a classic bizarre and extreme sect that goes on to become the mainstream of the mainstream (just as bizarre in the eighteenth century as Baptists and Quakers were in the seventeenth). In other words, they go on to be Microsoft.

There are a hundred other groups, including all sorts of communal sects, which were often mystical, celibate, or occult, and they lasted maybe ten years or a century. We see the remains of their settlements as tourist attractions around the country, like the Harmony settlements in Pennsylvania and Indiana, or the Ephrata commune in Pennsylvania, or the Shaker communes in New England. Wonderful, magical, evocative places.

America had Rosicrucians and alchemists before it had Methodists.

RK: I was fascinated by two related points you made: Most, if not all, mainstream religions started out as what could be called "cults." Similarly, many of today's "cults" have what you term "respectable lineages." Please elaborate.

PJ: One criterion that people try to use to differentiate cults from churches is that cults have no roots in a given society, that they are new outbreaks of alien ideas. By those standards, there are no cults. The example I use is that America had

Rosicrucians and alchemists before it had Methodists, so the occult is nothing new—we have groups organized by the 1690s. We have also had Hindus and Buddhists longer than we have had Pentecostals.

Virtually all the so-called "cults" grow out of mainstream organizations.

Also, virtually all the so-called "cults" grow out of mainstream organizations—the People's Temple (of Jonestown fame) developed from a respectable evangelical denomination, the Christian Church/Disciples of Christ, and Jim Jones was ordained in that group. Incidentally, the same group gave rise to the International Churches of Christ, which is today the main target of anti-cult critics. Another example I use in the book is Jeffrey Lundgren, whose group undertook several ritualistic slayings in the late 1980s: His origins lay in the Reorganized Church of Latter Day Saints, a sober and conservative branch of the Mormon tradition.

RK: Asian sects and gurus have been in America since way before the 1960s. When did they first make their mark on America?

PJ: This goes back at least to Thoreau and the Transcendentalists, basically the 1840s. In literally every generation since then, there have been new infusions of Hindu and Buddhist thought, often disguised in American mode—the New Thought movement of the late nineteenth century, Theosophy in the 1870s. With its cults, health fads, and wandering gurus, Boston in the 1880s looks a whole lot like San Francisco in the 1970s.

The Anti-Cult Attitudes, Then and Now

RK: You've noted that it's not only new sects that have been around since day one, but anti-cult groups as well. Every period has it opponents of new religions, and their basic charges and allegations have remained constant. Please elaborate.

PJ: The best account of an anti-cult movement I know is found in a work called the New Testament, where literally every single charge familiar today is made, specifically against Jesus. Take a look. Jesus is accused of being a drunkard and a crazy man, his family tries to drag him away from his group, and in return he insists that his followers have to *hate* their wives, parents, children etc. You can make a striking list of the New Testament passages calling believers to separate from the world, break from their families, separate from darkness, etc. In other words, cult scares and anti-cult reactions go back a very long way. Today, most of the issues concern Europe, where we are seeing the same kinds of panic that we saw in the US in the 1970s.

RK: I found it very interesting that a "Satanic Panic" occurred in the US before the famous one of the 1980s and early 1990s. Please tell us about the Satanic Panic of the 1930s.

PJ: I originally discovered this back in the late 1980s when I was trying to test the claims made by anti-satanic theorists

With its cults, health fads, and wandering gurus, Boston in the 1880s looks a whole lot like San Francisco in the 1970s.

that there were these old, established cults and covens in the US. I found that claims went back a long way, but in virtually every case, they could be associated with sensationalistic tabloid media, pulp fiction, etc. Interestingly, too, there has been a pattern whereby most anti-satanic claims originate as fiction and then find their way into the media as claims of facts. Most of the claims of the 1980s can be traced back to two fictional works, namely Herbert S. Gorman's novel *The Place Called Dagon* (1927) and the British thrillers of Dennis Wheatley, above all *The Devil Rides Out*.

RK: Another theme of your book is that the threat of "cults" is often extremely overblown. First of all, talk to me about the numbers of people involved in new religions in different periods, and how and why the "anti-cult" forces, the media, and the sects themselves often inflate their membership and influence.

The proportion of people living in cult communes was probably far less at any given moment in the twentieth century than in the nineteenth.

PJ: Without trying to evade the answer, it's almost impossible to know how many people are "involved" because it depends what we mean by "involved." If we include everyone who ever read a leaflet, bought a book, or attended a meeting, probably tens of millions of Americans now alive have been involved in "cults" of different kinds, but of course they didn't give up their lives and go join a commune.

Anti-cult people give ludicrously high estimates for this sort of activity, obviously to make the issue look as threatening as possible. The common figure in the 1980s was that two million Americans were full-time cult members at any given time, which is absurd. Probably, the proportion of Americans gener-

The idea of gullible, hysterical women is perhaps the commonest single strand in anti-cult fears over the centuries.

ally interested and active in cults and new religions—though not fully committed activists—was roughly the same at any given time in the twentieth century, whether we are looking at 1920, 1945, or 1980. That is of course counterintuitive, since we believe this all started in the 1960s. It didn't. The proportion of people living in cult communes was probably far less at any given moment in the twentieth century than in the nineteenth.

RK: Continuing on the theme of demonizing new religious groups, you say that although there are a few cases of sects and/or their leaders doing harmful things in every era, the vast majority are sincere and well-behaved. How and why is it that the few "bad apples," so to speak, are used to smear all new religions?

PJ: It's an obvious tactic, which we all use to some extent. If you want to attack the Christian Right, say, we focus on the bad apples, like Jim Bakker or Jimmy Swaggart. Such rhetoric is all the more important in religious matters, where we are setting claims of purity and morality against a sinful reality. Nobody was too surprised or shocked when Bill Clinton turned out to be a prize lecher, but if you could make the same claims against someone who was a great moral activist, it would be much more effective. Finding Hugh Grant with a hooker was a national joke; finding Jesse Helms with one would be a moment of ineffable joy for liberals across the nation.

RK: You make a point that mainstream organized religions often have the same problems (e.g. child abuse, misused funds) as some new religious sects, yet the former often get

off the hook. Although there may be some outcry about the specific incidents, no one in the mainstream uses these occurrences to smear organized religion as a whole. Why is that?

PJ: Things are changing here. Prior to 1980 or so, nobody but nobody published bad stories on mainstream religion, mainly because it was felt to be in atrocious taste, partly because of a well-substantiated fear of boycotts. Things changed with new media standards in the 1980s and the weakening of respect for church authority by believers. Hence the Catholic clergy scandals of the last few years. But generally, if (say) a rabbi sins, he is seen as a bad rabbi, not as proof of the evils of Judaism; if a "cult leader" sins, that is proof of the evils of cults. Jews (and other mainstream believers) buy newspapers and will complain if their religion is abused; whereas cults are not seen as a serious constituency.

RK: In *Mystics and Messiahs*, you wrote, "Racial factors are also significant in sculpting cult fears." Please explain that and give some examples.

PJ: Think of anti-cult charges over the years, which can be neatly divided into two categories: African stereotypes (primitivism, violence, sexual excess, savagery) and Asian stereotypes (passive obedience, mind control, brainwashing, slavish submission). These twin patterns run over the last century or so, back to the 1890s when the whole language of cult was invented. The same images emerge very strongly in the 1970s—the myth of brainwashing is a direct consequence of American nightmares of encounters with supposedly "Asian" mind-control and brutality in Korea and Vietnam. The fact that some of the most visible new cults were Asian—or even Korean, like the Moonies—was the icing on the cake.

RK: You also noted that gender politics plays a role in new religions. Please explain and show how that plays into anti-cult fears.

PJ: The idea of gullible, hysterical women is perhaps the commonest single strand in anti-cult fears over the centuries, and again I look at the charges against the early Christians, the myths about Mary Magdalene (hooker, crazy woman, etc). It

In many cases, such instances fall under what should be the constitutional right to fall victim to one's own stupidity.

emerges against literally every new religion, including Methodism and Pentecostalism, and the camp meetings in US history. Critics are quick to point out that emotional excesses in religion often look very much like orgasmic experiences. Equally, women frequently emerge as leaders of cults—Ann Lee of the Shakers, Elizabeth Claire Prophet, Mary Baker Eddy, and so on. The critics charge that any movements so led must be neurotic, fanatical, irrational, and unfit for rational believers. Though they don't overtly use words as coarse as "pussy whipped," that idea is strongly in the background.

Reality Check

RK: Do you feel that certain new religious movements are problematic in any way? What are your thoughts on charges of brainwashing, member abuse, etc.? Are they ever valid? If so, what can be done (and what should be done) about them? Obviously, the answer is not to fly into hysterics and slander new religions across the board, but how can a real problem be handled in a sane way?

> In religion, ideas like racial and gender equality were commonplace long before they got into the mainstream.

PJ: Absolutely, many fringe (and not-so-fringe) religions oppress and abuse their members. We can cite examples of fraud, rape, illegal imprisonment, and so on. In many cases, such instances fall under what should be the constitutional right to fall victim to one's own stupidity. If you choose to give all your money to a religious fraud, there's not much anyone can or should do to protect you. If you choose to go through Marine Corps training when no one is making you, that's your choice, and you have a right to do it. The problem, of course, is where we are dealing with children, who can't give legitimate consent to be exploited.

Normally, I feel that the battery of laws we already have is more than sufficient to deal with these problems: Just enforce them in a way that does not discriminate against religious groups, and within that broad category, just against new or fringe religious groups.

Religious Laboratories

RK: Finally, another major theme of your book is that new sects play an important and often positive role in the development of religion in the US. How has this occurred in the past, and how do you see it playing out in the future?

PJ: I cite lots of examples of cults and fringe religions serving as laboratories for mainstream religion or social thought. In religion, ideas like racial and gender equality were commonplace long before they got into the mainstream. Other ideas become mainstream without anyone realizing they are religious in origin, like 12-step groups or vegetarianism. And let's not forget washing machines and labor-saving devices! They began as a means for commune members to have enough time for prayer and religious exercises.

Next Up: The "Hidden Gospels"

RK: Your next book, which should be available by the time *You Are Being Lied To* is out, is titled *Hidden Gospels: The Modern Mythology of Christian Origins*. What is the main theme/focus of this book?

PJ: Over the last 20 years or so, we've heard a lot about supposed "hidden gospels" which have been recently discovered, like the Gospel of Thomas, which turned up in Egypt in 1945. The common belief is that these texts contain lost or suppressed secrets about the "real" Jesus, and this theme shows up a lot in popular culture, in movies like *Stigmata*, even in *The X-Files*.

I am arguing that nothing about these "new" texts is likely to be accurate or authentic. They are much later and more derivative than many people think, and most of their ideas have been known by scholars at least for well over a century. As a constructionist, what I am doing is trying to understand how and why these myths developed about these amazing "hidden gospels," and I try and explain it in terms of power shifts in Christianity, the rise of feminist scholarship, changes in the universities, etc.

Who's Who in Hell

His Secular Holiness
Reveals the Hidden Legacy of Non-Belief
Interview with Warren Allen Smith

During my last semester in college, I took a course on science fiction. Early on, the guy beside me said that he was sickened to find out that Isaac Asimov was an atheist. He had been reading *Foundation* at the time, and when he discovered Asimov's beliefs, he quit reading the book and vowed never to read anything by the prolific science and science-fiction author again.

That knucklehead dropped out of the class soon afterwards, but my nameless former classmate came to mind recently. I'd really love to call him on his bluff. If he refuses to read a book because the author is a non-believer, then I assume he refuses to read all books by non-believers. On top of that, following this principle, he should never again listen to music, watch a movie, look at art, or use an invention that was created by a non-believer. "Fine," he might say, thinking this only rules out a few minor things. Actually, he wouldn't be able to read a lot of science fiction, including *Brave New World*, *2001: A Space Odyssey*, *Stranger in a Strange Land*, *The Hitchhiker's Guide to the Galaxy*, *The Handmaid's Tale*, or *Fahrenheit 451* (how appropriate). For that matter, he couldn't read *Tom Sawyer* or *Huckleberry Finn*, "Kublah Khan," *Robinson Crusoe*, *Oliver Twist*, *A Tale of Two Cities*, *Les Miserables*, *The Three Musketeers*, *The Great Gatsby*, *Ulysses*, *The Call of the Wild*, *Moby-Dick*, *Death of a Salesman*, *Winnie-the-Pooh*, "The Raven," *Frankenstein*, "Ode on a Grecian Urn," *Prometheus Unbound*, *The Grapes of Wrath*, *Walden*, *Candide*, *Slaughterhouse-Five*, *The Color Purple*, *Leaves of Grass*, "My Luve Is Like a Red, Red Rose," *Don Juan*, *For Whom the Bell Tolls*, or the poetry of William Wordsworth, Emily Dickinson, and E.E. Cummings. Naturally, he also couldn't watch movies based on any of these works.

Speaking of movies, he won't be able watch *The African Queen*, *The Godfather*, the first *Star Wars* trilogy, the *Superman* trilogy, the *Die Hard* series, *Butch Cassidy and the Sundance Kid*, *The Sting*, *One Flew Over the Cuckoo's Nest*, *The Shining*, *Jurassic Park*, *The Silence of the Lambs*, *Chinatown*, or any of the films of Charlie Chaplin, W.C. Fields, Ingmar Bergman, Marlene Dietrich, or Uma Thurman.

According to his own rules, he couldn't enter a building designed by Frank Lloyd Wright, attend a ballet starring Baryshnikov, or gaze at *The Thinker*, "*Whistler's Mother*," or the paintings of Delacroix, Picasso, Wyeth, and Frida Kahlo. He wouldn't be able to listen to the music of Beethoven, Brahms, Debussy, Haydn, Mahler, Mozart, Verdi, or Wagner, not to mention R.E.M., the Beatles, or, um, Barry Manilow.

> Mostly the uncomfortable fact that these achievers don't believe in a god or gods is conveniently overlooked.

He can't look at any pictures sent back from the Hubble telescope, go to a Barnum & Bailey Circus, fly in a hot-air balloon, drink pasteurized milk, or use the services of the Red Cross.

And he wouldn't be able to watch CNN or an Atlanta Braves game. Or the original *Twilight Zone* series. He'd better be using a Mac, because Windows and DOS—not to mention Word, Hotmail, and Internet Explorer—are all owned by an agnostic. Of course, he wouldn't need to use Internet Explorer, because he couldn't surf the Web, which is the creation of a Unitarian. Come to think of it, he can't use a telephone or incandescent lighting, either. On top of all that, he'd have to leave the US, whose principal founders were deists.

The point of my little thought exercise, of course, is that non-believers of all stripes—atheists, humanists, naturalists, agnostics, deists, transcendentalists, Unitarians, and other freethinkers—have contributed an awful lot to civilization. It's easy to overlook this fact, though, since the beliefs of many famous freethinkers are not widely known. Once in a while,

Who's Who in Hell
His Secular Holiness Reveals the Hidden Legacy of Non-Belief
Interview with Warren Allen Smith

371

one of them—such as John Lennon or Jesse Ventura—will cause a shit-storm by bashing religion, but mostly the uncomfortable fact that these achievers don't believe in a god or gods is conveniently overlooked. Except by Warren Allen Smith, who has spent over 50 years compiling information on non-belief. The fruits of this effort have finally been borne in the form of the gargantuan, cheekily-titled *Who's Who in Hell: A Handbook and International Directory for Humanists, Freethinkers, Naturalists, Rationalists, and Non-Theists*, from which I gleaned all of the above info. Cleverly designed to look like a standard *Who's Who* volume, this weighty tome is the

Friends have found that provisions written in some freethinkers' wills were not carried out, because their families were believers.

first large-scale effort to catalog information on non-belief in 50 years and just might be the largest ever. I interviewed the author via email in August 2000.

Russ Kick: You mentioned to me that Christians try to claim Charles Darwin as one of their own, to the point of burying him in Westminster Abbey. This hits on the topic of historical individuals whose belief systems have been lied about. Tell me a little about this regarding Darwin, as well as other non-believers whose belief systems have been posthumously "revised."

Warren Allen Smith: Darwin was clearly an agnostic. "For myself," he wrote, "I do not believe in any revelation. As for a future life, every man must judge for himself between conflicting vague probabilities." In my book I cite his son's account of the last moments: "He seemed to recognize the approach of death, and said, 'I am not the least afraid to die.' All the next morning he suffered from terrible nausea and faintness, and hardly rallied before the end came."

Who's Who in Hell is an A-to-Z listing of individuals who, over the centuries and all over earth, have not been attracted to the concept of a personal God.

As for any last-minute conversion, Francis Darwin told T.H. Huxley in 1887 that any such allegations were "false and without any kind of foundation," calling such stories "a work of imagination." He affirmed that his father died an agnostic. Of his sons, Sir Francis became a leading botanist, Sir George Howard a distinguished astronomer at Cambridge, and two

others became successful engineers. All, stated Joseph McCabe [one of the greatest, most prolific writer-scholars of freethought], were agnostics.

Off the top of my head, I only recall one deathbed conversion (although there must have been many more): novelist Kay Boyle's. In her final months the elderly writer of short stories was tenderly treated by a kindly monk, and she agreed to becoming a Catholic as a special favor to him. Her son, Ian Franckenstein, wrote me the details, however, and confirmed that her entire life had been lived as a non-believer.

Also, Sinclair Lewis was rumored to have converted, but his wife Dorothy Thompson and I could point to a 1950 postcard in which he wrote to me, "Just back from Italy. I find your letter. Yes, I think naturalistic humanism—with dislike for verbalistic philosophy—is my category."

Also, friends have found that provisions written in some freethinkers' wills were not carried out, because their families were believers.

RK: On a related note, we have a case in which an entire nation's religious heritage has been lied about. Christians insist that the United States is a Christian nation, but the facts don't bear this out. Please tell me about this.

WAS: In my book I show how the Founding Fathers, no longer agreeable to having King George III their spiritual head, came up with a deistic solution: a Constitution that separates church and state and favors no one church. To deny this is to admit one's pre-judging the facts.

RK: Who are some famous people of the past and present who most of us would probably be surprised to learn are non-believers?

WAS: At the end of the book, I include over a dozen pages which organize many of the listees by occupation. In parentheses are some who surprised me that they are agnostics,

Unitarians, rationalists, or some kind of freethinker: Actors (Charles Chaplin, George Clooney, Marlene Dietrich, Phyllis Diller, Carrie Fisher, Katharine Hepburn, Paul Newman, Jack Nicholson, Christopher Reeve, Peter Ustinov); anthropologists (Carleton Coon, Weston LaBarre, Richard Leakey, Bronislaw

My intent has been to name every freethinker I could find.

Malinowski); architects (Buckminster Fuller, Cesar Pelli, Frank Lloyd Wright); artists (Marie Bonheur, Lucian Freud, Henri Matisse, Pablo Picasso, Auguste Rodin, James Whistler, N. C. Wyeth); astronauts (R.M. Bonner; Yuri Gagarin, Robert Jastrow); astronomers (Alan Hale, Edmund Halley, Fred Hoyle, Edwin Hubble, Carl Sagan, Harlow Shapley); authors (two entire pages!). And that's just the A's!

Other extensive listings of occupations include biologists, business executives, critics, dancers, economists, educators, encyclopedists, explorers, feminists, historians, humorists, inventors, journalists, jurists, mathematicians, musicians, Nobel Prize winners (over 50 of them), philosophers, physicians, physicists, playwrights, poets, psychiatrists, publishers, reformers, revolutionaries, satirists, scholars, science fiction writers, scientists, sexologists, soldiers, statesmen, television producers, and zoologists.

RK: Tell me about your book.

WAS: *Who's Who in Hell* is an A-to-Z listing of individuals who, over the centuries and all over earth, have not been attracted to the concept of a personal God. Admittedly, they are in a minority now and have been over the ages.

Corliss Lamont's *The Philosophy of Humanism* lists some of the early freethinkers: Protagoras, the fifth-century BCE agnostic; Lucretius and Spinoza, the naturalists; and Epicurus, who neither believed that deities intervene in human affairs nor that there is an afterlife after death. Then Voltaire, the Encyclopedists, and the deists; Kant, Coleridge, Emerson, and the transcendentalists. And today there are the existentialists, pragmatists,

Theism admittedly has been more popular than non-theism. As a result, most people use words that, according to the Principle of Verifiability, rationalists say are meaningless. In short, if something cannot be verified, it is considered meaningless. It is easy to verify, for example, that Prague is not the capital of Czechoslovakia—no such nation now exists. But theists come up with meaningless, or unverifiable, concepts such as sin, grace, baptism, God, Christ, Heaven, atheism, angel, transubstantiation. Philosophers, on the other hand, speak of logic, ethics, morality, epistemology (the nature of knowledge), and naturalism (as opposed to supernaturalism).

In addition to listing over 10,000 freethinkers by name, the book also lists, again alphabetically, hundreds of subjects of interest to freethinkers. Cannibalism, for example, is related to Christian communion and therefore to theophagy (the eating of god). The book lists as many international freethought organizations as I could find, so by looking under Nepal or New York, one can locate humanist chapters, often with their officers and snail-mail or email addresses.

The 1,237-page tome weighs over six pounds. I like to point out that it's "bigger than the Holy Bible...and far funnier." For example, a "fairy" was once linguistically connected with the god that vanquished a demon, and the Celts shrank the old gods into fairies, brownies, or "little people." Today, I quote a wag who said, "Large numbers of fairies have been seen in the rest rooms of churches, libraries...and even skirting about in offices of the most prestigious philosophy departments." Footwashing is a rite for Christians, a fetish for freethinkers. Although both a lama and a llama are wooly, the latter is pronounced YAH-ma in Spanish and is not a "superior one," whereas the former "is neither a beast of burden nor a ruminant." The only humor I could find in the entire Holy Bible—this says much about people who are attracted to its contents—was the verse alluding to a geographical location, "And Noah looked from the ark and saw..."

Footwashing is a rite for Christians, a fetish for freethinkers.

secular humanists, and other non-theists. My intent has been to name every freethinker I could find, including officers of atheist and humanist chapters or staff members of freethought publications.

In 1990 when I purchased an Apple Macintosh computer, I started alphabetizing all this. A year ago, when I submitted the proposed manuscript to Beacon Press, Open Court, Prometheus Books, and the Rationalist Press in England, I

Who's Who in Hell
His Secular Holiness Reveals the Hidden Legacy of Non-Belief
Interview with Warren Allen Smith

373

got immediate rejections. But when I approached Lyle and Carol Stuart of Barricade Books, I was signed up almost immediately and was even allowed to edit my own work using their QuarkXPress.

Theists who have corresponded included Faith Baldwin, Paul de Kruif, Alan Dowling, E.L. Mayo, Reinhold Niebuhr, J.B. Priestley, Dorothy Sayers, Karl Shapiro, and Richard Wilbur. Although some non-theists advised me not to include them, I not only did but also in the handbook attempted to define

Counts, Norman Cousins, E.E. Cummings, John Dewey, Paul Edwards, Albert Ellis, Royston Ellis, James T. Farrell, Erich Fromm, Allen Ginsberg, Emily Hahn, Nat Hentoff, Julian Huxley, Horace Kallen, William Heard Kilpatrick, Paul Kurtz, Corliss Lamont, Sinclair Lewis, Walter Lippmann, Vashti McCollum, Archibald Macleish, Butterfly McQueen, Cesar Pelli, Charles Francis Potter, James Randi, Ned Rorem, Alan Ryan, Charles Smith, Gordon Stein, Rob Tielman, Norman L. Torrey, Sir Peter Ustinov, Gore Vidal, Kurt Vonnegut Jr., Eva Ingersoll Wakefield, Ibn Warraq, Glenway Wescott, William Carlos Williams, and Edwin H. Wilson.

> ## Playwright Arthur Miller, for example, when asked what kind of humanist he is, replied that it depends on the day.

some of the strange terminology used by theologians. Not many humanists, for example, are aware that a theologoumenon is a theological statement or concept that is an individual opinion, rather than authoritative doctrine. Or that theodicy refers to a defense of God's goodness and omnipotence in view of the existence of evil; if bad things occur, in other words, God may have done them to illustrate His mysterious ways—rationalists are more apt to spell the word "idiocy." In addition, I have defined philosophic terms for the average layman, terms such as epistemology, metaphysics, logical atomism, pragmatism, evolution, Darwinism, process philosophy, phenomenalism, instrumentalism, and realism.

The book challenges creationism, homophobia, anti-abortionism, anti-euthanasia, and hatred in general. It is science-, feminist-, gay-, and rationalism-friendly. As Paul Edwards, editor-in-chief of *The Encyclopedia of Philosophy* has already noted, "Religious fanatics will hate it."

Many people, I have found, do not like to be labeled. Playwright Arthur Miller, for example, when asked what kind of humanist he is, replied that it depends on the day. "I'd call myself a secular humanist, excepting when the mystery of life is overwhelming and some semi-insane directing force seems undeniable." Thomas Mann granted me the right to label him whatever I wished. "Humanism is the most precious result of rational meditation upon our existence and that of the world," wrote Albert Schweitzer, avoiding my question. Robert Frost simply told me his mother was a Swedenborgian.

RK: What about your own beliefs?

WAS: I personally was raised a Methodist, but upon leaving Iowa's Bible Belt for college I moved progressively from nihilism to agnosticism to deism to Emersonianism to pantheism to transcendentalism to the Unitarian humanism of the John H. Dietrich-Curtis W. Reese vintage to freethought to rationalism, and then to naturalistic humanism and secular humanism. As the result of my 50 years of research, I now feel more comfortable being described as a "humanistic naturalist," which implies

RK: I noticed that you've actually corresponded with many of the famous people covered in your book.

> ## For theists to accuse non-theists of being atheists is analogous to soccer players accusing baseball players of lacking goal posts.

WAS: While I was studying with Lionel Trilling at Columbia University in 1948, Thomas Mann wrote me his ideas about "humanism," and to my surprise I later talked with or received correspondence about humanism over the years from James Truslow Adams, Conrad Aiken, Van Meter Ames, Maxwell Anderson, Isaac Asimov, Margaret Bourke-White, Paul Cadmus, John Cage, Brock Chisholm, Sir Arthur C. Clarke, George

that naturalism (not supernaturalism) is paramount but that my inspiration (not in any way connected to spiritualism) comes from the humanities (music, art, novels, poetry, drama, essays).

For theists to accuse non-theists of being atheists is analogous to soccer players accusing baseball players of lacking goal posts. When asked if I am an a-theist, I can honestly respond that I am and also that I am an a-vegetarian, an a-Texan, and an a-transgendered person. In short, I am *not* many things, although it escapes me why anyone should be interested in what I am *not*.

During the past five decades I also have experienced being on Omaha Beach, rioting in June 1969 at the Stonewall Inn, teaching several thousand teenagers, founding the recording studio in which Liza Minnelli made her first demo record, cre-

Atheists, humanists, and all other freethinkers have never received good press, of course.

mating after our 40 years of companionship a Costa Rican lover who founded the studio with me, writing a syndicated column in West Indian journals, and publishing numerous materials for skeptics and freethinkers.

Do I go to church? No, but on my way to Omaha Beach I left Fort Knox long enough to join the Unitarian Society in Louisville, Kentucky. I have since been a Unitarian in Des Moines, Iowa; Cedar Falls, Iowa; Nassau County, New York; and Westport and Stamford, Connecticut. The present leader of the Fourth Universalist Society of New York, which I attend with my present lover, knows that as a member I am active in various freethought, non-theist, rationalist, and humanist groups. Anyone who does not know me very well probably thinks I'm a left-of-center liberal, and I would not initiate litigation if so accused.

RK: Who are some of your heroes?

WAS: Well, Bertrand Russell is high on the list. A.J. Ayer, Antony Flew, and David Hume all rejected the gods and held that we only die once. In Sir Bertrand's words, we become "food for the worms." Historian Priscilla Robertson, Bangladesh physician Taslima Nasrin (upon whose head the Muslim fundamentalists have placed a *fatwa*, so whoever assassinates her will achieve Allah's approval and gain entry to Paradise once they die), Susan B. Anthony, and Elizabeth Cady Stanton are also high, because they are activists, not just theorists. I also prize the close friendship of freethinkers such as Taslima Nasrin, anthropologist H. James Birx, editor Timothy Madigan, and economics professor Robert Shirley.

RK: What are some of your thoughts on religion?

WAS: Well-known and apparently rational individuals ironically use opposite facts to reach conclusions. The Pope and Mother Teresa "believe" in the Holy Bible, in the supernatural, and in life after death. Freethinkers by the thousands do not make such "leaps of faith," and others such as Christopher Hitchens find the "presumably virgin" Teresa egregiously evil because of her views on India's caste system, her holding that the Inquisition was right and Galileo was wrong, her having buddied with dictators, and her views on how to treat HIV by preaching penance through suffering. Readers of American journals exalt the Pope and Teresa, but in Sri Lanka the former was snubbed when he last visited, and the latter was described by rationalists in Calcutta as a Nobel Prize winner "who is not at all any better than all the other godmen and godwomen, because she helps to place a more kindly mask on the overall exploitation in our society."

As for "belief," entertainer Steve Allen makes the point that he does not "believe" that 2 + 2 = 4. He knows it. Rationalists tend to avoid using "belief" and any words which are theological inventions.

RK: Do you think non-belief will ever become more accepted? Can we ever expect to see an atheist president, for example?

WAS: According to Sir Arthur C. Clarke's *3001*, anyone showing symptoms of religiosity in the year 3001 will be sent to a booby hatch for observation. Meanwhile, so long as the Religious Wrong holds sway in the United States, I see no atheist becoming president for a long, long time. The present President of Brazil, Fernando Cardosa, I've just learned (too late to include him) is a non-believer.

Other contemporary non-believers who are statesmen or stateswomen are Ms. Shulamit Aloni in Israel, Manuel Avila Camacho (president of Mexico in the 1940s), Fidel Castro of Cuba (whom many humanists find inhumane), Dobrica Cosic (a former President of Yugoslavia and a signer of the Humanist Manifesto 2000), Senator Alan Cranston of California (who also signed the Humanist Manifesto 2000), William Hayden (a Governor General of Australia), Lionel Jospin (a French Prime Minister), Neil Kinnock (former member of Britain's House of Commons), Aleksander Kwasniewska (the atheistic politician in Poland who defeated Lech Walesa), Eliot Richardson (a Unitarian who has served in more Cabinet positions than any other person in US

Who's Who in Hell
His Secular Holiness Reveals the Hidden Legacy of Non-Belief
Interview with Warren Allen Smith

375

history), Simone Vail (who was President of the European Parliament), and Jesse Ventura (the Minnesota Governor who has said, "Organized religion is a sham and a crutch for weak-minded people who need strength in numbers. It tells people to go out and stick their noses in other people's business.").

What alarms me these days is how difficult it is to find disinterested facts and opinions. I have to read several newspapers, including my mainstay *The Economist*, to figure out what is really going on. Corporations swallow newspapers, book publishing concerns, Internet concerns, show-business organizations, television programs, and magazines, and as the global corporate influence grows, it is questionable who is behind what a person is seeing or reading.

story (August 14, 2000) complete with my caricature and a photo. CNN correspondent Jeanne Moos not only televised an interview but then followed it up wittily by going to St. Patrick's Cathedral and inquiring of parishioners on camera if they were aware of the book and what they thought about the title. Various radio talk-show hosts have interviewed me, and I am being asked to travel for book-signings around the country. *Publishers Weekly* came out with a 101% favorable review. I've frankly been overwhelmed by the praise but, realistically, am expecting the brickbats to follow.

The bottom line? What I hope to accomplish is to have written something that will be consulted for decades to come, to gain the recognition that the work is in a category with Pierre Sylvain Maréchal's *Dictionnaire des Athées* (1798), J.M.

Ted Turner may once have described Christianity as "a religion for losers," but where is this viewpoint dramatized, described, and written about by the mass media?

Atheists, humanists, and all other freethinkers have never received good press, of course. If tomorrow a VIP dies, cameras will pan in on the church ceremony, implying that death and organized religion are in cahoots (except that freethinker François Mitterand's funeral featured not only his non-belief but also his wife and his mistress; and Isaac Asimov's memorial at the New York Ethical Society and Carl Sagan's memorial at St. John's Episcopal Cathedral in New York City both cited their non-theism).

Ted Turner may once have described Christianity as "a religion for losers," but where is this viewpoint dramatized, described, and written about by the mass media? Usually, it's a story about a lesbian atheist who gives birth and the father is unknown.

RK: What reactions has your book gotten so far? What do you hope to accomplish with *Who's Who in Hell*?

WAS: Like Topsy, the book just grew, so I never compiled the work for money. It clearly has been a labor of love. I have already been interviewed by Brazilian, British, Ecuadorian, and Indian journalists—I am pleased that already it is considered a handy international reference book.

Frank DiGiacomo of the *New York Observer* wrote a page-one

Wheeler's *Biographical Dictionary of Freethinkers of All Ages and Nations* (1889), and Joseph McCabe's *Biographical Dictionary of Ancient, Medieval, and Modern Freethinkers* (1945). If this is accomplished, I will settle for having made a little footnote in the study of intellectual history.

Meanwhile, I'm happy to report that having long since discarded Heaven and Hell, I almost never experience hell in my personal relations and, in fact, am enjoying this moment's heaven.

BLINDED BY SCIENCE

Confession of an "AIDS Denialist"

How I Became a Crank Because We're Being Lied to About HIV/AIDS

Henry H. Bauer

For decades I had taken an interest in scientific unorthodoxies. I had written books about them.[1] I had learned from Bernard Barber[2] that scientists always vigorously resist the great discoveries—almost every nineteenth-century advance in understanding electricity, for example—before accepting them. I had learned from Gunther Stent[3] that some discoveries come "before their time" and are long ignored—Mendel's genetics, Wegener's continental drift. I had learned from Thomas Kuhn[4] that science progresses by paradigm shifts in which the old worldview is overturned by one that seemed heretical or incredible just before the revolution—light as particles, or quantum mechanics.

I also learned that the history of science is largely silent about all the claimed discoveries that turned out to be spurious. Most unorthodox claims come to naught in the end, and so they were very properly ignored or resisted.

> Geniuses are cranks who happen to be right, and cranks are geniuses who happen to be wrong, and they all behave in the same way.

I learned much about heretics. I learned that one cannot easily or quickly distinguish cranks from geniuses. Geniuses are cranks who happen to be right, and cranks are geniuses who happen to be wrong, and they all behave in the same way. They stubbornly believe themselves right, no matter what others think. They know that their discovery is the most important thing under the sun, and they believe everyone should appreciate that. They so misunderstand the ways of the world that they are their own worst enemies. They press their ideas in ways that give them the least possible chance of being taken seriously. Failing to get favorable attention from the experts, heretics often fall into the company of other people who have

ideas that everyone else thinks absurd. Finding appreciative attention there, the heretics come to see more and more substance in all those other rejected ideas; whereby, little by little, a perfectly competent scientist may become progressively more and more gullible, forgetting the necessity of always being critical, always skeptical, of always checking theories against facts.

I understood all that, yet still I found myself going the same way, becoming a crank.

■ ■ ■ ■ ■ ■ ■ ■ ■

Contrary to what just about everyone knows, HIV doesn't cause AIDS. Billions of dollars are being misspent on misguided research and misguided aid; untold thousands of well-intentioned people are misled and are actively misleading others; and, what most haunts me, healthy people (including babies) who test positive on an "HIV" test are being made unhealthy by toxic "antiretroviral" drugs.

Here's what made me a crank: fully believing that I had stumbled upon *the proof* that HIV doesn't cause AIDS; proof so absolutely clear and decisive that everyone who looks at it is bound to concede to it, yet at the same time a proof that everyone else had somehow been overlooking, even the many competent people who have been arguing for twenty years that HIV doesn't cause AIDS.

Shades of Immanuel Velikovsky. He was the first crank whose story I looked into in any detail. One day he had been struck by a stunning insight: The ancients had described, in masked fashion—in legends and myths about the gods—actual events they saw taking place in the skies. Being a psychoanalyst, Velikovsky could decode these stories. The Red Sea's parting was owing to a comet passing close to earth; so were the plagues of Egypt; and so on, and so forth. Velikovsky had uncovered the hidden, repressed memories that cause human beings to lapse into traumas and behave badly toward one another. He could correct ancient history and save the world from itself, through the obviously correct insights that had evaded everyone else.

To ignore us cranks is to go very sensibly with the overwhelming odds.

One day I was struck by a stunning insight: Data from HIV tests prove that HIV is not a sexually transmitted virus. Somehow, everyone else had overlooked this for twenty years. Yet the proof is so absolutely clear and decisive that everyone who looks at it is bound to agree.

All I had to do was to get people to pay attention.

When I shared my insights with the US Military HIV Research Program, they ignored me.

The Centers for Disease Control and Prevention were more courteous. They acknowledged the great time and effort I had put in, agreed that I had the data right, agreed that the trends I saw really are there—but insisted they are compatible with orthodox HIV = AIDS theory.

That was my first great surprise. I had expected to be told that I had the data wrong, or that there were other sources that vitiated the trends I thought I had seen. I had expected denial, stonewalling, not the defending of insupportable inferences. Yet I shouldn't have been surprised; that's par for the course. For reasons of human psychology and sociology and material self-interest, astronomers and other scientists didn't accept Velikovsky's insights. For reasons of human psychology and sociology and material self-interest, the HIV/AIDS Establishment couldn't accept my insights.

■ ■ ■ ■ ■ ■ ■ ■ ■

To doubt that HIV causes AIDS is not merely to doubt a claim made by a few clinicians; it's to deny the authority of the National Institutes of Health, the Centers for Disease Control and Prevention, the World Health Organization, UNAIDS, the World Bank, and other powerful organizations. It is to question pledges by governments to spend billions of dollars in the fight against HIV/AIDS in Africa. It is to threaten the research grants needed by innumerable individuals and coveted by innumerable institutions. It is to suggest that the host of AIDS charities have been misled and misguided—charities established, supported, and advertised by such celebrities as Princess Diana, Nelson Mandela, Bill Gates, Sir Elton John, and many others.

Those institutions and those eminences are not going to admit they've been wrong before they absolutely have to. You don't have to be a conspiracy buff to suspect that they will find all manner of ways to prevent it from happening.

Paranoia comes readily to us cranks. It's a well-earned paranoia, as a friend and colleague remarked recently in connection with how the media treat us. Tell someone—almost anyone—that HIV doesn't cause AIDS, and you're immediately and automatically labeled a kook, not to be taken seriously. I've understood that for a long time, of course, and the seemingly good and ample justification for it: Out of all the many such claims—pyramid power, homeopathy, extrasensory perception, etc., etc.—only a very few will ever turn out to have

My "Eureka!" moment, my *satori*, had been the realization that the argument over HIV/AIDS could be settled by looking solely at the epidemiology of positive HIV-tests—no need to get into intricate technicalities of molecular biology.

real substance to them; that's what the history of science teaches. To ignore us cranks is to go very sensibly with the overwhelming odds.

Understanding that, I had acknowledged it when I approached the Centers for Disease Control and Prevention and the Military HIV Research Program: I noted that this sort of communication, from someone not known to them and making so startling a claim, would normally be the sign of a crank; but, please, just look at the data.

Confession of an "AIDS Denialist"
How I Became a Crank Because We're Being Lied to About HIV/AIDS
Henry H. Bauer

379

I was telling them, in other words, "*I am not a crank.*" Just as convincing, no doubt, as when a president assured the nation, "I am not a crook."

I realized how unconvinced they were when I read that brief but courteous letter from the Centers for Disease Control and Prevention. I recognized the style, because I'd written letters like that myself, as editor of the *Journal of Scientific Exploration*, responding to obvious cranks who wanted their stuff published and for whom I felt sympathy—nice old fellows lapsing into their dotage who wanted to do something really important before they passed on. I had observed the syndrome years earlier. Analogous to the mid-life crisis, it's the end-of-career crisis. It's seen, for example, in those Nobel-winners who then behave like all-purpose world-saving gurus, the physicist who discovers eugenics and reinvents the old erroneous wheels, the professor not of biology or anthropology or medicine who comes up with a new theory of human social evolution. Less kindly, the phenomenon has been described not as the end-of-career crisis but as the "old-man last-gasp syndrome."

Why are male babies infected about 25 percent more often than female babies?

I had understood all this for quite a while, yet here I was, exemplifying it. Having been retired for half-a-dozen years, I had now achieved the most important, the most consequential insight of my life. I could set straight what thousands of others, tens of thousands, had gotten wrong.

■■■■■■■■

I'd been haranguing friends and acquaintances to look at the data, to read my analyses, to tell me where I'd gone wrong or where I was unconvincing. I couldn't help being surprised—even as I ought to have known better—when they didn't think it all that world-shattering. To them, after all, HIV/AIDS is just another tsunami, earthquake, massacre, famine—the sort of thing that goes on all the time in some other part of the world. AIDS is devastating Africa, not the United States—or at least here it only affects those "others" who don't behave as responsibly as we ourselves do.

■■■■■■■■

Cranks suffer from a lack of constructive critiquing. Every researcher and every writer soon learns to value disinterested criticism—it helps in avoiding error and in enhancing the persuasiveness of what one later publishes. Heretics receive at best only cursory comments, so what we then publish tends to be anything but professionally polished, and that provides yet further ready excuse for not taking us seriously.

We cranks are also pushed into presenting ourselves as know-it-alls. My "Eureka!" moment, my *satori*, had been the realization that the argument over HIV/AIDS could be settled by looking solely at the epidemiology of positive HIV-tests—no need to get into intricate technicalities of molecular biology. But as I sought reactions from various people, I was constantly asked, "But then what *does* cause AIDS? What *is* HIV? How could everyone have been so wrong for so long?"

Those are red herrings. They're beside the point. The data show conclusively that "HIV" is not sexually transmitted, and didn't spread from the AIDS epicenters. Case closed.

But those questions are red herrings only intellectually, whereas the task is a matter of psychology, of how to persuade people to shed their beliefs, preconceptions, prejudices. People who have imbibed the standard view of HIV/AIDS *cannot* accept my analysis of the data. That's what Kuhn meant by "incommensurability"—radically unorthodox claims are not even understood by those vested in the conventional wisdom. Psychology calls it "cognitive dissonance." In Festinger's classic study,[5] the beliefs of cult members grew stronger rather than weaker when evidence contradicted their belief.

So, in order to be persuasive, I prepared answers to those red-herring questions: I explained what HIV really is, what really causes AIDS, how everyone could indeed have been so wrong for so long. I've got an answer to everything, in other words. I present myself as not just an iconoclast on a single point—the epidemiology of HIV, showing it isn't sexually transmitted—I present myself as a know-it-all about matters of medicine and about the history and sociology of science and medicine. One of the marks of the crank that I had identified in the Velikovsky affair is the brazen willingness to speak like an expert in any number of disciplines. Now here I am, doing that myself.

■■■■■■■■

Yet it's not only the questions raised by individuals that make it necessary to offer answers to those red-herring questions, it's also in the nature of how science works. A theory is never abandoned just because of accumulated conundrums that it can't explain; change comes only when it's seen that an alternative theory does the job better. To displace current beliefs about HIV/AIDS, there has to be offered a comprehensive framework for explaining what AIDS is, what HIV is, and how a wrong interpretation came about and persisted for so long. One who seeks to displace the current theory *must* act as a know-it-all.

■ ■ ■ ■ ■ ■ ■ ■ ■

So there we are. I have to behave like a crank even though I recognize that's what I'm doing and how counterproductive that is. We cranks are *incurably* naïve: We believe that the truth speaks for itself, and that therefore the truth will out. No matter how much we know about the ways of human beings and human groups, we continue to regard self-interested behavior as aberrant instead of recognizing it as the norm. No matter how much we've learned about the other cranks who were sure they were right, each one of us knows that he is different, unique—*I* know I'm different, because unlike all those other cranks, I *really* am right.

■ ■ ■ ■ ■ ■ ■ ■ ■

Time to cut to the chase: Could I perhaps interest you in looking into the data I've put together, just looking at it? No obligation to think about it, or to comment, let alone to buy into it. (Though secretly I know, if I can just get you to look, you're bound to get hooked, just as I was.)

Here's just a taste.

Since 1985, tens of millions of HIV tests have been done, mostly on people not really thought to be at risk of infection: blood donors, military personnel, women giving birth, many others.

Whenever and wherever tests were done, anywhere in the US, some HIV-positive people were found. Not many, just a few in every thousand or every ten thousand or so. But all over the place. If HIV started out—as the experts tell us it did—in San Francisco and New York and Los Angeles no earlier than the 1970s, then it couldn't have become so widely distributed by

1985. That's not enough time for a sexually transmitted bug to go from ghettos of gay men in a few big cities to become so widespread that some teenage Army recruits, males and females equally, from all over the country, turn up infected. But that's what the facts are. Among teenage applicants for military service between 1985 and 1989, equal numbers of males and females tested positive. And yet AIDS victims then were 95 percent males.[6]

The sex ratio for "HIV infection" is nothing like that, rarely more than two men for each woman, 65 percent against 95 percent—among blood donors and Army recruits, at hospitals and clinics. Among young teenagers, "HIV"-positive females often outnumber the males.

Why is it that drug addicts who shared needles showed *less* infection than those who used clean needles—at the same clinics and in two countries?

How do babies get infected? Through their mothers, of course. But why are male babies infected about 25 percent more often than female babies?

Infection by HIV is supposed to be permanent. Once you've got it, you never get rid of it. The prevalence of HIV can't go down; it can only increase in the population, under the accepted view. Yet the data show that it *did* decrease during the 1980s, in every state and in every tested group—blood donors, active-duty soldiers, applicants for military service, members of the Job Corps, people tested at all sorts of public clinics.

Drug addicts typically have a high rate of testing "HIV"-positive. But among those who stopped taking drugs, the rate was lower; and it was lower the longer the tested group had been off drugs. How did they become disinfected?

Babies test "HIV"-positive about four to ten times more often than children between about one and teenage years. How do those babies become disinfected?

Why is it that drug addicts who shared needles showed *less* infection than those who used clean needles—at the same clinics and in two countries? And why did those who *smoked* crack cocaine have a higher level of infection than those who

Confession of an "AIDS Denialist"
How I Became a Crank Because We're Being Lied to About HIV/AIDS
Henry H. Bauer

381

injected cocaine? And why did those who injected cocaine show a higher level of infection than those who injected heroin, who in turn had a higher rate of infection than those who injected amphetamine? Does amphetamine sterilize the needles?

In June 2005, a press release from the Centers for Disease Control and Prevention announced that the number of HIV-infected Americans had surpassed a million "for the first time." But two decades earlier, in 1986, their estimate had been

Why would patients at TB clinics and at clinics for sexually transmitted diseases be equally infected with HIV? Why would psychiatric patients be even more infected?

between a million and a million-and-a-half, refined a few months later to between 945,000 and 1,410,000. Those are rather precise figures, so they must have been rather sure of them. In 1990, they estimated that about 1 million Americans were infected but that at the beginning of 1986 there had been only about 750,000. In 1993, the flagship journal *Science* gave the estimate of >1 million. Now, a dozen years later, here we were again at about 1 million…"for the first time"?!

Whichever way you look at it, this is not a spreading, increasing epidemic. The numbers of infected haven't changed appreciably. But neither have the hysteria and fear-mongering changed, the propaganda that insists everyone is at risk and that sex isn't safe.

Nothing about HIV makes sense if you regard it as a sexually transmitted infection. Why would patients at TB clinics and at clinics for sexually transmitted diseases be equally infected with HIV? Why would psychiatric patients be even more infected?

How could HIV have remained distributed around the United States in exactly the same way for 20 years? And why is it distributed like that, anyway—more prevalent in the Atlantic Coast and Southern regions than in North-Central locales? In every group—Army recruits, the Job Corps, women having children, people getting tested at all sorts of clinics! What's so specially dangerous sexually about the Southeast and the Atlantic Coast?

Why are Asians always less infected than white people, who

are always less infected than Latinos, who are always less infected than black Americans? No matter what group you look at—soldiers, sailors, Marines, blood donors, women who have just given birth—always that same sequence! What sort of virus discriminates by race?

The reason is *not* that the minorities have been so long discriminated against that sexual diseases are naturally more common among them. Native Americans, who have been discriminated against as much as anyone, are less infected than Latinos, and much less infected than black Americans.

And why are Latinos on the West Coast infected about as little as Anglo Americans, while on the East Coast they are infected nearly as much as black Americans?

■ ■ ■ ■ ■ ■ ■ ■

As I've confessed, I'm a crank; and another crank characteristic is that we can't stop talking. I said I was going to give a taste, and here I am, spilling bean after bean.

Please, do just look at the data. They are in articles in respectable, peer-reviewed journals and official reports from the Centers for Disease Control and Prevention and the Department of Defense, all unclassified, all no further away than an Internet terminal.[7]

Nothing about HIV makes sense if you regard it as a sexually transmitted infection.

But be warned: If you do look at the data, you may stop thinking I'm a crank. You'll be well on the way to becoming one yourself.

Endnotes

1. *Beyond Velikovsky: The history of a public controversy* (1984); *The enigma of Loch Ness: Making sense of a mystery* (1986); *Science or pseudoscience: Magnetic healing, psychic phenomena, and other heterodoxies* (1992); all from University of Illinois Press. **2.** Barber, Bernard. (1961). Resistance by scientists to scientific discovery. *Science* 134, pp 596–602. **3.** Stent, Gunther. (1972). Prematurity and uniqueness in scientific discovery. *Scientific American*, December, pp 84–93. **4.** Kuhn, Thomas S. (1970). *The structure of scientific revolutions.* Chicago: University of Chicago Press (2nd ed., enlarged; 1st ed. 1962). **5.** Festinger, Leon, Henry Riecken & Stanley Schachter. (1956). *When prophecy fails: A social and psychological study of a modern group that predicted the destruction of the world.* Minneapolis: University of Minnesota Press. **6.** All the following assertions are fully supported by original sources in the mainstream medical-scientific literature. Those sources are cited in Bauer, Henry H. (2007). *The origin, persistence and failings of HIV/AIDS theory.* Jefferson, NC: McFarland. See <failingsofhivaidstheory.homestead.com>. **7.** A large number of these sources is also cited in the book mentioned in the previous endnote.

You Are Still Being Lied To

NutraFear & NutraLoathing in Augusta, Georgia

Alex Constantine

Mr. X of Augusta, Georgia, is unable to discuss a death he witnessed inside a local processing plant because he signed a secrecy oath. His silence has nothing to do with protecting state secrets or the "sources and methods" of the CIA. He was coerced into signing the agreement because the manufacturer of a common "food additive" does not want the public to know it is a potent toxin.

Mr. X made the grave error of walking into Augusta's NutraSweet plant "without a 'space suit,'" says Betty Martini, an anti-aspartame activist in Atlanta. (Workers at the plant wear protective clothing.) "It almost completely destroyed his lungs. A man who entered the plant with him—also without a suit—dropped dead."

The company attempted to discredit Mr. X by publicly dismissing the death as alcohol-related. NutraSweet executives offered him a settlement if he signed a secrecy agreement. He turned them down. He was shadowed for two years by corporate spies. He went to a local television station. A pair of reporters taped the interview.

"A week later the reporters were fired and NutraSweet somehow obtained the tapes," Martini recalls. Mr. X signed the secrecy agreement "to prevent the persecution of friends at the plant. He has little lung function left and probably won't live long.[1]

"We're used to stories like this," she reports with a shrug.

The company often contracts work to local engineers to spare NutraSweet the public embarrassment of admitting there is a high mortality rate among employees. Trucks idling up with incoming cargo do not dock to unload; an employee drives the trucks in. Visitors to the complex must don protective clothing to avoid contact with lethal waste.

Exactly what is aspartame (commonly known by its brand name, NutraSweet)? The aspartame molecule has three components: aspartic acid, phenylalanine, and methanol amino acids swimming in petrochemicals. Searle, Inc.—the developer of aspartame—was founded in 1888 on Chicago's North side and is a mainstay of the domestic medical establishment. The company's products range from prescription drugs to advanced medical technology. And, formerly, artificial sweeteners. In 1983 Denise Ertell, a public affairs director at Searle, offered: "Phenylalanine is a fermentation byproduct of soybeans and corn, and aspartic acid is a total synthesis from hydrocarbons, petrochemical derivatives." A petrochemical, like gasoline.

Monsanto—until recently, the producer of NutraSweet—is one of the leading chemical manufacturers in the country, based in St. Louis. The company has contracted with the US government in the past to produce chemical warfare agents in collaboration with I.G. Farben, a cartel that supported the rise of the Nazi Party under Hitler and manufactured Zyklon B, the gas used to decimate much of Europe's Jewish population. Another bridge to Farben and the Nazis was Monsanto's acquisition of American Viscose in 1949—20 years earlier, the US Commerce Department identified this company as a

"It is a powerful metabolic poison," Martini laments, "a witch's brew of breakdown products."

Fascist front. Monsanto's board of directors has long included officials of the CIA. The company claims on its website that their concoction is "made from peaches."

"It is a powerful metabolic poison," Martini laments, "a witch's brew of breakdown products. The methanol—wood alcohol—converts to formaldehyde and finally formic acid (ant sting poison). The breakdown product of diketopiperazine, DKP, is a tumor agent.

"I was lecturing one afternoon on NutraSweet," Martini recalls, "and a gentleman in the audience stood up and said he had prepared legal papers for a man who was killed at the plant. 'The papers are sealed,' he told me. 'I can't find anything out and it does no good to ask. That product is a poison.'"[2]

Many medical activists have arrived at the same conclusion. *Prescription for Nutritional Healing*, by James and Phyllis Balch, lists aspartame under the "Chemical Poison" category. Dr. Russell L. Blaylock, a professor of neurosurgery at the Medical University of Mississippi, drew upon some 500 scientific references to demonstrate, in *Excitotoxins: The Taste That Kills*, how a surplus of free excitatory amino acids, such as aspartic and glutamic acids, results in serious chronic neurological damage and a score of adverse reactions.

Dr. Walton wrapped up: "Individuals with mood disorders are particularly sensitive to this artificial sweetener; its use in this population should be discouraged."

Dr. Ralph G. Walton conducted an independent, double-blind study of subjects with mood disorders in 1993. NutraSweet Co. stonewalled, refusing to sell Dr. Walton the aspartame needed for his study. He was forced to turn elsewhere for the supply. He noted a sharp rise in symptoms among volunteers on aspartame. Some of the side-effects were so severe that the Institutional Review Board terminated the research project to safeguard the health of test subjects—three of whom complained they'd been "poisoned." Martini: "One [subject] was bleeding from the eyes (conjunctival bleeding) and one had a retinal detachment, common with aspartame."[3] Dr. Walton wrapped up: "Individuals with mood disorders are particularly sensitive to this artificial sweetener; its use in this population should be discouraged."[4]

"The Pepsi Generation is ill," says Carol Guilford, author of *The New Cookie Cookbook* and *Carol Guilford's Main Course Cookbook*. "Aspartame poisoning mimics MS [multiple sclerosis] and rheumatoid arthritis. Fibromyalgia is a catchall term for the excruciating joint pain endured when aspartame dries up the lubricating synovial fluid and turns the joints into plastic."[5]

Monsanto spokesmen swear the sweetener is no more toxic than a glass of orange juice: "The overwhelming body of scientific evidence establishes that aspartame is not associated with side effects. Specific research has been conducted in each of these areas. The results support the safety of NutraSweet brand sweetener," the company boasts.[6] On September 13, 1995, a Congressional environmental committee reported that of all food additive complaints filed with the FDA, "more than 95 percent have been about two products: the sweetener aspartame and sulfite preservatives. No firm evidence exists to prove that aspartame actually causes many adverse reactions."[7] This is dangerous rhetoric, obscuring the risks not only of aspartame, but also of scores of drugs allowed on the market by the Food and Drug Administration.

In February 1994, one study reported that 51 percent of all drugs approved by the agency had serious or fatal side effects.[8] But the FDA has received more complaints of aspartame poisoning than all other food additives combined, about 75 percent. In 1995 the FDA tabulated 10,000 consumer complaints, listing 92 documented symptoms, including death—so many, incidentally, that the FDA pulled the plug on its complaint lines and referred complainants to the AIDS Hotline.[9]

NutraSweet is an addictive drug. At its inception, scientists for Searle acknowledged that it was a drug (corporate revisionists have labeled it a "food additive"). Martha M. Freeman, M.D., from the FDA division of metabolic and endocrine drug products, wrote in an August 20, 1973, memo to Dr. C. J. Kokost, division of toxicology:

Conclusion:

1. The administration of aspartame, as reported in these studies at high dosage levels for prolonged periods, constitutes clinical investigational use of a NEW DRUG SUBSTANCE.

2. The information submitted for our review is inadequate to permit a scientific evaluation of clinical safety.

Recommendations:

1. An IND (notice of claimed investigations [exemption for a new drug]) should be filed, to include all required manufacturing controls, pharmacology and clinical information.

2. Marketing for use as a sweetening agent should be contingent upon satisfactory demonstration of clinical safety of the compound...

A quarter-century later, the complaints that have come Betty Martini's way are a grim commentary on the FDA's "regulatory" integrity. ("The FDA conveniently puts death in their report under 'symptoms,'" she points out, aghast):

William Reed, Pullman, Michigan:

I'm a diabetic. I used Equal in my coffee, a lot of diet soft drinks, and NutraSweet in many foods. I started having headaches all the time...seizures, up to eight seizures, one right after the another. I couldn't sleep, my mouth was dry all the time. I had sores on my tongue, I started having trouble with my memory. I had muscle spasms in my legs almost every night which cause my legs to be sore all day long, and my back was sore from seizures...

Alicia Morris, Doraville, Georgia:

I'm a 29 year old athletic female.... I began using it in the spring of 1990, and soon afterwards my condition began to deteriorate.... My eyesight began to fade until I was almost blind in one eye. Next my hearing became dull and my legs, feet and torso lost sensation and became numb...

Mark Motluck, Chicago, Illinois:

My wife wrote to you last year (Kelli Motluck). She told you her story about her use of aspartame and the subsequent onset of brain tumors. She died on April 21, 1998 at the age of 37. She left behind a grieving husband and an eight-year-old daughter. Our lives will never be the same. Tonight, the Chicago NBC affiliate ran a story on the ten o'clock news about the controversy surrounding aspartame. A spokesman for Monsanto spewed their garbage about aspartame's safety and the like. Fortunately, the reporter also mentioned that every report which showed aspartame as being safe to use was funded directly by Monsanto. Quite a coincidence. The FDA refused to comment, which is no surprise either.

And it's not as though the marketers of aspartame are insensible to the side effects despite 20 years of specious denials. (Monsanto: "Formaldehyde has been implicated as a possible carcinogen when inhaled, but this hasn't been shown to be the case when it's taken by mouth..."). Jonathan Leake, science editor of the London Times, reported in February 2000 that a suppressed report written in the early 1980s by researchers for the National Soft Drink Association (NSDA) "condemned" NutraSweet as a "dangerous" and "potentially toxic" neurochemical.

The FDA has received more complaints of aspartame poisoning than all other food additives combined, about 75 percent.

The same soda bottlers who suppressed the report on aspartame "now buy tons of it to add to diet drinks." They were warned at the outset that aspartame "can affect the workings of the brain, change behavior and even encourage users to eat extra carbohydrate, so destroying the point of using diet drinks. The documents were unearthed last week under freedom of information legislation. It follows a decision by researchers at King's College in London to study suspected links between aspartame intake and brain tumors." The NSDA's own scientific advisors stated, "We object to the approval of aspartame for unrestricted use in soft drinks." Their 30-page report listed the means by which aspartame was believed to affect brain chemistry directly, including the synthesis of serotonin and other crucial neurotransmitters. "Other papers obtained with the NSDA documents show the Food and Drug Administration also had misgivings. Despite this, it approved aspartame."[10]

"Coke knew," Martini observes, "and knowing, broke their good faith contract with customers, a breach exhibited by the recent plot to program vending machines to raise the price with the temperature. Dissatisfied with selling flavored sugar water plus phosphoric acid, they switched to pushing an addictive formula called 'Diet.' Addictive substances multiply markets, so Diet Coke soared off the sales charts."

Aspartame has become a staple of the American diet. And yet flies won't touch it, as a health columnist at the Boston Globe reported:

Q. Are insects attracted to artificial sweeteners as much as to sugar? —J.M., Boston

A. Linda Kennedy, assistant professor of physiology at Clark University in Worcester, says her studies indicate that flies have no reaction to aspartame, the basic ingredient in NutraSweet, although they are attracted to sugar. For more information on this tasty subject, she suggests you read Vincent Dethier's The Hungry Fly, published by the Harvard University Press in 1976.[11]

NutraFear & NutraLoathing in Augusta, Georgia
Alex Constantine

NutraDeath Comes for Santiago

The same lobbying group, the NSDA, now insists that aspartame is safe. So how, many consumer activists wonder, to account for the Niagara of complaints pouring into the FDA, the blindings, neurological symptoms, the abrupt rise in chronic fatigue, the headaches and memory loss—the swollen desk reference of adverse reactions associated with aspartame?

The most extreme case histories are warning flares in the night, sporadically reported by the corporate press. A rare exception was Janet Soto of Brooksville, Florida, who recently appeared on a local television news program to accuse the NutraSweet company of responsibility for her father-in-law's gradual decline.

The victim, Santiago "Chago" Echiverria, struggled with diabetes for fifteen to twenty years. Upon his retirement from the railroad, he moved from Ashtabula, Ohio, to Puerto Rico, where he continued his habitual swigging of diet cola and copious intake of coffee sweetened with Equal.

When Soto received word of Echiverria's death in June of 1994, she and her husband made arrangements to fly to Puerto Rico for the wake. The funeral director informed them that a surfeit of formaldehyde in the body made it necessary to close the casket.

The putrid chemical seeped through the cadaver's skin.

"His sisters, Minerva Ortiz and Nydia Colon, told me that the funeral director said he had never seen a body deteriorate as quickly, and was puzzled by the formaldehyde content even before embalming," Soto says. [12]

In a letter to Mission Possible, a registered nurse in Florida tells her own grim horror story of formaldehyde poisoning—diagnosed as the cause of death of a patient—from daily aspartame use. A physician at the hospital learned that the deceased had stored cases of diet drinks in his garage, and was poisoned by the petrochemical byproducts of heated aspartame released in the cola.

"The formaldehyde stores in fat cells," Martini explains. "Some undertakers tell me that bodies sometimes come to them reeking of formaldehyde." The chronic ingestion of formaldehyde at very low doses has, according to medical activist Mark Gold, "been shown to cause immune system and nervous system changes and damage as well as headaches, general poor health, irreversible genetic damage and a small medical grimoire of severe health problems. One experiment (Wantke, 1996) showed that chronic exposure to formaldehyde caused systemic health problems (i.e., poor health) in children at an air concentration of only 0.043–0.070 parts per million. Obviously, chronic exposure to an extremely small amount of formaldehyde is to be avoided. Even if formaldehyde adducts did not build up in the body from aspartame use, the regular exposure to excess levels of formaldehyde would still be a major concern to independent scientists and physicians familiar with the aspartame toxicity issue." [13]

Aspartame is a drug. It interacts with other drugs, alters dopamine levels and can cause birth defects. It has been known to trigger seizures. [14]

Nevertheless, as the tobacco industry soft-peddles the hazards of smoking, so do NutraSweet executives insist that

> Aspartame has become a staple of the American diet. And yet flies won't touch it.

aspartame is safely absorbed. But intake standard comparisons alone write another commentary: The EPA safety standard for methanol intake is 7.8 mg a day. A liter of diet soft drink contains 550 mg of aspartame, 55 mg of methanol.15 The methanol ingested by heavy consumers could easily exceed 250 mg daily—32 times the FDA's suggested limit.

The late Dr. Morgan Raiford, a specialist in methanol toxicity, circulated a fact sheet in 1987 deploring the sweetener's adverse effects on eyesight and the central nervous system. He found "toxic reactions in the human visual pathway, and we are beginning to observe tragic damage to the optic nerve, blindness, partial to total optic nerve atrophy. Once this destructive process has developed there is no visual restoration." (Mission Possible refers patients going blind on aspartame to the National Eye Research Foundation, a diagnostic lab outfitted to detect toxic reactions to methanol.) He described a second side effect "related to phenylalanine levels in the central nervous system…. Over the past year the writer has observed the fact that any portion of the central nervous system can and is affected." The chemical feast caused "sensations of dullness of the intellect, visual shadows, evidence of word structure reversing and some hearing impairment. This can and will in time cause problems in learning." [16]

Lennart Hardell, M.D., Ph.D., in 1999 reported in Sweden that both cell phone use and heavy aspartame use correlate with increased brain cancers.[17] Normally, the blood/brain barrier shields the user from excess aspartate and accompanying toxins—but is not fully developed during childhood, so the young are particularly at risk. Further, it does not fully protect all areas of an adult brain, so damage with chronic use is a distinct possibility. The barrier allows seepage of excess glutamate and aspartate into the brain even when intact, and gradually destroys neurons. Most of the neural cells, better than 75 percent, in one area of the brain are depleted before clinical symptoms of chronic disease are detectable. Some of the many illnesses attributable to long-term exposure to excitatory amino acid damage include MS, Lou Gehrig's Disease, memory loss, hormonal problems, hearing loss, epilepsy, Alzheimer's, Parkinson's Disease, hypoglycemia, AIDS dementia, brain lesions, and neuroendocrine disorders.[18]

Laboratory rats turn their noses up to any food with aspartame in it. Yet every single morning, millions wake up to a steaming cup of coffee, RNA derivatives, and petrochemicals.

Pass the ant poison, please. Splash of formic acid?

Endnotes

1. Betty Martini, Mission Possible, private correspondence forwarded to author, July 9, 1996. **2.** Martini, correspondence with author, July 9, 1996. **3.** Martini, letter to Robert Cohen, August 30, 1996. **4.** Ralph G. Walton, et al, "Adverse Reactions to Aspartame: Double-Blind Challenge in Patients from a Vulnerable Population," *Biological Psychiatry*, 1993:34: 13–17. **5.** Carol Guilford, "No Hoax, Crime of the Century," Internet posting. **6.** Company public relations release. **7.** Committee for the National Institute for the Environment, "Food Additive Regulations: A Chronology," Congressional Research Service, Updated Version, September 13, 1995. **8.** See *Omni* magazine, February 1994. **9.** Martini correspondence. **10.** Jonathan Leake, "Top sweetener condemned by secret report," *London Times*, February 27, 2000. **11.** *Boston Globe*, July 16, 1988. **12.** Janet Soto, letter to Martini, April 3, 1995. **13.** Mark D. Gold, "Scientific Abuse in Methanol/Formaldehyde Research Related to Aspartame," <www.holisticmed.com/aspartame/abuse/methanol.html>. **14.** *Ibid.* **15.** Dr. H.J. Roberts in a letter to Martini. Also see, H.J. Roberts, *Aspartame: NutraSweet, Is It Safe?* (Charles Press). **16.** "Nutrasweet Factsheet," original in possession of the author. **17.** <www.medscape.com/MedGenMed/braintumors>. **18.** Life Sciences Research Office, FASEB, "Safety of Amino Acids," FDA Contract No. 223-88-2124, Task Order No. 8.

Forbidden Archaeology
Michael A. Cremo

A couple of years ago, in the middle of my talk about my book *Forbidden Archeology* to students and professors of earth sciences at the Free University of Amsterdam, a professor stood up and said, "What you say is all very interesting, but how can we accept something that goes against what thousands of archaeologists and geologists and other scientists are telling us?"

Forbidden Archeology documents evidence for extreme human antiquity. Actually, over the past 150 years archaeologists have found abundant evidence showing that human beings like ourselves have existed for hundreds of millions of years. This evidence, practically unknown to both scientists and members

> Over the past 150 years archaeologists have found abundant evidence showing that human beings like ourselves have existed for hundreds of millions of years.

of the public, radically contradicts the picture of human origins that is presented to us by Darwin's modern followers, who say that we evolved fairly recently—within the past 100,000 years or so—from some more apelike ancestors.

So the professor was correct. I was indeed asking my audience to consider something that goes against what all the conventional experts are saying.

"You know," I responded, "it must have been quite interesting to have been a Darwinist in 1860, when hardly anyone accepted it. Even though I disagree with the Darwinists, I have a lot of respect for the early ones, because it must have taken a considerable amount of courage to stand up for Darwinism in the face of heavy opposition and disagreement from what was then the scientific establishment."

I then added, "I am especially surprised to hear such an objec-

tion from you, because Dutch scholars have an historic reputation for intellectual independence, and now you are saying that we can only accept ideas that have already been endorsed by thousands of experts."

At that point, sensing that the mood of the audience was against him, the professor bravely said, "I can also stand up against thousands," and sat down.

I returned to the Netherlands for another series of lectures to students and professors of archaeology, anthropology, and biology at the universities of Amsterdam, Utrecht, Leiden, Groningen, and Nijmegen, among others. After the lectures, during the question sessions, there were many kinds of reactions from my listeners. Sometimes they were shouting at me; sometimes they sat in shocked silence, not knowing what to say or think; sometimes they asked deep questions about the nature of our knowledge of humankind's hidden history.

Yes, the audiences were tough, unsympathetic, and skeptical, but that is to be expected when you present ideas as radical as mine. Nevertheless, despite all this, I did win some admissions that the case I was presenting was interesting, well-argued, and worthy of serious consideration. This reaction mirrors that of the scientific world in general, where *Forbidden Archeology* has attracted a great deal of attention. The book has been reviewed in most of the major journals of archaeology, anthropology, and history of science, not always unfavorably. I have also had the chance to speak about the book at international conferences, such as the World Archaeological Congress, held in New Delhi in 1994, the Twentieth International Congress for the History of Science, held in Liege in 1997, the World Archaeological Congress, held in Cape Town in 1999, and the European Association of Archaeologists annual meeting, held in Bournemouth, England, in 1999.

Not all of my audiences in the Netherlands were unsympathetic. I spoke about *Forbidden Archeology* at a lecture in Amsterdam organized by Herman Hegge of the Frontier Sciences Foundation, which publishes the bimonthly Dutch-language journal *Frontier 2000*. I also had the chance to talk to Theo Paijmans and his listeners on Talk Radio 1395 AM (Theo's show, *Dossier X*, focuses on scientific anomalies). But although I do like to speak to people who are already inclined to agree with me, I especially enjoy attempting to change the minds of people who are not so inclined.

My research into humanity's hidden history was inspired by my study of the ancient Sanskrit writings of India, collectively known as the Vedas. Among these Vedic writings are the Puranas, or histories, which tell of human civilizations existing on this planet for tens of millions, even hundreds of millions of years. My interest in India's Vedic writings is more than intellectual. For 25 years, I have been practicing the *bhakti* (devotional) school of Indian spirituality as a member of the International Society for Krishna Consciousness. Sometimes people are surprised to learn that the gray-haired person of over 50 years of age, lecturing before them in suit and tie, is a member of what is popularly known as the Hare Krishna movement. But indeed I am, and during my stay in Amsterdam, I took the chance to join the young local members in one of their Thursday evening chanting processions through the shopping streets of the city center. This clash of images—science and street religion—is nothing new. For ages, the *bhakti* tradition in India has always been a mixture of two seemingly contradictory elements—the emotional expression of *bhakti* through public chanting and profoundly deep scholarship.

One thing that such scholarship reveals is that time proceeds in cycles rather than in linear fashion. According to the Puranas, the basic unit of these time cycles is the day of Brahma, which lasts 4.3 billion years. The day of Brahma is followed by the night of Brahma. During the day of Brahma life is manifest, and during the night of Brahma life is not manifest. If we consult the ancient Sanskrit calendar of cosmic time, we learn that we are about two billion years into the current day of Brahma.

Now let's imagine that we have a "Vedic archaeologist." Based on the information given above, he or she would expect to see signs that living things have been present on earth for about two billion years. Interestingly enough, modern science says that the oldest signs of life on earth do indeed go back two or even three billion years. These signs of life include fossils of algae and other single-celled creatures. But our Vedic archaeologist would not be surprised to also find signs of more advanced life forms, including the human form. A conventional archaeologist, however, would not expect to find any such thing. According to conventional views, human beings like ourselves have appeared fairly recently on earth, within the last 100,000 years or so.

Taking all this into consideration, our Vedic archaeologist would make two predictions: First, scientists digging into the earth should find signs of a human presence going back hun-

In other words, if the facts do not agree with the favored theory, then such facts, even an imposing array of them, must be discarded.

dreds of millions of years. Second, this evidence will largely be ignored because it radically contradicts the ideas of human origins currently held by the scientific community.

This leads us the concept of what I call the knowledge filter. The knowledge filter represents the dominant ideas of the scientific community regarding human origins and antiquity. Evidence that conforms to these ideas passes easily through the filter. Evidence that varies slightly from these ideas may pass through the filter with some difficulty. But evidence that radically contradicts these dominant ideas will not pass through the filter. Such evidence is forgotten, set aside, or, in some cases, actively suppressed.

The existence of the knowledge filter is something that scientists themselves will admit. When archaeologist Wil Roebroeks of the University of Leiden visited me in Amsterdam, we had a long talk about it, and he shared with me some of his own personal experiences with knowledge filtration in treatment of evidence for the earliest occupation of Europe, particularly northern Europe. Of course, it goes without saying that I think the filter operates differently and to a greater extent than he would accept. For example, Roebroeks thinks the filter operates to unfairly include evidence for a very early occupation, whereas I believe it operates to unfairly exclude it.

Forbidden Archaeology
Michael A. Cremo

In *Forbidden Archeology,* I document two things:

1. Hundreds of cases of scientifically-reported evidence for extreme human antiquity, consistent with the account of human origins given in the ancient Sanskrit writings of India.

2. The process by which this evidence has been filtered out of normal scientific discourse.

Let's now look at some particular cases.

In the last century, gold was discovered in the Sierra Nevada mountains of California, and miners came from all over the world to extract it. At first they simply took the gold from streams, but afterwards they began to dig mines into the sides of mountains. Inside the tunnels where they were digging into solid rock, the miners found human skeletons, spear points, and numerous stone tools. These finds occurred at many different locations. One of them was Table Mountain in Tuolumne County, California.

According to modern geological reports, the rock in which the miners found the bones and artifacts at Table Mountain is about 50 million years old. Our Vedic archaeologist would not be surprised at this. But our conventional archaeologist would be very surprised, because his textbooks say that no humans (or even apemen) existed at that time.

The California discoveries were very carefully documented and reported to the scientific world by Dr. J. D. Whitney, a geologist for the state of California. His work (*The Auriferous Gravels of the Sierra Nevadas*) was published by Harvard University in 1880. So why do we not hear anything about these discoveries today?

Whitney's work was dismissed by Dr. William H. Holmes, a very influential anthropologist who worked at the Smithsonian Institution in Washington, D.C. He said in the Smithsonian Institution's annual report for 1898–99: "Perhaps if Professor Whitney had fully appreciated the story of human evolution as it is understood today, he would have hesitated to announce the conclusions formulated [that humans existed in very ancient times in North America], notwithstanding the imposing array of testimony with which he was confronted." In other words, if the facts do not agree with the favored theory, then such facts, even an imposing array of them, must be discarded. This is a good example of the operation of the knowledge filter.

And the knowledge filtration process continues to influence the California gold mine discoveries even today. I appeared on a television show called *The Mysterious Origins of Man,* produced by BC Video and broadcast by NBC, the largest television network in the United States. This show was based in part on my book *Forbidden Archeology.* The show also featured the work of other researchers who challenge the current ideas of human prehistory.

Among them was Graham Hancock, author of *Fingerprints of the Gods.* Graham and his wife Santha stopped to visit me in Los Angeles, on their way to Japan, where they were going to investigate some underwater pyramids, *apparently* of human construction. In the course of our conversation, we agreed that a lot of the really exciting scientific research is going on outside the normal channels.

In any case, when the producers were filming *The Mysterious Origins of Man*, I asked them to go to the museum of natural history at the University of California at Berkeley, where the California gold mine artifacts are stored.

The producers asked the museum officials for permission to film the artifacts. The museum officials, assuming that the producers were working on a tight deadline, said they could not bring out the objects on short notice. The producers then explained that they had six months time to finish their work. The museum officials then said they had another problem—a shortage of staff and money. They would have to pay their workers "overtime" to bring out the objects and could not afford to do it. The producers replied that they would pay the museum workers any amount of money required. But at that point the museum officials simply said they were not going to bring out the artifacts for filming. Finally, the producers just used some nineteenth-century photographs of the objects in the show.

When the show finally aired in February 1996, it inspired extreme reactions from the orthodox scientific community in

> At that point the museum officials simply said they were not going to bring out the artifacts for filming.

the United States. This was the first time that a major American television network had ever broadcast a show that seriously questioned the Darwinian account of human origins.

Why was the scientific community so angry? One reason is they did not like anti-Darwinian ideas reaching American schoolchildren through the popular medium of television. The president of the National Center for Science Education, as reported in the journal *Science,* complained that after *The Mysterious Origins of Man* was broadcast, the phones in his organization's headquarters were ringing constantly. Science teachers from all over the country were calling, saying that their students who saw the show were asking them difficult questions. Meanwhile, on the Internet, scientists wondered what effect such television programs might eventually have on government funding for certain kinds of scientific research.

Most of the opposition to the program came from what I call the fundamentalist Darwinian group within the scientific community. This group adheres to Darwinism more out of ideological commitment than scientific objectivity. If this group was disturbed when NBC showed *The Mysterious Origins of Man* in February 1996, they became even more disturbed when they learned that NBC was going to show it again, despite their protests. After the show aired the second time, Dr. Allison R. Palmer, president of the Institute for Cambrian Studies, sent an email message (dated June 17, 1996) to the Federal Communications Commission (FCC) of the United States government, asking the FCC to punish NBC for showing the program to the American people. This letter was circulated on scientific discussion groups by Dr. Jere Lipps, a paleontologist at the University of California at Berkeley, in order to generate more pressure from scientists on the FCC. Palmer and his supporters wanted the FCC to censure NBC for showing the program, compel NBC to repeatedly broadcast a public apology, and compel NBC to pay a substantial fine. Fortunately, this effort did not succeed.

What all this shows is that science does not always operate according to its high ideals. The way science works, we are normally told, is on the basis of free and open discussion of evidence and ideas. But in the case of *The Mysterious Origins of Man,* we see elements of the scientific community restricting access to evidence and preventing open discussion of it. Yes, there is in fact a knowledge filter. I have fully documented the

reactions to *The Mysterious Origins of Man,* along with other reactions to *Forbidden Archeology,* in a book titled *Forbidden Archeology's Impact.*

Now let's consider a case from the more recent history of archaeology. In 1979, Mary Leakey found dozens of footprints at a place called Laetoli, in the East African country of Tanzania. She said that the footprints were indistinguishable

Scientists who find things that should not be found sometimes suffer for it professionally.

from those of modern human beings. But they were found in layers of solidified volcanic ash that are 3.7 million years old. According to standard views, humans capable of making such prints should not have existed that long ago. So how do scientists explain the Laetoli footprints?

They say that there must have existed in East Africa 3.7 million years ago some kind of apeman who had feet just like ours. And that is how the footprints were made. That is a very interesting proposal, but unfortunately there is no physical evidence to support it. Scientists already have the skeletons of the apemen who existed 3.7 million years ago in East Africa. They are called *Australopithecus*, and their foot structure was quite different from that of a modern human being.

This question came up when I was speaking at the World Archaeological Congress in Cape Town, South Africa. Also speaking there was this scientist, Ron Clarke. In 1998, Clarke discovered a fairly complete skeleton of *Australopithecus* at a place called Sterkfontein, in South Africa. This discovery was widely publicized all over the world as the oldest human ancestor. It was 3.7 million years old, the same age as the Laetoli footprints. But there was a problem.

Clarke reconstructed the foot of his Sterkfontein *Australopithecus* in an apelike fashion, as he should have, because the foot bones were quite apelike. For example, the big toe is very long and moves out to the side, much like a human thumb. And the other toes are also quite long, about one and a half times longer than human toes. Altogether the foot was not very humanlike. So after Clarke gave his talk, I raised my hand and asked a question: "Why is it that the foot structure of your Sterkfontein *Australopithecus* does not match the footprints found by Mary Leakey at Laetoli, which are the same age, 3.7 million years old, but which are just like those of modern humans?" You see what the problem was for him. He was claiming to have the oldest human ancestor, but there is evidence from elsewhere in Africa that human beings like us were walking around at the exact same time. So how did he answer my question? He said that it was his *Australopithecus* who made the Laetoli footprints, but he was walking with his big toes pressed close in to the side of the foot, and with his other toes curled under. I did not find that to be a very satisfactory explanation.

Scientists who find things that should not be found sometimes suffer for it professionally. One such scientist is Dr. Virginia Steen-McIntyre, an American geologist whom I know personally.

In the early 1970s, some American archaeologists discovered stone tools and weapons at a place called Hueyatlaco, in Mexico. They included arrowheads and spear points. According to archaeologists, such weapons are made and used only by humans like us, not by apemen.

At Hueyatlaco, the artifacts were found in the bottom layers of the trenches. Of course, the archaeologists wanted to know how old the objects were. So when archaeologists want to know how old something is, they call in some geologists because the geologists will be able to tell them, "The layer of rock in which you found these objects is so-and-so thousand years old." Among the geologists who came to date the site was Virginia Steen-McIntyre. Using four of the latest geological dating methods, she and her colleagues from the United States Geological Survey determined that the artifact-bearing layer was 300,000 years old. When this information was presented to the chief archaeologist, the chief archaeologist said it was impossible. According to standard views, there were no human beings in existence 300,000 years ago anywhere in the world, not to speak of North America. The current doctrine is that humans did not enter the Americas any earlier than 30,000 years ago. So what happened? The archaeologists refused to publish the date of 300,000 years. Instead they published an age of 20,000 years for the site. And where did they get that date? It came from a carbon-14 date on a piece of shell found five kilometers from the place where the artifacts were found.

Steen-McIntyre tried to spread the word about the true age of the site. Because of this, she began to get a bad reputation in her profession. She lost a teaching position she held at a uni-

versity, and all of her opportunities for advancement in the United States Geological Survey were blocked. She became so disgusted that she went to live in a small town in the Rocky Mountains of Colorado and remained silent for ten years, until I found out about her case and wrote about it in *Forbidden Archeology,* giving her work some of the attention it deserves. Partly because of this, the Hueyatlaco site is now being studied by more open-minded archaeologists, and hopefully before too long her original conclusions about the age of the site will be reconfirmed.

An anatomically modern human skull was found by the Italian geologist Giuseppe Ragazzoni at Castenedolo, near Brescia, northern Italy, in the late nineteenth century. Ragazzoni found not only this skull, but the skeletal remains of four persons, in layers of rock which, according to modern geological reports, are about five million years old.

Sometimes when Darwinist scientists hear of modern-looking skeletons being found in very ancient layers of rock, they say: "There is nothing mysterious here. Only a few thousand years ago, someone died on the surface, and his friends dug a grave and placed the body down fairly deep. And that is why you think you have found a human skeleton in some very ancient layer of rock."

I learned that the layers of the earth in which the skeleton was found are about 300 million years old.

Such things, technically called intrusive burial, can certainly happen. But in this case, Ragazzoni—himself a professional geologist—was well aware of the possibility of intrusive burial. If it had been a burial, the overlying layers would have been disturbed. But he checked very carefully during the excavation, and found that the overlying layers were perfectly intact and undisturbed. This means that the skeletons really are as old as the layers of rock in which they were found, in this case five million years old.

Early in the twentieth century, the Belgian geologist A. Rutot made some interesting discoveries in his country. He found hundreds of stone tools and weapons in layers of rock 30 million years old. I mentioned in connection with the California gold mine discoveries that sometimes we are not allowed to see the ancient objects in the museum collections. In this case I was able to see the artifacts. Once when I was in Brussels for some newspaper interviews, a friend of mine was driving me around, and I suggested that we go to the Royal Museum of Natural Sciences, because that is where I thought Rutot's collection should be. The first museum officials we spoke to had denied having any knowledge of the collection, but finally we found an archaeologist who knew the collection. Of course, it was not being displayed to the public.

This archaeologist took me into the storerooms of the museum, and there I took photographs of Rutot's collection of hundreds of 30 million-year-old stone tools and weapons from Belgium.

Up to this point, all of the finds we've discussed were either made by professional scientists or were reported in the professional scientific literature. But if this evidence for extreme human antiquity really is there in the layers of the earth, then we might expect that people other than professional scientists might be finding it. And their reports, although they might not appear in the pages of scientific journals, might appear in the pages of more ordinary literature. I think we can predict that this should be happening. And in fact it does happen.

Let us consider an interesting report from the *Morrisonville Times,* a newspaper published in the little town of Morrisonville, Illinois, in the year 1892. It tells of a woman who was putting a big piece of coal into her coal-burning stove. The piece of coal broke in half, and inside she found a beautiful gold chain, ten inches long. The two pieces of coal were still attached to the ends of the chain, demonstrating that the chain had been solidly embedded in the coal. From the newspaper report we were able to determine the mine from which the coal came. According to the Geological Survey of the State of Illinois, the coal from that mine is about 300 million years old, the same age as the human skeleton found in the same state.

Let's go back to the scientific literature. In 1862, a scientific journal called *The Geologist* (volume 5, p 470) told of a human skeleton found 90 feet below the surface in Macoupin County, Illinois. According to the report, there was a two-foot thick layer of unbroken slate rock directly above the skeleton. From the government geologist of the state of Illinois, I learned that the layers of the earth in which the skeleton was found are about 300 million years old, making the skeleton the same age as the gold chain found in the same state. In 1852, *Scientific American* reported that a beautiful metallic vase came from five meters deep in solid rock near the city of Boston. According to modern geological reports, the age of the rock at this place is 500 million years old.

The oldest objects that I encountered in my research were some round metallic spheres found over the past 20 years by miners at Ottosdalin, in the Western Transvaal region of South Africa. The objects are one or two centimeters in diameter. Most interesting are the parallel grooves that go around the equators of the spheres. The spheres were submitted to metallurgists for analysis before they were filmed for the television program *The Mysterious Origins of Man.* The metallurgists said they could see no way in which the spheres could have formed naturally in the earth, indicating they are the product of intelligent work. The spheres come from mineral deposits over 2 billion years old.

We are nearing the end of this brief review of evidence for extreme human antiquity. I have given you only a small sample of this evidence. I could go on for quite some time, because there are hundreds of such cases from the scientific literature of the past 150 years.

I will end by saying this. We have been told by the Darwinists that all the physical evidence ever discovered by scientists supports their picture of human origins, which has human beings like us coming into existence about 100,000 years ago. I think we can safely say that is not true. There is a chain of discoveries going from 100,000 years ago all the way back to 2 billion years. I did not find any evidence older than that. I think it is, at the very least, an interesting coincidence that the ancient Sanskrit writings say humans have been present on earth for two billion years.

What does all of this suggest? It means we need an alternative picture of human origins, and I intend to present one of my own in my next book, *Human Devolution.* In that book, I will suggest that we have not evolved upward from the apes on this planet, as modern science tells us, but that we have devolved from an original spiritual position in higher levels of reality.

There Is So Much That We Don't Know

Selections from the *Science Frontiers* Book and Newsletter

William R. Corliss

From the Preface to *Science Frontiers: Some Anomalies and Curiosities of Nature*

The primary intent of this book is entertainment. Do not look for profundities! All I claim here is an edited collection of naturally occurring anomalies and curiosities that I have winnowed mainly from scientific journals and magazines. With this eclectic sampling I hope to demonstrate that nature is amusing, beguiling, sometimes bizarre, and, most important, liberating.

My view is that anomaly research, while not science per se, has the potential to destabilize paradigms and accelerate scientific change.

"Liberating?" Yes! If there is anything profound between these covers, it is the influence of anomalies on the stability of stifling scientific paradigms.

My view is that anomaly research, while not science per se, has the potential to destabilize paradigms and accelerate scientific change. Anomalies reveal nature as it really is: complex, chaotic, possibly even unplumbable. Anomalies also encourage the framing of rogue paradigms, such as morphic resonance and the steady-state universe.

Anomaly research often transcends current scientific currency by celebrating bizarre and incongruous facets of nature, such as coincidence and seriality. However iconoclastic the pages of this book, the history of science tells us that future students of nature will laugh at our conservatism and lack of vision.

Such heavy philosophical fare, however, is not the main diet of the anomalist. The search itself is everything. My greatest thrill, prolonged as it was, was in my forays through the long files of *Nature*, *Science*, *English Mechanic*, *Monthly Weather Review*, *Geological Magazine*, and like journals. There, anomalies and curiosities lurked in many an issue, hidden under layers of library dust. These tedious searches were hard on the eyes, but they opened them to a universe not taught by my college professors!

The Incorruptibility of the Ganges

The Ganges is 2,525 kilometers long. Along its course, 27 major towns dump 902 million liters of sewage into it each day. Added to this are all those human bodies consigned to this holy river, called the Ganga by the Indians. Despite this heavy burden of pollutants, the Ganges has for millennia been regarded as incorruptible. How can this be?

Several foreigners have recorded the effects of this river's "magical" cleansing properties:

- Ganges water does not putrefy, even after long periods of storage. River water begins to putrefy when lack of oxygen promotes the growth of anaerobic bacteria, which produce the telltale smell of stale water.

- British physician C.E. Nelson observed that Ganga water taken from the Hooghly—one of its dirtiest mouths—by ships returning to England remained fresh throughout the voyage.

- In 1896 the British physician E. Hanbury Hankin reported in the French journal *Annales de l'Institut Pasteur* that cholera microbes died within three hours in Ganga water but continued to thrive in distilled water even after 48 hours.

- A French scientist, Monsieur Herelle, was amazed to find "that only a few feet below the bodies of persons floating in the Ganga who had died of dysentery and cholera, where one would expect millions of germs, there were no germs at all."

More recently, D.S. Bhargava, an Indian environmental engineer measured the Ganges' remarkable self-cleansing properties:

Bhargava's calculations, taken from an exhaustive three-year study of the Ganga, show that it is able to reduce BOD [biochemical oxygen demand] levels much faster than in other rivers.

Quantitatively, the Ganges seems to clean up suspended wastes fifteen to twenty times faster than other rivers.[1]

Underwater Thumps

Scientists based on the central California coast are trying to identify the origin of a mysterious underwater sound that disturbed surfers and divers for three weeks—and then just as mysteriously disappeared.

> The sound, made up of thumps occurring at 10-second intervals, was compared by one diver to five or six giant bongo drums going off simultaneously. Most experts have concluded that it was of human origin.

As usual in such cases, no governmental or military sources knew anything about the thumps.[2]

The Earth Is Expanding and We Don't Know Why

Let us taunt the geologists now with an idea that many of them consider to be nonsense. The expanding earth hypothesis goes back to at least 1933, a time when the continental drift hypothesis was accorded the same sort of ridicule. Now, continental drift is enthroned, and many of its strongest proponents are vehemently opposed to the expanding earth theory, ignoring the lessons of history.

The data that suggest that the earth has expanded significantly over geological time come from the pleasant pastime of continent-fitting. If one takes the pieces of continental and oceanic crust and tries to fit them together at various times over the past several hundred-million years, taking into account the production of crust at the mid-ocean ridges, the fit gets worse and worse as one works backward in time. Great gaps (or "gores") appear between the pieces of crust which geologists believed existed at these periods. (Of course, one can play this

> "It's rare that archaeologists ever find something that so totally changes our picture of what happened in the past, as is true for this case."

puzzle-piece game only at passive continent-ocean boundaries where the oceanic crust has not slid under the continental crust. The South Atlantic is a good place to work.)

These embarrassing, grotesque gaps can be made to disappear almost as if by magic by assuming that the earth was smaller in the past. This seems, on the surface, to be a crazy idea. Why would an entire planet swell up like a balloon? Hugh Owen answers in this way:

> The geological and geophysical implications of such Earth expansion are so profound that most geologists and geophysicists shy away from them. In order to fit with the reconstruction that seems to be required, the volume of the Earth was only 51 per cent of its present value, and the surface area 64 per cent of that of the present day, 200 million years ago. Established theory says that the Earth's interior is stable, an inner core of nickel iron surrounded by an outer layer that behaves like a fluid. Perhaps we are completely wrong and the inner core is in some state nobody has yet imagined, a state that is undergoing a transition from a high-density state to a lower density state, and pushing out the crust, the skin of the Earth, as it expands.[3]

Reference. For more on the expanding earth hypothesis, see category ETL6 in *Carolina Bays, Mima Mounds, Submarine Canyons* (Sourcebooks, 1988).

About as Anomalous as Mounds Can Get

The title refers to a circle of eleven earthen mounds located near Monroe, Louisiana—the Watson Break site. Local residents have known about the mounds for years, but archaeologists weren't attracted to them until clear-cutting of the trees in the 1970s made the size and novelty of Watson Break all too obvious.

Just how anomalous is Watson Break? Archaeologist V. Steponaitis, from the University of North Carolina, opined:

> It's rare that archaeologists ever find something that so totally changes our picture of what happened in the past, as is true for this case.

On what does Steponaitis base such a powerful statement?

- Watson Break is dated at 5000–5400 BP (Before Present), some three millennia before the well-known mound-builders started piling up earthen structures from the Mississippi Valley to New York State. In other words, the site is anomalously early.

- Indications are that Watson Break was built by hunter-gatherers, but no one really knows much about them; there's an aura of mystery here.

- Watson Break consists of eleven mounds—some as high as a two-story house—connected by a peculiar circular ridge 280 meters in diameter. The back-breaking labor required to collect and pile up all this dirt is incompatible with the lifestyle of mobile bands of hunter-gatherers.

- The purpose of the Watson Break complex escapes us. Why the mounds? Why the circular ridge? Can we just shrug it off as a "ritual site"?[4]

Mysterious Swirl Patterns on the Moon

In at least three lunar locations, enigmatic bright-and-dark swirl patterns drape craters and mar terrains. Ranging from ten kilometers across to less than 50 meters, they may be ribbon-like, open-looped, or closed-looped. The swirls are sharply defined but do not appear to scour or otherwise disturb the terrains where they occur. Similar swirl patterns have been recognized on Mercury. Two intriguing characteristics of the lunar swirl patterns are that (1) they coincide with strong magnetic anomalies, and (2) they appear to be very young, being superimposed on top of essentially all lunar features of all ages. Schultz and Srnka suggest that recent cometary impacts created the patterns.[5]

Comment. The terrestrial implications are obvious: Our earth must have been hit, too. Perhaps at the Tunguska site there are similar swirl patterns—now obliterated by vegetation.

Reference. Lunar swirl patterns are cataloged in Section ALE5 of *The Moon and the Planets* (Sourcebooks, 1985).

Ten Strikes Against the Big Bang

T. Van Flandern, editor of the *Meta Research Bulletin*, has compiled a list of big bang problems—and it is not a short list. Can the big bang paradigm be *that* shaky? Like evolution and relativity, the big bang is usually paraded as a proven, undeniable fact. It isn't.

- Static-universe models fit the data better than expanding-universe models.

- The microwave "background" makes more sense as the limiting temperature of space heated by starlight rather than as the remnant of a fireball.

- Element-abundance predictions using the big bang require too many adjustable parameters to make them work.

- The universe has too much large-scale structure (interspersed "walls" and voids) to form in a time as short as 10 to 20 billion years.

- The average luminosity of quasars must decrease in just the right way so that their mean apparent brightness is the same at all redshifts, which is exceedingly unlikely.

- The ages of globular clusters appear older than the universe.

In at least three lunar locations, enigmatic bright-and-dark swirl patterns drape craters and mar terrains.

- The local streaming motions of galaxies are too high for a finite universe that is supposed to be everywhere uniform.

- Invisible dark matter of an unknown but non-baryonic nature must be the dominant ingredient of the entire universe.

- The most distant galaxies in the Hubble Deep Field show insufficient evidence of evolution, with some of them apparently having higher redshifts ($z = 6$–7) than the faintest quasars.

- If the open universe we see today is extrapolated back near the beginning, the ratio of the actual density of matter in the universe to the critical density must differ from unity by just one part in 1,059. Any larger deviation would result in a universe already collapsed on itself or already dissipated.[6]

Einstein's Nemesis: DI Herculis

DI Herculis is an eighth-magnitude eclipsing binary about 2,000 light years from earth. These two young blue stars are very close—only one-fifth the distance from earth to our sun. They orbit about a common center of gravity every 10.55 days. So far, no problem!

The puzzle is that, as the two stars swing around one another, the axis of their orbit rotates or precesses too slowly. General relativity predicts a precession of 4.27°/century, but for DI Herculis the rate is only 1.05°/century. This does not sound like a figure large enough to get excited about, but it deeply troubles astronomers. D. Popper, an astronomer at UCLA, says:

> The observations are pretty clear. I don't think there's any question there's a discrepancy and, frankly, it is an important one and it's unresolved.

Accentuating the challenge to general relativity is the discovery that a second eclipsing binary, AC Camelopardalis, also violates general relativity in the same way. It *seems* that wherever gravitational fields are extremely strong and space-time, therefore, is highly distorted, general relativity fails.

Ironically, it was a very similar sort of astronomical observation that helped make general relativity a pillar of the scientific edifice early in the twentieth century. The orbit of Mercury precesses a bit faster than Newtonian physics predicts. The application of Einstein's general relativity corrected the calculation of Mercury's rate of precession by just the right amount. Now we may need a new theory to correct Einstein—at least where time-space is sharply bent![7]

Where Have All the Black Holes Gone?

Like the big bang, black holes are an astronomical staple. Most scientists and laymen assume that black holes are proven, well-observed denizens of the cosmos. Certainly the media entertain no doubts! Let us take a skeptical look.

Does theory require black holes? In 1939 R. Oppenheimer and H. Snyder showed on paper that a massive star could collapse and create a black hole, *assuming* the correctness of stellar theories and General Relativity. Initially, scientists were skeptical about black holes because of their bizarre properties: They emit no light and inhale unwary starships. Black holes are also singularities, and singularities make scientists nervous. In the black-hole singularity, thousands of stars are swallowed and compressed into an infinitesimally small volume.[8] This grates against common sense.

All objects previously proclaimed to be small black holes have instead turned out to be neutron stars.

The philosophical uneasiness about black holes is worsened by the discovery that they:

> ...threaten the universe with an irreversible loss of information, which seems to contradict other laws of physics.[9]

Adding to these problems are nagging doubts about General Relativity, which underpins black-hole theory. Recently, some theorists have shown that General Relativity requires that two bodies of approximately equal size not attract one another![10]

Despite all these qualms, black holes have become a fixture of astronomy because they promise to explain the incredibly powerful energy sources seen in the cores of galaxies.

Do astronomers really observe black holes? The answer is: *maybe*. And even if yes, there are not nearly enough of them to satisfy theory.

To illustrate, according to present theory, when stars weighing in at less than three solar masses collapse, they become neutron stars; if larger, the stars turn into *small* black holes. Theoretically, there should be one small black hole for every three neutron stars. But with some 500 neutron stars already pinpointed, only three "possible" small black holes have been given votes of confidence; namely, Cyg X-1, LMC X-3, and AD 620-00. All objects previously proclaimed to be small black holes have instead turned out to be neutron stars.[11]

The case for *massive* black holes weighing in at millions of solar masses is not overwhelming either. These are supposed to lurk in the centers of galaxies. To find them, astronomers look for intensely bright spots in galaxies, around which stars swirl at speeds approaching the speed of light as they are sucked into the black hole's maw. Such fantastic celestial maelstroms *do* seem to exist, as evidenced by "something" in the giant elliptical galaxy M87.[12]

New claims for massive black holes are always being put forward. The spiral galaxy NGC 4328, for example, is thought to

All you have to do is cool helium down to almost absolute zero. It will liquefy but, unlike most other gases, it will not freeze. You are surprised at this, of course. Now, if you spin a bowl of this liquid helium around, you will be astounded. The liquid remains absolutely stationary in its spinning container— no centrifugal effects, no friction with the contained wall, *nada*! However, the strangest part comes when you:

> Draw a cupful out of the bowl, suspend it a few centimeters above the remaining liquid, then stand back and rub your eyes—the fluid in the cup will cheat common sense by pouring itself, drop by drop, back into the bowl. A drop climbs up the inside of the cup, then runs down the outside. When it falls, another begins climbing, and the magic continues until the cup is dry.[15]

The First Digit Phenomenon

Back in 1881, Simon Newcomb, the renowned Canadian-American scientist, published a provocative conjecture that was promptly forgotten by everyone. Newcomb had noticed that books of logarithms in the libraries were always much dirtier at the beginning. Hmmm! Were his fellow scientists look-

> One scientist has even despaired that "the stratigraphic record, as a whole, is so incomplete that fossil patterns are meaningless artefacts of episodic sedimentation."

harbor a super-massive black hole weighing in at 40 million solar masses![13] However, claims for massive black holes are also being shot down all the time. Several have thought they had found a massive black hole at the center of our own galaxy. This no longer seems likely.[14]

Conclusion. Don't be too quick to accept such bizarre constructs as black holes, whether small or massive.

More Quantum Weirdness

You have probably already heard how a change in one subatomic particle can cause an instantaneous change in another, even if the second particle is cruising along in another galaxy. That's quantum weirdness all right, but this weirdness can also produce effects we can see and hear.

ing up the logarithms of numbers beginning with 1 more frequently than 2, 3, etc.? It certainly seemed like it. He formalized his suspicions in a conjecture:

$$p = \log 10 \ (1 + 1/d)$$

where p = the probability that the first significant digit is d.

This (unproven) equation states that about 30 percent of the numbers in a table or group will begin with 1. Only about 4.6 percent will begin with 9. This result certainly clashes with our expectation that the nine digits should occur with equal probability.

Fifty-seven years later, F. Benford, a GE physicist who was unaware of Newcomb's paper, observed the same dirty early pages in the logarithm tables. He came up with exactly the

Single cells taken from multicellular organisms tend to inch along like independent amoebas—almost as if they were looking for companionship or trying to fulfill some destiny.

same conjecture. Benford didn't stop there. He spent several years collecting diverse data sets—20,229 sets, to be exact. He included baseball statistics, atomic weights, river areas, the numbers appearing in *Reader's Digest* articles, etc. He concluded that his (and Newcomb's) conjecture fit his data very well. There were notable exceptions, though. Telephone directories and square-root tables didn't support the conjecture.

Interestingly, the *second* digits in numbers are more equitably distributed; the third, even more so.

Mathematicians have never been able to prove the Newcomb-Benford conjecture. How could they if it doesn't apply to all tables? Nevertheless, it works for most data sets, and that's still hard enough to explain.[16]

All Roads Lead to 123

Start with any number that is a string of digits—say, 9,288,759—and count the number of even digits, the number of odd digits, and the total number of digits it contains. These are 3 (three evens), 4 (four odds), and 7 (seven is the total number of digits), respectively. Use these digits to form the next string or number, 347. If you repeat the process with 347, you get 1, 2, 3. If you repeat with 123, you get 123 again. The number 123, with respect to this process and universe of numbers, is a mathematical black hole.

We have a black hole because we cannot escape, just as spaceships are doomed when captured by a physical black hole! You end up with 123 regardless of the number you start with. Other sorts of mathematical black holes exist, such as the Collatz Conjecture, but we must not fall into them because our printer awaits.[17]

Poets at Sea: Or Why Do Whales Rhyme?

We found the following in *Newsweek*:

When scientists talk about whales singing songs, they're not talking about mere noise. They're talking about intricate, stylized compositions—some longer than symphonic movements—performed in medleys that can last up to 22 hours. The songs of humpback whales can change dramatically from year to year, yet each whale in an oceanwide population always sings the same song as the others. How, with the form changing so fast, does everyone keep the verses straight? Biologists Linda Guinee and Katharine Payne have been looking into the matter, and they have come up with an intriguing possibility. It seems that humpbacks, like humans, use rhyme.

Guinee and Payne suspect that whales rhyme because they have detected particular subphrases turning up in the same position in adjacent themes.[18]

Comment. This is all wonderfully fascinating, but why do whales rhyme at all, or sing such long, complex songs? Biologists fall back on that hackneyed old theory that it has something to do with mating and/or dominance displays. Next, we'll hear that human poets write poems only to improve their chances of breeding and passing their genes on to their progeny!

Reference. Whale "communication" is the subject of BMT8 in *Biological Anomalies: Mammals I* (Sourcebooks, 1995).

Eight Leatherback Mysteries

Our subject here is the leatherback turtle. Weighing up to 1,600 pounds, it is the largest of the sea turtles. It is also the fastest turtle, hitting nine miles per hour at times. But weight and speed are not necessarily mysterious; here are some characteristics that are:

- The leatherback is the only turtle without a rigid shell. Why? Perhaps it needs a flexible shell for its very deep dives. What looks like a shell is its thick, leathery carapace—a strange streamlined structure with five to seven odd "keels" running lengthwise.

- These turtles are *warm-blooded* and able to maintain their temperatures as much as 10°F above the ambient water, just as the dinosaurs apparently could.

- The bones of the leatherback are more like those of the marine-mammals (dolphins and whales) than the reptiles. "No one seems to understand the evolutionary implications of this."

- Leatherbacks dive as deep as 3,000 feet, which is strange because they seem to subside almost exclusively on jellyfish, most of which are surface feeders.

- Like all turtles, leatherbacks can stay submerged for up to 48 hours. Just how they do this is unexplained.

- Their brains are miniscule. A 60-pound turtle possessed a brain weighing only four grams—a rat's weighs eight!

- Leatherbacks' intestines contain waxy balls, recalling the ambergris found in the intestines of sperm whales.

- The stomachs of leatherbacks seem to contain nothing but jellyfish, which are 97 percent water. Biologists wonder how the huge, far-ranging leatherback can find enough jellyfish to sustain itself.[19]

The Ubiquity of Sea Serpents

Public interest is usually focused (by the media) upon the supposed monsters in Loch Ness, Lake Champlain, the Chesapeake Bay, etc. Actually, an immense body of sea-serpent reports also exists. B. Heuvelmans collected many of these in his 1965 classic *In the Wake of the Sea-Serpents.*

At one point during the last 400,000 years, the human population worldwide was reduced to only about 10,000 breeding men and women— the size of a very small town.

P.H. LeBlond, a professor at the University of British Columbia, is extending Heuvelman's work, concentrating on the thousand miles of Pacific Coast between Alaska and Oregon. Since 1812, there have been 53 sightings of sea serpents or other unidentified animals along this narrow strip of ocean. Some of these are very impressive. Take this one for example:

In January 1984 a mechanical engineer named J.N. Thompson from Bellingham, Washington, was fishing for Chinook salmon from his kayak on the Spanish Banks about three-quarters of a mile off Vancouver, British Columbia, when an animal surfaced between 100 and 200 feet away. It appeared to be about eighteen to twenty feet long and about two feet wide, with a "whitish-tan throat and lower front" body. It had stubby horns like those of a giraffe, large ("twelve to fifteen inches long") floppy ears, and a "somewhat pointed black snout." The creature appeared to Thompson to be "uniquely streamlined for aquatic life," and to swim "very efficiently and primarily by up and down rather than sideways wriggling motion…"

LeBlond and biologist J. Sibert have analyzed all of the 53 sightings in a 68-page report entitled "Observations of Large Unidentified Marine Mammals in British Columbia and Adjacent Waters," published by the University of British Columbia's Institute of Oceanography. Of the 53 sightings, 23 "could not definitely or even speculatively be accounted for by animals known to science." The authors of the report emphasize that the reports are of high quality, made by people knowledgeable about the sea and its denizens.[20]

Facing up to the Gaps

The textbooks and professors of biology and geology speak confidently of the fossil record. Darwin may have expressed concern about its incompleteness, but, especially in the context of the creation-evolution tempest, evolutionists seem to infer that a lot of missing links have been found. Some scientists, however, are facing up to the fact that many gaps in the fossil record still exist after a century of Darwinism. One has even despaired that "the stratigraphic record, as a whole, is so incomplete that fossil patterns are meaningless artefacts of episodic sedimentation."

D.E. Schindel, Curator of Invertebrate Fossils in the Peabody Museum, has scrutinized seven recent microstratigraphical studies, evaluating them for temporal scope, microstratigraphical acuity, and stratigraphical completeness. His first and most important conclusion is that a sort of Uncertainty Principle prevails such that, "a study can provide fine sampling resolution, encompass long spans of geological time, or contain a complete record of the time span, but not all three." After further analysis he concludes with a warning that the fossil record is full of habitat shifts, local extinctions, and general lack of permanence in physical conditions.[21]

Comment. This candor makes one wonder how much of our scientific philosophy should be based upon such a shaky foundation.

Polar-Bear Bones Confound Ice-Age Proponents

Given the unquestioning fealty accorded the Ice Ages, it is not especially odd that the information reported below has not received wider circulation.

In 1991 construction workers at Tysfjord, Norway, 125 miles north of the Arctic Circle, accidentally dug up polar-bear bones that were later radiometrically dated as at least 42,000 years old, probably 60,000. R. Lie, a zoologist at the University of Bergen, and other scientists subsequently found the bones of two more polar bears in the area. These were dated as about 20,000 years old. An associated wolf's jaw was pegged at 32,000 years.

> But it turns out that the healthy heart does *not* beat steadily and precisely like a metronome.

The problem is that Norway and many other northern circumpolar lands are believed to have been buried under a thick ice cap during the Ice Ages. In particular, northern Norway is thought to have been solidly encased in ice from 80,000 to 10,000 years ago. Polar bears could not have made a living there during this period. Clearly, something is wrong somewhere.[22]

An associated conundrum. Some authorities have stated that polar bears evolved *recently*—only 10,000 years ago! Polar bear evolution is discussed in more depth in *Biological Anomalies: Mammals II* (Sourcebooks, 1996).

Artificial Panspermia on the Moon

A colony of earth bacteria, *Streptococcus mitis*, apparently survived on the moon's surface between April 1967 and November 1969. The organisms were discovered in a piece of insulating foam in the TV camera retrieved from *Surveyor 3* by Apollo astronauts. [Note: Panspermia is the idea that life—particularly primitive life—does or at least can survive in outer space.][23]

Blebs and Ruffles

Single cells taken from multicellular organisms tend to inch along like independent amoebas—almost as if they were looking for companionship or trying to fulfill some destiny. This surprising volition of isolated cells becomes an even more remarkable property when the individual cells are fragmented. Guenter Albrecht-Buehler, at Cold Spring Harbor Laboratory, has found that even tiny cell fragments, perhaps just a couple percent of the whole cell, will tend to move about. They develop blebs (bubbles) or ruffles and extend questing filopodia. They have all the migratory urges of the single cells but cannot pull it off. Cell fragments will bleb or ruffle, but not both. Why? Where are they trying to go?[24]

Subversive Cancer Cells

It has been generally believed that most cancers originate in a single founder cell, which then multiplies to create the tumor. But cancer is more insidious than expected. A *precancerous founder cell may actually subvert nearby *non*cancerous cells and turn them into cancerous cells. In this sense, the first precancerous cell recruits and transforms healthy cells, enlisting them in its destructive operations, and thereby turning them against the body that produced them. No one yet knows how this subversion is effected or how it evolved. (Why is there cancer anyway?)

The basis for this claim involves a few rare human *mosaics*, whose bodies are built of cells with two different genetic complements. Cancers in human mosaics have been found to contain *both* types of cells and, therefore, did not grow from a single cell alone.[25]

Comments. Curiously, some "primitive" animals, such as sharks, seem to have evolved defenses against cancer that mammals lack.

Tobacco and Cocaine in Ancient Egypt

The current newsletter of the New England Antiquities Research Association has flagged an important anomaly that appeared on a 1997 TV program:

> In January [1997] the Discovery Channel broadcast a program stating that cocaine and tobacco had been found in Egyptian mummies known to be at least 3,000 years old. Tests used modern forensic methods and were repeated many times under carefully controlled conditions. Since coca and tobacco are not known to have grown anywhere other than the Americas, the evidence points to trade routes across the Pacific or Atlantic in those remote times. The program seemed to favor a Pacific crossing and then delivery via the Silk Route.

This news item continued with a reference to Dr. Balabanov's supporting tests on bodies from China, Germany, and Austria, spanning the years 3700 BCE to 1100 CE. These bodies contained incredibly high percentages of nicotine.[26]

Comment. In *Science Frontiers* #7/48, back in 1978, we reported that the mummy of Rameses II contained anomalous traces of nicotine.

American Pygmies

Today's anthropological texts say little about pygmies populating ancient North America, but a century ago, when tiny graves replete with tiny skeletons were discovered in Tennessee, controversy erupted. Were they the bones of pygmies or children of normal-sized tribes? The latter choice was made, and we hear no more on the subject—at least on the standard academic circuits.

But a few reverberations are still detectable elsewhere. V.R. Pilapil, for example, asserts that the disputed Tennessee graves *really* did contain pygmy remains. Not only that, but he hypothesizes that the pygmies arrived in ancient times from southeast Asia, probably the Philippines, where today's diminutive Aetas live.

To support his case, Pilapil recalls B. Fell's examination of the Tennessee skeletal material. Fell noted that:

- The skulls' brain capacity was equivalent to only about 950 cubic centimeters, approximately the volume of a non-pygmy seven-year-old.

- The teeth were completely developed and showed severe wear characteristic of mature individuals.

- The skulls were brachycephalic with projecting jaws. Fell had, in fact, described skulls very much like those of today's adult Philippine Aetas.

Another line of evidence adduced by Pilapil involved the traditions of British Columbia tribes, which recognized a tribe of very small people called the Et-nane. More significant is the oral history of the Cherokees, which mentions the existence of "little people" in eastern North America.[27]

When Humans Were an Endangered Species

At one point during the last 400,000 years, the human population worldwide was reduced to only about 10,000 breeding men and women—the size of a very small town. What caused this population "bottleneck"? Did a population crash engulf the entire globe? If not, who was spared?

"Women are more likely to die in the week following their birthdays than in any other week of the year."

Such questions arise from a surprising observation: Human DNA is remarkably uniform everywhere humans are found. This hidden genetic uniformity is difficult to believe if one strolls through a cosmopolitan city like New York or Paris. Nevertheless, compared to the DNA of the great apes, whose mutation rates *should* be close to ours, human genes on the average show far fewer mutations. Human DNA from Tokyo and London is more alike than that from two lowland gorillas occupying the same forest in West Africa. Harvard anthropologist M. Ruvolo has commented: "It is a mystery that none of us can explain."

The clear implication is that humans recently squeezed through a population bottleneck, during which many accumulated mutations were wiped out. In a sense, the human race began anew during the last 400,000 years. Unfortunately, DNA analysis cannot say where the very grim reaper came from.[28]

Comment. The hand that wiped the slate clean, or nearly so, might have been a meteor impact, a pandemic, the Ice Ages, a flood, volcanism, etc. Whatever it was, it seems to have largely spared Africa. The chimps and gorillas there apparently did not pass through the bottleneck. Even more interesting is the observation that the DNA of Subsaharan Africans does show more variability and therefore *seems* older than that from humans elsewhere on the planet. (See *Biological Anomalies: Humans III* (Sourcebooks, 1994).) Or perhaps Subsaharan DNA only seems older because it was not forced through that bottleneck. There are implications here for the African Eve theory.

Our Genes Aren't Us!

Almost without exception, biology textbooks, scientific papers, popular articles, and TV documentaries convey the impression that an organism's genes completely specify the living animal or plant. In most people's minds, the strands of DNA are analogous to computer codes that control the manufacture and disposition of proteins. Perhaps our current fascination with computers has fostered this narrow view of heredity.

Do our genes really contain all the information necessary for constructing human bodies? In the April 1994 issue of *Discover*, J. Cohen and I. Stewart endeavor to set us straight. The arguments against the "genes-are-everything" paradigm are long and complex, but Cohen and Stewart also provide some simple, possibly simplistic, observations supporting a much broader view of genetics:

■ Mammalian DNA contains fewer bases than amphibian DNA, even though mammals are considered more complex and "advanced." The implication is that "DNA-as-a-message" must be a flawed metaphor.

■ Wings have been invented at least four times by divergent classes (pterosaurs, insects, birds, bats); and it is very unlikely that there is a common DNA sequence that specifies how to manufacture a wing.

■ The connections between the nerve cells comprising the human brain represent much more information than can possibly be encoded in human DNA.

■ A caterpillar has the same DNA as the butterfly it eventually becomes. Ergo, something more than DNA must be involved. (This observation **does** seem simplistic, because DNA could, in principle, code for metamorphosis.)

Like DNA, this "something more" passing from parent to offspring conveys information on the biochemical level. This aspect of heredity has been bypassed as geneticists have focused on the genes.

Cohen and Stewart summarize their views as follows:

> What we have been saying is that DNA space is not a map of creature space. There is no unique correspondence between the two spaces, no way to assign to each sequence in DNA space a unique animal that it "codes for." Biological development is a complicated transaction between the DNA "program" and its host organism, neither alone can construct a creature and neither alone holds all the secrets, not even implicitly.[29]

Comment. If "genes aren't us," the billion-dollar human genome project cannot fulfill its promises.

You May Become What You Eat

When we scarf down a hamburger, we ingest bovine DNA. The textbooks say that this alien DNA is destroyed during digestion. Otherwise, it might "somehow" be incorporated into our own DNA, leading in time to our acquisition of some bovine characteristics! You'll recall that cannibals thought to acquire the virtues of their slain enemies by grabbing a bite or two. But this all sounds pretty farfetched, doesn't it?

Maybe not. When W. Doerfler and R. Schubert, at the

University of Cologne, fed the bacterial virus M13 to a mouse, snippets of the M13's genes turned up in cells taken from the mouse's intestines, spleen, liver, and white blood cells. Most of the alien DNA was eventually rejected, but some was probably retained. In any event, alien DNA in food seems to make its way to and survive for a time in the cells of the eater.[30]

Comment. We are only half-kidding when we ask if food consumption could affect the evolution of a species. After all, our cells already harbor mitochondria, which are generally admitted to have originally been free bacteria that were "consumed" by animal cells. The process even has a name: "endosymbiosis."

Organ Music

Your doctor is understandably concerned if he finds your heartbeat is irregular. But it turns out that the healthy heart does *not*

Monogrammic Determinism

About two years ago (*Science Frontiers* #108), we succumbed to the lure of "nominative determinism." The Feedback page of the *New Scientist* had been printing case after amusing case in which a person's occupation was described or suggested by his or her surname. A classic example is seen in a paper on incontinence published in the *British Journal of Urology* by J.W. Splatt and D. Weedon! Does a person's name exert a psychological force of the choice of a career? We have seen no formal studies of nominative determinism, but we have just discovered a closely-allied phenomenon that *has* been scientifically investigated. We call it "monogrammic determinism."

An individual's monogram does not seem to be associated with his or her occupation but rather with longevity. People with monograms such as ACE, WOW, or GOD tend to live longer than those with monograms like PIG, RAT, DUD, or ILL.

When a type of computer program termed an "artificial neural network" is "killed" by cutting links between its units, it in effect approaches a state which might be something like biological "death."

beat steadily and precisely like a metronome. In fact, the *intervals* between normal heartbeats vary in a curious fashion: In a simple, direct way, they can be converted to musical notes. When these notes (derived from heartbeat intervals) are heard, the sound is pleasant and intriguing to the ear—almost music—and certainly far from being random noise. In fact, a new CD entitled *Heartsongs: Musical Mappings of the Heartbeat*, by Z. Davis, records the "music" derived from the digital tape recordings of the heartbeats of fifteen people. Recording venue: Harvard Medical School's Beth Israel Hospital! This whole business raises some "interesting" speculations for R.M. May:

> We could equally have ended up with boring sameness, or even dissonant jangle. The authors speculate that musical composition may involve, to some degree, "the re-creation by the mind of the body's own naturally complex rhythms and frequencies. Perhaps what the ear and the brain perceive as pleasing or interesting are variations in pitch that resonate with or replicate the body's own complex (fractal) variability and scaling."[31]

The study was conducted at the University of San Diego, where 27 years' worth of California death certificates were examined. Only men were chosen, because their initials did not change with marriage. They were divided into three groups: (1) those with "good" monograms, (2) those with "bad" monograms, and (3) a control group with "neutral" monograms. Those men bearing "good" monograms lived 4.48 years *longer* than those in the control group; those with "bad" monograms, 2.8 years *less*.

Manifestly, being called DUD or PIG all your life can shorten it. Being addressed as ACE or GOD can give one a psychological boost that prolongs life.[32]

The Birthday: Lifeline or Deadline?

The following abstract is from a paper in *Psychosomatic Medicine*:

> This study of deaths from natural causes examined adult mortality around the birthday for two samples,

totaling 2,745,149 people. Women are more likely to die in the week following their birthdays than in any other week of the year. In addition, the frequency of female deaths dips below normal just before the birthday. The results do not seem to be due to seasonal fluctuations, misreporting on the death certificate, deferment of life-threatening surgery, or behavioral changes associated with the birthday. At present, the best available explanation of these findings is that females are able to prolong life briefly until they have reached a positive, symbolically meaningful occasion. Thus the birthday seems to function as a "lifeline" for some females. In contrast, male mortality peaks shortly before the birthday, suggesting that the birthday functions as a "deadline" for males.[33]

Addictions to Placebos

A 38-year-old married schizophrenic was in psychotherapy for severe depression and multiple suicide attempts. She was addicted to methylphenidate, taking 25 to 35 ten-mg pills per day. She was incredibly adept at persuading pharmacists to refill old prescriptions. With the help of her husband and a drug company, placebos were gradually substituted for the real pills to the point where only two real pills and 25–30 placebos were taken each day. The patient never noticed, indicating that the placebos satisfied the patient's real need—something to fill an inner void.[34]

Lacrima Mortis: **The Tear of Death**

It must be a heart-wrenching experience to see a single tear roll down the cheek of a person at the moment of his or her death. I. Lichter, medical director of the Te Omanga Hospice, in New Zealand, wondered how often this phenomenon occurred and why. Working with the Hospice nursing staff, Lichter followed 100 patients nearing death.

The results showed 14 patients shed a final tear at the time of death, and a further 13 within the last 10 hours of life.

In 21 of the 27 cases, the dying person was unconscious at the time of the last tear. And in all but one case the tear was shed by patients whose death was expected rather than sudden.

Lichter and colleagues wondered if the death-bed tears were emotional in origin or perhaps caused by a reflex action. Notes made by the nursing staff were inconclusive on this matter. Lichter thought of chemically analyzing some of the last tears, because emotional tears have a different chemical composition from those produced by irritation. Unfortunately, a single tear was insufficient for the analysis.[35]

Evolvable Hardware

First, you must envision a computer chip as an evolvable entity—an array of logic gates that can be connected in an almost infinite number of ways. A software instruction becomes the equivalent of a biological gene. Software instructions can be changed to achieve certain hardware goals just as genes can be rearranged to modify an organism. Furthermore, human operators can specify a hardware goal to the chip and let it evolve on its own, something it can do in microseconds rather than millions of years.

This is not a frivolous subject. D. Fogel, chief scientist at Natural Selection, Inc., in La Jolla, California, asserts:

Eventually, we will need to know how to design hardware when we have no idea how to do it.

A few demonstration devices have already been built, and in them we see something worthy of note for *Science Frontiers*. One such device, built by A. Thompson, University of Sussex, was tasked to identify specific audio notes by certain voltage signals. Given 100 logic gates, the device needed only 32 to achieve the result. The surprise was that some of these working gates were *not even connected* to others by normal wiring. Thompson admitted that he had no idea how the device worked. Something completely unexpected had evolved. Perhaps, thought Thompson, some of the circuits are coupled electromagnetically rather than by wires. Human engineers would never have tried this stratagem; it is not even in their computer-design repertoire.[36]

Comments. Evolvable hardware, like God and Nature, works in mysterious ways! As the above type of hardware evolves, it will probably leave a "fossil record" full of mysterious transitions.

What shall we call the units a cyberheredity? "Cyberenes" is too cumbersome. How about: "bytenes"?

Computers Can Have Near-Death Experiences!

When HAL, the treacherous computer of *2001: A Space Odyssey*, was being slowly disconnected, it began singing "A Bicycle Built for Two." In other words, the cutting of the computer's interconnections did not result in gibberish, but rather memories that were previously stored flashed through its data processors. Something similar seems to happen with nonfictional computers.

When a type of computer program termed an "artificial neural network" is "killed" by cutting links between its units, it in effect approaches a state which might be something like biological "death." S.L. Thaler, a physicist at McDonnell Douglas, has been systematically chopping up artificial neural networks. He has found that when between 10 percent and 60 percent of the network connections have been severed, the program generates primarily nonsense. But, as the 90 percent (near-death!) level is approached, the network's output is composed more and more of previously learned information, like HAL's learned song. Also, when *untrained* artificial neural networks were slowly killed, they responded only with nonsense.[37]

Endnotes

1. Kalshian, Rakesh. (1994). "Ganges has magical cleaning properties." *Geographic*, 66, April, p 5. **2.** Shurkin, Joel N. (1994). "Underwater thumps baffle ocean scientists." *Nature*, 371, p 274. **3.** Owen, Hugh. (1984). "The earth is expanding and we don't know why." *New Scientist*, November 22, p 27. **4.** Saunders, Joe W., et al. (1997). "A mound complex in Louisiana at 5400–5000 years before the present." *Science*, 277, p 1796; Pringle, Heather. (1997). "Oldest mound complex found at Louisiana site." *Science*, 277, p 1761; Stanley, Dick. (1997). "Finds alter view of American Indian prehistory." *Austin American Statesman*, September 19. Cr. D. Phelps. **5.** Schultz, Peter H. & Leonard J. Srnka. (1980). "Cometary collisions on the moon and Mercury." *Nature*, 284, p 22. **6.** Van Flandern, Tom. (1997). "Top ten problems with the big bang." *Meta Research Bulletin*, 6, p 64. (*Bulletin* address: P.O. Box 15186, Chevy Chase MD 20825-5186.) **7.** Naeye, Robert. (1995). "Was Einstein wrong?" *Astronomy*, 23, November, p 54. **8.** Parker, Barry. (1994). "Where have all the black holes gone?" *Astronomy*, 22, October, p 36. **9.** Flam, Faye. (1994). "Theorists make a bid to eliminate black holes." *Science*, 266, p 1945. **10.** *Ibid*. **11.** *Op cit.*, Parker **12.** *Ibid*. **13.** Cowen, R. (1995). "New evidence of a galactic black hole." *Science News*, 147, p 36. **14.** Goldwurm, A., et al. (1994). "Possible evidence against a massive black hole at the galactic center." *Nature*, 371, p 589. **15.** Brooks, Michael. (1998). "Liquid genius." *New Scientist*, September 5, p 24. **16.** Hill, T.P. (1998). "The first digit phenomenon." *American Scientist*, 86, p 358. **17.** Ecker, Michael. (1992). "Caution: Black holes at work." *New Scientist*, December 19/26, p 38. **18.** Cowley, Geoffrey. (1989). "Rap songs from the deep." *Newsweek*, March 20, p 63. Cr. J. Covey. **19.** McClintock, Jack. (1991). "Deep-diving, warm-blooded turtle." *Sea Frontiers*, 37, February, p 8. **20.** Gordon, David G. (1987). "What is that?" *Oceans*, 20, August, pp 44. **21.** Schindel, David E. (1982) "The gaps in the fossil record," *Nature*, 297, p 282. **22.** Anonymous. (1993). "Polar bear bones cast doubt on Ice Age beliefs." *Colorado Springs Gazette*, August 23. An Associated Press dispatch. Cr. S. Parker. (A COUDI item. COUDI = Collectors of Unusual Data, International) **23.** Anonymous. (1982). *Science Digest*, 90, April, p 19. **24.** Anonymous. (1981). "The blebs and ruffles of cellular fortune." *New Scientist*, 90, p 87. **25.** Day, Michael. (1996). "Cancer's many points of departure." *New Scientist*, June 1, p 16. **26.** Ross, Priscilla. (1997). *NEARA Transit*, 9, Spring, p 5. **27.** Pilapil, Virgilio R. (1991). "Was there a prehistoric migration of the Philippine Aetas to America?" *Epigraphic Society, Occasional Papers*, 20, p 150. **28.** Gibbons, Ann. (1995). "The Mystery of humanity's missing mutations." *Science*, 267, p 35. **29.** Cohen, Jack, & Ian Stewart. (1994). "Our genes aren't us." *Discover*, 15, April, p 78. **30.** Cohen, Philip. (1997). "Can DNA in food find its way into cells?" *New Scientist*, January 4, p 14. **31.** May, Robert M. (1996). "Now that's what you call chamber music." *Nature*, 381, p 659. **32.** Anonymous. (1998). "Do initials help some live longer?" *San Mateo Times*, March 28. Cr. J. Covey. **33.** Phillips, David P., et al. (1992). "The birthday: Lifeline or deadline?" *Psychosomatic Medicine*, 54, p 532. **34.** Muntz, Ira. (1977). "A note on the addictive personality: Addiction to placebos." *American Journal of Psychiatry*, 134, p 327. **35.** Morrison, Alastair. (1993). "The mystery of the deathbed tear." *Wellington Dominion*, August 11. Cr. P. Hassall. **36.** Taubes, Gary. (1997). "Computer design meets Darwin." *Science*, 277, p 1931. **37.** Yam, Philip. (1993). "'Daisy, Daisy'." *Scientific American*, 268, May, p 32

THE BIG PICTURE

Will the Real Human Being Please Stand Up?

Riane Eisler

What does it mean to be human? Is there really something terribly wrong with us? Or is the story about "human nature" we get from our education—both formal and informal—skewed toward a particular way of relating?

Our first inventions, we are told, were weapons, and the first human groups were organized by men to more effectively kill both animals and members of other human groups. Stanley Kubrick's film *2001: A Space Odyssey* (based on Arthur C. Clark's book) begins with a scene showing a hominid creature suddenly realizing that a large bone can be used as a weapon to kill another member of his species. The "innocent" cartoon (we think nothing of showing it to children) of a brutal caveman carrying a large club in one hand, dragging a woman around by her hair with the other, has this same message. Not only that, in a few "amusing" strokes it tells us that sex and male violence have always gone together, that this is just "the way it is."

> The invention of tools does not begin with the discovery that we can use bones, stones, or sticks to kill one another.

Although this story of an inevitably flawed humanity is still embedded in prevailing religious and scientific narratives about "original sin" and "selfish genes"—which also present male dominance as justified by either God or evolution—scholars from many disciplines tell us a different story of our cultural origins.

In this story, the invention of tools does not begin with the discovery that we can use bones, stones, or sticks to kill one another. It begins much earlier, with the use of sticks and stones to dig up roots (which chimpanzees do) and continues with the fashioning of ways to carry food other than with bare hands (rudimentary vegetable slings and baskets) and of mortars and other tools to soften foods.

In this story, the evolution of hominid, and then human, culture also follows more than one path. We have alternatives. We can organize relations in ways that reward violence and domination. But, as some of our earliest art suggests, we can also recognize our essential interconnection with one another and the rest of the living world.

The Two Chimps

In most nature documentaries, as well as in a huge body of sociobiological literature, we are led to believe that we are prisoners of our "unfortunate" evolutionary heritage. Just look at other primates, we are told, and you see why men are violent and women are subordinate to them.

But that's actually not what we see if we look at our species' two closest primate relatives: the common chimpanzees and the so-called pygmy chimpanzees or bonobos. The DNA of bonobos (pygmy chimpanzees) and common chimpanzees (who are actually no larger) is basically the same. Moreover, it is not very different from that of our own species. However, observations of both these species in the wild indicate that there are marked differences between the behaviors and social organizations of bonobos and common chimps.

In many ways, bonobo chimpanzees prefigure much of what we find in humans. They have what primatologists call a more

> To maintain social cohesion and order, this species, so closely related to us, relies primarily on the sharing of pleasure.

gracile (or slender) build, longer legs that stretch while walking, a smaller head, smaller ears, a thinner neck, a more open face, and thinner eyebrow ridges than most other apes. Of particular interest is that—also like humans but unlike most other species—bonobos have sex not just for reproduction but purely for pleasure, and even beyond this, pleasure-bonding.

In fact, this sharing of pleasure through the sharing of food as well as through sexual relations is a striking aspect of bonobo social organization. Just as striking is that even though theirs is not a violence-free social organization, their society is held together, far more so than among common chimps, by the exchange of mutual benefits characteristic of partnership relations. To maintain social cohesion and order, this species, so closely related to us, relies primarily on the sharing of pleasure—and not on the fear of pain (or violence) required to maintain rigid rankings of domination.

Equally striking is that, even though males are not dominated by females, in bonobo society females—particularly older females—wield a great deal of power. Moreover, it is through

men, although there are some notable exceptions, such as Mary Leakey, who found the first early human fossil in East Africa in 1959, and Adrienne Zihlman, who has proposed the bonobo chimpanzee as the most likely prototype for the "missing link" between hominids and earlier primates, and who has also helped to develop a theory about the origins of human tools in which women play an important role.[1]

Zihlman is among a growing number of scientists—most of them women in fields ranging from physical anthropology and biology to cultural anthropology, psychology, and sociology—who have over the last 30 years been developing a more gender-balanced narrative of early human evolution. As Zihlman notes, this has been an uphill struggle. No sooner are earlier male-centered accounts of human evolution contradicted by new evidence, than new theories are put forward to again render women invisible, or at best portray them as "handmaidens to men" and squarely place men—and with them an emphasis on aggression and competition—at the center of our human adventure.[2]

These contributions present a view of our human emergence in which more stereotypically "feminine" human characteristics, such as nurturance and nonviolence, are highlighted—*whether they reside in women or men.*

the association of females in groups that bonobo females seem to have avoided the kind of predatory sexual behavior that has been observed among common chimps, where males have been seen to force sexual relations on females.

In short, the bonobo chimpanzees rely more on bonds based on pleasure and the sharing of benefits than on rankings based on fear and force. (A good resource here is the article on the bonobos by the primatologist Takayoshi Kano in *Nature*. The difference between the bonobo chimps and common chimps is also discussed in detail in my books *Sacred Pleasure* and *Tomorrow's Children*.)

Were Women There?

Much of what is still written about the story of human evolution follows the old view that "man the hunter" was its main protagonist. Indeed, most of the scientists in this field have been

Not only that, these theories—which invariably portray male-dominance as natural—continue to be replicated in the vast majority of textbooks, as well as in visual representations of human evolution. Typical are museum dioramas where a male stands tall in the foreground while a group of females sits in the background, or where a male towers over a smaller crouching female, as in the dioramas of Neanderthals and *homo sapiens* at the American Museum of Natural History exhibit. (For a survey of such scenes in books, see Diane Gifford-Gonzales' "You Can Hide, But You Can't Run: Representations of Women's Work in Illustrations of Paleolithic Life," where she speaks of one classic pattern for depicting women sitting on or working with animal skins as the faceless "drudge-on-the-hide" distortion of women's roles as passive and peripheral).[3]

By developing more balanced, and accurate, narratives in which women, and not just men, play a major role in innovating and making hominid and human evolution happen, women scientists are making significant contributions to our understanding of how

Will the Real Human Being Please Stand Up?
Riane Eisler

we became human. These contributions present a view of our human emergence in which more stereotypically "feminine" human characteristics, such as nurturance and nonviolence, are highlighted—*whether they reside in women or men.*

For example, Zihlman goes beyond earlier accounts about what distinguishes our species: Our upright posture, which freed our hands for tool use, and on our large brains, which give us our great capacity to learn, making possible our immense behavioral flexibility. Like other theorists, such as Glynn Isaacs, Nancy Tanner, Ralph Holloway, Paul MacLean, and Humberto Maturana, she emphasizes the role of communication and caring in human evolution. The theory she developed together with Nancy Tanner also emphasizes our enormous human capacity for creativity. Indeed, Tanner and Zihlman propose that we have even to some degree been co-creators of our own biological evolution—and that females played a key part in this process.

As Tanner writes in *Becoming Human*, not only is it more than likely that females developed and used some of the earliest tools, such as slings and other means of carrying infants, baskets to carry gathered plants, and possibly also tools to dig for tubers and roots; these tools, in turn, also affected our evolution. "Tools for gathering meant mothers could collect more food for offspring who, then, could be supported longer before becoming independent"[4]—a longer period of dependency being a salient characteristic of our species. This also made it possible for children to have a longer period to "learn social and technological traditions"—another key development in human evolution, as it lead to the much greater role of culture in shaping behavior found in our species.[5]

One could even speculate that as we increasingly relied not on teeth, but on the use of tools and cooking methods to soften food, the huge molars characteristic of most other primates became less necessary, leaving more cranial room for larger brains. As many scientists have noted, it is our larger relative brain-size of an average of 1,350 cubic centimeters—a quantum leap from even our first hominid ancestors, who had already attained a brain size of 450 cubic centimeters—that characterizes our human emergence.[6] One could further speculate that this reduction in molar size also left more room for the voice boxes required for the complex verbalizations of human language—leading to the much greater capacity for communication

and symbolization that make possible the complex social, technological, and artistic development that we call human culture.

Indeed, as Paul MacLean also argues, it is highly probable that the most unique and important of human tools—our highly complex language—originated out of mother-child bonds; in other words, out of the bond of caring and love between mother and child.[7] Moreover, as Humberto Maturana and Gerda Verden-Zöller emphasize, writing about what Maturana calls the biology of love, one of the most important developments in our evolution is this human capacity for love.[8]

> It is highly probable that the most unique and important of human tools—our highly complex language—originated out of mother-child bonds.

This kind of approach to the study of human evolution makes it possible for people to refocus from selfishness and violence as the main themes in our evolution to caring and creativity as equally, and in some ways more important, themes. It also makes it possible for us to see that these qualities are part of the nature of both women and men. And it makes it possible to see that our primary and most meaningful identity is as human beings, regardless of gender, race, religion, or nationality. At the same time, this approach also helps us appreciate, and respect, other life forms and our Mother Earth, thus better equipping us to responsibly deal with the environmental challenges we face.

Our Neglected Mythic Heritage

The period after the gathering/hunting so-called Old Stone Age is known as the Neolithic or New Stone Age. It marks the beginning of what is perhaps the most important human invention: agriculture.

Here we are taught another interesting story of cultural origins. It is completely inconsistent with the one about violence and male dominance being "human nature," but it still conveys a similar message. Now we are told that chronic warfare and male dominance were ushered in by the agricultural age. That is, war and the subordination of one half of humanity are unfortunately the price we have to pay for civilization.

But what we are today learning about the Neolithic does not support this view. For example, the belief that the Neolithic was a male-dominated period is inconsistent with the myths found in many cultures throughout the world. Stories about female deities with great power and importance, as well as functioning partnerships between priestesses and priests, are found in many traditions. Female deities are also in many world traditions associated with important inventions that most texts still credit solely to men. In Mesopotamia, the Goddess Ninlil was revered for providing her people with an understanding of planting and harvesting methods. The official scribe of the Sumerian heaven was a woman, and the Sumerian Goddess Nidaba was honored as the one who initially invented clay tablets and the art of writing—appearing in that position earlier than any of the male deities who later replaced her. Similarly, in India, the Goddess Sarasvati was honored as the inventor of the original alphabet.[9]

That we find basic human inventions—from farming to writing—credited to female deities suggests that women probably played a key part in their development. That female deities are attributed so much power, including the power to create the world and humanity, also suggests a time when women occupied positions of leadership in their communities. And that we find these powerful female deities in ancient stories of every world region suggests that this was once widespread.

We find clues to this earlier period in the traditions of many indigenous North American tribes. As Paula Gunn Allen writes in *The Sacred Hoop: Recovering the Feminine in American Indian Traditions*, many Indian myths revolve around powerful female figures.[10] Serpent Woman is one. Corn Woman is another. Earth Woman is another. Still another is Grandmother of the Corn. As Allen writes, "Her variety and multiplicity testified to her complexity: she is the true creatrix for she is thought itself, from which all else is born…She is also the spirit that forms right balance, right harmony, and these in turn order all relationships in conformity with her law."[11] Similarly, central to Keres Pueblo theology is a Creatrix called She Who Thinks, who is the supreme spirit, both mother and father to all people and to all creatures.[12]

From China, too, we have myths about a time when the yin or feminine principle was not yet subservient to the yang or male principle. This is a time that the Chinese sage Lao Tsu, who dates to about 2,600 years ago, reports was peaceful and just. Likewise, one of the earliest known European writers, the Greek poet Hesiod, who lived approximately 2,800 years ago, tells us that there was once a "golden race" who lived in peaceful ease before

a "lesser race" brought with them Ares, the Greek god of war.

These stories were undoubtably greatly idealized folk memories of earlier times. Nonetheless, they tell us that, although most of the early agricultural era was not a violence-free utopian period, it was not the bloody time we have been led to believe.

The Metamorphosis of Myth—and Reality

Towards the end of the Neolithic period, however, we begin to see evidence of a fundamental social and cultural shift. In the Americas, even before the European conquests, there are indications that during a period of great drought there were incursions from warlike tribes. For example, such a drought is documented by dendrochronology in the western part of the American continent between approximately 1275 and 1290. There is also evidence of raiders who came down from the north and destroyed earlier Mogollan and Anasazi communities—highly developed cultures that represent a Golden Age of American Prehistory, the Anasazi later becoming the Hopi and Zuñi Pueblo Indians.[13]

> That we find basic human inventions—from farming to writing—credited to female deities, suggests that women probably played a key part in their development.

In Europe and Asia Minor, this shift occurred much earlier, approximately 5,500 years ago. At that point there appear, in the words of the British archaeologist James Mellaart, severe signs of stress. There are natural disasters and severe climate changes. Here, too, during a period of severe drought we begin to see invasions by nomadic herders, who bring with them a more warlike social organization.[14]

In the area the archaeologist Marija Gimbutas calls Old Europe (the Balkans and Northern Greece) we now, for the first time, find large stores of weapons. Often these are in a new type of burial: "chieftain graves." Horses, women, and children were often sacrificed and placed in these graves to accompany their masters into the afterworld.

In China, scholars at the Chinese Academy of Social Sciences in Beijing have also traced this shift from more peaceful and egalitarian societies in which women do not appear to have been subservient to men and female deities seem to have played leading roles to a later time when Chinese society oriented more to the dominator model.[15] For example, in his article "Myth and Reality: The Projection of Gender Relations in Prehistoric China," Professor Cai Junsheng writes: "NuWa is the most important mythological female figure handed down from the prehistoric age. NuWa was long considered by the Chinese as the creator/creatrix of the world. However, a careful examination of Chinese myths shows how, at the same time that the social structure changed to a patriarchal one, NuWa lost her power until finally there are myths where she dies."[16]

because the snake was viewed as one of the manifestations of the power of regeneration, since snakes shed and renew their skins. But in later Greek mythology, we have the monstrous Medusa, a terrible female with hair of coiled snakes. Significantly, she has been stripped of the power to give life, but still retains the power to take life, as she is said to turn men to stone.

Similarly, the Hindu Kali is noted for her bloodthirsty cruelty. Nonetheless there are also remnants in Hindu mythology of the female power to give life splintered off into a number of

For what is still seldom noted in conventional history texts and classes is that, as new technologies destabilize established institutional forms, there are opportunities to challenge entrenched systems of belief and social structures.

As Junsheng puts it, "due to the elimination and misinterpretation of information during the subsequent long period of patriarchal society" available data have to be carefully analyzed.[17] However, as he also notes, a careful analysis of myths provides clues to a massive cultural shift.

There are mythical clues to this shift from every world region. In Africa, the female status in sacred mythology deteriorated over time. This seems to follow the pattern found in other world regions, where female mythological figures start out as the Creatrix, then become a wife or mother of a male god, first in an equal role and then in a subservient role, are next demoted to nondivine status, and finally are demonized as witches or monsters. African goddesses can be found which run the gamut of these roles. The South African Ma is the "Goddess of Creation" and Mebeli (of the Congo) is the "Supreme Being;" Haine is the Tanzanian Moon Goddess whose husband is Ishoye (the sun); Dugbo (of Sierra Leone) is an Earth Goddess, responsible for all plants and trees, married to Yataa, the Supreme Being. There are also La-hkima Oqla (of Morocco), a female "jenn" who inhabits a river and rules over other evil spirits, Yalode (of Benin) who causes foot infections, and Watamaraka (of South Africa), the "Goddess of Evil" who is said to have given birth to all the demons.[18]

Today all these female mythic representations are found side by side. But if we do a little detective work, we can trace their origins and situate them in a sequence from Creatrix to subservience to conversion to a male deity or to a demonic witch or monster. For example, in the iconography of old Europe, the figure Gimbutas, called the Snake Goddess, plays a prominent role, probably

deities, including Parvati. Along a somewhat different trajectory, the early Greek Mother Goddess Demeter is first turned by Christian remything into Saint Demetra—and finally masculinized as Saint Demetrius. Following still another trajectory, female deities such as Athena in Greek mythology and Ishtar in Middle Eastern mythology are now goddesses of war and human sacrifice—reflecting the shift to a more violent, hierarchic, and male-dominated social structure.

Does this mean that societies ruled by women, matriarchies, are superior to societies ruled by men? Hardly. There is no evidence that these earlier societies were ruled by women.

But there is evidence that women and qualities stereotypically associated with women, such as caring and nonviolence, were not excluded from social governance. In other words, rather than patriarchies or matriarchies, these societies seem to have oriented more to what I have called a partnership rather than dominator model of organizing relations with other humans and with our Mother Earth.[19]

A New Look at Modern History

When we look at the last 300 years, taking our hidden cultural heritage into account, we see that the struggle for our future is not between right and left, religious and secular, or even industrial and pre- or postindustrial. It is rather between the two basic ways of organizing relations that—because there were no names to describe the configurations I discovered—I named the partnership model and the dominator model.

Another important aspect of modern history that then becomes visible is that during the great technological and social disequilibrium of the Industrial Revolution and now the postindustrial revolution of electronic, nuclear, and biochemical technologies, has come the opportunity for another major cultural shift: this time from domination to partnership. For what is still seldom noted in conventional history texts and classes is that, as new technologies destabilize established institutional forms, there are opportunities to challenge entrenched systems of belief and social structures.

century civil rights and women's liberation and women's rights movements. There is the nineteenth-century pacifist movement followed by the twentieth-century peace movement, expressing the first fully-organized rejection of violence as a means of resolving international conflicts. There is the twentieth-century family planning movement as a key to women's emancipation as well as to the alleviation of poverty and greater opportunities for children.

In basic respects, however, the dominator system remained firmly entrenched. Colonialism and the killing and exploitation of darker-skinned peoples continued the tradition of conquest

Regions ranging from the former Soviet Union to countries in Asia, Africa, and Latin America are being forced into a replay of the robber-baron days of early capitalism.

This leads to a completely different, more interesting, and more meaningful picture of the last 300 years: one with important practical implications for what we can do today.

Certainly the Enlightenment was a period where we begin to see a massive questioning of entrenched patterns of domination. The so-called rights of man movement of the late seventeenth and early eighteenth centuries eventually led to both the American and French Revolutions and to a gradual shift from monarchies to republics. Paralleling the challenge to the supposedly divinely-ordained right of kings to rule was the feminist movement of the eighteenth and nineteenth centuries, which challenged the supposedly divinely-ordained right by men to rule over women and children in the "castles" of their homes, bringing about a gradual shift to less autocratic and male-dominated families.

During both the nineteenth and twentieth centuries there were movements against slavery and against the colonization and exploitation of indigenous peoples. We see the rise of organized labor and socialism, followed by the toppling of feudal monarchies and warlords by communist revolutions in Russia, China, and other countries. In the United States, there is a gradual shift from unregulated robber-baron capitalism to government regulations—for example, anti-monopoly laws and economic safety nets such as Social Security and unemployment insurance.

There is the nineteenth-century feminist movement demanding equal education and suffrage for women and the organized movement by blacks for the vote, followed by the twentieth-

and domination on a global scale. There are also periodic backlashes; for example, Jim Crow laws passed after the abolition of slavery, anti-union violence during the first half of the twentieth century, and continuing anti-feminist agitation—from resistance to higher education and the vote for women in the nineteenth century to the defeat of the Equal Rights Amendment and renewed opposition to reproductive rights for women in the twentieth century.

The twentieth century also witnessed massive dominator regressions. In Europe, for example, we see Hitler's Germany (from the early 1930s to the mid-1940s) and Stalin's Soviet Union (the 1920s to the 1950s), in which the ideals of a more just society were coopted into a "dictatorship of the proletariat," creating still another version of a brutal dominator model.

And even after Western colonial regimes are overthrown in Africa and Asia, we see the rise of authoritarian dictatorships by local elites over their own people, resulting in renewed repression and exploitation, including the rise of so-called fundamentalist religious regimes that once again reinstate the domination of one half of humanity over the other as a cornerstone of a violent and authoritarian system.

During this modern industrial age we also see the use of ever more advanced technologies to more effectively exploit, dominate, and kill. Moreover, it is during the industrial age that high technology begins to be harnessed to further "man's conquest of nature"—wreaking ever more environmental damage.

Humanity at the Crossroads

Today the mix of the dominator model and advanced technology becomes increasingly unsustainable. The blade is the nuclear bomb and/or biological warfare and terrorism. Increasingly advanced technologies in the service of a dominator ethos threaten our natural habitat, as well as that of most species with whom we share our planet.

This postmodern period brings further challenges to traditions of domination. It brings a strong environmental movement: millions of people coming together to challenge "man's conquest of nature." It also brings a strengthening of the family-planning movement as integral to environmental sustainability; stronger movements against the domination and exploitation of indigenous peoples; a growing challenge by peoples in the "developing world" to its domination by the "developed world;" and thousands of grassroots organizations all over the world working toward political democracy, nonviolent ways of living, and economic, racial, and gender equity.[20]

Significantly, because these are foundational relations where we first learn and continually practice either domination or partnership, we now see a much more organized challenge to traditions of domination and violence in intimate relations. Child abuse, rape, and wife-beating are increasingly prosecuted in some world regions. A global women's-rights movement frontally challenges the domination of half of humanity by the other half, gaining impetus from the unprecedented United Nations conferences (1975–1995) that brought women from all world regions together around such pivotal issues as violence against women, equal legal rights and economic opportunities, and reproductive freedom.

However, precisely because the movement toward partnership is intensifying and deepening—for the first time focusing on the so-called private sphere of human relations that are the foundations for habits and attitudes we carry into all areas of life—the resistence to change stiffens. There is continued, and in some places increasing, violence against women and children. Some of the statistical increases are due to the fact that this violence was formerly unreported, as it was not prosecuted and was often instead blamed on the victims. But since violence is what ultimately maintains dominator relations, as women's and children's human rights are asserted, violence against them has also increased to literally "beat them back into submission." In some countries, this violence is perpetrated by government officials; for example, in Afghanistan, Algeria, Pakistan, Bangladesh, and Iran the stoning to death of women for any act perceived as countering male sexual and personal control—even a young woman exposing her ankles—is again being justified on "moral" grounds.[21]

There is also, under the guise of economic globalization, a recentralization of economic power worldwide. Under pressure from major economic players, governments are cutting social services and shredding economic safety-nets—"economic restructuring" that is particularly hurtful to women and children worldwide. In the developing world, this restructuring is enriching dominator elites through a shift from the production of food and goods for local consumption to products for the export trade. At the same time, it is contributing to the impoverishment of Third World people, who no longer produce what they need and are ever more dependent on jobs in urban centers.

Concurrently, high-paying jobs in postindustrial economies are shrinking, creating increased competition for low-paying jobs (generally without benefits) by workers in blue collar, pink collar, and middle management displaced by automation or corporate downsizing. Regions ranging from the former Soviet Union to countries in Asia, Africa, and Latin America are being forced into a replay of the robber-baron days of early capitalism, complete with sweatshops, forced child labor, rampant political corruption, and organized crime.[22] In short, there is a widening gap between haves and have-nots both within countries and between different world regions.

There is growing scapegoating of women (particularly single mothers living in poverty) and minorities, once again sometimes in the name of religious fundamentalism. There is an increase in terrorism, even in once supposedly impregnable nations such as the United States—some by its own citizens. There are "ethnic cleansings," such as those in Bosnia and Kosovo, and resurgent genocidal warfare, such as the carnage of Rwanda. In addition, in the name of entertainment, the mass media obsessively focus on violence—constantly emphasizing the infliction or suffering of pain that are mainstays of dominator politics and economics.

There is also burgeoning population growth. The world's population, which has doubled in the last 40 years—in only a few decades reaching more than 5 billion people, the vast majority in the poorest world regions—is projected to again double by the mid-twenty-first century, exacerbating hunger, violence, and other causes of human suffering, straining the world's natural resources. This unsustainable population growth is in large part also due to dominator systems dynamics: the continued denial of reproductive freedom to women (or the loss of gains already made) and the efforts, often violent, to deny women access to life options other than procreation.

In sum, the outcome of the tension between the partnership and dominator models as two basic human possibilities is far from settled. We are now at what scientists call a bifurcation point, where there are two very different scenarios for our future.

One is *dominator systems breakdown*: the unsustainable future of high technology guided by the dominator model. This is where high technology in service of the domination of nature despoils and pollutes our natural habitat. It is a future where advanced technologies will be used not to free our human potentials, but to more effectively control and dominate. And ultimately, it is a future of environmental, nuclear, or biological holocaust.

The other scenario is *breakthrough to partnership*: the sustainable future of a world primarily orienting to the partnership model. Here advanced technologies are developed and used in ways that promote environmental balance and the realization of our species' great untapped potentials. International regulations ensure corporate accountability to workers, communities, and our natural habitat. New economic institutions and rules recognize the value of the work of caring and caregiving, and discourage violence, exploitation, and the despoliation of nature.[23]

Although in this world, too, nation-states may continue to break down, instead of leading to genocidal ethnic civil wars, diversity is valued and our shared partnership heritage binds cultures together. Although there is still some violence, it is not built into the system as a means of maintaining rankings of domination. Although there is still conflict, as is inevitable in human relations, young people have the tools to resolve it in creative ways.

Women and men are equal partners in both the "private" or family sphere and the outside or "public" sphere. And children are valued and nurtured not only by their biological parents, but by the entire community—which recognizes that children are our most precious resource.

To move toward this world, however, requires fundamental changes, including changes in our education that make it possible for today's and tomorrow's children to see that if we work together we can create a more equitable, peaceful, and sustainable future—once we acquire the knowledge and skills to do so.[24]

Endnotes

1. Zihlman, Adrienne L. (1982). *The Human evolution coloring book*, with illustrations by Carla Simmons, Wynn Kapit, Fran Milner, and Cyndie Clark-Huegel. New York: Barnes and Noble Books. **2.** Zihlman, Adrienne. (1997). The Paleolithic glass ceiling: Women in human evolution. In Hager, Lori D. (Ed.) *Women in human evolution.* New York: Routledge, pp 91–113. **3.** Gifford-Gonzales, Diane. (1993). You can hide, but you can't run: Representations of women's work in illustrations of Paleolithic life. *Visual Anthropology Review* 9, pp 23–41. **4.** Tanner, Nancy M. (1981). *Becoming human.* Cambridge, Mass.: Cambridge University Press, p 274. **5.** *Ibid.*, pp 274–275. See also Zihlman, Adrienne & Nancy Tanner. (1974). Becoming human: Putting women in evolution. Paper presented at the annual meeting of the American Anthropological Society, Mexico City. **6.** Leakey, pp 44–48. **7.** MacLean, Paul. (1995). *The triune brain in evolution: Role in paleocerebral functions.* New York: Plenum, p 544; MacLean, Paul. (Sept 1996). "Women: A more balanced brain?" *Zygon*, 31:3, p 434. **8.** Maturana, Humberto R., & Gerda Verden-Zoller. (1998). *Origins of humanness in the biology of love.* Durham, NC: Duke University Press. **9.** Stone, Merlin. (1976). *When God was a woman.* New York: Harcourt Brace Jovanovich, p 3. This book is an excellent source of information about ancient female deities, its only drawback being that it does not make a distinction—which is critical—between the character of the female deities before and after the shift to a dominator model, when they often became goddesses of war and sacrifice. For a discussion of this, see *The Chalice & the Blade* and *Sacred Pleasure*, both by Riane Eisler. **10.** Allen, Paula Gunn. (1986). *The sacred hoop: Recovering the feminine in American Indian traditions.* Boston: Beacon Press. **11.** *Ibid.*, p 14. **12.** *Ibid.*, p 15. Herb Martin and Terri Wheeler of California State University at Monterey Bay contributed material on Goddess myths from Native American traditions. **13.** Gibson, Arrell Morgan. (1980). *The American Indian: Prehistory to the present.* Lexington, Massachusetts: D.C. Heath and Company, pp 30–34. **14.** Chapter 5 of Riane Eisler, *Sacred pleasure* (San Francisco: Harper Collins, 1996) explores some of the reasons that the culture of these herding people, who came from arid environments, may have evolved in a dominator direction. **15.** Jiayin, Min. (Ed.). (1995). *The chalice and the blade in Chinese culture.* Beijing: China Social Sciences Publishing House. **16.** Junsheng, Cai. "Myth and reality: The projection of gender relations in prehistoric China," in Jiayin (1995), p 44. **17.** *Ibid*, pp 34–35. **18.** Herb Martin and Terri Wheeler of California State University at Monterey Bay contributed material on Goddess traditions from Africa. **19.** For a detailed description of these societies and the factors behind the shift, see Eisler, Riane (1987, 1988). *The chalice and the blade.* San Francisco: Harper & Row; Eisler, Riane. (1995, 1996). *Sacred pleasure.* San Francisco: Harper Collins. For a work that incorporates this information into education, see Eisler, Riane. (2000). *Tomorrow's children.* Boulder, Colorado: Westview Press. **20.** For examples, see chapters 18 and 19 of *Sacred Pleasure*. **21.** Women Living Under Muslim Laws, an organization of Muslim women with offices in Pakistan and France, is an excellent source of information here. They can be reached at Women Living Under Muslim Laws, Boite Postale 23, 34790 Grables (Montpellier), France. Another excellent source is the quarterly *Women's International Network News*, which can be subscribed to by writing to Women's International Network News, 187 Grant Street, Lexington, MA 02173. **22.** Some good readings are Mander, Jerry & Edwin Goldsmith. (Eds.). (1996). *The case against the global economy and for a turn toward the local.* San Francisco: Sierra Club Books; Henderson, Hazel. (1991). *Paradigms in progress: Life beyond economics.* Indianapolis: Knowledge Systems, Inc.; Korten, David. (1995). *When corporations rule the world.* San Francisco: Barrett-Koehler; Peterson, The. Spike & Anne Sisson Runyan. (1993). *Global gender issues.* Boulder: Westview Press; Eisler, Riane, David Loye, & Kari Norgaard. (1995). *Women, men, and the global quality of life.* Pacific Grove, California: Center for Partnership Studies; *Human development report 1995.* (1995). Published for the United Nations Development Program (UNDP) by Oxford University Press (New York); *The world's women 1995: Trends and statistics.* (1995). New York: The United Nations. For a short piece that has some good statistics and could serve as a handout, see also Korten, David. (June 1997). A market-based approach to corporate responsibility. *Perspectives on Business and Global Change* 11: 2, pp 45–55. See also the Center for Partnership Studies' Website <www.partnership-way.org> to download "Changing the Rules of the Game: Work, Values, and Our Future," by Riane Eisler, 1997. **23.** See Riane Eisler, "Changing the Rules of The Game" on the CPS website <www.partnershipway.org>. **24.** These two scenarios are outlined in chapters 12 and 13 of *The Chalice and the Blade* and detailed in the closing chapters of *Sacred Pleasure*.

Adapted from Tomorrow's Children: A Blueprint for Partnership Education in the 21st Century *by Riane Eisler (Westview Press, 2000).*

Will the Real Human Being Please Stand Up?
Riane Eisler

New Thought vs. Holism

How Did "Oneness" Get Hijacked by Materialism?

Alexandra Bruce

Isn't it interesting that among the most influential movements in American culture, the origin of a specific way of thinking that pervades the very core of American identity remains largely undistinguished and is not commonly known? How many people have even heard of the New Thought Movement?

Who knew that the phenomenally successful *The Secret*, the *Christian Science Monitor*, the Unity Church, Alcoholics Anonymous, *A Course in Miracles*, and Norman Vincent Peale's *The Power of Positive Thinking* are all outgrowths of the New Thought Movement, which swept America starting in the mid-nineteenth century, a time when the much-vaunted "American Way" was beginning to be defined?

> The idea of self-improvement through changing one's thinking may not have been invented in America, or even be unique to America, but it sure did find fertile territory and a profusion of expressions in this land.

The idea of self-improvement through changing one's thinking may not have been invented in America, or even be unique to America, but it sure did find fertile territory and a profusion of expressions in this land.

Wallace D. Wattles' 1910 book, *The Science of Getting Rich*, is a classic exemplar of New Thought. Wattles cited his main influences as philosophers Ralph Waldo Emerson and Georg Hegel. These men in turn were heavily influenced by ancient Hindu and Buddhist texts, the Western translations of which had only recently become accessible during their lifetimes.

At the root of these Eastern spiritual philosophies is the concept of monism. In Wattles' words:

The monistic theory of the universe, the theory that One is All, and that All is One; That one Substance manifests itself as the seeming many elements of the material world—is of Hindu origin, and has been gradually winning its way into the thought of the western world for two hundred years. It is the foundation of all the Oriental philosophies, and of those of Descartes, Spinoza, Leibnitz, Schopenhauer, Hegel, and Emerson.[1]

In seventeenth-century Europe, the "All is One" concept was as heretical to the Abrahamic religions of Christianity, Judaism, and Islam as it remains today, and in 1656 the celebrated Dutch philosopher Spinoza was excommunicated from his Orthodox Jewish congregation because of the monistic expressions in his writings.

Similar to Spinoza before him, Wattles was fired from his Methodist ministry when his sermons were ruled un-Christian by the hierarchy. However, his compelling blend of American "can-do" with Eastern monism remains as appealing as ever to the silent majority of people around the world who are not fundamentalists.

Christianity vs. the Unity Church

Considered to be the weightiest exponent of New Thought in the present era and strongly endorsed by Oprah Winfrey, the Unity Church was founded in the 1880s in the Missouri frontier town of Kansas City by Myrtle and Charles Fillmore. It has a membership today of approximately 3,000,000.[2]

Like Wallace D. Wattles and the philosophers who had informed him, the Fillmores were greatly influenced by Eastern philosophy. In fact, some Christian fundamentalists actually describe the Unity Church as a Hindu sect(!). For its part, the Unity Church describes itself as "Practical" and/or "Positive" Christianity, and it uses the Bible as its central text.

The Unity Church and the New Thought Movement represent a revolt against what its founders viewed to be the negative dogmas of Christian fundamentalism. In kind, Christian fundamentalists to this day regard the monism of the Unity Church as Satanic because it instructs adherents to *see God in all things.*

The "All is One," monistic worldview espoused by New Thought runs 180 degrees counter to the doctrine of mainstream Christianity, where Christ died on the Cross for our sins and we must accept him as our Savior in order to go to Heaven. In a conversation I had with a Catholic priest, he explained the doctrine of God as the creator of the universe and how he set the universe into motion. The priest likened God's relationship to his creation to an author's relationship to her book: The book is *not* the author just as God is *not* the universe.

What this says to me is that from the Christian perspective, the very concept of a universe, the idea of "All That Is," does not exist.

David Bohm and the Implicate Order

Mainstream Christian doctrine conflicts not only with Eastern philosophy and with New Thought but also with the mathematical proofs and interpretations of quantum mechanics put forth in the twentieth century by physicists such as David Bohm. In his book *Wholeness and the Implicate Order*, Bohm describes how space, time, and physical objects belong to what he calls the "unfolded" explicate order, which is contained within the general totality of the "enfolded" implicate order, where:

> ...space and time are no longer the dominant factors determining the relationships of dependence or independence of different elements.[3]

In Bohm's view, infinite dimensions of space, time, and what-have-you are "enfolded" and are not all necessarily perceptible by humans or our instrumentation. However, this implicate order can be expressed in mathematical proofs, and he says that a form of the implicate order is actually experienced by human beings as consciousness. Bohm's work ultimately led

Wattles' The Science of Getting Rich speaks to a beaver-capped, musket-toting, rugged individualist pulling himself up by his bootstraps in a libertarian utopia on the frontier.

him to conclude: "Everybody not merely depends on everybody but everybody actually *is* everybody, in a deeper sense."[4]

The monism of American New Thought fails to truly apprehend this kind of holism, the Wholeness and the Oneness of All That Is, the very cornerstone of Buddhism and other Eastern spiritual philosophies—and of Bohmian dynamics.

Stuck in Materialistic Mode

The abiding duality of Western thinking and its preoccupation with the personal self continue to make both the consciousness and practice of true holism a tough maneuver for the Western mind. This is why the most common expression of New Thought is a means for personal gain. Forged as it was on the rugged American frontier, before 95 percent of the old-growth forest in this country had been razed, New Thought remains seemingly stuck in an era when resources appeared boundless and the world's population was less than third of what it is today.

Wattles' *The Science of Getting Rich* speaks to a beaver-capped, musket-toting, rugged individualist pulling himself up by his bootstraps in a libertarian utopia on the frontier. American monism does not represent the ancient, Eastern monism of acting within the greater good. To the contrary, it is extremely self-centered and alarmingly out of step with today's looming planetary environmental collapse.

The conflation of "spirituality" with "relentless materialism"[5] is what makes New Thought and self-help very compelling to some people and totally abhorrent to others.

New Thought vs. Holism
How Did "Oneness" Get Hijacked by Materialism? **Alexandra Bruce**

417

The equation of spiritual wealth with material wealth is abundantly evident in the bestselling DVD and book by Australian TV producer Rhonda Byrne, *The Secret*, which has sold well over 7 million copies. This is especially so of many of its abysmally money-grubbing spin-offs, such as the "SGR: Science of Getting Rich Seminar."[6]

This Internet venture between fellow *Secret* teachers Bob Proctor, Jack Canfield, and Michael Beckwith was produced and is being promoted by men for whom I have a great deal of respect. However, this package really just looks to me like an egregious pile of junk: The "Home Study Course with Full SGR Membership Benefits" consists of a copy of Wattles' *Science of Getting Rich* book, an MP3 player loaded with the three speakers' motivational lectures, ten CDs and printed transcripts of the same recordings, "vision boards" (which look

The conflation of "spirituality" with "relentless materialism" is what makes New Thought and self-help very compelling to some people and totally abhorrent to others.

exactly like the Quartet Dry-Erase Boards you can get from Office Depot), "a Rich, Supple Leather-Bound Briefcase" (during the making of which a Chinese slave laborer probably inhaled carcinogenic fumes, in order for her factory to sell it to the SGR folks for less than a tenth of its actual worth…), and "A Life-Changing Opportunity: Coaching Calls with Bob Proctor." All for just $1,995!

There is no doubt value to be found in the "SGR" package, but the naked money-grab by these teachers in the wake of *The Secret*'s success is, quite frankly icky. Further, the pile of stuff that comprises this product is not exactly environmentally friendly. (If we are to believe the statistics presented by Annie Leonard in her brilliant viral video, "Story of Stuff,"[7] 99 percent of everything Americans buy ends up in a landfill within six months of purchase!)

At a time of "Operation Iraqi Freedom," genocide in Darfur, and the unsustainable desecration of the planet's resources, *The Secret*'s message of visualizing your skinny body and attracting your brand-new BMW seems pathologically narcissistic and almost criminal in its degeneracy. Nonetheless, *The Secret* resonates powerfully with millions of Americans despairing over their credit card bills, dreaming of an escape from their financial enslavement, wishing only to pursue their shopping addictions with even greater freedom….

In his book *Against Happiness*, Eric G. Wilson argues that most Americans are so thoroughly programmed to "think positively" and to obsess on their personal desires, that it is precisely this ideological landscape that enabled the dismantling of the US Constitution and the prosecution of the war in Iraq, in the face of the ridiculously specious justifications of the Executive branch of the US government.

The financially thriving members of the success-coaching industry have grinned in silence on such matters, while the legal and economic environment, which has enabled them to prosper and to help others to do the same, has been slyly slipped out from under them. The rising pressure on America's middle class has actually been great for business. The unsurprising cynicism that exists towards the self-help industry exists quite simply because it is too selfish.

Isn't it ironic that although the concept of "holism" is the underlying principle of New Thought, it is so rarely the product that it sells. Come to think of it, true holism and mass marketing are almost mutually exclusive ideas—despite the growing market for upscale "holistic" products and services. As consciousness researcher Bill Harris—cocreator of Holosync meditation technology—said in a film which I am producing:

> The people who are known in human history for having the greatest amount of inner peace are those who finally realize that the separate self who they thought they were was actually just a conceptualization. And the most amazing thing happens when you actually realize that… you literally are connected to everything and everything is one system, one vast interconnected thing…
>
> The side effect…is that, since you're everywhere, there's nowhere to go. Since you're everything, there's nothing outside of you to get—also nothing outside of you to threaten you…. This intense peace comes over you.[8]

The underdogs of American society will likely be the first to experience the needed transformation of human values, when our backs are pressed against the walls of a paradigm whose chicanery can no longer hold up. In *Against Happiness*, Wilson writes:

> [S]ome people strain all the time to break through their mental manacles, to cleanse the portals of their perceptions, and to see the universe as an ungraspable riddle, gorgeous and gross. Happy types, those Americans bent only on happiness and afraid of sadness, tend to forgo this labor. They sit safe in their cages. The sad ones, dissatisfied with the status quo, are more likely to beat against the bars....
>
> We perhaps could be gentle toward these happy American types if their dreams were only abstract and predictable. But isn't there something else at work here, something potentially more pernicious? These dreams are ultimately delusional, and narcissistically so. Lopping off half the world with their one-sided responses, these American seekers of happiness are in danger of deluding themselves into believing that only one part of the world exists, the part that gladdens their egos.[9]

Until a better option can be agreed upon, the ego-gratification of consumerism *is* humanism. Institute of Noetic Sciences Fellow Peter Russell offers these thoughts in regards to what is lacking from the modern state of mind:

> We may think we are seeking an external goal, but in truth we are looking for something internal—a more satisfactory state of mind.... [Our true inner nature] is something that can never be taken away from us. But when we lose sight of it we begin looking for it in the world around us. And because we never find anything there of truly lasting satisfaction, we keep on searching. We keep on taking from the world, caught in a cycle of greed and fear....
>
> What we need today is not more things, but an awakening to our true inner nature.[10]

At a time of "Operation Iraqi Freedom," genocide in Darfur, and the unsustainable desecration of the planet's resources, *The Secret*'s message of visualizing your skinny body and attracting your brand-new BMW seems pathologically narcissistic and almost criminal in its degeneracy.

The "American Way" has given us many of the artifacts and the technologies that define contemporary Western civilization, but it may also have unwittingly brought the world to the precipice of mass extinction. It will take a lot of "can-do" to remove the global stranglehold of the petroleum cartels, for starters—and to make humanity's need for ego-gratification and its means of production and consumption sustainable before the manufacture of desire eats this planet alive. Using New Thought techniques to lose weight and acquire more consumer goods is not the answer.

Endnotes

1. Wattles, Wallace D. (1910). *The science of getting rich.* **2.** Adherents.com. **3.** Bohm, David. (1980). *Wholeness and the implicate order.* Routledge, p xv. **4.** David Bohm quoted in *From fragmentation to wholeness* (1990). Mystic Fire Video, Inc. **5.** Adler, J. (2007) "Decoding 'The Secret.'" *Newsweek*, March 5. **6.** www.thesgrprogram.com. **7.** www.storyofstuff.com. **8.** Bill Harris quoted in *The gift* (working title). (2008). Equilibrium Entertainment, LLC. **9.** Wilson, Eric G. (2008). *Against happiness.* Sarah Crichton Books. **10.** Russell, Peter (2001), "Sustainability: Waking up in time." Closing speech given at the Sustainability Forum, Zurich, Sept 25.

New Thought vs. Holism
How Did "Oneness" Get Hijacked by Materialism?   **Alexandra Bruce**

419

THE RELIGIOUS EXPERIENCE OF PHILIP K. DICK

PHILIP K. DICK WAS A WRITER OF SCIENCE FICTION. IN 1982 HE DIED SUDDENLY OF A STROKE. HIS BOOKS OFTEN DEALT WITH THE ILLUSORY QUALITY OF REALITY AS WE KNOW IT. IN MARCH, 1974 DICK SAW WHAT HE LATER DESCRIBED AS "A VISION OF THE APOCALYPSE," AND SPENT THE REST OF HIS LIFE TRYING TO UNDERSTAND WHAT HE HAD EXPERIENCED. WAS IT THE ONSET OF ACUTE SCHIZOPHRENIA, OR WAS IT A GENIUNE MYSTIC REVELATION, AND THEN AGAIN, IS THERE ANY DIFFERENCE ??

FULLERTON, CALIFORNIA, MARCH, 1974: "I HAD A WISDOM TOOTH EXTRACTED. THEY GAVE ME A TREMENDOUS AMOUNT OF SODIUM PENTOTHAL. I CAME HOME AND WAS IN GREAT PAIN. HE HADN'T GIVEN ME ANY PAIN MEDICATION AND MY WIFE CALLED THE PHARMACY."

"I WAS IN SUCH PAIN THAT I WENT OUT TO MEET THE GIRL WHEN SHE CAME. SHE WAS WEARING A GOLDEN FISH IN PROFILE ON A NECKLACE. THE SUN STRUCK IT AND IT SHONE, AND I WAS DAZED BY IT."

"FOR SOME REASON I WAS HYPNO-TIZED BY THE GLEAM-ING GOLD-EN FISH. I FORGOT MY PAIN, FORGOT THE MED-ICATION, FORGOT WHY THE GIRL WAS THERE. I JUST KEPT STARING AT THE FISH SIGN."

"'WHAT DOES THAT MEAN?' I ASKED HER. THE GIRL TOUCHED THE GUMMERING GOLDEN FISH WITH HER HAND AND SAID, 'THIS IS A SIGN WORN BY THE EARLY CHRISTIANS.' SHE THEN GAVE ME THE PACKAGE OF MEDICATION."

"IN THAT INSTANT, AS I STARED AT THE GLEAMING FISH SIGN AND HEARD HER WORDS, I SUDDENLY EXPERIENCED WHAT I LATER LEARNED IS CALLED *ANAMNESIS* — A GREEK WORD MEAN-ING, LITERALLY, 'LOSS OF FORGETFUL-NESS.'"

"I REMEMBERED WHO I WAS AND WHERE I WAS. IN AN INSTANT, IN THE TWINK-LING OF AN EYE, IT ALL CAME BACK TO ME. AND NOT ONLY COULD I REMEM-BER IT BUT I COULD SEE IT. THE GIRL WAS A SECRET CHRIST-IAN AND SO WAS I. WE LIVED IN FEAR OF DETEC-TION BY THE RO-MANS. WE HAD TO COMMUNICATE IN CRYPTIC SIGNS. SHE HAD JUST TOLD ME ALL THIS, AND IT WAS TRUE!"

"I SAW THE WORLD AS THE WORLD OF THE APOSTOLIC CHRISTIAN TIMES OF ANCIENT ROME, WHEN THE FISH SIGN WAS IN USE."

"IT ONLY LASTED A FEW SECONDS. I WENT IN AND TOOK THE PAIN MEDICATION. I WAS HEMORRAG-ING. I WAS BLEEDING BADLY, IN GREAT DISCOMFORT."

"AND THEN A MONTH LATER, IT ALL BEGAN TO SEEP THROUGH. THERE WASN'T ANY WAY I COULD HOLD IT BACK. THE TRANSFORMATION OC-CURED AND IT STAYED FOR A YEAR... I SAW THE WORLD UNDER THE AS-PECT OF THE CHRISTIAN APOCALYPSE."

The Religious Experience of Phillip K. Dick
R. Crumb

"IT WASN'T LIKE AN ALTERNATE REALITY, IT WAS LIKE WHAT I CALL 'TRANS-TEMPORAL CONSTANCY'... IT WAS AN ETERNAL TRUTH, LIKE PLATO'S ARCHETYPICAL WORLD, WHERE EVERYTHING WAS ALWAYS HERE AND ALWAYS NOW, AND HAD BEEN THAT WAY AND WOULD BE THAT WAY."

"BUT THERE WAS SOME KIND OF DYNAMISM, WHERE IT WASN'T STATIC. THERE WAS SOME KIND OF TIME, BUT IT WAS A DIFFERENT KIND OF TIME... A DREAM TIME, WHERE THE DEEDS OF HEROES OCCUR. IT WAS SOME KIND OF MYTHOLOGICAL TIME, EVERYTHING ASSUMED A MYTHOLOGICAL QUALITY."

"I WAS ABLE TO FUNCTION PERFECTLY, I WASN'T PSYCHOTIC. I WAS ABLE TO HANDLE ALL MY BUSINESS—IN FACT I HANDLED IT BETTER... I WASN'T SCREWED UP."

"IT INVADED MY MIND AND ASSUMED CONTROL OF MY MOTOR CENTERS AND DID MY ACTING AND THINKING FOR ME. I WAS A SPECTATOR TO IT... THIS MIND, WHOSE IDENTITY WAS TOTALLY OBSCURE TO ME, WAS EQUIPPED WITH TREMENDOUS TECHNICAL KNOWLEDGE. IT HAD MEMORIES DATING BACK OVER TWO THOUSAND YEARS...IT SPOKE GREEK, HEBREW, SANSKRIT, THERE WASN'T ANYTHING THAT IT DIDN'T SEEM TO KNOW."

"IT IMMEDIATELY SET ABOUT PUTTING MY AFFAIRS IN ORDER. IT FIRED MY AGENT AND MY PUBLISHER...MY WIFE WAS IMPRESSED BY THE FACT THAT, BECAUSE OF THE TREMENDOUS PRESSURE THIS MIND PUT ON PEOPLE IN MY BUSINESS, I MADE QUITE A LOT OF MONEY VERY RAPIDLY, WE BEGAN TO GET CHECKS FOR THOUSANDS OF DOLLARS—MONEY THAT WAS OWED ME..."

"I DIDN'T WANT TO INVOLVE MY WIFE IN THIS. SHE WAS A WITNESS ON ONE CRUCIAL MATTER. SHE WAS THERE WHEN ALL THAT INFORMATION ABOUT OUR LITTLE BOY'S BIRTH DEFECT WAS TRANSFERRED TO ME. SHE SAW ME SITTING THERE LISTENING TO THE BEATLES RECORD ON THE PHONOGRAPH."

"HE WOULD HAVE DIED...HE WAS IN IMMINENT PERIL. IT WAS JUST A MATTER OF TIME, ONLY A MATTER OF TIME... SO I WAS SITTING THERE LISTENING TO 'STRAWBERRY FIELDS FOREVER,' WITH MY EYES SHUT, WHEN ALL OF A SUDDEN THIS TREMENDOUS LIGHT HIT ME."

"LITERALLY, IN THE SENSE I SAW THE LIGHT. I WAS BLINDED...I THOUGHT, JESUS CHRIST! WHAT'S HAPPENING? I'M BLIND, MY HEAD HURTS, CAN'T SEE NOTHING. ALL I CAN SEE IS PINK...A PHOSPHENE AFTER IMAGE, LIKE YOU SEE WHEN A FLASHBULB FIRES OFF."

"ALL I COULD SEE WAS A PINK HAZE, AND THE WORDS OF THE BEATLES SONG GOT ALL CHANGED AROUND."

YOUR EYES ARE CLOSED TO YOUR SON'S BIRTH DEFECT... YOUR SON IS IN DANGER...HE HAS A RIGHT INGUINAL HERNIA THAT'S POPPED THE HYDROSEAL, AND GONE INTO THE SCROTAL SAC... YOU MUST GET HIM TO THE DOCTOR IMMEDIATELY.....

"ELOI, ELOI, LAMA SABACHTHANI"

"I LEAPED UP...TESS WAS IN THE OTHER ROOM CHANGING CHRISTOPHER—I WALKED IN AND SAID, 'TESS, HE'S GOT A BIRTH DEFECT, AND IT'S GOING TO KILL HIM. WE'VE GOT TO GET HIM TO A DOCTOR!'"

"I WAS SO UPSET I COULDN'T EVEN DRIVE, SO SHE CALLED THE DOCTOR AND SAID IT WAS AN EMERGENCY."

"SHE CAME BACK AN HOUR LATER AND SHE WAS ABSOLUTELY ASHEN. SHE SAID, 'HE DOES HAVE A RIGHT HERNIA, AND IT IS DOWN INTO THE SCROTAL SAC...I'VE GOT THE NAME OF A SURGEON...THE DOCTOR SAYS HE SHOULD HAVE SURGERY IMMEDIATELY.'"

"WE TOOK HIM INTO THE SURGEON'S THE NEXT DAY, AND SCHEDULED SURGERY IMMEDIATELY. THE SURGEON SAID, 'YOUR BABY COULD HAVE DIED ANY TIME.'"

"BUT THAT WAS ONLY ONE THING THAT HAPPENED...THERE WERE LOTS OF OTHERS. THAT WAS JUST ONE...I WOULD NOT BE SITTING HERE TALKING TO YOU TODAY * IF THAT WEIRD-LOOKING SHINY FIRE HADN'T COME AROUND AND ZAPPED ME...SHOOTING UP THE WALLS AND THROUGH THE APERTURES OF THE DOORS..."

*1981 INTERVIEW WITH GREGG RICKMAN

The Religious Experience of Phillip K. Dick
R. Crumb

"THERE IS NO REASONABLE ARGUMENT THAT WOULD ELUCIDATE WHAT THAT WAS THAT WAS FLOWING AROUND THE ROOM LIKE ST. ELMO'S FIRE... AND IT THINKS! IT GOT INTO MY BRAIN AND MADE ME THINK! ...IT DIDN'T THINK WHAT WE THINK...."

"...I WAS LOOKING AT MY NOTES—IT'S OVER SEVEN YEARS LATER, AND I'M STILL TAKING NOTES, IN AN EFFORT TO UNDERSTAND. IT DID NOT THINK IN THE SENSE THAT WE THINK. WE THINK IN DIGITAL, SYNTACTICAL, VERBAL INTEGERS... IT DID NOT THINK IN VERBAL TERMS... IT THOUGHT PURE CONCEPTS, WITHOUT WORDS. BUT IT KNEW WITHOUT RATIOCINATION. IT TRANSFERRED TO MY MIND CONCEPTS THAT IN SEVEN YEARS OF TRYING TO ARTICULATE THEM IN WORDS I'VE ONLY NOW BEEN ABLE TO REDUCE THEM~"

"I'VE FINALLY FOUND A MODEL THAT WAS SUGGESTED TO ME BY A PROFESSOR FRIEND. IT WORKED LIKE A BINARY COMPUTER, ON A FLICKER PULSATION OF 'OFF' AND 'ON'. IT JUST WASN'T A MIND LIKE WE HAVE MINDS."

"ONE OF MY EXPERIENCES—IT WAS '74—I BOUGHT ONE OF THOSE FISH SIGNS WITH THE GREEK LETTERS ON IT, AND PASTED IT UP ON MY WINDOW."

"I WAS SITTING THERE ONE DAY AND THE UPSILON, WHICH LOOKS LIKE A CAPITAL 'Y', SUDDENLY TURNED INTO A PALM TREE, AND THEN OPENED UP INTO THE ENTIRE MESOPATAMIAN WORLD, THE MIDDLE-EASTERN WORLD."

"...THAT PERSONALITY GRADUALLY TOOK ME OVER FOR A MONTH, AND THEN FOR ABOUT A YEAR I WAS THAT OTHER PERSONALITY... IT WAS SO FUNNY—I USED TO BE ABLE TO PICK UP HIS THOUGHTS WHILE I WAS FALLING ASLEEP.... AND I PICKED UP HIS THOUGHTS ONE NIGHT, AND HE WAS THINKING, 'THERE'S SOMEBODY ELSE INSIDE MY HEAD, AND HE'S LIVING IN ANOTHER CENTURY'...MEANING ME."

"I THOUGHT, 'TELL ME ABOUT IT! I CAN SAY THE SAME THING!' AT FIRST HE THOUGHT HE WAS STILL BACK IN ROME. HE HAD EVERYTHING WRONG. HE THOUGHT THE ROMANS WERE GOING TO COME AND GET HIM, THAT WE HAD TO DEVELOP ELABORATE CODES AND STUFF TO EVADE THE ROMANS."

You Are Still Being Lied To

"HE TRIED TO WORK THIS OUT WITH TESS, AND SHE KEPT SAYING, 'BUT THERE **ARE** NO ROMANS! ROME HAS BEEN GONE FOR 1600 YEARS!'"

"'NO, NOPE,' HE SAID, 'NOW, WHEN I PUT MY FINGER ON A BUTTON ON MY SHIRT, IT MEANS THAT WE'RE IN THE PRESENCE OF A BUTTON-DOWN MIND, AND WE CAN'T TALK.'"

"HE HAD THE SENSE OF A REGIME THAT WAS MURDEROUS, NOT JUST OPPRESSIVE, BUT MURDEROUS! HE THOUGHT CHRISTIANITY WAS AN ILLEGAL RELIGION. HE WAS AFRAID OF BEING KILLED FOR BEING A CHRISTIAN, THAT'S WHAT HE WAS AFRAID OF....DAMNEDEST THING..."

"HE WAS QUITE CONFUSED BY THE SOCIAL SITUATIONS AROUND HIM. HE KEPT INTERPRETING THEM IN GRECO-ROMAN TERMS... HE COULDN'T CONTROL THE CAR. HE COULDN'T FIGURE OUT WHAT THE PEDALS AND STUFF WERE FOR...SO I HAD TO GIVE UP DRIVING FOR AWHILE."

"I THINK THE SPIRIT OF ELIJAH CAME TO ME IN 1974. THAT HEART AND SPIRIT RETURNED TO ME...I DO BELIEVE THAT...BECAUSE IT WAS AT PASSOVER THAT IT HAPPENED, AND THERE WAS SOME KIND OF VIGOROUS SPIRIT IN ME, AND IT WAS NOT ME AND YET WAS HUMAN AND YET MORE THAN HUMAN."

"IT WAS TOM DISCH WHO FIRST SUGGESTED TO ME THAT THIS MIGHT BE THE CASE. AFTER HEARING MY DESCRIPTION IN LATE '74 OF MY EXPERIENCE HE SAID IT SOUNDS LIKE *ENTHOUSIASMOS** BY ELIJAH...AND I LIKE THAT IDEA... I FOUND THE IDEA PLEASANT..."

*ENTHOUSIASMOS: "ENTRY OF THE GODS INTO YOU," RECIEVING THE HOLY SPIRIT

The Religious Experience of Phillip K. Dick
R. Crumb

"IT'S BE-LIEVED THAT THE SPIRIT OF ELIJAH RETURNS TO EARTH PERIODIC-ALLY TO INFUSE ITSELF INTO HU-MAN BE-INGS, AND I KIND OF LIKE THAT IDEA... IT'S SORT OF, YOU KNOW, MEANING-FUL TO ME."

"IT'S THE SAME AS RECIEVING THE HOLY SPIRITS...I SUPPOSE IT COULD BE THAT...I COULD SIMPLY BE A CHARISMATIC CHRIST-IAN...I DONT KNOW. I JUST DON'T THINK IT *IS* THE HOLY SPIRIT...I THINK IT'S ELIJAH OR...THE SPIRIT OF GOD. WELL, MAYBE IT *IS* THE HOLY SPIRIT. I DON'T KNOW...HOW DO *I* KNOW? I MEAN, WHO CAN TELL ONE OF THEM? THERE'S NO REFER-ENCE BOOK THAT YOU COULD TURN TO TO SEE EXACTLY..."

"I JUST KNOW THAT SOME KIND OF SPIRIT TOOK ME OVER...THROUGH ITS HELP I WAS ABLE TO SOLVE PROBLEMS AND CONCERNS, THE THINGS I COULDN'T DO...IT SEEMED ABLE TO DISCERN ANY-THING IT LOOKED AT..."

"...I *DO* HAVE GRANDIOSE ILLU-SIONS THAT THE SPIRIT OF ELIJAH ENTERED ME AND I UTTERED PROPHESIES...AND FOR WHAT?"

"...BECAUSE THE PROPHECIES HAD TO BE FULFILLED, THAT ELIJAH COMES FIRST, AND SECOND, THAT THE NEWS BE RE-VEALED, AND THAT IS WHAT JOHN THE BAPTIST DID FOR JESUS...HAVING DONE SO HE FADED AWAY..."

"IN FACT THEY CUT OFF HIS HEAD, AND BY THE WAY I DREAMED A-BOUT THAT... I WAS IN A DUNGEON, A ROMAN DUNGEON, AND THEY CAME AND CUT OFF MY HEAD, TOOK A WIRE AND GARROT-ED ME. I DREAMED THAT, AND THAT WAS MY MEMORY OF MY LIFE...I WAS JOHN THE BAPTIST HAVING MY HEAD CUT OFF."

"I REMEMBER THEM COMING TO THAT CELL AND TAKING AND SLICING MY HEAD OFF...IT WAS HOR-RIBLE...AND YOU KNOW WHAT I DID WHEN THEY CAME THROUGH THE DOOR? I CURSED THEM WITH ALL THE FURY I HAD...THERE WAS NO LOVE IN ME FOR THEM AT ALL...JOHN WAS A VERY FIREY PERSON, WHO WAS VERY VULGAR. IT WAS ELIJAH, AND IT WAS ME."

You Are Still Being Lied To

"THE VOICE THAT I HEARD, THAT I CALL THE 'A. I.' VOICE *, IS THE VOICE THAT ELIJAH HEARD... THE STILL SMALL VOICE, THE LITTLE MURMURING VOICE... IT SPOKE IN A FEMININE VOICE... I HEARD IT SAY:"

THE TIME YOU'VE WAITED FOR IS COME... YOUR WORK IS COMPLETE, THE FINAL WORLD IS HERE... HE HAS BEEN TRANSPLANTED AND HE IS ALIVE!

*"ARTIFICIAL INTELLIGENCE"

"I ASKED THE I CHING IF INDEED THE 'PAROUSIA' (THE SECOND COMING) WAS HERE, CHRIST HAD RETURNED. I GOT 'DARKENING OF THE LIGHT', AND THE FOLLOWING LINE, THE ONLY TIME I EVER GOT THIS LINE..."

'DARKENING OF THE LIGHT INJURES HIM IN THE LEFT THIGH. HE GIVES AID WITH THE STRENGTH OF A HORSE, GOOD FORTUNE.'

"...HERE THE LORD OF LIGHT IS IN A SUBORDINATE PLACE AND IS WOUNDED BY THE LORD OF DARKNESS, BUT THE INJURY IS NOT FATAL. IT IS ONLY A HINDRANCE...THEREFORE HE TRIES WITH ALL HIS STRENGTH TO SAVE ALL THAT CAN BE SAVED... THERE IS GOOD FORTUNE. I INTERPRET THESE WORDS AS SAYING THAT INDEED CHRIST HAS RETURNED...THE LORD OF LIGHT IS THE CHRIST WHO HAS COME HERE AND SUBORDINATED HIMSELF...THE SAVIOR, YOU SEE?"

"THE LORD OF DARKNESS IS VERY POWERFUL. WE HAVE POWERFUL ADVERSARIES. THEY DON'T GIVE UP THEIR INTEREST IN POWER VOLUNTARILY. THEIR POWER MUST BE TAKEN FROM THEM. WE ARE IN A CRISIS SITUATION OF THE LIKE THIS PLANET HAS NEVER SEEN BEFORE. WE HAVE LUNATICS IN POWER WITH THE CAPACITY OF BLOWING UP THE PLANET. THEREFORE, IF WE ARE DELIVERED FROM THESE PEOPLE, THE PLANET SURVIVES; THE ECOSPHERE IS NOT DESTROYED.

"IN 1976 I TRIED TO KILL MYSELF BECAUSE ELIJAH HAD LEFT ME. I FELT HIM LEAVE AND IT WAS AWFUL...THERE IS NOTHING WORSE IN THE WORLD, NO PUNISHMENT GREATER THAN TO HAVE KNOWN GOD AND NO LONGER TO KNOW HIM...THE VOICES STOPPED TALKING TO ME... I DIDN'T CARE IF I LIVED OR DIED..."

'ELOI, ELOI, LAMA SABACHTHANI!'*

*"MY GOD, MY GOD, WHY HAVE YOU FORSAKEN ME?"

"IN ESSENCE, I HAD SERVED MY PURPOSE IN FLOW MY TEARS (ONE OF HIS BOOKS IN WHICH THERE IS A 'CIPHER', A SECRET PROPHETIC MESSAGE AIMED AT 'PARTICULAR PEOPLE', AND WHICH DICK WAS NOT EVEN AWARE OF WHEN HE WROTE THE BOOK IN 1974). I RALLIED BACK FROM THE SUICIDE ATTEMPT, BUT IF I HADN'T RALLIED IT WOULD HAVE ALL GONE ON WITHOUT ME."

IN THE LAST FEW MONTHS OF HIS LIFE DICK FINALLY LOCATED WHAT HE CONSIDERED THE LIKELIEST CANDIDATE FOR THE RETURNED CHRIST... ...THE SO-CALLED "MAITREYA"... IN THE MIDST OF THIS LAST FEVERISH ENTHUSIASM, HOWEVER, HE SUFFERED A STROKE, AND DIED SIXTEEN DAYS LATER, ON MARCH 2ND, 1982.

THE END

MOST DIALOGUE TAKEN FROM PHILIP K. DICK; THE LAST TESTAMENT, ©1985 BY GREGG RICKMAN; PUBLISHED BY FRAGMENTS WEST/THE VALENTINE PRESS

The Religious Experience of Phillip K. Dick
R. Crumb

A Sentient Universe

Peter Russell

> A nature found within all creatures
> but not restricted to them;
> outside all creatures,
> but not excluded from them.
>
> —*The Cloud of Unknowing*

What is consciousness? The word is not easy to define, partly because we use it to cover a variety of meanings. We might say an awake person has consciousness, whereas someone who is asleep does not. Or, someone could be awake, but so absorbed in their thoughts that they have little consciousness of the world around them. We speak of having a political, social, or ecological consciousness. And we may say that human beings have consciousness while other creatures do not, meaning that humans think and are self-aware.

The way in which I shall be using the word "consciousness" is not in reference to a particular state of consciousness, or a particular way of thinking, but to the faculty of consciousness—the capacity for inner experience, whatever the nature or degree of the experience.

The faculty of consciousness can be likened to the light from a video projector. The projector shines light on to a screen, modifying the light so as to produce any one of an infinity of images. These images are like the perceptions, sensations, dreams, memories, thoughts, and feelings that we experience—what I call the "contents of consciousness." The light itself, without which no images would be possible, corresponds to the faculty of consciousness. We know all the images on the screen are composed of this light, but we are not usually aware of the light itself; our attention is caught up in the images that appear and the stories they tell. In much the same way, we know we are conscious, but we are usually aware only of the many different perceptions, thoughts, and feelings that appear in the mind. We are seldom aware of consciousness itself.

Consciousness in All

The faculty of consciousness is not limited to human beings. A dog may not be aware of all the things of which we are aware. It does not think or reason as humans do, and it probably does not have the same degree of self-awareness, but this does not mean that a dog does not have its own inner world of experience.

When I am with a dog, I assume that it has its own mental picture of the world, full of sounds, colors, smells, and sensations. It appears to recognize people and places, much as we might. A dog may at times show fear and at other times, excitement. Asleep, it can appear to dream, feet and toes twitching as if on the scent of some fantasy-rabbit. And when a dog yelps or whines, we assume it is feeling pain—indeed, if we didn't believe that dogs felt pain, we wouldn't bother giving them anesthetics before an operation.

If dogs possess consciousness then so do cats, horses, deer, dolphins, whales, and other mammals. They may not be self-conscious as we are, but they are not devoid of inner experience. The same is true of birds; some parrots, for example, seem as aware as dogs. And if birds are sentient beings, then so, I assume, are other vertebrates—alligators, snakes, frogs, salmon, and sharks. However different their experiences may be, they all share the faculty of consciousness.

> For every psychological term in English there are four in Greek and forty in Sanskrit.
>
> —A. K. Coomaraswamy

The same argument applies to creatures further down the evolutionary tree. The nervous systems of insects are not nearly as complex as ours, and insects probably do not have as rich an experience of the world as we do, but I see no reason to doubt that they have some kind of inner experience.

Where do we draw the line? We usually assume that some kind of brain or nervous system is necessary before consciousness can come into being. From the perspective of the materialist metaparadigm, this is a reasonable assumption. If consciousness arises from processes in the material world, then those processes need to occur somewhere, and the obvious candidate is the nervous system.

But then we come up against the inherent problem of the materialist metaparadigm. Whether we are considering a human brain with its tens of billions of cells, or a nematode worm with a hundred or so neurons, the problem is the same: How can any purely material process ever give rise to consciousness?

Panpsychism

The underlying assumption of the current metaparadigm is that matter is insentient. The alternative is that the faculty of consciousness is a fundamental quality of nature. Consciousness does not arise from some particular arrangement of nerve cells or processes going on between them, or from any other physical features; it is always present.

If the faculty of consciousness is always present, then the relationship between consciousness and nervous systems needs

In philosophical circles the idea that consciousness is in everything is called *panpsychism*, from the Greek *pan*, meaning all, and *psyche*, meaning soul or mind. Unfortunately, the words "soul" and "mind" suggest that simple life-forms may possess qualities of consciousness found in human beings. To avoid this misunderstanding, some contemporary philosophers use the term *panexperientialism*—everything has experience. Personally, I prefer the term *pansentience*—everything is sentient.

Whatever name this position is given, its basic tenet is that the capacity for inner experience could not evolve or emerge out of entirely insentient, non-experiencing matter. Experience can only come from that which already has experience. Therefore the faculty of consciousness must be present all the way down the evolutionary tree.

We know that plants are sensitive to many aspects of their environment—length of daylight, temperature, humidity, atmospheric chemistry. Even some single-celled organisms are sensitive to physical vibration, light, and heat. Who is to say they do not have a corresponding glimmer of awareness? I am not implying they perceive as we do, or that they have thoughts or feelings, only that they possess the faculty of consciousness; there is a faint trace of sentience. It may be a billionth of the richness and intensity of our own experience, but it is still there.

According to this view, there is nowhere we can draw a line between conscious and non-conscious entities; there is a trace of sentience, however slight, in viruses, molecules, atoms, and even elementary particles.

What emerged over the course of evolution was not the *faculty* of consciousness, but the various qualities and dimensions of conscious experience—the *contents* of consciousness.

to be rethought. Rather than creating consciousness, nervous systems may be amplifiers of consciousness, increasing the richness and quality of experience. In the analogy with a video projector, having a nervous system is like having a lens in the projector. Without the lens there is still light on the screen, but the images are much less sharp.

Some argue this implies that rocks perceive the world around them, perhaps have thoughts and feelings, and enjoy an inner mental life similar to human beings. This is clearly an absurd suggestion, and not one that was ever intended. If a bacterium's experience is a billionth of the richness and intensity of a human being's, the degree of experience in the minerals of a rock might be a billion times dimmer still. They would possess none of the qualities of human consciousness—just the faintest possible glimmer of sentience.

The Evolution of Consciousness

If the faculty of consciousness is universal, then consciousness is not something that emerged with human beings, or with vertebrates, or at any particular stage of biological evolution. What emerged over the course of evolution was not the *faculty* of consciousness, but the various qualities and dimensions of conscious experience—the *contents* of consciousness.

The earliest living organisms, bacteria and algae, had no sensory organs and detected only the most general characteristics and changes in their environment. Their experience might be likened to an extremely dim, almost imperceptible hint of light on an otherwise dark screen—virtually nothing compared to the richness and detail of human experience.

With mammals the limbic system appeared, an area of the brain associated with basic feelings such as fear, arousal, and emotional bonding.

With the evolution of multicellular organisms came the emergence of specific senses. Some cells specialized in sensing light, others in sensing vibration, pressure, or changes in chemistry. Working together, such cells formed sensory organs, increasing the detail and quality of the information available to the organism—and enhancing the quality of consciousness.

In order to process this additional information and distribute it to other parts of the organism, nervous systems evolved. And, as the flow of information became more complex, central processing systems developed, integrating the different sensory modalities into a single picture of the world.

As brains grew in complexity, new features were added to the image appearing in consciousness. With mammals the limbic system appeared, an area of the brain associated with basic feelings such as fear, arousal, and emotional bonding. With time the mammalian brain grew yet more complex, developing a new structure around it—the cerebral cortex. With this came better memory, focused attention, greater intention, and imagination.

The picture appearing in consciousness had by now reached the richness of detail and diversity of qualities that we associate with our own experience. But this is not the end of the story. With human beings another new capacity emerged—speech. And with this, the evolution of consciousness took a huge leap forward.

For a start, we could use words to communicate experiences with each other. Our awareness of the world was no longer limited to what our senses told us; we could know of events occurring in other places and at other times. We could learn from each other's experiences, and so begin to accumulate a collective body of knowledge about the world.

Most significantly, we began to use language internally. Hearing words in our minds without actually saying them allowed us to talk to ourselves. An entirely new dimension had been added to our consciousness—verbal thought. We could form concepts, entertain ideas, appreciate patterns in events, apply reason, and begin to understand the universe in which we found ourselves.

Then came the most important leap of all. Not only could we reflect upon the nature of the world around us, we could also reflect upon thinking itself. We became self-aware—aware of our own awareness. This opened the door to a whole new arena of development. We could begin to explore the inner world of the mind and, ultimately, delve into the nature of consciousness itself.

"A Sentient Universe" is chapter 3 of *From Science to God: The Mystery of Consciousness and the Meaning of Light* by Peter Russell.

A Lost Theory?
Introduction to *Darwin's Lost Theory of Love*
David Loye

A "lost theory" of Charles Darwin's? How could this be? Don't we by now know Darwin from A to Z?

Certainly few other figures have been so comprehensively covered by biographies. And surely the story is one which we must by now know every detail. The amiable, indifferent student, cowed by a domineering father. The fervent collector of beetles. The year of trying out medicine at Edinburgh. The three years of tentative commitment to the ministry at Cambridge. How he then went off to sea in the *Beagle*. And how, transformed by this journey of journeys—which was also to transform the lives of every one of us living today—he became Darwin the ruminating, troubled, but ever steadily ascendant man of science.

We know seemingly everything about the long years of his immersion in the development of his theory of evolution—only to be nearly upstaged by Alfred Wallace. If we happen to be interested in the family life of the great figures of the past, we know of the sunny and quirky charm of the Darwin household and family orchestra—his wife Emma on the piano, son Francis on the bassoon, grandson Bernard with a whistle—to play to a dish of earthworms to see how they might respond to this form of cultural advancement.

Thereafter, it is true, to all but the most devout of Darwinians, the story fades away into the pleasant mush of a few more books after the pivotal *On the Origin of Species by Means of Natural Selection*, then death and a ceremonious burial in Westminster Abbey. But where in all this well-plowed ground could anything like a lost theory have been hidden?

Theories do not leap into being overnight. Indeed, the story of Darwin's development of what we know today as his theory of evolution has become the favorite story of how long theories take to build—at least eighteen years, in this case. It just does not seem possible to tuck away in all those years a lost theory that amounts to anything.

The fact is that, buried for 100 years within the lost theory, has been the proof that the beliefs of *both* regressive religion and reductionist science are gross distortions of what Darwin really believed.

what at times seems to have been dozens of children and pets. If we are interested in medical details, we also know that he was mysteriously sick for much of his working life.

If we are interested in science, we also know of the incredible range of his experiments with pigeons, barnacles, wild ducks, and lizard and snakes' eggs. Also: cabbage, lettuce and celery seeds, orchids, passion flowers, purple loosestrifes, wild cucumbers, Venus fly traps, and on and on. We may even have chuckled over the story of how he sought evidence of the roots of intelligence in earthworms, once even assembling a

And yet there was such a theory, and for over 100 years it was ignored—a theory that might have changed the course of the twentieth century in countless ways for the better. Could we have gone to war so often, or tolerated being globally inundated with television violence, had we believed we were not incurably selfish and vicious by nature? This, we were told, Darwin's theory proved.

Or could this theory—the core of modern science—have been attacked so successfully by right-wing religious forces as to endanger not only the teaching of science itself but also our hard-won heritage of free inquiry in a democracy?

It goes in and out of the news so fast as to hardly register, but the theory of evolution has been on trial again not only in Tennessee but elsewhere in the US. The decision in 1999 of the Kansas State Board of Education to drop the requirement that evolution be taught in schools sent out a shock wave that circled the educated world.[1] A few months later Oklahoma followed suit with a requirement that all new textbooks carry a disclaimer saying that evolution is a "controversial theory." This after more than 100 years of science to establish evolution theory as the floor under modern mind. Could this have happened had Darwin's theory been seen after all this time not merely as the "godless" plaything of "pointy head" scientists, but rather as something of practical value that could provide the growing child, as well as the rest of us, with some sense of dignity, purpose, direction, and meaning to life?

The fact is that, buried for 100 years within the lost theory, has been the proof that the beliefs of *both* regressive religion and reductionist science are gross distortions of what Darwin really believed.

Most meaningful today, as we emerge—still shellshocked—from the twentieth century, this lost theory is astoundingly attuned to both our deepest yearnings socially and our most advanced scientific probing. It is a theory, moreover, that in a time of increasing doubt and fear of the future offers a new burst of hope for the twenty-first century.

The Old Theory and the New Theory

How can I most quickly convey the nature of this "new" theory, or the startling story that lies ahead? Perhaps the best way is to briefly characterize Darwin's theory as it is known to us today and then go to the largest chunk of his writing, long ignored, in which he so radically departed from what we have been told.

One of the great difficulties holding back both advances in evolution theory and, I believe, the advance of humanity globally is the immense gulf between the social "footprint" and the scientific "head trip" of Darwinism. In other words, most scientists interested in evolution theory today are aware of many refinements, shadings, and qualifications of the prevailing Darwinian story line.[2] But what gets "out there" to us—or what we are generally told—has the raw psychological impact of the footprint of a King Kong. Everywhere the story is that science tells us that evolution is basically a matter of the great predatory force of natural selection that feeds on the wild output of random varia-

tion in order to pick out only the very best of organisms or efforts and discards the rest. This "footprint" theory is dressed up in much biology and paleontology, but at the core it seems to work very much like a giant motorized threshing machine moving through a wheat field. Through the front end it swallows up sheaf after hapless sheaf of wheat, and out the rear end it spews mountainous piles of the rejected straw and a thin stream of the precious grain.

In classrooms throughout our world, in an unending stream of beautifully packaged books, and routinely over television, we are shown what is further pursued here in chapter two—how this combination of forces has not just shaped every living thing prior to the emergence of the human, but also ourselves: our species, we humans, and everything about us. This theory is dressed up in ways to make it more palatable, and summaries such as this are always attacked as exaggerations. But basically we are told that this is why by necessity we are so aggressive and violent, or why by necessity we are driven by selfish genes, or why by necessity we must be ruthlessly competitive and exploitive. We are told that only in this way can our species evolve according to the sacred Darwinian principle of survival of the fittest.

We are also told that, with a few modern improvements, this was and is Darwin's one and only theory. But what happens if, with an open mind, we move from *Origin of Species*, where he first articulated this theory, to *The Descent of Man*, or to the early notebooks he filled out just after getting back from the famous voyage of the *Beagle*?

What became for me many years of exploration can be condensed into a simple bit of research toward the end of this process that I believe reveals it all in one fell swoop, as they say. In *The Descent of Man* Darwin moves on from the world of the "lower organisms" supposedly to show how the great threshing machine operates among us, at the human level. Now, for over 100 years the index at the back of the book—dutifully put to use by scholars as a guide to what is of importance in *Descent*—has shown but a single listing for "love." This, of course, is not unusual. Until quite recently, this simple word, which not only fills our songs but also our minds much of the time, was considered not only suspect but wholly outside the realm of science. "Love" was just not what science was all about. Yet through the use of a modern computerized search of the whole book, I discovered that in *Descent* Darwin is actually exploring the usage and evolutionary meaning for "love" 95 times![3]

What is going on here, one wonders? What could account for such a massive contradiction? And why should the discrepancy involve a concept that in a world everywhere now torn apart by hate has become of increasing scientific as well as popular interest?

I then tried searches for what we should, with more certainty, expect to find in *Descent*. According to what we have been told is Darwin's binding theory for us at the human level, we would, for example, expect to find much about the survival of the fittest. The computer found only two entries. And in one of the two he tells us he exaggerated its importance in *Origin of Species*! Or what about competition? Nine entries. From all we have been told, we would certainly *not* expect to find anything about cooperation. Yet for the nearest equivalent to this word for Darwin's time, "mutuality"—as in *mutual aid*, which Darwin coined as a phrase—there were 24 entries.

And if what primarily operates at our level is only the impersonal grinding of the great machine of natural selection and random variation, why do we find Darwin talking so often not of the power of the great machine? Why, instead, is he so often talking about the powers of the supposedly hapless organism at the heart of this process—that is of ourselves, of you and me? Why does he speak so often of the powers of our minds to perceive, and puzzle over what is going on, and decide what to do, and thereby make our way so effectively in this world? Why does he speak so often, for example, of our power of reasoning—24 entries? Or of imagination—24 entries? Or of sympathy for one another—which jumps to *61* entries?

And why do we find 95 entries for "habit," a concept explored by psychologists, as against 95 entries for "instinct," which used to be the biological equivalent for habit but was more often probed by psychologists than by biologists?

And why, if science has nothing to do with values, and what happens to us is up to the random action of a fate in which we supposedly have little voice, do we find the entries for Darwin's use of the word "moral"—or how we decide what is right and what is wrong for us to do—skyrocketing to a number just short of that for "love," *90* in all?

Why, in short, do we find this overwhelming interest on

Darwin's part in what in actuality most interests and concerns every one of us about ourselves at our level—not that of barnacle, finch, or amoeba? In contrast to what we have been told, why does he seem to find love, sympathy, reason, and morality of overriding importance for evolution at *our* level? Why do we find so much about the mind and the future for our species in this book that for over 100 years has been written off by evolution theorists as of little interest other than for its passages on sexual selection?

The Challenge for Twenty-First Century Science

The answers I found to these and many other questions can be put quickly and bluntly. Although present evolution theory represents a considerable and, I believe, an enduring achievement, because of a purblind immersion in a theory overwhelmingly fixated at the biological level we have overlooked something huge and meaningful for over 100 years. Through the research over a number of years reported in this book, I discovered there were actually two halves to Darwin's theory. There is the first half, or foundation, of a biological base for his theory, with which we are somewhat familiar. **But then Darwin went on to complete his theory with the superstructure of a psychological, systems-scientific, humanistic, and morally grounded "higher" half—of which today we know almost nothing**.

Moreover, the understanding of the lost Darwinian superstructure casts a wholly new and more hopeful light on the biological foundation. The biological picture, to put it quickly, looks more like a slate upon which each organism writes its own brief message than like the heedless rolling among us of first-half Darwinism's beloved threshing machine.

What this discovery can mean for science is a jolt of the earthquake proportion that is needed to speed up the all too slow-moving rearrangement of thinking and priorities for all scientific fields as we enter the twenty-first century. Within the comfortable, snail's-pace world of academia—and often plans to here, now, and ever after be—this matter of a so-called "lost theory" of Darwin may not seem to be of earthshaking importance. But what it can mean for every one of us—scientist, and layman and laywoman alike; that is, for every one of us with children

I discovered that in *Descent* Darwin is actually exploring the usage and evolutionary meaning for "love" 95 times!

A Lost Theory?
Introduction to *Darwin's Lost Theory of Love*
David Loye

433

and grandchildren or larger hopes for humanity—is something of exceptional urgency and meaning. In a world increasingly desperate for guidance out of science, it can mean that at last there may emerge an adequate theory of who we really are, and how to get from here to the better world we want to build.

It can mean that out of the science that gave us atomic bombs and pesticides and acid rain there might at last emerge a unified theory not of atoms, quarks, and strong and weak fields but of what accounts for what is *best* in us, rather than of excuses for what is *worst* in us. It can mean that out of science can emerge a theory that soars beyond so much that is secondary, trivial, and wasteful to show us how to achieve what is of first-rate importance and our highest aspirations. Of increasing importance in a world everywhere involved both in massive breakdown and the drive for the hopeful breakthrough, it can show us how to build the radically better world that we human beings have sought for thousands of years.

We hear much of chaos, complexity, or the abiding mystery of the cell these days, but in reality there are far more pressing challenges for science. As an evolutionary scientist myself, I express the conviction of increasing numbers of us about the one most urgent task today for all scientists. This is to find and advance whatever their field can do to better serve the needs of humanity as we enter a century in which, in terms of evolution, it seems evident we face a threat to the survival of our species.

What other conclusion can we come to? It does not take a scientist to read the handwriting on the wall. Who but the most blind among us can fail to see the warning in the widening global gap between rich and poor, the proliferation of nuclear and all other forms of superbomb, the polluting of sky, land, and water already beginning to silence the voices of the birds and frogs?

Yet at the same time—if we can find the vision and the courage of leadership—there opens before us a great new opportunity for long-term improvement of the human condition. It is here that the most unexpected thing of all rises out of the past here recovered—for in the pages that lie ahead we are to encounter not only the revolutionary implications of Darwin's lost theory, but also the grandeur, majesty, and humanity of Darwin's lost vision of the real nature and destiny of our species.

How urgent is the need for an updating of Darwin's theory of evolution can be seen from the cry for something better out of the very fields of biology and physics to which the task of building a modern theory of evolution was mainly relegated.

Those who are aroused—for example, the thousands of us responsive to the purpose of the Union of Concerned Scientists and similar professional bodies—write and speak out of a jolting recognition of the incredible danger our species faces at this juncture. Of the many questions that press upon us, one I believe is of overriding and inescapable meaning. After nearly 150 years since Darwin set the whole thing going, shouldn't we by now have a theory of evolution good for something more than scholarly squabbles and dubious mass entertainment? Shouldn't we by now have a theory of evolution that might provide us with *a source of guidance through these difficult years?*

A theory that can find a place for love as well as violence in our development? A theory offering hope rather than despair at the end of the line?

But instead we have this great, slick, gleaming, and entrancing package of a one-sided story of the past and the prehuman. We have the half-truth of this story out of which, pumped up by a global orgy of media feeding on fear, we are given the vision of killer apes, selfish genes, blind watchmakers, and an incurably violent species that continues to drive us toward destruction.

The main news of this book is the surprising new voice that has been added to the ignored voices of those who have been trying to reach their scientific peers and everybody else with a larger and more hopeful vision of human evolution—the voice of none other than Darwin himself.

In page after page out of his own long-ignored writings, he returns here to disavow much of what has been attributed to him by what is today known as the Darwinian tradition. He reaffirms the basic theory of his *Origin of Species*, of the centrality of natural selection and variation. But to this he now adds two startling departures.

One is his leap beyond biology and natural science into the psychology and the social and systems science that are the main focus for this book. We find ourselves able at last to marvel at the wonder of his lost leap to identify something far more important than natural selection and random variation at the human level. It is the power of moral sensitivity, he tells us—of love, mutuality, reasoning, imagination, habit, and education.

The other departure is even more surprising from the scientific standpoint. For I have brushed away the cobwebs from how Darwin discovered what is only today beginning to be explored as the possibility for a *new* major principle for evolution. As we enter the twenty-first century, in addition to natural selection and random variation, the focus is on *self-organizing* processes as a third candidate for being a prime shaper of our lives. This idea animates the new evolutionary theories of thermodynamacist Ilya Prigogine, biologists Stuart Kauffman and Humberto Maturana, and many others. And Darwin was already there more than a hundred years ago!

> After nearly 150 years since Darwin set the whole thing going, shouldn't we by now have a theory of evolution good for something more than scholarly squabbles and dubious mass entertainment?

And what emerges in his vision of the completed theory? Very much what progressive science—as well as progressive spirituality—has long dreamed of. It is very much what humanistic psychologists as well as humanistic biologists, systems theorists, chaos theorists, general evolution theorists—and moral and spiritual theorists, mothers, fathers, grandmothers, grandfathers, uncles, aunts, and everybody else concerned with how our species is to get better before it wipes itself out—have wished that his theory *could* have been.

The story, ramifications, and explanation of how all this was buried for over 100 years is covered in Part I: The Story. Part II: The Theory provides the reconstruction of his lost theory made possible by an editing that frees Darwin's own extremely readable and engaging writings from the murk of their long-time burial. Part III: The Vision then briefly explores the implications of what the story and theory have uncovered for the betterment of our lives during the twenty-first century.

A brief appendix takes the reader behind the scenes into the exciting new world of the advanced exploration of evolution theory for a glimpse at some of many new groups involved in this vital venture. In particular, I focus on the one I am best acquainted with. Drawn together by systems philosopher Ervin Laszlo, this is the General Evolution Research Group, of which I was a cofounder. This is a group composed of biologists; physicists; astrophysicists; mathematicians; systems, brain, social, and computer scientists; psychologists; historians; philosophers; and chaos, feminist, and management theorists. Working toward the development of an evolution theory that might better fit the needs of our time, these heirs and heiresses of the new Darwin live in or are from Germany, Italy, England, France, Sweden, Belgium, Chile, China, Finland, Hungary, Russia, Sri Lanka, Switzerland, and the United States.

This book is an independent work, representing my own research and my own conclusions. But I owe the inspiration, the perspective, and key aspects of the data out of which I write to some of the members of the General Evolution Research Group, as well as to others among the much larger group of scientists trying to build a better and more useful evolution theory.

Increasing numbers of us in these groups look to this new century as not only one of the very greatest of challenges but also of the greatest of opportunities—as something really special for our species. As I sketch in the last chapter, beyond its inevitable horrors, we look to the twenty-first century for the opening of windows and doors into springtime after a long winter.

In this regard, however fierce the howls or the drubbing of the brickbats this book may raise in certain quarters now, I feel confident that over time it will be met with increasing appreciation—and much relief.

Endnotes

1. See Sommerfeld, Meg. (June 5, 1996). "Lawmakers put theory of evolution on trial." *Education Week*; Johnston, Robert. (March 13, 1996). "70 years after Scopes, evolution hot topic again." *Teacher Magazine*; and Beem, Kate. (June 13, 1999). "Debates over evolution in the classroom rage country-wide." *Kansas City Star.* **2.** For good summaries of the varieties of evolution theory, see references for Ervin Laszlo's *Evolution*, and particularly for biologically-oriented questioning of the gross social "footprint," Peter Corning's "Holistic Darwinism," Stanley Salthe's *Development and Evolution*, or David Depew and Bruce Weber's *Darwinism Evolving.* **3.** A fascinating new resource for the researcher is *Darwin 2nd Edition*, a CD-ROM produced by Pete Goldie for Lightbinders, Inc., 2325 Third Street, Suite 324, San Francisco, CA 94107. Not only are the texts beautifully accessible but the reproductions of the original engravings and color plates in Darwinian works are amazing. Besides *The Descent of Man*, this CD-ROM offers *Origin of Species, The Voyage of the Beagle, The Expression of Emotions in Man and Animals*, and many other useful items.

Excerpted from *Darwin's Lost Theory of Love: A Healing Vision for the New Century* (iUniverse.com, 2000). That book is now out of print. David Loye is working on a new book, *Darwin's Unfolding Revolution*, that will recap and expand upon *Darwin's Lost Theory of Love*. Details are at <www.thedarwinproject.com>.

CONTRIBUTORS AND INTERVIEWEES

CONTRIBUTORS & INTERVIEWEES

Agent J (a/k/a Jay Parsons) is a hillbilly who grew up in bayou country and now lives on the Lower East Side of Manhattan. He is a freelance art director, full-time skeptic, part-time anarchist, amateur rabble-rouser, and student of history, politics, economics, media, and 8-ball.

Will Allen grew up on a small farm in southern California and served in the Marine Corps between the Korean and Vietnam wars. He received a Ph.D. in anthropology (focused on Peruvian tropical forest agriculture) and taught at the University of Illinois at Urbana-Champaign, and the University of California–Santa Barbara, before being fired and sentenced to a year in jail for civil-rights and antiwar activism. He returned to farming and farm labor full-time in 1972 and has been farming organically ever since in Oregon, California, and Vermont, where he now co-manages Cedar Circle Farm. He founded the Sustainable Cotton Project in 1991 and served as its executive director for thirteen years. He is currently a cochair of Farms Not Arms, is a policy advisory board member of the Organic Consumers Association, and serves on the board of Rural Vermont.

Paul Armentano is the Deputy Director of NORML and the NORML Foundation (1994–1999, 2001–present), a non-profit advocacy organization based in Washington, DC. Armentano is an expert in the field of marijuana policy, health, and pharmacology. His writing has appeared in over 500 publications, including more than a dozen textbooks and anthologies. He has spoken at numerous national conferences and legal seminars, testified before several state legislatures and federal bodies, and assisted dozens of criminal defense attorneys in cases pertaining to the use of medicinal cannabis, drug testing, and drugged driving. He may be contacted at <paul@norml.org>.

Normand Baillargeon is Professor of Education Fundamentals at the University of Québec in Montreal, where he teaches on the history of pedagogy and the philosophy of education. He is the author of *A Short Course in Intellectual Self-Defense* (Seven Stories, 2008).

Russell Banks is the author of sixteen works of fiction, many of which depict seismic events in US history, such as the fictionalized journey of John Brown in *Cloudsplitter*. His work has been translated into 20 languages and has received numerous international prizes, and two of his novels—*The Sweet Hereafter* and *Affliction*—have been made into award-winning films. His latest novel is *The Reserve*, and he is the author of *Dreaming Up America* (Seven Stories, 2008). A member of the American Academy of Arts and Letters, founding president of Cities of Refuge North America, and former New York State Author, Banks lives in upstate New York.

Henry Bauer is Austrian by birth, Australian by education, and American by choice. He is now Dean Emeritus of Arts and Sciences and Professor Emeritus of Chemistry and Science Studies at Virginia Polytechnic Institute and State University (Virginia Tech), where he had also been a founding member of the Center for the Study of Science in Society. Earlier, Bauer had taught at the Universities of Sydney (Australia) and Kentucky, and held visiting appointments at the Universities of Michigan and Southampton (England) and at Rikagaku Kenkyusho (Tokyo). Since the 1970s, his chief interest has been the role of heterodoxy in the progress of science and the "demarcation problem": what differentiates topics considered properly part of science from other topics—UFOs, psychic phenomena, and the like—that are shunned by mainstream science. Bauer founded and edited (1993–1999) *Virginia Scholar*, the newsletter of the Virginia Association of Scholars, and later served as editor-in-chief of the *Journal of Scientific Exploration* (2000–2007). Bauer's books range over chemistry, academic administration, the nature of mainstream science, and the critical assessment of scientific unorthodoxies (details at <www.henryhbauer.homestead.com>). His latest book is *The Origin, Persistence and Failings of HIV/AIDS Theory* (2007), which shows that official data about HIV prove that it is not contagious and doesn't correlate with the incidence of AIDS. For more on that, see Bauer's blog <http://hivskeptic.wordpress.com>.

Howard Bloom has been called "the Darwin, Einstein, Newton, and Freud of the Twenty-first Century" by Britain's Channel 4 TV and "the next Stephen Hawking" by *Gear* magazine. Bloom calls his field "mass behavior" and explains that his area of study includes everything from the mass behavior of quarks to the mass behavior of human beings. He is the founder of three international scientific groups: the Group Selection Squad (started in 1995), the International Paleopsychology Project (1997), and the Space Development Steering Committee (2007—a group that includes Buzz Aldrin, Edgar Mitchell, and reps from NASA, the National Science Foundation, and the Defense Department). And he's the founder of a mass-communications volunteer group that gets across scientific ideas using animation, the Big Bang Tango Media Lab (started in 2001). Bloom comes from the world of cosmology, theoretical physics, and microbiology. But he did 20 years of fieldwork in the world of business and popular culture, where he tested his hypotheses in the real world. In 1968 Bloom turned down four graduate fellowships and embarked on what he calls his Voyage of the Beagle, an expedition to the dark underbelly where new myths, new historical movements, and new shifts in mass emotion are made. The result: Bloom generated $28 billion in revenues for companies like Sony, Disney, PepsiCo, Coca-Cola, and Warner Brothers. He accomplished this by taking profits out of the picture and focusing on doing good. He applied the same principle to star-making, helping build the careers of figures like Prince, Michael Jackson, Bob Marley, Bette Midler, Billy Joel, Paul Simon, Billy Idol, Peter Gabriel, David Byrne, John Mellencamp, Queen, Kiss, Aerosmith, AC/DC, Grandmaster Flash and The Furious Five, Run DMC, and roughly 100 others. Bloom also plunged into social causes. He helped launch Farm Aid and Amnesty International in the United States, created two educational programs for the black community, put together the first public-service radio advertising campaign for solar energy, and founded the leading national music anti-censorship movement in the United States. A recent visiting scholar in the graduate psychology department at New York University and a former core faculty member at the Graduate Institute in two fields—conscious evolution and organizational leadership—Bloom is the author of three books: *The Lucifer Principle: A Scientific Expedition into the Forces of History* ("mesmerizing" —the *Washington Post*), *Global Brain: The Evolution of Mass Mind From the Big Bang to the 21st Century* ("reassuring and sobering" —the *New Yorker*), and *How I Accidentally Started The Sixties* ("a monumental, epic, glorious literary achievement" —Timothy Leary).

Alexandra Bruce. Author/filmmaker: • *The Gift*, co-executive producer/writer of documentary feature film about personal and planetary transformation, with Jack Canfield, Dr. Michael Bernard Beckwith, the Dalai Lama, and David Bohm. 2007–Present. • *Investing in Liquid Assets: Uncorking Profits in Today's Global Wine Market,* coauthor with David Sokolin (Simon & Schuster). A tiny group of investment-grade wines have reliably outperformed the stock market for over 60 years. Predicts which ones are likely to produce the highest financial returns in the long term. May 2008. • *Beyond "The Secret": The Definitive Unauthorized Guide to "The Secret"*, author (Disinformation). Explores how *The Secret* managed to top the nonfiction bestseller lists for over two years. December 2007. • *Beyond the Bleep: The Definitive Unauthorized Guide to "What the Bleep Do We Know!?"*, author (Disinformation). Makes sense of the quantum physics and neuroscience presented in the film. August 2005. • *The Philadelphia Experiment Murder: Parallel Universes and the Physics of Insanity,* author (Sky Books). Untangles some disinformation surrounding this urban legend. Discovers that the actual boat used in the so-called "Philadelphia Experiment" was not the *Eldridge* and concludes that the murder of the book's central character was covered up by officials in the State of Oregon. January 2001. • Director/producer/editor of over 40 music videos for the music conglomerates of the day, including Sony, Universal, Polygram, etc. through own production company. 1989–1996. • MTV, associate producer, and a creator of one of MTV's all-time highest-rated programs, *Yo! MTV Raps.* 1988–89. • Brown University, B.A. in Semiotics.

Chaz Bufe's most recent book is *Dreams of Freedom: A Ricardo Flores Magón Reader* (coauthor Mitch Verter; AK Press, 2005). He is currently revising his as-yet-to-be-titled science fiction novel.

Barry Chamish's book *Who Murdered Yitzhak Rabin* made the top of the Israeli bestseller lists and was translated into seven languages. His latest book is *Bye Bye Gaza* (Lulu.com), which exposes the deep corruption that culminated in 10,000 Israelis removed from their homes without compensation. A series of near-fatal experiences in Israel forced him to move to Florida, he hopes, temporarily. Visit his website at <www.barrychamish.com>.

Noam Chomsky was born on December 7, 1928, in Philadelphia, Pennsylvania. He received his Ph.D. in linguistics in 1955 from the University of Pennsylvania. During the years 1951 to 1955, Chomsky was a Junior Fellow of the Harvard University Society of Fellows. The major theoretical viewpoints of his doctoral dissertation appeared in the monograph *Syntactic Structure* (1957). This formed part of a more extensive work, *The Logical Structure of Linguistic Theory*, circulated in mimeograph in 1955 and published in 1975. Chomsky joined the staff of the Massachusetts Institute of Technology in 1955 and in 1961 was appointed full professor. In 1976 he was appointed Institute Professor in the Department of Linguistics and Philosophy. Chomsky has lectured at many universities here and abroad and is the recipient of numerous honorary degrees and awards. He has written and lectured widely on linguistics, philosophy, intellectual history, contemporary issues, international affairs, and US foreign policy. His most recent books are *A New Generation Draws the Line*; *New Horizons in the Study of Language and Mind*; *Rogue States*; *9-11*; *Understanding Power*; *On Nature and Language*; *Pirates and Emperors, Old and New*; *Chomsky on Democracy and Education*; *Middle East Illusions*; *Hegemony or Survival*; *Imperial Ambitions*; *Failed States*; *Perilous Power*; *Interventions*; *Inside Lebanon*; *What We Say Goes: Conversations on US Power in a Changing World*; and *The Essential Chomsky*.

Jeff Cohen, media critic and lecturer, is founding director of the Park Center for Independent Media at Ithaca College, where he is an associate professor of journalism. His latest book is *Cable News Confidential: My Misadventures in Corporate Media*. He has been a TV commentator at CNN, Fox News, and MSNBC, and was senior producer of MSNBC's Phil Donahue primetime show until it was terminated weeks before the Iraq invasion. Cohen founded the media-watch group FAIR <www.fair.org> in 1986. His columns on media issues have been published online at such websites as the Huffington Post, Common Dreams, and Alternet—and in dozens of dailies, including *USA Today*, *Washington Post*, *Los Angeles Times*, *Boston Globe*, *Atlanta Journal-Constitution*, and *Miami Herald*. More info at <www.jeffcohen.org>.

Alex Constantine is the author of *The Covert War Against Rock*, rated by the London *Observer* as among the 50 best books on music ever written. Constantine was a student of late anti-fascist researcher Mae Brussell and began writing on domestic fascism in 1988, when his radio program, *The Constantine Report*, was first broadcast over KAZU-FM in Monterey, CA. He has appeared on most cable television information channels, hosted a BBC documentary on the Kennedy assassination, and another on the mysterious death of rock virtuoso Jimi Hendrix. Constantine is also widely published. His first book, *Blood, Carnage and the Agent Provocateur*, was issued in 1993, followed by *Psychic Dictatorship in the USA* (1995), *Virtual Government: CIA Mind Control Operations in America* (1997), and several others. Alex Constantine has also edited an e-book of Ms. Brussell's essays and radio transcripts, entitled *Fascism in America: The Essential Mae Brussell*, available on CD from his core blog (he has four), Alex Constantine's Blacklist <http://aconstantineblacklist.blogspot.com>. Alex Constantine's Anti-Fascist Research Bin <www.alexconstantine. blogspot.com>.

William R. Corliss has been a freelance writer and researcher since March 1963. He is the author of more than 55 books, as well as several-dozen booklets and articles on such diverse subjects as electric-power generation, computers, space radiation, robotics, and telecommunications. He has also held consulting positions with Time-Life Books, General Electric Company, Martin-Marietta, and several other organizations. <www.science-frontiers.com>.

Michael A. Cremo was born in 1948, in Schenectady, New York. In 1966 he entered the George Washington University School of Foreign Affairs. After participating in the March on the Pentagon, he backpacked to Europe in 1968 to join the Czech anti-communist uprising. But by the time he arrived, the Russians had already moved in. He then embarked on a spiritual quest that eventually led him to India. When he was 27, he became a disciple of Krishna guru Bhaktivedanta Swami Prabhupada. In 1984 (coincidence?) he began work on *Forbidden Archeology*, with coauthor Richard Thompson. When the 900-page book came out in 1993, it quickly became an underground classic, and in abridged form has been translated into 20 languages. Cremo speaks regularly at mainstream and alternative science conferences, and has appeared on hundreds of radio and television shows worldwide.

Robert Crumb has been called "the Godfather of the underground comic," and since his first self-published comic appeared in the late 1960s, his work has been published in many different languages throughout the world and has appeared in publications from New York (the *New Yorker*) to Paris (*Libération*) to Tokyo. His characters, such as Mr. Natural and Fritz the Cat, and his autobiographical comics have influenced an entire generation of both cartoonists and readers, but his interest in other "non-comics" subjects is less well-known. He has illustrated stories by Charles Bukowski and Jean-Paul Sartre and collaborated on an introduction to Kafka. The work of great medieval artists such as Bosch and Breughel the Elder has inspired him, and he identifies with their humor and their power of expression. Crumb's cover for Janis Joplin's *Cheap Thrills* album is well-known among rock and roll fans, but less well-known perhaps is his love of blues and jazz from the 1920s and 30s, including the French *musette* style. He has done numerous illustrations and stories about blues, jazz, and country music. A native of the United States, Robert Crumb and his family have lived in France for many years.

Gregory M. Davis received his Ph.D. in political science from Stanford University in 2003. He has written for *Human Events*, WorldNetDaily, FrontPage Magazine, and JihadWatch, and has appeared as a guest commentator on Fox News and numerous radio programs across America. He is author of *Religion of Peace?: Islam's War Against the World* and producer and director of the feature documentary *Islam: What the West Needs to Know*.

Riane Eisler is an eminent social scientist, attorney, and social activist best known as author of the international bestseller *The Chalice and The Blade: Our History, Our Future*, hailed by Princeton anthropologist Ashley Montagu as "the most important book since Darwin's *Origin of Species*" and by novelist Isabel Allende as "one of those magnificent key books that can transform us." This was the first book reporting the results of Eisler's study of human cultures spanning 30,000 years, and is in 22 languages, including most European languages and Chinese, Russian, Korean, Hebrew, and Japanese. Eisler was born in Vienna, fled from the Nazis with her parents to Cuba, and later emigrated to the United States. She obtained degrees in sociology and law from the University of California, taught pioneering classes on women and the law at UCLA, and is a founding member of the General Evolution Research Group (GERG) and the Alliance for a Caring Economy (ACE), and a fellow of the World Academy of Art and Science and World Business Academy. She is also co-founder of the Spiritual Alliance to Stop Intimate Violence (SAIV) <www.saiv.net>. She is president of the Center for Partnership Studies <www.partnershipway. org>, dedicated to research and education. Her books include the award-winning *The Power of Partnership* and *Tomorrow's Children*, as well as *Sacred Pleasure*, a daring reexamination of sexuality and spirituality, *Women, Men, and the Global Quality of Life*, which statistically documents the key role of the status of women in a nation's general quality of life, and *The Real Wealth of Nations: Creating a Caring Economics*. <www.rianeeisler.com>.

Stan Goff is a retired Special Forces Master Sergeant. He is the author of several books: *Hideous Dream: A Soldier's Memoir of the US Invasion of Haiti* (Soft Skull Press, 2000), *Full Spectrum Disorder: The Military in the New American Century* (Soft Skull Press, 2004), *Energy War: Exterminism for the 21st Century*, *Sex & War*, and *My Year with the Liberals*. He is the former military-affairs editor for From The Wilderness and has written foreign-policy analysis for Sanders Research Associates. He also occasionally writes for Truthdig. He is a member of Vietnam Veterans Against the War (VVAW), Veterans for Peace (VFP), and Military Families Speak Out (MFSO). His oldest son is in the active-duty Army and has been deployed to Iraq four times; his youngest—likewise Army—has been to Iraq once.

Peter Gorman is a noted and award-winning journalist and adventurer. His feature writing has appeared in more than 100 major national and international magazines including *Omni*, *Playboy*, *Wildlife Conservation*, Spain's *Geo*, Mexico's *Geo Mundo*, Italy's *Airone* and *Sette*, Germany's *Die Zeit*, England's *World*, and the *Times of India*. Gorman's video work includes major pieces for the United Nations and the Salvation Army, as well as consulting assignments for National Geographic's *Explorer* and the BBC's *Natural World*. In Peru, Gorman has collected artifacts from the Matses Indians of the Rio Javari for the American Museum of Natural History in New York, as well as herpetological species and medicinal plants for FIDIA Research Institute of the University of Rome and Shaman Pharmaceuticals. For nearly 25 years, Gorman has worked with ayahuasca, the visionary vine of the Amazon. His work in the jungles of South America has been the subject of a feature in *Men's Journal* (May 2008). It was also the subject of a cover story in *New York Press* and has been covered in both *Newsweek* and *Science* magazine, among other places. He currently lives in Texas on a small ranch with his three kids, and when not there can be found investigating Drug War stories, running occasional tours to the jungle, and trying to get a new Cold Beer Blues Bar up and running in Iquitos.

Steven Greenstreet first became involved in documentary film with *Futonmaker* in 2001. That film explores the life of Melchizedek Todd, a young black man who found God while working in a futon factory in downtown Baltimore. Since moving to Utah in 2003, Greenstreet has worked extensively with the film community, recently working on *The World's Fastest Indian* with Anthony Hopkins, on HBO's hit show *Entourage*, and most recently on FOX's new science-fiction TV show, *Beyond*. In 2004, when Utah Valley State College invited liberal filmmaker Michael Moore to speak on campus, an explosion of outrage and protest descended on the college. Death threats, bribery attempts, and lawsuits all surged in an attempt to prohibit Moore from speaking. Greenstreet dropped out of school, quit his job, and dedicated all his efforts to making a film about the failure of civil discourse in America. That film, *This Divided State*, has garnered international acclaim as a riveting slice of American history. Critics have called it a "fascinating, infuriating story" (*TV Guide*) that is both "provocative" (*Variety*) and "extremely moving" (*NY Times*). In addition to the obesity documentary, *Killer at Large*, Greenstreet is currently producing and co-directing a follow-up to *This Divided State* about the unprecedented level of fury that arose on the most conservative college campus in the country when Vice President Dick Cheney was invited to speak at the spring commencement.

Daniel Grego is the executive director of TransCenter for Youth, Inc., the nonprofit agency that operates Shalom High School, the Northwest Opportunities Vocational Academy (NOVA), El Puente High School for Science, Math, and Technology, The CITIES Project High School, and the Technical Assistance & Leadership Center (TALC New Vision) in Milwaukee. One of his major interests is exploring the confluence of the ideas of Mahatma Gandhi, Ivan Illich, and Wendell Berry. He lives with his wife, choreographer Debra Loewen, and their daughter, Caitlin Grego, on a small farm in the Rock River watershed in Dodge County, Wisconsin.

Graham Hancock is the author of the major international bestsellers *The Sign and the Seal*, *Fingerprints of the Gods*, and *Heaven's Mirror*. His books have sold more than 5 million copies and have been translated into 27 languages. His TV appearances and lectures have put his ideas before audiences of tens of millions. "Hancock has invented a new genre" (London *Guardian*).

Judith Rich Harris is a former writer of college textbooks on child development who suddenly realized one day that much of what she had been telling her readers was wrong. She stopped writing textbooks and instead wrote a theoretical article on childhood, which was published by the *Psychological Review*. Her article received an award from the American Psychological Association; ironically, the award was named after the same prominent psychologist who had informed her, almost 30 years earlier, that Harvard had decided not to give her a Ph.D. because she lacked originality and independence. Harris's book *The Nurture Assumption*—a runner-up for the Pulitzer Prize in nonfiction—brings to life the ideas first presented in the *Psychological Review* article. *The Nurture Assumption* has been translated into 15 languages; a tenth-anniversary revised edition will be published in 2009. Harris has also written *No Two Alike: Human Nature and Human Individuality*, which focuses on the question of why siblings—even identical twins reared in the same home—are so different in personality. Further information about this author can be found on the Nurture Assumption website <http://xchar.home.att.net/tna/>.

John Major Jenkins has been researching Maya culture and cosmology since the 1980s. While undertaking careful archeo-astronomical investigations of ancient Maya sites, he was inspired in his work by living and working with the contemporary highland Maya. His pioneering works are internationally recognized and include *Tzolkin* (1994), *Maya Cosmogenesis 2012* (1998), *Galactic Alignment* (2002), and *Unlocking the Secrets of 2012* (2007). They document and explore the relationships between the 2012 cycle-ending of the Maya calendar and astronomy, prophecy, and spiritual teachings. John believes it is possible to reconstruct and give voice to ancient insights, addressing both spiritual and scientific considerations. In pursuing this, he focuses his analysis on Izapa, the early Maya ceremonial site that was involved in the formulation of the 2012 calendar as well as the Maya Creation Myth. Recently appointed a National Fellow member of Sir Edmund Hillary's Explorer Club for his work at Izapa, Jenkins has taught at conferences and universities throughout the United States, as well as in Central America, Mexico, Canada, and Europe. Sought after for his clarity and comprehensive understanding of a difficult topic, his work has been featured in many documentaries and on the History Channel, the BBC, and the Discovery Channel.

Philip Jenkins teaches at Penn State University. He has published more than 20 books, including *Synthetic Panics: The Symbolic Politics of Designer Drugs* (1999) and *Beyond Tolerance: Child Pornography on the Internet* (2001: both from New York University Press). His latest book is *The Lost History of Christianity* (HarperOne, 2008).

Alex Jones is an award-winning documentary filmmaker and political researcher. His news websites, <infowars.com> and <prisonplanet.com>, are at the forefront of the exploding alternative media. Jones is recognized by many as the father of the 9/11 truth movement, being the first to question the government's official story. His daily radio show is syndicated nationally.

The continuing journalistic adventure of **Peter Laufer** has already resulted in thousands of hours of network reporting from the front lines of conflict and social change around the world, and a growing shelf of books dealing with social and political issues: from immigration (*Wetback Nation*) to talk radio (*Inside Talk Radio*) to the pleasures of an intriguing American art form: neon signs (*Neon Nevada*, with Sheila Swan Laufer). Laufer's latest books include one that focuses on American soldiers who return from Iraq opposed to the war; *Mission Rejected* (Chelsea Green Publishing), and another, *Hope Is a Tattered Flag* (PoliPoint Press), written with Markos Kounalakis, offering scenarios for recovery post-Bush <www.hopeisatatteredflag.com>. Radio work by Peter Laufer includes the creation of a magazine show from around the world for National Geographic and a radio adaptation of his investigative reporting for *Mother Jones* magazine. He co-anchors a *Washington Monthly* magazine weekly radio talk show, and provides coaching and program consulting for talk radio shows and stations worldwide. In the past, he reported for NBC News, CBS and ABC radio, and was the Berlin voice of the public radio program *Marketplace*. Laufer's years in radio work resulted in his winning virtually every major award available to broadcast journalists. Articles and op-ed pieces by Laufer appear in a wide variety of publications, from the *San Francisco Chronicle* to *Mother Jones* magazine, from the *Washington Monthly* to *Penthouse*. On television, Peter Laufer has produced and directed an award-winning documentary film on immigration in Europe (*Exodus to Berlin*) and anchored national television talk shows such as LinkTV's *FAQs*. Laufer is a frequent lecturer on the role of talk radio in American society and the crisis on the US-Mexican border. Laufer anchored the live Sunday morning KPFA (94.1 Berkeley) current affairs program which features guest interviews and interaction with the audience, a show he moved to Sunday mornings on Green 960 (960-AM in San Francisco). <www.peterlaufer.com>.

Earl Lee is a librarian at Pittsburg State University in Pittsburg, Kansas. He is the author of numerous articles and several books, including *Libraries in the Age of Mediocrity* (1998). His latest book is the satire *Raptured!: The Final Daze of the Late, Great Planet Earth* (2007).

James Loewen. A sociologist who spent two years at the Smithsonian surveying twelve leading high-school textbooks of American history only to find an embarrassing blend of bland optimism, blind nationalism, and plain misinformation, weighing in at an average of 888 pages and almost five pounds. A bestselling author who wrote *Lies My Teacher Told Me: Everything Your High School History Textbook Got Wrong* and *Lies Across America: What Our Historic Sites Get Wrong*. A researcher who discovered that many, and in many states *most*, communities were "Sundown Towns" that kept out blacks (and sometimes other groups) for decades. (Some still do.) An educator who attended Carleton College, holds a Ph.D. in sociology from Harvard University, and taught race relations for 20 years at the University of Vermont.

Social psychologist, systems-theorist, and futurist **David Loye** is the author of widely respected books on the use of the brain and mind in prediction, political leadership, race relations, and is the developer of new theories of moral sensitivity and evolution. His psychohistory *The Healing of a Nation*—which *Psychology Today* called "a work of uncommon humanity and vision"—received the Anisfield-Wolfe Award for the best scholarly book on race relations in 1971. *The Leadership Passion: A Psychology of Ideology* was hailed by *Contemporary Psychology* as a "major advance" in its field. *The Knowable Future: A Psychology of Forecasting and Prophecy* is recognized as a pioneering work of unusual stature in the field of futures studies. *The Sphinx and the Rainbow: Brain, Mind, and Future Vision* gained an international readership through Japanese, Dutch, Portuguese, and two German editions. Loye is the editor of *The Evolutionary Outrider: The Impact of the Human Agent on Evolution* (Praeger, 1998). He is also the coauthor, with Riane Eisler, of *The Partnership Way* (Harper San Francisco, 1990; Holistic Education Press, 1998). A former member of the psychology faculty of Princeton University, Loye for nearly a decade was a professor in the research series and Director of Research for the Program on Psychosocial Adaptation and the Future at the UCLA School of Medicine.

Thomas Lyttle has published eight books and 100+ articles for the popular and academic press. His work focuses on SOCs (states of consciousness) and psychedelic substances. His books include *Psychedelics: A Collection of the Most Exciting New Materials on Psychedelic Drugs* (Barricade Books, 1994) and *Psychedelics ReImagined* (Autonomedia, 1999). Thomas Lyttle's works have been profiled in newspapers, radio, television, and in courtrooms. He was admitted into Marquis' *Who's Who in America* in 1996 for his unusual publishing contributions. Lyttle passed away in September 2008.

A native of Fort Worth, Texas, **Jim Marrs** has worked for several Texas newspapers, including the *Fort Worth Star-Telegram*, where beginning in 1968 he served as police reporter. Since 1980, Marrs has been a freelance writer and public relations consultant. Since 1976, Marrs has taught a course on the assassination of President John F. Kennedy at the University of Texas–Arlington. In 1989 his book, *Crossfire: The Plot That Killed Kennedy*, was published to critical acclaim and within three years had gone into an eighth printing in both hardbound and softbound editions. It became a basis for the Oliver Stone film *JFK*. Marrs served as a chief consultant for both the film's screenplay and production. In May 1997, Marrs's in-depth investigation of UFOs, *Alien Agenda*, was published by HarperCollins Publishers, and in early 2000, HarperCollins published *Rule by Secrecy*, in which Marrs traced the hidden history that connects modern secret societies to the ancient mysteries. He is also the author of *The Terror Conspiracy, The Rise of the Fourth Reich* and *Above Top Secret*. An award-winning journalist, Marrs is listed both in *Who's Who in the World* and *Who's Who in America*. Marrs also produced *Texas Roundup* for cable television, two popular videos on Lee Harvey Oswald, and has written several television, video, and film scripts and treatments.

Jim Martin founded Flatland Books <www.flatlandbooks.com> in 1984; he also publishes *Flatland*—a semiannual "review of the suppressed and secret evidence." Last radio contact indicated his position somewhere beyond the Three Mile Limit off the coast of northern California.

Paul McMasters, now retired, is the former First Amendment Ombudsman at Vanderbilt University's First Amendment Center <www.firstamendmentcenter.org>.

Known for her health and science reporting, **Terri Mitchell** has been delivering cutting-edge reports on dietary supplements, drugs, and more for over a decade. Mitchell goes after the corporate corruption seeping from the edges of today's "official reports." Armed with a tenacious desire for the truth, and a scientist's perspective, she consistently delivers the shocking underbelly of modern medicine. Mitchell is peer-review published in *Medical Hypotheses* and other journals. She graduated *cum laude* from the University of Southern California.

Cletus Nelson is a freelance writer from the Los Angeles area whose writings have appeared in several online and print publications. He is currently working on his second book.

Christian Parenti is an author and journalist, a contributing editor at the *Nation*, and has reported extensively from the Middle East, Africa, and Latin America. His most recently published book is *The Freedom: Shadows and Hallucinations in Occupied Iraq* (2004). His two previous books are *The Soft Cage: Surveillance in America from Slavery to the War on Terror* (2003) and *Lockdown America: Police and Prisons in the Age of Crisis* (1999).

Michael Parenti received his Ph.D. in political science from Yale University and has taught at a number of colleges and universities. His twenty-one books include *The Culture Struggle*; *Superpatriotism*; and *The Assassination of Julius Caesar* (which was selected as Book of

the Year 2004 by the Online Review of Books). His most recent book is *Contrary Notions: The Michael Parenti Reader*. Portions of his writings have been translated into some 20 languages and have been used extensively in college courses. He lectures frequently across North America and abroad. Tapes of his various talks and interviews have played widely on community radio stations and public-access television. More than 300 articles of his have been published in scholarly journals, magazines and newspapers, books of collected readings, and online publications. He has won awards from various academic and social-activist organizations, and serves on advisory boards for Project Censored, Education Without Borders, the Jasenovic Foundation, and several publications. For further information, visit his website <www.MichaelParenti.org>.

Elias Pate has been working in the film industry for close to a decade. He has co-directed two feature films—*Missy* (1999) and *The Fleapit Three* (2007)—and a feature-length documentary, *The Misbehavers* (2004). He has also produced and/or assistant-directed numerous films, including the award-winning documentary *This Divided State* (2005). Along with Bryan Young, he's written more than a dozen screenplays, two of which are at the top two agencies in the world. He also cowrites (with Bryan Young and artist Derek Hunter) the comic book *Pirate Club*, which is released quarterly from Slave Labor Graphics. Aside from producing duties on *Killer at Large*, he's producing and co-directing *The BYU 25*, about the unprecedented level of fury that arose on the most conservative college campus in the country when Vice President Dick Cheney was invited to speak at the spring commencement.

Congressman **Ron Paul** is the leading advocate for freedom in Washington, DC. As a member of the US House of Representatives, Dr. Paul tirelessly works for limited constitutional government, low taxes, free markets, and a return to sound monetary policies. He is known among his congressional colleagues and his constituents for his consistent voting record. Dr. Paul never votes for legislation unless the proposed measure is expressly authorized by the Constitution. In the words of former Treasury Secretary William Simon, Dr. Paul is the "one exception to the Gang of 535" on Capitol Hill.

Preston Peet is a NYC-based freelance editor and investigative journalist. He has edited two anthologies for the Disinformation Company: *Under the Influence: The Disinformation Guide to Drugs* and *Underground: The Disinformation Guide to Ancient Civilizations, Astonishing Archaeology and Hidden History*. He is the author of *Something in the Way: A True Life Misadventure Tale of One Drug (Ab) User's Life on and off Streets Around the World*. A long-time contributor to *High Times* magazine and website, he also has more than 60 articles archived at <www.disinfo.com>.

Peter Rost, M.D., is a former Pfizer Marketing Vice President providing services as an expert witness, speaker, and writer. According to

Fortune, "Peter Rost has become the drug industry's most annoying—and effective—online scourge…. Rost's blog is one part mocking rant, two parts investigative chronicle…. Even his critics admit that when Rost is on his game, he is a force to be reckoned with." He is the author of *The Whistleblower: Confessions of a Healthcare Hitman* (Soft Skull, 2006) and the thriller *Killer Drug*. His blog: <http://peterrost.blogspot.com>.

Douglas Rushkoff is the author of a dozen books, most recently *Life Incorporated*. He made the *Frontline* documentaries *Merchants of Cool* and *The Persuaders*, and he speaks around the world about media, culture, and change. He is host of *RadioBottomUp* and blogs at <rushkoff.com>.

Dan Russell entered the University of Buffalo in 1963. His anthropological historiography was learned in the wildly creative 1960s, as was his interest in the archaic techniques of ecstasy and automatic creativity. This interest was politicized by the fascists who have engineered the current Inquisition, which he has chosen to deconstruct. He is a 1970 graduate of the City College of New York and a 1972 graduate of the streets of New York. Since then he has sold books in Pittsburgh and manufactured candy bars in North Central New York State, where he currently lives with his wife and three children. He and his son Joshua are retailers of Frontier Herbs, the largest herb and health-food distributor in the US. Frontier's full line, drop-shipped direct from the Frontier warehouse, is available from their website <www.kalyx.com>. His books, *Shamanism and the Drug Propaganda* and *Drug War: Covert Money, Power & Policy*, are available at <www.drugwar.com>.

Peter Russell, M.A., D.C.S., gained an honors degree in physics and experimental psychology at the University of Cambridge, England, and a postgraduate degree in computer science. He studied meditation and Eastern philosophy in India, and on his return conducted research into the neurophysiology of meditation at the University of Bristol. As an author and lecturer, he has explored the potentials of human consciousness—integrating Eastern wisdom with the facts of Western science—and shared with audiences worldwide his discoveries and insights about the nature of consciousness, global change, and human evolution. Russell was one of the first to present personal development programs to business. Over the past 20 years, he has been a consultant to IBM, Apple, American Express, Barclays Bank, Swedish Telecom, Nike, Shell, British Petroleum, and other major corporations. His books include *The Brain Book*, *The Global Brain Awakens*, *The Consciousness Revolution*, *Waking Up in Time*, and *From Science to God*. He also created the award-winning videos *The Global Brain* and *The White Hole in Time*.

Sydney H. Schanberg, a journalist for nearly 50 years, has written extensively on foreign affairs—particularly in Asia—and on domestic issues such as ethics, racial problems, government secrecy, corporate excesses, and the weaknesses of the national media. Most of his journalism career has been spent on newspapers, but his award-winning work has also appeared widely in other publications and media. The 1984 movie *The Killing Fields*, which won several Academy Awards, was based on his book *The Death and Life of Dith Pran*—a memoir of his experiences covering the war in Cambodia for the *New York Times* and of his relationship with his Cambodian colleague, Dith Pran. For his accounts of the fall of Cambodia to the Khmer Rouge in 1975, Schanberg was awarded the Pulitzer Prize for international reporting "at great risk." He is also the recipient of many other awards—including two George Polk awards, two Overseas Press Club awards, and the Sigma Delta Chi prize for distinguished journalism.

Warren Allen Smith is a roué and sybarite currently living in New York's Greenwich Village. Drafted into the Army and wearing identifying "dog tags" which listed his religion as "None," Acting First Sergeant Smith led his company onto Omaha Beach in 1944, experienced being an atheist in a foxhole. Upon returning home unwounded, Smith used the G.I. Bill of Rights to study philosophy with logician Charner Perry and metaphysician Charles Hartshorne at the University of Chicago. At the University of Northern Iowa, he majored in English and in 1948 founded the first Humanist Club on any college campus. Smith signed the Humanist Manifesto II and the Humanist Manifesto 2000, has been a director of the Bertrand Russell Society of America since 1967, and has headed Mensa's oldest interest group, the Investment Club (1967 to date). He is the author of *Who's Who in Hell* (Barricade Books, 2000). <http://wasm.us>.

Norman Solomon is a nationally syndicated columnist on media and politics. He has been writing the weekly "Media Beat" column since 1992. His latest book is *Made Love, Got War: Close Encounters with America's Warfare State* (2007). Solomon's book *War Made Easy: How Presidents and Pundits Keep Spinning Us to Death* was published in 2005; the *Los Angeles Times* called that book "brutally persuasive" and "a must-read for those who would like greater context with their bitter morning coffee, or to arm themselves for the debates about Iraq that are still to come." The newspaper's reviewer added: "Solomon is a formidable thinker and activist." The *Humanist* magazine described the book as "a definitive historical text" and "an indispensable record of the real relationships among government authorities and media outlets." A documentary based on *War Made Easy* was released in 2007. His book *Target Iraq: What the News Media Didn't Tell You* (coauthored with foreign correspondent Reese Erlich) was published in 2003 by Context Books. *Target Iraq* has also been published in German, Italian, Hungarian, Brazilian, and South Korean editions. A collection of Solomon's columns won the George Orwell Award for Distinguished Contribution to Honesty and Clarity in Public Language. The award, presented by the National Council of Teachers of English, honored Solomon's book *The Habits of Highly Deceptive Media*. In the introduction to that book, Jonathan Kozol wrote: "The tradition of Upton Sinclair, Lincoln Steffens, and I.F. Stone does not get much attention these days in the mainstream press…but that tradition is alive and well in this collection of courageously irreverent columns on the media by Norman Solomon…. He fights the good fight without fear of consequence. He courts no favors. He writes responsibly and is meticulous on details, but he does not choke on false civility."

David Steinberg writes frequently on the culture and politics of sex in America, edits and publishes a variety of sexual and erotic material intended as an alternative to commercial pornography, and is experimenting with imaginative sexual photography. His books include *Erotic by Nature: A Celebration of Life, of Love, and of Our Wonderful Bodies*, *The Erotic Impulse: Honoring the Sensual Self*, and *Photo Sex: Fine Art Sexual Photography Comes of Age*. He is a regular columnist for *Spectator*, US photo representative for *Cupido* (Norway/Denmark), and associate editor of *Sexuality and Culture*. His writing has also appeared in such journals as Salon, *Playboy*, *Boston Phoenix*, *Los Angeles Weekly*, *Cupido*, the *Sun*, *Libido*, the *Realist*, CleanSheets, Scarlet Letters, and *Anything That Moves*. He is currently completing a book of essays, *This Thing We Call Sex: Reflections on the Culture and Politics of Sex in America*. He lives in Santa Cruz, California. If you would like to receive David Steinberg's columns regularly via email (free and confidential), send your name and email address to him at <eronat@aol.com>.

Tristan Taormino is an award-winning author, columnist, editor, sex educator, and pornographer. She is the author of four books: *Opening Up: A Guide to Creating and Sustaining Open Relationships*, *True Lust: Adventures in Sex, Porn and Perversion*, *Down and Dirty Sex Secrets*, and *The Ultimate Guide to Anal Sex for Women*. She is series editor of sixteen volumes of the Lambda Literary Award–winning anthology *Best Lesbian Erotica*. She runs her own adult film production company, Smart Ass Productions, and is currently an exclusive director for Vivid Entertainment. She wrote the popular syndicated sex column "Pucker Up" for the *Village Voice* and other alternative weeklies for nine years. Her official website is <puckerup.com>.

Dave Thomas is a physicist and mathematician. He received bachelor degrees in mathematics and in physics and a master of science in mathematics from the New Mexico Institute of Mining and Technology, where he was awarded the Brown Medal and the Langmuir Award. Dave is president of the science group New Mexicans for Science and Reason <www.nmsr.org> and also is a Fellow of CSI (Committee for Skeptical Inquiry), the publishers of *Skeptical Inquirer*. He has published several articles in *Skeptical Inquirer* on the Roswell and Aztec UFO Incidents, as well as on the Bible Code. Dave has also published in *Scientific American* (Dec. 1980 cover article) and has several patents. He received the National Center for Science Education's Friend of Darwin Award in 2000. Dave is married and has two sons. He enjoys playing bluegrass and performs juggling and magic shows for elementary schools and other groups. Dave is past presi-

dent of the Coalition for Excellence on Science and Math Education (CESE) and past president of the New Mexico Academy of Science. Heworks in Socorro, New Mexico.

Josh Tickell, director of the eco-documentary *Fields of Fuel*, has been on a mission to promote biodiesel and sustainable fuels for the past ten years. <joshtickell.com>.

In 1980, **Seth Tobocman** was one of the founding editors of the political comic book *World War 3 Illustrated*. His illustrations have appeared in the *New York Times* and many other periodicals. Tobocman is the author/illustrator of the graphic books *You Don't Have to Fuck People Over to Survive*, *War in the Neighborhood*, and *Disaster and Resistance: Comics and Landscapes for the 21st Century* (AK Press, 2008). He has shown his work in streets and galleries across the globe—including Exit Art, the Museum of Modern Art, and the New Museum of Contemporary Art.

Steve Watson is webmaster and analyst at InfoWars <www.infowars.net>, the news website belonging to independent journalist, political activist, and documentary filmmaker Alex Jones. Watson is also a regular editor of Jones' Prison Planet site <prisonplanet.com>. Watson was a cinematographer for and appeared in the documentary *TerrorStorm: A History of Government-Sponsored Terrorism*, released in 2006. Watson has a Masters Degree in International Relations from the Department of Political Sciences at Nottingham University in England.

Gary Webb was an investigative journalist for around 25 years, focusing on government and private sector corruption. His controversial 1996 newspaper series "Dark Alliance"—which exposed the sale of cocaine and weapons by CIA-supported rebels to the street gangs of South Central Los Angeles—caused a nationwide outcry that is still reverberating today. His 1998 book, also called *Dark Alliance*, has received critical acclaim in the *San Francisco Chronicle*, the *Baltimore Sun*, and the *Nation*, along with several literary awards. Webb wrote for the *San Jose Mercury News* from 1988 to 1997. He worked as a statehouse correspondent for the *Cleveland Plain Dealer* and the *Kentucky Post* before that, and won more than 30 journalism prizes. He was part of the *Mercury News* team that won the 1989 Pulitzer Prize for general news reporting. He appeared on *Dateline NBC*, the *Montel Williams Show*, CNN, National Public Radio, C-SPAN, CBS *Morning News*, MSNBC, the BBC, British, Australian, and French TV, and dozens of syndicated and local talk radio shows from Bogota, Colombia, to British Columbia. He also worked as a consultant and researcher for the California Assembly. He died in December 2004 of allegedly self-inflicted gunshot wounds.

Bryan Young has been working in the film industry for close to a decade. He has co-directed two feature films—*Missy* (1999) and *The Fleapit Three* (2007)—and a feature-length documentary, *The*

Misbehavers (2004). He has also produced and/or assistant-directed numerous films, including the award-winning documentary *This Divided State* (2005). Along with Elias Pate, he's written more than a dozen screenplays, two of which are at the top two agencies in the world. He also cowrites (with Elias Pate and artist Derek Hunter) the comic book *Pirate Club*, which is released quarterly from Slave Labor Graphics. Aside from producing duties on *Killer at Large*, he's producing and co-directing *The BYU 25*, about the unprecedented level of fury that arose on the most conservative college campus in the country when Vice President Dick Cheney was invited to speak at the spring commencement.

Michael Zezima (a/k/a Mickey Z.) is a relentless purveyor of stand-up tragedy and can be found on the Web at <www.mickeyz.net>.

Howard Zinn grew up in New York City of working-class parents, was a shipyard worker at the age of eighteen, a bombardier in the Air Force at 21 (European theater, World War II), and went to NYU and Columbia under the G.I. Bill of Rights, receiving his Ph.D. in history and political science from Columbia in 1958. His doctoral dissertation, *LaGuardia in Congress*, was a Beveridge Prize publication of the American Historical Association. His first teaching job was at Spelman college in Atlanta, Georgia, a black women's college, where he taught for seven years. After that he taught at Boston University, becoming a professor emeritus in 1988. He has written over a dozen books, his best known being *A People's History of the United States*, which has sold over 700,000 copies. His most recent books include *A People's History of American Empire* (with Paul Buhle and Mike Konopacki), *Voices of a People's History of the United States* (with Anthony Arnove), *Howard Zinn on Democratic Education*, and *Terrorism and War*. He has been active in various social movements for civil rights and against war.

ABOUT THE EDITOR

Russ Kick has been dubbed an "information archaeologist" by the *New York Times*, "a happily maladjusted and radically tolerant Renaissance man" by *Details*, and one of "50 visionaries who are changing your world" by *Utne Reader*.

Besides the books below, Russ has written articles and a column for the *Village Voice* and several independent magazines. The Memory Hole <www.thememoryhole.org>, a website devoted to rescuing knowledge and freeing information, is his labor of love. His personal website is <www.mindpollen.com>. Russ made world headlines in April 2004 when his Freedom of Information Act request/appeal resulted in the release of 288 photos of the US war dead coming home in flag-draped coffins. The previous Halloween, Russ had made the front page of the *New York Times* when he digitally uncensored a heavily redacted Justice Department report. The Memory Hole was also the first to post the uncut 5-minute footage of George W. Bush doing nothing in a Florida classroom as the 9/11 attacks raged, Martin Luther King's entire FBI file (16,000+ pages), and over 400 internal forms used by the National Security Agency, among other exclusives.

Books as Author

- *Outposts: A Catalogue of Rare and Disturbing Alternative Information*
- *Psychotropedia: Publications from the Periphery*
- *50 Things You're Not Supposed to Know*
- *The Disinformation Book of Lists: Subversive Facts and Hidden Information in Rapid-Fire Format*
- *50 Things You're Not Supposed to Know, Volume 2*

Books as Editor

- *Hot Off the Net: Erotica and Other Sex Writings From the Internet*
- *You Are Being Lied To: The Disinformation Guide to Media Distortion, Historical Whitewashes and Cultural Myths*
- *Everything You Know Is Wrong: The Disinformation Guide to Secrets and Lies*
- *Abuse Your Illusions: The Disinformation Guide to Media Mirages and Establishment Lies*
- *Everything You Know About Sex Is Wrong: The Disinformation Guide to the Extremes of Human Sexuality (and Everything in Between)*
- *Everything You Know About God Is Wrong: The Disinformation Guide to Religion*

ARTICLE HISTORIES

"AA Lies" by Charles Bufe was originally published in *You Are Being Lied To*.

"Amnesia in America" by James Loewen was originally published in *You Are Being Lied To*.

"Art and the Eroticism of Puberty" by David Steinberg originally appeared in *Spectator* magazine <www.spectatormag.com> and was included in *You Are Being Lied To*.

"Bedouin Blues" by Seth Tobocman originally appeared in *Disaster and Resistance: Comics and Landscapes for the 21st Century* by Seth Tobocman (AK Press, 2008).

"The Bible Code" by David Thomas originally appeared in shorter form in *Skeptical Inquirer* magazine <www.csicop.org/si/>. It was expanded for *You Are Being Lied To* and has been updated for this volume.

"Cheap, Crappy Food = A Fat Population" by Steven Greenstreet, Bryan Young, and Elias Pate was written for this volume. The title is the editor's.

"Chemicals Are Killing You" by Terri Mitchell was written for this volume.

"Colony Kosovo" by Christian Parenti was originally published in *You Are Being Lied To*.

"Columbus and Western Civilization" by Howard Zinn was originally published under the title "Christopher Columbus & the Myth of Human Progress" as part of the Open Magazine Pamphlet Series and was included in *You Are Being Lied To*.

"Confessions of an 'AIDS Denialist'" by Henry H. Bauer was written for this volume.

"The Constitution, War, and the Draft" by Ron Paul is an excerpt from *The Revolution: A Manifesto* by Ron Paul (Grand Central Publishing, 2008). The title is the editor's.

"Crushing Butterflies With Iron Boots" by Peter Gorman was originally published in *Cannabis Culture*.

"Dear Deluded Mass Media, North American Union Agenda Exists" by Alex Jones and Steve Watson was originally published in slightly different form on InfoWars.net.

"Digital Seductions" by Norman Solomon is a remix of two previously published articles, written for this volume.

"Don't Blame Your Parents," the interview with Judith Rich Harris, was originally published in *You Are Being Lied To*.

"Dreaming up America, Reel One" by Russell Banks is the first chapter of *Dreaming up America* by Russell Banks (Seven Stories, 2008).

"Drug War Mythology" by Paul Armentano was originally published in *You Are Being Lied To*. The postscript was written for this volume.

"The Eurabian Revolution" by Gregory M. Davis was originally published in *Chronicles* magazine.

"Fear And Lying in 2012-Land" by John Major Jenkins was written for this volume.

"Fields of Fuel" by Josh Tickell was written for this volume.

"Forbidden Archaeology" by Michael A. Cremo was originally published in *You Are Being Lied To*.

"From Untouchables to Conscientious Objectors" by Daniel Grego was originally published in *Everywhere All the Time: A New Deschooling Reader*, edited by Matt Hern (AK Press, 2008).

"How the People Seldom Catch Intelligence" by Preston Peet was originally published in *You Are Being Lied To*. It has been updated for this volume.

"The Information Arms Race" by Douglas Rushkoff was originally published in *You Are Being Lied To*.

"John McCain and the POW Cover-up" by Sydney H. Schanberg was originally published as "The War Secrets Senator John McCain Hides" on the defunct APBnews.com and was included in *You Are Being Lied To*. It was heavily expanded and updated for the Nation Institute website, and it is this new version that appears in this volume.

"A Lost Theory?" by David Loye originally appeared as the introduction to *Darwin's Lost Theory of Love: A Healing Vision for the New Century* by David Loye (iUniverse.com, 2000) and was included in *You Are Being Lied To*.

"The Man in the Bushes," the interview with Philip Jenkins, was originally published in *You Are Being Lied To*.

"The Martin Luther King You Don't See on TV" by Jeff Cohen and Norman Solomon was originally published as a "Media Beat" column. It has been updated for this volume.

"The Media and Their Atrocities" by Michael Parenti was originally published on the Michael Parenti Political Archive Website <www.michaelparenti.org> and was included in *You Are Being Lied To*.

"Mission Rejected: Clifton Hicks" by Peter Laufer is a chapter from *Mission Rejected: US Soldiers Who Say No to Iraq* by Peter Laufer (Chelsea Green, 2006).

"Moral Imperialism and the Iron Logic of War" by Stan Goff is a chapter from *Full Spectrum Disorder: The Military in the New American Century* by Stan Goff (Soft Skull, 2004).

"Mystics and Messiahs," the interview with Philip Jenkins, was originally published in *You Are Being Lied To*.

"New Rules for the New Millennium" by Gary Webb originally appeared as the introduction to *Censored 1999: The News That Didn't Make the News* by Peter Phillips and Project Censored (Seven Stories Press, 1999). It was revised and expanded by the author for *You Are Being Lied To*.

"New Thought Vs. Holism" by Alexandra Bruce was written for this volume.

"NutraFear & NutraLoathing in Augusta, Georgia" by Alex Constantine was originally published in *You Are Being Lied To*.

"A Panic of Biblical Proportions over Media Violence" by Paul McMasters originally appeared on the Freedom Forum Website <www.freedomforum.org> and was published in *You Are Being Lied To*. It has been updated for this volume.

"Pharmaceutical Crimes and Misdemeanors" by Peter Rost, M.D. is a chapter ("Crimes and Misdemeanors") from *The Whistleblower: Confessions of a Healthcare Hitman* by Peter Rost, M.D. (Soft Skull, 2006).

"The Puppets of Pandemonium" by Howard Bloom was originally published in *You Are Being Lied To*. It has been updated for this volume.

"The Rabin Murder Cover-up" by Barry Chamish was originally published in *You Are Being Lied To*.

"Reality Is a Shared Hallucination" by Howard Bloom was originally published in *You Are Being Lied To*. It has been updated for this volume.

"Reassessing OKC" by Cletus Nelson was originally published in *You Are Being Lied To*. The postscript was written for this volume.

"The Religious Experience of Philip K. Dick" by R. Crumb was originally published in *Weirdo*, issue 17.

"Saving Private Power" by Michael Zezima is comprised of excerpts from the author's book *Saving Private Power: The Hidden History of "The Good War"* (Soft Skull, 2000). The author created the article version for *You Are Being Lied To*.

"School Textbooks" by Earl Lee was originally published in *You Are Being Lied To*. It has been updated for this volume.

"A Sentient Universe" by Peter Russell originally appeared in *From Science to God: The Mystery of Consciousness and the Meaning of Light* by Peter Russell (prepublication edition; see the author's Website <www.peterrussell.com>) and was published in *You Are Being Lied To*.

"There Is So Much That We Don't Know" by William R. Corliss is comprised of selections from the author's book *Science Frontiers* (Sourcebooks, 1994) and his newsletter of the same name. It was originally published in *You Are Being Lied To*. The title is the editor's.

"Toad-Licking Blues" by Thomas Lyttle is a condensed version of the article "*Bufo* Toads and Bufotenine: Facts and Fiction Surrounding an Alleged Psychedelic," which originally appeared in the *Journal of Psychoactive Drugs*. It was originally published in its current form in *You Are Being Lied To*.

"Treacherous Words" by Normand Baillargeon is a chapter from *A Short Course in Intellectual Self-Defense* by Normand Baillargeon, translated by Andréa Schmidt (Seven Stories, 2008).

"The Truth About Corporations" by Agent J was written for this volume.

"The Unconscious Roots of the Drug War" by Dan Russell is comprised of excerpts from *Shamanism and the Drug Propaganda: The Birth of Patriarchy and the Drug War* by Dan Russell (kalyx.com, 1998). It was originally published in *You Are Being Lied To*.

"The Unkindest Cut" by Tristan Taormino was originally published as "Schlong Song" in the *Village Voice*. The title is the editor's.

"The War on Bugs: Pesticide Spray Devices, Household Poisons, and Dr. Seuss" by Will Allen is a chapter from *The War on Bugs* by Will Allen (Chelsea Green, 2008).

"The War on Consciousness" by Graham Hancock was written for this volume.

"We Were Silenced by the Drums of War" by Jeff Cohen was originally published as "Inside TV News: We Were Silenced by the Drums of War" on Truthout.org.

"What I Didn't Know About the Communist Conspiracy" by Jim Martin was originally published in *You Are Being Lied To*.

"What Makes Mainstream Media Mainstream" by Noam Chomsky originally appeared on the ZNet Website <www.zmag.org>. It was revised by the author for inclusion in *You Are Being Lied To*.

"What's Missing from This Picture?" by Jim Marrs was originally published in *You Are Being Lied To*.

"Who's Who in Hell," the interview with Warren Allen Smith, was originally published in *You Are Being Lied To*.

"Why Did the Iraqi Government Want Blackwater Banned?" by Jim Marrs was written for this volume.

"Will the Real Human Being Please Stand Up?" by Riane Eisler was originally published in *You Are Being Lied To*.

"'A World That Hates Gays'" by Philip Jenkins was originally published in *You Are Being Lied To*. It has been updated for this volume.